Ministry and the American Legal System

Ministry and the American Legal System

A GUIDE FOR CLERGY, LAY WORKERS, AND CONGREGATIONS

RICHARD B. COUSER

FORTRESS PRESS   MINNEAPOLIS

MINISTRY AND THE AMERICAN LEGAL SYSTEM
A Guide for Clergy, Lay Workers, and Congregations

Interior design: Publishers' WorkGroup

Library of Congress Cataloging-in-Publication Data

Couser, Richard B., 1941-
  Ministry and the American legal system / Richard B. Couser.
      p. cm.
    Includes bibliographical references and index.
    ISBN 0-8006-2603-6 :
    1. Corporations, Religious—Law and legislation—United States.
2. Church and state—United States. 3. Church management—Law and legislation—United States. 4. Clergy—Legal status, laws, etc.—
United States. I. Title.
KF4865.C68 1993
346.73'064—dc20
[347.30664]   92-34214
                                                                              CIP

The paper used in this publication meets the minimum requirements of American National Standard for Information Sciences—Permanence of Paper for Printed Library Materials, ANSI Z329.48-1984. ∞™

Manufactured in the U.S.A.   AF 1–2603
  97   96   95   94   93   1   2   3   4   5   6   7   8   9   10

To Lindie

My wife, best friend, and fellow pilgrim,
whose prayers, spiritual and practical counsel,
encouragement, and support
have made this book and so many other things possible

Contents

Preface

Pastors and priests, trustees and deacons, members of lay councils or presbyteries, directors and administrators of counseling centers, schools, conference centers, and camps, boards of directors, and all religious workers in the United States, whether full- or part-time, paid or volunteer–all need to understand the shape and nature of the American legal system, not just its rules, but how it was formed, how it operates, and how it relates to religious persons and their goals. This book not only promotes an understanding of the practical elements of the American legal system but also provides a context in which specific questions that are integral to the life of the church today can be explored.

Perhaps little needs to be said about the urgency of promoting greater understanding. Twentieth-century America has experienced an explosion of legislation, regulation, and litigation. The legal system has often entered parish doors, even though the United States Constitution forbids any law that prohibits the "free exercise" of religion. The life of the church and the legal system intersect at every turn. Federal and state laws and regulations govern every facet of employment; land use is controlled by local boards and ordinances; courts hear damage suits arising out of pastoral counseling, sexual or financial misconduct, church discipline, or slips and falls in church buildings. Increasingly, the church needs to deal with such questions as sales taxes on sales of Bibles and religious literature, property taxes on church camps, and health regulations in the church kitchen. In every community, clergy, Christian workers, and laity make decisions regarding the affairs of congregations and parachurch organizations without a clear knowledge of the legal system by which they are governed.

My thinking about this book developed during years of work as a lawyer and lay leader with churches and religious organizations. It came into symbolic focus as I revisited, now as a parent, the scene of my own undergraduate education—Yale University. The Yale Divinity School, with its gold-crowned tower and Georgian brick buildings, is connected to the rest of the Yale campus by a thread of science labs strung along the steady rise of Prospect Street that expire, as if tired of the climb, just before reaching it. The stranger seeking the school must search for the entrance with care. The Yale Law School, by contrast, occupies an entire, albeit small, city block central to the New Haven campus, surrounded by libraries, the freshman dining hall, and the Hall of Graduate Studies. These two centers of their respective discipline's claim to light and truth on the Yale campus are an allegory of the relationship of the two disciplines in the larger world. The world of law is central to the life of the larger society; indeed, it writes the very rules by which the society lives. The world of divinity often seems remote, removed from the civil society, and unrelated to such rules of law.

Because the law may seem formidable or inaccessible to many, this book is divided into three parts. Part 1 discusses the U.S. Constitution and religion. After a review of the pre-constitutional history in chapter 1, chapter 2 describes the American constitutional system, with its separation of powers among the state and federal governments and the three branches of the government: legislative, executive, and judicial. This constitutional system in action is illustrated by a review of how the legal system has dealt with the abortion controversy. Chapter 3 focuses on the two religion clauses of the First Amendment—the Establishment Clause and the Free Exercise Clause. The chapter describes the history of religious liberty both before the Constitution and after its adoption, the meaning the courts have given to the religion clauses, particular application of the clauses in such areas as government funding, the right to witness, and equal access to public facilities, and how the constitutional rights of religious organizations can be used to obtain remedies that transcend mere recognition of rights.

Part 2 focuses on the important legal concepts and principles that are of interest to religious ministries. The organizational form of ecclesiastical bodies as jural entities and their treatment in the courts is discussed in chapter 4. Chapter 5 addresses the legal privileges and obligations of clergy. Chapter 6 sets forth the rules of law in two of the broad areas in which most legal liability arises—contracts and torts—and discusses the liability of the religious organization for the acts of its employees or others in these areas. Regulation of the church as an employer—including such issues as antidiscrimination laws, minimum wages, and labor organization—is covered in chapter 7. Chapter 8 discusses the law of property ownership; chapter 9, copyright law; and chapter 10, other areas of government regulation, including the church's obligation as a taxpayer, child abuse reporting, securities regulation, food laws, and public accommodations.

Part 3 expands on Part 2 by addressing risk management issues—how the church or religious organization can and should conduct itself to live within the rules set forth in Part 2, minimize its liability exposure, and use its assets and contributions most effectively. Chapter 11, on organization and governance, expands in practical detail on the discussion of ecclesiastical organization in chapter 4. Chapter 12, on hiring, supervising, and firing employees, addresses the employment contract, expand-

ing on the general discussions of contract law in chapter 6 and employment regulation in chapter 7. Chapter 13 discusses the church's role as wagepayer, and chapter 14, that of the pastor as taxpayer, expanding on the discussion of the privileges and obligations of clergy in chapter 5. Chapter 15 provides practical advice on property ownership, including such matters as purchasing property or goods, construction contracts, and the liability of a property owner to persons injured on its property, expanding on legal concepts of property ownership set forth in chapter 8 and torts in chapter 6. Chapter 16 discusses acquisition and management of funds and trusts. Chapter 17, on social events, child care, and trips, and chapter 18, on the counseling relationship and church discipline, are further risk management expansions of the tort concepts of chapter 6. Chapter 19 considers the church in the position of litigant, approaches to alternative dispute resolution, and hiring a lawyer; and chapter 20 closes the risk management part of the book with a discussion of liability insurance.

Included as appendices are the U.S. Constitution, an explanation of legal citations, conciliation provisions for contracts and wills developed by the Association of Christian Conciliation Services, and selected resources for further information.

One caveat is in order: This book is intended to help readers involved in religious ministries to understand the American legal system and its practical application to their work. But the law is a moving target. As time passes and society's perceptions change, old laws are modified, and legal principles evolve to fit the contemporary context. New needs arise, giving birth to new statutes, regulations, court decisions, and constitutional interpretations. Decisions cited that have not reached the highest level of judicial authority are appealed and sometimes modified or overturned. Books of law must be constantly updated as legislatures pass statutes and written decisions pour out of the nation's appellate courts. Because our legal system consists of fifty separate sovereign states as well as the federal government, different principles may apply to the same facts, depending on where, as well as when, the facts occur. No book can cover all of these variables or anticipate the infinite variety of situations that may cause religious ministries to need legal advice.

Some books may help people improve their physical health or recognize when they should seek qualified medical assistance, but such knowledge is not a substitute for getting the needed medical advice. Nor is this book a substitute for getting qualified legal help when a ministry has a legal problem. Rather, this book should be used as a tool to understand the legal system and the issues that need to be addressed in avoiding or dealing with legal problems in ministry. *Always get specific qualified legal advice when dealing with specific problems.* The material contained here is only a guide and does not provide definite or all-inclusive answers. The author and publisher make no warranty, express or implied, that the information contained herein is correct, complete, or current. Independent verification is essential. Any statutes, cases, or other legal reference material cited should be checked to determine if they are current or have been reversed, amended, repealed, or modified. This book is a beginning for understanding legal issues, not definitive or final advice.

Since I made my commitment to bring the worlds of law and church closer in understanding, several persons have assisted me to clarify and develop this book.

My partners at Orr and Reno Professional Association allowed me the necessary extended leave from a busy law practice. The faculty and staff of Santa Clara University and especially its vice-president, Ralph Beaudoin, assisted in making facilities available for research and writing and provided support and encouragement. A number of members of the Christian Legal Society and other Christian attorneys of my acquaintance suggested topics to be covered and directed me to research materials. And, most importantly, my wife, Linda, mastered the computer and showed boundless skill, patience, and faithfulness in preparation of the manuscript. I would be remiss if I did not also acknowledge my debt to my late mother-in-law, Adelia Gelatt, to whose tireless prayers I attribute much of God's grace in my life and that of my family; my children, Alison and Jonathan, who provide constant encouragement and spiritual support; my parents, Thomas and Winifred Couser, who saw to it that my childhood was rooted in a church that taught the Bible to its children; and the Reverend Cornelius Fersch, former minister of the First Congregational Church of Lebanon, New Hampshire, who first taught me the words of John 3:16: "For God so loved the world that he gave his one and only Son, that whoever believes in him shall not perish but have eternal life."

Religion and Its Legal Context

Today, clergy, lay workers, and congregational leaders need to understand the American legal system in relation to their ministries. Because few clergy or lay leaders have legal training, their knowledge of the law and its effect on their work is often gained by hearsay, media accounts, or an occasional, and perhaps unpleasant, encounter with regulators, taxing authorities, or the courts. Lack of knowledge or naiveté is sometimes compounded by theologies of separation from the world or religious convictions that claim to transcend, but may in fact conflict with, civic obligations. Ministry effectiveness is impaired by unnecessary conflict with civil authorities and by the failure to order church business to minimize liability exposure and maximize use of the church's financial and organizational resources. Integrating practical legal knowledge with the work of religious ministries cannot be ignored if ministries are to function effectively in the contemporary American milieu of pervasive regulation and liability consciousness.

Religious persons and religion as a collective expression of relationship to the transcendent and ineffable exist today, as they always have, in a societal context—an ordered relationship of people and groups held together by law. In American society, that law is comprised of the body of juridical principles set forth in the U.S. Constitution, state constitutions, statutes, court decisions, and administrative regulations that are binding upon citizens—those rules that can be and ultimately are enforced by the power of the state through its courts, court officers, and law enforcement agencies. The legal system is the civil government that makes and enforces the law and resolves disputes that arise under the law.

A brief and selective look at how religious people have historically integrated their spiritual world with civil law may remove some of the mystery from the relationship between the secular and the religious, provide perspective to the modern context, and offer insight into the source of many of our legal principles—their origins and the importance of these origins to religious life. Most of the topics discussed here have roots in both the Bible and post-biblical history, reflecting the integration of civil law with the lives of people of faith.

CONTRACTS

Contracts or covenants are as old as the Bible, and, likely, as old as the human race. The Old and New Testaments or old "covenant" and new "covenant" are said to have the nature of contracts,[1] The Old Testament contains a number of covenants, sometimes with Yahweh as a party (e.g., in the Noachian, Abrahamic, and Davidic covenants), other times between governments or individuals.[2] Both the Ten Commandments and the book of Deuteronomy have been viewed as forms of covenant.

The covenant as a binding promise, or contract, that regulated behavior and brought predictability to social and political relationships is known from Sumerian archaeological evidence from the mid-third millennium B.C. These ancient covenants were usually made under oath and called upon the gods of the participating parties as witnesses who were expected to punish the party who failed to perform an obligation. The prohibition that forbade the Israelites from making treaties with the Canaanites may reflect the danger to the people of Yahweh of recognizing foreign gods that is implicit in such a covenant relationship.

A vestige of ancient covenant practice survives today in the traditional oath taken by witnesses in court to tell "the truth, the whole truth and nothing but the truth, so help me God."

LAW CODES

Law codes that govern civil affairs such as marriage, divorce and adultery, assault and battery, injuries to persons and property, and inheritance are known from patriarchal societies, for example, the Sumerians and Hittites, and from the Babylonian Code of Hammurabi. Although most of the content of these codes is secular, reflecting the lawgiver's rules to establish order and justice among the people, the source of authority is typically the choice of the king as ruler by the regnant deities. Sometimes the gods play a role in the administration of justice as, for example, in the provision of the Code of Hammurabi which called, for a wife accused of adultery, for trial by the ordeal of being cast into the river where her survival would be the gods' testimony to her innocence. A biblical permutation of the idea of trial by ordeal appears in Daniel 6, in which Daniel is thrown into the lions' den for violating the decree of King Darius by praying to God instead of the king. The king expresses the hope to Daniel that Daniel's God will rescue him. When Daniel is unharmed, he explains to the king, "They have not hurt me, because I was found innocent in his sight. Nor have I ever done any wrong before you, O king" (Dan. 6:22). Trial by ordeal was known in England and the early American colonies, particularly for such theologically related offenses as witchcraft.

PROPERTY

An account of a property transfer appears in Jer. 32:8-14: "I knew that this was the Word of the Lord; so I bought the field at Anathoth from my cousin Hanamel and weighed out for him seventeen shekels of silver. I signed and sealed the deed, had it witnessed, and weighed out the silver on the scales. I took the deed of purchase—the unsealed copy—and I gave this deed to Baruch . . . I gave Baruch these instructions: '. . . take these documents . . . and put them in a clay jar so they will last a long time.'"

Jeremiah's account of his purchase of his cousin's field at Anathoth bears a striking resemblance to modern American conveyancing. The deed is signed, sealed, witnessed, paid for, delivered, and put in a place where the record will be preserved. The deed contains terms and conditions, which might now be called "covenants" or "restrictions," and is purchased under a right of redemption—another familiar concept in American law.

Yet Jeremiah's purchase of his cousin's field is not just a property transfer; it is an event of theological and prophetic significance. The Babylonian army is besieging Jerusalem and Jeremiah is confined in the royal palace for prophesying that the city will fall—scarcely a propitious time for real estate investments. By obeying the Lord's word and purchasing the field, Jeremiah uses the civil legal system to carry out an act symbolizing the Lord's promise of restoring the people to the land. God's wrath will not last forever.

Modern American property law was borrowed from English common law as it existed before the American Revolution. Its history contains a mixture of theological and secular concepts dating to medieval times and to the Norman conquest of Anglo-Saxon England in 1066. At that time, William the Conqueror introduced the feudal system of the continent to the British Isles: the king ruled by divine right. All land held by subordinate nobility was subject to the king's authority or ultimate right to the land. A vast pyramid of descending vassals, in turn, were lord over subordinate vassals, down to the one who actually possessed and used the land. The feudal system involved mutual obligations: the lord provided security and protection in exchange for the vassal's provision, depending upon the nature of his tenure, of such support as military service, money, or agricultural services. The analogy to ancient Israel, which was provided land by its Lord who required certain sacrifices of the people, is not remote. Church land in feudal society was held in a form called "frankalmoyn," which required spiritual services for assurance of the lord's eternal life. Feudalism was both a system of land ownership and a system of government—hence, rent and taxes come from the same source.[3]

Although English land law had progressed beyond feudal concepts by the time of the settlement of America, colonial lands were originally held as grants from the king.[4] The proprietors of the colonies, in laying out new towns, often set aside certain land for the "first settled" minister. This was done to help the town get started by encouraging a clergyman to settle. To be entitled to the property, a minister had to have a lifelong contract to live and preach in the town, but he often took absolute title to the land and could pass it to his heirs.[5] Lands were also settled on a town for church purposes and were in the nature of permanent endowments. Towns had a parochial as well as a municipal character, at least until a separate parish was formed within them. Then the parish took the lands that had been granted for parochial use or appropriated to such use by the town and assumed the town's parochial rights, such as taxing inhabitants for its support. This is the source of real estate title for many older churches in New England.[6] Older churches in other areas of the United States may trace their title to grants from Russian, Spanish, Mexican, other colonial, or the federal (mostly in favor of Indian missions) governments.[7]

TAXATION

Taxation is also as old as organized societies with central governing institutions, and it has often been interrelated with religious concerns. The Bible reports on the taxation systems of the Egyptian and Roman Empires (Gen. 47:26; Matt. 22:17; Luke 20:22; 23:2). The fulfillment of the prophecy in Micah 5:2 of the birth of Christ in Bethlehem is set in motion by the decree from Caesar Augustus, reported in Luke 2:1, that a census of the Roman world be

taken for military and taxation purposes. The apostle Paul enjoins believers to be faithful in payment of taxes (Rom. 13:6-7). Tension between the Roman taxation system and the Jewish people is evident in the Gospels, for example, in Matthew 22, in the inquiry of the Pharisees' disciples and Herodians to Jesus about the legality of paying taxes to Caesar.

A question that is often related to taxation today is the identity of those entitled to the status of clergy. In Old Testament times, too, although for different reasons, the people required instruction on how to identify God's spokespeople and distinguish them from false prophets. So Moses taught them that "if what a prophet proclaims in the name of the Lord does not take place or come true, that is a message the Lord has not spoken" (Deut. 18:22). The struggle between true and false prophets is a recurring Old Testament theme, as in Elijah's confrontation with the prophets of Baal on Mount Carmel (1 Kings 18) and Jeremiah's struggles with the false prophets of the days before the exile. The problem recurs in the New Testament, requiring the discernment of Jesus with respect to the man driving out demons in his name (Mark 9:38-41), and Peter with respect to Simon the Sorcerer (Acts 8:9-25).

CHURCH ORGANIZATION

The early church had little need to concern itself with the civil law governing corporations, or aggregates of people who functioned collectively in a legal existence separate from their individual identities. The Apostles' Creed, still recited in many churches, states simply, "I believe in . . . the holy catholic church." The language echoes through the years, from the ninth century, when the Eastern and Western churches viewed themselves as one. The Nestorian and Monophysite churches had separated after the Council of Chalcedon in A.D. 451 and disappeared in lands largely swallowed up by Islam.[8] The Protestant Reformation was still five hundred years in the future. The church fathers of the time were confident that the catholic, or universal, church that they led was the church which Christ promised to build on "this rock" (Matt.

16:18). But the politics and history of the church and the lands within which it existed have contributed much to the legal needs of the church in our time.

In 1054, a long-simmering dispute between Rome and Constantinople erupted in a schism when Cardinal Humbert, the papal legate, laid a bull excommunicating the Patriarch Cerularius on the altar of the Church of the Holy Wisdom in Constantinople. Later efforts at reunion were half-hearted and ultimately unsuccessful. The schism was based on several factors—prominent among them the claim of the Bishop of Rome, in a hierarchical church, to have authority "over all the earth, that is, over *every* Church."[9] The Orthodox were unwilling to grant Rome more than a *primus inter pares* (first among equals) status with the ancient patriarchates of Constantinople, Alexandria, Antioch, and Jerusalem.

Orthodoxy, more conciliar in church governance at the top but scarcely less hierarchical than Rome, came under political pressure, and the church formed relationships with states and emperors that led to autonomous national churches headed by their own patriarch, catholicos, archbishop, or metropolitan. These national churches separated from one another as Byzantium itself broke up. In modern times the Orthodox diaspora in the new world has strained the authority of the national churches, leading to breakaway groups and a self-governing Orthodox Church in America, not universally recognized by the national churches. Issues of the control of orthodox churches and church offices have been seminal in U.S. Supreme Court decisions on the degree of autonomy of the church from secular authority.

Martin Luther's and Henry VIII's breaks with Rome and the subsequent balkanizing of Protestantism in England and Europe in the sixteenth century preceded American colonization and resulted in a proliferation of religious groups willing to settle the new world, some fleeing persecution by established churches and governments that had once supported them. Congregationalists abounded in New England; Anglicans in the South; Quakers, Baptists, and Presbyterians in the mid-Atlantic states. Larger numbers of immigrants from the older churches came later—Irish, Italian, Polish, and French-Canadian Catholics; Greek, Russian, and other Slavic Orthodox; German and Scandinavian Lutherans and Anabaptists. And the next several hundred years provided plenty of time for the flourishing of religious groups born in the new world—Adventists, Christian Scientists, Jehovah's Witnesses, Mormons, and others. The freedom and independence of thought and action that existed in America permitted people to have their own church wherever "two or three come together in my name" (Matt. 18:20). America has thousands of independent churches unaffiliated with any denomination. Each of these, consistent with its theology, faces organizational and operational problems within the legal system.

Although religion and religious groups necessarily and universally relate to their contextual legal systems, in the United States that relationship differs in one very significant aspect from most societies in history, including most post-Constantinian Christian societies. The American constitutional mandate that there be no "establishment of religion"—the separation of church and state—has required an accommodation between the religious and civic spheres through our legal system that is historically unique. Although there is some limited precedent, as in the Persian and Roman Empires, for allowing some subject peoples to retain their own religion, in most societies, as in the Israel of the Pentateuch, civic and religious obligations are intertwined. In Calvin's Geneva and Zwingli's Zurich, as in Catholic Europe of the time, religious leaders often defined civic duty, and heresy was punishable by the government. While most of the countries that are heir to the Judeo-Christian tradition practice religious tolerance today, the strict separation of church and state remains a foreign concept in most of the countries with which we share the closest kinship as well as in those more culturally distant. To many Americans also, it is a separation that is confusing and often unwelcome. It may account, more than any other factor, for the estrangement and often reciprocal ignorance and confusion between the church and the legal system that I seek to redress here.

This confirmation was brought home to me in the circumstances of a meeting I scheduled with town officials to discuss a church camp's property tax exemptions. After settling into the conference room, I observed a handwritten scroll on the mantel over the fireplace. It read, "If we hung the Ten Commandments here, somebody would sue us for discriminating against sinners." The reference to the Constitution was, to be sure, garbled—the Supreme Court case prohibiting the posting of the Ten Commandments in a public school classroom[10] is based on the First Amendment's prohibition of laws "respecting an establishment of religion," not on the Fourteenth Amendment's requirements that the government afford "equal protection of the law" to its citizens. Perhaps the anonymous author knew that and simply lumped into a single aphorism his or her frustration with a variety of judicial decisions that seemed to undermine a way of life. Whatever the motive, it seemed ironic that we, representatives of a religious organization, were meeting our government adversary in a government building under a constitutionally rebellious banner that inferentially endorsed the moral code represented by the Ten Commandments.

In another incident, a local high school teacher invited a witch to make a presentation to his class, ostensibly to enact religious ceremonies that the witch attributed to Native American religion. The presentation occurred near Halloween. Students who might be offended by the exercise were offered the opportunity to leave the class. When this episode came under attack, the witch defended the conduct of the school officials as upholding her constitutional right freely to exercise her religion. It did not seem to occur to her or the teacher that the exercise of religion in a public school classroom encountered another constitutional principle—separation of church and state.

The separation of church and state is part of the American constitutional system, but it no more insulates religious ministries from the operation of law than do separatist theologies. Just as people of faith have integrated their religious life with law in other historical and contemporary biblical and post-biblical societies, so must modern American religious ministries understand and integrate their activities with American law of today.

THE U.S. CONSTITUTION AND RELIGION

CHAPTER 1

Pre-Constitutional History

A. Before Independence
B. The Declaration of Independence
C. The Articles of Confederation

Most Americans have some notion of what the wallpaper looks like in at least some parts of the American legal system. They receive some general secondary or college education on the structure of government, read media accounts of civil and criminal trials, and perhaps either voluntarily or involuntarily become involved in the legal system, appearing before a zoning board to protest a proposed intrusion into the neighborhood, buying a house, signing a will, appearing in traffic court, or pursuing or defending a damage claim arising out of an auto accident. All of these activities provide some external learning about the legal system. They are unlikely, however, to reveal its foundations and bearing walls.

The American legal system is built upon the United States Constitution, its defining document. The Constitution, in turn, was constructed by men whose thought was shaped by nearly two centuries of colonial experience. The history and experience of the colonial leaders who wrote the Constitution, and their constituents who approved it, help us understand what the Constitution is and why it was written as it was. The tension between central and provincial governments, the identity of sovereignty, the relation of legislative to executive power, and the preservation of individual rights perceived as fundamental to a free people are all themes that appear in pre-constitutional American history.

Before doing an architect or engineer's examination of some of the rooms of interest in the American house of law in order to learn how to engage in some climate control and make the amenities work, it would be well to spend a little time becoming familiar with the structure and foundation on which it is built. To do this, one must become, for a bit, a student of history and recall how the American republic came together. In the early history appear many of the themes later articulated in the Constitution and litigated thereafter between parties with different views of the Constitution's meaning for the new republic.

A. BEFORE INDEPENDENCE

Jonathan Edwards (1703–58) has been called the "greatest divine . . . that America ever produced."[1] Edwards, preaching at Northampton, Massachusetts, was instrumental in the extraordinary religious revival—the Great Awakening—that took place in the 1730s and 1740s in colonial America. His life spanned much of the pre-revolutionary eighteenth century. In Jonathan Edwards's time, the word "Americans" meant "Indians," that is, Native Americans. Edwards, like most colonials, identified his own nationality as English.

Edwards's Massachusetts began in 1620 with the Mayflower pilgrims, blown off course from their destination of "Virginia" (they held a patent on a tract near the mouth of the Hudson, then within what was loosely called Virginia), who settled in Plymouth. They entered the new land where "none had power to command them," a remark rooted in the shipboard agreement known as the Mayflower Compact, an exercise in self-government that reflected their English heritage and convictions. Through the Puritan migrations of the 1630s, the Massachusetts Bay Colony became a colony that sought to implement its founders' vision of a city of God, where the passion to know and do God's will would order social behavior as well as personal life.

Each colony likewise had its own charter and unique history, the details of which are beyond our scope here. As Massachusetts Bay was founded to build a Puritan vision of the good life, so Virginia was founded firm in the embrace of Anglicanism, Pennsylvania in Quakerism, and Rhode Island in the Baptist tradition.

Each colony began with a royal grant or charter to a group or company that usually hoped to profit from the trade and produce of the New World and had varying degrees of independence from the English Crown. Charters were bought and sold, and grants were often sold back to the Crown. Boundaries were moved and territories changed to create new colonies or add to already-existing ones. New Hampshire and Maine began as proprietary grants, of, respectively, Captain John Mason and Sir Ferdinando Gorges. Mason sold his New Hampshire grant back to the Crown; Gorges' heirs sold theirs to Massachusetts. Maryland was chartered as a proprietary grant to Sir George Calvert, a Roman Catholic convert who in compensation for the loss caused by his new religion was given, by his friend King Charles I, a large portion of Virginia. "Carolina" began in 1663 as a grant from Charles II of all the land from Virginia to Spanish Florida. With whatever checkered and unique history each colony possessed, they all grew through the seventeenth and eighteenth centuries not as a nation occupied, governed, or controlled by a foreign power, but as separate colonies of Englishmen, colonies that shared a common heritage, culture, language, and law, and that looked, with whatever degree of self-government they exercised, to London as the center and source of authority. The colonial grants from a central authority, from which the grantees' descendants later separated, laid the foundation for what became our federal system.

The decade and a half that preceded the American Revolution saw a series of poorly managed attempts by England to assert imperial control over people who treasured their rights as free English citizens. Despite occasional points of friction, before 1763 a passable compromise generally existed between home rule and the authority of London. Colonial assemblies enjoyed the right to tax, to appoint officials, to raise military forces, and to control their schools, churches, and land. Parliament and the king made the rules of war, foreign affairs, and trade. This compromise began to unravel in the mid-1760s, after the enforcement of various measures, the most notable of which was the Stamp Act of 1765, the first direct internal tax to be levied on the colonies by Parliament. The act taxed a variety of legal documents, newspapers, college diplomas, land deeds, liquor licenses, and playing cards. It was widely resisted and ultimately repealed, but not before bringing about the Stamp Act Congress, a gathering of delegates from nine colonies, held in New York but summoned by Massachusetts, in October of 1765. It was the first such gathering and the beginning of the movement toward colonial union.

The repeal of the Stamp Act was a short-lived victory. It was followed by the Townshend Acts of 1767, which imposed custom duties on a number of English imports. In response to the colonial argument against Parliament-imposed internal taxes that was raised in the Stamp Act debate, the Townshend Acts imposed a tax the colonials conceded lay in Parliament's power—a tax on trade with the colonies. With the tax came, however, an onerous but efficient system of collection, replacing the lax earlier system. Offenses were to be tried in admiralty courts, without a jury. These administrative provisions were more burdensome than the tax itself and called forth from John Dickinson, a conservative, English-educated Philadelphia lawyer, a series of "Farmer's Letters," published in colonial newspapers that expressed colonial concerns. In one passage, Dickinson wrote: "We are but parts of a whole; and therefore, there must exist a power somewhere to preside, and preserve the connexion in due order. This power is lodged in the Parliament: and we are as much dependent on Great Britain as a perfectly free people can be on another."[2]

Historian Samuel Eliot Morison observes that this remark "shows that Dickinson was moving, somewhat fumblingly, toward the principle of Federalism which became implicit in the American Revolution and explicit in the Constitution of 1787. 'We are as much dependent on Great Britain as a perfectly free people can be on another.' In other words, Parliament as the supreme legislature of the Empire has certain distinct powers over the Colonies; but they retain the residue, corresponding to state rights."[3]

The Townshend Acts proved to be the spark that began the fire of anti-British sentiment, especially in Massachusetts where such revolutionary thinking by agitators such as Samuel Adams, promulgated through the Sons of Liberty, and supported by familiar names such as Paul Revere, John Hancock, Joseph Warren, and James Otis, became dominant. The years 1768 to 1770 saw the rise of the nonimportation movement, an effort to boycott British goods that spread throughout the colonies. Yale students renounced imported wines, Harvard students gave up tea, and students at the College of New Jersey (later Princeton) wore homespun rather than imported cloth.

The Townshend Acts were repealed in 1770, with the exception of the tax on the importation of tea. Ironically, the repeal of the acts occurred on the same day as a confrontation in Boston between about twenty British soldiers and a taunting, stone-throwing mob of several hundred men and boys who so provoked the patience of the Redcoats that several fired on the mob, killing three and mortally wounding two. "The Boston Massacre," as it was quickly termed by the colonial radicals, escalated the bad feelings to new heights of animosity.

When news of the repeal of the Townshend duties reached the colonies and the nonimportation acts collapsed as a result, a new wave of prosperity set in, and a few years of relative calm followed. The calm was a temporary lull, however, as political disagreements between the more radical leaders in Boston and the Royal Governor, Thomas Hutchinson, led to the appoint-

ment by the Boston Town Meeting of a "Committee of Correspondence" whose duty was to coordinate, with similar committees elsewhere, the defense of the colonists' liberty. The Committees of Correspondence spread rapidly after the *Gaspee* affair, the burning of a British revenue cutter that ran aground in Narragansett Bay and the beating of her crew by local patriots. The *Gaspee* incident provoked a strong reaction from British law enforcement agencies and an effort to find the culprits and send them to England for trial. The British response was perceived by the colonists as a violation of one of their most sacred rights of English liberty, the right to a trial by a jury of their own community. This provoked the Virginia House of Burgesses to appoint a Committee of Correspondence that included Patrick Henry, Thomas Jefferson, and Richard Henry Lee; by 1774 twelve of the colonies had similar committees. The committees functioned as an extra-legal organization ready to promote insurrection when the normal means of government failed.

The ongoing irritation relating to the importing of tea led, in December of 1773, to the Boston Tea Party, which goaded the British Parliament, in 1774, into the punitive and repressive responses known as the Coercive Acts, blockading Boston to exact a payment for lost tea and empowering the Royal Governors to quarter British soldiers in private homes. Such British insensitivity and the repeated impositions by England on what were viewed by the colonists as their English rights were directly responsible for incorporation into the Constitution of the Bill of Rights, the first ten amendments, which set forth such fundamental rights as freedom of speech, press, assembly, and religion, and trial by jury.

The effect of the British legislation was to galvanize the Committees of Correspondence to organize such effective resistance that (1) the authority of the Royal Governor was for practical purposes confined to Boston, and (2) the commonwealth was virtually independent beyond his immediate reach. It also rallied the other colonies to send relief assistance in the form of food and money to the beleaguered Bostonians. The Virginia Assembly, before being dissolved by the Royal Governor, denounced the occupation of Boston as a "hostile invasion" and "an attack made on all British America," and through its Committee of Correspondence, which it had directed to exchange views with similar committees in the other colonies, it summoned the First Continental Congress, which met at Philadelphia on September 5, 1774. This assemblage, representing all of the colonies but Georgia, was comprised of members chosen by revolutionary conventions or committees and "evolved into a federal government of a nation at war."[4]

Other efforts to reconcile the issue of power between Great Britain and its rebellious colonies died when, on the night of April 18–19, 1775, Governor Gage dispatched a detail of Redcoats to destroy patriot arms in Concord, an event immortalized in Longfellow's poem, "The Midnight Ride of Paul Revere." By the time the Second Continental Congress met on May 10, Ethan Allen and his Green Mountain Boys had crossed Lake Champlain, taken Fort Ticonderoga and Crown Point, and sent a stand of British colors to decorate Independence Hall. Independence itself, however, was still nearly fourteen months away. The Second Continental Congress created a provincial army and navy, sent diplomatic agents to Europe, and assumed power over Indian relations; but it continued to work and hope for a change of heart, or government, in Great Britain that would bring the incipient conflict to a satisfactory end. The English ties that bound American society and the biblical command to submit to God-ordained governments and honor the king were more troubling to our revolutionary forebears than we often imagine. The Battle of Bunker Hill, the lifting of the British siege of Boston by the efforts of the Continental Army commanded by General Washington, and the unsuccessful invasion of Quebec by General Richard Montgomery and Benedict Arnold all occurred before the colonies declared their independence.

B. THE DECLARATION OF INDEPENDENCE

The failure of both military and diplomatic efforts to bring about a reconciliation and the escalating independence fervor in the colonies concluded on July 4, 1776, with the adoption by the Second Continental Congress of the Declaration of Independence. The stirring words have been often read and recited, inspiring the best in patriotism and commitment to human rights and ideals. Our purpose for examining the Declaration of Independence, however, is not to examine the political philosophy, patriotic inspiration, or ideals reflected in this most remarkable document but rather to see what it reveals about the origins of the American legal system.

The Declaration of Independence twice refers to "the United States of America," the first time these words are used. Whether the authors' intent was to use the term as a singular or plural noun remains unclear. The Preamble refers to the colonists as "one people," but the conclusion declares in the plural, "That these United Colonies are, and of Right ought to be Free and Independent States: that they are Absolved from all Allegiance to the British Crown, and all political connection between them and the State of Great Britain, is and ought to be totally dissolved: and that as Free and Independent States, they have full Power to levy War, conclude Peace and contract Alliances, establish Commerce, and to do all other Acts and Things which Independent States may of right do."

Did the colonies, now states, by the Declaration become thirteen sovereign nations who later submitted by voluntary delegation to the limited authority of the federal government, or did they declare a new nation which assumed immediately the sovereign authority of a central government? The growth of national sentiment, exigent needs for national government over the next two centuries, the success of the North in the American Civil War, and later decisions of the United States Supreme Court support the latter view. For many of the purposes of the American legal system, the former view was from the beginning and is still the governing rule. One of the most fundamental principles of understanding the American legal system is understanding that the sovereign and final authority in most fields of law with which Americans deal in their everyday lives, subject to certain limitations imposed by the U.S. Constitution, is the state, not the federal, government. These original thirteen, now fifty, sovereignties retain and act upon today, for most purposes of the legal system, the power "to do all other Acts and Things which Independent States may of right do."

C. THE ARTICLES OF CONFEDERATION

The Second Continental Congress, with no formal authority, did those things necessary to conduct a war that, despite the popularity of the cause of independence, was unpopular among the people. Lacking the power to draft, it set quotas for each state. The states, in general, passed the responsibility to counties or towns, which often bid against each other to fill their quotas. Rhode Island bought slaves to fill its quota and sent the bill for them to Philadelphia. Nevertheless, local militia and farmers often turned out to fight whenever the British army put in an appearance, a phenomenon unknown to European armies, and this was a major factor in the colonial military success.

The Continental Congress also lacked the power to tax, and the Continental Army was often poorly fed and clothed. The war was financed largely by bills of credit issued by the Continental Congress or the states, domestic loans, and requisitions from the states. In short, it was financed on borrowed money by a revolutionary government that was at war and had no guarantee that it would survive and no clear authority to raise the money if it did.

The informal union, which had no clearly stated authority for the central government, carried the states through the war almost to the surrender of Cornwallis at Yorktown in November of 1781. In March of that year, the Maryland legislature became the last to ratify the Articles of Confederation, which had been adopted by Congress in 1777. The Articles did little more than ratify what the Continental Congress had been doing all along. It provided for the representation of each state by from two to seven members of its choice but with only one vote per

state. Nine votes were required for deciding important issues such as declaring war, making treaties, borrowing money, and raising an armed force. Five executive departments were created under the power of Congress: Foreign Affairs, Finance, War, Admiralty, and a Post Office. Consistent with the "states' rights" view of the Declaration of Independence, the independence and sovereignty of the states were preserved and the central government received only certain limited powers that the colonies had acknowledged belonged to the king and Parliament. It did not acquire the power to tax or to limit the states' rights to set customs duties. There was no federal judiciary and no means created to enforce such powers as the central government had. Unanimous consent of the members was required for any amendment.

The difficulties inherent in the Confederation and the paralysis resulting from the need for unanimity became apparent in the course of the 1780s. The absence of a power to tax and the states' possession of the power to impose customs duties impeded any effective functioning of the central government and created disunity among the states. On February 21, 1787, Congress invited the states to appoint delegates to a convention to be held in Philadelphia "for the sole and express purpose of revising the Articles of Confederation." This led to the Federal Convention which met in Philadelphia from May 25 to September 17, 1787, and drafted the Constitution, which came into effect when New Hampshire became the ninth state to ratify it on June 21, 1789. Virginia, New York, and North Carolina had ratified the Constitution and joined the union by the end of the year. Rhode Island did not address the issue until 1790 but became at that time the last of the thirteen states to approve the federal Constitution.

REFERENCES

Morison, Samuel Eliot. *The Oxford History of the American People* (New York: Oxford University Press, 1965).

Peltason, J. W. *Corwin and Peltason's Understanding the Constitution* (New York: Holt, Rinehart & Winston, 1985).

CHAPTER 2

The U.S. Constitutional System

A. THE CONSTITUTIONAL FOUNDATION: SEPARATION OF POWERS

When religious people and institutions meet their government, it may wear a variety of hats. Authority may be state or federal, enacting or enforcing laws with either national, state, or more local application. In either case, it may be executive power in the form of the law enforcement and administrative agencies that implement laws; legislative power that enacts, modifies, and repeals laws; or judicial power that resolves controversies. Where legal authority resides with respect to a given issue is determined, in the first instance, by the United States Constitution, which must be understood to understand the American legal system.

The Constitution is the legal system's foundational defining document, the source to which one turns when fundamental questions need to be answered, the limits of acceptability defined, and the first principles analytically applied to deal with new issues.

Some would draw an analogy between the Constitution and the Bible, but such a comparison is imperfect. The Constitution can be amended, although the process is arduous and has seldom been successfully accomplished, whereas the canon of Scripture, even if a point of disagreement among Christians, is closed. The Constitution has a final arbiter, the United States Supreme Court, but there is no human authority universally acknowledged to have the last word on scriptural interpretation. Both must be, and have been, applied to give guidance to situations never dreamed of by their human authors, but notions of constitutional law and the meaning of constitutional language have undoubtedly altered with time in ways that orthodox Christians, at least, would never find acceptable for the Bible.

Much has been written, and appropriately so, on the wisdom and perspicacity of the authors of our Constitution who gave the new republic what is today the oldest written constitution among nations, a document that has served the nation well for over two hundred years, and, with the exception of the Civil War period, has been the foundation of a broad consensus among the American people on the nature of their government. The success of the Constitution may rest in large measure on its authors' understanding of the concept of inherent human sinfulness.

James Madison did not doubt that sinfulness. The man who became our fourth president and was one of the principal architects of the United States Constitution and the Bill of Rights was one of the authors of a series of papers, published in 1787 and 1788, that became known as the *Federalist Papers*. They discussed the proposed new Constitution and whether or not the pivotal state of New York should ratify it. Consider Madison's words in *The Federalist,* No. 51:

But the great security against a gradual concentration of the several powers of the same department, consists in giving to those who administer each department the necessary constitutional means and personal motives to resist encroachments of the others. The provision for defence must in this, as in all other cases, be made commensurate to the danger of attack. Ambition must be made to counteract ambition. The interest of the man must be connected with the constitutional rights of the place. It may be a reflection on human nature, that such devices should be necessary to control the abuses of government. But what is government itself, but the greatest of all reflections on human nature? If men were angels, no government would be necessary. If angels were to govern men, neither external nor internal controls on government would be necessary. In framing a government that is to be administered by men over men, the great difficulty lies in this: you must first enable the government to control the governed; and in the next place oblige it to control itself. A dependence on the people is, no doubt, the primary control on the government; but experience has taught mankind the necessity of auxiliary precautions.

This policy of supplying, by opposite and rival interests, the defect of better motives might be traced through the whole system of human affairs, private as well as public. We see it particularly displayed in all the subordinate distributions of power, where the constant aim is to divide and arrange the several offices in such a manner as that each may be a check on the other—that the private interest of every individual may be a sentinel over the public rights. These inventions of prudence cannot be less requisite in the distribution of the supreme powers of the State. . . .

There are, moreover, two considerations particularly applicable to the federal system of America, which place that system in a very interesting point of view.

First. In a single republic, all the power surrendered by the people is submitted to the administration of a single government; and the usurpations are guarded against by a division of the government into distinct and separate departments. In the compound republic of America, the power surrendered by the people is first divided between two distinct governments, and then the portion allotted to each subdivided among distinct and separate departments. Hence a double security arises to the rights of the people. The different governments will control each other, at the same time that each will be controlled by itself.

Second. It is of great importance in a republic not only to guard the society against the oppression of its rulers, but to guard one part of the society against the injustice of the other part. Different interests necessarily exist in different classes of citizens. If a majority be united by a common interest, the rights of the minority will be insecure. There are but two methods of providing against this evil: the one by creating a will in the community independent of the majority that is, of the society itself; the other by comprehending in the society so many separate descriptions of citizens as will render an unjust combination of a majority of the whole very improbable, if not impracticable. The first method prevails in all governments possessing an hereditary or self-appointed authority. This, at best, is but a precarious security; because a power independent of the society may as well espouse the unjust views of the major, as the rightful interests of the minor party, and may possibly be turned against both parties. The second method will be exemplified in the federal republic of the United States.[1]

More than a faint echo of Paul's letter to the Romans can be heard: "There is no one righteous, not even one" and "all have sinned and fall short of the glory of God" (Rom. 3:10, 23).

The Constitution addresses this defect in the nature of man by two distinct separations of power: (1) between the states and the federal government; and (2) between the branches of the federal government.

Every state, in turn, has its own constitution which follows (or, for the original thirteen colonies, generally precedes) the federal model in the separation and balance between the branches of the government.

An examination of these two fundamental separations of power will provide an understanding of how the legal system comes together.

B. FEDERALISM: THE SEPARATION OF POWERS BETWEEN THE STATE AND FEDERAL GOVERNMENTS

Federal law may command the headlines, but it remains a fact that much—probably most—of the law that religious people encounter in establishing and maintaining their institutions is state law. This law, covering much of the day-to-day business of life, has no national uniformity and has developed separately in the fifty sovereign states. While there is much commonality of principles between them, and all are subject to the overriding principles of the U.S. Constitution, each state is free to, and does, develop and implement its own law in such areas as incorporation, liability for personal injuries, property transfer, land use, and contracts. Where state and federal authority divide is determined by the separation of powers between them established by the U.S. Constitution.

A copy of the Constitution is included in this book as Appendix A. The reader may want to take a few minutes to read it now. It is not very long. Some parts are archaic and of no current concern—who now worries about letters of marque and reprisal?[2] Other parts are embarrassing—the apportionment of representatives is according to population, which is counted by adding "the whole Number of free Persons including those

bound to Service for a Term of Years and excluding Indians not taxed," and "three fifths of all other Persons," that is, slaves.[3] It would be another half-century before the ringing principles of the Declaration of Independence would come into focus in the American mind with respect to slavery.

The Constitution consists of seven articles and twenty-seven amendments, the first ten of which, known as the Bill of Rights and consisting of a statement of certain fundamental freedoms presumed in the fight for liberty, were adopted within two years after the Constitution itself was ratified. The seven original articles set forth the executive power (Article I), the legislative power (Article II), the judicial power (Article III), relations between the states and the state and federal governments (Article IV), the process of amending the Constitution (Article V), a collection of measures the most important of which is the Supremacy Clause (Article VI), and the ratification provision (Article VII).

Among the amendments, the most important after the Bill of Rights is the Fourteenth Amendment, one of a series enacted after the Civil War to ensure the rights of the newly freed slaves. It contains the language requiring states to extend "equal protection of the law" to all and forbidding them to "deprive any person of life, liberty, or property, without due process of law." The principal clauses defining the separation of powers between state and federal governments are contained in Article VI and the Tenth Amendment.

1. The Tenth Amendment

The Tenth Amendment, the last entry in the Bill of Rights, reads as follows:

The powers not delegated to the United States by the Constitution, nor prohibited by it to the States, are reserved to the States respectively, or to the people.

The principle succinctly stated in the Tenth Amendment is implicit in the entire Constitution. Just in case some future generation should miss the point, however, the Bill of Rights concludes by making it clear. The federal government is a government of delegated powers. Those powers that are not delegated to it by the Constitution (and nothing else), it does not have. All of those powers that the Constitution does not give the federal government remain in the states (unless the Constitution prohibits that power) or the people. Since many areas of law and functions of the legal system are not delegated to the federal government by the Constitution, this amendment makes it clear that they repose in the states. The federal government is a created sovereign which was created by thirteen independent sovereigns and possesses only the powers upon which those thirteen independent sovereigns agreed. The powers reserved to the states are often called the "police powers." The term has nothing to do with law enforcement officers. It refers to the inherent power of the people acting through their state governments to legislate measures for the health, safety, welfare, and morals of the populace. One check on the validity of state legislation is to ask whether it is truly within the police power. Despite the breadth of the power, laws of states or their subordinate units have occasionally failed the test.[4]

The history of the understanding of the Tenth Amendment by the Supreme Court in some measure reflects the development of the nation. Early construction of the Constitution upheld an expansive view of federal authority under the delegated powers of the Constitution, notwithstanding the Tenth Amendment. Chief Justice John Marshall in the 1819 case of *McCulloch v. Maryland*,[5] upheld the power of Congress to create a national bank despite the absence of any express power in the Constitution to do so, finding that the Constitution granted the federal government implied power to do so in order to carry out its specifically delegated powers to "raise and support armies" and "borrow money on the credit of the United States." He found constitutional support for his approach in the grant to Congress of the power to "make all Laws which shall be necessary and proper for carrying into execution the foregoing Powers."[6]

Marshall's expansive view of federal power did not prevail on the Court for another century. He was succeeded by states' rights–oriented judges who took a narrower view of federal power, striking down much congressional legislation addressing social and economic problems which the Congress viewed as within its power under the provision known as the Commerce Clause: "to regulate commerce . . . among the several states. . . ." In the Court's view, this referred only to goods actually in transit across state lines. The factories that produced them were not engaged in interstate commerce and not subject to federal regulation, nor were the myriad other activities affecting, and affected by, interstate commerce.

The growth and complexity of an interdependent national economy created an ever-growing need for regulation at the federal level. The Great Depression of the 1930s brought the issue to a crisis point. The Court, against increasing political resistance and resentment, had found unconstitutional various New Deal regulatory plans to address the problems. In 1937, the constitutional dam broke with the decision in *National Labor Relations Board v. Jones and Laughlin Steel Corp.*[7] There the Court upheld, as a constitutional exercise of congressional power under the Commerce Clause, legislation establishing the National Labor Relations Board and authorizing it to regulate labor relations. The Court gave a broad reading to the right to regulate commerce, extending it to activities within a state that "have such a close and substantial relationship to interstate commerce that their control is essential or appropriate to protect that commerce from burdens or obstructions."[8] With this expansive view of its power constitutionally legitimized by the Court under the Commerce Clause, the Congress embarked on a broad range of regulatory legislation and expansion of the activities of the federal government well familiar to us today. Thus for the last half century, the applicability of the Tenth Amendment has been limited to its original intent, and the Court has been more willing to find elsewhere in the Constitution express or implicit delegations of power to the federal government to regulate an increasingly integrated and complex national economy.

2. The Supremacy Clause and the Problem of Preemption

Article VI contains in the Supremacy Clause the counterpoint to the Tenth Amendment:

This Constitution, and the Laws of the United States which shall be made in Pursuance thereof; and all Treaties made, or which shall be made, under the Authority of the United States, shall be the supreme Law of the land; and the Judges in every State shall be bound thereby, any Thing in the Constitution or Laws of any State to the Contrary notwithstanding.

Article VI goes on to require, among other things, that members of state legislatures and executive and judicial officers of the several states "shall be bound by Oath or Affirmation, to support this Constitution." Federal law is the supreme law of the land and the executive, legislative, and judicial authorities of the states as well as the federal government are bound by oath to uphold it.

The integration, interdependence, and complexity of national life in a technological age have resulted in the tilting of the scales of federalism toward the Supremacy Clause and away from the reserved powers of the states. Courts have found it easier to find national powers implied from those expressly granted, resulting from the combination of enumerated powers, or inherent in the very existence of the national government. Nonetheless, it remains that much of the law that religious people may encounter in their administration of religious organizations will be state laws enacted under the states' reserved or police powers functioning in areas in which the federal government may not act or has not acted. The legislatures of the original thirteen, now fifty, sovereigns still write the laws that govern most areas of their citizens' lives, and their courts shape and form the law of each of these sovereigns to their own design.

a. The Problem of Preemption

But although federal law and the federal Constitution make up the supreme law of the land to which all state laws and constitutions are subject, it is not always clear whether federal authority or legislation in a particular field is exclusive of that of the states, that is, that it precludes any right of the states to enact their own laws in the field altogether, or whether federal law is merely supreme in the sense of having priority where laws may conflict. This is the problem of preemption.

The preemption problem has been resolved by courts on a case-by-case basis. In general, the issue turns on an analysis of whether the federal statute has "occupied a field in which the States are otherwise free to legislate" by a "scheme of federal legislation" which "is so pervasive as to make reasonable the inference that Congress left no room for the States to supplement it" or whether the federal statutes "touch a field in which the federal interest is so dominant that the federal system [must] be assumed to preclude enforcement of state laws on the same subject," or whether enforcement of state law would present "a serious danger of conflict with the administration of the federal program."[9] In many fields, for example, including most areas of environmental and health and safety regulation, states are free to enact legislation in the field and indeed may regulate more stringently than the federal government has chosen to do.

3. No Other Sovereignties

There are no other sovereigns in this country than the state and federal governments, and there are no other sources of governmental power. When we move from the state level of government down to municipal, county, and other local governmental units, it is a universal rule that all such entities are the creatures of the state, that is, they are created by the sovereign state, subordinate to it, and possess only such powers as are granted to them by the state. Municipal laws that do not act within the power granted by the state are invalid. Unlike the delegated powers of the federal government, powers granted to the subordinate units of the state may be altered or taken away at will by the state.[10] Indeed, the state can create new subordinate units of government and divide or consolidate those that exist. The problem of preemption discussed above with respect to the authority of the state and federal governments arises again with respect to local governmental bodies making law in the same field as the state and is resolved in the same way.

4. Relations between the States

The Constitution also has something to say about how the states are to relate to each other. Article IV, Section I provides "Full Faith and Credit shall be given in each State to the public Acts, Records, and judicial Proceedings of every other State. And the Congress may by general Laws prescribe the Manner in which such Acts, Records, and Proceedings shall be proved, and the Effect thereof."

Section II of Article IV provides, in part, that "the Citizens of each State shall be entitled to all Privileges and Immunities of Citizens in the several States."

The Full Faith and Credit Clause has its greatest application with respect to judicial decisions. A party who has otherwise properly obtained a judicial decision in his or her favor in one state is entitled to have that decision enforced or given "full faith and credit" by the courts of all the states without having to relitigate the matter again. The issue in such cases is not whether the court rendering the decision made a right or wrong decision but, rather, whether it had the authority to render the decision at all, that is, whether it had jurisdiction over the matter and the party against whom the decision is later sought to be enforced.

The Privileges and Immunities Clause, which is essentially repeated in the Fourteenth Amendment, simply guarantees that states will not discriminate against citizens of other states, although states can have laws that apply differentially when there are otherwise valid reasons for doing so.

To summarize then, our Constitution creates a federal government, sovereign in the spheres delegated to it in the Constitution by the sovereign states. Power not delegated to the federal government remains in the states. Since 1937, Supreme Court rulings have greatly expanded the scope of federal power as set forth in the Constitution, enabling the federal government to bring within national regulation and control those areas of national life affecting, even if indirectly, interstate commerce and other constitutionally delegated powers. States retain the right to enact laws in all areas not exclusively delegated to the federal government. Unless Congress has enacted pervasive federal legislation that preempts the states' dual or concurrent power, states may regulate along with the federal government and more stringently.

Where there is constitutionally acceptable federal law, it is supreme, that is, it governs over any contrary state law. There are no sovereignties other than the state and federal governments; county, municipal, and other lesser units of government are creations of the states and possess only such powers as the states give them. States are required to honor judicial decisions made in the other states if the deciding court had the power to do so.

While federal regulation has had an ever-increasing reach into church affairs, many areas of law remain primarily or entirely governed by state law.

C. SEPARATION OF POWERS: THE THREE BRANCHES OF GOVERNMENT

Just as religious people may encounter either state or federal laws, enacted and administered by separate but sometimes overlapping sovereignties, so may they encounter the legal process in any of the three governmental branches—executive, legislative, and judicial.

James Madison's second device to prevent the undue concentration or the arbitrary exercise of power was the division of powers within the national sovereignty among the legislative, executive, and judicial branches. The powers of each are articulated respectively in the First, Second, and Third Articles of the Constitution. This separation of powers is among departments of the government that are constitutionally and politically independent of one another in some respects, but dependent in others. Federal judges, for example, are appointed by the president with the consent of the Senate, but, once appointed, have no obligations to either. Congressional legislation can be vetoed by the president, but the veto can be overridden by a sufficient majority. The three branches and the relations between them constitute the "checks and balances" that prevent an excessive accumulation of power by any person or group.

1. The Legislative Power: Article I

Article I of the Constitution vests "all legislative powers herein granted" in the Congress consisting of a Senate and House of Representatives. The function of the legislative branch is to legislate, to write the laws or statutes. Section 8 of Article I enumerates specific powers of the Congress, the source of federal authority to legislate in such areas as bankruptcy, patent law, copyright law, and postal service. These enumerated powers do not include many areas in which the federal government has in fact legislated and regulated. There is, for example, no reference to the environment, labor laws, Social Security, antidiscrimination provisions, or subsidized housing. The power to legislate in these areas is largely the result of the expansion and reach of federal law under the Commerce Clause, which has provided sufficient rationale for the intrusion of federal legislation into innumerable areas of endeavor, as growth in population, communication, and transportation has made the nation an increasingly interrelated and integrated economic entity. Few indeed are the areas of activity that are fully contained within a single state, the impact of which on interstate commerce is so remote as to preclude federal regulation. The power of regulation does not depend upon physical movement between states but extends to activity that concerns more states than one, or burdens or impacts that activity sufficiently. Activities may be in "commerce" although noncommercial.

Among the activities regulated by Congress under the Commerce Clause are navigation and navigable waters; interstate carriers of all kinds, including trains, airplanes, buses, trucks, and pipelines; racial and other forms of discrimination; protection of workers; regulation of the sale of goods; controlling crop production and marketing of agricultural products; controlling labor relations and standards; and protecting consumers against dangers to health and pocketbook.

2. The Executive Power: Article II

When does the church meet the administrative agencies of the executive branch? In licensing, health, and safety regulation of church-supported schools, day care centers, or providers of social services;[11] in compliance regulations related to government grants for services that can constitutionally be funded through religious organizations;[12] in reporting requirements related to child abuse;[13] in building, zoning, planning, landmark, and other land-use control agencies;[14] in taxing agencies administering and interpreting the scope of taxation and, especially, exemptions;[15] in the plethora of agencies concerned with employment issues—minimum wages, antidiscrimination, occupational safety, and health.[16] When the government knocks on the church door, it is usually the hand of the executive branch that is knocking.

The executive branch is headed by the president, whose task is to execute faithfully the laws passed by the Congress. To do so, the executive branch requires millions of employees; in fact, the largest number of employees of the federal government are employed by the executive branch. The Defense Department, the Internal Revenue Service (IRS), the federal law enforcement agencies—the Federal Bureau of Investigation (FBI) and the Department of Justice, the Environmental Protection Agency (EPA), and the Social Security Administration (SSA) are parts of the executive branch of the government.

One of the most significant functions of the executive branch is broadly known as "administrative law." It has become common for Congress, recognizing the need for a system of implementation, regulation, and enforcement of the legislation which it passes, to establish administrative agencies in the executive branch and empower them to adopt rules and regulations. The rules or regulations adopted by administrative agencies must implement the statutes under which they are adopted. Agencies cannot write new laws; that is the Congress's job. Frequently, however, the law is written very broadly, and an agency has great discretion in the rules and regulations promulgated to implement it. Federal legislation, for example, sets forth extensive regulatory responsibilities with respect to hazardous waste but does not specify what waste is hazardous. Identifying the specific materials considered to be hazardous waste is left, in this case, to the EPA to develop by its rules and regulations.

This process allows administrative agencies to use their expertise to develop detailed rules implementing legislation that Congress lacks the time and expertise to do. Before finalizing the rules, agencies publish drafts, receive comments, and allow input from the interested public. Administrative law is a growing part of the legal system because of the proliferation of such agencies and the increasing complexity of the laws they administer.

Administrative agencies often have hearings and render decisions on issues and parties that are subject to their regulation. Here they are acting in a "quasi-judicial" capacity. As with rule making, quasi-judicial activities of the agencies serve a dual function: (1) they enable the decision makers to bring technical expertise in the regulated field, expertise not possessed by a court, to bear on the issues; and (2) they relieve courts of the substantial burdens this highly specialized workload would impose. Administrative agencies are not required to follow the rules of evidence that are binding on courts or the rules of "due process" that apply to courts, although they may do so if they choose. They are, however, required to meet such minimum standards of "administrative due process" as insuring that parties have notice of proceedings and an opportunity to be heard on matters affecting them, and they may not act beyond their jurisdiction, that is, beyond their legislative or statutory authority. Agencies may have investigatory powers to initiate proceedings themselves. A party may also be required to ask for an agency's action, when seeking approval required for a regulated action the party wants to take. Agency decisions are appealable

to courts—sometimes for a "trial de novo," that is, a complete rehearing of the issue, but more often for the same kind of review given by appeals courts to trial court decisions—to determine if the agency correctly followed the law, acted within its power, was unaffected by bias or prejudice, and had a rational basis for its decision.

3. The Judicial Power: Article III

Article III, Section 1 provides that "the judicial power of the United States shall be vested in one Supreme Court, and in such inferior courts as the Congress may from time to time ordain and establish."

The judicial power of the United States, like the legislative power, extends only to those areas delegated by the Constitution. For the most part, these fall into two broad categories:

1. *Federal question.* Cases and controversies arising under the Constitution or laws of the United States.
2. *Diversity jurisdiction.* Controversies between citizens of different states, currently limited by Congress to matters in which the amount at issue is at least $50,000.

State courts have the right to hear these cases also, except in a few limited areas in which Congress has given exclusive jurisdiction to the federal courts. Parties sued in a state court in a case that could have been brought in federal court have the right to "remove" their case, that is, have it transferred, to federal court if they act promptly when the suit is brought.

Congress has implemented its power to create inferior courts and tribunals by instituting a three-tiered federal judicial system. The lowest tier or level is the United States District Court, sometimes called the Federal District Court. There are over ninety federal judicial districts in the United States, at least one in each state. If there is only one, it coincides with the state boundaries. Judicial districts do not overlap state boundaries, with minor exceptions. Populous states such as New York and California have several United States

District Courts, each with authority over a geographically distinct area identified in its title. The United States District Court for the District of Northern California, for example, sits in San Francisco; the United States District Court for the Southern District of New York sits in Manhattan. Each court sits in a courthouse or federal building located in a convenient municipality within the geographical district, typically either the state capital or the city that is the population center of the district.

The United States District Courts are the trial courts of the federal system. With the minor and limited exception of some cases in which the United States Supreme Court has original jurisdiction, within the federal court system it is only in the United States District Courts that lawsuits originate, evidence is taken, and facts contested. Federal jury trials occur only in the district courts.

Final judgments of the U. S. District Courts are subject to appeal to the middle level of the federal judicial system, the Courts of Appeals. The Courts of Appeals are divided into numbered "circuits" or geographic districts and are often referred to as Circuit Courts of Appeals. The "circuit" title harks back to the days when judges "rode circuit," moving about, literally riding in circuits from place to place within the territory of their jurisdiction to hear cases. In those days it was considered easier to move the judge to the people than to move the people and their attorneys to the judge. Each Circuit Court of Appeals hears cases appealed from the U.S. District Courts in the states constituting its designated area. The First Circuit Court of Appeals, for example, hears cases appealed from the U.S. District Courts in Maine, New Hampshire, Massachusetts, Rhode Island, and Puerto Rico. The Second Circuit Court of Appeals embraces Vermont, Connecticut, New York, and the U.S. Virgin Islands, and so on across the country for eleven geographic circuits. There is also a Circuit Court of Appeals for the District of Columbia, and one known as the Federal Circuit, which hears certain cases of unique federal jurisdiction, such as patents and federal trademark issues.

Appeals from the Circuit Courts of Appeals go to the final and highest tier of the judicial system, the U.S. Supreme Court. In certain cases, such as when a state court declares a federal law unconstitutional or a federal court declares a state law unconstitutional, the aggrieved party has a right to appeal to the Supreme Court. In most cases, however, appeal is by a procedure known as *certiorari,* in which the appealing party petitions the Supreme Court to hear the matter, presenting the reasons it is appropriate for consideration. Granting certiorari simply means the Supreme Court will hear the appeal. Certiorari is granted in only a small percentage of the cases in which it is requested, when at least four of the justices consider the issue to be of sufficient importance to merit the Court's attention. Because the same or similar issues often arise in more than one circuit and the circuit courts do not always agree on the answer, there are occasionally situations in which the law in the federal courts of one or more circuits is in conflict with the law in another circuit or circuits. The Supreme Court may grant certiorari in matters which may not be of compelling public interest to resolve conflicts between the circuits and establish a uniformity of federal law.

a. The Power of Judicial Review

The election of 1800 was as raucous and scurrilous a campaign as can be imagined. The Federalist Party had renominated President John Adams, the Republicans, Thomas Jefferson. In those days, politicians did not make speeches or even release press statements. They played coy, waiting for the call to service from their country. Their surrogates, however, did the mudslinging for them; they accused Jefferson of being a Jacobin,[17] an atheist, and a French agent, and Adams of being an autocrat and admirer of the British monarchy. When the dust had settled, the Republicans had triumphed, and Jefferson was to succeed Adams as president. The Federalists, before leaving office, provided for their supporters by creating a number of new judicial posts, including forty-two justices of the peace for the District of Columbia to which the retiring President Adams, in a series of "midnight appointments," appointed forty-two Federalists, among them one William Marbury. Some of the commissions for these new appointments, Marbury's among them, were not delivered before Jefferson assumed office. The new president instructed his secretary of state, James Madison, not to deliver certain of these commissions, Marbury's being again among them. Marbury sought the release of the commission by a suit initiated in the Supreme Court under the authority of the Judiciary Act of 1789, which had given the Supreme Court power to issue writs of *mandamus* to persons holding office under the authority of the United States.[18] It was not clear that the Republican administration would obey a court order to deliver the commission even if Marbury's suit succeeded. The Court, speaking through Chief Justice John Marshall, who, ironically, had been Adams's secretary of state, resolved the political crisis by finding the section of the Judiciary Act that granted the Supreme Court authority to issue writs of *mandamus*, on which Marbury relied, to be in conflict with the Constitution which in Article III, Section 2, limited the Court's original jurisdiction[19] to cases affecting "ambassadors, other public Ministers and Consuls, and those in which a State shall be Party." Because it was unconstitutional, it was unenforceable and of no effect, and Marbury lost his suit.

The result of the Federalist chief justice denying the congressionally mandated rights of the Federalist would-be justice of the peace and leaving Republican defiance intact was to establish another of the most fundamental principles of our constitutional government—the principle of judicial review. This principle asserts that the power to determine whether a law is in keeping with the Constitution is a power that resides in the courts and, ultimately, of course, in the Supreme Court. For the first fourteen years of the nation's existence under the Constitution, the issue of who was the final arbiter of the constitutionality of laws was unresolved, although it is widely thought that most of the framers intended the result Marshall reached. While Marshall's 1803 decision in *Marbury v. Madison* has been criticized on a variety of logical, legal, and

political grounds, it has become one of the most fundamental tenets of the legal system. The Supreme Court is the final arbiter of what is and is not constitutional under the U.S. Constitution, whether the rules are written by Congress or the states, as much today as in 1803. The principle is so well-established and accepted that it may as well be directly written into the Constitution. Thus litigation has often played as important a role in policy making as legislation, and advocates who have lost a battle against new laws in the legislative arena can have another bite at the apple in the judicial arena by attacking the constitutionality of the legislation. The Supreme Court is the last arbiter, the plate umpire, as it were, in the constitutional system, whose final unappealable decision declares the policy "safe" or "out" when the runner slides into home plate.

b. The Common Law and the Value of Precedent

Courts are responsible to heed, first, the Constitution and, second, any applicable statutes, in resolving the cases and controversies that come before them. Often, however, the meaning of those written guides is unclear, and it is the business of the courts to interpret as well as apply them.

Frequently, however, issues arise that the Constitution and legislation simply do not address. These are resolved by looking to the *common law*, the record of court decisions and opinions on similar facts and issues that have previously arisen. The common law developed in the English courts and was brought here by the colonists, where it took root and grew quite independently of its English forebears. For the most part, the common law deals with the areas of law people have always encountered in day-to-day life, matters such as contracts, negligence, real estate, and inheritance. It is almost entirely state law and differs in some particulars from state to state.

Prior to 1938, federal courts often endeavored to apply their own notion of common law, deriving it from the idea still popular among those not legally literate that there is a "general law" that transcends the law of the state in which they are located. In the 1938 case of *Erie Railroad Co. v.*

Tompkins,[20] the Supreme Court put an end to the fiction of "general law," declaring that there is no federal common law, because the subjects of common law are not specifically delegated to the national government. With the exception of those limited areas controlled by the Constitution or when federal legislation has been introduced that may modify common-law rules, the common law still governs and is the law formed by state—not federal—courts. The obligation of a federal court dealing with a common-law issue is to follow the state law that applies, not to decide on a rule for itself. If the state courts have not established a rule, the federal court must examine all relevant state law and decide what it believes the state courts would do if faced with the issue. Even the U.S. Supreme Court may not decide what the law of a state will be; it must follow the state court's interpretation of its own law.

Higher court decisions on issues, whether of constitutional or statutory interpretation or common law, have value as *precedent*; that is, the principles established by the case must be followed to the extent that they are applicable, not just in further proceedings on the litigated case but in all similar cases that arise in the future, by all lower courts in the jurisdiction. Thus all courts must follow the interpretation the U.S. Supreme Court makes of the federal Constitution, federal statutes, and federal law. Decisions of a federal circuit court of appeals must be followed by all federal district courts within the circuit. Decisions by a state's highest court must be followed by all lower courts in the state, and federal courts must follow the highest state court's interpretation of state law.

When a lower court is obliged to follow the law set forth by a higher court to which it is responsible, the precedent is "binding," that is, the lower court has no discretion in the matter. When the decision of interest is from some other court, however, as, for example, if a California decision is used to persuade a Texas court as to the result it should reach, the California decision may be of interest to the Texas court in seeing how another court decided a like situation, but it is not binding. The Texas court can reach an entirely contrary result, concluding that the rule established by the California decision will not be the common law of Texas. Courts are much influenced by precedent, however, even when they are not bound by it. The accumulated wisdom of the thinking of numerous courts on issues and articulated reasons for deciding one way rather than another can be persuasive. Sometimes, however, there are clear policy reasons for different results, and courts may disagree on which is more important, just, or consistent with their own precedent. Much time is spent by lawyers finding precedent that supports the result their client hopes to reach in a case.

c. Law and Equity

There is a distinction still recognized in the American legal system between suits at law and suits in equity. An *action in* or *at law* is simply one in which the relief requested by the plaintiff or complaining party is an award of monetary damages. Typical litigation involving personal injuries, breaches of contract, and the like fall into this category.

A *suit in equity* is a suit in which the complaining party asks the court to enter an order or decree compelling the other party to do or refrain from doing something other than the payment of money. *Injunction* is a term often used for such an order—the court enjoins a party to do or refrain from doing the act in question. A temporary restraining order or preliminary injunction is such an order issued on a temporary basis, to preserve the status quo until the court can more fully evaluate the claim. Courts will usually issue injunctions only when there is "no adequate remedy at law" and the complaining party will suffer "irreparable injury" if the injunction is not granted. This usually this means that monetary damages cannot compensate the complaining party, as in cases involving ownership of unique items of property. Real estate by its nature is considered unique since no piece of real estate is just like another. Hence, disputes over the ownership of real estate can always be the subject of equity cases. For both practical and legal reasons, injunctions are more often issued to prevent a party from taking an action than to compel a party to do so.

In legal history, equity arose out of the authority of the lord chancellor and the ecclesiastical courts in England. In the English system this was a totally separate court system from the law courts. Since most of the American states carried over the English legal system, although without the lord chancellor and ecclesiastical courts, law and equity were separate concepts in the American legal system, and in some states separate courts existed for the two types of suits. Today in most states the same court hears cases in law and equity, usually under the same rules for the legal process. Equity cases are decided by judges, not juries, although parties are in some instances entitled to have an advisory jury to decide on certain issues of fact. An order, decree, or injunction in an equity case, however, is always issued by the judge.

D. STATE GOVERNMENT AND COURTS

Every state has a constitution that establishes state government on a parallel basis to the federal government, with the separation of powers between the three branches and the protection of fundamental rights. A state constitution is as supreme as the federal Constitution, with respect to matters of state law, as long as it does not contradict the U.S. Constitution or laws properly enacted by the U.S. Congress within its constitutional authority. States may *enlarge* people's rights beyond those provided by the U.S. Constitution, but they may not *diminish* the rights it grants. State legislatures are not constrained by the requirement that they act within their delegated powers; they have plenary authority to make law within the broad ambit of the police power unless the U.S. Constitution or their own state constitution forbids it or congressional legislation has occupied the field. State executive branches have the same proliferation of administrative agencies as the federal executive branch, with the same sort of regulatory and quasi-judicial powers as granted by the state legislature and the same limitations on those powers that apply to federal agencies. Commonly, parallel state and federal agencies regulate the same subject matter, some-

times dividing their jurisdiction according to whether the particular matter is interstate or intrastate (within the state) in nature, and sometimes imposing dual layers of regulation on the same subject matter. Often they cooperate in the delegation of regulation from one to the other (usually federal to state) so that the state agency administers federal regulations or their state equivalent.

In the judicial branch, there is always a highest state court and a trial level court where jury trials are held—the state equivalent of the U.S. Supreme Court and federal district courts. Terminology, however, may vary; in New York, for example, the state supreme court is the trial court, and the highest state court is called the Court of Appeals. In smaller states appeals often go directly from the trial court to the state's highest court with no intermediate level appeals court. Larger states, such as New York, Illinois, and California, have intermediate appellate courts that parallel the federal structure.

The principles discussed above for the federal system—judicial review and the value of precedent—apply with equal force in state courts. State courts have much broader jurisdiction than federal courts, however, being empowered to hear all matters properly in the judicial system except in the limited areas in which Congress or the U.S. Constitution have given federal courts exclusive jurisdiction, for example, cases arising under certain federal laws such as antitrust laws. The state's trial level court where jury trials are held is called the "court of general jurisdiction"; it hears all matters not allocated to some other court.

An understanding of the structure of the judicial system and the significance of precedent enables one to keep the meaning of judicial decisions in focus. The state and federal court systems coexist like a family of pyramids—one large federal pyramid and fifty independent state pyramids, each supreme in its sphere of jurisdiction. Only decisions at the top of the federal pyramid—by the U.S. Supreme Court—bind all Americans. Decisions of the highest court of each state bind all lower courts in that state only. Decisions of state or federal intermediate appeals courts bind only the trial courts that report to that particular appeals court. And decisions of trial courts bind no one but the parties to the case and the deciding judge to the extent the judge is likely to act consistently with his or her own decisions in future cases. Often a remarkable decision made by a trial-level court has no ultimate impact on anyone but the parties to the case in which it was made.

E. OTHER COURTS

A variety of other courts have been created by the U.S. Congress and state legislatures to hear special issues. In the federal system there are, for example, a tax court, a court of claims, a trademark trial and appeals board, and a court of patent claims, each of which is a non-Article III court, which means each court is not part of the general judicial system created by Article III of the Constitution but is a specially mandated court with limited functions in a specific area.

There are also bankruptcy courts, which are special branches of the United States District Court, that operate with their own judges and their own set of rules.

In state legal systems, probate courts deal with matters of the administration of wills, trusts, estates, and the like. There may be separate family courts that deal with divorce, child custody, and similar domestic issues. There will also be a court system that is subordinate to the trial courts of general jurisdiction and that operates on the local or municipal level to hear minor traffic violations and minor civil and criminal matters. These courts may also conduct preliminary hearings on major criminal matters such as arraignments and preliminary hearings to determine if sufficient evidence exists for a prosecution to go forward.

F. OUR CONSTITUTIONAL SYSTEM IN ACTION: THE ABORTION CONTROVERSY

The abortion controversy provides a good illustration of our constitutional system in action. Few constitutional decisions have had such a direct and widespread impact on American society, and few have been as divisive or have aroused more intense emotion. Before the 1973 *Roe v.*

Wade decision,[21] abortion was a matter entirely regulated by the states, most of which prohibited it or restricted it in some manner. Most of these laws had been in place for a century or more and reflected a widely prevailing moral code. *Roe v. Wade* came to the Court as an attack on the Texas criminal statutes forbidding abortion. Because the Texas legislature had addressed the issue by statute, there was no occasion for the Court to make a common-law ruling, and, in any case, the U.S. Supreme Court has no authority to make Texas common law. Nor does it have any authority to interpret Texas statutes or the Texas constitution. There were no federal statutes involved, which left the sole authority of the Court to speak to the matter resting on the question of whether or not anything in the U.S. Constitution was offended by the Texas law, an authority that rested on the Supremacy Clause and the power of judicial review.

The Court, in striking down the Texas statutes forbidding abortion, based its ruling on a constitutional "right of privacy" that it acknowledged is not explicitly mentioned in the Constitution. Here, the Court exercised its authority to interpret the Constitution, finding sufficient basis in the Fourteenth Amendment's concept of personal liberty to find a right of privacy that "is broad enough to encompass a woman's decision whether or not to terminate her pregnancy."[22] Absent any direct precedent in its own decisions, the Court looked for guidelines in other right of privacy cases it had decided. The closest precedent the Court could point to for its conclusion was its 1965 decision in *Griswold v. Connecticut*,[23] in which the Court struck down a Connecticut statute that criminalized artificial methods of birth control as a wrongful invasion of marital privacy. That decision itself had been based on nothing explicit in the Constitution but on rights which the Court found in the "penumbras" of the document. The power of judicial review and the interpretation of precedent had a long-enough reach to extend a right of privacy, recognized for people seeking to prevent conception that had not occurred, to people wishing to terminate the result of the conception which had occurred.

As set forth in *Roe,* the right of a woman to terminate her pregnancy is not absolute. The state may properly "assert important interests in safeguarding health, and maintaining medical standards, and in protecting potential life."[24] The state interest must be shown to be compelling, however, and the law implementing it must be narrowly drawn to express only the legitimate state interest at stake. The Court then announced what has been called "the trimester system," in which no regulation of abortion would be permitted whatsoever during the first trimester; thereafter, until the fetus was viable (usually considered to be around the late part of the second trimester), regulation could only be such as is "reasonably related to maternal health";[25] and after viability the state may regulate or proscribe abortion except for the preservation "of the life or health of the mother."[26]

In finding the unarticulated penumbral constitutional right of privacy to allow a mother to abort her fetus, the Court found irrelevant what some thought the most obvious constitutional language addressing the subject—the Fourteenth Amendment's prohibition on depriving "any person of life . . . without due process of law." Despite the fact that both tort and probate law had long accorded certain rights to the unborn, the Court found that the unborn were not "persons" within the meaning of the Fourteenth Amendment and thus defined them out of the Constitution. The decision was seven to two. Justice White, in dissent, described the decision as "an exercise of raw judicial power."

Following *Roe,* a number of state legislatures tested its limits by passing laws that imposed various restrictions and regulations on abortion and by limiting or prohibiting the use of public funds or facilities for the procedure. The constitutionality of these, in turn, was tested in the court system, with most restrictions and regulations being struck down under the precedent of *Roe.*

Since *Roe* had been based on the Court's reading of the Constitution, a political effort to amend the Constitution and reverse *Roe* began. Short of a change of heart by the Court and a reversal of *Roe,* this was the only available solution to those Americans who believed *Roe* to be not just unwise but immoral at the most profound level. Constitutional amendments require a two-thirds vote by both houses of Congress and ratification by three-fourths of state legislatures or conventions. The necessary political support for the two-thirds vote in Congress was never obtained.

Enter the executive and legislative branches and the checks and balances on this exercise of "raw judicial power." As abortion cases rose through the judicial system in the aftermath of *Roe,* the philosophical composition of the Court began to shift under the influence of appointments by more conservative presidents, approved, under the Constitution, by the Senate. *Roe's* seven to two majority fell to six to three when the Court struck down Ohio's abortion regulations in the 1983 case of *Akron v. Akron Center for Reproductive Health, Inc.*[27] and slipped to a mere five to four in striking down Pennsylvania's regulations in the 1986 decision of *Thornburgh v. American College of Obstetricians and Gynecologists.*[28] When Justice Lewis Powell, who was part of the pro-abortion majority, retired, President Reagan nominated Judge Robert Bork, whose views made it highly likely that he would tip the balance to a five to four anti-*Roe* majority. Abortion proponents, perceiving that *Roe* itself was in jeopardy, mounted a massive, bitter, and ultimately successful political fight to defeat Bork's nomination in the Senate. Anthony Kennedy was finally approved for the seat on the Court.

When the next abortion case came to the Court, *Webster v. Reproductive Health Services,*[29] a five to four majority, joined by Justice Kennedy, upheld Missouri's prohibition on the use of public employees and facilities for performing or assisting in nontherapeutic abortions and its regulations requiring viability testing whenever a doctor had reason to believe that the unborn child might be viable. The Court declined, however, an invitation from certain of the parties to overrule *Roe* directly, asserting that the cases were sufficiently different so that there was no occasion to do so. The assertion was questionable but perhaps prudent given the intensity of the abortion controversy.

Webster signalled that at least a majority of the Court was prepared to be deferential to state legislative attempts to regulate or restrict abortion, if not to overrule *Roe* outright. An outright reversal of *Roe* would not have the effect of outlawing abortion by Supreme Court decision. Only if the Court were prepared to adopt the position that it had specifically rejected in *Roe*, that the unborn are "persons" entitled to constitutional protection in their own right, would that result obtain. Otherwise a reversal of *Roe* would simply put things back where they were in 1973. Each state could address the issue through its own political, legislative, and judicial process and reach its own conclusion based on state laws and constitutions.

In the 1992 decision of *Planned Parenthood of Southeastern Pennsylvania v. Casey*,[30] the court did address the continuing vitality of *Roe v. Wade*. A five to four majority, consisting of the remaining justices from the old liberal block, Stevens and Blackmun, and a new centrist block including Justices O'Connor, Kennedy, and Souter, reaffirmed the central holding of *Roe v. Wade* but reformulated its application. The old trimester formula was dropped, and the concept of viability, which the court recognized could be a moving target, was substituted as a dividing line in the extent to which the state may interpose its interest on behalf of the unborn. Prior to viability, the state's "profound interest in potential life" may be implemented only if it does not place an "undue burden" on the right of a woman to choose an abortion. Measures designed to ensure that the woman's choice is well-informed and to persuade her to choose childbirth over abortion are permissible throughout pregnancy, as are measures to further the health or safety of the woman that do not have the purpose or effect of presenting a substantial obstacle to her right to have an abortion. Subsequent to viability, the state may regulate and even forbid abortion except in cases in which appropriate medical judgment deems it necessary to preserve the life or health of the mother.

While *Roe v. Wade* was reaffirmed, the court also approved most of the Pennsylvania regulatory measures that the case challenged, including requirements of parental notification for minors and a twenty-four-hour waiting period. It struck down a spousal notification provision as being an undue burden. This reaffirmation of *Roe v. Wade* found in *Roe* new vitality for the language which it contained but which had often been overlooked in subsequent cases, recognizing the state's interest in what the court referred to as "potental life."

The majority opinion in *Casey* leaned heavily on the importance of precedent and what it viewed as a threat to the Court's institutional integrity, were important and controversial decisions to be overruled simply as a result of the changing composition of the Court, following an appointment and confirmation process that had become increasingly politicized as a result of the abortion controversy. The three members of the new centrist block did not express personal approval of *Roe* and hinted that they might have voted differently had they been on the court in 1973; but they viewed the continuity of the legal rule as superseding whatever doubts they might have had as to the wisdom of the original decision.

The minority opinions pointed out that the Court's eloquent defense of precedent was made in the context of an opinion in which the court not only reformulated the rules laid down in the case it was affirming but explicitly overruled aspects of two of its subsequent abortion decisions disapproving state regulatory measures, *Akron* and *Thornburgh*, discussed above. In the minority's view, the only way to remove the Court from its role as ongoing referee of the minutiae of abortion regulations would be to overrule *Roe* outright and leave abortion rights to the political process. Abortion was not, the minority pointed out, a national controversy before *Roe v. Wade*. The Court had placed itself in the position that it now found undermined its institutional integrity and had an obvious route to escape from its discomfort.

The five to four decision in *Casey* that affirmed *Roe* was in reality a seven to two decision in favor of allowing states significant regulatory activity with respect to assuring informed consent for women choosing abortion, and it frankly approved the states' implementing policies designed to encourage women to choose childbirth. With four members of the court still advocating the overturning of *Roe*, future Supreme Court nominations are likely to be as invested with the abortion controversy as those of the recent past.

The aftermath of *Webster* and *Casey* promises both a renewed interest in finding a more expansive right to abortion in state constitutions than the Supreme Court may permit under the U.S. Constitution and an intense interest in the state political and judicial processes whereby state legislatures and governors will shape the scope of permissible regulatory activity on a state-by-state basis. State legislatures pass measures seeking both to expand and restrict abortion rights, and state governors have to decide to sign or veto them. The issue is present in virtually every political contest for state executive or legislative office. After 1973, the relatively absolutist language of *Roe* shielded the state political process and its participants from the need to take positions and make decisions. To the extent that *Webster* and *Casey*, and future cases reaching the Supreme Court, retreat from this, the void will be filled by the powers reserved to the states under the Tenth Amendment.

Meanwhile, the tenuous five to four balance on the Court in its most recent decisions on abortion, coupled with the intensity and passion of the national debate on the issue, have made it almost impossible for a president to nominate a Supreme Court justice who has a clearly stated position on the issue. President Bush's nomination of David Souter to fill the seat vacated by Justice Brennan was at least partly motivated by the fact that Souter's outstanding intellectual and judicial credentials were not compromised by a position on the issue; and the next nominee, Clarence Thomas, professed no position on abortion in his confirmation hearings.

REFERENCES

Barron, Jerome A., and C. Thomas Dienes. *Constitutional Law: Principles and Policy* (Charlottesville, Va: Michie Co., 1982).

Corwin, Edward S. *The Constitution and What It Means Today.* Revised by Chase and Ducat. (Princeton: Princeton University Press, 1974).

Cox, Archibald. *The Court and the Constitution* (Boston: Houghton Mifflin, 1987).

Curtis, George Ticknor. *Constitutional History of the United States* (New York: DeCapo Press, 1974).

Peltason, J.W. *Corwin and Peltason's Understanding the Constitution* (New York: Holt, Rinehart & Winston, 1985).

CHAPTER 3

The Religion Clauses of the First Amendment

A. THE TWO RELIGION CLAUSES

The religion clauses of the First Amendment to the Constitution read: "Congress shall make no law respecting an establishment of religion, or prohibiting the free exercise thereof."

The language of the religion clauses contains two distinct prohibitions:

1. "Congress shall make no law respecting an establishment of religion." In other words, Congress may not institute a state church, compel any particular belief or worship, nor aid, finance, promote, or endorse any particular religion or religions in general. This is known as the Establishment Clause.
2. "Congress shall make no law . . . prohibiting the free exercise [of religion]." In other words, Congress may not ban religious exercise or impede religious freedom. This is known as the Free Exercise Clause.

The Establishment Clause prevents the government from imposing religion on people; the Free Exercise Clause prevents the government from interfering with the religion people exercise of their own choice.

These two clauses are the two sides of the coin of religious liberty. Yet these sixteen words that express the American legal system's commitment to religious liberty have not always spoken clearly as to their application. In fact, these words have generated more litigation, confusion, frustration, and uncertainty in recent decades than almost any other words found in the U. S. Constitution.

B. RELIGIOUS LIBERTY BEFORE THE CONSTITUTION

The religion clauses, like the Constitution as a whole, did not arrive in the American legal system unannounced. The concepts they represented were grounded in the development of American thought over most of the two previous centuries before the Constitution was written.

The seventeenth-century English colonies spread along the east coast of the North American continent had a variety of approaches to religious establishment and toleration. Most of the settlers came to the colonies from an England that was experiencing an unhappy century of religious struggle and intolerance. The Church of England, which had suppressed both Roman Catholics and Protestant separatists, was itself dissolved after Charles I was deposed in the English Civil War, but the purported free exercise of religion that followed did not extend to "papists, the adherents of prelacy and the advocates of 'blasphemous, licentious or profane' doctrines."[1] With the restoration of the monarchy in 1660, the Church of England was reconstituted, but Catholics continued to be suppressed, as were Protestant dissenters.

In the New World, several points of view, carried out of the English strife, flourished in different locales.

As an overview (although history is always more complex than overviews), the New England colonies, with the exception of Rhode Island, were settled by English Calvinists and Puritans who had a vision of a Christian commonwealth and saw little need for religious pluralism or even tolerance, despite their own origins as separatists and dissenters. Their churches were highly decentralized and congregational in church polity, each town constituting a congregation which selected its own minister on a democratic basis with a high degree of autonomy from civil control. Dissenters were actively persecuted in Massachusetts; Baptists were banished in 1644, and Quakers were expelled and even, on at least one occasion, hanged. These extremes of intolerance were largely ended by the late 1600s, but some level of religious establishment in New England—such as support for churches by government funds or allowing territorial parishes the power to tax—persisted well into the nineteenth century.

The southern colonies by contrast had, by and large, an Anglican establishment, by order of the Crown, that was maintained by government authorities and the local upper classes. There were few dissenters in the seventeenth century, but when Presbyterians, Baptists, and Quakers entered the colony of Virginia in the eighteenth century, it proved as intolerant as Massachusetts. Baptists were met with violence, horsewhipped, and jailed. The Virginia system, with varying degrees of rigidity, was extended to the more southerly colonies of the Carolinas and Georgia and also to Maryland.

Maryland, begun by Catholic gentry, endeavored to foster religious toleration. The first use of the term "free exercise," which found its way into the Constitution nearly a century and a half later, came from a 1649 Maryland statute that provided that at least a person "professing to believe in Jesus Christ" would not be "troubled . . . for . . . his or her religion nor in the free exercise thereof."[2] By 1689, however, an Anglican establishment was in power, and Maryland followed Virginia into intolerance toward dissenters, including Catholics.

It was in the middle colonies that tolerance and religious freedom flourished. New York and New Jersey had nominal Anglican establishments in some areas but a sufficiently diverse population so that they in fact pursued a policy of benign neglect toward the various sects. Pennsylvania and Delaware, founded by the Quaker William Penn, and Rhode Island, founded by Baptist Roger Williams, affirmatively protected liberty of conscience and protected religious dissenters.[3]

Various colonies shifted between degrees of establishment and toleration from time to time, and even in the most tolerant colonies there were exceptions. Pennsylvania, for example, restricted public offices and franchises to Christians at least until 1701.

The religious establishments and intolerance of the seventeenth century were shaken by the Great Awakening of the 1730s, which originated in New England and spread south into the middle and southern colonies. Led by itinerant English preacher George Whitefield and Northampton, Massachusetts, pastor Jonathan Edwards, the Great Awakening was an evangelical revival that drew large numbers of people away from established churches and advocated a theology of salvation, a renewed puritanism, and a moral protest against what was perceived as increasing commercialism and corruption in much of society.

Another major impetus toward religious freedom was the influence of Enlightenment thought and, particularly, English philosopher John Locke on American thinkers, especially on Jefferson, Madison, and the Massachusetts Baptist Isaac Backus. Locke became an advocate of a widespread toleration toward religion, although even he excepted Catholics and atheists. His perception of the separation of church and state would confine the state to the "care of the things of this world" and give the churches no "jurisdiction in worldly matters."[4] Locke's notion of toleration did not, however, extend to permitting people to be exempted on the grounds of religious conscience from generally applicable laws that did not directly discriminate against any particular sect. Locke's views on separation of church and state and his lack of sympathy for the idea that "free exercise" rights be exempt from nondiscriminatory laws heavily influenced the thinking of Jefferson, who advocated both of Locke's positions.

There is good reason to believe, however, that Jefferson's younger colleague, James Madison, who was the principal drafter of the First Amendment, was much more sympathetic to religious exemptions from general legislation. Such exemptions were commonplace in the colonies on matters such as conscientious objection to military service, assessments for support of clergy of established churches, and allowing affirmations in lieu of oaths (which were particularly offensive to Quakers). The affirmation alternative to oaths was written into the U.S. Constitution in three places.[5]

The American Revolution discredited the Anglican establishment in the southern states, and the states for the most part disestablished the Anglican Church in their state constitutions, written from 1776 to 1778. By the time of the adoption of the U.S. Constitution in 1789, only Connecticut, Massachusetts, New Hampshire, and Vermont retained any actual legal and financial support for the church. The constitutions of the original thirteen states, all written before the federal, generally provided for some level of free exercise or "liberty of conscience," some in broader terms than others. Some extended the right, for example, only to "worship," while others limited it only by conduct that jeopardized the "peace and safety" of the state.

Perhaps the most significant pre-constitutional religious liberty issue occurred in Virginia, which was later than its fellow southern states in disestablishing the Anglican Church. In 1783, with the active support of Patrick Henry, a bill was introduced in the Virginia House of Delegates which called for a tax or contribution for the support of the Christian religion, the proceeds to be made available to Presbyterians and Baptists as well as Anglicans. People would pay taxes only for the church of their choice, and if they had no church the money was to go to education. The purpose of the bill in Henry's view was not to support religion but to assist the state by promoting religion, which kept people virtuous and law-abiding. Thomas Jefferson opposed the bill but left the country to become the minister to France, and the opposition leadership fell to James Madison. Madison authored a petition captioned *A Memorial and Remonstrance against Religious Assessments,* which has become a monument in the history of religious liberty in America. It was widely circulated throughout Virginia and led to the defeat of Henry's bill and the adoption of a statute supporting religious freedom, originally authored by Jefferson. The flavor of the *Memorial and Remonstrance* may be taken from the following exerpts:

> The Religion then of every man must be left to the conviction and conscience of every man; and it is the right of every man to exercise it as these may dictate. This right is in its nature an unalienable right. It is unalienable, because the opinions of men, depending only on the evidence contemplated by their own minds cannot follow the dictates of other men: It is unalienable also, because what is here a right towards men, is a duty towards the Creator. It is the duty of every man to render to the Creator such homage and such only as he believes to be acceptable to him. This duty is precedent, both in order of time and in degree of obligation, to the claims of Civil Society. Before any man can be considered as a member of Civil Society, he must be considered as a subject of the Governour of the Universe: And if a member of Civil Society, who enters into any subordinate Association, must always do it with a reservation of his duty to the General Authority; much more must every man who becomes a member of any particular Civil Society, do it with a saving of his allegiance to the Universal Sovereign. We maintain therefore that in matters of Religion, no man's right is abridged by the institution of Civil Society and that Religion is wholly exempt from its cognizance. True it is, that no other rule exists, by which any question which may divide a Society can be ultimately determined, but the will of the majority, but it is also true that the majority may trespass on the rights of the minority. . . . Who does not see that the same authority which can establish Christianity, in exclusion of all other Religions, may establish with the same ease any particular sect of Christians, in exclusion of all other Sects? that the same authority which can force a citizen to contribute three pence only of his property for the support of any one establishment, may force him to conform to any other establishment in all cases whatsoever? . . . Whilst we assert for ourselves a freedom to embrace, to profess and to observe the Religion which we

> believe to be of divine origin, we cannot deny an equal freedom to those whose minds have not yet yielded to the evidence which has convinced us. If this freedom be abused, it is an offence against God not against man: To God, therefore, not to man, must an account of it be rendered . . . the establishment proposed by the Bill is not requisite for the support of the Christian Religion. To say that it is, is a contradiction to the Christian Religion itself, for every page of it disavows a dependence on the powers of this world: it is a contradiction to fact; for it is known that this Religion both existed and flourished, not only without the support of human laws, but in spite of every opposition from them, and not only during the period of miraculous aid, but long after it had been left to its own evidence and the ordinary care of Providence. Nay, it is a contradiction in terms; for a Religion not invented by human policy, must have pre-existed and been supported, before it was established by human policy. It is moreover to weaken in those who profess this Religion a pious confidence in its innate excellence and the patronage of its Author; and to foster in those who still reject it, a suspicion that its friends are too conscious of its fallacies to trust it to its own merits . . . . What influence in fact have ecclesiastical establishments had on Civil Society? In some instances they have been seen to erect a spiritual tyranny on the ruins of the thrones of political tyranny: in no instance have they been seen the guardians of the liberties of the people. [6]

Thus, in Madison's view, religious liberty was born not from a merely civil, political, or philosophical base of justice or toleration, but from a theological necessity. For if the universe does, or may, have a "governour," it follows that there is a sovereign whose claim on people's allegiance is superior to that of civil society. It is to protect that allegiance that religious liberty is required, since people have not agreed on what that allegiance demands of them. Those who fail of that superior allegiance will be accountable to God, not to other human beings.

C. ORIGIN OF THE FIRST AMENDMENT

The First Amendment is part of the Bill of Rights, the first ten amendments to the Constitution. It was proposed before ratification of the Constitution by the states was even complete. The protections of the Bill of Rights were not included in the Constitution by the federal convention of 1787, "partly because the Constitution set forth limited and specific powers for which no Bill of Rights was logically necessary; but mostly because members were worn out and wanted to go home when they got around to the subject."[7] But lack of a Bill of Rights was a major argument used by the anti-Federalists to oppose adoption of the Constitution, and, as the Constitution circulated among the states for ratification, it became increasingly clear that such an addition would be needed. President Washington urged it in his inaugural address on April 30, 1789, and Madison, who had authored the *Memorial and Remonstrance*, took the lead in putting it together. The amendments were approved by Congress on September 25, 1789, and by December 15, 1791, with ratification by Virginia, the approval of the eleven states necessary for amending the Constitution were in place and the Bill of Rights was part of the Constitution.

As written and adopted, the First Amendment bound only "Congress," that is, the federal government. It had no application to states or subsidiary governmental units, some of which retained established churches and most of which acted on religious matters in various ways not necessarily consistent with the religion clauses.

The First Amendment contains other freedoms than the religious, and these have had their role in protecting religious freedom. Although the religion clauses are set forth first, the amendment also precludes Congress from making any law "abridging the freedom of speech, or of the press, or the right of the people peaceably to assemble, and to petition the government for a redress of grievances." Archibald Cox, Harvard Law Professor Emeritus and former Watergate special prosecutor and solicitor general of the United States, believes the order is significant:

The Framers put first the prohibition against any law respecting an establishment of religion, or prohibiting the free exercise thereof. To those guarantees of spiritual liberty they next linked their indispensable prerequisite, freedom of speech, or of the press. Then on the far side of the freedoms of expression one finds the political rights of free assembly and free petition for redress of grievances. The progression recalls that the Constitutional guarantees of freedom of speech and of the press are also indispensable to self-government. Both aspects of the guarantees seem rooted in a single source. Both the concern for spiritual liberty and the commitment to self-government rest on faith in the potential flowering of the human spirit in a society where an individual is accorded both dignity and the power and the responsibility of choice. . . .

History made it natural for the authors of the Amendment to move from freedom of religious belief and worship to "the freedom of speech, or of the press." The one church was breaking up in late-sixteenth- and seventeenth-century Britain. New faiths were emerging, based upon individual study of the Holy Word. The man or woman who has discovered the road to salvation has a need, even feels a duty, to bring the Gospel to others. But the goal was not simply the freedom of the speaker. Liberty of expression was essential to all who wished to hear and read the Word of God and thus to discover the road to salvation. Modern legal analysis recognizes the importance of the hearers' and readers' access to information and ideas in cases allowing them to bring suits challenging a government restriction on freedom of expression.[8]

D. 1791 TO THE 1940S: EARLY HISTORY AND THE INCORPORATION DOCTRINE

The religion clauses received little attention from the courts for the first one hundred fifty years of their existence as part of the U.S. Constitution. From their adoption in 1791 until 1940, only ten cases in which these two clauses were in issue reached the

U.S. Supreme Court. Several cases were efforts by Mormons to use the Free Exercise Clause to defend their practice of polygamy, but these met with no success. This paucity of cases left the doctrines and application of the religion clauses largely undeveloped before 1940. Thereafter, an explosion began. By 1990, over one hundred additional religion clause cases had reached the Court, half of them in the 1980s.

This geometric increase in First Amendment religion clause litigation began with an invitation from the U.S. Supreme Court to extend application of the First Amendment from "Congress," that is, the federal government, to the states. In the course of its opinion in the 1937 case of *Palko v. Connecticut,* in which religion was not at issue, the Court stated:

> On the other hand, the due process clause of the Fourteenth Amendment may make it unlawful for *a state* to abridge by its statutes . . . the free exercise of religion. . . . In these and other situations immunities that are valid as against the Federal government by force of the specific pledges of particular amendments have been found to be implicit in the concept of ordered liberty, and thus, through the Fourteenth Amendment, become valid as against the states.[9]

The statement was *dictum,* comment by the Court unnecessary to the opinion in the case before it, and therefore not binding precedent. But it sent a clear signal as to how the Court thought about the matter: "implicit in the concept of ordered liberty" to which the states were bound by the Fourteenth Amendment were the specific rights of the religion clauses.

With the 1940 Supreme Court decision in *Cantwell v. Connecticut,*[10] the Free Exercise clause emerged through *Palko's* dictum. The *Cantwell* case began in the Roman Catholic neighborhoods of New Haven, Connecticut, where Newton Cantwell and his sons, Jesse and Russell, all ordained ministers of the Jehovah's Witnesses, went door-to-door distributing literature and, when allowed entrance to the house, played a recorded attack on organized religion in

general and denounced Roman Catholicism as "an instrument of the devil." Arrested and convicted in the New Haven Court of Common Pleas on a charge of soliciting without a permit, the Cantwells took their case to the United States Supreme Court, which unanimously announced for the first time (with respect to the religion clauses) the "incorporation doctrine."

The incorporation doctrine recognizes that the First Amendment, by its terms, applies only to Congress (the federal government) and neither has nor ever claimed to have any control over state governments and their local municipal and other subdivisions. In 1868, following the Civil War, the Fourteenth Amendment to the Constitution was adopted. Its purpose was to assure the rights of the newly freed African Americans, although the generality of its language has since then permitted a much broader application. The Fourteenth Amendment is the basis of the incorporation doctrine. The amendment reads as follows:

> All persons born or naturalized in the United States, and subject to the jurisdiction thereof, are citizens of the United States and of the State wherein they reside. No State shall make or enforce any law which shall abridge the privileges or immunities of citizens of the United States nor shall any State deprive any person of life, liberty, or property, without due process of law; nor deny to any person within its jurisdiction the equal protection of the laws.

"Incorporation" means simply that in the words of the Fourteenth Amendment, in particular, the "liberty" of which no state shall deprive any person "without due process of law," are embodied the concepts of the religion clauses found in the First Amendment. Thus did the right of free exercise and the prohibition against establishments of religion become extended from the acts of the United States to the acts of the now fifty states and all subordinate governmental entities. Because municipalities and other governmental entities within a state are creatures of the state, every school board, city council, and other state or local government subdivision or agency is as subject to the First Amendment as is the Congress of the United States. The Cantwells, who appeared to have no applicable federal constitutional rights before, went free. The Connecticut law under which they had been convicted was declared a violation of their constitutional right freely to exercise their religion.

A few years later, in the 1947 case of *Everson v. Board of Education*,[11] the Court extended the incorporation concept explicitly to the Establishment Clause. In a five to four opinion written by Justice Hugo Black, the Court set forth some of the most oft-quoted language about the meaning of the Establishment Clause:

> The "Establishment of Religion" Clause of the First Amendment means at least this: Neither a state nor the Federal Government can set up a church. Neither can pass laws which aid one religion, aid all religions, or prefer one religion over another. Neither can force nor influence a person to go to or to remain away from church against his will or force him to profess a belief or disbelief in any religion. No person can be punished for entertaining or professing religious beliefs or disbeliefs, or church attendance or non-attendance. . . . In the words of Jefferson, the clause against the establishment of religion by law was erected to set up a "wall of separation between church and state."

In spite of this ringing separatist language, the majority of the Court found that the use of a New Jersey township school board's tax funds to pay bus fares for children attending a Catholic school did not violate the Establishment Clause.

The proliferation of religious freedom cases in the courts after the incorporation decisions of the 1940s probably can be attributed, at least, to the following reasons:

1. The incorporation doctrine made the religion clauses applicable to all government entities at every level, thus greatly multiplying the opportunity for conflict to arise.
2. The great increase in the nature and extent of government regulation in recent decades has further multiplied the opportunities for conflict.
3. The Warren and Burger Courts, during the period from the 1950s to the early 1980s, each functioned as a Court that perceived its role, and was perceived by litigants, as an activist guardian of individual rights against majoritarian oppression, thereby encouraging those offended by majoritarian practices to take their grievances to the judicial system.
4. Changes in perspective after the Second World War and especially since the mid-1960s have brought into constitutional question many government practices long taken for granted, such as school prayer, and have given rise to more individuals and organizations willing to challenge them. At the same time, the proliferation of nontraditional religious groups and practices creates conflict with government laws and programs that would not have existed in a more traditional society.

The "wall of separation" metaphor employed by Justice Black in the *Everson* case came into the American lexicon from a letter that Thomas Jefferson, while president, wrote to the Danbury, Connecticut, Baptists in 1802, expressing his view of the meaning of the religion clauses. Jefferson was of the rationalist enlightenment school of thought, a deist, and a unitarian who believed that if only all people were well-enough informed and left without coercion, the entire nation would be unitarian within a hundred years. His concern was likely more to prevent religion from controlling or interfering with government than the reverse. Ironically, and probably unknown to Jefferson, the "wall of separation" metaphor had been used a century earlier by the Baptist religious dissenter Roger Williams, who believed, from the reverse perspective, that the wall was necessary, in view of the hazards to the church from interference by the government, "to protect the garden of the church from the wilderness of the world."

These two perspectives translate loosely into the concepts that became, respectively, the Establishment and the Free Exercise Clauses. The wall of separation has in fact been an unsteady one, described by former Chief Justice Burger in the 1971 decision of

Lemon v. Kurtzman as "a blurred, indistinct, and variable barrier depending on the circumstances of a particular relationship."[12]

The religion clauses are not like a set of traffic lights with a red or green signal telling the citizen or government official what to do in relatively simple and predictable patterns of activity. In the myriad of relationships in which church and state intersect one another at every level of government, church, and individual life, the facts are often not simple or the answers obvious. Applying the First Amendment to a rapidly changing society proves the impossibility of having a static body of law. Social, economic, and technological change may make formerly relevant answers unsatisfactory. New Supreme Court justices, appointed through the political process by presidents who may disagree with former interpretations by the Court, bring new insights and perceptions to constitutional interpretation. The cases that reach the Supreme Court and thus become the occasions for the Court to articulate standards that will govern future cases and lower courts are often among the most complex, presenting clashes of values in the gray areas of the Constitution.

Nevertheless, the Supreme Court, as the promulgator of the rules of interpretation and the arbiter of the application in the constitutional arena, does not wish citizens to be confused. Judges recognize that the perception of the legitimacy of the legal process, the value of judicial precedent as a guide to conduct, and the understanding of those governed by the legal system, depend on the law being a continuing body of neutral and predictable governing principles, values, policies, or standards that have a separate existence and command a greater allegiance than does the government or any individual who occupies a position in the government. It must govern everyone equally, "the judges as well as the judged."[13] In the constitutional interpretation of the First Amendment religion clauses, the Court seeks to articulate standards by which the two broad concepts, succinctly expressed in the sixteen words of the First Amendment, can be understood and consistently applied in the myriad clashes between the government and the governed that stream into the nation's courtrooms.

E. THE ESTABLISHMENT CLAUSE

Establishment Clause litigation has brought about some of the most visible and controversial Supreme Court decisions of recent decades. Deep-rooted practices in the public schools, such as Bible reading[14] and school prayer,[15] have been struck down as Establishment Clause violations. So have, more recently, legislation that attempted to avoid the effects of Supreme Court decisions or to combat perceived secular biases in public education, such as moment-of-silence laws[16] and laws to require teaching of creationism.[17] The legitimacy of Christmas crèche displays on public property is an Establishment Clause issue, and decisions have gone both ways, depending on (1) the extent of the secular symbols surrounding the displays, and (2) whether or not the government displays them or merely permits private groups access to public property for temporary displays, with appropriate disclaimers of government sponsorship.[18]

Yet the Court does not understand the Establishment Clause as requiring a hostility to religion. It is not prepared to cast out of our national life the symbols of what Justice O'Connor has called "ceremonial deism" which "serve the secular purpose of 'solemnizing public occasions,' and 'expressing confidence in the future,' . . ."[19] The Court has noted with apparent approval presidential proclamations of Christmas and Thanksgiving as national holidays, a national day of prayer, commemoration of Jewish heritage week and Jewish High Holy Days; government-funded chaplains and chapels for the Congress and the military; the national motto of "In God We Trust"; the "one nation under God" language in the Pledge of Allegiance; the display of religious art in public museums; the opening of Court sessions with "God save the United States and this Honorable Court"; and the imagery of Moses with the Ten Commandments in the Supreme Court chamber itself.[20] None of these official acknowledgments of religion by the government struck the court as an

Establishment Clause violation. "We are," wrote Justice Douglas, "a religious people whose institutions presuppose a Supreme Being."[21]

1. The *Lemon* Test

After a quarter of a century of Establishment Clause cases following the incorporation decision in *Everson*, the Court endeavored to articulate the test by which it would measure whether or not a particular government action offended the Establishment Clause. The occasion was the 1971 opinion in *Lemon v. Kurtzman*,[22] a consolidated case that brought First Amendment challenges to state statutes in Rhode Island and Pennsylvania that provided state aid to private schools and teachers.

The Rhode Island statute provided for a salary supplement to teachers of secular subjects in nonpublic elementary schools. The statute was carefully crafted in an attempt to avoid the Establishment Clause challenge. It applied only when the teacher was employed in a nonpublic school in which the average per-pupil expenditure on secular education was less than the public school average; the school's financial records were subject to audit by the state; the teacher was required to teach only those subjects offered in the public schools, to use teaching materials used in the public schools, and to agree in writing not to teach a course on religion while receiving salary supplements. The only teachers who applied for such supplements were teachers from Roman Catholic schools.

The Pennsylvania statute provided for state reimbursement to the nonpublic elementary and secondary schools for teachers' salaries and certain materials used in teaching certain secular subjects, but it did not permit reimbursement for teaching subject matter with religious teaching and morals or forms of worship. Prescribed accounting procedures had to be maintained, and the schools were subject to audit. Reimbursement would only apply to courses presented in the public school curricula, and textbook and instructional materials were subject to approval by the state. Both states had large parochial school populations (20 to 25 percent of school-age

children) and legitimate concerns for both the quality of education these children were receiving and, perhaps more importantly, the potential burden on the public treasury if the schools failed.

The Court summarized its decisions over the years by gleaning from them three tests, or criteria, to measure the validity of a statute against the Establishment Clause. These criteria, which have since been known in constitutional jurisprudence as the *Lemon* test, are:

1. The statute must have a secular legislative purpose.
2. The principal or primary effect of the statute must neither advance nor inhibit religion.
3. The statute must not foster excessive government entanglement with religion.

Applying these criteria to the facts in the *Lemon* case, the Court (1) was satisfied that there was a secular legislative purpose—enhancing the quality of secular education in all schools covered by the laws; (2) declined to decide whether or not the statutes restricted the principal or primary effect of the programs to the point where they did not offend the religion clauses; and (3) concluded that the "cumulative impact of the entire relationship arising under the statutes in each State involves excessive entanglement between government and religion,"[23] based on the elaborate procedures undertaken by both states to assure that state funds were not, in fact, used for religious purposes. Thus, in a Catch-22, the very procedures Pennsylvania and Rhode Island had instituted to avoid an Establishment Clause problem were found to be the constitutional violation.

Since then, Establishment Clause cases have continued to adhere to the *Lemon* test, although it has been much criticized by commentators and even by the Court itself. One of the more significant criticisms is that the second part of the test, regarding effects that inhibit religion, and the third part of the test, regarding excessive entanglement, are more properly understood to be free exercise concepts. By making them Establishment Clause concepts, it is argued, the Court permits nonbelievers or those who are not affected by the purported entanglement to bring suit to prevent the problems, whether or not the religious institution wants to be saved from them.

Criticism of the *Lemon* test within the Court has led Justice O'Connor to develop a clarification of the Establishment Clause doctrine in the concept of "endorsement," essentially a clarification of the first and second parts of the *Lemon* test, which require a secular purpose and prohibit the government from acting in a way that either advances or inhibits religion. Justice O'Connor's concept of endorsement would prohibit the government from "making adherence to a religion relevant in any way to a person's standing in the political community" by action which would be perceived as conveying that a religion or a particular religious belief is endorsed or disapproved.[24] The *Lemon* test, with whatever modification may be added by the concept of endorsement, remains the basic test in an Establishment Clause case. The concepts of the *Lemon* test, however, are elastic, and the consistency of application from case to case is not always self-evident.

2. Alternatives to the *Lemon* Test

The Court has often spoken of *Lemon* as a guideline rather than a mechanistic formula. In at least two instances, the Court has departed from *Lemon*.

a. The Historical Test

Although the Court has observed that unconstitutional practices do not become constitutional by long observance, in the 1983 case of *Marsh v. Chambers*,[25] it found constitutional, based on an alternative historical test, the practice of a state legislature having a paid chaplain who opened each session with a prayer. Because this practice was followed by the very U.S. Congress that wrote the Establishment Clause, it could not be credibly claimed that it violated that clause. In upholding religious property tax deductions as part of a larger plan of tax deductions for nonprofit institutions the Court also emphasized the long history of the practice, dating to colonial times, although it did not justify the practice constitutionally on that ground alone.[26]

These cases are consistent with the oft-quoted words of Justice Douglas in *Zorach v. Clauson*:

> When the state encourages religious instruction or cooperates with religious authorities by adjusting the schedule to sectarian needs, it honors the best of our traditions. For it then respects the religious nature of our people and accommodates the public service to their spiritual needs. To hold that it may not would be to find in the Constitution a requirement that the government show a callous indifference to religion and religious groups. It would be to prefer those who believe in no religion over those who do believe. . . . We find no constitutional requirement which makes it necessary for government to be hostile to religion and to throw its weight against efforts to widen the effective scope of religious influence.[27]

b. The Discrimination Test

In a second departure from the tripartite test, the 1982 case of *Larson v. Valente*,[28] the Court addressed a state charitable registration statute that exempted from the registration requirement religious organizations that receive more than half their total contributions from members or affiliated organizations. The Court found that this registration violated the Establishment Clause because it discriminated between religions and created a denominational preference. The Court departed from its usual Establishment Clause analysis and used an Equal Protection Clause analysis to find that the denominational preference constituted a suspect classification so that strict scrutiny must be applied.

3. Establishment Clause Applications

The Establishment Clause is of principal practical concern to the functioning of church and parachurch institutions that receive, or whose clients receive, some form of government aid for services the organization provides. This occurs, in some instances, with respect to government-funded relief or social services provided by religious organizations. Government support for day care is an increasing area of practical application. Most of the litigation in this area to date, however, has involved aid to private schools (most of which are, inevitably, religious) and to families whose children attend those schools. A review of decisions in these areas will illustrate the difficulties the Court has had in drawing clear lines in Establishment Clause cases.

a. Government-funded Relief or Social Services

In the 1899 decision of Bradfield v. Roberts,[29] the Court permitted government funding of a new building that was part of a religious hospital. That the hospital was affiliated with the Roman Catholic church was considered irrelevant to the secular purpose of the funding.

The modern equivalent of Bradfield is Bowen v. Kendrick,[30] a 1988 decision in which the Adolescent Family Life Act was challenged as a violation of the Establishment Clause. The act provided for grants to both public and nonprofit private organizations for services and research in the area of adolescent premarital sexual relations and pregnancy. Grants had been made to organizations with institutional ties to religious denominations, although they were not the primary recipients in number of grants or dollars. The act provided that funded services should promote the involvement of religious organizations, along with parents and other family members and charitable and voluntary organizations, in addressing the problems at which the act was aimed.

Bowen upheld the constitutionality of the act under a straightforward Lemon analysis. It had no difficulty finding a sincere and legitimate secular purpose in dealing with problems of adolescent sexuality. Most of the analysis was devoted to the second part of the Lemon test—whether the act had the impermissible effect of advancing religion. That the act encouraged grant recipients to involve religious organizations, among others, in addressing the problem was considered to have too incidental and remote an effect of advancing religion to be a constitutional problem. The Court viewed as neu-

tral the fact that religious institutions could apply for grants along with secular institutions: "This Court has never held that religious institutions are disabled by the First Amendment from participating in publicly sponsored social welfare programs."[31]

The Court did caution that a different effect might be found if the aid flowed to "pervasively sectarian" institutions, which it had earlier defined as institutions "in which religion is so pervasive that a substantial portion of its functions are subscribed in the religious mission."[32] In such an institution, even aid designated for secular purposes "may nonetheless advance the pervasively sectarian institution's 'religious mission.' "[33] The risk of such inappropriate grants, however, did not justify striking down the act as unconstitutional, although it would justify further inquiry into actual grants that had been made.

Alignment of the government's secular concerns, as expressed in the statutory objectives, with religious views of the grantees did not destroy the religious neutrality of the act. Matters such as pregnancy testing, adoption counseling, and prenatal and postnatal care "are not themselves 'specifically religious activities,' and they are not converted into such activities by the fact that they are carried out by organizations with religous affiliations."[34]

Finally, the Court addressed the third part of the Lemon test—the excessive entanglement of government and religion. Noting the Catch-22 that the government's very supervisory efforts to assure proper secular use of funds become too religiously entangling to be constitutionally permissible, the Court observed that this problem arose primarily in parochial schools, which it viewed as "pervasively sectarian." The limited amount of grant monitoring required to assure proper use in organizations not "pervasively sectarian" would not require excessive government entanglement with religion.

The Court made a distinction between the act's being "facially" unconstitutional and unconstitutional as applied. Had it been facially unconstitutional, which it was not, it would have been struck down. Were unconstitutional applications being made, they could be dealt with on a case-by-case basis, by invalidating the applications rather than the act. The case was remanded to the district court to determine (1) if aid was in fact flowing to pervasively sectarian institutions, not those merely religiously inspired or affiliated with a religious institution; or (2) if the act was funding specifically religious activities that used materials with explicit religious content, rather than presenting views of sexuality that coincided with the act.

The issues raised by *Bowen* are likely to receive more attention in the near future. For example, the Child Care and Development Block Grant of 1990[35] provides federal funds for child care for low-income families, either by direct grants to eligible child care facilities or by certificates to eligible parents that can be used for services at eligible child care facilities. Certificates can be used for religious providers of child care. Direct grants may also be made to religious providers if the funds are not used for religious purposes. This use of funds for religious child care providers will likely be challenged under the Establishment Clause. If it survives, it may portend a growth in funding of social services through the existing nonprofit sector, including the religious nonprofit sector.

In summary, religiously inspired or affiliated institutions that are not pervasively sectarian can receive public funds for secular purposes without violating the Establishment Clause. The coincidence of their religious views with the secular purpose of the funding does not make the funding unconstitutional. The limited government monitoring necessary to ensure proper use of the funds does not constitute an excessive entanglement. Grants to persons to pay for services that may be provided by secular or religious institutions and that allow the recipient to choose where to use them will probably be acceptable under the Establishment Clause. Grants to pervasively sectarian institutions for secular purposes will be subject to continuing Establishment Clause challenges.

b. Public Aid to Sectarian Schools

Beginning with *Everson*,[36] the issue of public aid to sectarian schools has been one of the most persistent and difficult areas of application of Establishment Clause principles. A thorough analysis of the numerous such cases decided by the Supreme Court is beyond the scope of this work, but the following summary of results will help:

(i) Higher Education

In a series of cases, the Court has upheld government aid to higher educational institutions that are not pervasively sectarian, so long as the aid is not used for sectarian purposes.[37] It did strike down, in the 1971 *Tilton* case, a provision that could have removed, after twenty years, government sanctions for violating the restrictions on religious use of funds.

The Court has also ruled that scholarship aid available to an individual for secular training can be used for religious training.[38]

(ii) Elementary and Secondary Schools

The Court assumes that elementary and secondary religious schools, unlike religiously affiliated universities, are pervasively sectarian. Notwithstanding their pervasively sectarian character, they provide an education in secular subjects for students who are entitled to a free public education and meet many secular requirements imposed, or provide secular services made available, by the state. The persistent interest of state and local governments in assisting them stems from a consciousness of the heavy burden they lift from the public educational system, as well as concern for the quality of education and services available to their students. It is here that the Court has had its most difficult Establishment Clause struggles.

(a) Released Time. A released-time program, in which released-time classes were conducted in the regular classrooms of a school building while children whose parents had not given them permission to attend those classes were required to go to separate classrooms to pursue secular studies, was held unconstitutional in the 1948 case of *McCollum v. Board of Education*.[39] A released-time program in which students were released during the school day to go to religious centers for religious instruction and devotional exercises

was upheld in the 1952 case of *Zorach v. Clauson.*[40]

(b) Transportation. A reimbursement to parents for the cost of bus transportation to public and private schools was upheld in the 1947 case of *Everson v. Board of Education.*[41] Using state money to pay for field trip transportation of private school students was struck down in the 1977 case of *Wolman v. Walter.*[42]

(c) Shared Time. A shared-time program which permitted public school teachers to teach secular courses in private religious schools was found unconstitutional in the 1985 decision of *Grand Rapids School District v. Ball.*[43]

(d) Testing, Reporting, Diagnostic, Remedial, and Guidance Services. It is unconstitutional to use state money to supply guidance counseling to students in church-related schools.[44] The Court has, however, approved the use of state funds for therapeutic guidance and remedial services; speech, hearing, and psychological diagnostic services; standardized tests and scoring as used in public schools;[45] and state-mandated testing and reporting services.[46] Guidance counseling, remedial instruction, and other therapeutic services are permissible if provided by public school teachers away from the religious school campus[47] but not if provided on the campus.[48]

(e) Textbook Loans. Loans of state-approved secular textbooks to students in church-related schools are constitutionally permissible.[49] The state, however, cannot loan maps, projectors, or other instructional materials to the school.[50]

(f) Tuition Deductions, Reimbursements, and Credits. In the 1973 case of *Sloan v. Lemon* the Court found it unconstitutional to reimburse parents for costs of nonpublic school tuition.[51] In the same year, in *Committee for Public Education v. Nyquist,*[52] tax credits for parents having children in nonpublic schools were also found unconstitutional. State income tax deductions for private school tuition, however, are acceptable according to the 1983 case of *Mueller v. Allen.*[53] As with the certificates for child care that can now be used at religious facilities under 1990 funding legislation, there is a growing trend for federal, state, and local governments to seek constitutional means to strengthen and use existing institutions, including the religious, to provide needed services and allow users choice in those services.

While one can recite the results of these cases, they are difficult to reconcile on a consistent basis. Douglas Laycock, of the University of Texas School of Law, has identified six theories that have been articulated by various justices from time to time. They may be summarized as follows:

1. The no-aid theory. No state money may be paid to a religious school or its students. Any money so paid expands the school's budget and aids religion.
2. The purchase-of-services theory. State money paid to a religious school is simply a purchase of educational service which the state is obliged to provide for free to all of its children anyway and can do so through independent contractors as long as it is only paying for the secular part of the education.
3. The equal-treatment theory. Government is either obligated or permitted to pay for the secular aspects of education in religious schools, because children have a constitutional right to attend such schools and their exercise of that constitutional right forfeits the state subsidy of their education, thus penalizing the exercise of their constitutional right and discriminating against religion.
4. The child-benefit theory. The state can provide educational benefits directly to children or their parents, even if used at or in connection with the religious school so long as the aid is not provided directly to the school.
5. The tracing theory. Activities of the religious school are divided into the wholly secular and those that are or may be affected by religion. Government money is traced to be sure that it is used for a wholly secular expenditure.
6. The little-bit theory. A little bit of aid

to religious schools is all right, but too much is not. Laycock suggests that this theory "may explain more of the Court's results than the theories it relies on more often. . . . Perhaps, in general, the Court believes that a little bit of government support for religion is unobjectionable."[54]

In these difficult and sometimes divisive issues that arise in gray areas where government and religion meet, despite the various tests that have been articulated by the Court and principles that it attempts to follow, perhaps the only final answer is that lines must be drawn somewhere and this is where the judges responsible for the final judgment have drawn them.

c. Other Important Establishment Clause Cases

In the 1990 decision of *Mergens v. Board of Education*,[55] discussed below, the Court found no Establishment Clause violation in the Equal Access Act,[56] which permitted student religious groups to meet on public school premises, if the school had a "limited open forum" that permitted noncurriculum-related groups meeting on school premises during noncurriculum hours.

The Court has upheld the granting of local property tax exemptions to buildings used for religious worship, as part of a broad statutory scheme of exemptions that included charitable and other nonprofit organizations;[57] has struck down a state sales tax exemption limited to religious publications;[58] and has upheld the constitutionality of the exemption from the Civil Rights Act of 1964 for religious institutions that discriminate in employment on the basis of religion.[59] These cases are discussed below in more detail in the sections dealing with their subject matter.[60]

F. THE FREE EXERCISE CLAUSE

1. History and Meaning of Free Exercise

"Congress shall make no law . . . prohibiting the free exercise [of religion]."

Adele Sherbert, a Seventh Day Adventist, was discharged by her employer for her refusal to work on Saturday, which was her Sabbath. She applied for unemployment compensation from the state of South Carolina, which denied the application on the grounds that her refusal to work Saturdays disqualified her for failing to accept suitable work.

Jonas Yoder, an Amish parent in Wisconsin, where the compulsory school attendance law required children to attend school to age sixteen, refused to send his children to school beyond the eighth grade. Yoder believed it contrary to the Amish faith to expose his children to worldly beliefs that contradicted central Amish religious values. He was prosecuted under Wisconsin's truancy laws.

Alfred Smith, a Native American, ingested peyote as part of the sacraments of the Native American church in Oregon, where possession of peyote is a crime. Fired from his job as a drug rehabilitation counselor, Smith sought unemployment compensation. Oregon denied the compensation on the ground that his discharge was due to work-related "misconduct."

Adele Sherbert, Jonas Yoder, and Alfred Smith have something in common. Each of them was a litigant in a major Free Exercise Clause case that reached the United States Supreme Court and shaped Free Exercise jurisprudence. Establishment Clause cases, as the reader will have noted, are populated with school boards, municipalities, and assorted government officials defending the validity of laws or practices of the government or a government agency that are alleged to be "respecting an establishment of religion" against attacks by individuals or groups who do not share the faith position that it is claimed the law or practice in issue endorses.

Free Exercise cases, in contrast, have been populated by members of religious groups that have typically been perceived, at least at the time of each case, as outside the mainstream of American religious life: Mormons, Jehovah's Witnesses, Amish, Seventh Day Adventists, Orthodox Jews, Moslems, members of the Native American church.

Adele Sherbert, Jonas Yoder, and Alfred Smith were each part of such religious groups whose beliefs and practices were in certain respects outside the American mainstream. These religious practices brought them into conflict with laws of general application, that is, laws that do not discriminate against religion in the sense of singling out a particular sect, sects, or religion in general for special treatment but apply to all citizens regardless of sect and do not prohibit any religious belief. As they apply to the religious practices of these particular people of faith, however, these laws of general applicability either prohibit their religiously motivated conduct or deprive the religious person who exercises that conduct of benefits provided by the government to everybody else. Their cases pose the paradigmatic issue of the rights of religious people in our constitutional democracy and the essential issue litigated under the Free Exercise Clause: When, if ever, does religious conviction excuse a person from having to obey the same law that everyone else has to obey?

The English philosopher John Locke clearly stated the concerns that our forebears later expressed in the Declaration of Independence, the Constitution, and the Bill of Rights. Jefferson, Madison, and others were intimately familiar with Locke's work. He was a zealous advocate of religious toleration and the separation of church and state. He would not, however, have allowed any exceptions on the basis of religious conscience to the obligation of citizens to obey the law.

Jefferson and Madison, perhaps the two most prominent thinkers and writers among the American founders, and both of whom were influenced in many ways by Locke, appear to differ from each other on this issue. Even though allusions can be found in the writings of each to lend support to either position, Jefferson appears to have subscribed to Locke's view that the natural rights of a person did not extend "in opposition to his social duties."[61] Madison, in contrast, in *A Memorial and Remonstrance against Religious Assessments,*[62] recognized the prior claim of the "Universal Sovereign" on a person's conscience.

The history of religious tolerance in the colonies before the Constitution was adopted was mixed. Despite widespread intolerance,

particularly in the seventeenth century, there were in fact a number of practices common in the colonies that evidenced the colonials' acceptance of the principle that religious conscience stood above generally applicable laws in many instances—for example, regarding conscientious objection to military service, religious assessments for the support of established churches, and the requirement of oath taking. All of the original states' constitutions made some provision for religious freedom, but the language differed. Some extended it only to specifically religious activity such as worship, while others granted a general free exercise right subject only to exceptions for conduct that endangered the "peace and safety" or some similar behavior.

Before the incorporation cases of the 1940s extended First Amendment obligations to the states, any issues of religious liberty relative to state action were determined under the states' laws and constitutions, which often differed in interpretation as well as language. Two interesting cases, from New York and Pennsylvania, illustrate early American legal attitudes toward the free exercise issue of exemptions in the context of the privacy of the confessional. De Witt Clinton, mayor of New York City and, later, governor of New York and presidential candidate against Madison, hearing an 1813 case in which a Catholic priest was subpoenaed to testify to matters heard in confession, declared, "This important branch [confession and penance] of the Roman Catholic religion would be thus annihilated. . . . This court can never countenance or authorize the application of insult to their faith, or of torture to their consciences."[63] John Bannister Gibson, chief justice of the Pennsylvania Supreme Court, on the other hand, addressed the same question in 1831 when Clinton's opinion was presented to him in a case requiring a Jew to testify on his Sabbath against his conscience: "No one is more sensible than I, of the benefit derived by society from the office of the Catholic clergy, or of the policy of protecting the secrets of auricular confession. But . . . were the laws dispensed with, whenever they happen to be in collision with some supposed religious obligation government would be perpetually falling short of the exigence."[64] In Gibson's Pennsylvania courts, no recognition would be accorded the privacy of the confessional.

The earliest free exercise cases involved the Mormon practice of polygamy.[65] In the first of these cases, the *Reynolds* case in 1878, the U.S. Supreme Court articulated the distinction between belief and action in a free exercise case. The Court has repeatedly held from its earliest decisions on the subject that the Free Exercise Clause affords an absolute protection to *beliefs* but that religious *actions* are subject to some regulation notwithstanding the clause. The need for the distinction is self-evident. The society could hardly tolerate an absolutist interpretation of the clause in the face of a sect that insisted on practicing, for example, human sacrifice.

In *Reynolds*, the Court found no free exercise protection for the polygamous conduct at issue, rejecting the notion that conduct (as opposed to belief) would ever be entitled to protection. That position was repudiated in the 1940s. A series of cases, most of them involving Jehovah's Witnesses, addressed the right of states and municipalities to license or regulate public religious meetings, the distribution of religious literature, and religious solicitation. In virtually all of these cases, the Court found the municipal action in denying a license or seeking to regulate or criminalize such activity unconstitutional, often resting its decisions on the freedoms of speech and/or the press in lieu of or in addition to freedom of religion.

Adele Sherbert's case[66] in 1963 and Jonas Yoder's case[67] in 1972 became the occasions for the Court to articulate a three-pronged test for measuring free exercise cases, a free exercise counterpart to the *Lemon* test for Establishment Clause cases; the *Sherbert/Yoder* test stood until the 1990 decision in Alfred Smith's case (see pp. 46–49, below). It set forth the test for the validity of a free exercise claim as follows:

1. *Does the claimant have a sincerely held religious belief that is at issue?* Free exercise cases have occasionally compelled the Court to address what constitutes a "religion" for free exercise purposes. In most cases the sincerity of the belief has not been questioned by the Court or the government, although one can discern, or at least suspect, a tendency to be more deferential to government regulation with respect to beliefs more remote from the American mainstream, as in the Mormon polygamy case or several more recent cases involving the Native American church. It may be easier to define what religion is not than what it is. In the *Yoder* case, the Court had no doubt of the sincerity and religious nature of Yoder's belief. But it noted that:

A way of life, however virtuous and admirable, may not be interposed as a barrier to reasonable state regulation of education if it is based purely on secular considerations; to have the protection of the Religion Clauses, the claims must be rooted in religious belief. Although a determination of what is a "religious" belief or practice entitled to Constitutional protection may present a most delicate question, the very concept of ordered liberty precludes allowing every person to make his own standard on matters of conduct in which society as a whole has important interest. Thus, if the Amish asserted their claims because of their subjective evaluation and rejection of the contemporary secular values accepted by the majority, much as Thoreau rejected the social values of his time and isolated himself at Walden Pond, their claims would not rest on a religious basis. Thoreau's choice was philosophical and personal rather than religious, and such belief does not give rise to the demands of the Religion Clauses.[68]

In the 1961 case of *Torcaso v. Watkins*[69] the Court indicated that nontheistic religions such as "Buddhism, Taoism, Ethical Culture, Secular Humanism and others"[70] would be considered religions for purposes of the religion clauses.[71]

The Court will not, however, inquire into the truth or falsity of the belief as such, although one can imagine a belief so bizarre as to raise a serious issue as to whether it could be sincerely held by anyone. Nor does the entitlement of the belief to free exercise protection depend on it being shared by all, or even any, of the members of a particular sect. It may be entirely unique to the individual so long as it is "religious" and sincere.[72]

> [T]he determination of what is a "religious" belief or practice . . . is not to turn upon a judicial perception of the particular belief or practice in question; religious beliefs need not be acceptable, logical, consistent, or comprehensible to others in order to merit First Amendment protection. . . . The guarantee of Free Exercise is not limited to beliefs which are shared by all of the members of a religious sect. Particularly in this sensitive area, it is not within the judicial function and judicial competence to enquire whether the petitioner or his fellow worker more correctly perceived the commands of their common faith. Courts are not arbiters of Scriptural interpretation.[73]

2. *Does the law at issue unduly burden the free exercise of the claimant's religion?* While the Court has had difficulty on the question of whether it can properly assess the centrality of a belief to a free exercise claimants' religion without impermissibly inquiring into the truth of the religion and has been deferential to claimants' positions in this area, it is clear that not every incidental or remote burden on religion will give rise to a free exercise right.

3. *Is there a compelling governmental interest in the burden imposed by the law or regulation? As a corollary to this, if such a compelling interest is found, has it been implemented by the least restrictive means available with respect to the First Amendment interest at issue?* It is this third part of the free exercise test that has generated the most attention in litigation. Most free exercise cases involve sincere religious beliefs that are significantly burdened by a law of general applicability. Since *Sherbert*, most cases have turned on an analysis of how compelling the government's interest is in enforcing the law with respect to the particular free exercise claim and whether the claim could be accommodated by some less restrictive regulation. Such an accommoda-

tion appears in the Constitution itself in the allowing of affirmations instead of oaths for public office.[74]

Applying the three-part test, the Court found the free exercise claim of the Amish parents in *Yoder* overcame Wisconsin's compulsory attendance law, and it allowed the unemployment compensation claims of the Sabbatarian in *Sherbert*. Similar free exercise claims were allowed in three later unemployment compensation cases, *Thomas v. Review Board* (1981), involving a pacifist's objection to manufacturing military equipment, *Hobbie v. Unemployment Commission* (1987), another Sabbatarian case, and *Frazee v. Illinois Department of Employee Security* (1989), which held that the religious belief in question could be unique to the individual.[75]

In recent years the Court has analyzed certain types of free exercise claims by a less demanding standard than the compelling government interest test. This has included cases involving prisoners and the military, in which the Court has required only that the government show a "rational relationship" between the government conduct or regulation and a legitimate government interest, as opposed to a compelling interest accomplished by the least restrictive means. The Court has also denied relief in cases in which free exercise claimants have sought to reshape the government's way of conducting its business to accommodate their religion as opposed to the government compelling the religious claimants to follow practices that offended their religion. One case allowed a government road to be placed through public land used by Native Americans for religious purposes.[76] Another upheld a state rule requiring families seeking child welfare benefits to obtain a Social Security number for the child over religious objections to both applying for and government use of the number.[77]

The three-pronged free exercise test articulated in *Sherbert* and *Yoder* guided the courts and was considered settled First Amendment law, with the limited exceptions noted above, until Alfred Smith's case was decided in June of 1990.[78] In *Employment Division v. Smith,* the Court issued an opinion that effected a sea change in free exercise jurisprudence. Abandoning the third prong of the *Sherbert* and *Yoder* test—that governmental actions that substantially burden a religious practice must be justified by a compelling governmental interest and must be the least restrictive means to accomplish that interest—the Court found that the Free Exercise Clause did not compel it to conduct such a balancing test or determine whether the religious freedom claimant's burden was justified by a compelling governmental interest.

Breathing new life into the old *Reynolds* rule,[79] the Court retreated from both its role as the protector of religious minorities and the notion that religious claims to exemptions from laws of general applicability were entitled to any constitutional protection. *Smith* found the interest in religious freedom to be less than other freedoms, such as freedom from racial discrimination and freedom of speech, which it acknowledged were areas in which the compelling governmental interest test had been applied. It left to the political process the accommodation of an individual's religious beliefs to generally applicable legislation, noting that some states had exempted sacramental peyote use such as Smith's from their drug laws.

> It may fairly be said that leaving accommodation to the political process will place at a relative disadvantage those religious practices that are not widely engaged in; but that unavoidable consequence of democratic government must be preferred to a system in which each conscience is a law unto itself or in which judges weigh the social importance of all laws against the centrality of all religious beliefs.[80]

Smith's deference to the legislative branch and its abandonment of the "compelling governmental interest" test disturbed a broad spectrum of groups concerned with religious liberty from a wide range of political and religious perspectives. Absent the protection of the compelling governmental interest test, a variety of common religious practices could come into question. The possibilities include creating legislation that prohibits alcoholic beverages without making an exemption for sacramental use of wine; landmark preservation statutes that restrict the use of religious sanctuaries; health- or humane-based laws that ban certain types of ritual slaughter or circumcision; compelling public or private school students to be exposed to sex education and AIDS-prevention classes that their religion finds morally offensive; applying employment discrimination laws to require religious bodies to hire employees who are not members of their religion or whose conduct is offensive to the teachings of the religion; compelling doctors and nurses to perform abortions even if their religious principles would be offended by doing so; forbidding sexual segregation in the Orthodox synagogue; invading the privacy of the confessional; and the list goes on. In a secularized society in which the moral consensus may have a decreasing sensitivity to the unique claims of religion on individual conscience, the protection of religious practices from majoritarian regulation must be the concern of all religious groups.

Although the decision was five to four with a strong dissent by Justice O'Connor, most of the dissenters were the older justices and two—Brennan and Marshall—have since retired. And although the case involved a criminal, not civil, law of general applicability, the Court gave no signal that the abandonment of the compelling governmental interest test was limited to free exercise claims that contravened only criminal statutes. The opinion generated a petition for rehearing which brought together such diverse groups as People for the American Way, the Unitarian-Universalist Association, the Baptist Joint Committee, the Christian Legal Society, the Lutheran Church-Missouri Synod, and the National Association of Evangelicals, as well as mainstream religious groups such as the National Council of Churches and the American Jewish Committee. The petition was signed by fifty-four American constitutional scholars, including such well-known and often-referenced professors as Gerald Gunther of Stanford, Laurence Tribe of Harvard, Douglas Laycock of the University of

Texas, and Michael McConnell of the University of Chicago. The petition was denied.

Smith did not revise all previous free exercise law. It apparently leaves intact the series of unemployment compensation decisions, at least so long as the grounds for denying compensation are not the violation of a criminal statute. It reaffirms the absolute protection of religious beliefs as opposed to conduct. And, importantly, it purports not to change the numerous free exercise cases in which other constitutionally protected rights were involved along with religion, such as the right of parents to direct the education of their children and religious freedom assertions that involve communicative activities such as speech, press, or assembly, which the Court labeled "hybrid" rights. Thus Jonas Yoder, Adele Sherbert, and the Jehovah's Witnesses might achieve the same result under the *Smith* rule as when their cases were litigated. Other cases not within these exceptions, however, would not.

Smith has caused free exercise lawyers and constitutional law professors to throw away their notes. In its aftermath the content of the Free Exercise Clause will be shaped by litigation that yet lies ahead. Early results show that lower courts, no longer bound to give as much deference to religious objections to generally applicable laws, are increasingly rejecting free exercise claims. Whatever the future of free exercise jurisprudence, at least two directions are already clear: (1) a greater reliance on legislation to accommodate religious conscience, and (2) a new emphasis on state constitutions as sources of free exercise rights and state courts as protectors of those rights.

Legislative accommodation to religious freedom concerns can be approached on a generic basis by passing federal legislation which would write into law as a statute the *Sherbert* and *Yoder* standards for government restrictions on the free exercise of religion, including the compelling governmental interest test. Such legislation, known as the Religious Freedom Restoration Act, has been introduced in Congress. While some have expressed reservations about the wisdom or desirability of relying on legislation to implement constitutional freedoms thought to be above majoritarian control, there is much support in the political and religious liberty communities for moving in this direction.[81] Legislative accommodation can also be specific; it can, as has occurred in other areas of law, address particular issues on a case-by-case basis in response to political disagreement with the Court's seeming retreat in recent years from its role as the guardian of religious freedom.[82]

The second inevitable consequence of the *Smith* decision will be to cause free exercise claimants to look to their state constitutions for protections no longer available under the U.S. Constitution. Such cases are already reported in Minnesota and Massachusetts. In *Minnesota v. Hershberger,* decided by the Minnesota Supreme Court in November of 1990,[83] the Court considered a religious freedom claim by the Amish in which they objected on religious grounds to compliance with a state statute requiring them to display an SMV symbol on their slow-moving vehicles; they proposed instead to use silver reflective tape in conjunction with lighted red lanterns. An appeal to the U.S. Supreme Court had resulted in the vacating of an earlier judgment in favor of the Amish and a direction that the Minnesota Supreme Court reconsider the case in light of the *Smith* decision. In response, the Minnesota court ignored *Smith* and turned instead (as it is constitutionally entitled to do) to the Minnesota Constitution which, it found, afforded Minnesotans "greater protection for religious liberty against governmental action under the State Constitution than under the First Amendment of the Federal Constitution."[84] The Minnesota court said that in order to infringe upon the asserted religious freedoms, the state must demonstrate that public safety could not be achieved through reasonable alternative means—essentially the *Sherbert/Yoder* test. Since the state had failed to make such a demonstration in this case, the Amish again prevailed.

Hershberger was followed by the December 1990 decision of the Massachusetts Supreme Judicial Court in *Society of Jesus v. Boston Landmarks Commission.*[85] The Society of Jesus (Jesuits) wanted to renovate the historic Church of the

Immaculate Conception in Boston's South End, whose attendance was declining, to provide office, counseling, and residential space. The Boston Landmarks Commission, acting under state statutes, gave landmark designation to portions of the interior, including the nave, chancel, vestibule, and organ loft, and refused to permit the alterations. The trial court had decided in favor of the Jesuits on the basis of the federal Free Exercise Clause. The Massachusetts high court, like Minnesota's, deciding the appeal after *Smith*, ignored the First Amendment and found for the Jesuits based on the Massachusetts Constitution. Interestingly, although the Massachusetts Constitution did not protect free "exercise" of religion but only "worshipping" and "religious profession and sentiments," the court read the word "worship" broadly to include "religious practice." The *Society of Jesus* case evidences the reality that, in a post-*Smith* world, mainstream religious groups and practices are as vulnerable as the less common or less understood groups.

Two other states have since had occasion to reconsider their state constitutional religious freedom protection in view of *Smith*. In *Donahue v. Fair Employment and Housing Commission*,[86] a California intermediate appellate court concluded that California's understanding of its state constitution continued to be determined by pre-*Smith* rules and upheld the religous freedom claim of a Roman Catholic couple to violate the nondiscrimination in housing law by refusing to rent to an unmarried couple. And the Maine Supreme Court, in *Rupert v. City of Portland*,[87] while declining to decide if it would follow *Smith* in its interpretation of the Maine Constitution, in fact applied the old *Sherbert/Yoder* standards to find that a religious freedom claim did not protect a Native American from the seizure of a marijuana pipe under the Maine Drug Paraphernalia Act.

Hershberger, *Society of Jesus,* and their progeny, which will continue to develop in the state courts, along with proposed federal legislation, demonstrate that the free exercise values developed over the last fifty years of Supreme Court jurisprudence have become normative in the minds of the American people to the extent that state courts and the political process may perpetuate those values for the time being even when the Supreme Court retreats from its recent historic role as the protector of the liberty of religious minorities. People of faith must be concerned, however, about subjecting those values to the variant interpretations of the highest courts of fifty states and to the majoritarian rule of legislation. Free exercise has lost the shining gleam of a priority constitutional right and must beg for its continued vitality among the state courts and politically sensitive legislators, state and federal. How long the normative consensus will last remains to be seen.

2. Free Exercise Applications

a. Private Schools and Day Care Centers

In the 1800s, Roman Catholic immigrants came to America in large numbers and faced the problems of preserving their culture and religion in an often-hostile Protestant milieu that included the public schools, where the Protestant Bible was read and Protestant notions taught. In response, they began the parochial school system in which millions of Catholic children received their elementary and often their entire education. In recent decades, as the public schools have become ever more secularized under the twin pressures of Establishment Clause litigation that suppresses the vestiges of religious observance and cultural and philosophical shifts that leave public schools largely bereft of the will to inculcate values, conservative Protestant Christians have followed the Catholic example by creating a nationwide system of Christian schools. Jewish and other groups also have sectarian schools, and many parents have taken to "home schooling" their children for similar reasons.

Day care centers, often housed in religious premises or run by religious groups, have been born of related social conditions. Social inhibitions and legal restrictions on divorce have collapsed in recent decades. Nearly one in two marriages ends in divorce. Single-parent families, usually headed by women, make it an economic necessity to be a working mother. Married women are more likely to want—or need—a career or job than in the past. Churches and church groups across the religious spectrum have moved into the child-care gap, helping to fill a genuine need in a manner consistent with their beliefs or lending little-used facilities to other groups to do so.

Both phenomena have tested the free exercise limits of the power of government to regulate religious institutions.

The significant legal history goes back to 1925 when the state of Oregon tried to force all of its school-age students to attend public schools. In *Pierce v. Society of Sisters*,[88] the U.S. Supreme Court determined that parents had a constitutional right to select religious education, a right the state could not usurp. This and *Yoder*, discussed above, which established a limited free exercise exception to compulsory attendance laws, have been the only cases with respect to government regulation of religious schooling that have reached the Supreme Court. Following principles set forth in these and other free exercise cases, however, a substantial body of cases in lower courts have established that although there is a parental right to control a child's religious education, there is also a compelling governmental interest in both the health and safety and the quality of education of students in private schools. State regulation of private schools has generally been upheld and has covered a variety of areas—licensing, compulsory attendance, minimum hours of instruction, teachers with specified qualifications, secular curriculum content, and health, fire, and safety laws. Schools in churches have been held to regulations applicable to schools instead of churches.

The state may not, however, overregulate in an unreasonable manner or in a way that destroys the distinctiveness of the private school, as by requiring so much secular curriculum that no time is left for religious studies, or by rules that are so pervasive and all-encompassing that private schools and parents are deprived of any discretion in the education of children in such schools. And, again, some states may find free exercise rights in the state constitution that prohibit a level of regulation that would not offend the federal Constitution.[89]

Day care centers, operating outside the orbit of mandatory education, present a different set of problems.[90] Health and safety regulations are universal, although the ambit of them may vary considerably. Child-to-staff ratios, personnel qualifications, nutrition, discipline, and record keeping may add to such basic regulations as fire codes and building safety. Some states provide less stringent measures for regulating church-sponsored centers. Sometimes administrative interpretation by state regulators accommodates free exercise concerns of church-sponsored day care centers without forcing confrontation.

Churches may object to being subject to any regulation or may object only to certain specific regulations that are claimed to violate their free exercise rights. In those instances when churches have objected to any regulation, they have met with little success. The compelling governmental interest in children's health and safety is sufficient to overcome the objection that any regulation violates the church's religious interest.[91] Objections to specific regulations are handled on a case-by-case basis. When administrative agencies have interpreted regulations to accommodate the free exercise claim, the courts have not thrown out the regulation just because it could be interpreted otherwise. For example, a Michigan requirement that day care center directors have completed a minimum of credits at an accredited college or university presented a problem to a center that hired most of its staff from Christian colleges that objected to accreditation. The Michigan Department of Social Services did not enforce the rule against church-sponsored day care providers, instead developing a special set of criteria to measure competence of graduates of nonaccredited colleges.[92]

Church-sponsored or church-operated day care centers have not had much success in their religious objections to bans on corporal punishment. Despite such centers' espousal of the "spare the rod, spoil the child"[93] biblical mandate as religiously compelled, courts have generally upheld restrictions on corporal punishment as part of the state's compelling interest in the physical and emotional treatment of children.[94]

Churches or church-related institutions troubled on religious grounds by government regulation of school, day care, or other programs should seek legal advice and evaluate their concerns with at least the following considerations:

1. Does the regulation truly contradict a specific religious belief, or does it merely inconvenience the activity or make it more expensive? What is the biblical or other principle of faith that is offended? Be sure its source and binding authority are understood. Can the regulation be obeyed without a true violation of duty to God?
2. Is the belief that is offended central or important, or is it peripheral?
3. Is the burden of the regulation significant, or is it remote or incidental?
4. Consider prayerfully the mandate of Romans 13 and other Scripture to submit to governing authorities.
5. Consider the purpose of the regulation and whether that purpose is not shared by the religious group itself.
6. Is there a way to accomplish the purpose of the regulation without offending the requirements of religious conscience?
7. Talk the issues through with the regulators concerned. Explain your religious objection in depth. Explore alternatives. See if an accommodation can be reached that satisfies the legitimate concerns of both sides.
8. Only after all efforts have failed to find a reasonable accommodation to a religious belief that cannot be compromised should the issue be taken to court.

b. The Right to Witness

The Christian church is a unique organization. It is, in thoughts and words, if not in deeds, a band of thieves and whores who have come to know the meaning of repentance and forgiveness and are commanded to bring that good news to all the other thieves and whores outside. A primary reason for its existence is to benefit those who do not belong to it. While the means of communicating the good news differs from group to group, to many, witnessing or proselytizing is important, not just to growth or financial health but to obedience to their understanding of Scripture or the requirements of their faith. Door-to-door calling, speaking, and distributing literature in public places are the usual forms of public exercise of these requirements. The history of the practice is at least as old as the ministry of Jesus himself. New and unpopular groups often test the legal limits of public witnessing, as did the apostles as recounted in the book of Acts.

In American constitutional history, the principal definers of the right to witness have been the Jehovah's Witnesses. Bursting onto the American legal and public scene in the mid-twentieth century with intolerant and often virulently anti-Catholic messages, they provoked state and local officials to seek tactics to stop them. They were aggressively litigious and prevailed in all but twelve of eighty-seven cases they appealed to the Supreme Court from 1937 to 1977.[95] Many of the cases were decided on the basis of free speech or press in lieu of or in addition to the Free Exercise Clause. These cases established that religious speech and press are entitled to the same free speech and press protection as any other speech or writing, in addition to whatever protections they are entitled to under the religion clauses. Because these cases fall into the "hybrid rights" category, their ongoing validity is apparently not affected by *Smith*.[96]

The Jehovah's Witnesses are no longer the primary litigants in this area. The rules established by their cases have filtered into the legal fabric of government and are largely accepted and followed. New groups continue to press the limits of these rights, however. In the 1980s, one was more likely to see Hare Krishnas, Jews for Jesus, or anti-abortion protesters invoking the regulatory wrath of local officials, and these groups continue to shape the law and the limits of governmental action. The sum of the Jehovah's Witness and other similar cases involving witnessing, distribution of literature, picketing, or solicitation covers certain specific areas and may be stated as follows:

(1) Door-to-Door Activities

Government may not prohibit door-to-door witnessing, including sales of literature or solicitation of contributions. It may not license such activities on a discretionary basis. It may not tax such activities or prohibit people engaged in them from summoning inhabitants of a home to the door. It may not discriminate among groups engaged in such activities, as by limiting solicitation to groups that use a certain percentage of their contributions for charitable purposes.

Government may, however, act to prevent fraud, as by requiring people to establish their identity and authority to represent the organization or cause for which they claim to speak as long as it does not inquire into the truth of the religious claims.[97] It may impose reasonable regulations to preserve public safety, health, order, and convenience. It can, for example, prosecute the use of "fighting words" that may provoke breaches of the peace, and it can apply child labor laws to prevent the use of children in distributing religious literature. And it may protect people in their homes from unwanted speech that intrudes into their privacy, such as targeted residential picketing.

(2) Witnessing in Public Places

Government is subject to the same restrictions in regulating witnessing activities in public places as it is with respect to door-to-door witnessing. It may not prohibit, tax, license on a discretionary basis, or discriminate among groups conducting such activities. Nor may it ban the use of loudspeakers, although it can regulate their sound level.

Government may, however, require a license or permit as long as the conditions to obtain it are specific, thus removing discretion from the issuing officials; those conditions are directed to meeting the constitutionally permissible objectives of preserving public peace, order, safety, health, or convenience in the least restrictive manner, and regulating the time, place, and manner of use of public streets and places to prevent disorder and scheduling conflicts. Moreover, provision must be made for action on applications in a reasonable time period, with the burden on the government to show why the permit should be denied; a prompt, final judicial resolu-

tion must be available. Trespassing and blocking access to facilities will receive no First Amendment protection, however, no matter how firmly or on what religious or other grounds the protester believes in his or her cause.

In assessing government restrictions on public expression, the courts often distinguish between three categories of public property: (1) the traditional public forum such as the streets, sidewalks, and public square; (2) the public forum by government designation, where the government has permitted First Amendment activities although it may not have been required to do so; and (3) the nonpublic forum. In the first two categories, the government may not ban all communicative activities and may regulate only in a narrow manner to serve a compelling interest, as with time, place, and manner regulations that are not based on speech content. An important factor in evaluating the reasonableness of time, place, and manner regulations is the extent of alternative means of communication. When these are available, government regulation of communicative activities will be viewed leniently. In the nonpublic forum, access may be reasonably restricted by regulations not intended to suppress expression. The government may not, however, discriminate against religious communicative activities when it allows such secular activities.

In practice, these rules have had recent application in several cases that have reached the United States Supreme Court. An attempt by the Los Angeles Board of Airport Commissioners to ban all First Amendment activities in the central terminal of the Los Angeles Airport was found invalid on its face.[98] In New York airports, the distribution of literature has been allowed but the solicitation of funds prohibited.[99] The Minnesota State Fair was allowed to restrict the Hare Krishnas' solicitation and distribution of literature on the fair grounds to a booth.[100] Ordinances forbidding targeted residential picketing that intrudes on home privacy have been found valid.[101] A crèche scene funded by a private group with an appropriate disclaimer may be placed for a limited time in a public park that has been used as a public forum.[102]

The degree and nature of acceptable regulation will depend on the nature of the public forum in question. The broad protection afforded to activities in the public square or on the sidewalk narrows to be nearly impassable at the schoolhouse door. What may be acceptable in the street may not be acceptable in the reading room of the library. Significant protection of public schools from outside First Amendment activity has been allowed,[103] although public universities may be limited to rules that protect the opportunity of their students to receive an education.[104] Cases are decided on a fact-specific basis, and the detailed circumstances are always important.

c. Access to the Nonpublic Forum

Evangelistic crusades or religious speakers come to town and need a place to speak to larger crowds than the local churches can accommodate. Conventions and conferences of church groups or on religious subjects are organized to bring believers together to share information and inspiration. Church and parachurch groups run programs that need specialized facilities they do not have. New churches spring up, sometimes planted as an outreach of existing groups or denominations, sometimes spontaneous gatherings of believers departing from or feeling a need to gather outside existing local churches. Often the only suitable facilities available for such activities are publicly owned. In these and other situations, religious people may seek access to publicly owned property—stadiums, civic centers, auditoriums, schools with cafeterias and gymnasiums—for religious activities, even worship services. Although few cases dealing with these issues have reached the U.S. Supreme Court (a limited exception is *Widmar v. Vincent*, discussed on p. 55, which deals with the rights of student religious groups in a public university),[105] lower courts have defined the rules governing them based on principles laid down by the U.S. Supreme Court.

The rules are as follows: Government is not required to make its nonpublic facilities, such as schools, available to others for use. If it does so, however, it must act on a neutral basis, making them available to religious as well as nonreligious groups on the same basis. It may not discriminate based on the content of the speech or activity. It is not an Establishment Clause violation for religious groups to be allowed the same access to public facilities as nonreligious groups, even for worship services. Government may, of course, impose reasonable time, place, and manner regulations, and such groups must reimburse the public owner for out-of-pocket expenses and pay fair rental value. Long-term use of public facilities for religious services with no evidence of intent by the group to acquire its own facilities, or more than occasional use for speakers, crusades, and the like, might be impermissible although there is little law dealing with such situations.

d. What Is Public Property?

Both a company town[106] and a federally owned town[107] have been found sufficiently public to give rise to First Amendment rights of door-to-door distribution of religious literature despite the owner's objection. Shopping centers, however, are not subject to those First Amendment rights[108] unless the activity directly concerns what is going on at the shopping center.[109] State constitutions, however, may extend a state constitutional right to engage in such activities at shopping centers even though the First Amendment does not require it.[110] An interesting question is the extent to which a public or private university may prohibit religious witnessing by outsiders on its campus. A public university, the Court has noted,[111] possesses many of the characteristics of a public forum; but it clearly has an educational mission that it has a right to protect by reasonable regulation, and it need not make its campus equally available to all, both students and nonstudents, or grant free access to all of its grounds and buildings. It is likely that similar rules would govern on a university campus as in other public forums, subject to the right to impose such additional time, place, and manner of use regulations as may be necessary to protect the opportunity of its students to receive an education.

The private college or university lacks the constitutional status of being itself an arm of the state and, hence, directly subject to constitutional limitations on state action. Residential higher educational institutions are, however, much like company towns and might be required to permit witnessing activities on their campuses, subject to the restrictions discussed above.

G. TENSION BETWEEN THE CLAUSES

The Free Exercise and Establishment Clauses have often been viewed as being in tension with one another. Excessive accommodation of the free exercise rights of some by exempting them from generally applicable laws may be viewed as government establishment of their religion. On the other hand, excessive zeal to remove religion from public life may intrude on legitimate free exercise claims.

Many scholars and commentators have endeavored to find a unifying theory for the two religion clauses. It has been advocated that they should be best understood as "co-guarantors of the core value of liberty of conscience in religious matters."[112] This view contends that "religious liberty is the core value of the religion clauses" and that the Court's "rigid dichotomy between the establishment and free exercise clauses, without reference to this unifying value, would appear to be flawed historically."[113] Other commentators would suggest that Establishment Clause values should yield to free exercise claims, that the free exercise claim should be interpreted broadly to protect religious minorities and the Establishment Clause construed narrowly to permit cultural expression of majority religions, or that tension between the clauses should be resolved in favor of the Establishment Clause.[114] One commentator has proposed the principal of "equality of religious liberty," or nondiscrimination, the "equal protection of everybody's freedom in matters of religion," as the reconciling principle.[115]

The Court itself has not endeavored to find a unifying theory but has viewed the two clauses as polar opposites. In the 1970 decision of *Walz v. Tax Commission*,[116] the Court stated, "The Court has struggled to find a neutral course between the two Religion Clauses, both of which are cast in absolute terms, and either of which, if expanded to a logical extreme, would tend to clash with the other."

The Court's actual decisions have moved back and forth between concepts of "separation" and "neutrality," on the one hand, both sometimes referred to as "strict,"[117] and the neutrality sometimes referred to as "benevolent" and a notion of "accommodation," on the other hand.[118] While much of the free exercise notion of accommodation as a matter of constitutional interpretation may be gone in the aftermath of *Smith*, the Court has been deferential to legislative accommodation to concerns of religious conscience, and *Smith* indicates it will continue to be so.

In its 1987 opinion in *Presiding Bishop v. Amos*,[119] the Court upheld the exemption of religious organizations from the ban on religious discrimination in employment in the Civil Rights Act of 1964 as applied to nonreligious activity of nonprofit religious corporations. The Court noted that it "has long recognized that the government may (and sometimes must) accommodate religious practices and that it may do so without violating the Establishment Clause."[120] It went on to quote *Walz* that "it is well established, too, that '[t]he limits of permissible state accommodation to religion are by no means co-extensive with the non-interference mandated by the Free Exercise Clause.'"[121] "There is ample room under the Establishment Clause for 'benevolent neutrality which will permit religious exercise to exist without sponsorship and without interference.'"[122] Although "[a]t some point, accommodation may devolve into 'an unlawful fostering of religion,'"[123] the secular legislative purpose test of *Lemon* means not that the purpose must be unrelated to religion, which would amount to a requirement that the government "show a callous indifference to religious groups"[124] but that it merely prevent the Congress from abandoning neutrality and acting to promote a particular point of view in religious matters. "Under the *Lemon* analysis, it is a permissible legislative purpose to alleviate significant governmental interference with the ability of religious organizations to define and carry out their religious missions."[125] A law is not unconstitutional simply because it allows churches to advance religion, which is their very purpose. For a law to have forbidden effects under *Lemon,* the government itself must be advancing religion through its own activities. Perhaps the last word on the relationship between the clauses should go to Chief Justice Burger, speaking in *Walz:*

> The general principle deducible from the First Amendment and all that has been said by the Court is this: that we will not tolerate either governmentally established religion or governmental interference with religion. Short of those expressly proscribed governmental acts there is room for play in the joints productive of a benevolent neutrality which will permit the religious exercise to exist without sponsorship and without interference.[126]

H. RELIGIOUS LIBERTY IN ACTION: THE EQUAL ACCESS CONTROVERSY

Christian students in public high schools and universities often want to form Christian groups or organizations for such activities as Bible study, prayer, or fellowship, and they want these groups to meet on the public campus as other extracurricular groups do. To school authorities gun-shy of litigation by organizations vigilant to exclude religion from the public square, permitting such activities on school premises looks like an Establishment Clause violation—an endorsement or advancement of, or excessive entanglement with, religion. To the students, refusing to accommodate their request to meet and use school facilities on the same basis as other groups looks like discrimination against religion and a violation of their free exercise rights. This very real conflict became known as the "equal access controversy" and illustrates live application of the religion clauses.

The issue began at the university level. In *Widmar v. Vincent,*[127] the University of Missouri, a public university, had denied a student group use of its facilities for religious purposes, although it had made its facilities generally available for student use. The student group challenged the university policy as a violation of its free exercise and free speech rights. The university contended that to permit its facilities to be so used by a religious group would violate the Establishment Clause. The Court sidestepped the free exercise issue. The students' religion might compel them to pray and read the Bible but not necessarily on university premises. Instead, it found that the students' right of free speech and association was denied by the university policy, because religious speech was entitled to the same protection as other forms of speech. As to the Establishment Clause concerns, it found that the university's objective of achieving a greater separation of church and state was not a sufficiently compelling state interest under the Establishment Clause to justify the discrimination against religious speech and association.

The issue, being thus resolved at the university level, then moved to the high school level where the different level of maturity of the students arguably justified a different result. In the case of *Bender v. Williamsport Area School District,*[128] a student religious group at a public high school sought to meet during a regularly scheduled school activity period in which pupils were generally free to pursue personal interests or participate in student clubs or groups. More than forty such groups had been allowed to meet. The state trial court followed the *Widmar* analysis and ordered the school district to permit the group to meet. The court of appeals reversed, holding that "the presence of religious groups within the school during the curricular day has the effect of advancing religion, in that it communicates a message of government endorsement of such activity" and that "prayer in the public schools segregates students along religious lines."[129] On appeal to the U.S. Supreme Court, the court of appeals decision was reversed on procedural grounds, thereby leaving in effect the trial court decision that permitted this particular group to meet, but also leaving the underlying issue unresolved on a broader level.

Perceiving a discrimination and hostility toward religious speech in the public schools, Congress then, by an overwhelming margin, enacted the Equal Access Act.[130] It requires public secondary schools that receive federal assistance and have a "limited open forum" to permit equal access to that forum to students who wish to conduct meetings on the basis of religious, political, or other content of speech. A "limited open forum" exists when the school allows "non-curriculum related student groups" to meet on school premises during noninstructional time. School employees can only be present for custodial or nonparticipatory purposes.

In Omaha, Nebraska, a young woman named Bridget Mergens requested that her high school let her and a group of students form a Christian club to meet at the school for the purposes of reading and discussing the Bible and having fellowship and prayer together. School officials refused and challenged the act as an Establishment Clause violation. Bridget became the named party in *Board of Education v. Mergens,*[131] which traveled through the federal court system to the Supreme Court to test the validity of this legislative accommodation to high school students' free exercise rights. In June of 1990, the Court, with a single dissent, found that the Equal Access Act was not a violation of the Establishment Clause, thereby giving the act a broad construction. The Court opined that "secondary students are mature enough and are likely to understand that a school does not endorse or support student speech that it merely permits on a nondiscriminatory basis."[132] There is a "crucial difference between *government* speech endorsing religion, which the Establishment Clause forbids, and *private* speech endorsing religion, which the Free Speech and Free Exercise Clauses protect."[133] Thus the principle of equal access carried the day through a combination of legislative action, court approval of free speech rather than free exercise rights for religious speech, and deference to Congress with respect to the establishment issue.

The equal access story is not over. In a case filed in Oklahoma in 1991,[134] a fifth grader complained that her free speech, associational, and equal protection rights were violated because she was being prevented from meeting voluntarily with other students during recess to discuss the Bible and pray. The case was settled with a recognition of the child's right to continue her activities and to engage in a peaceful, nondisruptive expression of her religious views, and her agreement not to communicate her views unless invited.[135] It remains to be seen if fifth graders will achieve the same constitutional rights of equal access as their elders in the student population.

Finally, in attempting to prevent the exercise of religion on school premises, some school districts have invoked state constitutions to bar voluntary student religious activity. The legal issue is whether the Supremacy Clause of the U.S. Constitution requires states to follow the Equal Access Act even if the activity would be forbidden by the state constitution. A federal district court in Idaho has said that it does and allowed the meeting.[136] A federal district court in the state of Washington reached the opposite result, finding that the Equal Access Act did not preempt contrary state law,[137] but the court did not consider whether the U.S. Constitution required permitting the students to meet. Like crèches and abortion, legal issues surrounding equal access will continue to play out through legislation, court decisions that interpret the legislation, and state and federal constitutional provisions for years to come.

I. SECTION 1983: CONSTITUTIONAL RIGHTS AS A SWORD

People deprived of their constitutional rights may have remedies that go beyond merely requiring the recognition of those rights. A federal statute, 42 U.S.C. Sec. 1983, reads in part as follows:

Every person who, under color of any statute, ordinance, regulation, custom, or usage, of any State or Territory or the District of Columbia, subjects, or causes to be subjected, any citizen of the United States or other person within the jurisdiction thereof to the deprivation of any rights, privileges, or immunities secured by the Constitution and laws shall be liable to the party injured in an action at law, suit in equity, or other proper proceeding for redress.

This statute was originally enacted in 1871 and was part of a series of statutes, along with the Thirteenth, Fourteenth, and Fifteenth Amendments to the Constitution, that were designed to protect the rights of African Americans. It has been rediscovered in the civil rights–conscious atmosphere of the last several decades and has been the source of prolific litigation. The collection, organization, and brief description of Section 1983 cases alone that appear in the United States Code Service, which provides such annotations to federal statutes, consume an entire volume of approximately one thousand pages.

Most Section 1983 litigation has nothing to do with religion. Since, however, First Amendment religious rights are among the rights "secured by the Constitution," any person who is deprived of those rights "under color of" any state law can seek redress of his or her injury by an action at law, for damages, or in equity, for an injunction. Religious litigants too have begun to discover their rights under Section 1983. In a number of cases, plaintiffs have been asserting violations of the Establishment Clause from municipal or school activities. Usually the only relief sought or obtained is injunctive relief. In at least several recent cases, however, the courts have considered or awarded damages under Section 1983 to religious plaintiffs deprived of their free exercise constitutional rights.

One such plaintiff was the Burlington Assembly of God Church, which owned 106 acres of land in New Jersey on which it operated a church, a school with three hundred students, and a garage for a fleet of thirty-five buses. Its desire to operate a radio station on the property required the construction of two 184-foot tall antenna towers, which required a zoning variance. The local zoning board denied the variance but was reversed by the superior court. The church then pursued its damage claims under Section 1983. The superior court allowed the church to collect such damages as it could prove.[138]

A similar case with a different result is *Love Church v. City of Evanston*.[139] The plaintiff challenged the constitutionality of an ordinance that required a special-use permit for a church and sought damages under Section 1983. The trial court had rejected the plaintiff's First Amendment claims but had entered judgment for the plaintiff on claims of equal protection, because churches were treated differently under the Evanston zoning ordinance than were other, similar gathering places, such as movie theaters, funeral homes, hotels, and community centers. The court awarded approximately $18,000 in damages. The appeals court reversed the decision, finding that the church did not have standing to bring the suit since there was no evidence that the Church's difficulty in finding quarters was caused by the zoning ordinance, which had never been enforced against any religious organization. The Love Church had never even applied for a special-use permit, much less been denied one, and in fact had met in various locations over a period of several years with no municipal enforcement against it. In the court of appeal's judgment, enjoining enforcement of the Evanston zoning ordinance would do nothing to help the church establish itself.

These cases illustrate that religious groups with real injuries due to deprivations of their constitutional rights under color of state law can seek and obtain monetary damages. Section 1983 may be of particular importance to smaller churches and religious groups with limited resources, because the right to collect damages includes the right of the prevailing party to receive reasonable attorneys' fees.[140] Legal cost is often the biggest barrier to the protection of rights of smaller groups and individuals—the very parties who may be least able to protect their interests in the political process. Court decisions on attorneys' fees have generally awarded them to successful plaintiffs in the absence of exceptional circumstances. The "prevailing party" that may be entitled to attorneys' fees can also be a successful defendant in a Section 1983 claim, but the courts have generally only allowed attorneys' fees to defendants if the original action was frivolous, unreasonable, or without foundation.

A second right under Section 1983, developed by court decisions, is to obtain punitive damages, that is, damages intended to punish a wrongdoing defendant rather than compensate for the loss to the plaintiff. The U.S. Supreme Court has allowed punitive damages in a Section 1983 action, following decisions in virtually all of the circuit courts of appeals to the same effect, when the defendant's conduct is shown to be motivated by evil motive or intent or when it involves reckless or careless indifference to federally protected rights.[141] Punitive damages cannot be assessed against municipalities but can be assessed against officials in their personal capacities.[142]

Thus financially strapped religious litigants or those who would pursue a more aggressive vindication of religious rights are armed by Section 1983 with the prospect of being made financially whole if successful. Whether or not to pursue these damage remedies must, of course, be guided by the litigant's theological understanding of the appropriateness of such litigation. A second, very practical consideration in such litigation is good will and public relations with the defendant, often a local government or regulatory board or its officials. A church that wants to be a witness to the world may wish to give careful consideration to the effect of aggressive litigation and collecting damages from governments or government officials, often local. And, as a practical matter, local boards and officials have a good deal of discretion in many areas. It is

not necessarily in a religious organization's best interest to be at sword's point with people it will continue to live with regardless of the outcome of the litigation. Nonetheless, a Section 1983 claim may be a useful tool when rights are abused.

REFERENCES

Adams, Arlin M., and Charles J. Emmerich. *A Nation Dedicated to Religious Liberty* (Philadelphia: University of Pennsylvania Press, 1990).

Bird, Wendell K. "U.S. Supreme Court Decisions on Freedom of Religion." Vol. 5, *Religious Freedom Reporter*, nos. 6 and 7 (June/July 1985).

Goldberg, George. *Church, State and the Constitution* (Washington, D.C.: Regnery Gateway, 1987).

Laycock, Douglas. "A Survey of Religious Liberty in the United States." 47 *Ohio State Law Journal* 409 (1986).

McConnell, Michael W. "The Origins and Historical Understanding of Free Exercise of Religion." 103 *Harvard Law Review* 1409 (1990).

———. "Free Exercise Revisionism and the Smith Decision." 57 *University of Chicago Law Review* 1109 (1990).

Payne, Lucy Salsbury. "Uncovering the First Amendment: A Research Guide to the Religion Clauses." 4 *Notre Dame Journal of Law and Ethics* 825 (1990). This valuable article collects the numerous publications dealing with the religion clauses of the First Amendment and has a selective bibliography of particularly pertinent sources.

U.S. LAW
AND RELIGIOUS BODIES

CHAPTER 4

Ecclesiastical Organization and the Courts

A. History
B. Contemporary Forms of Organization
  1. The Corporation Sole
  2. The Trustee Corporation
  3. The Membership Corporation
  4. The Unincorporated Religious
     Association
C. Church Organization and the Courts

A. HISTORY

In late-twentieth-century America, there are nearly three hundred thousand local church bodies.[1] These can be broadly grouped into twenty-two "families" of liturgy and belief.[2] Local churches are organized into well over two hundred denominations, either from the bottom up by affiliation of local churches or from the top down by establishment of churches within an existing hierarchy.[3] Every denomination, local church, and affiliated or independent religious group—schools, colleges, universities, seminaries, hospitals, nursing homes, day care centers, retirement communities, publishing houses, camps, conference centers, counseling centers, organizations advancing evangelism, missionary activity, youth work, and numerous other facets of ministry—must interface with the legal system in carrying out its affairs as an aggregate entity. To do this, most (but not all) have organized themselves as corporations or in a form that achieves the objectives of incorporation.

The necessity of the law to recognize the functioning of people in groups is said to be

as old as the Code of Hammurabi[4] (ca. 2083 B.C.) and was developed in Roman law, which fostered the idea that corporate or legal groups could only come into existence by imperial fiat or the creative touch of sovereign power.[5] Pope Innocent IV is credited with developing the notion under canon law of the *persona ficta,* or artificial person, which, by analogy to the Roman approach, was created and controlled by the pope.[6] Over the centuries, the exigencies of commerce developed a body of law known as the Law Merchant, or *Lex Mercatoria,* that provided for the recognition of commercial groups. The Law Merchant transcended local law and was generally recognized by the European countries.

By the fourteenth century English law recognized ecclesiastical and charitable corporations as well as temporal or governmental corporations, and in the sixteenth century commercial corporations arose in response to urbanization, wider trade, and the Law Merchant. Domestic trading groups such as medieval guilds, markets, and fairs contributed to the development of the law pertaining to organizations. English kings revived the Roman and papal notions that a corporation could only be established by royal authority as manifested by a charter or special act of Parliament, thus increasing governmental control. The principal feature of such corporations was their perpetual succession. Since they typically had the power to assess shareholders for money to pay debts—a power that could be used to satisfy their creditors—insulation from liability was not a primary concern in their formation. The Pilgrims who landed at Plymouth Rock in 1620 were granted their privileges by one such early trading company known as the Treasurer and Company of Adventurers and Planters of the City of London, for the First Colony of Virginia, or, simply, the Virginia Company, chartered in 1609. The Massachusetts Bay Company, chartered in 1629, which founded the Massachusetts Bay Colony, was another such company, as was Hudson's Bay Company.

While some English corporations carried on business in the American colonies, there was little demand for corporate status before the American Revolution. At the Constitutional Convention in 1787, Madison proposed a federal incorporation provision which was defeated. As a result, the ability of the federal government to incorporate a body is limited to the implied power to do so when necessary and proper to carry out certain express federal powers, such as the fiscal and war powers, and is seldom exercised. Virtually all American corporate law, whether business, nonprofit, or religious, is state law established by the statutes and court decisions of the fifty states. While corporations are subject to federal regulation in certain specific areas, such as the issuing of securities in interstate commerce and federal taxation, their basic organization, structure, and government are matters of state, not federal, law.

Early American law carried forward the English notion that corporations could exist only by express grant of the state. Initially these grants were made by special acts of state legislatures. With the industrial revolution, this process created both a burden on the legislatures and a nagging problem of bribery and corruption. As a result, states began enacting general incorporation statutes that allowed corporations to be formed without special legislative acts. Most states by the end of the nineteenth century had amended their constitutions to prohibit special incorporation by the legislature and to require that all corporations be formed under the general law, although some types of corporations, whose objects would be inconsistent with the general law, were excepted from such provisions.

In the English colonies, the English pattern of granting special charters to religious corporations was generally followed, and the practice paralleled the history of special grants to business corporations. Between 1769 and 1862, for example, 288 corporate charters were granted to religious bodies in Rhode Island. This practice caused occasional problems due to the existence of established churches. In one such instance, in July of 1767, the Lords of Trade in London denied a corporate charter to the Presbyterians of New York due to a concern that this might constitute an impermissible establishment of dissenters.[7]

An interesting variant of the religious corporation, known as the "territorial parish," occurred in New England. The parish was a public corporation, like a town or school district is today, whose purpose was to provide for the support and maintenance of religious instruction and worship. Initially virtually identical with the town, the territorial parish evolved into a distinct political entity but nevertheless included in its membership all residents within its boundaries, whom it had the power to tax and who were individually liable for its debts. Parishes had no power of excommunication although provision was made for separation from the parish of those who joined independent religious societies. As the spiritual arm of the state, the parish had the power of eminent domain and could even tax business corporations, nonresidents, and unbelievers who owned property within its limits. During the first half of the eighteenth century, through progressive exceptions and the process of disestablishing Congregationalism in New England, the territorial parish disappeared, at least as an arm of the government. As a nonterritorial religious corporation without governmental power, it has survived in some New England towns.

Another form of religious corporation that has not disappeared, although its use is much changed today, is the "corporation sole." The corporation sole is a corporation that consists of the occupant of a given office. The Queen of England, for example, is a corporation sole. In the New England colonies, the parish minister was often a corporation sole for the purpose of holding title to parish property. This the minister did as a trustee and not for personal benefit. The corporation sole was also widely used in the southern states for Episcopal clergy. The old corporation sole that developed in connection with the territorial parish is no longer with us, but, in its modern form, it is in wide use as an organizational device for hierarchical churches.

B. CONTEMPORARY FORMS OF ORGANIZATION

Churches formed early enough in our history may still exist in corporate form through an early legislative act. Such churches should be aware of the provisions of the statute incorporating them and how it relates to present law governing religious associations. In contemporary form, religious organizations exist under one of four forms of organization:

1. the corporation sole
2. the trustee corporation
3. the membership corporation
4. the unincorporated association

State laws differ on which of these forms of organization are permitted; to whom and under what conditions they may be permitted; how such an organization comes into existence; the powers, rights, and privileges attendant upon its existence; how its form of government should work; and in various other particulars. Virginia and West Virginia, for example, prohibit incorporation of churches or religious denominations, an anachronism that dates back to the separatist philosophy of Thomas Jefferson and James Madison, who viewed state incorporation of churches as establishments. Madison, as president, vetoed a bill incorporating the Episcopal church for the District of Columbia on these grounds.[8] New York, on the other hand, has statutes making special provision for the incorporation of several dozen religions and denominations. It is necessary to examine individual state law with care to determine what options are available to a religious organization in a given state and the most prudent choice for the form of organization.

1. The Corporation Sole

The corporation sole in its modern form is a creature of statute but retains its essential nature as the incorporation of an office occupied by a single individual. It is most widely used by religious organizations that aim, on a prudential or theological basis, to retain management and control in the clergy; often the denomination is more hierarchical in nature, such as the Roman Catholic or Episcopal churches. While its use is most common in hierarchical churches, most of the legislation allowing corporations sole to exist would not so restrict them. Some states, however, limit their use to Roman Catholic or Episcopal churches or to churches with bishops or presiding elders or they require evidence of hierarchical authority before incorporating. Usually some evidence that the office holder is elected or appointed according to the governing instruments of the denomination is required, and some public notice of the existence of the corporation must be filed with an appropriate governmental officer. The corporation sole is permitted in at least seventeen states.[9]

2. The Trustee Corporation

The trustee corporation, initially formed by special charter and later by incorporation statutes, is a corporate form in which the church as a whole is not incorporated; instead, certain designated officers are incorporated as a body with perpetual succession, the power to hold the church property in trust for the body, and such other corporate powers as the statutes give them. The trustee corporation arose, in part at least, as a response to the legal inability of unincorporated associations to own and transfer real estate. The incorporated officers may be known as trustees, the vestry, the deacons, or as some other group of officers. Provision must be made for filling the office, most typically by vote of the members of the association. The trustees are themselves the body corporate, however, and can act in that capacity subject to whatever limitations on their action may be placed by the law or the governing instruments of the church. Eighteen American states recognize religious trustee corporations.[10]

3. The Membership Corporation

The membership corporation is by far the most common form of religious organization and is recognized in most American jurisdictions. In many states, there are specific statutes applicable to religious corporations in general or to religious corporations of particular denominations or types. Religious organizations may also be able to incorporate under a state's statutes that provide for the incorporation of any type of nonprofit or charitable organization, not merely religious. These statutes generally follow the pattern of business corporation statutes, without the extensive provisions in business corporation statutes for protection of shareholders in enterprises in which they have invested money and are entitled to certain information and control. The statutes generally assume a democratic government in church affairs, in which the members are akin to shareholders in a business corporation and are entitled to control the affairs of the corporation by voting through appropriate procedures set forth in the governing corporate documents or statutes.

4. The Unincorporated Religious Association

The unincorporated religious association is simply a religious association that has taken no steps to incorporate itself under any of the incorporation laws that may be available to it. A number of states have, however, provided for some recognition of such religious associations and invested them with certain rights generally incident to a corporation, such as the right to take and hold real property either in the organization's name or through trustees. These organizations are sometimes called "quasi-corporations." In the absence of any action by the state, an unincorporated association has no legal existence as an entity separate from its members, although such associations may adopt their own governing rules in the form of by-laws, constitutions, charters, or other sets of rules and regulations.

These will be viewed as a contract between the members of the association as to matters covered by them.[11]

C. CHURCH ORGANIZATION AND THE COURTS

The internal organization of churches and religious denominations, apart from the civil law governing religious corporations or associations, is generally viewed by the courts as falling into one of two types: (1) the hierarchical model, in which the local church is part of a larger denomination or body to whose supervision it is subject in various particulars of church polity and government; and (2) the congregational model, in which the members of the local church are entirely autonomous with respect to their own church government. While churches of a congregational polity may affiliate themselves with other like-minded churches in a denominational structure, the denominational body typically exists as an independent corporation or organization with no authority over its member or affiliated churches.

This twofold division of church polity is an oversimplification, and actual church structures are often hybrids. The hierarchical model includes a number of variants. In the Roman Catholic church, for example, authority passes up through a clerical chain of command from the parish priest to the bishop or archbishop of the diocese to the pope, as the Bishop of Rome, mediated by various collegial or conciliar structures. In the Orthodox churches, a highly structured hierarchy exists, but it is more conciliar at the top and permits the entry of laity in certain positions. Some Lutheran and Brethren groups are hierarchical in organization. Episcopal and Methodist polity provide further variations with descending levels of authority in the clergy from the House of Bishops as the highest Episcopal authority or General Conference as the highest Methodist authority. Laypeople have roles in the government of both churches but are generally involved to a greater degree in the Methodist church and more limited to the local level in the Episcopal church. The Presbyterian church has an elected representative type of hierarchy in which each local church or assembly elects elders or presbyters who form a presbytery of churches grouped in a geographical territory. The presbyteries in turn are grouped into synods which in turn are subject to the authority of the General Assembly, which is the highest legislative and judicial body of the church. Laypeople can be elected to the various levels and have much involvement in Presbyterian polity. Many so-called hierarchical churches are in reality more "synodal" or "connectional," with little or no central authority over regional organizations. These churches include the several Reformed churches and the Methodists.

Congregational forms of polity, such as Baptists, Assemblies of God, Congregationalists, Quakers, Disciples of Christ, Churches of Christ, and some Lutheran and Adventist churches, as well as Jewish and other denominations such as Unitarians, are very democratic at the local church level, being theologically based on the concept of the priesthood of believers, with each believer seeking a personal understanding under the guidance of the Holy Spirit. The autonomy of the local congregation in such churches is protected so rigorously that, for example, Southern Baptist churches insist that representatives to its regional or national conventions be called messengers rather than delegates or representatives so that no inference can be drawn that such groups have any authority over the local church.[12]

The tension between the hierarchical and congregational models of church polity also affects churches unaffiliated with a denomination or larger body. A local church is free to choose that its own internal governing structure be hierarchical or congregational, and both models may be found in independent churches, along with a full range of composites.

The various forms of polity present a spectrum of theological understandings. Each form can appeal to aspects of Scripture and has a tradition of usage. All polities have been affected by the American context—its disinterest in establishing any state church, its democratic form of governance, its voluntary form of participation, and even the legal structure of its nonprofit corporations. Thus most denominational structures are influenced to a degree by this context and tradition and are adjusted to civil ideals. Yet the issue of church polity is religious, not civil, and the tension between each traditional form and its context needs to be viewed as a religious tension.

The best approach to fitting the square peg of church polity into the round hole of the forms of legal organization available is not always obvious, and denominations do not always have consistent practices. One might think, for example, that the Roman Catholic church, which is hierarchically organized, has been in existence for so long, and has access to the best legal advice, would have clearly established the form of organization of the church as a jural entity in the American legal system. But this is not the case. Roman Catholic dioceses are organized, in various states, as trustee corporations, membership corporations, corporations sole, and unincorporated associations. In some states, the bishop or diocese is the only Roman Catholic corporation and as such owns all of the schools, churches, and other property in the diocese. In other states, each parish may be separately incorporated, along with the bishop or diocese itself.[13] If this much variation prevails in the way the Roman Catholic church is organized under the American legal system, it is scarcely surprising to find enormous variation in less hierarchical or congregational, and independent, churches.

Issues of church government have been brought to the courts as a result of disputes and schisms arising from both profound historical movements and events and mundane local disputes. The Civil War divided churches and denominations in the border states and across the Mason-Dixon Line. The triumph of communism in the Soviet Union and Eastern Europe raised troubling and divisive questions of control and authority in Russian Orthodox churches in this country as well as other orthodox national churches in countries that fell behind the Iron Curtain. In the 1950s and 1960s, civil rights issues again caused church divisions. In more recent years, as churches have been confronted by sweeping social changes concerning such matters as women's rights, homosexual rights, and abortion rights, which often stir deeply held moral and religious convictions, further divisions have arisen. On the more mundane level, the termination of clergy is perhaps the most common source of church disputes.

Divided congregations usually fight about property—which group is the real church, and who is entitled to continue to occupy the real estate. In 1 Cor. 6:1-7 the apostle Paul enjoins lawsuits among believers: "If any of you has a dispute with another, dare he take it before the ungodly for judgment instead of before the saints? . . . The very fact that you have lawsuits among you means you have been completely defeated already." Court opinions frequently betray an almost equal reluctance to judge church disputes. Nevertheless, the disputes roll on and, with distressing predictability, present themselves to the civil courts for resolution. In resolving them, the courts must consider both the form of organization of the church from a civil perspective and the church polity, as discussed above.

Church polity, like many issues involving churches, is inherently religious, and the Free Exercise Clause is frequently invoked by one or another of the parties in an attempt to limit or prevent the court from taking action. For this reason, the U.S. Supreme Court has decided a series of cases in which it has attempted to set forth guidelines as to how disputes within religious organizations may or must be decided within the court system without violating the First Amendment. Contemporary understanding of the meaning of the Free Exercise Clause has been significantly impacted by the 1990 *Smith* case, discussed in chapter 3 (pp. 46–49),[14] which abandoned the requirement that the government show a compelling interest addressed by the most narrow means available in order to justify regulation by laws of general applicability that significantly burden a sincere religious belief. However, the free exercise cases involving internal church disputes appear to invoke an understanding of the Free Exercise Clause that stands outside the *Sherbert/Yoder* test addressed in *Smith*. There is no indication in *Smith* that the law in these "church autonomy" cases is modified.

The Supreme Court's most recent, and therefore most pertinent, pronouncement on church disputes was in *Jones v. Wolfe* in 1979.[15] That case, like most of the church autonomy cases that have come to the court, involved a property dispute—who owns the church?—that followed a schism in a local Presbyterian church. If churches owned no property, it is likely that few church schism disputes would reach the courts. An unpropertied group could simply divide and go its way. But when a propertied church divides, both factions cannot continue to meet in the church building despite the fact that members of each have likely contributed to creating the asset. A church building is not divisible; these are fights that someone must win and someone must lose.

Jones v. Wolfe is worth examining with some care. Although it is a church property case, there is no particular reason to suppose that the principles set forth therein would not apply to many other kinds of church disputes. The property at issue was acquired in three conveyances to the trustees of or for the local church or to the church in its own name. The church was a member of the Presbyterian Church in the United States, a hierarchical church in which actions of the local church (or assembly or court) are subject to review and control by higher church courts—in order, the presbytery, synod, and general assembly. A majority of the local church had voted to separate from the denomination. The presbytery had investigated the matter and determined that the minority faction constituted the true congregation of the church. The majority, which took no part in the inquiry, did not appeal its ruling to higher church tribunals. The minority then sought possession of the church by court order.

The Georgia Supreme Court chose to resolve the issue by applying "neutral principles of law." In an earlier Georgia case involving a Presbyterian schism,[16] the court had rejected Georgia's previous approach—what was known as the "implied trust theory." By that approach, the property of a local church that is part of a hierarchical organization was considered held in trust for the general church, provided the general church had not departed from church doctrines that existed at the time of affiliation. The "departure from doctrine" approach was considered unacceptable because it required courts to determine church doctrine.

In the neutral principles of law approach, the courts are permitted to examine deeds to the property, state statutes, and church-governing documents to see if the dispute can be resolved without examining religious doctrine. The Georgia court, having examined the deeds conveying the property to the local church, state statutes, the corporate charter of the church, and the Book of Church Order which was the constitution of the denomination, found nothing to indicate that there was any trust in favor of the general church with respect to the ownership of the property and determined that the property was vested in the local congregation.

The U.S. Supreme Court entertained no doubt that the civil courts had authority to resolve the issue: "The State has an obvious and legitimate interest in the peaceful resolution of property disputes, and in providing a civil forum where the ownership of church property can be determined conclusively."[17] The First Amendment, however, "prohibits civil courts from resolving church property disputes on the basis of religious doctrine and practice" and "requires that civil courts defer to the resolution of issues of religious doctrine or polity by the highest court of a hierarchical church organization."[18] States are constitutionally free to adopt any approach in settling disputes that involves no inquiry into doctrine, ritual, liturgy, or tenets of the faith.

The Supreme Court recognized that scrutinizing church religious documents such as church constitutions runs the inherent risk of placing a court in the position of making religious judgments, and it cautioned that "a civil court must take special care to scrutinize the document in purely secular terms, and not to rely on religious precepts in determining whether the document indicates that the parties have intended to create a trust."[19] If the civil courts were required to resolve a religious controversy to interpret the documents, "then the court must defer to the resolution of the doctrinal issue by the authoritative ecclesiastical body."[20] Although the state is free to resolve the issue of church property disputes by compulsory deference to religious authority, when no doctrinal controversy is involved and the issue can be resolved by neutral principles of law, the court is free to do so.

Applying these principles, the Court was satisfied that the Georgia court had correctly determined that the local body, not the denomination, was indeed the owner of the church. There was, however, another issue the Georgia court had inadequately addressed. It had assumed that the majority vote of the local church had determined which body constituted the local church, although the Presbyterian church tribunal had determined that the minority was in fact the "true congregation" of the church. The question of who constituted the true congregation, the minority faction argued, was itself an ecclesiastical question concerning which the civil courts are obliged to defer to the ecclesiastical tribunal.

The Supreme Court noted the general rules that majority rule is usually employed in the governance of religious societies and that majorities can usually be identified without resolving any question of religious doctrine or polity. Religious societies, however, are not obliged to conduct their affairs by majority rule. It would be consistent with the First Amendment for Georgia to adopt a presumptive rule of majority representation "defeasible upon a showing that the identity of the local church is to be determined by some other means."[21] The case was remanded to the courts of Georgia to determine whether or not there was a presumptive rule of majority representation in Georgia and, if so, how that presumption would be overcome and whether it had been in this case. If the outcome of Georgia law were that the identity of the true congregation of the church was to be determined according to the laws and regulations of the denomination, then the courts would be obliged to give deference to the Presbyterian tribunal's determination of the church identity.

The decision was five to four with a vigorous dissent championing the rule of deference to church tribunals and pointing out the difficulty of administering neutral principles of law in church disputes: "Disputes among church members over the control of church property arise almost invariably out of disagreements regarding doctrine and practice."[22] While two of the five-member majority in *Jones* had retired from the Court by 1992, so also had three of the four dissenters. *Jones* is likely to continue to be the constitutional guide in this area for the foreseeable future.

In summary, *Jones v. Wolfe* permits courts, based on state law, to resolve church property disputes, and perhaps all church disputes, by (1) neutral principles of law, as long as they can be applied without examining religious doctrine, practice, polity, ritual, liturgy, tenets of faith, and the like; (2) deference to the highest church tribunal that has examined the issue; or (3) any other means (although none have been suggested) that would enable courts to resolve the issue without getting into religious questions. In earlier cases, the Court had deferred to decisions of hierarchical church tribunals which, it held, were subject only to marginal civil review for fraud, collusion, or arbitrariness. The Court has never addressed what might constitute fraud or collusion sufficient to overcome the deference to church tribunals. It has found that the "arbitrary" exception to such deference does not permit courts to examine whether or not the church complied with its own rules in reaching the decision. Internal organization, ecclesiastical rule, custom, and law are among the religious matters that may not be examined by the court. Constitutional notions of fundamental fairness or due process have no place in examining church procedures.[23]

Lower courts, attempting to apply constitutional principles set forth in *Jones v. Wolfe* and earlier cases, have found difficulty in achieving consistent results. For example, in the 1981 New Jersey case of *Elmora Hebrew Center v. Fishman,*[24] a rabbi termination case, the synagogue claimed to be independent and congregational in government, whereas the rabbi claimed that the Code of Jewish Law applied and that the issue was under the jurisdiction of the Beth Din, an ecclesiastical tribunal

of the Union of Orthodox Rabbis. The court abstained from deciding the matter, finding that determining whether the Jewish law applied and whether the issue was subject to the jurisdiction of the Jewish ecclesiastical tribunal would involve questions of a religious nature. By contrast, in *Atterberry v. Smith,* a 1987 Pennsylvania case,[25] the court found that it could determine whether or not the church in question was hierarchical and what the highest ecclesiastical tribunal was.

In a 1987 Alaska case, *Herning v. Eason,*[26] the court permitted proxy voting in a church dispute in which the state nonprofit statute permitted it, despite a claim that proxy voting interfered with the church's free exercise rights; the court found that no free exercise right had been shown. In a 1989 New York case, *Frankel v. Kissena Jewish Center,*[27] the court refused to allow proxy voting, despite the fact that the nonprofit corporation law permitted it, because the church by-laws, which could supersede the corporate law, adopted Robert's Rules of Order which did not allow a proxy in the situation.

Frankel presents another issue on which court decisions have divided: whether or not courts will review the church's adherence to Robert's Rules of Order in its proceedings when the by-laws call for their application. *Frankel* did so. So did the 1988 Arizona decision of *Blanton v. Hahn,*[28] which interpreted the by-laws under Robert's Rules to determine whether a provision that required three-fourths of the voting members present to vote to oust a pastor meant three-fourths of the voting members who were at the meeting or three-fourths of the voting members who voted, finding that it required a vote of three-fourths of those present, whether or not they voted. But in *Crowder v. Southern Baptist Convention,* a 1987 case decided by the Eleventh Circuit Court of Appeals,[29] the court deferred to the convention's interpretation of its own church governance in the face of a claim that the convention had violated Robert's Rules of Order, finding that the major doctrinal controversy resolved by the highest church tribunal was only one step removed from the dispute over Robert's Rules of Order. Despite the ruling of the U.S. Supreme Court in a hierarchical church case[30] that courts are not, under the guise of determining whether a church tribunal has acted arbitrarily, to look into whether or not the tribunal followed its own rules, lower courts dealing with actions of churches with congregational-type polities frequently have not deferred to the congregational decision but have examined whether or not the meeting was called and held in accordance with state statutes or church rules of proceeding.[31] Other courts, however, have declined to review even whether a church with a congregational polity has followed its own rules.[32]

When issues arise as to who is a member and thus entitled to vote in a congregational-type polity, a particular conundrum occurs. Determining membership in a church almost invariably involves issues of religious faith, doctrine, or practice. In a congregational polity, it is the members who decide who is a member. If there is a difference of view as to who is a member, the mechanism of government collapses completely.[33] Perhaps in response to this obvious Catch-22, courts have occasionally intervened in church disputes when the method of church governance was unclear and have resolved conflicts forcefully. In the 1988 Louisiana case of *First Union Baptist Church v. Banks*,[34] a dispute over the removal of a pastor from office, the articles of incorporation and by-laws were inadequate in informing the governing body of the church as to how its affairs were to be handled. The court order declared all prior meetings of trustees and members to be null and void; ordered a general membership meeting to be held on a specific date with written notice to the members; ordered the election of a nine-member board of directors; ordered a panel of three persons, one of whom was to be designated by the court to preside over the meeting, at which voting was to be limited to those who were at least eighteen years of age and had been members of the church for the preceding six months; and empowered the newly elected board of directors to adopt by-laws that included provisions for the calling and dismissal of the pastor. This extraordinary foray into church government by a trial judge was upheld by the Louisiana appel-

late court, which presumably despaired of the church's ability to govern itself and perceived the practical necessity of putting church affairs in order.

The U.S. Supreme Court in *Jones v. Wolfe* fairly cried out to churches to organize their church polity and governance to avoid the necessity of involving courts:

> Through appropriate reversionary clauses and trust provisions, religious societies can specify what is to happen to church property in the event of a particular contingency, or what religious body will determine the ownership in the event of a schism or doctrinal controversy. In this manner, a religious organization can ensure that a dispute over the ownership of church property will be resolved in accord with desires of the members. . . .[35] [O]ccasional problems in application . . . (of the neutral principles approach) . . . should be gradually eliminated as recognition is given to the obligation of "States, religious organizations, and individuals [to] structure relationships involving church property so as not to require the civil courts to resolve ecclesiastical questions." . . .[36] At any time before the dispute erupts, the parties can ensure, if they so desire, that the faction loyal to the hierarchical church will retain the church property. They can modify the deeds or the corporate charter to include a right of reversion or trust in favor of the general church. Alternatively, the constitution of the general church can be made to recite an express trust in favor of the denominational church. The burden involved in taking such steps will be minimal. And the civil courts will be bound to give effect to the result indicated by the parties, provided it is embodied in some legally cognizable form.[37]

More than a century earlier, in the 1872 case of *Watson v. Jones*,[38] the first church property dispute to reach the Supreme Court, the same Court had said:

> We have held it under advisement for a year; not uninfluenced by the hope that since the civil commotion, which evidently lay at the foundation of the trouble, has passed away, that charity, which is

so large an element in the faith of both parties, and which, by one of the apostles of that religion, is said to be the greatest of all the Christian virtues, would have brought about a reconciliation. But we have been disappointed. It is not for us to determine or apportion the moral responsibility which attaches to the parties for this result. We can only pronounce the judgment of the law as applicable to the case presented to us.

In forming their government and polity, churches and religious organizations should do what they can to accommodate the desire of the courts, as well as the biblical mandate of 1 Corinthians 6, to keep disputes among believers out of court.

Despite the courts' desire to avoid ecclesiastical disputes, they do arise both within the church body and between the body and outsiders. The resolution of those disputes may turn on how the church is organized and governed. I examine these issues further in the context of risk management in chapter 11.

REFERENCES

Gaffney, E., and P. Sorensen. *Ascending Liability in Religious and Other Nonprofit Organizations*, ed. H. Griffin (Macon, Ga: Mercer University Press, 1984).

Hammar, Richard R. *Pastor, Church and Law*, 2d ed. (Matthews, N.C.: Christian Ministry Resources, 1991).

Henn, Harry G. *Handbook of the Law of Corporations*, 2d ed. (St. Paul, Minn.: West Publishing Co., 1970).

Kauper, Paul G., and Stephen C. Ellis. *Religious Corporations and the Law*. 71 *Michigan Law Review* 1499 (1973).

Lincoln, C. *The Civil Law and the Church* (New York: Abingdon Press, 1916).

Mead, Frank S. *Handbook of Denominations in the United States*, 9th ed. (Nashville: Abingdon Press, 1990).

Melton, J. Gordon. *The Encyclopedia of American Religions* (Detroit: Gale Research Co., 1987).

Zollmann, C. *American Church Law* (St. Paul, Minn.: West Publishing Co., 1933).

CHAPTER 5

Legal Privileges and Obligations of Clergy

A. THE LEGAL NEED TO IDENTIFY CLERGY

It is occasionally necessary to determine who has the status of clergy (priest, minister, or pastor) for the purpose of applying some right, privilege, or obligation imposed by law. In colonial times, land was often set aside out of land grants for new townships for the "first settled minister," to encourage a minister to settle and to help the settlers afford the costs. To qualify the minister needed to settle for life, have a contract with the town for service, and be ordained; and old cases from the New England states report litigation over the privilege.[1] In modern times, the issue is most likely to arise in determining rights and obligations under federal tax law and in certain ministerial functions under state law.

The contemporary issue will not arise with respect to clergy who have both obtained their status through the normal course of training and recognition followed in most Christian denominations, in which the practicing clergy go through a period of formal education and training at a seminary or divinity school and are then formally licensed, commissioned, or ordained by the denomination as a recognition of their status; and who are carrying out duties customary to pastoring a congregation, including leading public worship, administering sacraments, and the like. Rather the issue will arise on the fringes and in the gray areas of clerical practice: when the individual comes to the position in a nontraditional manner; when the duties performed are something other than the normal sacerdotal duties of a pastor of a congregation; or when the church itself is organized in a manner that makes it difficult for the legal system to recognize the equivalent of the traditional pastor, priest, or rabbi in more familiar settings.

In some churches, it is customary to identify all members as "ministers," that is, servants of the Word, distinguishing the servanthood of all believers from the specifically shepherding duties of the cleric who is likely to be referred to as the "pastor." Such self-designations have little relationship to the legal consequences of status, however, as the law will look to its own definitions in applying the terms when they have legal significance.

We can group the issues involved in determining who has the status of clergy into two categories, which follow the structure of the legal system:

1. Federal laws and definitions which have uniform applicability throughout the country;
2. State laws and definitions which will differ in particulars from state to state, the law of each state requiring examination

with respect to the particular issue involved.

B. FEDERAL LAW

Federal law raises the issue in what are probably the two most significant contexts in practical application: (1) federal income taxes, and (2) application of the social security laws.

Federal income tax law allows a unique tax benefit to qualifying clergy in the housing allowance, an opportunity to avoid federal income taxes on either the rental value of a parsonage or living quarters provided or on a financial allowance by the church to meet housing expenses. As this is a unique and valuable tax benefit, it is not surprising that many have sought to participate in it, requiring the Internal Revenue Service and the courts to give attention to the scope of the allowance.

Another federal income tax provision exempts clergy from having income taxes withheld from their wages (but not for paying them). This provision also necessitates that clergy be identifiable.

The issue under Social Security arises because the Social Security system is in fact a system of two taxes—(1) the Federal Insurance Contributions Act (FICA) applicable to those employed by an employer; half of this tax is paid by the employer and the other half is paid by the employee; and (2) the Self-Employment Contributions Act (SECA) applicable to self-employed persons who are liable for paying all of the tax. Clergy are always considered self-employed for Social Security tax purposes with respect to ministerial services, irrespective of the reality of their status as employed or self-employed, which gives rise to the necessity of identifying clergy for purposes of administering Social Security law. Certain clergy, moreover, may qualify under certain conditions for exemption from Social Security coverage altogether, further necessitating a distinction among religious workers between clergy and nonclergy.

A more detailed description of these four provisions—housing allowance, clergy exemption from withholding, treatment of clergy as self-employed for Social Security pur-

poses, and clergy who may under certain conditions exempt themselves from the Social Security system—is contained in chapters 13 and 14. For now we are only concerned with the definitions that bring clergy within these provisions. Happily, federal law is uniform in this respect, and the same standards apply for all four of the special treatment areas of clergy under federal income tax and social security law.

The benefits or privileges are only available to "ordained, commissioned, or licensed ministers of a church with respect to services performed in the exercise of ministry." This definition then has two components:

1. It applies only to "ordained, commissioned, or licensed ministers of a church."
2. It applies only "with respect to services performed in the exercise of ministry."

In the 1989 decision of *Knight v. Commissioner,*[2] the Tax Court[3] clarified the issue of identifying a minister for tax purposes. Five factors are considered significant. They are:

1. Is the person ordained, commissioned, or licensed?
2. Does the person administer sacraments?
3. Does the person conduct worship services?
4. Does the person perform services in the control, conduct, or maintenance of a religious organization?
5. Is the person considered to be a spiritual leader by his or her religious body?

The first requirement, that the individual be ordained, commissioned, or licensed, must be present. The remaining four factors are considered not an arithmetical but a balancing test.

The issue in Knight's case was whether he was subject to self-employment tax (which he had not paid). Hence he hoped to be classified as a nonclergy for application of the federal laws. Knight was a licentiate of a Presbyterian church, a pre-ordination status. He had served as a minister of a local church and had preached and conducted worship services, visited the sick, performed funerals, and ministered to the needy, but, lacking ordination, could not vote in the local church's governing body, administer the sacraments, or solemnize marriages. The Tax Court found that he met three of the five criteria it set forth and was therefore a minister, notwithstanding that he lacked ordination and was not qualified to administer the sacraments.

The five-factor decision in the *Knight* case was a liberalization of the definition and a useful clarification of prior law. Just before the decision, the IRS had issued a Technical Advice Memorandum,[4] following an earlier tax court ruling,[5] which required that a minister perform functions 2, 3, and 4 from the *Knight* decision to qualify. Under the earlier decision and the technical advice memorandum, Knight would not have been a qualified minister because he did not administer sacraments or participate in church governance.

Since decisions of the Tax Court, although they carry significant weight, are subject to appeal to the court of appeals and ultimately to the U.S. Supreme Court, *Knight* is not necessarily the last word on this issue. The IRS may accept the decision notwithstanding its pre-*Knight* memorandum to the contrary, or it may litigate the issue another day and hope for a different result in a higher court.

1. Ordained, Commissioned, or Licensed Minister of a Church

Ordination is the form used by most churches and denominations to recognize by ceremony and in status the clothing or investing of the individual with ministerial functions and sacerdotal power. Sacerdotal power is the authority to perform functions normally reserved to the priest, minister, or similar recognized religious leader of the body and includes, but is not limited to, performing the sacraments. Ordination occurs in accordance with the ceremony or discipline of the church or sect, based on its community of faith, belief, doctrines, and practices, and normally follows a prescribed course of study. It clothes the individual with the right or power to lead a congregation in worship and life as a pastor, to

preach and teach the doctrines of the church or sect, to administer its rites and ceremonies, and to administer its ordinances of public worship and sacraments. It constitutes a setting apart or consecration to the service of living and teaching the religion.

Many religious bodies license ministers prior to ordination. Licensing is usually a status inferior to ordination and may initiate a time period within which the individual can give evidence of ability and suitability for ordination.

Commissioning is a procedure which may be followed by independent churches that do not conduct formal ordination. It is an investiture of authority to perform religious functions on behalf of the congregation and is analogous to ordination. The important criterion from the legal perspective is that commissioned or licensed individuals perform substantially the same religious functions as an ordained minister. There are instances of persons who are functional equivalents of ordained, commissioned, or licensed ministers being included in that classification.[6]

Those who are not ordained, commissioned, or licensed will not qualify, no matter what duties they perform in the church. Ministers of music, ministers of visitation, youth pastors, ministers of administration, teachers at religious schools, or even the senior or sole pastor of a church will not qualify if they are not licensed, commissioned, or ordained.

The church can, of course, always commission an individual who might otherwise qualify but for a lack of commissioned status. However, a commission given solely to receive benefits under the Social Security Act and Internal Revenue law that does not in fact change the individual's status is likely to be viewed with skepticism by the IRS and the courts and fail in its purpose.[7] Commissioning should recognize the status and privileges of an individual as a religious leader and not be a piece of paper handed out in the hope of enabling a person to obtain tax benefits.

Ministers employed by nonprofit religious organizations not directly affiliated with a church, who perform religious worship and sacerdotal functions for the organization, including such duties as Bible teaching, spiritual counseling, and speaking engagements, can qualify.[8]

The terms "ordained minister," "commissioned minister," and "licensed minister" are not, of course, limited to Christian ministers. In the 1966 case of *Salkov v. Commissioner*,[9] the Tax Court found that a Jewish cantor who otherwise met the qualifications was the equivalent of a commissioned minister and recognized as a religious leader by his congregation. In a religious discipline lacking a central ecclesiastical organization, ministerial authority could be conferred by the church or congregation itself and, in the *Salkov* case, was. In the 1972 case of *Silverman v. Commissioner*,[10] a Jewish cantor was again found to meet the qualifications because he participated with a rabbi in conducting religious services, weddings, funerals, and youth education; had his title bestowed by his congregation as its religious leader in liturgy and prayer; and performed on a regular and full-time basis substantially all the religious worship, sacerdotal, training, and educational functions of the religion's tenets and practices.

Christian Science practitioners, which include Christian Science Readers, practitioners of healing according to the teachings of Christian Science, and Christian Science teachers and lecturers, are treated the same as ordained, commissioned, or licensed ministers.

2. Service Performed in the Exercise of Ministry

The federal tax and Social Security benefits to or obligations of ordained, commissioned, or licensed ministers of a church apply only to services performed by the minister in the exercise of his or her ministry. These include sacerdotal functions, the conduct of religious worship, and the control, conduct, and maintenance of religious organizations under the authority of a religious body that constitutes a church or denomination. Sacerdotal functions include performing such ministerial duties as baptisms, marriages, funerals, and communion and other religious leadership activities normally provided by clergy invested with

authority to do so by the body they lead or of which they are a part. A minister performing sacerdotal functions or conducting religious worship will be considered to be in the exercise of her or his ministry with respect to these functions, whether or not they are performed for a religious organization. Whether the service constitutes a sacerdotal function or religious worship will depend on the tenets and practices of the particular religious body that constitutes the minister's church or denomination. Service in the control, conduct, and maintenance of a religious organization relates to directing, managing, or promoting the activities of the organization.

Services performed for an integral agency of a religious organization in the conduct of religious worship, ministration of sacerdotal functions, or the control, conduct, and maintenance of the organization is in the exercise of ministry. Thus ministers performing service for integral agencies of religious organizations under the authority of a religious body that constitutes a church or church denomination will qualify in the same manner as a church's ministers. This poses the further issue of identifying an integral agency of a church or religious denomination. The criteria set forth by the IRS in considering this issue are:[11]

1. Whether the religious organization incorporated the institution;
2. Whether the corporate name of the institution indicates a church relationship;
3. Whether the religious organization continuously controls, manages, and maintains the institution;
4. Whether the trustees or directors of the institution are approved by or must be approved by the religious organization;
5. Whether the trustees or directors may be removed by the religious organization or church;
6. Whether annual reports of finances and general operations are required to be made to the religious organization or church;
7. Whether the religious organization or church contributes to the support of the institution;
8. Whether in the event of dissolution of

the institution, its assets would be turned over to the religious organization or church.

It is not necessary that all eight criteria be present in every case.

Under these provisions, clergy serving in faculty and administrative positions in church-related colleges and universities that qualify as integral agencies of religious organizations have been found to meet the qualifications for the housing allowance.[12] If the college or university, however, is not an integral agency of the church, clergy serving in faculty and administrative positions do not qualify unless they can meet the *Knight* test.

Clergy working in administrative capacities in religious denominational offices will normally qualify because they are engaged in the control, conduct, and maintenance of a church organization.[13]

If a minister's church or religious body assigns or designates the minister to perform a service for an organization that is not a religious organization or an integral agency of one, that service is nevertheless in the exercise of his or her ministry even if it does not include conducting worship services or ministration of sacerdotal functions. This is true, for example, in the case of the minister who is assigned or designated to teach at a college or university that does not meet the integral organization test. However, the assignment must be a true and substantive one, not made merely to assist the minister in getting a tax benefit for doing what she or he would have been doing otherwise.

In one case, an ordained minister who had obtained employment as an instructor in computer programming at a nonreligious state college arranged for the governing body of his church to assign him to the task. The Tax Court was unimpressed by this "perfunctory ratification by religious authority of secular employment" and concluded that there is an implicit requirement that the assignment by the church must further the church's purposes.[14] The services must be specifically assigned to the minster and must directly further the purposes of the church. In another case, a minister who established a counseling practice in a sepa-

rate organization from the church, although it had originally been associated with it and purported to be commissioned and endorsed by it, failed to qualify. Despite the fact that the church stated that it commissioned and endorsed the service, the IRS found that the church had not specifically assigned the minister to perform counseling services on its behalf. Although the church may benefit from the counseling, the services were not done to further directly the church's purposes, and although the minister used the principles and teachings of the church in his counseling, it was performed free of the church's control.[15]

Members of religious orders are subject to special rules with respect to Social Security status which are not covered herein.

The requirements of these provisions are technical and the meaning of the terms and their application not always self-evident. Clergy and churches concerned with these issues should seek qualified counsel and consult a more specialized work in this area, such as *Church and Clergy Tax Guide,* listed in the references below.

3. Other Federal Laws

Exemptions from the unemployment compensation law also include services performed by a duly ordained, commissioned, or licensed minister of a church in the exercise of her or his ministry or by a member of a religious order in the exercise of duties required by the order.[16]

Regular or duly ordained ministers of religion are exempted from military training and service under the Military Selective Service Act.[17] Most of the cases that developed the law with respect to this exemption, which does not track the language applicable to federal income tax, social security, or unemployment compensation exemptions, was developed during the time of the Vietnam and Korean wars. In the era of the volunteer army, it is of little concern and is not discussed further here.[18]

Certain ministers may be entitled to "special immigrant" status and may be admitted to the United States without being subject to the usual numerical limitations. This requires that they show the following:

1. They were continuously carrying on their ministerial vocation for at least two years immediately preceding their application to be admitted to the United States as an immigrant.
2. They seek to enter the United States for the sole purpose of carrying on their ministerial vocation.
3. A religious denomination with a bona fide organization in the United States needs their services.[19]

This provision requires a definition of the term "minister." The Immigration and Naturalization Service has determined that it means "a person duly authorized by a recognized religious denomination having a bona fide organization in the United States to conduct religious worship and to perform other duties usually performed by a regularly ordained clergyman of the denomination."[20] This is a much more restrictive definition than applies under the federal income tax and social security laws. Thus an individual who might qualify for the benefits those laws afford to ministers might not qualify for admission to the United States as an immigrant. For example, the provision has been strictly construed to deny admission to an applicant who had not functioned as a minister for two years immediately preceding his application notwithstanding the fact that he had been unable to do so because the Turkish government had outlawed the sect.[21] It has also been used to deny admission to an ordained minister of music because she did not perform sacerdotal functions notwithstanding the fact that she may have had the authority to do so.[22]

Ministers of religion can be provided free or discounted transportation by common carriers under the Interstate Commerce Act, although such carriers would normally be precluded from discriminating among customers.[23]

C. STATE LAWS

State laws also provide certain rights, privileges, and duties to clergy, although specific laws and applications vary from state to state. The most important are (1) confiden-

tial communications, and (2) performance of marriage.

1. Confidential Communications

Most if not all states have some form of the clergy-penitent privilege, which is discussed in more detail in chapter 18. A common version provides that a person has the privileges of refusing to disclose and of preventing another from disclosing a confidential communication made by that person to a cleric acting in the professional role of spiritual advisor. Clergy may include ministers, priests, rabbis, accredited Christian Science practitioners, or other similar functionaries of a religious organization, or an individual reasonably believed so to be by the counselee.

Court interpretations have not been entirely consistent. Communications made to elders in the Presbyterian church[24] and lay religious counselors whose services are necessitated by the number of people needing counseling[25] have been within the privilege. Communications made to other lay religious counselors,[26] an elder and deacon in the Christian church,[27] and nuns[28] have been found outside the privilege.

The definition of "clergy" for purposes of applying the confessional privilege in federal courts will be the same as in the relevant state court in any case in which state law is applicable. In other cases, such as federal criminal trials that are governed by federal law, the issue is to be "governed by the principles of the common law as they may be interpreted by the courts of the United States in the light of reason and experience."[29] This is one of the few areas in which there is a "federal common law."

2. Performance of Marriages

States have an obvious interest in the proper solemnization and legitimization of marriage. Despite the fact that officiating at marriages is a traditional role of the clergy, it is subject to state law and can only be performed pursuant to that law. It may be a criminal offense for an unauthorized person to perform a marriage ceremony.

Thus clergy must understand the law applicable to performing marriage ceremonies in the jurisdiction in which the ceremony is to be performed and be sure they are acting consistently with it.

Some of the points on which state laws may vary are:

1. The authority of out-of-state clergy. Some states make no distinction between the right of resident and nonresident clergy to solemnize marriages. Others have a different authorizing procedure, for example, requiring nonresident clergy to obtain a special license to perform only the particular marriage. Still other states limit authority to conduct marriages to resident clergy.

2. The necessity for a cleric. While most states specifically authorize clergy to perform marriages, some simply allow for marriages to be solemnized in accordance with the mode recognized by a religious denomination. In other states, special statutes authorize that marriage be solemnized in accordance with the rules of particular groups such as the Friends (Quakers), the Baha'i faith, the Church of Jesus Christ of Latter Day Saints (Mormons), German Baptists, Buddhists, Muslims, and others.

3. The significance of ordination. In some states, only ordained clergy can perform marriages; in others, licensed clergy can, as well, sometimes subject to special requirements such as posting a bond. Still other states simply refer to the usages of the church for the authorization or do not qualify the authority at all, authorizing statutes that simply refer generically to priests, ministers, and rabbis.

4. The public filing required to evidence the individual's authority. Some states require a public record of the cleric's authority, which may need to be filed in a court or some other public office. Such filings may be limited to the non-ordained who perform marriages. In many states, there is no such public filing requirement.

There is no uniformity or consistency to state laws in this area. Ascertaining the requirements of the state in which the marriage is performed is essential. Denominational resources may help clergy to understand the requirements of particular jurisdictions.

Performing a marriage ceremony usually requires the officiating cleric to perform certain reporting or record-keeping functions to insure that the married persons are legally capable of marrying and have a marriage license, and that the record of the marriage is properly recorded with public authorities. Failure to comply with the record-keeping and reporting requirements may also carry criminal penalties.[30]

In performing marriages, clergy are considered to function as public officers for limited purposes. The concept is a carry-over from English law and the notion of established churches. It seems to have been universally accepted and apparently never challenged as a violation of the Establishment Clause. In this particular area, a religious ceremony results in a valid civil marriage that carries rights and responsibilities enforceable by the secular legal system. Performance of the marriage ceremony stands as a universally accepted reminder that "we are a religious people"[31] and also recalls the time when established churches in America had public functions as arms of the state.[32]

3. Miscellaneous State Laws

Ministers may be exempted from jury duty.[33] They may have visiting privileges at penal institutions, subject to the discretion of the prison authorities.[34] As in federal law, state law may permit common carriers to provide them free or discounted transportation.[35]

At one time, the fear of ecclesiastical domination of government gave rise to various state statutes and even constitutional provisions that prohibited clergy from holding certain public offices.[36] This concern has long since disappeared from the public mind and the world of politics and government, and any such provisions that remain on the books may be disregarded as unconstitutional.[37]

Finally, state property tax statutes may make exemptions for parsonages dependent upon their being made available to or occupied by clergy. Such exemptions will generally depend upon whether the property is owned by the church, and not the cleric. Examination of particular state statutes for this exemption is necessary. Property tax exemptions are discussed in more detail in chapter 8.

REFERENCES

Bush, John P., and William Harold Tiemann. *The Right to Silence: Privileged Clergy Communication and the Law*, 3rd ed. (Nashville: Abingdon Press, 1989).

Buzzard, Lynn, and Dan Hall. *Clergy Confidentiality: "A Time to Be Silent, and a Time to Speak"* (1988). Available from Christian Ministries Management Association, P.O. Box 4638, Diamond Bar, Calif. 91765.

Hammar, Richard R. *Pastor, Church and Law*, 2d ed. (Matthews, N.C.: Christian Ministry Resources, 1991).

———. *Church and Clergy Tax Guide*. Published annually. Available from Christian Ministry Resources, P.O. Box 2301, Matthews, N.C. 28106 (704–846–2507).

Liability for Contracts and Torts

A. AN OVERVIEW OF LIABILITY

"Liability" is the legal, enforceable responsibility to pay someone money. It usually arises from either a contract—a consensual relationship that creates the obligation—or a tort—a civil (not criminal) wrong that causes injury to persons, property, economic well-being, or reputation.

Corporations, despite the fiction of corporate personhood, act only through the people who conduct their affairs. People who do things that injure other people cannot avoid responsibility for their acts because the act occurred when they were acting in the course of their employment by a corporation or other organization, reli-gious or otherwise. A priest or pastor who en route from the church to the hospital to visit the sick goes through a red light and injures someone is responsible for the resulting damages. The rare exception is confined to a situation in which the employee carries out an employer's instructions without knowledge that the instructions included a wrongful act. An example of this would be an employee who trespasses on property without being aware that he did not have a right to be there.

The same result does not necessarily follow for employees who sign contracts on behalf of their corporate employer. Employees who are properly authorized to make the contract will not be personally liable for its performance. But if they are not so authorized, they may be personally liable to the other party for the obligation.

When the organization is directly responsible, whether for a tort or a contract, it is liable, just as an individual who breaks a contract or commits a wrong is liable.

Often, however, the question of who is liable is complex. Is it the individual, the employing organization, or both? Are there other layers of authority where legal responsibility can be assigned?

Usually the individuals who cause the damage do not have the personal financial resources to pay a major damage claim, particularly one not covered by insurance. Hence the search for the "deep pocket," an organization that can be held financially accountable for and is able to pay the damages. Churches and other religious organizations, and each ascending level of organization in a religious hierarchy, are potential "deep pockets." You may be sure that a plaintiff's attorney in a damage suit will assert the plaintiff's claim against every organization or level of the hierarchy that can in any way be held responsible.

Employers may also have a right to recover damages from employees who create liability if the employees do so by acting outside their authority. Employees who negligently injure a third person while acting in the scope of their employment may not only be liable to the third person but also liable to their employer if the employer is required to pay damages. Because employees rarely have assets to pay damage judgments and suits by employers against employees do not make for good personnel relations, suits of this nature are rare.

The field of law that addresses questions of who is responsible for the acts of another is called "agency law" or "the law of principal and agent." An agent is a representative, someone acting for another. A principal is the one for whom the agent acts. Employment relationships are always agency relationships, the employer being the principal and the employee being the agent. These are not the only kind of agency relationships, however; agents may be volunteers or others who act on the principal's behalf.

The principles of contract, tort, and agency law that govern the liability of churches for the acts of their agents are issues of state law. While some states have legislated in these areas, the rules are largely determined by common law decisions of the highest courts of each of the states. For the most part, the general principles are long-established, universally followed rules of common law. Application of these principles by courts, however, has not given uniform results. They are usefully considered separately with respect to contracts and torts.

This chapter summarizes the law of contracts and torts, the two major liability-generating relationships. With respect to each it also considers who else may be responsible for damages caused by another and how far up the organizational structure liability can be pushed.

B. CONTRACTS AND THE AUTHORITY TO MAKE THEM

1. The Nature of Contracts

When I visit my barber, Dick Terrill, I take a seat in his chair when my turn comes, receive my haircut, and pay him $5.50 when he is through, although we have no written agreement about his services or the price, and the entire transaction occurs with no discussion between us of what he is to do or what I am to pay. Despite the lack of direct communication about what is going on, however, I am obliged to pay for the haircut, and to pay $5.50 and not some other amount.

The reason is that Dick and I have formed a contract. A contract is a consensual relationship between two people, corporations, or other legal entities—an agreement.

Contrary to popular opinion and notwithstanding Samuel Goldwyn's adage that "a verbal contract isn't worth the paper it's written on," most contracts do not need to be in writing to be enforceable, although they often are and, in important or complex matters, should be as a matter of prudence to avoid misunderstanding. There are a few exceptions to the rule that contracts need not be in writing. These fall within universally adopted or recognized standards which are misnamed the "statute of frauds." The statute of frauds has nothing to do with fraud. It says that only certain contracts must be in writing to be enforceable. Those few limited contracts that must be are of a sort important enough so that people should not be held to the obligation unless they have committed themselves in writing. They include contracts for such matters as the purchase and sale of real estate, contracts that cannot by their terms be performed within one year, or contracts to pay the debts of another. The statute of frauds is state law but, with minor variations and interpretation from state to state, is virtually universal.

My contract with Dick Terrill is not subject to the statute of frauds. It could have been formed orally, as if I came into the barbershop and asked him how much he would charge me for a haircut and, upon being told, said "Okay, go ahead and give me a haircut and I'll pay you $5.50." That would be an express oral contract. Absent that conversation, my contract with him arises by implication rather than expression, but it is no less binding because of that. The agreement is implicit in my conduct and his. The understanding and the amount of the compensation may arise from our past conduct—we have done this many times before; from my observation of the conduct of others; from our knowledge that this is the custom and practice in the situation; or from a sign on the wall that informs any who care to read it that haircuts are $5.50. Contracts may be formed by express written or oral communcation between the parties or may be formed implicitly by the situation.

The subjects concerning which parties may contract are limited only by the requirement that the contract have a lawful purpose, rarely a problem for religious organizations. In order to be enforceable, there must be some mutual understanding reached, often called by lawyers "offer and acceptance" or a "meeting of the minds." The offer and acceptance must involve "consideration" on both sides, meaning that each party must give something up or make some sort of commitment. Promises to make a gift are not normally enforceable although they may become so in some instances, such as where the person to whom the promise was made has taken certain action in reliance on the promise.[1]

The terms of the contract must be sufficiently definite so that a court asked to enforce the contract can understand what the transaction really was. Promises to reach an agreement on something in the future are not normally enforceable because they are simply agreements to agree and provide no basis for determining what the future agreement is to be. Contract terms that are not part of the express understanding of the parties may sometimes be supplied by other means, such as a course of dealing by the parties over a period of time, customs or usages of the trade, or reasonableness.

Parties who have actually performed a contract or part of it for the benefit of the other, even though the contract is too vague to be enforced, are still entitled to recover the reasonable value of their performance.

When the terms of the contract are ambiguous, the meaning of the contract is determined insofar as possible by determining what the parties mutually intended, based on all of the circumstances surrounding the contract, although the uncommunicated intention of one party cannot bind the other party. In the absence of any evidence of what the parties intended, a court will construe a contract to give it a just and reasonable meaning. The contract itself may be made up of a number of documents or communications between the parties, some verbal and some written. In such instances all of these communications must be construed together to find the meaning of the contract. Written contracts, however, may contain provisions stating that the written document is the entire contract and that neither party is relying on any representations or statements not contained in the written document.

Most written contracts do not require any special formality of execution such as witnesses, seals, or notarization, although such formalities may be followed to provide assurances of the binding nature of the contract or for other reasons.

Parties who breach contracts without a legal justification are liable to the other party for the foreseeable damages to that party. The party making a contract cannot avoid the obligation to perform because performance becomes more difficult or expensive than anticipated at the outset, although the party may be excused because performance becomes impossible due to circumstances beyond his or her control.

Parties who are victims of another party's wrongful breach cannot just sit back and collect their damages. They must attempt to mitigate damages, that is, to do what they reasonably can to avoid the damages and charge the breaching party only for the difference. For example, if one party agrees to buy goods from another at a certain price and then wrongfully refuses to accept them, the seller must make reasonable efforts to sell the goods elsewhere and can only charge the breaching party for his loss on the transaction. Similarly, employees who are wrongfully discharged cannot sit back and let the damages pile up; they must make reasonable efforts to find alternative employment and can only claim the difference between what they actually earned and what they would have earned.

Employees cannot be compelled to carry out an employment contract. This is considered involuntary servitude, which is barred by the Thirteenth Amendment to the United States Constitution. But if it costs the employer more to get the services performed by someone else, they may be charged with the difference.

2. Authority to Contract for the Church

Contracts must be made in managing the day-to-day business affairs of the church. Maintenance and repairs are required; furniture, furnishings, equipment, and supplies must be purchased; staff members are hired; services from outside consultants such as accountants, attorneys, or engineers are procured. The church may also from time to time enter into transactions that are more far-reaching. Real estate may be purchased or sold, buildings constructed, funds borrowed, organic church changes, such as merger or consolidation with another religious organization, carried out. The rules that govern authority within churches with respect to both routine and extraordinary transactions are not generically different from those that govern business corporations or other nonprofit organizations.

The source of authority to enter into contracts with respect to a church's management and business affairs is found in the church's governance documents and in the state statutes. Unless the church has established a different governance procedure, as in some hierarchichal churches, there is normally a board or committee (usually called a board of directors in corporate parlance but in churches more often a board of trustees, deacons, or the like) given authority for the business management of the church. Depending on the church's governance procedure, this may or may not be the same board or committee that has spiritual authority in the church.

The board of directors or its equivalent must hold its meetings and exercise its authority in accordance with the by-laws or other church governance documents or state statutes. It may delegate its authority in a particular situation. Individual members of the board, however, have no authority to act on its behalf, nor does the pastor by virtue of that office have any authority over the business and property affairs of the church. Unless the minister's employment contract, the church governance documents, or specific authority delegated from the governing board with authority has given that authority to the minister, the minister is not the business manager of the church.

In most churches with a congregational polity and, again, unless the church governance documents provide otherwise, major transactions such as the purchase or sale of real estate, construction of a building, major capital expenditures, and merger or consolidation with another church require a vote of the membership, as does the calling of a pastor or minister. In more hierarchical churches, such authority may be distributed less democratically. In churches that are organized as trustee corporations, there is some authority that the trustees must act unanimously, although normally a majority vote of the authoritative body is sufficient. When a person who is not authorized to do so acts on behalf of the organization, the properly authorized body may ratify the action, that is, approve it retroactively. And if it does not ratify the action expressly, but knows about it and takes no contrary action within a reasonable period of time, it will undoubtedly be considered to have ratified it implicitly.

Suppose the church board, being authorized by the congregation or its governance documents to sell a parcel of real estate owned by the church, gives the pastor authority to act for the church to sell it and tells a local realtor that she may deal exclusively with the pastor on the matter. Later, troubled by the pastor's apparent eagerness to sell for what the board views as too low a price, it passes a resolution revoking the pastor's authority but does not communicate the revocation to the real estate agent. The pastor, ignoring this limitation of authority, enters into a contract with the agent to sell the property. The board refuses to go through with the transaction, citing the pastor's lack of authority. In this scenario, the church would certainly be liable to the real estate agent for a commission and likely could be compelled to transfer the property to the prospective buyer as well. This is because the church board let the real estate agent, and through her the buyer, believe that the pastor had authority to act in the matter and, having done so, must be held to the consequences of its action. The equity of the result is apparent. In law, this is known as "apparent authority." The principle has broader application than just the failure to communicate a revocation of authority; it applies whenever the church or religious organization acts so as to lead another to believe that someone has authority to act for it, whether or not that person actually has such authority. A similar principle known as "estoppel" would hold the church liable if it intentionally or carelessly caused a third party to believe that the agent had authority or if it knew that the third party held such a belief and that the third party might change their position in reliance on that belief, yet did nothing to correct it. Churches and religious organizations may be bound by the apparent authority of their representatives or by estoppel if they let third persons dealing with them believe that the representatives are authorized to act when they are not.

A similar result would be reached if the person who purported to act on the church's behalf was not actually authorized to do so but had in fact been acting in such a manner as a matter of custom or over a period of time. Suppose, for example, that the pastor had signed a contract at the beginning of every winter with the same contractor for snowplowing services for the church parking lot. Even though it may be clear under the church by-laws that the pastor has no authority to bind the church by such a contract and the governing board has never granted the pastor authority to do so, the church will almost certainly be held to the contract. The result could be rationalized in several ways—as an implicit authorization of the pastor to act, as an implicit ratification of the pastor's acts or

authority, as an instance of apparent authority manifested to the snowplow contractor, or as an estoppel. Absent some course of conduct or acquiescence that may mislead others, however, religious organizations are not bound by the unauthorized acts of their representatives. The representatives themselves normally will be bound and may be liable to the other party for acting outside their authority.

There are three parties involved in any agency contractual relationship: the principal, being the church or religious organization represented by its governing body with respect to the matter at issue; the agent, being the cleric or other employee or representative conducting the transaction; and the outside party entering into a transaction with the body. Prudence dictates that all three communicate and understand clearly the scope of authority. Governing boards should keep track of what their organization's representatives are doing, be clear as to who is authorized to do what, not allow unauthorized persons to act as if they have authority when they do not, and promptly communicate any revocation or limitation of authority to those who may be relying on it. Significant transactions in churches organized as membership corporations should be submitted to the membership for approval according to church governance documents or state statutes. When authority is unclear, membership approval should be sought. Persons in the position of agents should be sure that they understand their authority and any limitations on it and do not act beyond it, no matter how tempting the opportunity may appear to be. When in doubt, they should consult the governing body or authority to whom they report. Third persons dealing with religious organizations should be sure that they are dealing with persons authorized to take the action in question.[2] When in doubt, they should not rely on the representation of the agent but should receive direct confirmation from the agent's principal, normally the governing body.

Naturally the same principles govern in reverse. Religious organizations dealing with other organizations should assure themselves that commitments are made by those with authority to do so.

Sophisticated business institutions, such as banks and lawyers who deal with significant transactions like real estate transfers, mergers, or consolidations, will normally ask for and receive evidence of authority for a specific transaction as, for example, by a certified copy of a corporate resolution or vote of the governing body. Less sophisticated parties, however, may rely on their assumption that they are dealing with an authorized person without evidence and do so at their peril.

C. TORTS AND THE CHURCH'S LIABILITY FOR THEM

1. The Nature of Torts

What's a tort? is the second most common question I am asked by nonlawyers. (The first is, How could any lawyer defend a person she knows is guilty?) Most people have a general and instinctive understanding of what contracts are all about. Few have the same insight into torts.

A satisfactory dictionary definition of a tort is "a legal wrong committed upon the person or property independent of contract."[3] The word comes from the Latin *torquere*, meaning to twist, and, hence, in the evolution of word usage, means something that is twisted or not right. It came into English through old French and middle Latin and appears in other familiar terms such as torte, tart, tortellini, tortuous, and torture. One commits a tort when one damages another person's physical or emotional well-being, property, freedom, or reputation by means which the law views as improper. A person who commits a tort is called a "tortfeasor." Tort law is broadly divided into negligence and intentional torts.

Negligent torts are unintentional. Negligence is "the omission to do something which a reasonable man, guided by those ordinary considerations which ordinarily regulate human affairs, would do or the doing of something which a reasonable and prudent man would not do."[4] Courts have defined the scope of tort law in terms of duty, determining that a duty does or does not exist to act without negligence in a given situation. Jurors who must decide tort cases when a duty exists are asked to determine whether or not the defendant acted in accordance with the standards of the hypothetical "reasonable and prudent man" in determining whether or not there is liability. For there to be liability, of course, not only must the defendant have acted negligently, but the plaintiff must have been damaged and the damage must have been caused by the defendant's negligence. Violation of a criminal statute that results in injury to someone's person or property is almost always a tort, whether the violation is negligent or intentional. The reverse is not true; criminal conduct is not an element of a tort. The most familiar form of negligence case is the automobile accident, but the types of negligence claims that are brought are limited only by the imagination of plaintiffs' attorneys and the tolerance of courts.

No one is liable just because an accident happened and someone was injured. Nor is the fact that they have been sued evidence that they are liable. Before the church or its workers can be held liable, the plaintiff must prove that there was indeed negligence on the part of the defendants (or someone for whom the defendants are responsible) and that the negligence caused the plaintiff's damages. In addition, there are a number of defenses that may be available, depending upon the state and the situation. The more common are (1) contributory or comparative negligence; (2) assumption of risk; (3) intervening and superseding cause; and (4) forseeability.

1. Contributory or Comparative Negligence. When I was a teenager learning to drive, my father observed one of my slightly older friends driving after he had just obtained his license and said, "Accidents happen when drivers like him meet drivers like you." Courts have recognized that injury-causing accidents are not always the exclusive fault of one party. No matter how negligent the defendant may be, the injured person has often contributed to the accident through negligence as well. The unfairness of letting a plaintiff recover money from a defendant when the plaintiff's own negligence contributed to the accident led to the rule

known as "contributory negligence," which prevented plaintiffs from recovering anything if their negligence, however slight, contributed in any way to their injury.

The result of this rule was equally unfair—plaintiffs whose negligent contribution to the injury may have been trivial and whose injuries may have been overwhelming were prevented from any recovery at all. Most states, either by legislation or by court decision, have now adopted some form of comparative negligence that allocates responsibility for the damages in some fashion proportionate to the contribution of the respective parties. States which have "pure" comparative negligence will do just this—a defendant is liable for whatever proportion his causal negligence contributed to the accident and no more. Other states may limit recovery to plaintiffs whose negligence did not exceed 50 percent of the causation of the accident and reduce their recovery by whatever percentage it did contribute. There are other variations. Comparative negligence will usually be the defense which, if it does not eliminate liability altogether, may most significantly reduce the damages.

2. Assumption of Risk. While similar to contributory or comparative negligence, the notion of assumption of risk goes to the adventuresomeness of the injured plaintiff rather than the plaintiff's negligence. Certain situations involve hazards that are or should be apparent. A plaintiff who puts himself or herself in these situations may be said to have assumed the risk of injury. Some states do not recognize the assumption-of-risk defense, but the facts that support it can usually be characterized as contributory or comparative negligence as well.

3. Intervening and Superseding Cause. Occasionally, even though one person is negligent and sets a cause in motion, another cause, later in time, comes along and supersedes the first negligence in leading to the accident. Such an intervening or superseding cause would relieve the original tortfeasor of liability. An example would be when a defendant negligently sets a fire and a strong wind comes up later which causes it to damage property that might not otherwise be damaged. The notion of intervening and superseding causes is not very clear. Usually the facts will fit into some other understanding, for example, that there was no negligence because the damage was not foreseeable.

4. Foreseeability. Suppose you run a railroad. While a passenger is running to catch one of your trains, one of your employees tries to assist him in getting on, knocking a package from his arms which falls onto the rails. Suppose that the package contains fireworks which cause a great explosion. Suppose that the force of the explosion overturns some scales some distance away which fall onto a bystander and injure her. She then brings suit against you, the railroad.

This unique set of facts is not a hypothetical but an actual case presented to the highest court of New York, the New York Court of Appeals, and decided in an opinion by Benjamin Cardozo, who was later appointed to the United States Supreme Court. It is known as *Palzgraf v. Long Island Railroad Co.*[5] The 1928 decision by Judge Cardozo found that the railroad was not liable to the plaintiff because there was no negligence toward her. The injury to her was simply not foreseeable in the situation.

Palzgraf is a well-known case taught in every law school torts course and discussed in every legal text on the subject. Not every court has adopted its reasoning, but it illustrates important points that most courts follow in one form or another: (1) liability for negligence is not unlimited, and (2) there must be some not unduly remote relationship between the act of the defendant and the injury to the plaintiff for there to be liability. Some courts characterize this as "proximate cause." Others may cast it in terms of whether or not there is a duty owed. Cardozo called it "foreseeability." Whatever the legal buzzword, the result is the same: some injuries are simply too remote from the original act for courts to make the actor liable. Negligence is still a fault system.

Intentional torts, like negligence, must fit within certain specific categories. Common intentional torts include assault, battery, trespass, defamation, and invasion of privacy. Religious organizations encounter claims of intentional tort when problems arise such as the sexual misconduct of church workers or volunteers toward minors or counselees, and church discipline issues. The courts have developed rules to determine when a person may recover for each type of intentional tort.

Another type of tort which is not based on either negligence or intent is called *strict liability*. It refers to certain types of tort claims in which a person may be held liable "strictly," that is, even though the person neither acted negligently nor intended to cause an injury. The most familiar form of strict liability is the field of products liability, in which a manufacturer or other party in the chain of distribution may be held liable if the product is "in a defective condition unreasonably dangerous to the user or consumer or to his property"[6] and the product thereby causes harm to a user or consumer. Strict liability may also apply to keeping animals or to abnormally dangerous things (such as explosives or inflammable liquids stored in quantity) or activities (such as blasting, pile driving, or crop dusting). Strict liability is rarely applicable to religious organizations and is not discussed further herein.

Tort law is almost entirely state law. Thus, while there are certain common principles that are widely recognized, the law of every state must be consulted for a detailed application to any given situation. For the most part it is common law, that is, law that is determined by courts rather than by legislatures, although legislative intervention in the court system is not uncommon, particularly in "tort reform" legislation enacted in many states in response to a perceived insurance crisis in the mid- to late-1980s.

Once upon a time, churches and other charitable organizations and enterprises were immune from being sued. The rationales for the immunity were various: the assets were provided by public support and for public benefit; charities should receive the same immunity as the government; trust funds should not be diverted to purposes other than that intended by the donors; the charity derives no gain or benefit from the services of its employees; beneficiaries of the charitable services implicitly waive any liability claim against those who provide them; those who render gratuitous aid should not be held to undue responsibility for their efforts; donors will be discouraged and charities crippled. Whatever the merits of the rationales, since the early 1940s the notion of charitable immunity has been rejected by court decision in almost every state. Even in its heyday, it never applied to commercial or profit-making activities of a charitable organization. Today, in most American jurisdictions, churches and religious organizations, along with other charities, are as liable as any secular or commercial organization for their tortious acts. Some states continue to allow immunity from claims by those who are the beneficiaries of the organization's services, such as youth campers, attendees at worship services, wedding guests, scout troop members meeting on the premises, and the like. And there are recently enacted, but limited, statutory immunities in many states (discussed on p. 95, below). But churches and religious organizations today will normally be as liable as any other defendant, and need to conduct themselves accordingly.

Assuming that a church's employee or representative has committed an act that injured another for which the employee is legally liable, is the church liable as well? And how far up the organization, if it is hierarchical in any sense or if the church is part of any larger denomination or affiliation, does the liability ascend? It is useful to consider this issue at two levels, liabilities of the religious employer and liability of the denomination or parent institution, although both will often be sued in the same action.

2. Liability of the Religious Employer: Respondeat Superior

Courts in times past liked to put Latin names on things and some of these have stayed with us. The term "respondeat superior" is such Latin legal jargon. It means, literally, "let the master respond." In practical terms, it means that the "master," that is, the employer, is, under certain circumstances, responsible or liable for injuries caused by his "servants" or employees. The rule applies to religious employers as well as secular. The idea is sometimes referred to as "vicarious," or "substitutionary," liability. It parallels the biblical teaching of substitutionary atonement for sin fundamental to understanding the work of Christ on the cross.

Because this term is also used of Christ's atonement, perhaps the analogy needs to be drawn out. Some Christians understand that, for believers, Jesus took on the punishment for sin in his suffering and death, thus relieving the believer of his or her liability to be punished by God. Employers in this analogy function as Christ figures, but, unlike Christ, they do not relieve employees from liability for any wrongs committed. The employers' presence, however, means that the employee is less likely to pay directly for the offense; the wronged party will likely collect from the employer or employer's insurance company.

Several rationales have been offered for respondeat superior liability. It is said to be desirable to spread the risk or cost from the single or limited number of victims who suffer to a broader base of those who can absorb it; to encourage employers to prevent harm by doing a better job in hiring, training, and supervising their help; to reflect the true cost of doing business in the form of the damage to the victim by placing the burden on those who get the profit or benefit from the business; and, sometimes, simply and frankly, to reach a "deep pocket." While some of the rationales have limited or questionable application to religious organizations, in American law today religious organizations are generally subject to the same vicarious liability for the wrongs of their employees as are other organizations.

The issue in a vicarious liability or respondeat superior case is usually twofold:

1. Was the wrongdoer in fact an employee of the church or religious organization?
2. Was the wrong done in the course of his or her employment?

In addition the plaintiff has to show the same requisites to recovery he would have to show in a case not involving vicarious liability, that is, that he had an injury that was caused by a negligent or otherwise wrongful act of the person or persons claimed to be an employee.

a. Was the Wrongdoer an Employee?

The central issue in identifying who is employed by the church for purposes of vicarious liability is whether "with respect to the physical conduct in the performance of the services" the individual "is subject to the other's control or right to control."[7] Note that the employment relationship can be established by the "right to control." Actual control of the physical conduct of the work is not necessary. The right to terminate services is often regarded as adequate evidence of right to control. The following factors are often considered to determine doubtful cases:[8]

1. the extent of control which, by the agreement, the master may exercise over the details of the work;
2. whether or not the one employed is engaged in a distinct occupation or business;
3. the kind of occupation, with reference to whether, in the locality, the work is usually done under the direction of the employer or by a specialist without supervision;
4. the skill required in the particular occupation;
5. whether the employer or the worker supplies the instrumentalities, tools, and the place of work for the person doing the work;
6. the length of time for which the person is employed;
7. the method of payment, whether by the time or by the job;
8. whether or not the work is a part of the regular business of the employer;
9. whether or not the parties believe they are creating the relation of master and servant;
10. whether the principal is or is not in business.

Applying these principles, employees will

normally include church administrative staff and secretaries, regular or full-time maintenance personnel, teachers and administrators in church schools, staff and administrators in church camps and conference centers—in short, virtually all full-time regular staff of religious organizations and institutions. People who maintain their own trade or business and are engaged by the church from time to time for special services, whether religious, such as music, speaking, or evangelism, or secular, such as maintenance, repair, construction, or janitorial services, would not be employees. Such workers are self-employed and are sometimes referred to as "independent contractors." The characterization that the parties give to their own relationship is not determinative although it will be considered. For many workers in a religious organization, the distinction will be clear enough, but gray areas will remain for others.

Volunteers can be considered to be employees for purposes of vicarious liability. Sunday School teachers and youth group leaders are generally subject to the right of the church to control their conduct and can create liability for the church.[9] A wrinkle arises with respect to clergy. By the ordinary understanding of who is and is not an employee, most clergy would be considered employees of their church or religious organization. There is, however, a history and tradition in the United States of clergy being considered self-employed. This finds expression in the Social Security law, which in section 1402(c) of the Internal Revenue Code treats all ordained, commissioned, or licensed ministers of churches in the exercise of their ministry as self-employed for Social Security purposes whether or not they are considered employees for other purposes. Since the conduct of clergy is frequently the conduct that gives rise to the most substantial liability claims, it is also the area that has gotten the most attention from the courts. However the parties characterize their relationship, a court will look at the reality of the relationship to determine whether or not the church has the requisite control or right to control the cleric's services for him or her to be considered employed for both tax (except Social Security) and liability purposes. The reverse is also true. The fact that the church or denomination treats the cleric as employed for tax or other purposes is not binding on a court in a liability suit if the evidence indicates that the true nature of the relationship is self-employment.

Despite the extensive litigation of respondeat superior issues with respect to clergy, there is little consistency in the law. Three recent cases involving Roman Catholic priests, all decided in 1988, illustrate the contrasting applications of these principles in determining who is sufficiently controlled to be an employee for purposes of respondeat superior liability. In a Kansas case, *Brillhart v. Scheier*,[10] the priest had been involved in an automobile accident in which the occupants of another vehicle were injured. In an Alabama case, *Wood v. Benedictine Society*,[11] the priest had injured a woman while destroying equipment with a sledgehammer in an abortion clinic. The third case, the Washington state case of *Does 1–9 v. Compcare, Inc.*,[12] involved a priest charged with sexual abuse committed in the course of his job as a counselor of adolescents in an alcohol and drug rehabilitation center in a private hospital. The diocese was sued in the Kansas and Washington cases and the Benedictine Order in the Alabama case, all on a respondeat superior theory that the priest was their employee. However, in both the automobile accident and abortion clinic cases, the courts in Kansas and Alabama found that the priests were not employees and, therefore, their diocese and order had no vicarious liability for the priests' actions. In the Kansas automobile accident case, the court found that the diocese did not have the requisite right to control the priest's work since his day-to-day activities were within his own discretion and control; he was authorized under canon law to do whatever he felt necessary to carry out his duties; he established his own working hours and vacation time; he made out his own paycheck and hired and fired nonclergy workers in the parish; he had complete discretion in purchasing church supplies and paying bills out of parish funds; his work required a high level of skill and experience and was generally performed without supervision; and he was driving his own car at the time of the accident and had obtained his own insurance on the vehicle. (Who owned and insured the vehicle would seem to be of little relevance to the employed/self-employed issue but might be relevant to whether or not the accident occurred in the course of the priest's employment if the employer provided transportation for job-related travel.) The bishop's control over the priest was viewed by the court as purely "ecclesiastical control" and not relevant for determining legal liability. The "self-employed" determination was made by the court notwithstanding that the diocese issued a W-2 form to the priest, treating him as an employee for federal income tax purposes.

In *Wood,* the abortion case, the Alabama Supreme Court also found that the relationship between the priest and the society was ecclesiastical and not a secular controlling relationship. The fact that he was subject to the orders of the society twenty-four hours a day did not make the society liable for his actions. Existence of ecclesiastical authority alone in a hierarchical denomination is insufficient to make a cleric an agent of the denomination for liability purposes. The court analogized the relationship between the priest and his order to that of a minister and his seminary. The decision does not seem entirely consistent with established agency law, and the analogy to a seminarian seems inappropriate because seminary students would not by virtue of their status as such be employees of the seminary in the same way that a cleric of a hierarchical denomination or religious order may be related to his or her ecclesiastical order or authority.

A different result was reached in the Washington case involving sexual abuse, *Does 1–9 v. Compcare, Inc.* There the Louisiana Roman Catholic diocese had suspended the priest from performing priestly duties after admitted incidents of sexual misconduct. While the principal discussion in the case is about the scope of employment issue, the court found that notwithstanding the priest's employment with the private hospital, the employment relationship between the priest and the diocese continued and that he owed the diocese a duty of obedience encompassing all phases of his

life, thus extending the diocese's authority beyond the customary employer/employee relationship. The case carries the troubling implication, at least for as hierarchical a body as the Roman Catholic church, that the priest who remains such may be a liability burden to his ordaining bishop, diocese, or order for the rest of his life, no matter where he is, what kind of employment he is actually engaged in, or how remote he may be from any practical control of his activities by his ecclesiastical superior.

Although these cases come from three different jurisdictions, they apply the same rules in determining whether Roman Catholic priests are employees or self-employed for purposes of attributing liability to the ecclesiastical organization which governed them. Reading the cases side-by-side, one is inclined to think that all three are wrongly decided: the priest who was most removed from ecclesiastical control was found to be employed, while the two priests who remained in a much more direct-control relationship to their ecclesiastical superiors were found to be self-employed. Perhaps the difference in the decisions reflects a propensity in the three highest courts of the states that decided them to tilt in one direction or the other, exercising their own views of good policy and a just result. Whatever the reason, the cases vividly illustrate that churches and religious organizations facing liability claims for the conduct of clergy, whether negligent or intentional acts, should not presume that a liability-creating employment relationship exists but should, rather, consider their position on the issue carefully with the advice of counsel.

b. Was the Act Committed within the Course of Employment?

The second condition for vicarious or respondeat superior liability is that the act committed by the employee be committed "in the scope of" or in the "course of" employment. This is usually the more difficult issue.

Conduct that is in the course of employment for purposes of liability does not mean conduct that the employee was specifically engaged or instructed to do. Employees are rarely under their employer's direction to perform negligent or intentional acts that create liability; and, if they were, the liability would be direct, as the act of the employer, and not vicarious. Vicarious liability presumes that the employer is innocent. Even if the employer has expressly forbidden the conduct in question, it may still be held liable. The general standards for conduct within the scope of employment are as follows:

1. It is of the kind the servant is employed to perform.
2. It occurs substantially within the authorized time and space limits.
3. It is actuated, at least in part, by a purpose to serve the master.
4. If force is intentionally used by the servant against another, the use of force is not unexpectable by the master.[13]

Acts "which are so closely connected with what the servant is employed to do, and so fairly and reasonably incidental to it, that they may be regarded as methods, even though quite improper ones, of carrying out the objectives of the employment", will make the employer liable.[14] Thus an employee's negligence by which the employee injures another while engaged in his or her employment will be considered in the course of employment.

Employees, however, who go on what is sometimes referred to as a "frolic and detour," that is, who step outside of their employment to act for themselves rather than for their employer, are not acting in the course of employment. Frolic and detour cases are very fact-specific. If the deviation from employment purpose is minor or is a foreseeable deviation, the act is still considered in the course of employment for liability purposes. For example, if a church employee is running an errand on church business but deviates from the normal route to run a personal errand as well and gets in an automobile accident on the personal detour, the church will still be liable. If, on the other hand, the employee has no purpose of church business but is simply off on an entirely personal errand, the church may be able to avoid liability.

Intentional conduct, such as the sexual molestation of a minor, which is often a criminal offense as well, will not usually be imputed to the employer unless there is some element of foreseeability or a close connection to furthering the employer's business, although liability may be predicated on other than vicarious grounds, such as negligent hiring or supervision, discussed in chapter 12. Even in respondeat superior cases, however, the actual results are not consistent. Most cases that have addressed issues of sexual misconduct have found that religious employers are not vicariously liable for such acts because they are matters of personal gratification which are unusual, inappropriate, and not motivated by a purpose to serve the employer.[15] A recent case in Alaska, however, finds respondeat superior liability appropriate for a pastoral counseling center in a sexual seduction claim. Even intentional and unauthorized sexual misconduct was found to be a basis for respondeat superior liability if it "arises out of and is reasonably incidental to the employee's legitimate work activities."[16] The state court was impressed with the thought that imposing such liability would encourage prevention (notwithstanding that the event had occurred in disregard of all standards of professional conduct); that compensation for victims would be assured; and that such liability would distribute the costs of the enterprise among its beneficiaries. Cases such as these depart from more established standards of vicarious liability to broaden the opportunity for victims to recover, and they illustrate the importance of vigilance and prevention activities for all churches and religious organizations in which counseling or youth work is any part of the program.

The question of what is within or without the course of employment is considered by most courts to be a jury question. Hence if a plaintiff properly sets forth a claim for sexual abuse, there may be no other way to win the case than in a courtroom with a jury.[17] Trial procedure is discussed in detail in chapter 19.

3. Liability of the Denomination or Parent Religious Institution

If the church or religious organization that is asserted to be the employer of the wrongdoer is not liable, it is unlikely that a higher organization would be, because it would presumably exercise even less control over the individual. Nonetheless, plaintiffs often seek to impose "ascending liability"[18] on other levels of the organizational hierarchy. Ascending liability may be an attempt to make a regional or national organization liable for the acts or liability of a local organization or individual, or it may seek to make any higher level of the organization liable for any lower level or affiliated organizational entity.

Ascending liability is plainly contrary to the interests of the higher organizational levels targeted. The lower levels may be happy to have other targets to share the potential liability, but the price of sharing may be the acknowledgment of control that is not present, or desired, for theological or other reasons. American church organizations have "diverse, complex and confused structures,"[19] which may lend themselves to claims of ascending liability if only because the courts themselves are confused and may tend to view the aggregate institution as a single entity even though it is not so organized either in civil or ecclesiastical law.

Denominations with true congregational polities have generally been successful in avoiding denominational liability for acts of local church bodies.[20] Cases have involved such matters as fund-raising activities of a local church to finance a new building and facilities, a life-care contract for nursing home residents, and sexual misconduct toward a minor. The church governance documents and the theology of the church polity as well as church practice will be important in such cases in demonstrating that the necessary control does not exist to make a denomination or higher entity liable for a subsidiary or affiliated entity.

In the 1990 case of *Eckler v. The General Council of the Assemblies of God,*[21] a child sexual molestation case, the issue of apparent agency or authority was also raised by the plaintiff but rejected by the court. A plaintiff claimed that the ordination and licensing of clergy by the national denomination, the contribution of the local church to the national church, the use of the "Assembly of God" name, and the circulation of a denominational magazine created

a sufficient holding out by the national church of the authority of the local church to act in its behalf to make the denomination liable. The court rejected all of the arguments. It may have aided the court in reaching its conclusion that the plaintiff was closely associated with the local church and could reasonably be expected to have had notice of the limitations on denominational authority.

Other cases in less clearly congregational denominations or in cases involving relationships between affiliated organizations within a denomination rather than with a local church have led to different results. In the 1979 case of *Barr v. United Methodist Church,*[22] a California Court of Appeals found sufficient control in the United Methodist church as a hierarchical denomination to make it responsible for fraud and breach of contract claims for a subsidiary nursing home corporation. The decision was reached despite the fact that the religious self-understanding of Methodism was that no one was authorized to act on behalf of the United Methodist church except members of a quadrennial gathering known as the General Conference, and hence that it was not suable as a jural entity.[23]

Churches and religious organizations must be alert to the differences between their ecclesiastical and their civil organizations as well as the precise nature of the control exhibited by the ecclesiastical polity. This distinction was recognized in a suit against the Central Florida Diocese of the Episcopalian church that involved personal injuries that occurred on the premises of a local Episcopalian church. In the 1985 case of *Folwell v. Bernard,*[24] the court distinguished obedience and control involving ecclesiastical dogma, discipline, and authority from control over the everyday secular affairs of the church under the separate civil incorporation of the local church from the diocese. The ecclesiastical relationship should not, and in *Folwell* did not, serve as a bridge for liability to cross to the parent organization.

Chapters 4 and 11 discuss the relationship between the ecclesiastical polity and the civil polity of churches and religious organizations and the frequent difficulty of determining how best to organize the civil polity to reflect ecclesiastical as well as civil concerns. We also discussed in chapter 4 the constitutional protections of church autonomy that prevent courts from ruling on matters of ecclesiastical doctrine and polity. A serious First Amendment issue is raised when courts apply civil law notions of agency to ecclesiastical polities to find, control, and transmit liability when the organization does not perceive itself as having the same control relationships in the secular functioning between its components. Religious organizations and their counsel should eliminate from church governance documents all references to control in civil or secular matters that does not reflect the intent or actual functioning of organizational relationships. When taking other actions with legal consequences, regard must be given to the potential liability consequences of expressions of control relationships. For example, including subordinate organizations in a group exemption letter given to a central organization by the IRS to establish federal tax-exempt status requires verification that the subordinate is subject to the general supervision or control of the central organization[25]— often the very proposition the central organization wants to refute in an ascending liability case. When suits seek to impose liability on higher organizations in denominational or hierarchical churches or parent or affiliated entities of the organization actually involved in the act, it is imperative to communicate in the most effective way in court the secular divisions of function, the lack of control of or limitations on relationships where applicable, and the constitutional limitation on courts inquiring into theological organization and relationships. With such communication, courts are less likely to reorganize the corporate relationships within a larger religious organization de facto based on impermissible inquiries into theological matters or in contradiction to the organization's self-understanding.

D. PIERCING THE CORPORATE VEIL

A discussion of agency law would be incomplete without some discussion of the notion of "piercing the corporate veil,"

another favorite lawyers' phrase. The imagery is biblical. It refers to the rending in two, at the moment of Jesus' death, of the great veil in the temple which separated the Holy Place from the Most Holy Place, symbolizing the ability of the believer, through the death of Jesus, to enter into God's presence.[26] In corporate litigation, it refers to fastening liability on a parent corporation for the acts or obligations of a subsidiary. The notion is akin to the notions of authorization and control in agency law but is basically intended to allow the court to disregard a corporation. When a corporation creates sham subsidiaries for the sole purpose of shielding itself from liability but, in fact, conducts the basic operations of the subsidiary corporation centrally, the corporate "veil" may be "pierced" to make the parent corporation directly liable for the subsidiary without recognizing any corporate distinction.

To protect parent corporations from veil-piercing liability for a subsidiary, the subsidiary corporation(s) should have a bona fide purpose for existing as a separate corporation with a real and substantial function which should be reflected in actual practices and activities. It should not function as a mere arm or integral part of the parent or be so controlled by the parent that it can be considered as a single entity. The parent should not be involved directly in its day-to-day operation. It should maintain its corporate separateness through formalities of corporate meetings. Overlapping officers and directors should be minimized where possible. If employees share duties between the corporations, time records should be kept and arm's-length arrangements made for sharing personnel expense fairly. Other business relationships should also be at arm's length and should reflect reasonable business judgments by each side, with clear records of any such arrangements, for example, the transfer of goods and services or leases. Board meetings should be conducted separately, and corporate records should be separately maintained. Funds should not be commingled. The parent should not pay the subsidiary's bills and certainly not its wage expense. These rules prevent neither parent nor subsidiary from supporting one another financially within their respective corporate purposes, just as unrelated corporations can contribute to or support one another for whatever business or charitable purposes may be served in doing so. The important point is that the subsidiary be operated in fact as a separate entity for the law to recognize its separateness.

E. STATUTORY LIMITS ON LIABILITY

As part of the wave of "tort reform" legislation, a number of states in recent years have enacted provisions limiting the liability of churches and other charitable organizations.[27] Typically these statutes immunize either uncompensated directors and officers, or all volunteers, although in some states employees or compensated officers or directors may have some immunity. Immunity may be only for "ordinary negligence" or for acting in good faith and within the scope of their office, and it frequently excludes liability for conduct that is willful, wanton, or gross negligence. Immunity may be limited to claims from beneficiaries of the organization. It may not apply to commercial activities. In most instances, it will not extend to the organization itself, only to the individual participants, although a few states have statutes that provide some limitations on liability for the organization. The immunity may not be applicable if there is liability insurance and may not include operation of motor vehicles. It may limit damages to specified amounts and exclude recovery of punitive damages.

Most of these laws have not been constitutionally tested and may be vulnerable, because other legislative attempts to limit liability in specific situations or with respect to certain classes of tortfeasors have been struck down by courts.[28] Some recent cases, however, have upheld the constitutionality of statutes limiting the liability of charitable organizations for their workers.[29] Religious organizations should understand what, if any, the liability limitations are in

their state and should be guided by them as appropriate in purchasing liability insurance and other actions. Where, for example, the pastor is also an officer or member of a governing board and immunity applies only to uncompensated personnel, board minutes can make clear that the pastor's compensation is only for pastoral duties, not for service as an officer or board member; this will enhance the prospect of immunizing the pastor's conduct in the latter capacities. Churches should realize the limitations and vulnerability of immunity statutes, however, and should not rely on them for protection with respect to liability-generating conduct.

REFERENCES

American Bar Association. *Tort and Religion.* Publication of Section of Tort and Insurance Practice, Section of Individual Rights and Responsibilities of the Division for Professional Education of the American Bar Association, 1990.

Buzzard, Robert A., and Lynn R. Buzzard. *"Render unto Caesar"—Unrelated Business Income Tax: Liabilities of Churches and Charitable Ministries* (Buies Creek, N.C.: Church-State Resource Center, Norman Adrian Wiggins School of Law, Campbell University, 1990), 105–16.

Gaffney, Edward McClynn, and Philip C. Sorenson. *Ascending Liability in Religious and Other Nonprofit Organizations.* Howard R. Griffin, ed. (Macon, Ga.: Center for Constitutional Studies, and Mercer University Press, 1984).

Hammar, Richard R. *Pastor, Church and Law,* 2d ed. (Matthews, N.C.: Christian Ministries Resources, 1991).

Moots, Philip R. *Ascending Liability—A Planning Memorandum* (Macon, Ga.: Center for Constitutional Studies, 1987).

Prosser, William L. *The Law of Torts*, 4th ed. (St. Paul, Minn.: West Publishing Co., 1971), sects. 69 and 70.

Restatement, Second Agency (St. Paul, Minn.: American Law Institute, 1958).

CHAPTER 7

The Church as Regulated Employer

A. INTRODUCTION

Virtually all churches and religious organizations are employers. Although the employment relationship is a private contract and is subject to the same rules of law as any other private contract, employment is also one of the most highly regulated forms of consensual relationship. Whether an employer has one employee or thousands, it must be aware of and comply with laws applicable to employment.

Federal legislation imposes a uniform nationwide set of regulations on employers, although not all employers are subject to every regulation. Perhaps the most comprehensively applicable is the obligation to withhold from employees' pay, set aside, and pay to the government federal income taxes (see the discussion in chapter 14). Most other regulations are part of two broad legislative waves: (1) the worker security and protection legislation that came out of the Great Depression (Social Security, unemployment compensation, workers' compensation, union organizing and collective bargaining, minimum wages, and overtime pay, among others); and (2) the antidiscrimination legislation that began with the Civil Rights Act of 1964 and has since then been continuously augmented (forbidding discrimination on the basis of race, color, religion, national origin, citizenship, sex, age, and disabilities). Most states have parallel regulations in some or all of the areas regulated by federal law, and some municipalities also have ordinances that ban employment discrimination or otherwise affect the employment relationship.

To determine if an organization or activity is subject to federal jurisdiction with respect to any particular regulatory act, several levels of analysis are required.

First, federal regulation must be premised on federal jurisdiction over the activity. This requires that the employer be engaged in interstate commerce or in activity affecting interstate commerce (see the discussion in chapter 2) or that the regulation address some other subject delegated to the federal government in the U.S. Constitution. There is no question about federal authority to impose federal tax and Social Security law on churches and religious organizations. With respect to other federal regulatory legislation, whether or not the organization is engaged in commerce in such a way as to bring it within federal jurisdiction will depend on how broadly the statute and court interpretations of it define "commercial" activity, how large the organization is, and the nature of its activities. Small local churches engaged in no collateral activities may be sufficiently noncommercial and intrastate to avoid federal regulation that turns on Commerce Clause authority, although even activities such as using the telephone or buying gas or electric utility services have been held by some courts to involve a religious organization in interstate commerce. However, even if not subject to federal regulation, churches and religious organizations must consider state and local regulation that is not dependent on the Commerce Clause or the U.S. Constitution for its applicability to them.

Second, the definitional terms of the statute in question must be considered. Many statutes define "employer" so as to exclude those who employ fewer than a certain number of employees. Others may apply only to employers engaged in certain activities such as "trade or business" that may be interpreted effectively to exclude certain churches or religious organizations.

Third, does the statute have any religious exemptions? Recognizing the potential First Amendment problems with, or religious sensibility in, regulating religious organizations, Congress and state and local legislative bodies often provide religious exemptions in regulatory statutes, such as the exemption in the federal employment discrimination law that allows religious employers to discriminate on the basis of religion as discussed below, in section B of this chapter. If there is an exemption, it may be subject to constitutional challenge as a violation of the Establishment Clause by employees or other advocacy groups.[1] That challenge would not be made by the regulatory agency itself, whose task it is to carry out the mandate of the legislation, or by the religious organization. Unless successfully challenged, the exemption will be effective.

Fourth, if application of the statute *raises* First Amendment problems, it may be sub-

ject to a court-made exemption. The U.S. Supreme Court, in the 1979 case of *National Labor Relations Board v. Catholic Bishop,*[2] held that the National Labor Relations Act, which requires employers to permit union organizing activity and to collectively bargain with duly selected unions, did not cover lay teachers in church-run schools. The Court did not decide that there *was* a First Amendment violation, only that the matter would present "a significant risk that the First Amendment will be infringed,"[3] not only by the conclusions of an inquiry but by the very process of inquiry into school labor practices which would "inevitably . . . implicate sensitive issues that open the door to conflicts between clergy-administrators and the Board, or conflicts with negotiators for unions."[4] In view of these sensitive First Amendment problems and potential conflicts, the Court ruled that the National Labor Relations Board did not have jurisdiction over the church school teachers in the absence of some affirmatively expressed intention of Congress to assert such jurisdiction. The Court found no such affirmative intent expressed in the National Labor Relations Act or its legislative history. Had such an affirmative intention been found, the Court would have been required to determine whether there was an actual First Amendment violation in applying the statute to the employer in question. By deciding the issue on a jurisdictional basis, it avoided the constitutional question. The *Catholic Bishop* case provides a model from the U.S. Supreme Court for addressing the jurisdiction or application of any statute that regulates any employment practices of a religious institution. If applying the statute would implicate sensitive First Amendment issues and the statute does not express an affirmative intention to regulate such employers, a court may find that there is simply no jurisdiction of the regulatory agency or statute over the religious employer.

Fifth, does the law or regulation, either on its face or, more likely, as applied to the particular situation, violate the religious organization's constitutional rights? Both the Free Exercise and Establishment Clauses of the U.S. Constitution, which would apply to regulatory legislation by any level of government, and comparable provisions under the applicable state constitution that could invalidate state or local, but not federal, regulation must be considered.

The resolution of free exercise claims with respect to government regulation of employment by churches or religious organizations can be approached at several conceptual levels. In one approach, churches would receive the maximum insulation from government regulation if the courts view the issue as one of church autonomy, with all church employees treated similarly to members whose functions are invariably related to the organization's religious mission, regardless of whether their specific tasks are religious. This model is advocated by Douglas Laycock of the University of Texas.[5]

A second approach might be called the "concentric circles approach"; it examines the function of the job in question for its traditionally religious content. Thus, clergy in their traditional roles of, for example, administering the sacraments, leading worship, and teaching religion would occupy the inner circle and be most protected from government regulation. In the outermost circle would be employees of enterprises owned by religious organizations but used only for investment or profit-making purposes. Each case would require an evaluation of the religious function of the particular employment situation and how it would be affected by application of the law.[6]

The least insulating approach to government regulation of church and religious organizations as employers would defer to government regulation except with respect to belief or issues in which other constitutional rights, such as speech, assembly, press, or parents' rights to supervise the education of their children, are implicated. In deciding free exercise claims by religious employers, most courts have considered the religious function of the job and the burden of specific religious conduct on the employer, rather than a more general protection of church autonomy in its employment relationships. The U.S. Supreme Court and some lower courts have held that there is no constitutional violation in a state agency investigating whether unlawful discrimination has occurred, even if the religious

organization asserts a protected religious reason for its employment action.[7]

Sixth, the institution must consider whether it has been subjected to federal regulation by receiving federal funds that carry with them certain conditions that might not otherwise be applicable.

The discussion that follows covers primarily the major federal employment regulation statutes. One must always consider, however, whether there are any applicable state or local regulations. State statutes often parallel, and may expand on, federal law with respect to nondiscrimination and other regulatory requirements. Exemptions in state law may be broader or narrower for religious organizations, and state law often reaches employers with a smaller number of employees than would be covered under federal law. State or municipal law may ban discrimination in some categories not covered by federal law, such as marital status[8] and sexual orientation or gender preference. It may also impose additional regulatory requirements, such as smoking policies, that are not included in federal law.

B. ANTIDISCRIMINATION LAWS

Several federal laws prohibit employment discrimination against certain groups. The most important federal law prohibiting discrimination in employment practices is Title VII of the Civil Rights Act of 1964, the key provision of which is as follows:

(a) It shall be an unlawful employment practice for an employer—

(1) to fail or refuse to hire or to discharge any individual, or otherwise to discriminate against any individual with respect to his compensation, terms, conditions, or privileges of employment, because of such individual's race, color, religion, sex, or national origin; or

(2) to limit, segregate, or classify his employees or applicants for employment in any way which would deprive or tend to deprive any individual of employment opportunities or otherwise adversely affect his status as an employee, because of such individual's race, color, religion, sex, or national origin.[9]

An employer, to be subject to the act, must

be "engaged in an industry affecting commerce," which is defined as "any activity, business, or industry in commerce or in which a labor dispute would hinder or obstruct commerce or the free flow of commerce."[10] To be subject to the act, the employer must also have "fifteen or more employees for each working day in each of twenty or more calendar weeks in the current or preceding calendar year."[11] These definitional provisions exclude many churches and religious organizations from the Civil Rights Act of 1964, but they may not be similarly exempted from a parallel state statute.

We will consider below application of the Civil Rights Act of 1964 and other federal antidiscrimination laws to religious organizations based upon the type of discrimination.

1. Religion

The Civil Rights Act of 1964 contains a specific exemption for religious discrimination by religious employers. The act does not apply to "a religious corporation, association, educational institution, or society with respect to the employment of individuals with respect to a particular religion to perform work connected with the carrying on by such corporation, association, educational institution, or society of its activities."[12] It further provides that it is not an unlawful employment practice for "a school, college, university, or other educational institution or institution of learning to hire employees of a particular religion if such school, college, university, or other educational institution or institution of learning is, in whole or in substantial part, owned, supported, controlled, or managed by a particular religion or by a particular religious corporation, association, or society, or if the curriculum of such school, college, university, or other educational institution or institution of learning is directed toward the propagation of a particular religion."[13] The specific exemption for schools, colleges, universities, or other educational institutions or institutions of learning was included to cover all employees of the numerous such institutions with religious affiliations.

In order to be a religious organization within the Title VII exemption, there must be a specific religious purpose and activity as such. The Salvation Army has been found to be a religious corporation;[14] and the exemption has been applied to the *Christian Science Monitor,* which is controlled by the Christian Science church and has a religious purpose: "Merely because it holds some interest for persons not members of the faith, or occupies a position of respect in the secular world at large does not deprive it of religious status."[15] But a United Methodist children's home was not a religious corporation because its day-to-day life for the children was found to be "practically devoid of religious content or training as such" notwithstanding that it had a board of trustees who were members of the United Methodist church.[16]

The religious exemption permits a religious employer to discriminate on the basis of not only the employee's religion but also the employee's adherence to the employer's religious doctrine. A Roman Catholic school, for example, has been permitted to refuse to renew the contract of a teacher who remarried after a divorce without following the proper canonical process.[17]

For a number of years, there was a debate as to whether the religious exemption could constitutionally be applied to permit religious organizations to engage in religious discrimination with respect to nonreligious functions. No one ever questioned that such discrimination was permissible with respect to religious functions—the Catholic church can hire only Catholics as priests, and Jewish congregations are entitled to be sure the rabbi is a Jew. Indeed, such a result would undoubtedly be compelled by the First Amendment if the statute did not contain the exemption. Many, however, believed that with respect to employees whose duties included no specifically religious functions—for example, secretarial and administrative personnel, maintenance and custodial personnel, and the like—discrimination in employment by a religious organization on the basis of religion was not constitutionally permissible and should not, as a matter of simple justice, be permitted.

Such a view seriously misunderstood the

faith perceptions of many religious groups. These groups view the organization as a whole as a part of the body of Christ in the world, and they understand their church's ministry as being exercised by all of its employees, regardless of whether their particular function would, from a secular perspective, be deemed religious. The cook and the maintenance man are engaged no less than the cleric, teacher, counselor, or administrator in carrying out the organization's ministry and communicating the good news of God's love and the path to salvation.

In 1987, the Supreme Court put the issue to rest, construing the exemption broadly to apply to all employees of religious organizations, whether or not their jobs were specifically religious. The case was *Corporation of the Presiding Bishop v. Amos.*[18] The context was the discharge by the Deseret Gymnasium, a nonprofit facility run by a corporation of the Mormon church, of a building engineer and other nonreligious employees for failing to obtain a "temple recommend" (i.e., a certificate that they were members of the church and eligible to attend its temples). The Court clearly recognized the difficulty of ascertaining which activities were religious in the view and understanding of a religious organization:

> Nonetheless, it is a significant burden on a religious organization to require it, on pain of substantial liability, to predict which of its activities a secular court will consider religious. The line is hardly a bright one, and an organization might understandably be concerned that a judge would not understand its religious tenets and sense of mission. Fear of potential liability might affect the way an organization carried out what it understood to be its religious mission.[19]

Because of the *Amos* decision, it is no longer necessary to address free exercise issues in the context of religious discrimination by religious employers, at least under federal legislation. Religious employers should note, however, that:

1. *Amos* is construing federal legislation that could be amended. Indeed, the exemption that it was construing was amended by Congress in 1972 to broaden the application of the exemption from purely religious employees to all employees of religious organizations. What Congress has granted, Congress can take away; and the Court even suggested that the Free Exercise Clause may have required no more than the pre-1972 exemption, although it did not decide that issue.

2. *Amos* does not preclude state laws or constitutions from reaching a different result. The legislative accommodation provided by the federal government and upheld under the U.S. Constitution cannot be taken away by the state, but the state can enact a law with a narrower exemption or none at all, the validity of which would be unaffected by *Amos*. That law would have to be tested by a constitutional challenge under the Free Exercise Clause or the state constitution.

3. The Court emphasized in *Amos* that the Deseret Gymnasium was a nonprofit organization. The question of the constitutionality of the exemption as applied to for-profit activities remains open at this writing, but it appears likely that the Court would find the exemption unconstitutional if applied to profit-making activities of a religious organization.

4. *Amos* and the Title VII exemption *only* allow a religious organization to discriminate for *religious* reasons. It does not exempt a religious organization from any other aspect of the antidiscrimination law or from other common-law or statutory obligations with respect to its employees. A church or religious organization is not likely to win a wrongful discharge case just because it is a religious organization.

The federal district court in Utah reached the logical conclusion that the religious exemption is not limited to discriminating in favor of members but that religious employers may also discriminate *among* members based upon their degree of involvement, that is, upon how good a member each one is.[20]

The 1964 Civil Rights Act also provides some protection to employees whose religiously motivated conduct conflicts with job demands. Employers are required to make reasonable accommodations to the religious needs of their employees where they can do so without undue hardship on the conduct of the employer's business.[21] Such reasonable accommodations could include, for example, scheduling adjustments or reassignments for employees whose religious beliefs prevent them from working on certain days of the week. A state law prohibiting any employer from requiring an employee to work on that person's sabbath, however, was found unconstitutional by the Supreme Court in the 1985 case of *Thornton v. Caldor, Inc.*[22] Other religious accommodations in employment cases have dealt with issues such as religious garb on the job.

Is a religious employer that hires without religious discrimination then obliged to make reasonable accommodation to its employee's religious needs? One federal district court, faced with this intriguing conundrum, decided that the obligation to make religious accommodations to employees does not apply to religious employers in view of the religious exemption in the statute.[23]

Since these issues almost invariably arise in the context of secular employment, they are not discussed further here.

a. Bona Fide Occupational Qualification (BFOQ)

Title VII contains another exemption that may rarely be needed by religious organizations in view of the exemption for religious discrimination upheld in *Amos* but which could occasionally be important. It is called the Bona Fide Occupational Qualification (BFOQ) and is expressed in the statute as follows:

It shall not be an unlawful employment practice for an employer to hire and employ [an] employee . . . on the basis of his religion, sex, or national origin in those certain instances where religion, sex, or national origin is a bona fide occupational qualification reasonably necessary to the normal operation of that particular business or enterprise.[24]

Bona fide occupational qualifications based on sex or national origin will be hard to

establish. If the exemption for religious organizations that discriminate for religious reasons were not contained in Title VII and upheld as applied to jobs that are not specifically religious by *Amos*, this section would undoubtedly be the focus of much litigation to determine how far a religious organization could go in making adherence to its religion a bona fide occupational qualification. It had, for example, before *Amos*, been used to justify a Jesuit university retaining a certain number of positions in its philosophy department for Jesuits.[25] The bona fide occupational qualification may have its greatest potential application to religious organizations in clashes between employees who claim sex discrimination and religious organizations that claim that the discrimination is justified on a bona fide occupational qualification basis because of the religious nature of the enterprise. Such cases are discussed in the next section (pp. 103–4).

2. Sex

Title VII of the Civil Rights Act of 1964 also prohibits discrimination on the basis of sex. There is no exemption for religious organizations. Unless the discrimination can be justified on a constitutional basis that overrides the statute or as a bona fide occupational qualification, religious organizations have no more right to engage in gender-based discrimination than do secular organizations. Discrimination does not mean just hiring and firing but includes all aspects of the employment relationship, including pay, benefits, and working conditions. It would be a violation of the statute to categorically exclude women from particular jobs—for example, those that require heavy manual labor—or to similarly exclude males from more traditionally female jobs, such as secretary or nurse. It would also be unlawful to impose an additional qualification or condition on one sex that does not apply to the other, such as refusing to hire a woman with young children but not applying the same limitation to a man, again absent an overriding constitutional justification or bona fide occupational qualification.

Sexual harassment is a particular form of

sex discrimination that is prohibited by Title VII. Sexual harassment occurs not only when unwanted physical contact or sexual favors are demanded as a condition of employment or basis for employment decisions but also when sexual conduct interferes with an employee's job or creates a hostile, offensive, or intimidating atmosphere. The harasser may be male or female, a supervisor, co-worker, agent, or even a nonemployee if the situation is tolerated by the employer; and harassment may be directed to the same or opposite sex. Interference with the victim's work or the creation of an offensive atmosphere will give rise to a claim even if there has been no financial loss. Religious employers should be aware that even if they do not fit within the definition of an employer for purposes of the Civil Rights Act of 1964, they may be subject to state laws, which vary widely in specifics but would prohibit sexual discrimination and sexual harassment. Such laws also may create liability independent of the statutes prohibiting such discrimination or harassment, for example, for wrongful discharge, as discussed in chapter 12.

Employers are potentially liable for sexual harassment and should protect themselves as well as the working conditions of members of both sexes in the workplace by (1) adopting a policy that clearly and explicitly prohibits all forms of sexual harassment; and (2) providing a mechanism for workers with complaints to report them. Any such complaints should be handled confidentially and sensitively in accordance with the discussion in chapter 12. Just because the complaint has been made does not necessarily mean it is justified.

Sexual harassment does not include conduct that is not unwanted as long as it does not interfere with others' work and does not create an offensive working environment. Normal dating relationships off the job between co-employees do not constitute sexual harassment as long as no employment-related decisions turn, explicitly or implicitly, on the fact of the date, the relationship, or the conduct of parties on the date or in the relationship. Relationships between subordinates and their superiors in the organizational structure, however,

have great potential to create misunderstanding and should be approached with the greatest caution.

A further refinement of Title VII is the Pregnancy Discrimination Act of 1978.[26] The essence of this act is (1) to define discrimination because of or on the basis of sex in Title VII to include discrimination based on pregnancy, childbirth, or related medical conditions; and (2) to require that women with these conditions be treated for all employment-related purposes, including benefits, the same as any other worker who has a similar ability or inability to work. This applies to such things as disability or medical benefits, the accrual of benefits during leave, and the ability to return after leave. It is best understood by comparing the woman's situation to that of a male worker with a physical or medical disability for the same duration; all rights and benefits of employment should be the same.

The final federal law that prohibits sex discrimination is the Equal Pay Act of 1963.[27] This act is part of the Fair Labor Standards Act, although it is enforced by the Equal Employment Opportunity Commission rather than by the Department of Labor which normally enforces the Fair Labor Standards Act.[28] The Equal Pay Act simply prohibits employers from paying a lower wage or rate to employees of one sex than the other for equal work at jobs requiring the same skill, effort, and responsibility and performed under similar working conditions. Religious organizations cannot pay female employees at a lower rate for the same work because it is traditional or because the woman may not be the "breadwinner" in the family and may be perceived as having less need. Objective non-sex-related bases for pay differentials such as merit systems, production-based systems, or seniority systems are acceptable.

While no cases of sex discrimination involving religious organizations have thus far led to a substantive decision on the merits by the Supreme Court, lower courts have found gender-based salary scales[29] and differences in employment benefits prohibited.[30]

Religious organizations that are subject to Title VII should be sure that their job application forms and hiring procedures are consistent with the requirements of the law. Questions such as marital status or child-bearing intentions must be avoided. Advice and publications to assist employers in complying with the law may be available from the federal Equal Employment Opportunity Commission, state agencies enforcing state antidiscrimination laws, and private counsel. Further suggestions are made in chapter 12, below.

Sex discrimination does not include discrimination based on sexual preference.[31]

See section B.6 of this chapter for special considerations in the case of federal funding or a federal contract.

a. Constitutional Exception for Clergy

Constitutional considerations have provided religious organizations absolute protection against discrimination claims in the selection and treatment (salary, benefits, termination, etc.) of clergy, whether or not the organization claims a religious basis for discrimination.[32] It is not always self-evident who fits within this exception. Because the church–minister relationship is the lifeblood of the church and the content of that relationship is a prime ecclesiastical concern, Title VII cannot be applied to that relationship without violating the Free Exercise Clause of the First Amendment.[33]

A series of decisions in the Fifth Circuit Court of Appeals has drawn a line in sex discrimination cases against religious organizations between ministers and other church support personnel. With respect to a seminary whose functions were wholly religious, the Fifth Circuit found that the faculty and some administrative personnel, such as deans, were ministers with traditionally ecclesiastical and ministerial functions to whom Title VII could not be applied; but it also found that financial and nonacademic staff were not outside its reach.[34] With respect to a college that was religiously affiliated, however, even though it was pervasively sectarian and faculty members were expected to serve as exemplars of practicing Christians, the terms and conditions of their employment were not considered matters of church administra-

tion or purely ecclesiastical concern, and Title VII applied.[35] Title VII is not avoided by calling employees "ministers," however sincere the church may be in applying the title, who do not perform traditional ministerial functions such as administering sacraments, leading worship, or teaching religious doctrine.[36]

b. The Role Model Rule

An area that has received little attention from the higher courts to date is the ability of a religious organization to discriminate on the basis of moral conduct. The classic example is the unmarried pregnant teacher in a religious school. Religious organizations will take some comfort from the 1987 decision in the Eighth Circuit Court of Appeals that upheld the "role model rule" in a girl's club organization.[37] The Omaha Girl's Club was a nonprofit corporation that offered programs for girls between the ages of eight and eighteen. Their programs were intended to help the girls understand sexual, social, and emotional development in order to maximize their life opportunities. Many of their activities were aimed at pregnancy prevention. The club had a "role model rule" that banned single-parent pregnancies among its staff and subjected violators to immediate discharge. The rule was upheld as a bona fide occupational qualification. Although the case raised no First Amendment issues, it supports the idea that bona fide occupational qualifications can include moral conduct in certain circumstances in which that conduct is reasonable for the role model position occupied by the individual. One court has held, however, that even if a role model rule is a bona fide occupational qualification, it cannot be applied in a discriminatory manner. Allegations that male teachers in a Catholic high school who were known to have engaged in premarital intercourse were not fired entitled a single, pregnant female teacher to a discrimination trial.[38] However, religious organizations that apply a role model rule in a gender-neutral fashion should have little difficulty justifying discharge or disciplinary practices based on that rule. Maintaining such a position will be greatly aided by:

1. Explicit employment conditions that state specific conduct that can result in discipline or discharge, thus making it a matter of contract and providing clear notice of the job requirements.
2. Treating males and females alike for comparable known conduct, even though the men do not get pregnant.

c. Young Mothers with Children

Another issue that causes a clash between the constitutional right to religious freedom and the ban on sex discrimination arises from the position of some churches that mothers of young children, even if married, should be in the home and not the workplace. Such churches may discriminate in hiring mothers of young children or by terminating them following a successful pregnancy. This is an issue that has not been well-tested in the courts. In the 1985 decision of *Dayton Christian Schools v. Ohio Civil Rights Commission,*[39] the Sixth Circuit Court of Appeals upheld on constitutional grounds the right of a school and parents to have such a rule. The decision seems a less obvious application of the role model rule. The U.S. Supreme Court reversed on procedural grounds but did not indicate whether or not it agreed with the Sixth Circuit's analysis of the constitutional issue.[40] If the religious organization can make a case that this position is grounded in its sincere religious beliefs and not merely in its policy preferences, it should be able to maintain its position under the religious exemption from Title VII, as a bona fide occupational qualification or in a free exercise claim.

d. Factors in Resolving Issues

Sincerity of Belief. Several reported cases (*Fremont, Pacific Press, Shenandoah Baptist*) are clearly influenced by the lack of a sincere, central religious belief in gender discrimination. Moreover, inconsistent application of purported beliefs undermines the constitutional claim. The general notion of church autonomy has not carried the day in these courts when the church could not defend the specific practice on *religious* grounds. These courts viewed the constitutional issue as narrowly addressed

to the practice in question, not broadly to government regulation of the church.

Contracts. While contracts cannot deprive employees of rights given by statute for their protection, they can and often do incorporate specific religious criteria in defining the employee's duties that courts are unlikely to be willing, or constitutionally able, to evaluate.

Church Membership. This is within the exemption that allows religious employers to discriminate for religious reasons. Deprivation of church membership for conduct which the church does not allow (for example, suing the church) may result in loss of employment even if the conduct would be protected under employment law.

3. Race, Color, or National Origin

The Civil Rights Act of 1964 also bans discrimination in employment by covered employers on the basis of race, color, or national origin. At least two other federal statutes have related discrimination bans:

1. Section 1981 of the Civil Rights Acts of 1866 has been interpreted by the Supreme Court to prohibit racial discrimination in private employment.[41] It contains no limitations on the employers to which it applies.
2. The Immigration Reform and Control Act of 1986[42] bans discrimination on the basis of intended citizenship or national origin by employers of four or more workers, although the employer may select a citizen or intending citizen over an alien if both are equally qualified.

If reported court cases are any indication, there is no significant problem of religious organizations' discriminating on the basis of race, color, national origin, citizenship, or intended citizenship. Religious employers should, however, be careful that no inference of discrimination arises by avoiding hiring processes that, for example, test applicants for higher levels of skill than the job requires. Job qualifications can have the effect of being discriminatory even if they appear to be even-handed if they have a discriminatory impact, because they set job requirements that are not directly related to job performance and that disqualify a disproportionate number of minority applicants. Recruiting policies that have a racially discriminatory effect, such as word-of-mouth recruiting, preferential hiring of relatives of present employees, or recruiting only at predominantly white educational institutions, can be part of a hiring policy that has a discriminatory effect.

Although the case was not employment related, the United States Supreme Court in the 1983 decision of *Bob Jones University v. United States* held that a religious school or university that practiced racial discrimination could be deprived of its federal tax-exempt status notwithstanding a bona fide sincere religious belief that formed the basis for the discrimination.[43] The *Bob Jones University* case is discussed further in chapter 10.

4. Age

The Age Discrimination in Employment Act[44] (ADEA) bars discrimination against individuals over the age of forty as follows:

(a) It shall be unlawful for an employer—

(1) to fail or refuse to hire or to discharge any individual or otherwise discriminate against any individual with respect to his compensation, terms, conditions, or privileges of employment, because of such individual's age;

(2) to limit, segregate, or classify his employees in any way which would deprive or tend to deprive any individual of employment opportunities or otherwise adversely affect his status as an employee, because of such individual's age; or

(3) to reduce the wage rate of any employee in order to comply with this act.[45]

A covered employer is one "engaged in an industry affecting commerce who has twenty or more employees for each working day in each of twenty or more calendar weeks in the current or preceding calendar year."[46]

Mandatory retirement for persons over the age of seventy is not permitted except for (1) individuals in bona fide executive or high policy-making positions who have at least certain minimum retirement benefits provided for in the statute; and (2) certain tenured employees of institutions of higher education.

Efforts by religious organizations to exempt themselves from application of the ADEA by using a *Catholic Bishop*[47] analysis (as discussed on p. 97 of this chapter) have generally been unsuccessful because age discrimination in employment raises no apparent religious freedom issues.[48] One federal district court, however, reached a different conclusion with respect to a religious seminary. In the 1989 case of *Cochran v. St. Louis Seminary,*[49] the court found that application of the ADEA to a seminary that was primarily a religious institution whose objective was preparing students for the priesthood and disseminating religious values would raise serious constitutional questions, because courts would have to inquire whether dismissal was based on religious considerations or age; hence, by a *Catholic Bishop* analysis to the application, the court declined to apply the ADEA. The Circuit Court of Appeals for the District of Columbia reached a similar result in an ADEA claim by a Methodist clergyman,[50] as did the United States District Court for the Eastern District of Missouri with respect to an Episcopal priest who was a hospital chaplain.[51] It appears that courts are as reluctant to get into age discrimination claims as sex discrimination claims when the claimants are clergy or employees such as seminary faculty whose duties are in some sense specifically religious. Absent such specific religious or ecclesiastical focus in the employment situation, religious organizations will generally be held to the requirements of the ADEA if they are within its jurisdictional limits.

See section B.6 of this chapter for special considerations when federal funding or federal contracts are involved.

5. Disabilities

In 1990, Congress enacted the Americans with Disabilities Act (ADA),[52] a law that gives sweeping civil rights protection to people with disabilities. A disability is a physical or mental impairment that substantially limits a person in some major life activity but does not include physical characteristics, cultural or economic disadvantages, prison records, age, or homosexuality. Qualified individuals with disabilities may not be discriminated against in any aspect of employment. A person is considered qualified who can perform essential job functions with reasonable accommodation, which may include such matters as making facilities accessible, restructuring jobs, providing modified work schedules, acquiring or modifying training materials, and the like. Reasonable accommodations need not be made if they would impose undue hardship, that is, significant difficulty or expense. Undue hardship would be measured by the nature and cost of the accommodation, the overall size and financial resources of the employer, the number of people employed, the type of operation, and the impact of the accommodation on the operation. Reasonable accommodation does not require an employer to provide a rehabilitation program for drug or alcohol dependence. Employers are not required to hire or retain people who pose a direct threat to the health or safety of other employees, that is, a significant risk ιο their health and safety that cannot be eliminated by reasonable accommodation. Alcoholics, drug addicts, people with psychological problems, and people with AIDS are otherwise covered. It is not a violation of the ADA to act against an applicant or employee currently engaged in the illegal use of drugs, but the act does cover people who are off drugs and participating in supervised rehabilitation programs. The employment provisions in this act applied initially to employers of twenty-five or more persons, but starting in 1994 apply to employers of fifteen or more. The law borrows many definitions from Title VII. There is no general religious exemption, but the act does exempt religious organizations with respect to preferential hiring based on the applicant's adherence to the religious tenets of the organization.

Religious employers must inform themselves on this law and its application to them if they are subject to it. They may wish to seek specialized advice about compliance. The result of noncompliance can be expensive litigation with court orders to restore people to jobs, awards of lost wages or back pay, interest, benefits and seniority, and, in some instances, attorney's fees and even punitive damages. Adverse publicity can damage public image as well. While these issues are more likely to concern religious organizations that are or operate larger institutions and institutions that provide services other than the directly religious—such as schools, publishing houses, health care, retirement services, and the like—all religious employers should be familiar with them. The federal Equal Employment Opportunity Commission enforces the law under Title VII but often allows state agencies charged with enforcing similar state laws to investigate discrimination charges.

The Rehabilitation Act of 1973[53] also requires certain employers who receive federal aid or have government contracts to take affirmative action to employ qualified handicapped persons to carry out the contract, including anyone with a physical or mental impairment that substantially limits one or more of such a person's major life activities. Drug or alcohol addiction is not protected. This act is discussed further in section 6 below.

6. Federal Funding or Contracts

With the acceptance of federal funds, an organization must submit to a certain level of federal control. This is true of religious as well as secular organizations, as discussed in chapter 3.[54]

Receipt of federal financial assistance may impose an obligation not to discriminate on organizations not otherwise subject to such obligations or may impose more extensive obligations on organizations with existing obligations. Churches and religious organizations that participate in the federal commodities program to operate schools or camps, feed the homeless or the needy, and the like, or that receive school lunch-program support, disaster relief, refugee relief, low-income housing support, HUD loans, or federal child care assistance would be recipients of federal financial assistance. Institutions receiving Medicaid or Medicare funds, such as hospitals and nursing or retirement homes, would also be receiving such assistance.

Religious organizations do not receive federal funds because contributors or people who pay for the organization's services (such as school tuition) do so with general purpose governmental assistance such as, for example, Social Security, AFDC payments, food stamps, and welfare payments. Nor does the exemption from federal income taxation make a religious organization a recipient of federal financial assistance—to do so would make virtually every religious and nonprofit organization in the country a recipient of federal financial assistance.[55]

Religious organizations receiving federal funds should be sure they know what discrimination is prohibited as a result, what the compliance requirements will be, and should assure themselves that compliance presents no doctrinal or theological difficulties. Major federal aid programs that carry antidiscrimination obligations are the following:

1. Title IX of the Education Act Amendments of 1972.[56] This law prohibits sex discrimination in any educational program or activity that receives federal funds, although educational institutions controlled by a religious organization are exempted from this antidiscrimination provision if subjecting it to the requirement would not be consistent with the religious tenets of the organization, an exemption that applies to the entire institution.[57]

2. The Rehabilitation Act of 1973 prohibits discrimination based on handicap in any program or activity that receives federal funding.[58] Churches and religious organizations receiving federal financial assistance may be required to construct ramps and make other structural alterations to accommodate handicapped persons. Recipients with fewer than fifteen employees, however, are not required to make significant structural alterations to existing facilities if services are available by alternative means. Recipients of federal funding who are not subject to the Americans with Disabilities Act

(discussed in section B.5, above) may have to meet similar requirements under this act.

An alcoholic or drug abuser "whose current use of alcohol or drugs prevents such individual from performing the duties of the job in question or whose employment, by reason of such current alcohol or drug abuse, would constitute a direct threat to property or the safety of others" is not considered handicapped.[59]

While it is virtually certain that homosexuality is not considered a handicap, one federal district court has found that transvestites, who experience a strong social rejection in the workplace due to their cross-dressing lifestyle, are handicapped.[60] One trial court decision does not make a rule, however, and it is not clear that this decision will be followed by any other court.

AIDS victims present a different case. Handicapped persons do not include "an individual who has a currently contagious disease or infection and who, by reason of such disease or infection, would constitute a direct threat to the health or safety of other individuals or who, by reason of the currently contagious disease or infection, is unable to perform the duties of the job."[61] An AIDS victim who is not a direct threat to the health or safety of others and who is able to perform the duties of the job, however, could be classified as handicapped and be entitled to the protection of the Rehabilitation Act of 1973; and at least one court has so found.[62]

3. The Age Discrimination Act of 1975 which prohibits age discrimination in any program or activity receiving federal funding,[63] as discussed in section B.4 of this chapter.

4. Title VI of the Civil Rights Act of 1964 which bans race discrimination by any program or activity receiving federal funding.[64]

All of these acts were amended by the Civil Rights Restoration Act of 1987 to make it clear that if any program or activity of an institution receives federal financial assistance, the nondiscrimination provisions apply to the entire institution. The law was passed in response to the 1984 Supreme Court decision in *Grove City College v. Bell,*[65] which had limited the antidiscrimination provisions to the specific program or activity receiving the funding rather than the entire institution. All of the operations of colleges, universities, or other postsecondary institutions receiving federal aid are covered. If federal financial assistance is extended to another type of religious organization *as a whole* or if it is *principally* engaged in providing education, health care, housing, social services, or parks and recreation, the organization as a whole is subject to federal antidiscrimination law. A church that is principally engaged in providing religious services should not be covered under these provisions, even if it does provide covered services because the provision of religious services would still be its principal business. If the religious organization does not fit within these circumstances, only the specific "plant or other comparable geographically separate facility to which federal financial assistance is extended" will be subjected to the federal antidiscrimination law. For example, a church that operates a physically separate school would not be subject to the law, although the school would be. But if the school is located within the church building, the church as a whole would be subject to the law.

It should be noted that none of the above antidiscrimination laws affect religious discrimination by religious organizations; and First Amendment considerations should continue to give churches a high degree of protection in the selection of clergy and employees who perform specifically ecclesiastical functions. The federal district court in Mississippi, however, in a decision with troubling facts and implications, has found that a religious organization that accepts federal funds can no longer constitutionally claim the religious exemption. The employer was the Salvation Army, and the employee was a member of the Wiccan religion who was alleged to have been involved in the reproduction and dissemination of satanic manuals and rituals at work, contrary to the religious purposes of the Army.[66]

There is one clear exception to the general principle that religious recipients of federal funding can still discriminate in employment based on religion. Church child care facilities for which grants or certificates under the Child Care and Development Block Grant of 1990[67] comprise 80 percent or more of total revenue may not engage in religious discrimination in employment. With funding comes control.

Under Executive Order 11246, federal government contractors are required to take affirmative action to insure employment of individuals without regard to race, color, religion, sex, or national origin. Few religious organizations will be government contractors. Any who are should be sure they understand the requirements of this executive order.

Under the Vietnam Era Veterans Readjustment Assistance Act of 1972 (as amended in 1974),[68] employers may be required to take affirmative action to employ certain qualified disabled veterans and veterans of the Vietnam era under some contracts.

C. NATIONAL
LABOR RELATIONS ACT

We have already discussed the National Labor Relations Act[69] (NLRA) twice—in chapter 2, section A, and in section A of this chapter. Passed in 1935, it addressed the labor unrest of the Great Depression by assuring employees federally protected rights to join a union and to engage in collective bargaining through elected representatives. The act creates the National Labor Relations Board (NLRB) to supervise the process, certify union representatives as collective bargaining agents, and investigate disputes. It was the National Labor Relations Act that led to the landmark 1937 United States Supreme Court decision in *Jones v. Laughlin Steel Corporation*[70] which, in upholding the act's constitutionality, greatly broadened the definition of interstate commerce to enable federal regulation to occur on a much more far-reaching basis. In the 1979 case of *National Labor Relations Board v. Catholic Bishop,*[71] which we discussed at the beginning of this chapter, the Supreme Court discussed the applicability of the NLRA to workers in religious organizations and in so doing set a standard for determining when federal regulatory acts will apply. If subjecting the religious organization to the jurisdiction of the statute would give rise to delicate constitutional questions of religious freedom, the statute will not be applied unless there is a clearly expressed affirmative intention of Congress to do so. If such an intent appears, then the constitutional issue must be examined. The *Catholic Bishop* analysis can be applied in considering the extent to which many federal and state regulatory statutes reach religious organizations.

Catholic Bishop is the only NLRA case involving a religious organization to reach the Supreme Court. The Court declined to apply the act to lay teachers in Roman Catholic parochial high schools because of the substantial religious activities and purposes of such schools and the religious authority that necessarily pervades them. Intruding the government, in the form of the NLRB, into the collective-bargaining process between teachers and clergy-administrators would implicate sensitive religious issues.

The NLRA does not have any specific religious exemption, nor does it exclude employers with fewer than a certain number of employees. However, it applies only to employment relationships that affect commerce, meaning "in commerce, or burdening or obstructing commerce or the free flow of commerce, or having led or tending to lead to a labor dispute burdening or obstructing commerce or the free flow of commerce."[72] Commerce means trade, traffic, commerce, transportation, or communication among the several states.[73] Activities as trivial as local telephone calls or the purchase of gas and electricity from a company engaged in interstate commerce have been held to be sufficient, however, to cross this barrier.[74]

The significant issue in NLRA cases involving religious organizations is whether application of the act would raise serious constitutional questions under the First Amendment and thus require the NLRB and the courts to abstain from exercising jurisdiction. The NLRB and the lower courts that have reviewed its decisions have generally upheld its jurisdiction over organizations engaged in substantial commercial activities when this can be done without interfering with religious practices. The "commercial" activities do not need to be profit making.

Thus a Christian evangelistic organization engaged in substantial commercial activities,[75] a church-operated home for neglected children,[76] and church-affiliated hospitals[77] and nursing homes[78] have all been held subject to the NLRA. Factors that will be considered in determining whether or not a religious organization is subject to the NLRA include the source of funding; whether or not employees are hired on the basis of religious affiliation; the extent to which the institution is affiliated with and controlled by a church; the extent to which the church's religious tenets or beliefs are actively propagated; and the nature and extent of commercial activities. The more the religious organization operates like a secular institution, the more likely it is to be treated as such for NLRA purposes.

Churches and their affiliated organizations, other religious organizations involved in the direct propagation of religious teaching, doctrine, and practice as their primary mission, and those engaged in no significant commercial activities will not be subject to the NLRA. Religious organizations that engage in commercial activities, including nonprofit activities similar to those engaged in by secular profit or nonprofit organizations in which propagation of doctrine, belief, and religious practice is not a pervasive part of the mission—such as hospitals, nursing homes, and universities—will be subject to it. Institutions such as children's homes are likely to be exempt from the act if they are operated in a pervasively sectarian manner, but subject to it if they are run more like a secular institution.

A provision of the act which will be primarily of interest to secular employers but is potentially relevant to any employer subject to the act is the section which exempts from union membership "[a]ny employee who is a member of and adheres to established and traditional tenets or teachings of a bona fide religion, body, or sect which has historically held conscientious objections to joining or financially supporting labor organizations."[79] One circuit court of appeals has found this accommodation to be unconstitutional because it creates a denominational preference under the Supreme Court's decision in *Larson v. Valente*.[80]

As with other areas of employment law, some states have parallel state labor relations acts which are not necessarily governed by the same standards as the National Labor Relations Act. In *Christ the King Regional High School v. Culvert*, a 1987 case decided by the Second Circuit Court of Appeals,[81] the court found that the NLRA did not preempt the New York State Labor Relations Act[82] and that the states were free to supplement the NLRA with state legislation where the NLRA did not assert jurisdiction. The case, like *Catholic Bishop*, involved lay teachers at a Catholic high school and hence had a fact pattern precisely parallel to *Catholic Bishop,* in which the U.S. Supreme Court declined to impose federal jurisdiction due to the delicate constitutional questions that would arise. *Christ the King* follows an earlier case that limited the state labor act to jurisdiction over secular issues.[83] But the result of these cases is that the dividing line between secular issues and those delicate constitutional questions will have to be addressed by the courts in New York under the state labor relations act. In a later case in Minnesota, the same result was reached—application of the Minnesota Labor Relations Act to secular employment issues in a Catholic school was held not to violate either the Minnesota or the U.S. constitutions.[84]

D. FAIR LABOR STANDARDS ACT

The Fair Labor Standards Act,[85] passed in 1938, was another piece of legislation from the Great Depression that intended to protect workers from substandard wages and excessive hours, and to regulate child labor.[86] It prescribes a maximum forty-hour work week unless the employee is paid time-and-a-half for hours over forty, and it sets a minimum wage for employees that has been increased over the years. We have already noted that it includes the Equal Pay Act, added in 1963, which requires paying persons of different sexes the same pay for the same work.[87] In order to be covered by the act, the employer must have employ-

ees "engaged in commerce or in the production of goods for commerce" or "in an enterprise engaged in commerce or in the production of goods for commerce"[88] If the employees are not directly engaged in commerce or the production of goods for commerce, the enterprise must fall into one of two categories: (1) it must have at least two employees engaged in commerce or the production of goods for commerce or handling, selling, or working on goods or materials moved in or produced for commerce *and* have annual gross sales in excess of a prescribed amount (currently $500,000); or (2) it must be of a nature specifically identified in the act which is covered without regard to sales volume or employee participation in commerce. This second category includes hospitals and schools. Hence, most private religious schools will be covered by the act.[89] The act does not contain any general exemption for religious or nonprofit organizations. It does exempt employees of religious or nonprofit camps and conference centers which do not operate for more than seven months in any calendar year or in which average receipts for any six months of the preceding calendar year were not more than one third of its average receipts for the other six months of the year.[90] This limited exemption has the useful function of exempting institutions that operate primarily in the summertime and are staffed largely with high school or college students, who are often motivated to work for the religious organization as part of summer ministry and are happy to work for a limited period of time for less than the minimum wage or more than forty hours a week without overtime.

The Fair Labor Standards Act also exempts employees "employed in a bona fide executive, administrative, or professional capacity" if certain minimum income tests are met.[91] This will exempt most clergy, executives, and administrators of religious organizations.

The application of the Fair Labor Standards Act to religious organizations has been tested only once in the U.S. Supreme Court. In the 1985 case of *Tony and Susan Alamo Foundation v. Secretary of Labor*[92] the act was applied to employees, who were called "associates," of a foundation; they received food, shelter, and clothing but not cash wages for their work in a variety of foundation-run commercial enterprises, such as service stations, retail clothing and grocery outlets, hog farms, roofing and electrical construction companies, a record-keeping company, a motel, and companies engaged in the production and distribution of candy. The employees or associates were mostly drug addicts, derelicts, or criminals who had been converted and were being rehabilitated by the foundation, the purposes of which were to "establish, conduct and maintain an Evangelistic Church; to conduct religious services, to minister to the sick and needy, to care for the fatherless and to rescue the fallen, and generally to do those things needful for the promotion of Christian faith, virtue, and charity."[93] In analyzing the application of the act to this situation, the Court declined to follow *Catholic Bishop* because it found no significant risk of an infringement of First Amendment rights. The Court noted that the businesses in which the *Alamo Foundation* was engaged served the public in competition with ordinary commercial enterprises. Despite the foundation's argument that the businesses functioned as "churches in disguise" for preaching and spreading the gospel to the public, "the payment of substandard wages would undoubtedly give petitioners and similar organizations an advantage over their competitors," which was part of what the Fair Labor Standards Act was intended to prevent.[94] Despite the fact that none of the associates or employees viewed their work as other than volunteering, the noncash benefits made the economic reality of the situation one of employment. If the associates were opposed to receiving cash for their efforts, they were free to voluntarily return the cash as a donation to the foundation. The Court found that the commercial activities of the foundation were subject to the act notwithstanding its religious character and First Amendment claims.

The Fair Labor Standards Act has similarly been applied in lower courts to a publishing plant, even though its purpose was to "glorify God, publish the full Gospel to every nation, and promote the Christian religion by spreading religious knowledge."[95]

The 1990 Fourth Circuit Court of Appeals decision of *Dole v. Shenandoah Baptist Church*[96] well illustrates the application of the Fair Labor Standards Act. Shenandoah Baptist Church was a fundamentalist church which ran a private school with a full-time curriculum that included both Bible instruction and traditional academic subjects taught from a Christian point of view. The church paid a salary supplement to married male but not married female teachers, which it justified on the basis of the biblical teaching that the husband is the head of the wife and family. It also paid less than minimum wage to a number of support personnel such as bus drivers, custodians, kitchen workers, bookkeepers, and secretaries. It defended these practices against the Fair Labor Standards Act claim by contending that it was not covered by the act, that its employees were "ministers" and therefore excluded from coverage, and that application of the act to the school would violate the First Amendment guarantee of religious freedom. Since the act does specifically cover schools, the argument that it was not covered by the act was unavailing. The fact that the church and school shared a common building and payroll account and that school employees had to subscribe to the church's statement of faith did not alter the fact of coverage. The argument that employees were "ministers" was also unavailing. However the church and the individuals characterized their service in this regard, they could not be considered ministers for legal purposes because they performed no sacerdotal functions, did not govern the church, and belonged to no clearly delineated religious order. To permit them to be exempted from the act as ministers, in the court's view, would have eviscerated the act, which specifically intended to reach schools, by creating an exception that would swallow the rule. As to the free exercise claims, the burden on religion from requiring equal pay and minimum wages was considered to be outweighed by the government's compelling interest in implementing the policies of the Fair Labor Standards Act.

The church's testimony on the biblical grounding of its policies was weak. Church members testified that the Bible does not mandate a pay differential based on sex and that church doctrine does not prevent a school from paying women the same as men or paying the minimum wage. The religious freedom objection appeared to be based primarily on the notion that the church rather than the government, acting under divine guidance, should determine the wages of its employees and that the head-of-household supplement for married male teachers could be traced to a sincerely held biblical notion. As with *Alamo Foundation*, the court noted that employees whose religious convictions prevented them from accepting the additional wage could pay it back or serve the school as volunteers, and it was unwilling to exempt it from the law.

Most, if not all, states have state wage and hour legislation that parallels the Fair Labor Standards Act. In one case, the state of New Hampshire attempted to assert a minimum wage claim against a church conference center with respect to its summer employees. The conference center was owned by a corporation that was part of a religious denomination. Its summer program included specific religious programming with speakers, music, and Bible study, in each of the nine program weeks of the summer, each centering around a particular biblical theme and featuring a guest pastor or speaker. Morning and evening worship services were held and attended by all. Recreational activities and programs were also included. Children received special religious and recreational programming. The staff subject to the minimum wage claims were summer staff, mostly high school and college students, and included both staff with specific job responsibility for religious teaching and inculcating biblical understanding and support service staff, such as kitchen, dining room, maintenance, and housekeeping workers. Most of the support staff had additional responsibilities that included program work with minors. The state statute contained a conference center exclusion similar to the federal statute, but there was sufficient off-season activity at the conference center so that the exemption was not applicable. The statute also allowed for a room-and-board allocation at an arbitrary thirty dollars per week as a

contribution to the minimum wage, although the actual cost was over ninety dollars a week.

The conference center made a number of arguments in objection to the minimum wage claim, including religious freedom arguments under the state and federal constitutions; constitutional objections to the artificially low and statutorily fixed allowance for food and lodging; the argument that a "summer camps for minors" exemption in the statute should apply to the conference center in view of the extensive services for minors; and the point that the conference did not fit within the statutory jurisdictional definitions because it was not engaged in "an industry, trade or business or branch thereof."[97] The New Hampshire Department of Labor accepted the latter argument, finding that the conference center was not in competition with private industry because it served only persons who came because of their religious beliefs and for participation in religious functions.[98]

The Fair Labor Standards Act also regulates employment of minors. Use of children in a commercial enterprise is subject to the act notwithstanding religious freedom claims.[99]

Churches and religious organizations performing entirely religious functions and not engaged in any commercial activities or activities covered by the act, such as operating schools and hospitals, are usually not subject to the Fair Labor Standards Act. Religious organizations that are subject to the act but have a financial problem in meeting its requirements can address them by such practical methods as reducing overtime, rescheduling employees who must work outside the normal business day to limit their work hours to a forty-hour week, reducing wages as long as the reductions are within the limitations of the act, reducing hours, and the like.

Organizations that are subject to the act are subject to record-keeping requirements to document wages, hours, and other conditions and practices of employment. Records must document the value of non-cash payments and include payroll records, collective bargaining agreements, employment contracts, and pension and employee-benefit plans.

E. IMMIGRATION

Except for our Native American population, the United States is a nation of immigrants. The open invitation of the Statue of Liberty, however, began to be limited in 1875 with a law barring the admission of prostitutes and convicts. From then until 1986, the grounds of exclusion enlarged to include some thirty-three reasons, and numerical limitations on immigration and the admission of refugees were established. Exemptions are allowed for immediate relatives of U.S. citizens, including their spouses, children, and the parents of adults. As many as a million illegal aliens are deported or leave voluntarily each year. It has been estimated that the number of illegal aliens in the United States could be as high as twenty million.

To address this growing problem, the Congress enacted the Immigration Reform and Control Act of 1986.[100] The act addresses the problem of illegal aliens by focusing on what is the greatest attraction to illegal immigration—the American job. It accomplishes its result primarily by making the employer a deputy immigration agent, charged with the duty of verifying the status of all new employees. The job applicant must present satisfactory documents enabling the employer to verify the applicant's employment eligibility within three days of hire. Documents that may be used to verify employment eligibility include passports, driver's licenses, birth certificates, social security cards, and resident alien cards. Employer and employee must then sign form I–9 under penalty of perjury, and the form must be retained by the employer until three years after the date of hire or one year after the date of termination, whichever is later. It is advisable to photocopy the verification documents and staple them to the I–9 form as evidence of compliance. Employers must verify employment eligibility for all applicants, even if they are certain that the applicant is eligible due to appearance or personal acquaintance. To fail to do so can lead to fines of up to one thousand dollars for each employee.

There are no religious exemptions from the act. Free exercise challenges have thus far met with no success in the courts.[101]

The act imposes civil and criminal penalties on employers who knowingly employ illegal aliens, and employers with a pattern or practice of hiring illegal aliens can even be imprisoned. It is also an offense to hire a contractor who is known to be supplying unauthorized aliens.

The new immigration act had an amnesty provision that enabled illegal aliens who had been continuously in the country since before January 1, 1982, to apply for legalization and had certain special provisions for agricultural workers. Amnesty has now expired.

Finally, as noted previously,[102] the act eliminates discrimination against noncitizens. This aspect of the act applies only to the employers of four or more workers.

F. OCCUPATIONAL SAFETY AND HEALTH ACT

The Occupational Safety and Health Act (OSHA),[103] passed in 1970, imposes certain obligations on employers to maintain safe and health-protecting working conditions in the workplace. An employer subject to OSHA jurisdiction is one "engaged in a business affecting commerce who has employees."[104] Commerce is defined as "trade, traffic, commerce, transportation, or communication among the several States, or between a State and any place outside thereof, or within the District of Columbia . . . or between points in the same State but through a point outside thereof."[105] There are no exemptions for religious organizations or limitations of application of the act to employers with more than a certain number of employees. Whether or not a church or religious organization is subject to OSHA jurisdiction will depend on whether or not it is considered to be engaged in commerce within the meaning of the act, whether or not application of OSHA standards would raise sufficient constitutional implications so that a court should abstain from applying them under a *Catholic Bishop* analysis, and whether it would be a free exercise violation to apply the act. At this writing, OSHA issues have not had significant exploration with respect to religious organizations in reported court decisions.

G. SEXUAL ORIENTATION

No federal law presently bans discrimination based on homosexuality, gender preference, or sexual orientation. A growing number of states[106] and municipalities, however, do ban discrimination on these grounds. Religious organizations may be specifically exempted from these laws, or exemptions may be limited to clergy. When there are no exemptions, reported cases have upheld the First Amendment right of churches to discriminate on these grounds.[107] The full scope of a religious organization's right to discriminate on the basis of homosexuality remains to be explored.

H. JURY DUTY AND MILITARY RESERVE TRAINING

Employees are generally protected from discrimination because of jury duty or military reserve training. Check with a competent local attorney if you have an employment problem in these areas when situations arise.

I. SMOKING

State and local law may require employers to establish certain policies with respect to smoking. Local counsel should be consulted.

REFERENCES

Bagni, Bruce N. "Discrimination in the Name of the Lord: A Critical Evaluation of Discrimination by Religious Organizations," 79 *Columbia Law Review* 1514 (1979).

Bloss, Julie L. *Employment Law: A Guide for Churches* (1990) (Church Management, Inc., P.O. Box 162527, Austin, Texas 78716). Twenty-eight pages of text and sample employment forms. Good summary of applicable statutes and personnel management. No information on federal payroll issues such as federal tax withholding or Social Security.

Boyle, John P. *Religious Employers and Gender Employment Discrimination*, 4 *Journal of Law and Inequality* 637 (1986).

Hammar, Richard R. *Pastor, Church and Law*, 2d ed. (Matthews, N.C.: Christian Ministry Resources, 1991).

Kaspar, Dennis R. *Selective Hiring by Religious Organizations* (1984 with 1987 supplement on *Amos*). A forty-seven page memorandum by a private attorney. Available from Christian Legal Society (CLS Memo Bank #8-231), P.O. Box 1492, Merrifield, Va. 22116.

Laycock, Douglas. "Toward a General Theory of the Religion Clauses: The Case of Church Labor Relations and the Right to Church Autonomy," 81 *Columbia Law Review* 1373 (1981).

Lupu, Ira C. "Free Exercise Exemptions and Religious Institutions: The Case of Employment Discrimination," 67 *Boston University Law Review* 391 (1987).

Moots, Philip R., and Edward McGlynn Gaffney. *Church and Campus: Legal Issues in Religiously Affiliated Higher Education* (Notre Dame: University of Notre Dame Press, 1979).

Payne, Lucy Salsbury. "Uncovering the First Amendment: A Research Guide to the Religion Clauses," 4 *Notre Dame Journal of Law and Ethics* 825 (1990). This valuable article collects the numerous publications dealing with the religion clauses of the First Amendment with a selective bibliography of particularly pertinent sources.

CHAPTER 8

The Church as Property Owner

A. REAL ESTATE LAW AND THE CHURCH

Despite the interesting historical and even biblical features of property law which pertain to them, for most churches and religious organizations today, property ownership is a function of modern property law, which, with limited exceptions, applies to religious landowners the same as it does to secular landowners. Exceptions arise when issues of church property ownership turn on ecclesiastical considerations or when the application of normal rules governing real property raise significant issues of religious freedom. Growing churches are most likely to have to deal with issues of property ownership as they move, build, expand, or add services.

Property ownership is granted by a deed from the prior owner. Deeds, like wills, are formal legal documents, the validity and effectiveness of which depend upon their compliance with the requisite formalities. Hence they should always be prepared by an attorney. Deeds are either warranty or quitclaim. A warranty deed "warrants," or guarantees, that the seller has good title. A quitclaim deed conveys only whatever title the grantor has but does not guarantee that he has any. Deeds and other land records are recorded in a registry of deeds or other public office as provided by the laws of your state. To determine if title is good, one searches the registry records to follow the chain of title back, making sure all deeds in the chain are proper, that no part of the property was conveyed away, and that there are no mortgages, liens, attachments, or other encumbrances or burdens on the property, or at least none you do not know about and are not willing to accept.

Real estate transactions should always be handled by an attorney. There are too many traps for the unwary. This chapter reviews areas of law pertinent to property ownership—land-use controls, environmental concerns, eminent domain, adverse possession, leases, and property taxes. Chapter 15 discusses practical suggestions for acquiring property, construction contracts, and liability for maintenance of the premises.

B. LAND-USE CONTROLS

The "police power," as discussed in chapter 2, is the inherent power of the sovereign state to enact laws to promote public health, safety, morals, or the general welfare, and as such antedates the U.S. Constitution.[1] The regulation of land use falls within the police power.

In seventeenth-century New England, local land committees restricted building and farming sites and banned wooden chimneys and thatched roofs as fire hazards; and town ordinances prohibited the sheltering of strangers without the permission of town officials.[2] However, the rise of mercantile cities and increasingly individualistic, market-oriented agriculture overtook the close-knit ordering of small-town colonial life, and there were few attempts to regulate land use in the late colonial period and into the 1800s. As American cities continued to grow, with resulting chaos and congestion, so did an increasing recognition that the individualistic right of citizens to pursue their happiness and use their property without government restraint required modification in recognition of the interdependent reality of urban life. By the early twentieth century, many American municipalities had enacted local ordinances that regulated a variety of land uses, prohibiting or limiting to certain districts noxious uses, billboards, discharge of smoke and disposition of garbage; imposing lot size, setback, and type and height restrictions on structures; and providing for beautification. Comprehensive zoning codes were in place in many American cities by the 1920s, although they were often considered a radical departure from traditional concepts of private property. State courts generally upheld such ordinances as within the police power—meeting a need to prevent congestion, secure quiet residential areas, and segregate in an orderly fashion industrial, commercial, and dwelling areas as a result of the increasing density of urban populations, growing industry, and the general complexity of urban life.

The question of the constitutionality of a comprehensive zoning ordinance was put to rest by the U.S. Supreme Court in 1926 in the case of *Village of Euclid v. Ambler Realty Co.,*[3] which took a broad and expansive view of the police power regulation in upholding a zoning ordinance. The concept of the police power with respect to land-use control has continued to broaden. In the 1954 case of *Berman v. Parker,*[4] the Court said:

> The concept of the public welfare is broad and inclusive. . . . The values it represents are spiritual as well as physical, aesthetic as well as monetary. It is within the power of the legislature to determine that the community should be beautiful

as well as healthy, spacious as well as clean, well-balanced as well as carefully patrolled.[5]

In the 1974 case of *Village of Belle Terre v. Boraas,*[6] the Court stated that the police power was "ample to lay out zones where family values, youth values, and the blessings of quiet seclusion and clean air make the area a sanctuary for people," and enabled a municipality to make zones that were a "quiet place where yards are wide, people few, and motor vehicles restricted."[7] The notion of land-use regulation under the police power has continued to expand and is now recognized to include landmark and historic district restrictions, architectural controls and other esthetic regulations, limits on coastal development, regulation of subdivisions, and a variety of other restrictions.

Constitutional issues in land-use regulation no longer focus on the scope of the police power. Specific regulations are, however, successfully challenged in some instances as violations of the guarantee of due process where there is no rational or substantial relation between the regulation and the purposes for its enactment, and on an equal protection basis which requires some rational basis for justifying different treatment of similarly situated owners or groups. Restrictions are also occasionally challenged as violating freedom of speech or the right of privacy or, if excessive in the restriction of property use, as taking property under federal or state constitutions, which requires compensation. For churches and religious organizations, imposition on the free exercise of religion may provide an additional basis for challenging the application of an ordinance.

Land-use controls are almost entirely in the form of local ordinances. Since municipalities are creatures of the state[8] and have no inherent police power themselves but only such as is granted by the state, such ordinances must be enacted pursuant to state law. Usually the state law takes the form of an "enabling" statute which authorizes municipalities to regulate land use. Local ordinances that are inconsistent with the state enabling legislation may be attacked on this ground.

Most land-use regulation will consist of

zoning ordinances, planning regulations, and building codes, each of which is treated hereafter.

1. Zoning

Zoning ordinances began in the larger municipalities and proceeded outward to more rural areas as the need for land-use controls was locally perceived. Such ordinances in major cities may be complex codes; in small towns, a few pages of simple rules; and in some rural areas, still nonexistent.

The typical zoning ordinance divides the municipality into zones or districts which are defined by reference to a map. In each district, certain uses that are characteristic of the district are permitted as a matter of right, such as residences, agriculture, commercial establishments, and industry. Certain uses that are not permitted as a matter of right may be allowed in the district under a "special exception" or "special use permit" or similar terminology if they meet specific criteria generally aimed at insuring that they do not have a significant adverse impact on the character of the neighborhood. These permits are relatively easy to obtain. Uses which are allowed neither as a matter of right nor by a special permit may also be allowed through a more stringent procedure, which may be termed a "variance" in some areas, which generally requires a showing that the property in question is unusable for the purposes for which it is zoned, a showing which is difficult to make for most properties. A third means of authorizing a use which otherwise would not be permitted as a matter of right by the terms of the ordinance is a "grandfathered use," usually referred to as a "nonconforming use." It may be maintained in the form that existed at the time of adoption of the ordinance, although changes or expansions of the use may be limited or prohibited and the right to maintain it may be lost if the use lapses for a period of time.

Zoning ordinances may include within the right to make a "principal" use the right to make any normal "accessory" uses that would accompany it; or accessory uses may be a subject of separate regulation. Accessory uses would apply to such things as having an office or other commercial activity on residential property incidental to the principal use of the property for a residence.

Zoning ordinances may regulate not only the uses to which land is put but also the nature and design of structures on the land. Such matters as front, back, and side yard requirements or setbacks for buildings, minimum area or street frontage for various uses, parking requirements, regulation of signs, drives entering on streets, open space in multiple-unit developments, and height are commonly regulated by zoning ordinances.

Zoning ordinances may also include special "overlay" districts which impose particular requirements on certain areas of the municipalities that overlap and exist independent of use districts. This may include such things as historic preservation districts, flood way and flood plain districts, and wetland or other conservation districts. The ordinance is usually administered by a zoning board or commission which grants permits, exceptions, or variances and hears appeals from decisions of the building inspector or other municipal officials as to whether or not a particular use is permitted. It functions as a quasi-judicial administrative agency. Its decisions are appealable through the court system. Violations of zoning ordinances can lead to fines and injunctive relief compelling a landowner to bring the property into compliance.

Every church or religious organization that owns or leases property and engages in any use of real estate must be concerned with compliance with its local zoning ordinance. Compliance is usually an issue when property is acquired for new or expanded uses or uses on existing property are to be changed or expanded. In any such instance, the organization should examine the local zoning ordinance to determine its rights and responsibilities.

The Supreme Court has never had occasion to rule directly on the applicability of zoning ordinances to churches. It has, however, referred in "dicta" (discussion not necessary to the conclusion in the case before it) to zoning as one of the government regulatory powers that do not offend the religion clauses of the First Amendment.[9]

Hence, there is no generic federal constitutional right for churches and religious organizations to be free of zoning regulation with respect to their religious activities.

It is equally clear, however, that it would be a violation of the First Amendment and, undoubtedly, other constitutional provisions as well for a municipality to adopt a zoning ordinance that excluded churches and religious uses altogether. Since religious worship is an integral part of every community, this is rarely a problem. Most litigation involving religious organizations under zoning ordinances involves the right of the religious use in a particular zone and the scope of uses permitted where the ordinance allows a church.

No two zoning cases are identical. While there are some generally applicable principles in zoning law, every zoning ordinance and every property is unique; and each case has its own special set of facts. Hence court decisions that appear to reach conflicting results may simply reflect the fact that they are decided under different ordinances and on the basis of different circumstances. Nevertheless, the varying results reached by courts in evaluating church rights under zoning ordinances may also reflect the difference in value that different courts attribute to the governmental interest in a strict enforcement of the ordinance as opposed to the church's interest in the free exercise of its religious rights.

Most courts have held that churches cannot be excluded from residential areas, either as a matter of religious freedom or because such an exclusion exceeds permissible exercise of the police power. The common provisions in zoning ordinances that permit churches in residential areas reflect the pre–World War II American community: most people walked to church and most churches were located in residential areas for that reason. With the suburbanization of America and the proliferation of the automobile, few people walk to church anymore, and local political pressures are more likely to come from neighbors unhappy with the intrusion of traffic, parked cars, noise, and associated inconveniences related to the presence of a church than from parishioners who expect the church to be within walking distance of their residences.

Despite the majority rule, there appears to be an increasing tendency of reported cases to uphold zoning ordinances that ban churches from certain districts or affirm denials of use permits for churches.

For example, in the 1988 case of *Jehovah's Witnesses v. Woolwich Township*[10] the New Jersey Appellate Court reversed a lower court ruling that the First Amendment barred zoning churches out of residential districts and remanded the case with instructions for the lower court to consider whether the activity burdened was truly religious, whether the zoning ordinance imposed a significant burden on religion, what alternative locations and zoning options were available to the church, and what the government's interest was in maintaining the zoning plan. The Ninth Circuit Court of Appeals in the 1990 case of *Christian Gospel Church v. City and County of San Francisco*[11] upheld the denial of a conditional-use permit for a church in a single-family residential district where the church had previously been meeting in rented hotel space. The court found that the state interest in the integrity of residential neighborhoods outweighed the religious freedom interest and that denial restrained not the church's practice of religion but only a change of location. The Tenth Circuit Court of Appeals in the 1988 case of *Messiah Baptist Church v. County of Jefferson*[12] similarly upheld a zoning ordinance that did not allow churches to be located in agricultural areas, finding there was no direct burden on religious belief or doctrine in refusing the church's request for a special-use permit to build at a particular site.

A reversal of the usual pattern occurred in *Cornerstone Bible Church v. City of Hastings,*[13] where a church was refused permission to build in a commercial zone when the city zoning ordinance allowed churches only in residential zones, despite the fact that in three years of looking, the church had been unable to find any locations in the town outside of the commercial zone. The case was reversed on appeal, the higher court finding that the church's rights of free speech and equal protection were implicated and that the city had not provided factual support and a rational basis for the speech-based exclusion and disparate treatment from other noncommercial uses. The invocation of constitutional rights other than free exercise, such as free speech and equal protection rights, that prevailed in this case are likely to increase in the future in light of the Supreme Court's *Smith* decision, discussed in chapter 3.

Many courts have continued to provide churches with a high degree of protection under zoning ordinances. A New York court found that a rejection of a special-use permit for a church that wanted to build a new sanctuary was improper, noting that churches have a presumptively favored status under zoning law;[14] and another New York court overruled a local board's refusal to let a home be used as a church in a residential district in which churches were allowed, finding there was no substantial evidence of significant adverse effects.[15] In *Love Church v. City of Evanston*, a 1987 decision by the Federal District Court for the Northern District of Illinois,[16] a court found that the Equal Protection Clause was violated by a city zoning ordinance which required a conditional-use permit for a church in any district when similarly situated uses such as theaters, schools, and meeting halls were permitted as a matter of right. Several courts have overturned denials of church-use permits when the only apparent significant basis for the denial was the neighbors' objections.[17]

The right to exist in a given district, whether by virtue of the zoning ordinance or for constitutional reasons, does not necessarily exempt the church from other requirements of the ordinance. In the 1986 case of *Lakeshore Assembly of God Church v. Village Board of the Village of Westfield*,[18] a church was required to comply with limitations on the size of a sign imposed by the local zoning board.

Where churches are allowed as a matter of right, most courts have allowed a variety of related uses, on the theory that either they are part of the church or that they are uses that are permitted as accessory to the principal use of the property as a church. Free exercise claims have protected churches in operating a soup kitchen[19] and a parking lot.[20] Permissible accessory uses have been found to include day care centers[21] and homeless shelters.[22] Radio

towers have been both allowed[23] and disallowed,[24] as have parochial schools.[25]

Religious counseling has been upheld as a church use,[26] but pastoral counseling conducted in space leased from a church that was open to the general public and not just to members of the church or believers, that involved no proselytizing, and in which religious doctrine was subordinated and played no role in the counseling was found to have no religious purpose and was not allowed as part of a church use.[27] In the 1988 Connecticut case of *Daughters of St. Paul v. Zoning Board of Appeals*,[28] the court found that the presence of a bookstore and audiovisual center on the premises of a chapel and convent did not change the character as a church permitted under the zoning ordinance. The books and materials were related to education and were sold solely to supplement religious activity. This court defined a church broadly for purposes of zoning to avoid constitutional questions. In the 1989 Arizona case of *Cochise County v. Broken Arrow Baptist Church*,[29] however, the Arizona Court of Appeals found that a 5,000-square-foot building intended for the printing of Bibles was not permitted as part of the religious worship of a church but instead constituted manufacturing.

Private schools have usually been allowed on church-owned property either as part of the church, as a permissible accessory use, as a school use under the ordinance, or on the ground that exclusion of such use bears no reasonable relation to the values protected by the police power of public health, safety, morals, or general welfare. Private schools cannot be excluded from an entire municipality or subjected to conditions so burdensome that the effect is the same, nor can they be excluded from districts where public schools are permitted. Requirements for special permits for church schools, however, are usually upheld, although schools are often successful in overcoming permit denials based on an adverse effect on neighboring property values, loss of tax revenues, increase in noise, traffic hazards, or other inconveniences, and neighborhood opposition.[30]

Religious retreat centers have been held permissible as a "church,"[31] although camp meetings, a religious retreat house and property used as a conference center, leadership training center, and children's retreat have been found not within the zoning ordinance's meaning of a church.[32]

One zoning ordinance that prohibited "other religious use" without a special permit was found to be invalid as being unconstitutionally vague when the municipality sought to apply it to home meetings of followers of The Way, International, for prayer and discussion.[33]

Some zoning ordinances impose restrictions on other uses based on their proximity to churches. The Supreme Court has invalidated an ordinance that permitted churches to veto liquor license applications for facilities located within five hundred feet of a church[34] but has upheld a zoning ordinance that prohibited the location of adult theaters within a thousand feet of a church, residential zone, single- or multiple-family dwelling, park, or school as a reasonable time, place, and manner regulation aimed not at speech but at the effect on the surrounding community. It was important that the "speech" interest represented by the adult theater could be located elsewhere in the community.[35] Other courts, as well, have upheld ordinances that ban adult bookstores or theaters within a given proximity of a church, at least as long as the ordinance does not unduly restrict their location elsewhere in the municipality.[36]

An interesting case which illustrates the application of several zoning principles in the context of a religious institution is the 1959 decision of the Supreme Court of Wisconsin in *State ex rel Covenant Harbor Bible Camp v. Steinke*.[37] The case involved a Bible camp that constituted a nonconforming use under the zoning ordinance. Several camp-type buildings had been built over the years. A large family residence that had been used to house campers was totally lost in a fire, and the camp proposed to erect six cabins identical to those which had been erected at an earlier time that would house the same number of campers as the burned-out residence. The zoning ordinance prohibited restoration of a damaged nonconforming use if more than 50 percent of the assessed value was lost. The court found that the original establishment of the camp was not a nonconforming use

since the city had expressly permitted building construction for Bible camp use, presumably either as an authorized special permit or by administrative construction of ordinance language that permitted uses for a residence, rooming or boarding house, church, and school. Further cabin construction by permit at a time when the ordinance allowed churches, boarding and lodging parochial schools, and organized quasi-public recreational buildings and grounds was also considered administrative construction of the ordinance, and not a nonconforming use. Subsequently, the zoning ordinance was amended to make the camp a nonconforming use at a time when its capacity was approximately the same as at the time of the fire. At that time, the ordinance would allow the camp use to be continued but not extended.

The court resolved the case by concluding that the 50 percent limitation applied not to the residence but to the total use of the property. Hence, if the value of the residence destroyed was less than 50 percent of the value of all of the buildings on the premises used for camp purposes, the camp would be permitted to restore the destroyed building. The court was also of the view that a restored structure did not need to be identical to the one destroyed, although it would not be a matter of right to replace it with different buildings at different sites.

In the late 1970s and early 1980s, in a series of incidents across the country, local authorities sought to prohibit Bible study groups and religious worship activity conducted in private homes, or to require a permit based on local zoning ordinances to conduct such activities.[38] These actions were explained as being based on (1) ordinance requirements that called for special permits for religious uses, or, (2) in the case of a Bible study group led by a cleric, that such use constituted a "home occupation" that could not be conducted without a special permit. The cases were generally resolved without involving the court system.

There are several sound legal reasons why home gatherings for Bible study, fellowship, or worship should not be subject to zoning regulation. First, any such regulation would be a serious imposition on the free exercise of religion and should be viewed as a violation of state and federal constitutional guarantees. Notwithstanding the *Smith* decision,[39] a home Bible study or religious gathering may be constitutionally defended as an exercise of free speech and assembly as well as religion and, hence, may continue to be subject to the requirement that before such gatherings can be banned or regulated the government show a compelling interest in regulation that cannot be furthered by any less restrictive means. Second, home gatherings for religious purposes may be considered an integral, traditional, and normal use of residential property and, hence, simply part of a permitted residential use. Third, serious constitutional issues of discrimination against religion would arise if local authorities banned home gatherings for religious purposes but not for any other purpose such as social or political clubs, meetings of other nonprofit groups and committees, or even the normal gatherings of friends and family that create traffic, noise, and congestion. Fourth, zoning regulation can only be justified under the police power if it bears at least a rational relationship to protecting the health, welfare, safety, and morals of the people. While this authority has been viewed broadly to include esthetics, peace and tranquility, and other community interests, it would be difficult to make a rational argument that the police power requires regulation of home Bible study.

If in fact the religious use of the property is so extensive that it becomes the principal use, and the residential use is incidental, a different situation is presented. And if the nature of the gathering is such that significant intrusions are being made on the tranquility of the neighborhood, for example, by loud music or singing or by cars being parked inappropriately to impede neighbors' access or trespass on their property, the application of the zoning laws becomes more reasonable. Christians should, when gathering at one another's homes, be at least as sensitive to their neighbors' legitimate concern to be free of disturbance as they would wish their neighbors to be to them.

Some practical suggestions for addressing zoning issues are contained in chapter 15.

2. Planning

In many municipalities, separate planning boards or commissions impose additional land-use regulations that function either in tandem with or independent of the zoning ordinance. Planning regulations may require permission for the subdivision of land (the division of an existing lot into two or more lots for the purpose of sale). They may also impose regulations on various types of community growth and property development which may include expansion or improvements planned by religious organizations. Planning board review is generally a review of specific plans for development; it is more subjective than zoning permit hearings and is intended for the purpose of insuring the development and growth of the municipality in accordance with a long-range, master plan. There are few reported cases dealing with religious institutions and planning regulations. However, all purchases, construction, and expansion plans should be reviewed with the planning ordinance and zoning requirements in mind.

All fifty states have enabling legislation for municipal planning. Municipal planning is generally entrusted to a planning board or commission whose duties include the preparation or adoption of master plans for the municipality; the review of proposed zoning ordinances or amendments before they are acted upon by the legislative body; the review of changes in the official map to lay out new streets, highways, or drainage systems, or to expand or close existing ones; general investigations in the preparation of maps, reports, and recommendations with respect to planning and development of the municipality; and the review and approval of certain specific land-use or development actions by landowners, such as subdivision approval or site-plan review. It is in the latter functions that churches and religious organizations that are acquiring, selling, or developing property may encounter planning regulation.

Site-plan review is the regulatory function of the planning board. Certain types of development may be subject to a requirement that a plan be submitted and approved that shows the proposed location of buildings, parking areas, and other installations and their relation to existing conditions such as roads, neighboring uses, natural features, and the like. The purpose of site-plan approval is to insure that the details of the plan will be compatible with the public interest, taking into account such matters as traffic access, circulation and parking, the use of open space, the arrangement of buildings, and other adjacent uses, the zoning district and natural features of the area. The types of uses that require site-plan approval vary greatly but in most instances would not include single-family residences. Site-plan review, like other local land-use control, must be consistent with both constitutional limitations and state enabling legislation. In some instances, site-plan review is advisory only, but planning boards often do have authority to impose reasonable conditions that are consistent with their authority and are not confiscatory, discriminatory, or vague.

Municipalities that have adopted planning regulation almost universally require approval by the planning board or commission for the subdivision of land, including the division of a tract into two or more parcels for purposes of sale or development. Subdivision regulation is intended to insure that the development of lots for uses permitted by the zoning ordinance is done in such a way that the lots may be safely and properly used for the permitted purpose without imposing a burden on the community or creating health or other hazards. Building and planning approval are separate municipal functions, and many land-use plans require approval from the municipal board administering each of these regulatory functions.

Subdivision is controlled by requiring that subdivision plans be approved by the municipal planning board or the agency with planning authority. Among the considerations relevant to approval are compliance with the zoning ordinance, with the municipality's comprehensive or master plan, with a statewide or regional plan, and with various environmental considerations. The nature of the streets, roads, and highways providing access to and within the subdivision, drainage control, water supply and sanitary sewer provision, public facilities

and amenities, and open space may all be considered. Subdivision authority must be exercised in accordance with adequate standards set forth in the enabling legislation or consistent municipal ordinance.

Site-plan review and subdivision requirements will not normally be set forth in an ordinance with specific reference to churches or religious institutions. However, purchase, sale, and development plans of such institutions will often be subject to them.

3. Building Codes

Most municipalities have building codes that describe construction standards for purposes of health, safety, and sanitation. Such codes may require that construction be done with certain materials or methods and may impose certain design standards. Churches are subject to building codes in the same way secular organizations are, and they can be compelled to comply with them. Church buildings that have dual uses are required to comply with the more stringent requirements, for example, a church building that functions also as a school must comply with requirements applicable to schools, and such requirements are enforceable even if the result means closing the school.[40] After one congregation had completed a remodeling project that did not include a sprinkler system, it was required to comply with a building code that required the installation of a sprinkler system, even though it had obtained a building permit before commencing construction; the cost of adding the system after the remodeling was double what it would have been had it been done originally.[41]

The Americans with Disabilities Act (ADA), discussed in chapter 7 with respect to employment, imposes certain standards for handicapped access on certain "public accommodations" but does not apply to "religious organizations or entities controlled by religious organizations, including places of worship."[42]

Churches, like other building owners, rely on building permits at their risk. Permits issued in error can be subsequently revoked, or the church can be made to comply with additional requirements, even if it obtained the permit in good faith with full disclosure of its construction plans. If there is any question about what is required, the church may want to obtain independent advice in addition to relying on a municipal building permit. In significant projects, the responsibility for insuring compliance with the building code should rest by contract on the design professional with respect to matters of design, and on the contractor with respect to construction methods.

4. Landmark Designations

Many municipalities have enacted landmark ordinances under state enabling statutes in recent years. The ordinances enable the municipality or an agency established for the purpose to designate certain properties as landmarks that reflect significant aspects of the cultural or historic heritage of the city. The result of designation is that the property cannot be structurally altered without approval. Landmark designation may be an honor to the historic heritage of the church but can impose significant burdens on the ability of the body to manage its property to its desires. Three recent decisions show an interesting pattern of court analysis of such ordinances as they apply to churches.

In *First Covenant Church v. City of Seattle*, a 1990 decision of the Washington state Supreme Court,[43] the court held that the constitutional protection of the free exercise of religion and the public benefits associated with the practice of religious worship within the community outweigh the state interest in the preservation of historic landmarks; and it invalidated landmark designation for the Seattle church. The court found that the Landmark Preservation Ordinance, in imposing controls on the alteration of the church's exterior, failed to further a compelling governmental interest. The court applied the general understanding of the Free Exercise Clause as it existed before the *Smith* decision.[44] The church's success in the case was based on claims of (1) impairment of religious freedom by Seattle's applying the requirement of city approval to the church's request to structurally alter its worship facility, and (2) the decrease in the value of church property by the landmark designation and

reduction of the ability of the church to sell its property. The case was appealed to the U.S. Supreme Court, which remanded it for reconsideration in light of *Smith's* abrogation of the compelling governmental interest test. On remand, the church, state, and federal constitutional position was upheld.[45]

In a decision rendered after *Smith* by the Second Circuit Court of Appeals, *Rector of the Vestry of St. Bartholomew's Church v. City of New York*,[46] the church, which did not oppose the landmark designation at the time it was made, applied for permission to tear down a community house next to the church and to replace it with a forty-seven-story office tower. The church claimed that the property was inadequate to carry out the activities that comprised the church's present religious mission and charitable purposes and that it needed the revenue from the office tower to repair and renovate the church. The Second Circuit followed the *Smith* decision, finding that the landmark law was a valid neutral regulation of general applicability and, therefore, did not impinge on the church's free exercise right. It also found that the landmark law was not a taking of the property without just compensation under the Constitution because the church could continue its existing activities in its existing facilities. Church claims of the development of church property interferes with religious freedom by barring a church's ability to develop property for investment purposes that had previously been used for religious purposes have met with little sympathy in the courts.[47]

In the third of this trilogy of recent cases, also post-*Smith*, the Massachusetts Supreme Judicial Court addressed church objections to the Boston Landmarks Commission's attempt to regulate renovations inside a church building in *Society of Jesus of New England v. Boston Landmarks Commission*.[48] Ignoring *Smith*, the Massachusetts court found, under the state constitution rather than the U.S. Constitution, that the governmental interest in historic preservation was not sufficiently compelling to justify the restraints on the free exercise of religion. *Society of Jesus* illustrates the turn to state constitutions after *Smith* for churches and religious organizations and for people seeking free exercise protection. This trend will likely continue as long as *Smith* states the test under the federal Constitution.

Land-use regulation is one area of law in which the altered rules of the Free Exercise Clause that resulted from the *Smith* decision will be played out. Planning, building, and landmark regulations are likely to be neutral laws of general applicability with respect to which it will be increasingly difficult to make a federal free exercise claim. This is because the government need no longer show a compelling state interest to overcome the religious freedom right involved, although some uses may be an exception to *Smith* if "hybrid" constitutional rights of speech or assembly are involved. Zoning laws, however, usually make specific provision in some form for churches, and application of the *Smith* rules in this area will be more problematic. Zoning laws also give rise to constitutional issues unrelated to religion, as we have noted. In any event, churches will continue to have the traditional issues of zoning law available, under which many cases have been decided without any constitutional claim, such as whether or not a particular use is within the definition of a church or is an accessory use to the principal use of a church.

Land-use regulation is conducted almost entirely on the local level and is one of the most pervasive fields of law. Definitions and standards in zoning and planning ordinances are often subject to much administrative interpretation, and the application of ordinances to particular requests for approval are often inherently and largely subjective. When does a particular use, subdivision, or improvement change the character of the neighborhood, and how much traffic is permitted before a local land-use agency can find that there is too much congestion and refuse to permit the use? Being a good neighbor and acting as a good citizen within the community can go a long way toward success when a church or religious institution has to go before a zoning or planning board. Friendly neighbors and municipal officials who view the institution as a benefit rather than a bane to the community can be an immeasurable aid in obtaining the right result.

C. ENVIRONMENTAL CONCERNS

Prior to 1970, although the Boy Scouts, Girl Scouts, conservation organizations, and other charities taught conservation, there was no widespread awareness of the hazards of environmental pollution. Rivers in which earlier generations had found their swimming holes had turned foul with industrial waste and sewage. Industrial plants, electrical generating stations, and millions of personal and commercial motor vehicles were unrestrained in their release of noxious fumes and particulates into the atmosphere. Solid and liquid waste products from industrial and commercial activities were dumped in municipal landfills, in private dumps, or out the back door of the plant with little concern or awareness for the environmental consequences. Underground storage tanks sprang leaks of which no one was aware or were abandoned with no effort to pump them out or remove them. Asbestos, which was valued for its fireproofing and insulating qualities, was widely used in building construction.

This period of blissful ignorance began to end in the early 1970s with the dawning awareness of the magnitude of environmental desecration that had occurred in the country. The Love Canal disaster in New York state in the mid-1970s raised the specter of whole neighborhoods being abandoned because the soil was unsafe to live on and was a national consciousness-raising exercise in the problems of hazardous waste.

Beginning in the early 1970s, Congress passed a series of major environmental regulation statutes governing air and water pollution, handling and disposing of hazardous waste and toxic substances, management of leakage or spillage of petroleum products, and regulation of underground storage tanks and asbestos abatement. Most of these laws are administered by the Environmental Protection Agency (EPA), which enacts regulations to implement them. Most state legislatures have enacted parallel and sometimes more rigorous regulatory schemes, with state environmental agencies promulgating their own administrative regulations and enforcing them, sometimes with delegated power from the

EPA to enforce the federal regulations as well. Most of the regulated activities and associated liability arise from the ownership and use of land. There are no statutory exemptions for churches or religious organizations and no obviously compelling religious freedom arguments to be made for such exemptions on a constitutional basis.

Churches and religious organizations are not normally engaged in activities that generate hazardous waste or cause air or water pollution. It would be a mistake, however, to be ignorant of environmental obligations in the acquisition and utilization of real property on the assumption that these regulations have nothing to do with the church. Examples of some situations in which a church could incur environmental obligations are:

1. Acquiring property with existing hazardous waste or petroleum contaminants on it, which may make the new owner liable for cleanup costs even if the new owner did not cause the contamination. Such contaminants can come from a former owner, perhaps well in the past, or the former use of the property as a waste dump site, however casually or informally. It may also come from activities of neighboring landowners. Industrial installations, laundries, gas stations, auto repair shops, and metal-working shops are only a few examples of common property uses accompanied by a high incidence of resulting soil or ground water pollution. Any property located in an area that is or has ever been used for commercial or industrial purposes or in which such uses are or have ever been made in the general vicinity should not be purchased or a deed to it accepted, even by gift, without an environmental assessment. Such concerns are not necessarily limited to urban, industrial, or commercial areas. In numerous cases rural areas have been used for the disposal of hazardous waste. Even the most apparently pristine environment can have hidden problems.
2. Leaking underground storage tanks, usually containing fuel oil or gasoline, are a common source of contamination of the soil and ground water. Underground storage tanks exist at many religious institutions.
3. The presence of asbestos in buildings. Many older buildings contain asbestos—in insulation, wall and ceiling board, floor and roof tiles. Exposure to this widely used fireproofing mineral is now known to cause several types of cancer and other fatal diseases. Not all asbestos in buildings is dangerous, and removal may not be regulatorily required, as with hazardous waste remediation; but buyers of existing buildings must be alert to this potential problem.

These three examples can apply to every church and religious institution in the country. One Catholic school system with forty-seven schools, for example, estimates the cost of asbestos compliance at $1.25 million or approximately $25,000 per school.[49]

Those religious or religiously affiliated institutions that do engage in activities that cause them to be normal generators of hazardous waste should, of course, have specific advice as to how properly to deal with their obligations. Such institutions may include, for example, hospitals, schools, colleges and universities, printing plants, and property owned by a church or religious organization on which commercial or industrial activities may be conducted by a lessee or by the organization itself as an unrelated trade or business for purposes of investment management or for rehabilitation of the organization's clientele.

The major federal environmental laws can be summarized as follows:

1. *The Comprehensive Environmental Response, Compensation, and Liability Act of 1980.*[50] This law, known as CERCLA, or the Superfund Statute, aims at the cleanup of hazardous waste sites. As amended by the *Superfund Amendments and Reauthorization Act* (SARA) in 1986,[51] it has the following significant provisions:

a. In response to an emergency the federal government is authorized to enter property where hazardous substances are located and may remove hazardous material or take other abatement action.

The cost of cleanup is funded by the Superfund, which is generated by taxes on industry, but the private parties responsible for site contamination are obliged to reimburse the Fund for its expenses.

b. Parties liable for cleanup costs of a site, called Potentially Responsible Parties, or PRPs, include anyone who contributed to the contamination, the owners and operators of the facility presently or at the time of any disposal, any off-site entities whose hazardous substances were ultimately disposed of at the site, and anyone who transported hazardous substances to the site. The government can perform remedial work itself and recover its costs from the PRPs, or it can order the PRPs to do the work. The PRPs are liable not only for the cost of removal or remedial action, known as response costs, but also for damages to natural resources and for the costs of any health assessments done to determine human health risks from the contamination.

CERCLA liability is strict, that is, it is not dependent on fault. The present owner of the site is strictly liable, even if it did not contribute to the contamination, unless the contamination and damages resulted solely from an act of God, an act of war, or an act or omission by a third party—other than an employee or agent of the PRP—provided that the PRP exercised due care with respect to the hazardous substance and took precautions against foreseeable acts or omissions of such a third party.[52]

SARA clarifies the position of a present owner when the contamination was caused by a prior owner or operator by adding the so-called innocent purchaser defense.[53] This provides a defense to the innocent later purchaser if (1) at the time the property was acquired, the purchaser not only did not know but "had no reason to know" that any hazardous substance, which later became released, was disposed of at the site; *and* (2) at the time of the acquisition, the present owner undertook "all appropriate inquiry into the previous ownership and uses of the property consistent with good commercial or customary practice in an

effort to minimize liability."[54] This statute establishes a standard of care to be followed by all parties in the acquisition of real property and virtually mandates that an environmental assessment be conducted when property is acquired to assure that the defense will apply.

Under CERCLA, the liability for hazardous waste cleanup in a site is "joint and several," meaning that each contributor to the site is legally responsible for the entire cost. While dump site cleanup is customarily managed by negotiation between the government and the PRPs as a group or between the government and groups within the PRPs, the risk of major liability in these matters is real and the exposure can be in the millions of dollars.

In addition, individual managers who have any responsibility for illegal disposal of hazardous materials may be found civilly or even criminally liable. Cases of individuals receiving jail sentences for environmental violations are increasing.

Exposure to environmental liability may also occur when a church or religious institution becomes a lender. Although CERCLA excludes from the definition of an owner or operator "a person, who, without participating in the management of a . . . facility holds indicia of ownership primarily to protect a security interest,"[55] lending institutions that have placed officers on a borrower's board[56] or exerted control over them risk liability, as does a foreclosing mortgagee.[57] This potential lender liability is one that religious institutions must be aware of if they are or are considering becoming lenders and holding security interests in real estate. It may also affect their ability to borrow for acquisition or construction projects, because commercial lending institutions are increasingly wary of potential liability themselves.

Anyone who knows about the release of hazardous substances in reportable quantities (which depend upon the substance) must report such information on penalty of a fine or imprisonment or both. Civil penalties of up to $25,000 per day for violations of the statute may be assessed, with subsequent violations penalized up to $75,000 per day.[58]

SARA also contains provisions for emergency planning and a Community Right-to-Know Act, which imposes additional requirements on anyone operating a regulated facility.

2. *The Resource Conservation and Recovery Act (RCRA).* This statute, enacted in 1976 and amended several times thereafter, establishes a comprehensive program for regulating the treatment, storage, and disposal of hazardous waste. It has no application to normal activities of churches and religious organizations. Any religiously affiliated institution that is involved in the treatment, storage, or disposal of hazardous waste, however, must be familiar with its provisions and be sure that it is in compliance. The act defines hazardous waste in general terms, with certain specific substances being identified as hazardous by EPA regulation. Facilities that treat, store, or dispose of hazardous waste must obtain permits that establish operating conditions. Those who generate hazardous waste in sufficient quantities must obtain EPA identification numbers and comply with regulations for handling such waste. Hazardous waste is tracked on a "cradle-to-grave" system by a manifest that is completed by the generator. The manifest bears the generator's EPA identification number and other information that is subsequently signed by both the transporter and the treatment facility; completed copies are filed with the EPA and the relevant state agency. This provides the government with a record of whom to deal with as a potentially responsible party if a problem arises.

Of particular interest to churches and religious organizations are the 1984 RCRA amendments that regulate underground storage tanks, leaks from which are a major source of groundwater contamination. The owners of underground storage tanks in which particular substances are stored must register with the state and/or federal authorities and specify the age, size, type, and uses of the tank; new tanks may not be installed unless certain design and construction standards are met. The definition of underground storage tanks in the statute excludes a "tank used for storing heating oil for consumptive use on the premises where

stored" and a "farm or residential tank of 1,100 gallons or less capacity used for storing motor fuel for noncommercial purposes."[59] Churches with underground storage tanks should be alert, however, to the possibility that they are subject to regulation and be aware of any state regulations that may not have the same exclusions. EPA regulations require that existing tanks be tested, that leak detection systems be installed and maintained, that leaks be reported, that certain procedures for corrective action be followed, and that owners and operators be liable for damages to others or to the environment from leaks. Substantial penalties follow from the failure to comply, and the EPA has broad powers to enter and inspect, sample, and monitor the site; review records; and issue compliance orders or bring civil actions against violators. Some states have petrochemical superfunds to assist landowners in covering expenses related to leaking underground tanks and other environmental cleanup matters.

3. *The Clean Air Act.*[60] This 1977 legislation is the federal government's comprehensive regulation of air pollution. It includes a series of interrelated regulatory programs implemented by various levels of government, the principal enforcement tool being a state implementation plan adopted by each state. The EPA adopts regulations under the Clean Air Act for National Ambient Air Quality Standards for significant pollutants that may endanger public health or welfare; New Source Performance Standards for various categories of industrial sources; and National Emission Standards for Hazardous Air Pollutants which regulate particular pollutants at the point of emission.

Among the now-established National Emission Standards for Hazardous Air Pollutants are standards for asbestos at the point of emission. This is the aspect of the Clean Air Act most likely to impact religious organizations.

The state implementation plan translates the federal regulatory scheme into specific limits and reduction measures for both categories of sources and individual sources in a state. State and federal regulatory agencies have broad powers to permit and regulate new air pollution sources, to enter and inspect premises and records, and to require that those subject to the act install monitoring equipment, do emission sampling, and provide other information. Violations can result in administrative orders, including civil penalties of up to $25,000 per day and criminal penalties for knowing violations of up to $25,000 per day and one year imprisonment for the first offense and $50,000 per day and two years imprisonment thereafter. Emission standards can be enforced by suits filed by citizens, who may be awarded the costs of litigation.

4. *The Clean Water Act.* The Clean Water Act regulates discharges into surface water, ground water, and navigable water by establishing a National Pollutant Discharge Elimination System (NPDES). NPDES is a permit system that imposes effluent limitations for discharges by permit and makes unpermitted discharges unlawful. As with other environmental statutes, it provides for administrative compliance orders, injunctive relief, and civil and criminal penalties, including imprisonment, and for citizens' suits to remedy violations. The Clean Water Act rarely applies to a religious organization.

5. *The Toxic Substances Control Act.*[61] This comprehensive 1976 law governing toxic substances grants the EPA broad regulatory authority over chemical substances and mixtures produced in, used in, or imported into the United States for their entire life cycle, from initial manufacture to ultimate disposal. The act permits testing, record keeping, reporting, and direct regulation of management and handling of the chemical. To be regulated, a substance must present an unreasonable risk of injury to health or the environment, but once such a finding is made, a substance may be regulated to the extent necessary, and using the least burdensome method, to protect adequately against the risk. Regulations may prohibit or restrict the amount manufactured, processed, or distributed or the uses or concentrations thereof; require warnings and instructions, and record

keeping; prohibit or regulate various methods of disposal; impose quality control requirements; or require recalls. This legislation is the source of authority for regulation of asbestos in schools, its most likely applicability to religious institutions. Civil and criminal penalties and administrative orders can be assessed for violations.

6. *The Asbestos Hazard Emergency Response Act of 1986*[62] empowers the EPA to promulgate regulations for the inspection of schools and to define appropriate response actions in circumstances that involve actual or potential damage to a covering or material containing friable (easily crushed or crumbled) asbestos-containing material. The act applies to all schools, including private religious schools. As noted above, one Catholic school system with forty-seven schools estimates the cost of compliance at $1.25 million, and the EPA estimates the nationwide expenditure for compliance at approximately $6 billion.[63]

The liability for asbestos removal when a building is altered or demolished is not limited to schools; the liability includes all buildings and extends to the property owner as well as the contractor, even though the property owner may have no direct control over the contractor's demolition methods.[64] It is imperative that any church or religious organization that is engaged in renovation or demolition work that may involve asbestos removal be sure that it has a reliable, responsible, and bonded contractor to carry out the work. If the contractor violates the law, the church can be held responsible.

It is also important to know where removed asbestos is going. If the asbestos is improperly disposed of, the church or religious organization whose asbestos is the subject of necessary cleanup can be charged for the costs.

Asbestos manufacturers have been sued often by persons who have suffered personal injuries due to asbestos, as well as by schools and other organizations forced to bear significant costs for corrective actions because of asbestos. A church or religious organization with an asbestos removal problem should, in addition to hiring an expert consultant on handling the removal, consider with its counsel whether it has any claim against an asbestos manufacturer or prior owner for recovery. In a 1989 decision by the Fourth Circuit Court of Appeals, a Methodist church was unable to obtain such a recovery because too much time had passed since the installation.[65]

While litigation under liability insurance contracts for pollution claims is common and insureds have prevailed in many suits, the church or religious organization should not assume that its insurance policy covers such matters. If it is engaged in specific activities or uses that come under the environmental laws, it may wish to explore the availability and cost of coverage for pollution incidents with its insurer. Environmental claims are often uninsured under normal liability insurance contracts, which frequently contain specific "pollution exclusion" clauses, although the meaning and applicability of such clauses are often litigated and insureds have sometimes prevailed. Other defenses under the insurance contract may apply as well.

D. EMINENT DOMAIN

In the theocracy of ancient Israel, the land was ultimately the Lord's,[66] a belief adopted by later earthly rulers and recognizable today in the right of the sovereign to take land by eminent domain and by escheat.[67] Eminent domain is the power of the government, both federal and state (and municipal and other subdivisions of the state where properly authorized by the state), to take private property for its own use to enable it to perform proper functions. The right has been said to be "essential to its independent existence and perpetuity," "the offspring of political necessity," and "inseparable from sovereignty."[68] Eminent domain authority flows also from the "necessary and proper"[69] clause of the Constitution, read together with other granted powers.[70]

In order to be taken, property must be for a public use or purpose, although courts have been deferential to legislative determinations of such uses and purposes and do not usually judge the necessity of condemning a particular property (as opposed to some other property) for accomplishing the purpose.

Property may not be taken without "just compensation,"[71] which normally means the fair market value of the property.

Churches and religious organizations are not immune from having their property taken by the government under the eminent domain power, but the right of religious freedom introduces a competing constitutional issue in some cases. In the 1973 Colorado case of *Pillar of Fire v. Denver Urban Renewal Authority*,[72] an urban renewal project proposed to take a building that a Pentecostal sect asserted was its mother church, birthplace, symbol of its creed, and unique; it resisted the taking on free exercise grounds. The court held that "the State must show a substantial interest without a reasonable alternate means of accomplishment" to take such a religious property constitutionally.[73] On remand, the church was, on the evidence, unable to sustain its position that the building was as unique as it claimed, and the taking was confirmed and upheld when the case was appealed again to the Colorado Supreme Court.[74]

The free exercise test adopted in *Pillar of Fire* was also applied in another Colorado case, *Order of Friars Minor v. Denver Urban Renewal Authority*,[75] with respect to the condemnation of a parking lot that the church contended was essential because without it the parishioners would be discouraged from attending church due to their need to use mass transit or walk through high-crime areas. The court was influenced by the fact that the church itself was a historical landmark. It allowed the condemnation, however, because there would be public parking across the street from the church under the urban renewal plan.

The decision to exclude church property from taking as part of a park, even though the park would surround the church, has been found not to be an establishment of religion.[76] Religious property received protection also in the 1988 Second Circuit decision of *Yonkers Racing Corporation and St. Joseph's Seminary v. City of Yon-*

kers,[77] where the city had been directed through other court proceedings to construct public housing in nonminority areas of the city. It proposed to condemn a two-acre portion of a Catholic seminary's forty-four acre property. The seminary objected, claiming that the tract was necessary to the quiet, reflective atmosphere essential to prepare young men for the priesthood, and pointed out that this was the only seminary in the archdiocese. The court, in a pre-*Smith* decision that applied the compelling state interest test, rejected the city's claim that there were no politically acceptable alternatives to acquiring the seminary's property. It concluded that the city would not have a compelling interest if alternative building sites in nonminority areas were available.

A variation on the government's obligation to provide just compensation for the taking of property occurs when the government, by its actions, actually takes or deprives a landowner of the use of property without going through the formalities of an eminent domain proceeding. This is called "inverse condemnation," and the landowner can sue for compensation even if the government has not condemned the land. One case has found that there was no inverse condemnation in regulatory action that prohibited the construction or reconstruction of property in a flood zone.[78]

Inverse condemnation claims are often raised in landmark designation cases with mixed results. In the 1974 case of *Mayor and Aldermen of the City of Annapolis v. Anne Arundel County,*[79] the Maryland Supreme Court found that preventing demolition of a church was not a taking for public use without payment of just compensation under the state constitution. In the same year, the New York Court of Appeals in *Lutheran Church in America v. New York*[80] reached the opposite result.

E. ADVERSE POSSESSION

Adverse possession occurs when a party is in open, notorious, exclusive possession of property under a claim of right. Ownership of land can be obtained by adverse possession or can be lost to the adverse posses-

sion of another. Adverse possession has no unique application to churches but is an aspect of land law of which they should be aware. One church was pleasantly rewarded by the doctrine. The church was occupying a property under a deed, but there was an earlier deed to another organization. The earlier deed had been unrecorded, however, until the period of adverse possession had expired. The church, although its deed was later, prevailed over the other claimant.[81]

F. LEASES

A lease is a contract for the use of real estate. It should be reviewed by counsel and treated with the same attention to legal rights and obligations as with any other contract. In some states, certain leases, or notices or summaries of them—such as leases for more than one year—may require recording as with a deed. Or recording may be permitted to protect the lessee. Leases may involve rights and obligations that pertain to the use, maintenance, and repair of the premises, insurance for liability or damage to the premises, compliance with zoning or other land-use regulations, responsibility for property taxes, allocation of values in the event of eminent domain taking, and provisions for renewal, termination, rent adjustments, and other financial obligations that will be of the utmost importance to the parties. As with other contracts, leases should not be signed blindly, but, rather, should be read with care, understood, thought through with respect to the needs and objectives of the organization, and reviewed by an attorney. This advice applies with equal force whether the church is the lessor or the lessee.

Any church that owns rental property for any purpose, including future expansion, may be subject to nondiscrimination provisions in the sale or rental of dwellings. Such provisions may ban, among other things, discrimination against persons with children under the age of eighteen or the handicapped, including alcoholics and persons with AIDS. A church may, however, discriminate in favor of persons of the same religion if membership in the religion is not restricted on account of race, color, or national origin, and in the sale or rental of a single-family house if it does not own more than three single-family houses and is not using a real estate broker for the sale or rental.[82]

Churches or religious organizations that own residential rental properties should be familiar with their responsibilities under state, local, and federal law with respect to such leasing. Leasing church property to nonreligious groups, for example, may subject the church to antidiscrimination laws. In one such case, the Minneapolis Commission on Civil Rights fined an organization of the Roman Catholic archdiocese and required it to pay damages for refusing to renew the lease of an organization of gays that refused to acknowledge Catholic teaching on homosexuality. The decision was reversed on appeal, however.[83] Use of church property for nonchurch uses may subject the church to secular nondiscrimination laws.

Leasing church property for nonchurch uses may raise other issues, such as the need to pay federal or state taxes on unrelated business income, discussed in chapter 10, or the qualification of the property for property tax exemptions, discussed in section G of this chapter.

G. PROPERTY TAXES

The notion of exempting churches from taxation did not begin in the United States. Medieval Europe, the Roman Empire under Constantine, and even Egypt in Joseph's time exempted church property from taxation.[04]

All fifty states provide for tax exemption for places of worship, and many of them also provide it for parsonages or other property dedicated to religious use. The constitutionality of the exemption was upheld in the 1970 U.S. Supreme Court decision of *Walz v. Tax Commission of the State of New York,*[85] where the tax exemption was part of a broad class of property tax exemptions that included other non-profit and quasi-public corporations such as hospitals, libraries, playgrounds, and scientific, historic, and patriotic groups. Tax exemption was not considered to constitute

the kind of sponsorship, financial support, or involvement of the sovereign in religious activity that was prohibited by the Establishment Clause. Tax exemption does not need to be justified on the basis of social welfare services or good works performed by many churches. "Few concepts are more deeply imbedded in the fabric of our national life, beginning with pre-Revolutionary colonial times, than for the government to exercise at the very least this kind of benevolent neutrality toward churches and religious exercise generally so long as none was favored over others and none suffered interference."[86] "History," the Court found, "is particularly compelling in the present case because of the undeviating acceptance given religious tax exemptions from our earliest days as a Nation. Rarely if ever has this Court considered the Constitutionality of a practice for which the historical support is so overwhelming."[87]

Specific provisions of state law or constitutions as to the scope and extent of the religious property tax exemption vary, and this is one of the most frequently litigated issues in reported court decisions that involve religious organizations. Exemption may be limited to houses of religious worship or may extend to any property used exclusively for religious purposes. Parsonages are often exempt, but usually only if owned by the church and not privately. Sometimes there are limitations as to the amount of land or the dollar amount that may be exempt. The issue is raised, with varying results, as to whether the exemption of the parsonage applies only if a full-time minister inhabits the building; whether the exemption can include dwellings owned by religious denominations and used by denominational executives, church planners, evangelists, and others; and whether a church parsonage includes dwellings occupied by, for example, ministers of music, church school superintendents and instructors, and youth ministers.

Property that is unoccupied or used for income-generating purposes but not for direct religious activities is usually not exempt, although exceptions exist. For example, property with significant use for recreational activities associated with religious and charitable activities has been found exempt. And the active preparation for construction of a house of worship has been sufficient to permit the exemption in some cases.

Church campgrounds or retreat centers are likely to qualify for tax exemption if the jurisdiction exempts property used exclusively for religious purposes and if all the activities on the property are directly related to such purposes. They may be denied exemption in whole or in part under more limited statutes that exempt only actual places of worship, in cases where nonexempt uses are substantial, or when the campground is not owned or controlled by a church or religious denomination. Privately owned property on a campground will not be exempt even if it is owned by individuals who are members of the church that owns the property. An important line of cases in New Hampshire has found that although the religious property tax exemption is limited to houses of worship, parsonages, and property used for religious purposes, church camps and conference centers can be exempt under a broader exemption for properties owned, occupied, and used for charitable purposes.[88]

Cases involving other religious facilities—such as printing and publishing facilities, regional and national administrative offices of denominations, religious bookstores, church retirement homes, parochial schools, credit unions, recreational facilities, broadcasting facilities, and Salvation Army thrift shops—have reached mixed results, depending largely upon whether the applicable statute limited the exemption to houses of religious worship or more broadly exempted property used exclusively for religious purposes. Statutes requiring the "exclusive" use of property for religious purposes are generally interpreted to mean that the religious use must be the primary use. In some states, a partial exemption will be allowed if the property has both exempt and nonexempt uses.

Church property tax exemption cases continue to pour out of the courts based on both religious and charitable tax-exemption statutes, on the interpretation of "places of worship" and "religious use," and on other statutory provisions in much greater num-

ber than it is practical to summarize here. Recent cases have denied tax-exempt status to a caretaker's residence at a convent[89] and a child care facility;[90] a residential facility for the elderly and handicapped sponsored by a Lutheran organization;[91] unused land for which the church claimed to have future building plans although it had no reasonable expectation of fulfilling them and was not actively working toward that goal;[92] property owned by a nonprofit corporation that published religious materials;[93] low-rent housing operated in connection with a Lutheran nursing home;[94] a training center for religious counseling which the court found was operated essentially as a private practice with only slightly lower fees than in the private sector;[95] property that had been vacated and was for sale but on which some maintenance materials were stored;[96] a parking lot leased to a commercial lessee during the week;[97] and Salvation Army property used for a thrift store.[98]

On the other hand, courts have allowed tax-exempt status to property in which the church's interest was under a land sale contract but title had not passed;[99] an apartment building owned by a religious broadcasting organization and occupied by its workers;[100] a Baptist nursing home;[101] subsidized apartments;[102] land owned as a buffer to a worship center and used for recreational and retreat purposes;[103] a campground used as a place of religious worship;[104] a nursing home, even though one-third of the patients were full-pay patients not receiving Medicare or Medicaid benefits;[105] a religious park used for retreats and services;[106] an apartment building used for missionaries on furlough;[107] land surrounding a synagogue, the utility of which was principally for esthetic purposes;[108] camp property owned by Young Life;[109] and property owned by a trustee in trust for an unincorporated church.[110]

The foregoing cases are illustrative, and different results may be reached in different jurisdictions. It is hard to make generalizations about the outcome of property tax cases, because they depend on the particular facts and circumstances of the use, the language of local statutes, and court interpretations of the statutes.

A church's failure to pay taxes or to take

adequate steps to protect itself may result in the church losing the property altogether. In the 1990 Maryland case of *St. George Antiochian Orthodox Christian Church v. Aggarwal*,[111] that is just what happened. The church received a parcel of vacant land as a gift and assumed that it was tax exempt. The legal name of the church on the deed was different than the name the church used in the telephone directory and on its church sign. Tax bills were sent to the title insurance company, which was the only address on the deed. Taxes went unpaid, and a tax sale resulted. The church was unaware of the tax sale because it had received no notice of the sale, although notice had been published in a newspaper. The court had little sympathy for the church because (1) the vacant land was not tax exempt under Maryland law, and its assumptions in that regard were not reasonable; (2) the church had been less than diligent in failing to ascertain its position with respect to the taxes; and (3) the newspaper notice was sufficient as there were no other reasonable means of contacting the church under the circumstances. This case illustrates the hazards of ignorance and of using a different name and address on a deed than that which appears in a telephone directory and is otherwise normally used by the church. This church may, however, have a claim against its title insurance company for failing to transmit the tax bill and information.

Churches and religious organizations often make voluntary payments to municipalities in lieu of taxes, typically in amounts significantly less than the taxes that would be assessed if the property were not tax exempt. These may be negotiated and may or may not reflect such factors as the percentage of the municipal budget devoted to such services as fire and police protection that directly benefit the property owner. The motivation to make such payments may be partly moral, reflecting a feeling that the organization is in fact getting some benefit from the municipality and should, therefore, make some contribution even though it is not legally required to do so; and partly a matter of good public relations which can prove helpful in dealing with local land-use boards and municipal officials often hard-pressed for revenue.

Tax-exempt status has, however, been granted to such organizations throughout our history by constitutional and legislative policy that recognizes the unique status of religious and charitable organizations and the undesirability of subjecting them to the burden of supporting the government. Churches and religious organizations that wish to make a contribution in lieu of taxes should be careful to recognize that their ability to make such a contribution may not always be what it is now, that the contribution should not be made in such a way that the municipality comes to assume it is its due, and in full recognition that the larger society has freely exempted them from this obligation.

REFERENCES

Burkholder, John David. *Church and Land Use Law: A Research Guide* (1987). Available from Christian Legal Society, 4208 Evergreen Lane, Suite 222, Annandale, Va. 22003–9974.

Cunningham, Paige, and Samuel E. Ericsson. *Zoning Ordinances, Religious Uses of Land, and the Free Exercise of Religion.* Available from Christian Legal Society, 4208 Evergreen Lane, Suite 222, Annandale, Va. 22003–9974.

Hammar, Richard R. *Pastor, Church and Law*, 2d ed. (Matthews, N.C.: Christian Ministry Resources, 1991).

Ziegler, Edward H., Jr. *Rathkopf's the Law of Zoning and Planning.* 5 vols. (New York: Clark Boardman Co., 1990).

CHAPTER 9

Copyright Law and the Church

A. SOURCE OF COPYRIGHT LAW

Copyright law is federal statutory law. It is authorized by the language of the Constitution that vests in Congress the power to secure "for limited Times to Authors and Inventors the exclusive Right to their respective Writings and Discoveries."[1] The most recent enactment of copyright law is the Copyright Act of 1976, codified as Title 17 of the United States Code, Sections 101–810. Prior to the Copyright Act of 1976, state common-law copyright law had a concurrent role to play with federal statutes. The Copyright Act of 1976, however, pre-empts most state common-law copyright law with respect to "all legal or equitable rights that are equivalent to any of the exclusive rights within the general scope of copyright as specified by Section 106 in works of authorship that are fixed in a tangible medium of expression and come within the subject matter of copyright as specified by Sections 102 and 103."[2] Hence, almost all considerations of copyright law today are based on the federal copyright law and court interpretations thereof.

B. PURPOSE OF COPYRIGHT LAW

The purpose of the copyright law, as expressed in the Constitution, is "to promote the Progress of Science and useful Arts." It is a recognition, in short, that creators of musical, literary, artistic, and other works entitled to copyright protection require some inducement to carry on their craft; this inducement is the protection of their right to be compensated for the fruit of their labor. Since most persons who engage in such creative work do so as part of their occupation and are dependent on the commercial success of their endeavors to earn a living, creativity would be greatly reduced if artists, writers, musicians, and the like were unable to claim such rewards. Promoting the investment of resources in such creative effort is a matter of public good, fueling the "engine of free expression."[3]

The principle has equal validity and legal effect with respect to creative religious works, whether they are writings, musical works, dramatic productions, new translations of the Bible, or other works protected by copyright. The church community is the beneficiary of the effort and creativity of those producing such works. Worship and understanding are enhanced. Protection of the right of authors, artists, and composers to be compensated for the investment of their time and resources benefits the body as a whole by encouraging such activity.

C. PENALTIES FOR VIOLATION

Apart from the public purpose or moral justification for the copyright law, violations of the law carry potentially severe penalties. Courts have the power to enjoin copyright infringements,[4] to impound materials claimed to have been made or used in violation of copyright law, and, if it is determined that an infringement has occurred, to destroy those materials.[5] In addition, the infringer may be liable for either the actual damages of the copyright owner plus any additional profits of the infringer or for statutory damages of between $500 and $20,000 "for all infringements involved in the action," plus an additional $100,000 if the infringement was committed willfully. The damage award against an infringer, however, is limited to these amounts, no matter how many acts of infringement of a single work were committed by the infringer.[6] Infringers may also have to pay costs and attorney's fees to the prevailing party.[7] Thus, churches and religious organizations have not only the moral compulsion of honoring the law and the self-supporting efforts of those engaged in creative religious expression, but the prospect of significant financial penalties for violation as an incentive to adhere to copyright law.

D. MATERIAL SUBJECT TO COPYRIGHT

Materials that can receive copyright protection are "original works of authorship fixed in any tangible medium of expression, now known or later developed, from which they can be perceived, reproduced or otherwise communicated, either directly or with the aid of a machine or device." They include:

"(1) literary works;
(2) musical works, including any accompanying words;
(3) dramatic works, including any accompanying music;
(4) pantomimes and choreographic works;
(5) pictorial, graphic, and sculptural works;
(6) motion pictures and other audiovisual works; and
(7) sound recordings."[8]

Copyright protection does not, however, extend "to any idea, procedure, process, system, method of operation, concept, principle, or discovery, regardless of the form in which it is described, explained, illustrated, or embodied in such work."[9] In short, there is no protection before the idea or concept becomes fixed in a tangible medium of expression. Materials that may be subject to copyright include books, periodicals and articles appearing in them, poems, videotapes, the music and lyrics (separately and together) of musical pieces, records, tape recordings, hymnals, computer software, cartoons, and translations of the Bible other than the King James version.

E. EVIDENCE OF COPYRIGHT

For works published before March 1, 1989, copyright protection was obtained by placing on the work a defined notice that consisted of the word "copyright," "©," or the abbreviation "Copr"; the year of first publication (with certain exceptions); and the name of the owner of the copyright, an abbreviation by which the name can be recognized, or a generally known alternative designation of the owner, all affixed "in such manner and location as to give reasonable notice of the claim of copyright."[10] Failure to include a copyright notice on the first published copies has, since January 1, 1978, been correctable if the work was registered with the copyright office within five years of first publication and a reasonable effort was made to include notice on future copies distributed. Before 1978, failure to include copyright notice in the first published copies placed the work in the public domain; the omission could not be amended by later registration.

Lack of a copyright notice, even when

required, does not necessarily prove that the work is in the public domain. If the work has been copied illegally and without reproducing the notice (as, for example, might occur in a camp songbook), it is still protected. At best, a new user who innocently takes the work from an illegal publication may have an innocent infringement defense.

For works first published on or after March 1, 1989, the notice requirements no longer apply because the United States then became a party to the Berne Convention. This was an international agreement with the useful purpose of protecting the works of American artists and authors abroad. It required the United States to bring its law into accord with laws of other countries. The changes in the law as a result of the Berne Convention do not have retroactive effect. The copyright notice continues to be required for works first published before the effective date of the Berne Convention changes. And, notwithstanding the fact that the copyright notice is no longer required for copyright protection, affixing the notice is, for later published works, a sound practice and is strongly encouraged by the Copyright Office. If a proper notice appears on the published work, an infringer cannot in most cases take advantage of the defense of "innocent infringement." Regrettably, the new law has the negative effect of making it difficult to know whether a particular work is copyrighted because the absence of a copyright notice can no longer be taken as proof that the work is not subject to copyright.

Regulations of the Copyright Office make specific provisions as to the manner and location in which the notice is to be affixed.

While not a prerequisite of copyright protection, the statute requires the deposit of two complete copies of the best edition in the Copyright Office for the use or disposition of the Library of Congress, with certain exceptions. Failure to make the deposit when requested can lead to a fine.[11] Copyright owners may also register their copyright with the copyright office by depositing a copy of an unpublished work or two complete copies of the best edition of a published work with an application and fee.[12]

F. OWNERSHIP AND TRANSFERABILITY

A copyright in a work is a property right or ownership right that can be transferred like any other form of property. The initial owner is, of course, the author, with an important exception: "In the case of a work made for hire" which includes, among other things, "a work prepared by an employee within the scope of his or her employment" and specially ordered or commissioned works, "the employer or other person for whom the work was prepared is considered the author . . . and, unless the parties have expressly agreed otherwise in a written instrument signed by them, owns all of the rights comprised in the copyright."[13] We have discussed the definition of an employee in chapter 6, and the same principles apply in copyright law. Work created during regular working hours on the premises of the employer and using the employer's facilities is likely to be considered within the scope of employment. Clergy and other employees of churches and religious organizations engaged in writing, composing, or other creative activity which they expect to own should have a written agreement with their employer to that effect.

G. EXCLUSIVE RIGHTS OF THE COPYRIGHT OWNER

The owner of the copyright has certain exclusive rights with respect to the copyrighted work. These include:

"(1) to reproduce the copyrighted work in copies or phono records;
(2) to prepare derivative works based upon the copyrighted work;
(3) to distribute copies or phono records of the copyrighted work to the public by sale or other transfer of ownership, or by rental, lease, or lending;
(4) in the case of literary, musical, dramatic, and choreographic works, pantomimes, and motion pictures and other audiovisual works, to perform the copyrighted work publicly; and
(5) in the case of literary, musical, dramatic, and choreographic works, pantomimes, and pictorial, graphic, or

sculptural works, including the individual images of a motion picture or other audiovisual work, to display the copyrighted work publicly."[14]

H. VIOLATIONS OF COPYRIGHT

What acts violate these exclusive rights of reproduction, adaptation, publication, performance, and display? Clearly, copying is an infringement, and copying includes not only photocopies or other direct reproductions but also handcopies, copies into a different medium as by making a printed work, a transparency, and making only one copy for private purposes. A transformation or adaptation of a work, for example, setting a poem to music or making a play out of a story, is likewise within the exclusive right of the copyright owner. The copyright owner has the exclusive right to distribute copies of his or her work, although the purchaser of a copy is authorized to sell or dispose of a particular copy properly acquired. Exclusive copyright rights also include the right of public performance or display, which means "to perform or display it at a place open to the public or at any place where a substantial number of persons outside of a normal circle of a family and its social acquaintances is gathered."[15] Infringement of the copyrighted work may occur when the work is paraphrased or reproduced in substantially similar form, even if the reproduction is not identical.

A large area of uncertainty exists in cases when small portions of copyrighted material are reproduced. Whether or not an infringement has occurred will depend upon (1) how much of the infringing work consists of copied material and how much of the copyrighted work was copied, and (2) the significance of the copied material to both works.

I. DEFENSES

Not every reproduction, adaptation, distribution, performance, or display of a copyrighted work will be an infringement. Several defenses to or justification for what might otherwise be a copyright violation are discussed below. These are some of the defenses that are likely to be pertinent to churches and religious organizations, not an exhaustive list.

One of the most common copyright defenses, although it is not as broadly applicable as is often thought, is the "fair use" defense. This allows use of a copyrighted work by reproduction "for purposes such as criticism, comment, news reporting, teaching (including multiple copies for classroom use), scholarship, or research." "In determining whether a particular use is fair use, the factors to be considered shall include:

(1) the purpose and character of the use, including whether such use is of a commercial nature or is for nonprofit educational purposes;
(2) the nature of the copyrighted work;
(3) the amount and substantiality of the portion used in relation to the copyrighted work as a whole; and
(4) the effect of the use upon the potential market for or value of the copyrighted work."[16]

Guidelines for the use of books and periodicals exist with respect to classroom copying, use by not-for-profit educational institutions, and for the educational uses of music. They should be consulted where applicable.[17]

A second limited defense permits the owner of a lawful copy or a person authorized by the owner of the copy without the authority of the copyright owner "to display that copy publicly, either directly or by the projection of no more than one image at a time, to viewers present at the place where the copy is located."[18] This permits the projection or display of a slide or transparency that was lawfully acquired; for example, a church that purchased a transparency or slide of a song could project it at worship services or gatherings. The projection of a reproduction of a copyrighted work when the reproduction was not lawfully made or acquired would not be protected, however. Moreover, the privilege of displaying a lawfully made copy does not "extend to any person who has acquired possession of the copy or phono record from the copyright owner by rental, lease, loan, or otherwise, without acquiring ownership of it."[19] For example, the display of a rented video "at any place where a substantial number of persons outside of a normal circle of a family and its social acquaintances is gathered" or that is "open to the public"[20] is a violation unless governed by one of the other exemptions.

A further exception is for the "performance or display of a work by instructors or pupils in the course of face-to-face teaching activities of a nonprofit educational institution, in a classroom or similar place devoted to instruction, unless, in the case of a motion picture or other audiovisual work, the performance, or the display of individual images, is given by means of a copy that was not lawfully made under this title, and that the person responsible for the performance knew or had reason to believe was not lawfully made."[21] It is not clear if this definition would include a Sunday School. This exception does not authorize reproduction of copyrighted materials, only performance and display.

A further important exception for churches is the "performance of a nondramatic literary or musical work or of a dramatico-musical work of a religious nature, or display of a work, in the course of services at a place of worship or other religious assembly."[22] This exception permits choirs, groups, and soloists to perform copyrighted music in church. The work must be performed from a lawful copy, and the exemption does not authorize the reproduction of copyrighted works. It extends only to works of a religious nature and does not authorize radio or television transmission or the duplication and sale of audio or video tapes of the performance.

Another important exception is for the "performance of a nondramatic literary or musical work otherwise than in a transmission to the public, without any purpose of direct or indirect commercial advantage and without payment of any fee or other compensation for the performance to any of its performers, promoters, or organizers." For a performance to be within the exception, there must be no admission charge, direct or indirect, or the net proceeds must be used exclusively for the nonprofit purposes of the institution and not for private gain. In cases of an admission

charge the copyright owner may serve notice of objection to the performance under certain conditions.[23] While this exception authorizes such performances, it does not appear to authorize the making of taped copies of a worship service or performance for use by shut-ins or others.

J. DURATION OF COPYRIGHT

Copyrights do not last forever. For works copyrighted after January 1, 1978, the duration of copyright is for the life of the author or creator plus fifty years. If the work was made for hire or is anonymous, the copyright will last for the shorter of seventy-five years from first publication or one hundred years from creation. The time period is likely to include the duration of any utility of this book.

For works copyrighted before January 1, 1978, the copyright lasted for a first term of twenty-eight years, renewable for a second term during the twenty-eighth year of the first term. Before the Copyright Act of 1976 was enacted, Congress lengthened the renewal term from twenty-eight years to forty-seven years. Renewal is now automatic but certain incentives exist for filing for renewal. Works in which a copyright was obtained as late as 1918 may have copyright protection through the end of 1993. Older copyrighted works, however, may be republished in a revised form with new authorship (such revisions are known as derivative works) and be entitled to a new copyright, which would provide a further duration of protection to the work in question. Works published on or after March 1, 1989, may be subject to copyright protection even though the work itself does not contain any copyright notice as indication to that effect.

K. COMMON COPYRIGHT ISSUES

From this brief review of copyright law, some common church copyright issues can be addressed. Consider the following examples:

1. Unauthorized Reproduction of Copyrighted Music

A sunrise service is planned for Easter morning on a lovely point of land at a nearby lake. The worship leaders want to have the worshipers sing familiar Easter hymns and praise music, but they do not want to go to the trouble of hauling the hymnbooks from the church or risk exposing them to inclement weather. They solve the problem by photocopying for distribution the music they want to use. Have they done anything wrong?

The first question is, Is the hymn protected by copyright? Older hymns may be beyond copyright protection. The fact that it is included in a hymnal that is itself copyrighted does not extend copyright protection to the hymn if its copyright has expired. If the copyright is more than seventy-five years old, it is almost certainly unprotected. No copyright violation occurs if the copied and performed music is unprotected.

The performance of the musical work is not a violation of the Copyright Act, whether or not the work is protected. That is covered by the religious services exemption.

Assuming the copied work is subject to copyright protection, the unauthorized copying and distribution is an infringement unless it can be justified by the "fair use" doctrine. That requires an analysis of four factors:

a. The purpose and character of the use. It is helpful but not conclusive that the use was not commercially motivated. It is not helpful that the use of the work is for its intrinsic purpose and does not add any original or different material to it. Whether the use is, in a more general sense, ethical or equitable is another factor and may be viewed as pointing either way.
b. The nature of the copyrighted work. Certain kinds of works, such as dictionaries and encyclopedias, may lend themselves to fair use more than others. The nature of a copyrighted piece of music cuts against a fair use argument.
c. The amount and substantiality of the portion used in relation to the copyrighted work as a whole. If the music is copied in its entirety, it is difficult to make a fair use defense.
d. The effect of the use upon the potential market for or value of the copyrighted work. If the music is available as a separate publication or if permission is available for a fee, any copying has an adverse effect on the market. The fact that the piece of music was reproduced in its entirety makes it difficult to defend. While copyrights can be infringed by copying a chorus, a few verses, lyrics without music, or music without lyrics, the fair use argument in these circumstances would be stronger if only a brief excerpt of one stanza of the lyrics was reproduced. On balance, reproducing the entire copyrighted work in this circumstance is likely to be considered an infringement not protected by the fair use doctrine.

How can this dilemma be resolved? The hymnbooks can be brought to the service; a leader can speak the lines in advance to lead the congregation; or singing can be restricted to music familiar enough so that the music and lyrics do not have to be reproduced. Alternatively, churches can obtain authorization from the copyright owner. Music publishers have generous policies with respect to the use of church music. Some grant blanket licenses to churches for a modest annual fee. Contact the publisher for more information.[24]

2. Computer Software and Instructions

A member of the congregation volunteers to provide secretarial help to the pastor. Both have home computers, and it is inconvenient for the parishioner to do all of the work in the pastor's office. To enable the secretary to work at home, the pastor copies the necessary software and the instructions that go with it so the parishioner can do the work at home. Is there a copyright problem?

This is a plain violation of the copyright law, although there would no violation if the original, properly acquired software were used by different persons at different places and times. Nor is it a violation to make a single, backup copy of the software for archival purposes, provided that archival copies are destroyed if the continued possession of the computer program should cease to be rightful. And it is not an infringement to make a new copy or adaptation "as an essential step of the utilization of the computer program in conjunction with a machine and that it is used in no other manner" (for example, to input software into the computer's random access memory). This must be done by the owner of the software.

Suppose, however, that the church owns several computers. Is there anything wrong with its using a single, lawfully acquired software program in multiple computers, under its ownership, by its employees? The widely held view is that the law permits an owner to make a single copy into a single machine and that the permitted copying must be confined to the smallest single unit of use.[25] If the use of a computer software program is confined to a single computer of the owner, it follows, of course, that the program cannot be loaned out to the church secretarial volunteer to install in a home computer, even for church business. If the secretary's computer is the only one in which the program is used, however, and the program is used exclusively for the business of the lawful owner (the church), there is probably no violation.

Photocopying a copyrighted instruction manual without permission is certainly a violation.

The solution to the copyright problem presented by multiple computers is simple: purchase multiple programs. If in doubt as to whether your proposed use is a copyright violation, you can consult counsel or ask the copyright owner for permission to use the material as you propose.

3. Use of Transparencies

You have started a new church or worship group. It meets in rented quarters and does not own hymnbooks, perhaps because it cannot afford them or perhaps because it is not permitted to store them on the premises where it meets. Or perhaps it wants to use an eclectic variety of praise music that does not appear in a single source, or it believes praise and worship singing is more worshipful if the members of the congregation do not have their heads buried in a hymnbook. Or perhaps the youth group is going on retreat and wants

to have music available at its destination. The church solves any or all of these practical problems or concerns by writing or typing out the lyrics of the music it wishes to use and reproducing them on transparencies which it projects on a wall or screen using an overhead projector. Is this solution acceptable under copyright law?

Making an unauthorized transparency of a copyrighted work, whether it is a photocopy of the work in its entirety or a handwritten or typewritten reproduction of the work in whole or in part, is a copyright violation on its face. This is true whether the transparency is made for regular, ongoing use in a church service, as in the case of projecting lyrics on a screen for use by the entire congregation, or for one-time use, as in the example of making transparencies to take on a retreat where it is not feasible to bring hymnbooks. A fair use defense to the copyright infringement would have more validity in the nonrepetitive-use situation but would be unlikely to prevail if the work was copied in its entirety or if a substantial portion of it, such as the lyrics or chorus, was copied. This is fundamentally the same problem presented by the Easter morning sunrise service example.

One solution to the problem is for the church to purchase transparencies of the music it wants to use in this manner. Another is to obtain the permission necessary to make such a transparency, if one is not available for purchase. A lawfully acquired transparency can be displayed. The church may also be able to obtain permission from the copyright owner for a nominal or reasonable fee to make photocopies of the song for those attending.

4. A Poem in
the Church Bulletin

The pastor or the person responsible for preparing the Sunday morning bulletin is moved by a poem and reproduces it in its entirety in the church bulletin. Is this a violation of copyright law?

The reproduction of a poem in its entirety in the church bulletin is a copyright infringement if the poem is subject to copyright protection. As with hymns, some older poems will no longer be subject to copyright. Reproducing a few lines, a verse from a lengthy poem, or a brief excerpt from a work of prose, may, however, be defensible as fair use, because the purpose is noncommercial and has no effect on the potential market for value of the copyrighted work. The less of the copyrighted work that is reproduced, the better the fair use defense will be. If the reproduced portion is critical to the original work, however, even small excerpts may not qualify as fair use. And, to compound the uncertainty, some cases have found fair use in the copying of an entire work when the value to the defendant outweighed any loss to the owner of the copyright and when in the circumstances it would be impractically expensive to bargain for a license.[26] Prudent and conservative practice would be to seek permission for such use of any copyrighted work.

5. Reproduction of Scripture

Your church camp wants to make the book of Colossians the subject or theme of a week-long study around which the program for the week will be built. You reproduce Colossians in its entirety from a contemporary translation of the Bible as part of a booklet of program materials for use by staff and campers in the course of the week. Is this acceptable?

The King James Bible is in the public domain. Most newer versions are subject to copyright protection, and each copyright holder has its own policies as to the number of verses that may be copied without obtaining permission. The New International Version Study Bible, copyrighted in 1985, for example, permits the quoting and reprinting of as many as one thousand verses without express written permission of the publisher, provided the verses do not amount to a complete book of the Bible or count for 50 percent of the total work in which they are used. If the reproduction of the entire book of Colossians is outside such blanket permission granted by the copyright owner of the version of the Bible from which the reproduction is to be taken, specific permission should be obtained from the copyright owner.

6. Videotapes Used for Childsitting or Sunday School

The church has an adult Sunday School hour before the normal service. It lacks a fully staffed Sunday School or holds Sunday School for younger children during the church worship time. To free parents of young children to attend the adult Sunday School, the church rents videotapes from a local Christian bookstore to entertain the children during the adult Sunday School. May it do so without breaking copyright law?

The use of a video in the normal fashion by projecting the image on a television screen in conjunction with a video cassette recorder is, by the definitions of the Copyright Act,[27] considered to be performance, as opposed to display, of a work. Videotapes are normally copyrighted, and it is a copyright infringement to perform them "publicly," that is, in a place open to the public or where a substantial number of persons outside of a normal circle of a family and its social acquaintances are gathered.[28]

There are several exemptions from the apparent infringement that may be applicable, depending upon the circumstances:

a. "Performance or display of a work by instructors or pupils in the course of face-to-face teaching activities of a nonprofit educational institution, in a classroom or similar place devoted to instruction"[29] is lawful, provided that the copy was lawfully made. It is not entirely clear if this exemption would include a normal Sunday School. While it would seem to be a reasonable construction of the law that it would, in view of the obvious educational function of a Sunday School, this exemption may be limited to institutions that are primarily and directly engaged in instruction, a definition probably not broad enough to include a church, even in a Sunday School situation.[30] The exception would not include pure entertainment functions where there were no face-to-face teaching activities or the teaching was not conducted in a place devoted to instruction. Examples include showing videos to youth groups at retreats or using them to "babysit" young children during congregational meetings or worship services.

b. The religious exemption applies only to the "performance of a non-dramatic literary or musical work or of a dramatico-musical work of a religious nature . . . in the course of services at a place of worship or other religious assembly."[31] While some videotapes might constitute musical or dramatico-musical works of a religious nature, many would not. Literary works do not include audiovisual works. For this exemption to apply, the video would have to be used "in the course of services" at the place of worship or religious assembly. It is doubtful if a purely entertainment showing could constitute "in the course of services," even though it would likely fit within the exemption if it were part of a special service for children or other religious services.

c. If the performance is not "public" (being public requires that it be "at a place open to the public or at any place where a substantial number of persons outside of a normal circle of a family and its social acquaintances is gathered"), it is not a violation. Most churches, however, are probably "open to the public" in the sense that members of the public are free to enter without restrictions other than rules of comportment.[32] If it is not open to the public, a performance is still considered public if it is at a place where a "substantial" number of persons outside of a normal circle of a family and its social acquaintances is gathered. The law gives no definition of what constitutes "substantial."

d. One can argue that the fair use exception would apply, although the case is weak since the work is being used in its entirety and the showing of a videotape to a group may have a negative impact on the commercial market for it.

Unless the rental contract or the video includes a license permitting more than the usual at-home viewing of a rented movie, there is probably a copyright violation. The best resolution of this problem is to obtain permission for the desired use.[33] Before entering into any blanket license to perform videos, be sure that it covers the videos you

intend to show. Even a blanket license does not cover all videos or all uses.

Music, in particular, is a constant source of temptation to violate copyright laws. It may be a violation not only directly to copy music for use by a choir or congregation, including copying by transparencies, but also to make arrangements or derivative works from a musical composition. The right to do this is one of the exclusive rights of the copyright owner. And while the performance of copyrighted works by choir or congregation in a religious service is not a violation of the law as long as lawfully obtained music is used, it is a violation to make video- or audiotapes for resale, distribution, or broadcast. Radio and television stations normally have their own licenses for this purpose. However, making an unauthorized video or audio recording of a copyrighted work is a copyright violation, as is the further sale or distribution of the reproduction. Churches that record services can address this problem by avoiding copyrighted music in a recorded service, turning off the recording devices (or at least the sound recording) while copyrighted music is being performed, or obtaining permission for the recording and distribution.

L. SOLUTIONS TO COPYRIGHT PROBLEMS

1. Know the law and stay within it. The Copyright Office makes available many free circulars on specific aspects of copyright law. Write to Copyright Office, Library of Congress, Washington, D.C. 20559. Many books are available on copyright law, including Richard Hammar's *The Church Guide to Copyright Law*.

2. Secure permission from the copyright owner. This requires contacting the copyright owner directly for permission on a case-by-case basis.

3. Consider obtaining a blanket license to photocopy materials. If your congregation regularly copies music owned by a particular copyright holder, it may be cost-effective to purchase a license to do so. Look closely to see that the license you are considering actually includes the material you wish to copy and covers

the type of use you have in mind. Even a blanket license does not cover all songs and uses. Some organizations, acting as middlemen, have obtained the right from copyright holders to grant blanket licenses to users for a fixed fee to use musical works in copyright holders' repertory for a certain period of time.

4. Obtain a compulsory license to record music.[34] Compulsory licenses are available under certain conditions for the reproduction and distribution of nondramatic musical works by phono records of such works, which includes audiotapes but not videotapes. A recording license typically involves providing an advance notice to the copyright owner, the payment of royalties (mechanicals) at certain fixed rates, and the filing of monthly and annual statements of account with respect to the royalties.

5. Turn off the audio or video recorder when copyrighted music is being performed if the church makes and distributes audio and video cassettes of services containing copyrighted music.

6. Avoid the use of copyrighted music when audio or video recordings are being made of the service.

REFERENCES

Eidsmoe, John. *The Christian Legal Advisor* (Milford, Mich.: Mott Media, 1984).

Goldstein, P. *Copyright*, 3 vols. (Boston: Little, Brown & Co., 1989).

Hammar, Richard R. *The Church Guide to Copyright Law* (Matthews, N.C.: Christian Ministry Resources, 1990).

———. *Pastor, Church and Law*, 2d ed. (Matthews, N.C.: Christian Ministry Resources, 1991).

CHAPTER **10**

Other Government Regulation

A. THE CHURCH
AS FEDERAL TAXPAYER

1. The Exemption from Federal
Income Taxes

Nonprofit charitable, religious, and educational organizations have had federal tax-exempt status throughout our history. This status is a recognition by the government of the charitable functions, social benefits, and useful public purposes performed by such organizations, in some instances including or consisting of services which relieve the government of burdens. The Constitution permits such status, at least as long as it is not confined to religious organizations but includes a broad scope of nonprofit and charitable organizations.[1] Tax-exempt status is not a constitutional right, however, but a privilege. Religious and other nonprofit organizations must take the proper steps to obtain tax-exempt status and can lose it by failure to comply with government requirements to maintain it.

Section 501(c)(3) of the Internal Revenue Code is the principal federal statute that creates tax-exempt status for religious organizations. It exempts organizations "organized and operated exclusively for religious, charitable, scientific, testing for public safety, literary, or educational purposes, or to foster national and international amateur sports competition or for the prevention of cruelty to children or animals." The advantages of recognition as a Section 501(c)(3) exempt organization are (1) the exemption of the organization from liability for federal income taxation, and (2) the deductibility of gifts to the organization by donors, subject to rules governing deductibility discussed hereafter (pp. 157–62).

a. Filing for Tax-Exempt Status

Obtaining recognition as a Section 501(c)(3) organization is accomplished by filing an Application for Recognition of Exemption under Internal Revenue Code (IRC) Section 501(c)(3), otherwise known as Form 1023. The IRS then issues a determination letter granting or denying the request.

The requirement of filing an application for tax-exempt status began in 1969. Organizations formed on or before October 9, 1969, are exempt if they meet the requirements of the IRC without having filed the application. The application requires the organization to submit various documents such as the corporate charter and by-laws, financial statements, and descriptions of proposed activities, and obtain an employer identification number by filing Form SS–4. Applications must be filed within fifteen months from the end of the month in which the organization began for exempt status to be retroactive to the date of founding; otherwise, it is effective only from the date of filing. If filed in advance of actual operations, the IRS may decline to rule until it has a record of actual operations and an advance ruling will only be effective for the first two taxable years plus ninety days.

Certain organizations, including churches and many other religious organizations, are not required to file for exemption. These are:

1. churches, conventions and associations of churches, interchurch organizations of local units of a church, and integrated auxiliaries of a church. Integrated auxil- iaries are those subdivisions of a church which carry out one or more of the church's purposes and are integrated with the parent organization. Men's and women's organizations, mission societies, youth groups, and seminaries may qualify as integrated auxiliaries.

2. any organization that is not a private foundation and whose gross receipts in each taxable year are normally not more than $5,000.

Private foundations are certain 501(c)(3) organizations that are not "public charities" and that are subject to various special regulations relating to such things as investment income, distribution of funds, excess business holdings, and self-dealing. Private foundations are defined as those 501(c)(3) organizations that do not fit within certain exceptions. The exceptions include churches, hospitals, educational organizations, and certain governmental agencies; organizations that are publicly supported, meaning that they normally receive more than a third of their support from grants, gifts, and membership fees, and less than a third from investments; organizations closely affiliated with the preceding groups; and organizations for public-safety testing.

3. subordinate organizations within a church or denominational structure covered by a group exemption letter. The group exemption letter for subordinate organizations enables larger organizations with many financial or administrative subordinate units, which may be separately incorporated, to qualify under a single exemption without requiring each subordinate unit to apply separately for a determination letter.[2] To qualify for a group exemption, the subordinate units must be under the supervision and control of a central organization. Thus the principal utility of the group exemption procedure is for more hierarchical church organizations, in which a central organization exercises general supervision and control over subordinate churches and other units. While group exemption letters have been used for denominations of a more congregational polity, where there is little or no central

supervision and control, such use of the procedure requires a somewhat loose construction of current law. Use of a group exemption procedure when there is in fact no supervision and control may invite ascending liability for subordinate organizations under the principles discussed in chapter 6 and should be approached with caution for that reason.

A group exemption procedure does not automatically exempt incorporated units of a denomination or religious organization just because they are part of an organization that holds a group exemption letter. Such units must be specifically identified to the IRS, which will then issue a letter recognizing a subordinate unit as being within the group exemption letter. Unfortunately, IRS responses to denominational letters updating the list of subordinate units subject to a group exemption typically acknowledge the denominational letter and entitlement of the new units identified in it to coverage under the group exemption letter without specifically referring to the units. Hence, to show that a subordinate unit is within the group exemption letter, one must preserve both the letter to the IRS that identifies the group specifically by name and the IRS response that acknowledges the new unit's status as covered by the group exemption letter. Alternatively, subordinate units can simply file their own 1023 and obtain their own determination letter.

Organizations that are not required to file a Form 1023 to establish recognition of their exempt status may wish to do so anyway. The principal advantage is that they become listed in IRS Publication 78, a cumulative listing of organizations determined to be exempt from federal income tax, which is published annually with quarterly supplements. Donations to an organization listed in Publication 78 will not be questioned by the IRS, and some donors may be reluctant to contribute to a nonlisted organization.

b. Filing Information Returns

Many exempt organizations are required to file an annual information return, Form 990, with the IRS. Form 990 provides certain information on the finances, services, and administration of the organization.[3] Exempt organizations required to file a Form 990 may lose exempt status by failing to do so and may be subject to significant penalties for delinquent filing, including criminal penalties for the willful failure to file. Exempt organizations other than private foundations are required to make their Form 1023s and Form 990s for tax years beginning in 1986 available for public inspection. Churches and many religious organizations are exempt from the requirement of filing Form 990.

Religious organizations exempt from the requirement of filing Form 990 include:

1. A church, convention or association of churches, an interchurch organization of local units of a church, and some church-controlled organizations.[4]
2. A school below the college level that is affiliated with a church or run by a religious order.
3. A mission society more than half of whose activities are conducted in or directed at persons in foreign countries and are sponsored by or affiliated with one or more churches or denominations.
4. Exclusively religious activities of a religious order.
5. A religious or apostolic organization as described in the Internal Revenue Code, Section 501(d).
6. Exempt organizations whose annual gross receipts are normally $25,000 or less.

c. Certificate of Racial Nondiscrimination for Schools

Organizations that operate, supervise, or control a private school or schools and claim Section 501(c)(3) exemption must file an annual certificate of racial nondiscrimination (Form 5578) by the fifteenth day of the fifth month after the end of the organization's fiscal year. Private schools are educational organizations that normally maintain a regular faculty, curriculum, and enrolled body of pupils or students in attendance at the place where its educational activities are regularly conducted. They include schools from the preschool through the college and university level.

d. Qualifying for Exempt Status

Tax-exempt organizations use revenues in excess of expenses for the charitable purposes for which they are organized. These revenues are not diminished by federal taxes on the organization if it maintains exempt status. It has no "profits" to tax and no owners or shareholders who benefit financially from its revenue. For-profit organizations, in contrast, are operated for the financial benefit of their owners and are subject to tax on their profits.

Loss of tax-exempt status would have the most severe consequences for a church or religious organization. Its net income would become subject to federal and, possibly, state taxation. Its contributors and donors could no longer deduct their contributions. It would face the possibility of the loss of a number of other valuable benefits, including property and sales tax exemptions, preferential mailing rates, housing allowance exclusions for its ministers, and the eligibility to establish certain tax-sheltered annuities. Hence, it is important that all churches and other tax-exempt religious organizations be aware of and adhere to the limitations and requirements for maintaining tax-exempt status. There are approximately 460,000 tax-exempt organizations in the United States, and approximately two hundred of them lose their tax-exempt status each year.[5]

Whether these limitations are wise or good policy or, in some instances, even constitutional, is another matter. As long as they exist they must be followed.[6]

To achieve and maintain tax exempt status, the organization must be both organized and operated for exempt purposes.

(1) The Organizational Test

The organizational test involves the corporate governance documents and the formal statements and structure of the organization. The IRS will not recognize exempt status if the governance documents do not limit the organization's purposes and activities to exempt purposes or if they permit nonexempt activities such as substantial lobbying or participation in a political campaign.

The IRS will normally require not only a clear commitment to exempt purposes that is acceptable under Section 501(c)(3) but also provision for the distribution of assets upon dissolution consistent with the exclusive commitment to exempt purposes. This normally means a commitment that assets be distributed to another qualified 501(c)(3) organization. A prohibition on impermissible political activities is also normally required. These provisions will normally need to be included in the incorporation documents, not just in the by-laws.

(2) The Operational Test

The organization must not only be organized for exempt purposes but must actually operate or function for such purposes. Although the statute requires that operation be "exclusively" for exempt purposes, this has generally been understood by the IRS and the courts to mean "primarily." In recent years, much attention has focused on whether religious organizations are being operated primarily in ways or for purposes that disqualify them for tax-exempt status. The principal activities that threaten exempt status are racial discrimination, private inurement, and political activities.

(a) Racial Discrimination. The IRS has focused on concerns about racial discrimination in tax-exempt organizations. In Bob Jones University v. United States,[7] the U.S. Supreme Court upheld the revocation of exempt status for a religious college that forbade interracial dating. The national policy against racial discrimination supersedes any religious conviction, however sincere, on such an issue, and justifies denial of exempt status. Any racially discriminatory policy of a religious organization puts its exempt status in the most serious jeopardy.

(b) Private Inurement. The prohibition on private inurement simply means that the organization may not be run for the personal benefit of persons associated with it. This does not prohibit compensating staff for services, but salaries and other financial benefits to individuals must be reasonable in relationship to the actual value of services performed. Highly publicized compensation excesses in some televangelist ministries in recent years has focused attention on this issue.

How much compensation is too much? There is no clear answer to this question. Many denominations produce salary and compensation guidelines and have minimum standard salaries for newly ordained clergy. These should be consulted by those in denominations and may also be a useful reference for others not subject to them.

In one case, a combined annual income of $115,680 paid to the founder and wife of a religious organization was determined not unreasonable.[8] In another case, the Tax Court determined that there was no unreasonable or excessive compensation in the case of a church that provided a pastor a car and a free apartment; and provided a custodian and a caretaker, who worked twenty hours a week, a free apartment on the church's property, when the church's annual contributions received ranged from $10,700 to $16,200, most of which were used to pay mortgage, utility, and maintenance expenses on the church building.[9] In the PTL bankruptcy case,[10] the court found that during the years 1984 to 1987 reasonable compensation for Jim Bakker would have ranged from approximately $133,000 to $177,000. His actual compensation for those years totaled more than $7.3 million. In reaching its conclusion, the court considered that the salary of the president of the University of South Carolina, who was identified as the highest paid head of a government agency in the state, was under $100,000, and it also considered the testimony of expert witnesses that normal salaries of the most highly compensated clergy would be in the range of $75,000 to $120,000 and that bonuses were almost unheard of in the religious field although fringe benefits could be in the order of 30 percent of salary. The court rejected testimony that the Bible requires that a minister receive 10 percent of all donations and a high priest 20 percent. While few employees of churches and religious organizations are in this enviable position, the message of the PTL case is that compensation in excess of $100,000 for any clergy or other employees of churches or religious organizations should be subjected to a most careful review for its reasonableness. One of the most important factors to be considered in determining reasonableness is the compensation level of persons in positions of comparable responsibility in the religious, nonprofit, and public sector.

Religious organizations should also be aware that unreasonable compensation includes not just direct salary but all financial benefits, including bonuses, use of vehicles, contributions to retirement funds, payment of utilities, housing allowance, any expenditures of organizational funds for the personal benefit of the individual or for which there is inadequate documentation to substantiate that it is a business expense, cash advances or loans that are written off, and other economic benefits.

(c) Political Activities.[11] The involvement of churches and religious organizations in social and moral issues, ranging from abortion to sheltering illegal aliens, may involve taking positions on legislation or political campaigns. The 1988 presidential campaign saw two ordained ministers, Jesse Jackson and Pat Robertson, running for the highest office in the land. Church involvement in and publicized church positions on social and political issues have led to attacks on tax-exempt status by opponents of the positions espoused by the churches.[12] The attacks rest on the ban on tax-exempt organizations participating in certain political activities.

There are two restrictions on political activities. First, an exempt organization is only that organization "no substantial part of the activities of which is carrying on of propaganda, or otherwise attempting to influence legislation." This is sometimes referred to as the "lobbying restriction." Organizations with substantial lobbying activities are considered to be "action" organizations not entitled to 501(c)(3) status. They may be entitled to tax exemption under other 501(c)(3) categories, but contributions to them are not tax deductible.

The second political limitation is that the organization not "participate in, or intervene in (including the publishing or distributing of statements) any political campaign on behalf of (or in opposition to) any candidate for public office."[13]

The lobbying proscription apparently had its origin in the activities of the predecessors of Planned Parenthood, which lobbied and disseminated propaganda aimed at repealing birth control laws.[14] The proscription on participating in political campaigns arose from Senator, later President, Lyndon Johnson's taking offense at the activities of a Texas foundation which provided financial support to an opponent.[15] Both prohibitions have the underlying purpose of preventing organizations that benefit from the receipt of tax-exempt funds from skewing the political process with this advantage. The lobbying restrictions were upheld by the Supreme Court in the 1983 decision of *Regan v. Taxation with Representation of Washington,*[16] which rejected a constitutional attack on the restrictions as a violation of the First Amendment free speech right. The Court found that the restrictions were content-neutral, not aimed at any particular ideas, and did not penalize lobbying but merely denied it a government subsidy through tax exemption and deductions. The Court rejected the idea that the Constitution requires First Amendment rights to be subsidized by the state.[17]

(d) Substantial Lobbying Activities. An organization whose principal purpose is to influence legislative action or whose purpose can only be achieved by legislative action would be considered an action organization and would not qualify for tax-exempt status. The prohibited activity must be activity conducted by the organization. Its members and employees are not prohibited from conducting activities in their private status that would be forbidden to the organization.

The forbidden activity must also constitute "lobbying," which includes attempts to influence legislation by attempting to affect the opinions of the general public or any segment thereof or by communicating with a member or employee of a legislative body or governmental official or employee who may participate in drafting or formulating the legislation. It also includes communicating with members of the organization directly to encourage them to lobby or to encourage others to lobby.[18] Educational activities on issues of general public concern do not constitute forbidden lobbying when they are not advocacy of specific legislation.

Activities that have been found not to constitute lobbying include nonpartisan study, research, or analysis and making the results available to the general public; providing technical assistance or advice to a governmental body or committee in response to a written request; communicating with a legislative body with respect to decisions which affect the existence, powers, duties, exempt status, or deductibility of contributions to the organization (which may include initiating legislation but may not include grass-roots lobbying); communicating with members of the organization on legislation of interest to the organization and its members as long as they are not asked to communicate with legislators or legislative staff or encourage other members to do so; communicating with other government officials when the principal purpose is not to influence legislation; discussing social, economic, and other problems of broad or general concern as long as the discussion does not address specific legislation; soliciting funds for the exempt purpose of the organization, including funds from government grants or funding; and advocacy of viewpoints on controversial issues as long as there is a full and fair exposition of pertinent facts so that the activity is "educational." Revenue Procedure 86–43 lists four criteria to use to determine whether an activity is sufficiently educational to qualify: (1) are significant portions of the communication unsupported by facts; (2) are the facts put forth to support the viewpoint distorted; (3) does the presentation make substantial use of inflammatory or disparaging terms in expressing conclusions more on the basis of strong emotional feelings than objective evaluations; and (4) is the approach not aimed at developing an understanding by the audience, as evidenced by the lack of consideration of their background or training in the subject matter.

Activities that do constitute lobbying include activities connected with voter referendums or initiatives; formulating, discussing, and developing positions to be taken in supporting or opposing legislation; lobbying with respect to legislation that is for the benefit of all citizens; having a primary purpose which can only be achieved by the passage or defeat of legislation; retaining lobbyists; testifying before legislative committees or providing them written submissions; appearances in response to invitations arranged by the organization itself; informal meetings with legislators or committee staff; encouraging others to lobby; and seeking to influence legislative bodies with respect to confirmation of judicial nominees.

Improper activity must be directed at "legislation," meaning action by legislative bodies at any level, including local legislative bodies such as city councils or boards of selectmen and including public referendums, initiatives, constitutional amendments, and the like. It does not include activity directed at actions of the executive and judicial branches, or at administrative or quasi-judicial bodies such as local land-use boards and commissions, school boards, housing authorities, and the like. Action directed at legislation is lobbying no matter whom the communication is directed to. Action unrelated to legislation is not lobbying.

Use of litigation as a tool for achieving charitable purposes is an acceptable exempt activity if directed to a diffuse public interest and conducted in a way that sets it apart from the ordinary practice of law.[19]

It may not always be easy to separate advocacy undertaken on behalf of an organization from the expression of individual opinion. Where speech is involved rather than the application of funds, there are no clear guidelines. Clergy and other leaders of churches and religious organizations would be well advised to make the distinction explicit when expressing personal opinions on political or legislative matters so that the inference that they are speaking for the organization can be avoided. When speaking in a situation in which they would normally be understood to be speaking for the organization or using its facilities and resources to put forward their opinion, as from the pulpit, it would be prudent to avoid statements that could be construed as improper lobbying or advocacy of a political campaign.

Activities done to influence legislation are not absolutely banned to 501(c)(3) organizations. To jeopardize their exempt status, the lobbying must be "substantial." There is no clear definition of "substantial," although it has often been thought that organizational expenditures for lobbying which do not exceed 5 percent of the organization's total expenditures cannot be considered substantial.[20] Courts have not limited themselves to a pure mathematical formula, however, and have balanced political activities against the larger pattern of the organization's objectives and circumstances.[21]

Certain religious organizations, not including churches and their integrated auxiliaries and conventions or associations of churches, have the option of electing to be governed by the provisions of Section 501(h) of the Internal Revenue Code which replaces the "substantial" test with specific dollar limits on expenditures, depending upon the total of exempt expenditures. As much as 20 percent may be spent on lobbying for total exempt expenditures of $500,000 or less, with lower percentages for higher expenditures, a limit on grassroots lobbying of 25 percent of the lobbying amount, and a maximum of lobbying expenditures of a million dollars a year. Minor violations trigger penalties rather than the loss of exempt status. The 501(h) status must be elected by filing IRS Form 5768 during the first year in which the organization wants the election to apply and can be revoked with respect to future tax years.

(e) Ban on Political Campaign Activities. This ban is absolute. It is not subject to any substantiality requirement, as is lobbying. To violate this ban, the organization must intervene or participate in a campaign for or against a candidate for public office. Candidates for public office are not just those running for national or state offices but include anyone running for any elective public office, including such local offices as school boards.

Activities that constitute intervention or participation in a campaign may include such things as publishing or distributing statements for or against candidates; endorsing candidates or slates even if on the basis of a neutral assessment of professional qualifications rather than partisan analysis; opposing a candidate without endorsing the opponent; providing financial support, volunteers, mailing lists, or facilities to a campaign; establishing or supporting a political action committee (a committee not organized by the candidate or party but having the purpose of election of an individual to office); communicating with the public at large to support or oppose certain candidates; and soliciting funds on behalf of the candidate.

Activities that do not necessarily constitute forbidden participation or intervention include making facilities available to persons engaged in political campaigning; providing facilities for a campus newspaper that publishes an editorial opinion; voter education efforts that do not advocate specific candidates or slates; criticizing public officials outside the context of a political campaign; and encouraging voters to concern themselves with ethical and moral standards of campaign conduct.

Voter education efforts that are partisan in effect are suspect and may be considered campaign intervention. Public forums, debates, and lectures where speakers present their views or all candidates are invited and a broad range of issues are covered are not interventions so long as the organization does not indicate its views, comment on candidates' presentations, or indicate bias for or against a candidate. Neutrality is the key to such activities. Voter report cards evaluating candidates' responses to questionnaires or voting records may be impermissible activity if they evidence bias or focus on a single or narrow range of issues and are broadly distributed during an election campaign.

Organizations that wish to engage in activities prohibited by these rules can of course do so by forgoing their exempt status. With respect to lobbying (but not participating in political campaigns), they may also organize a subsidiary qualified under Section 501(c)(4) of the Internal Revenue Code to conduct such activities. Such organizations would need to maintain a primary focus on nonlobbying activities, apparently more than 50 percent. Recognition as a 501(c)(4) organization requires a procedure similar to recognition as a 501(c)(3) organization. The form filed is Form 1024.

Some other suggestions to enable those churches that understand their mission as being to call the public sector to align law and public policy with their understanding of biblical standards of morality and society are:

1. Focus activity on providing education to the organization's members or constituency rather than direct action.
2. Focus on issues rather than on specific legislation or candidates who have taken positions on issues.
3. Speak publicly and consistently on issues of concern to the church, not just when specific legislation or political campaigns are involved.
4. Keep a careful accounting of staff time and funds directed to lobbying activity so as to be able to document that such activity is not substantial.
5. Do not provide a favored political candidate exclusive access to church meetings, mailing lists, or facilities. Avoid any activity that favors or supports or opposes a particular candidate directly or indirectly.
6. Avoid inadvertent violations by developing a theological rationale, consistent with the governing documents of the church and implemented by authorized persons within the church, on any activities that may infringe the limitations on political activities of tax-exempt organizations. Provide for deliberate decision making and review of decisions. When in doubt, act with the advice of counsel.

Churches have been at the forefront of many of the great movements for justice in this country, including the abolition of slavery and the Civil Rights movement of the 1960s. Biblical commands must often be acted out in the public arena. If the religious organization wants to engage in overtly political activities such as supporting or opposing particular candidates for public office, its members or constituency are free to form separate political organizations to do so or to join or participate in other organizations which have that purpose. It need not be done from the pulpit or through the use of the facilities and organization of the church.

2. Unrelated Business Income[22]

Exempt organizations are, despite their exempt status, subject to taxation on "unrelated business income." The tax on unrelated business income is intended to prevent abuse of tax-exempt status by non-profit organizations that are substantially involved in business enterprises and unfair competition by exempt organizations with nonexempt businesses subject to taxation.

Exempt organizations may conduct unrelated businesses and receive unrelated business income so long as those unrelated activities do not become substantial and supplant the organization's primary exempt purpose. Should the unrelated business activity become too substantial, however, the organization's exempt status may be endangered and audits by the IRS may be triggered.

Unrelated business income issues challenge religious organizations to do effective legal planning. Are such activities included in the statements of purpose in their corporate governance documents? Are they organized and managed in the most appropriate manner to deal with tax liability issues? Are adequate records kept to provide the information necessary to relate such activities to the exempt purposes of the organization, to substantiate deductible expenses, or to allocate income appropriately? Should activities producing unrelated business income be segregated in separate corporate entities? Do unrelated business income activities have implications for state income tax or local property tax liability? Sound planning may result in important tax and other advantages and avoid particularly unpleasant consequences. Religious organizations with income should review the structure of their arrangements and the correct legal characterization of these sources of income to determine if they qualify as unrelated business income. Churches with income from debt-financed property should consult counsel for specific advice on their situation. This is an area of technical rules, the specific application of which is important to the result.

To be unrelated business income, the income must be from (1) a trade or business activity, (2) regularly carried on, and (3) not substantially related to the exempt purposes of the organization.[23] All three of the criteria must be met for the unrelated business income tax to apply.

A trade or business is an "activity which is carried on for production of income from the sale of goods or the performance of services."[24] Whether or not a trade or business is involved is determined on the facts of each case, considering such factors as whether or not there is intention of making a profit or producing income; how extensive the activity is and over how substantial a period of time; when the activity began; and whether or not the entity represents itself as being engaged in the selling of goods and services.[25] If the activity is carried out in what appears to be a commercial manner, it is likely to be construed as a trade or business. This may involve evaluation of whether there is competition with profit-making firms, whether profits are made and accumulated, whether workers are paid or volunteer, what formal contractual relationships exist, whether goods and services are sold, and how the organization is controlled.

The requirement that the activity be regularly carried on will not be met by activities that are one-time or sporadic. Activities that are conducted on an annual, seasonal, or intermittent basis may be considered regularly carried on if they are conducted in the same manner as similar activities by nonexempt organizations. For example, sales of Christmas cards or trees may be considered regularly carried-on activities because commercial enterprises engaged in similar activities would carry them on at the same time.[26]

Income from activities that are related to the exempt purpose of the organization will not be considered unrelated business income even if regularly carried on and constituting a trade or business. Wording in the corporate governance documents including the activity as part of the corporate purposes can be an important assistance in relating the income to the corporation's exempt purpose. There must be a substantial and causal relationship between the activity and the exempt purpose; that is, the activity must make an important contribution to the accomplishment of the organization's exempt purposes other than by producing revenue to support it. The size and extent of the activity may be important in evaluating the relationship between the activity and the organization's exempt purposes. Activities conducted on a larger scale than reasonably necessary to perform the organization's exempt functions may result in unrelated business income to the extent that the activities exceed the organization's exempt functions. Operating an activity simply to make profit for the organization would generate unrelated business income.

Identifying activities that may or may not be related to the purpose of a religious organization may involve theological considerations. Churches and religious organizations dealing with such issues should be mindful of the constitutional limitations on courts or governments making such determinations for a church.[27]

Activities that have been considered not to generate unrelated business income include the sale of religious items in connection with a church; the sale of items produced in a sheltered workshop or rehabilitation training program; cafeteria income at institutions where it may be important for people to be able to eat, such as hospitals and museums; sale of merchandise related to the exempt purpose, such as art books or reproductions in an art museum or books in a university bookstore; food services available at a Christian coffee house ministry; and university travel tours if serious educational components are included. Activities that have been subject to unrelated business income include such things as the production of nonreligious items as part of religious life, as by a religious order which provides food, shelter, and necessities to its participants; business operations run by a school to instill a work ethic in its students (although a farm used for such purposes has been ruled to be exempt);[28] university travel tours with no educational component; a tree-planting project by a religious organization; and the operation of a miniature golf course by a youth welfare organization and a health spa by another youth organization where fees were comparable to those of commercial establishments.

Certain other income is exempted from the definition of unrelated trade or business regardless of whether it meets the criteria set forth above. This includes, in particular, the following:

a. Income derived from volunteer work. To meet this exclusion, substantially all the work must be performed by volunteers who receive no compensation for their services. In one case, the IRS and the Tax Court held that providing workers with free beverages while working at a bingo game, a value of about $2.20 per worker per night, was sufficient compensation to take the activity out of the volunteer exemption; but the Fifth Circuit Court of Appeals overturned the ruling on this point.[29] The involvement of paid workers to organize volunteer networks may not destroy the exemption, depending upon the extent of the paid workers' contribution to the total effort. The Tax Court has denied the volunteer exemption where volunteers were provided with room and board.[30]

b. Income from activities engaged in for the convenience of members. This exemption allows activities for the convenience of members and employees, including students or others directly related to or involved in the organization's work. It has been used to exempt such activities as nonprofit laundries serving student and faculty, gift shops, cafeterias, parking lots, vending machines, and university golf courses not open to the public. University stores carrying a broad range of items have been controversial. The sale of items such as books, records, tapes, clothing with university emblems, and toiletries and the leasing of refrigerators and televisions have been found exempt; but the sale of gift items, plants, goods with a life of over one year, and watches is not exempt.

Churches and religious organizations, such as camps and conference centers, that operate shops or stores should be sensitive to whether the inventory carried is truly related to their exempt purposes or is for the convenience of their members, employees, or participants.

c. Sale of donated merchandise. Income from sales of donated merchandise, whether new or used, as in thrift shops, will not generate unrelated business income unless the goods have been refurbished by nonvolunteer labor before sale.

d. Bingo games and games of chance. Bingo games are not unrelated trade or business, if the work is done by volunteers. If done by paid workers, they may still be excluded if they are not operated in violation of state or local law and do not compete with similar commercial profit-making games. Games of chance are excluded from unrelated trade or business also if they do not violate state or local law where played and if a state law has been in effect since October 5, 1983, in the state where the game is played, permitting the playing of such games only by nonprofit groups.

Certain other kinds of income are also excluded from unrelated business income. These include:

a. Passive income (dividends, interest, royalties, rent, and the like), provided they are not financed by debt or received from controlled organizations, even if the activity generating the income is unrelated.

b. Gains or losses from the sale, exchange, or disposal of investment property such as real estate. This exception does not apply if the property is held primarily for sale or is stock in trade, inventory, or cut timber.

c. Rental income is not unrelated business income unless it is debt-financed, received from a controlled organization, or determined in whole or in part by the lessee's net income or profits. There are certain exceptions to the inclusion of income from debt-financed property as unrelated business income that may be important to churches. This would be the case if substantially all of the property is used for exempt purposes; or where real property adjacent to other exempt property has been acquired for use for exempt purposes within ten years (or fifteen for churches) and such use will involve the removal or demolishing of buildings on land; or where income from

the property would be exempt by virtue of the exemption for income from donated goods, the product of volunteer labor, or activities for the convenience of members. Personal property rented with real property is exempt if it is incidental to and in connection with the rental of real property and the income from the rental of personal property is 10 percent or less of the total income. If 50 percent or more of total rents are from personal property, the real property rentals may also be taxed. If unrelated business income services are provided along with the rental, the rental exclusion will not apply.

Leases of excess real property for parking lots will generally not result in unrelated business income unless the organization provides services in connection with the lease that cause the income to lose its passive character. Such services could be, for example, cleaning, providing of attendants, and security services at a parking lot.

Income from church camps and retreat centers is generally within the exempt purpose of the organization and, therefore, not unrelated business income. Income from meals service, vending machines, and camp stores will generally be for the convenience of the patrons and similarly not unrelated business income. Utilization of such an organization's facilities combined with services for a fee to the general public or organizations unrelated to the exempt purpose of the owning organization may, however, give unrelated business income. The problem arises when the property is debt-financed or when services are provided; otherwise, rental income would be passive income not subject to the unrelated business income tax. To show that the use is substantially related to the organization's purposes, it is best if the leasing or using organization has an institutional relationship with the owning organization or if the use includes a significant religious element consistent with the owning organization's purposes. Income generated by nonreligious groups making nonreligious use of property owned by religious organizations where services are provided is generally unrelated business income.

Income from child care or day care programs which contain significant religious components will usually be substantially related to a church's ministry and, therefore, exempt. In the absence of such specific religious training, the program may be considered unrelated business income.

Other areas that may be of specific concern to churches include leases of excess capacity, such as printing or computer use, cemetery income, dues income, publications income, mailing list rentals, affinity credit cards, insurance operations, and sale of advertising. Churches and religious organizations having income from any of these or from other sources not directly related to their exempt purpose should carefully examine their obligations under the unrelated business income tax provisions.

Unrelated business income is reported on IRS Form 990–T, which must be filed if the organization has gross (before deductions) unrelated business income over $1,000. Such organizations must report even if there is no actual liability after deductions. The return is due by the fifteenth day of the fifth month after the close of the organization's taxable year, which would be May 15 for organizations with a calendar tax year.

3. Tax Audits of the Church

Concerned that the IRS was inappropriately aggressive in its investigation of churches, the Congress passed protective legislation, codified as Section 7611 of the Internal Revenue Code, which is effective for inquiries or examinations that began after December 31, 1984. This legislation provides that the IRS may only begin a "church tax inquiry if an appropriate high-level Treasury official reasonably believes (on the basis of facts and circumstances recorded in writing) that the church" may not be exempt by reason of its status as a church from tax under Section 501(a), may be carrying on an unrelated trade or business, or may be otherwise engaged in activities subject to taxation. An appropriate high-level Treasury official means the secretary of the treasury or a delegate with a rank no lower than that of the principal Internal Revenue officer for an Internal

Revenue region. A church "for purposes of Section 7611 includes any organization claiming to be a church and any convention or association of churches." It does not, according to IRS interpretation, include separately incorporated church-supported schools or other organizations incorporated separately from the church.[31]

Section 7611 requires the IRS initially to send a written inquiry notice explaining the concerns which give rise to the inquiry, its general subject matter, a general explanation of the statutory provisions authorizing the inquiry and the applicable administrative and constitutional provisions, and the right to a conference with the IRS before the examination occurs. If the church requests a conference, the examination may not occur until the conference has been held. A further examination notice, at least fifteen days after the inquiry notice, must be sent for the examination to occur. It must, among other things, describe the church records and activities which the IRS seeks to examine, offer to have a conference to discuss an attempt to resolve concerns about the examination, and include a copy of all documents collected or prepared by the IRS for use in the examination, a disclosure required by the Freedom of Information Act.

The examination is limited to the extent necessary to determine if the church is liable for tax and, if so, how much; it may look into religious activities solely to the extent necessary to determine whether the organization is in fact a church. Examination must be completed within two years unless extended by mutual consent or as a result of certain judicial proceedings or failure of the church to comply with a reasonable request for records or other information. The IRS may not take adverse action without a written determination from the appropriate regional counsel that there has been substantial compliance with Section 7611. If no adverse result is reached, the church is protected from an inquiry examination involving the same or similar issues for five years, unless the examination is approved in writing by the assistant commissioner for employee plans and exempt organizations.

Certain procedures are exempted from

these requirements, including criminal investigations, willful attempts to defeat or evade taxation, and knowing failure to file a return. Certain routine inquiries are also exempted from these requirements. Routine inquiries are such things as inquiry into the filing of or the failure to file a tax or information return; compliance with income tax or FICA withholding responsibilities; supplemental information needed to complete processing of an incomplete or incorrect return; information necessary to process applications for exempt status, letter-ruling requests, or unemployment tax exemption requests; information identifying a church that is used by the IRS to update its cumulative list of tax-exempt organizations and other computer files; and confirmation that a specific business is or is not owned or operated by the church. Even if the protections of the statute do not apply, the church can still raise constitutional objections.[32] The statute is not intended to inhibit IRS investigations into tax protestors or tax avoidance schemes posing as religious organizations, such as mail-order ministries.[33] Section 7611 has been upheld by the courts to protect a church when the IRS has failed to demonstrate a legitimate purpose for its tax inquiry or to allege sufficiently a necessity of examining a document sought for a legitimate purpose.[34]

4. What Is a Church?

It is occasionally necessary to determine what constitutes a church under the Internal Revenue law. In the 1990 decision of *Spiritual Outreach Society v. Commissioner,*[35] the Tax Court addressed the issue. The organization in question was recognized as a 501(c)(3) organization and sought to be excepted as a church from being categorized as a private foundation, which had certain adverse tax consequences.

The term "church" is not defined in the Internal Revenue Code. The Tax Court defined a church as follows:

Although fundamental to determining whether an organization is a church, religious purposes alone do not serve to establish it as a church. Equally important are the means by which its religious purposes are accomplished. We take a common sense approach and posit our conclusion on the meaning of "church" in ordinary, everyday parlance. The word "church" implies that an otherwise qualified organization *bring* [*sic*] *people together as the principal means of accomplishing its purpose.* [citations omitted] Thus a church is a cohesive group of individuals who join together to accomplish the religious purposes of mutually held beliefs. "In other words, a church's principal means of accomplishing its religious purpose must be to assemble regularly a group of individuals related by common worship and faith. . . . To qualify as a church, an organization must serve an associational role in accomplishing its religious purpose." Church of Eternal Life v. Commissioner [Dec. 43,028] 86 T.C. 916, 924 (1986).[36]

The Spiritual Outreach Society maintained a facility at which it conducted musical programs on Saturdays, so that people could attend their own churches on Sunday; it had a published schedule of "donations" akin to admissions charges. It also held other events and gatherings, including several retreats where followers of different religions gathered for purposes of meditation, study, and spiritual advancement, and a revival conducted by a guest minister; and it maintained a chapel open to the public for meditation and individual prayer. Musical programs were religious in nature.

The court was of the opinion that the organization did not meet the "associational requirement" described above. It also discussed a set of fourteen criteria by which the IRS endeavors to determine what a church is, finding them helpful but not decisive:

1. a distinct legal existence
2. a recognized creed and form of worship
3. a definite and distinct ecclesiastical government
4. a formal code of doctrine and discipline
5. a distinct religious history
6. a membership not associated with any other church or denomination
7. an organization of ordained ministers
8. ordained ministers selected after completing prescribed studies

9. a literature of its own
10. established places of worship
11. regular congregation
12. regular religious services
13. Sunday Schools for religious instruction of the young
14. schools for the preparation of its ministers

The court recognized that some of the factors were inapplicable, particularly to a newly formed organization, and that the organization met some others. It found that the musical festivals and revivals, even if principally involving religious singing, and the gatherings for individual meditation and prayer by those who do not regularly come together as a congregation for such purposes do not satisfy the cohesiveness factor required for a church.

The IRS's fourteen criteria have been criticized as favoring denominational or hierarchical churches. There are of course many religious organizations that will qualify for Section 501(c)(3) status as exempt organizations, contributions to which are tax deductible, without being a "church."

A number of cases have dealt with attempts by mail-order ministries or individuals with tax avoidance motivation to organize themselves or claim to be churches or religious organizations. Such tax avoidance schemes will fail when challenged and are not further discussed herein.

5 Tax Treatment of Gifts to the Church

Most churches and religious organizations receive much of their income from donations. Deductibility of those donations for federal income tax purposes will be important to many donors, and the recipient organization is often asked and sometimes required to participate in substantiating the deductibility or amount of the gift. Hence, the importance of attention to the requirements for deductibility of charitable contributions under federal tax law.

Charitable deductions are allowed by Section 170 of the Internal Revenue Code. The following seven requirements must be met for deductibility:

1. The gift must be of cash or property. Contributions of cash or property are deductible. Contributions of services are not. Unreimbursed expenses incurred by the taxpayer while performing services for the church, however, may be deducted, such as out-of-pocket transportation expenses, reasonable meal and lodging expenses while away from home, and a standard mileage deduction for transportation costs.[37] Charitable contributions can include any kind of property contributed so long as the donor contributes the entire interest in the property.

Contributions of partial interests in property are deductible only if they fit within certain specific exceptions. For example, the contribution of a remainder interest following a life estate will be deductible. A "life estate" is the retained interest of an owner to occupy a property for life. A "remainder interest" is the right to own the property thereafter. The income tax regulations set forth a method for valuing remainder interests for contribution purposes.

A donation of an undivided interest in property is also deductible although it is only a partial interest. For example, if a donor gives a half interest in a piece of real estate to a church, the value of that interest can be deducted.

Finally, Section 664 of the Internal Revenue Code provides for the deduction of the contribution of an irrevocable remainder interest in property to a charitable remainder trust. This is a device in which the donor puts the property in trust to provide income payments to himself with a provision that the charity will receive the property at some specified future date. Such trusts are subject to specific rules and should be created and used only with the advice of competent counsel.

Partial interests that do not fit within any of these exceptions, such as a donation of rent-free use of a portion of a building, are not deductible.

2. Contributions are deductible in the year in which they are made. Contributions made by mail are considered to be made on the date of mailing. Pledges or promissory notes are not deductible

until actual payments are made, although credit card charges can be deducted in the year that the charge was made. Pre-dating checks or delivering checks after the year end that have been dated and completed before the year end do not qualify as contributions in the prior year, but only in the year of actual delivery.

3. The contribution must be unconditional. If the contribution is dependent on the performance of a particular act or the occurrence of some event, or if it will be voided if some specified future event occurs, then the deduction is not allowed unless the possibility of the future event occurring is so remote as to be negligible.

4. The contribution must be without personal benefit. Any "contribution" for which the taxpayer in fact received some personal benefit is nondeductible. For example, payment of tuition at a religious school or payment to the church or school in exchange for a reduction or elimination of tuition is nondeductible to the extent of the tuition paid or waived. Similarly, payment to a church in exchange for performing a marriage ceremony on the premises is nondeductible,[38] as is a contribution to obtain a preferential position with respect to the purchase of land or a reduction of the purchase price.[39]

Merchandise received in exchange for a contribution will reduce the deductibility of the contribution to the extent of the fair market value of the merchandise. Charities offering merchandise in exchange for contributions are encouraged by the IRS to determine in advance the amount attributable to the purchase of the item and to indicate the purchase and contribution amounts on any receipt or other evidence issued to the donor.

In Revenue Procedure 90–12, issued in 1990, the IRS set forth guidelines to permit charities that offer small items or items of token value to treat the benefits as having insubstantial value so that they may advise contributors that the contributions are fully deductible under Section 170. Benefits received in connection with a payment to a charity are considered to have insubstantial fair market value, for purposes of advising patrons, if the payment occurs in the context of a fund-raising campaign in which the charity informs patrons how much of their payment is a deductible contribution and one of the two following requirements is met:

a. The fair market value of all of the benefits received in connection with the payment is not more than 2 percent of the payment or $50, whichever is less, or

b. The payment is $25 (adjusted for inflation) or more, and the only benefits received in connection with the payment are such token items as bookmarks, calendars, key chains, mugs, posters, or tee-shirts bearing the organization's name or logo. Newsletters or program guides which are not commercial publications and are not available to nonmembers by paid subscription or newsstand sales are treated as not having measurable market value or cost. Certain other limitations apply.

The U.S. Supreme Court's 1989 decision in *Hernandez v. Commissioner*[40] addressed the question of the deductibility of amounts paid to a church for which specific benefits were provided in return. In *Hernandez* the contributions were made to the Church of Scientology for services known as auditing and training. In auditing, a church official acts as a counselor with a counselee, utilizing an electronic device to identify areas of spiritual problems by measuring skin responses during a question-and-answer session. The training sessions are doctrinal courses. Auditing and training sessions were offered, for published charges, for various lengths of basic and specialized sessions, with discounts for advanced charges and refunds available for unused portions of prepaid charges. The Court found that the payments for auditing and training services were not deductible charitable contributions since they were reciprocal exchanges in which the church had established fixed price schedules, calibrated prices to sessions, returned refunds if services were unperformed, given people account cards to keep track of unclaimed services, and barred providing such services for free. Since the benefits or services were not available without the prescribed payment and fees were specified for specified services, the requirement that a charitable contribution be made with no expectation of return benefit was not met.

Contributions to churches for which donors receive benefits, such as participation in worship, preaching, sacraments, counseling, teaching, and the like, remain deductible since there is no quid pro quo exchange in the transaction and the religious benefits are not limited to those who pay specified fees. Payments to religious institutions for such services as education at a parochial school, medical care, or counseling at church-affiliated institutions would not be deductible.

Certain other forms of contributions are more troublesome. The IRS and the Court have upheld the deductibility of pew rents, building fund assessments, and periodic dues; and specified payment for attendance at Jewish high holy day services, tithes for Torah readings, and memorial plaques. Fixed payments necessary by Mormons to obtain a temple recommend or stipends by Catholics for the saying of a mass would seem to be in the same category. If the specified service or benefit would be provided whether or not the specified fee was paid, a fee would undoubtedly qualify as a charitable contribution, but mandatory or specified fees for certain religious services may not, under *Hernandez*, be deductible.

5. Contributions must be made to or for the use of a qualified organization. Qualified organizations include those created or organized in the United States or its possessions, organized and operated exclusively for religious, educational, or other charitable purposes, no part of the net earnings of which inures to the benefit of any private individual and which are not disqualified for tax-exempt status under Internal Revenue Code Section 501(c)(3) by reason of attempting to influence legislation, and do not participate or intervene in political campaigns on behalf of candidates for public office.

Churches and religious organizations whose tax-exempt status has been recognized by the IRS under Section 501(c)(3) will normally be qualified organizations.

To be deductible a contribution must be made to the organization. Contributions directly to individuals are not deductible. The nondeductibility of gifts to individuals was affirmed in the 1990 Supreme Court decision of *Davis v. United States*.[41] At issue were funds paid directly by parents to their sons for the sons' support as Mormon missionaries, a practice encouraged by the church to reduce administrative and bookkeeping requirements and to foster the church doctrine of sacrifice and consecration. The church exercises a great deal of control over each missionary's life and limits supervision over his use of donated funds. A legal issue in contention was whether the funds were "for the use of" a qualified charitable organization. Alternatively, the parents claimed that the payments were deductible as "unreimbursed expenses" incurred in performing services for a charity. The court interpreted the phrase "for the use of" to mean donations made in trust or in a similar legal arrangement. The church's guidelines for the use of the funds or the reasonable ability to supervise them is not sufficient. An enforceable legal arrangement for the benefit of the church is required. In so ruling, the Court was clearly troubled by the administrative difficulties and the opportunities for tax evasion that would be present if it followed the parents' interpretation.

With respect to the parents' claim that the funds should be deductible as unreimbursed charitable expenses, the Court found that such deductions were only allowable for expenditures made in connection with the taxpayer's own contribution of services, not those of a third party. Again, the Court was clearly concerned that any other rule would invite tax abuse.

The *Davis* decision does not affect the deductibility of contributions made directly to churches or mission organizations that designate that a particular missionary be supported by the contribution.

Such designated contributions are tax deductible as long as the church or mission organization has full control of the donated funds and full discretion as to their use to insure that they will be used to carry out the organization's functions and purposes. They would not be deductible if the designation required that the funds be used only for the individual rather than manifesting the donor's desire that they be so used.[42] The sponsoring organization must require detailed accountings from the missionary, documenting amounts, dates, and the nature of expenditures to insure that funds are being used for religious purposes (which would include ordinary and necessary travel and living expenses as a missionary as well as directly religious expenditures). Contributions made to a church that designate a particular missionary not associated with a sponsoring organization are not deductible unless the church exercises the same control over the use of the funds. The *Davis* decision will have the effect of making it much more difficult to deduct contributions for support of independent missionaries.

There is, of course, nothing wrong with making direct payments to individual missionaries or religious workers. Such payments are perfectly proper—they are just not tax deductible.

Contributions made to a charitable organization for the benefit of specific individuals who are selected by the donee organization in a way to insure objectivity and preclude any influence by individual donors in the selection (for example, to support a needy child or family in a foreign country) are allowed by the IRS.[43]

Undesignated contributions to church benevolence funds that are used to assist needy persons, such as the unemployed, families burned out by fire, people with catastrophic illnesses, accident victims, and the like, are deductible. Contributions to such a fund that are intended to benefit a designated individual and use the church only as an intermediary are not deductible. The test is whether the church or organization has full control of the donated funds and full discretion as to their use to insure they will be used to carry out the organization's functions and purposes.[44] The fact that the donor mentions a beneficiary or makes a suggestion or recommendation as to a beneficiary is not necessarily fatal to a deduction if the donor's recommendation is advisory only and the donor understands that the church retains full control and authority to accept or reject the recommendation. This can be established by adopting a benevolence fund policy that gives the organization unrestricted control and discretion of distributions and of communicating the policy to prospective donors.

In Revenue Ruling 83–104, the IRS discussed the deductibility of payments made by a taxpayer to a church-operated private school or to the church that runs the school when the taxpayer's child attends the school. Such payments, even if not designated for the particular child, will only be deductible if "a reasonable person, taking all the facts and circumstances of the case in due account, would conclude that enrollment in the school is in no manner contingent upon making the payment, that the payment was not made pursuant to a plan (whether express or implied) to convert nondeductible tuition into charitable contributions, and that receipt of the benefit was not otherwise dependent upon the making of the payment."[45] The existence of such factors as a contract under which the taxpayer agrees to make a contribution and which insures the admission of the child, a plan allowing taxpayers to pay tuition or make contributions in exchange for the schooling, earmarking the contribution for the benefit of an individual child, or, without other explanation, denying admission or readmission to children of taxpayers who do not contribute will create a presumption that the payment is not a deductible contribution. Other facts that may be significant are the absence of a significant tuition charge, pressure to contribute applied particularly to parents of children attending the school, appeals for contributions made as part of the admissions process, the absence of significant revenues for operating the school other than parental contributions, or other factors suggesting that a contribution policy has been created to avoid characterizing payments as tuition.

6. The amount deductible by taxpayers is subject to certain limitations. For donations to most churches and religious organizations, the limitation will be up to 50 percent of the adjusted gross income of the taxpayer. Donations to certain "nonpublic" charities (i.e., those which do not receive a substantial part of their support from public contributions) may be deductible only up to 20 percent of adjusted gross income. Contributions for the use of a qualified organization rather than to it may be deductible only up to 30 percent of adjusted gross income. Special rules may apply to contributions of appreciated property. Contributions in excess of the ceilings may be carried over and deducted in the following five years until they are used up.

Special rules also apply in the case of "bargain sales," that is, sale of property to a church at less than its fair market value.

Taxpayers whose contributions may exceed the applicable limits or who are contributing appreciated property or engaging in bargain sales with the church should receive tax advice specific to the transaction.

7. Charitable contributions are only deductible if they are adequately verified or substantiated. This means the maintenance of reliable written records demonstrating that the contribution was made and the amount or value of it. Contributions of cash are evidenced by canceled checks or receipts showing the name of the donor, the amount, and date of the contribution or other reliable written records containing this information. For a written record to be reliable it should be made at or near the time of the contribution or as part of the regular bookkeeping procedures of the donor. Reliance on memory or oral information is unlikely to be sufficient to qualify.[46] In one case, the Tax Court allowed notations on a kitchen calendar of cash contributions as an adequate record, the contributions having been substantiated by other corroborative evidence.[47] Con-

tributors who itemize deductions would be well advised to make contributions to churches and other religious and charitable organizations by check rather than cash and to maintain the canceled checks as evidence of the contribution. The donee organizations, for their part, should maintain a record of donations and provide receipts or, in the case of churches receiving weekly or regular donations, periodic or annual summaries to donors. Donors making cash contributions can facilitate this process by using church envelopes.

Contributions of noncash property valued at $5,000 or less must be substantiated by a receipt from the donee showing the name of the donee, the date and location of the contribution, and a detailed description of the property. Churches can list in their receipts the value of the property as determined by the donor but should not specify its value other than to give a general description of the property and its condition. The donor is expected to maintain reliable written records which include the name and address of the church; the date and location of the contribution; a detailed description of the property; the fair market value of the property at the time of contribution including a description of how the value is determined; the cost or the basis of the property; an explanation of the amount claimed as a deduction in the current year if it is less than the donor's entire interest in the property as donated; and the terms of any agreement between the donor and the donee concerning the use, sale, or disposition of the property. If the property has a value in excess of $500, the donor must also maintain written records explaining the manner of acquisition of the property and the cost or other basis of the property immediately preceding the date of the contribution. Noncash property contributions valued between $500 and $5,000 are also subject to reporting by the donor on IRS Form 8283, which must be submitted with the federal income tax return.

Still more stringent requirements apply for contributions of noncash property valued at more than $5,000. The $5,000 limit applies not only to a single item of property but also to similar items donated within the same calendar or fiscal year, the combined value of which claimed by the donor exceeds $5,000. The donor must obtain a qualified appraisal, and must complete and enclose an appraisal summary with the tax return. The donee church or religious organization must sign the Form 8283 submitted with the donor's tax return indicating the date of the contribution and, if it disposes of the property within two years, must file a Donee Information Return Form 8282. The appraiser must also sign the form certifying that he or she is a qualified appraiser. The donor must also maintain records similar to those required for donations of noncash property of a value of less than $5,000. Again, the church's obligation is to sign the part of the Form 8283 that acknowledges the date of the contribution and to file the Donee Information Return Form 8282 if it sells, exchanges, or disposes of the property within two years of the date of the contribution.

B. STATE INCOME TAXES

Most states impose income taxes. Churches and religious organizations, as well as their clergy and other employees, must be aware of their liability and responsibilities with respect to state taxes. Many states follow the federal tax system and simply impose an additional state tax on whatever the taxpayer's federal taxable income may be. Others have state income tax laws that differ in various particulars from the federal.

Religious organizations that are exempt from federal income tax will usually be exempt from state income tax as well, either because the state recognizes the same exemptions as the federal government or because the state has a parallel system that reaches the same result. Likewise, unrelated business income is usually taxable under state income tax statutes, because the state either follows the federal procedure or has a state procedure which is similar.

Organizations subject to state income tax on unrelated business income face an additional complication if the unrelated busi-

ness is generated from activities in more than one state. If each state in which the business was done could impose its tax on the organization's entire income, this would be multiple taxation. Indeed, it is conceivable that an organization doing business in a number of states could owe more taxes than it had income. There are both constitutional and fairness problems with such multiple taxation. The problems are solved by formula allocations in state income tax statutes that form a basis for allocating the income taxable by a given state. Many of these formulas are uniform among the states and usually involve allocating a proportion of the organization's income to each state based on the proportion of its assets, sales, and wages paid within the state.

C. STATE SALES AND USE TAXES

Tangible personal property sales and services provided for compensation are subject to sales tax in most states. There is usually a corresponding use tax assessed against property purchased in another state by a resident of a taxing state for use within the taxing state. The use tax, while difficult to enforce, is directed at residents who seek to avoid state sales taxes by purchasing property in a state with a lower sales tax or no sales tax to avoid the sales tax in their state of residence, where the property will be used.

State sales taxes may exempt sales made to religious organizations, sales made by religious organizations, or both. The exemption for sales made to religious organizations may be limited to sales of property used for exempt purposes, sales to domestic religious corporations, sales of religious materials such as Bibles and hymnals, or items used in religious worship or education. Prudent planning may avoid taxes in some instances. One Minnesota Lutheran church, for example, had to pay a sales tax on purchases of construction materials by its contractor.[48] Although the state of Minnesota exempted sales made to churches, it did not exempt construction materials purchased by a contractor as part of a lump-sum contract with a guaranteed maximum price for labor and materials.

The liability would have been avoided if the church had purchased the materials directly. This illustrates the importance of addressing such issues in construction contracts.

Exemptions of sales made by the religious organization may also be subject to various restrictions. State statutes may restrict such exemptions to sales made to members in furtherance of the exempt purposes of the organization, sales of products not competing with taxable organizations, or fund-raising sales.

Eligibility for exemption generally requires an application and demonstration that the organization is in fact a religious organization. In the 1990 Ohio case of *The Way International v. Limbach,*[49] the Ohio Supreme Court upheld the exemption from state sales taxes of "The Way," finding that it was a church because it had adherents, adopted the Bible as its main source of dogma, propagated a comprehensive set of religious objectives and beliefs that attempted to answer its adherents' religious concerns, conducted services, employed ministers who presided at sacramental ceremonies, operated schools to train ministers, and sent forth missionaries to spread its beliefs. The court also ruled that The Way's sale of tapes and records did not constitute a nonexempt trade or business under Ohio law because, although The Way made some profit on the sale of these items, (1) the sale advanced its religion, (2) the profit was not distributed to individuals but was used to expand its operations, and (3) its prime source of funding was from voluntary contributions.

Two recent U.S. Supreme Court cases address the constitutional issues arising out of state sales taxes from two different perspectives: (1) when state sales taxes may constitutionally be imposed on a religious organization, and (2) when state sales tax exemptions for a religious organization are unconstitutional.

Jimmy Swaggart Ministries v. Board of Equalization of California,[50] decided by the U.S. Supreme Court in 1990, addressed the constitutionality of imposing the California sales and use tax on the religious organization's retail sale of religious materials. The religious organization had held evangelistic crusades in California, at which it had sold religious books, tapes, records, and other religious and nonreligious merchandise. In addition, it had mail order sales of similar material from its out-of-state location, advertised through a nationwide magazine sold by subscription as well as through radio, television, and cable TV broadcasts, some of which were made on local stations in California. The state took the position that sales of religious materials were not exempt from the California sales tax and that Jimmy Swaggart Ministries was required to register as a seller and report and pay sales taxes on sales made at its California crusades. The state also asserted that the Swaggart organization had a sufficient nexus or connection with California for the state to require it to collect and report use taxes on its mail-order sales to California residents. Jimmy Swaggart Ministries contended that the First Amendment exempted it from such taxes but did not contest the assessment to the extent that it related to nonreligious merchandise such as tee shirts, mugs, bowls, plates, pen and pencil sets, bud vases, and communion cups, and replicas of such religious items as the crown of thorns, the Ark of the Covenant, a Roman coin, and prints of religious scenes.

The free exercise argument was based on cases that found unconstitutional flat licensing fees for soliciting and distributing religious literature and for booksellers to sell books.[51] The Court, however, pointed out that the earlier cases found the flat license taxes unconstitutional as a prior restraint on the constitutionally protected exercise of religious liberty but did not free religious groups or clergy from all financial burdens of government, such as income or property taxes, to which other citizens may be subject as part of a general plan of taxation. The Court noted (1) that the California sales and use taxes were not preconditions to distributing a taxpayer's religious message; (2) that payment of the tax did not itself violate any religious beliefs; and (3) that the tax rate was only a small part of the amount of the retail sale and applied to the religious organization in the same way it would apply to a bookstore selling a Bible. The Court also found that the administrative and record-keeping regulations imposed by the state for compliance with the tax law did not constitute such an excessive entanglement between church and state as to violate the Establishment Clause, particularly because it did not require any inquiry by the state into the religious content of the items sold or motivation for selling or purchasing them.

A sales or use tax could still be considered unconstitutional if it imposed a precondition or prior restraint on the exercise of religious beliefs or practices; if it was so large as effectively to choke off religious practices; or if it was not generally applicable but singled out religious organizations for different or more burdensome treatment.

The sales tax is not collected from the organization's revenue but, rather, is added to the price of the product. Hence, it is ultimately paid not by the organization itself but by the purchaser of goods and services. The burden on the organization is primarily one of administration and record keeping, although an organization subject to tax liability for sales or use taxes that it has not collected may have at least a one-time, significant, additional, financial burden until it begins collecting the taxes on its sales from its purchasers. The Court declined for procedural reasons to rule on the ministry's claim that it was not subject to use taxes on mail-order sales because it lacked sufficient nexus or relationship to the state to be subject to the state's jurisdiction for this purpose.

The *Swaggart* decision was unanimous, emphasizing the clarity of the Court on the constitutional principles in question.

Normally some presence in the taxing state other than advertising and mail-order sales is required for a seller to be subject to state use taxes.[52] In a series of cases, the Court has defined when sellers who conduct an interstate sales business are subject to the jurisdiction of other states for purposes of collecting the use tax.[53] At issue is the Interstate Commerce Clause, which requires that taxes on interstate commerce be designed "to make such commerce bear a fair share of the cost of the local government whose protection it enjoys."[54]

Sellers whose sole contact with another state is a mail-order business conducted by United States mail or common carrier lack sufficient nexus with the taxing state to be subject to its use tax provisions: "Those who do no more than communicate with customers in the state by mail or common carrier as part of a general interstate business" are not subject to state use taxes.[55] On the other hand, sellers who have a presence in the taxing state, even if that presence has nothing to do with the mail-order sales, are subject to state use taxes. In the 1977 case of *National Geographic Society v. California Board of Equalization,*[56] the National Geographic Society was held responsible for California use taxes because it maintained two offices in the state that solicited advertising for its magazine, even though those offices had nothing to do with the mail-order sales conducted by the National Geographic Society to California buyers. What was required was simply "some definite link, some minimum connection, between [the State and] the person . . . it seeks to tax."[57] Obviously, any presence in the taxing state of property, employees, or offices that generate or service the sales business to customers within the state would justify imposing the use tax responsibility on the out-of-state seller. General advertising in the state by newspaper, radio, and mail is not sufficient, however.

In the 1992 decision of *Quill Corp. v. North Dakota,*[58] the U.S. Supreme Court held that the constitutional prohibition on mail-order sales was grounded solely on the Commerce Clause and not also, as earlier cases had held, on the Due Process Clause. Since Congress can regulate under the Commerce Clause, future federal legislation could remove or qualify the exemption and establish a national system for state taxation of such sales.

In the 1989 case of *Texas Monthly v. Bullock,*[59] the Supreme Court addressed another constitutional aspect of sales taxes: whether the Texas sales tax exemption, which was granted for religious literature but not for other literature, violated the Establishment Clause. Six of the nine justices held that it did, although no more than three joined in any one opinion on the reasoning.

The *Texas* statute exempted from sales tax periodicals "published or distributed by a religious faith and that consisted wholly of writings promulgating the teaching of the faith and books that consist wholly of writings sacred to a religious faith."[60] Because the Texas sales tax exemption lacked the breadth of the property tax exemption approved in *Walz*,[61] it failed the Establishment Clause test of having a primary secular purpose. Had the exemption included nonsectarian groups and had it had a legitimate secular objective, the fact that religious organizations fell within the perimeter of the group and were benefited by the exemption would not disqualify it. The scope of the group would depend on the secular objective pursued by the legislature in granting the exemption. The exemption limited to religious groups lacked a secular objective, however, and effectively endorsed religious belief. It was, accordingly, unconstitutional. As in the later *Swaggart* decision, the Court in *Bullock* noted that the Texas sales tax was not a flat tax, did not constitute a prior restraint on the exercise of First Amendment rights, and was only a small fraction of the value of the sale and payable by the buyer; hence, it posed little danger to propagation of religious views. Bringing the Texas law into compliance with the Constitution was a matter for the Texas Legislature. It could be done by eliminating the exemption, eliminating the tax, or broadening the exemption to a wide-enough class with legitimate secular purposes for the exemption so that the exemption no longer constituted an establishment of religion.

D. REPORTING OF ABUSE

Concern for the problem of child abuse arose in the 1960s when the "battered child syndrome" was recognized by the medical profession and publicized by the media. Increasing public awareness of the widespread existence of child abuse and the genuine threat to the health, safety, emotional well-being, and sometimes even the lives of defenseless children has led all fifty states to enact child abuse legislation. There is no federal legislation in this area, and the state laws are not uniform, showing wide variance in many aspects of their application. The essence of abuse-reporting laws is to require certain categories of persons to report to public authorities any actual or suspected abuse of which they have knowledge within a fixed period of time after having reason to suspect the abuse. The public authorities are then responsible for whatever investigation or intervention is appropriate to the situation. The person giving the report is generally exempted from civil or criminal liability so long as the report is made in good faith. A person may be subject to criminal penalties for failure to make a report.

Because of the wide variation in child abuse–reporting statutes, it is only possible in a work of this nature to identify some of the issues that need to be understood by persons who may be subject to the obligation to report. There is no substitute for or alternative to each church and religious organization informing itself on the obligations it has in its state and being guided accordingly. Following are some of the major issues.

1. Who Is Required to Report?

Physicians and other health care workers and child care workers or custodians are covered in most states. Health care workers may include, in addition to physicians, psychiatrists, psychologists, dentists, residents, interns, podiatrists, chiropractors, licensed nurses, dental hygienists, optometrists, licensed and unlicensed counselors, public health employees, coroners, and religious practitioners. Child care workers or custodians may include teachers, teachers' aides or assistants, other school employees, day camp administrators, day care workers, Head Start workers, foster parents, social workers, youth pastors or directors, and various public employees with responsibilities related to children.[62]

Some statutes specifically apply the reporting obligation to clergy; the New Hampshire reporting law, for example, includes priests, ministers, rabbis, and Christian Science practitioners among persons required to report.[63] Clergy or religious counselors, even if not specifically referenced in the statute, may be swept up in broad statutory definitions of persons required to report, such as "social worker." In the 1990 state of Washington case of *State of Washington v. Motherwell*,[64] for example, the Washington Supreme Court found that two religious counselors who were not ordained ministers were within the state's definition of "social worker," which was defined as "anyone engaged in a professional capacity during the regular course of employment in encouraging or promoting the health, welfare, support or education of children, or providing social services to adults or families, whether in an individual capacity, or as an employee or agent of any public or private organization or institution."[65] The result was to uphold a criminal prosecution of unordained religious counselors for failure to report suspected child abuse of which they became aware in the course of their counseling responsibilities. The court exempted an ordained clergyman from application of the statute, however, because the Washington legislature had deleted an express reference to "clergy" from the statute.

Some statutes go so far as to include, in addition to the enumerated categories of people required to report, a catchall such as "any other person having reason to suspect that a child has been abused or neglected,"[66] thus removing any limitations and making it necessary that all employees of institutions dealing with children or others who may be subject to abuse-reporting statutes be aware of the reporting obligations.

Statutes often allow permissive reporting of abuse by persons not subject to the mandatory reporting requirements of the statute. Such permissive reporting enables persons who are not required to report to do so and gain the protection of the statute against civil liability if the report is made in good faith.

2. Who Is Subject to Reportable Abuse?

Most statutes will define a "child" or "children," about whom the suspicion of abuse must be reported, as those under eighteen years of age. Some statutes may also require reporting of abuse of elders or other dependent or disabled persons.[67]

3. What Information Triggers a Reporting Requirement?

Under most statutes the obligation to report abuse is triggered by reasonable suspicion or having reason to suspect that abuse has occurred. This does not require absolute knowledge and does not make the reporter judge and jury of whether or not abuse has occurred. Investigation and intervention as appropriate are the responsibilities of public authorities after a report of suspected abuse has been rendered.

Abuse is defined in the statutes and is likely to include such things as sexual abuse, intentional or other than accidental physical injury, and psychological injury such that the child exhibits symptoms of emotional problems generally recognized to stem from consistent mistreatment or neglect. Child abuse is also likely to be defined to include neglect, or neglect may separately trigger a reporting requirement under the statute. Neglect will also be defined by statute and will include such things as negligent failure to provide adequate food, clothing, shelter, medical care, or supervision; being abandoned; or being without proper parental care, control, subsistence, education, or other care and control necessary for physical, mental, or emotional health when the child's health has suffered or is likely to suffer serious impairment. Treatment by spiritual means through prayer, in accordance with the tenets and practices of a recognized church or religious denomination, and by a duly accredited practitioner thereof, is often an exception to definitions of abuse or neglect.

The statutory definitions are often not very helpful in drawing the line as to when an obligation to report is triggered. Pastors and religious counselors often hear about ordinary physical discipline of children as well as situations that may constitute abuse. When are they to report?

While some contemporary social workers and theorists may view any corporal punishment as abuse, differing with the historical notions of parent-child discipline embodied in the adage "Spare the rod, spoil the child," normal spanking of a misbehaving child by a parent who disciplines out of love and not anger will rarely constitute legal child abuse. In many states, statutes make specific provision for such ordinary parental discipline. Most reported child abuse cases involve injurious conduct. For example, beating a child with a belt on the back, arms, and shoulders was considered "malicious punishment" and a violation of Florida law;[68] and beating a child with a belt and hitting the child in the face with a hand that wore a ring, leaving bruises on the legs, thighs, and face, was considered a violation of South Carolina law despite the parents' claim of a religious justification.[69]

Child abuse is not necessarily limited to such egregious cases, however, and acts which might not be abusive taken alone can be part of an overall pattern that is abusive. The prevailing hostility in many state agencies that have responsibility for child welfare toward all corporal punishment of children and especially toward religiously motivated parental discipline creates a potential hazard for those who choose not to report marginal cases. Clergy and other church workers who are subject to a mandatory abuse-reporting requirement should familiarize themselves with the law and consult counsel promptly with respect to the specific situation if they are in doubt as to their obligation to report.

4. Who Must Be Reported as an Abuser?

Some statutes limit the reporting obligation to abuse by parents, guardians, or other custodians. Other statutes may be broader. Again, familiarity with local law is required. Child abuse–reporting statutes have been upheld against claims that they were so vague as to make it unconstitutional for them to be the basis for criminal prosecutions.[70]

5. How and When Are Reports Made?

Abuse-reporting statutes will give specific directions in this regard. Normally, reports are made to the state agency responsible for child welfare, although reports may sometimes be made to other law enforcement agencies. Reports must be made within fixed and *short* periods of time after the suspicion of abuse arises—typically thirty-six or forty-eight hours. Statutes may provide that reports be made immediately by phone with a follow-up written report within a fixed time period.

6. What Is the Potential Liability for Reporting or Failing to Report?

All abuse-reporting statutes provide immunity from civil or criminal liability, at least for reports made in good faith, and some provide absolute immunity. Since the statutes require only the reporting of reasonable suspicions of, or a reason to suspect, abuse, good faith does not require that the reporter have personally concluded that there is abuse, only that he or she has sufficient information to arouse a reasonable suspicion.

Failure to report is a criminal offense punishable by fines and sometimes by imprisonment. Failing to report could also cause civil liability to persons injured by such failure, although some courts have refused to allow such a suit in the absence of any specific statutory authorization.[71] Negligence or recklessness in reporting has been found not to be a cause for a civil suit,[72] although one suit against a reporter of abuse was allowed to proceed to trial when the parents alleged that the report was not made in good faith.[73] Suit has been allowed against a state agency and its workers for negligently interfering with parental relationships by removing children from a home without substantiating the complaint of child abuse by obtaining a doctor's opinion, discussing the matter with the parents, or examining the file, which would have revealed that there had been a prior false accusation of abuse by one of the children.[74]

7. What about the Clergy-Penitent Privilege?

In chapter 5 we discussed the clergy-penitent privilege, which protects the confidentiality of certain communications made to clergy in the course of their religious counseling. Some child abuse–reporting statutes affirm the privilege; others specifically eliminate it; and others do not address the issue. In states whose statutes do not address the issue, clergy who may be within the privilege should determine if communications to them that give them reasonable suspicion of child abuse are communications that would be privileged except for the child abuse–reporting statute. If not, they must report. If they would otherwise be privileged, they should consult counsel with respect to the application of the statute. The clergy privilege normally applies only to being compelled to testify in a court proceeding and may not be in conflict with a mandatory child abuse–reporting statute. The civil liability protection contained in reporting statutes takes care of liability concerns that might otherwise arise from violating a counselee's expectation of confidence.

8. Can Child Abuse–reporting Requirements Be Avoided If They Conflict with the Reporter's Religious Beliefs?

The unequivocal answer to this question, given by the Washington State Supreme Court in the *Motherwell* case,[75] is No. Applying the pre-*Smith* free exercise analysis, the court had no difficulty finding that the state had a compelling interest implemented by the least restrictive means in the child abuse-reporting statute and that there was no violation of the Free Exercise Clause of the First Amendment or of the Washington state constitution. The court was clearly skeptical of the sincerity of the religious freedom argument, because the counselors testified that they sought to address the problem initially through prayer and counseling and to inform secular authorities only when religious procedures proved ineffective. One exhibit in evidence was a memorandum from one of the defendants to all counselors which unequivocally stated that Washington law required them to report suspected child abuse to government agencies. *Motherwell* was a weak case on its facts to make a religious freedom claim for exemption from reporting requirements. Those who can show a more compelling religious belief not

to report may have a better result in other states. While *Motherwell* is binding only in the state of Washington, the *Smith* case[76] will make it considerably harder to make a free exercise argument under the U.S. Constitution. Churches and religious organizations who have a sincere, religiously grounded belief that prevents them from reporting child abuse as required by the statutes in their state should consult counsel in advance to develop an approach to addressing the legal dilemma presented.

9. How Should a Church Manage Its Responsibilities under the Abuse-reporting Laws and with Its Counselees?

a. Train staff members who may be encountering facts that give rise to a reasonable suspicion of abuse in the requirements of the law and how to recognize abuse. This should include all staff engaged in counseling and direct child custodial functions such as teaching or day care, as well as their supervisors and administrators.
b. Resolve religious freedom or confidentiality problems by developing a policy with advice of counsel that is consistent with the church's theology.
c. In counseling situations, communicate to counselees, in advance of counseling, the church's obligation to report abuse. This may be included in a specific counseling agreement or statement reviewed by the counselee before counseling begins that may address other issues in which the normal expectation of confidentiality may not be binding. Develop such an agreement with the advice of counsel. Have the counselee sign it, acknowledging that he or she has read and understands it.
d. If in doubt as to whether a particular set of facts is such as to require reporting, consider the following options:
    (1) Discussing the facts with the state agency personnel to whom reporting must be made, without disclosing names, to obtain their views as to whether or not a report is required;
    (2) Making a report that qualifies your opinion by indicating that you have "reason to suspect" abuse but stating in the

report that you have not formed a personal conclusion that abuse has occurred;

(3) Keep in mind that the responsibility to determine whether a problem that requires intervention really exists is not yours but the public authorities'. Your legal responsibility is only to report your suspicion.

E. SECURITIES LAW

Both federal and state law regulate certain matters pertaining to the sale of securities. The term "security" is broadly defined.: "The touchstone is the presence of an investment in a common venture premised on a reasonable expectation of profits to be derived from the entrepreneurial or managerial efforts of others."[77] Thus securities may include such investment mechanisms as notes, stocks, bonds, debentures, treasury stock, evidence of indebtedness, certificates of interest or participation in profit-sharing agreements, collateral trust certificates, preorganization certificates or subscriptions, transferable shares, investment contracts, voting trust certificates, certificates of deposit for a security, certificates of interest or participation in an oil, gas, or mining title or lease or in payments out of production under such a title or lease, or any interest generally known as a security.[78] Churches and religious organizations that finance anything through arrangements in which people invest with an expectation of return are likely to be dealing with securities.

Federal and state securities laws generally function by (1) requiring the registration of securities subject to the law with certain disclosures and the filing of certain sales and promotional literature; (2) the registration of those who will be selling the securities; and (3) prohibiting fraud, deceit, and misrepresentation in marketing these securities.

Organizations that are organized and operated exclusively for religious, educational, and charitable purposes and not for profit, and no part of whose net earnings inures to the benefit of any person, private stockholder, or individual, are exempt from registration under federal law.[79] Many but not all state laws contain a similar exemption, but some make the exemption conditional or require application and approval. Where registration is required, it generally involves filing a registration statement and providing information required by the law with the regulatory agency, including information identifying the organization, its operations, and properties; information concerning the management of the organization and what compensation it receives from the organization; and information pertaining to the securities offered. It also includes filing copies of sales literature and the like, a sample of the registered security, organizational documents, legal opinions, and financial statements. Registration may be good for a year or may expire when the securities have been sold. Registration can be revoked by the state regulatory agency for such grounds as fraud, illegality, or violation of agency orders. Some state laws that may exempt registration may nevertheless require the filing of advertising literature.

Formal offering literature is usually referred to as a "prospectus" or "offering circular." Guidelines exist for the contents of such literature, which should be prepared only with the advice and assistance of counsel familiar with the handling of such matters.

The exemption of religious organizations from the registration requirements of the security laws does not necessarily extend to an exemption for those who sell or offer to sell the exempt securities. Such persons may be required to register.

Both state and federal securities laws prohibit fraud, deceit, or misrepresentation in connection with the offer, sale, or purchase of securities. There are no religious exemptions from this and the anti-fraud provisions apply whether or not the securities are required to be registered, literature to be filed, or persons selling these securities to be registered.

Satisfying the anti-fraud provisions means more than being truthful in what is said. It also requires that disclosure be complete. Fraud can be committed by omitting important information that investors would want to know as well as by presenting false information to them.

An illustrative case is the 1976 decision

of the U.S. Court of Appeals for the First Circuit in *Securities and Exchange Commission v. World Radio Mission, Inc.*[80] World Radio Mission was a religious organization that engaged in worldwide evangelical religious activities and proselytizing through a radio program and the magazines, books, and pamphlets it published and distributed. In addition to soliciting donations, which were not at issue, the mission raised money through two investment plans. One was a "loan plan" in which interest-bearing notes were issued that paid 8 to 12 percent interest, some with the option of early withdrawal on ninety days notice and others not, with the principal payable at the end of seven years and a minimum required investment of $1,000. The second investment vehicle was called a "land bonus loan plan." In it, the Mission gave a five-year $10,000 note at 9 percent interest with a bonus of an acre of land at the Mission's headquarters in the White Mountains of New Hampshire. It raised nearly $1,400,000 through these plans.

The Securities and Exchange Commission, the federal agency responsible for securities regulation, asked the United States District Court in New Hampshire to enjoin violations of the anti-fraud provisions of federal securities law by the Mission, notwithstanding that the securities were exempt from the registration requirements of federal law because they were issued by a nonprofit religious corporation. The federal district court declined to issue a preliminary injunction (an injunction that would be in effect from the start of the case until it reached a point of finality or was modified by the court during the case). Although it found a prima facie showing of a violation of federal securities law and a likelihood that future violations would occur, the court was concerned about the impact of an injunction on the functioning of the Mission, which, it had concluded, was a bona fide religious organization. The Securities and Exchange Commission appealed to the First Circuit Court, which reversed the district court's opinion and ordered the preliminary injunction.

The First Circuit had no trouble identifying the offerings as securities, despite the Mission's claim to the contrary. It was likewise unimpressed by the claim that the Mission was entitled to First Amendment protection. The sale of the loan plans was not part of the Mission's religious creed, and the securities were offered to the general public, not just to believers. However, even if the offering had been made solely to believers, the promotional literature and 12 percent interest rate belied any claim that the investors were motivated to lend with no real expectation of recovery. "The fact that the investors may also have had religious motives is irrelevant. . . . Having solicited funds on economic grounds, defendants must justify on those grounds. The acts contain no exception for 'in house' deception."[81]

The actual fraud involved was, in its most important aspects, deceit by omission. The Mission had failed to disclose that it had a substantially increasing operating deficit. It had stated that it had "proven over the years [that] we are well able" to "generate revenue enough to pay interest, repay principal and still provide funds for the ministry,"[82] without disclosing that the repayment of previous debt was being accomplished only by more borrowing. As an example of its ability to generate revenue it noted the sale of a piece of literature for $1.25 that was produced at a cost of $.15, but it did not disclose that its actual revenue from its printing operation was on the order of $2,000 to $4,000 annually, a trivial amount in the context of the funds it was raising by borrowing. While presenting this to the court as a "planned deficit operation," the Mission had failed to disclose its planned deficit to those who were investing their funds with it. While clearly skeptical of the Mission's good faith with respect to its conduct, the court found that its state of mind or intent to deceive was irrelevant when actual violations of the securities law were occurring. The court was also unimpressed with the Mission's argument that its assets were sufficient to satisfy all of its investors, because the nature of its activities was to increase the number and amount of investments, and entitlement to a share of the assets of a defunct entity would not be satisfactory protection for an investor who thought he was investing in a going enterprise. The Mission's expectations of future prosperity would also not suffice. Investors are entitled to be fairly apprised of current facts, and dreams or hypotheticals are not facts.

As *World Radio Mission* illustrates, the offering of securities, which may be any form of investment vehicle in which the investor(s) expects to obtain a return, must be approached with full disclosure and advice of counsel to be sure the offering organization is in compliance with law. Failure to do so can subject the offering organization to both governmental action and civil lawsuits by disappointed investors if it is unable to meet their expectations.

F. FOOD AND HEALTH LAWS

Does your church or its affiliated organizations, such as the women's auxiliary or youth group, raise money by selling food? Do you have bake sales? Christmas fairs or church bazaars at which food is sold? Saturday night baked-bean suppers?

If you are selling food to the public, you may be subject to state or local regulation to insure that your premises are safe for the preparation of food for sale. And the government may be able to tell you what you can and cannot sell. One Connecticut Episcopal parish was told that it could no longer sell homemade preserves, jellies, and pickles, although homemade baked goods could still be sold, and chili could be sold only if it was prepared on the premises and not at home.[83]

There is little doubt about the right of state and municipal governments to impose reasonable regulations to assure the safety of food sold to the public. As long as the government is not interfering with religious practices such as communion, the church is subject to regulation by the food and health laws just as are commercial establishments or other nonprofit food vendors. Such regulations may be extensive and detailed. In institutions such as camps and conference centers, there may be state licensing and inspection from the state health or youth services department. The local church, depending on its activities and the source

and extent of regulaton in its state, may be subject to state or local laws administered by building inspectors, health inspectors, or code-enforcement officers. There is no substitute for local knowledge on the source, nature, and extent of applicable food and health laws. If the regulation is unduly intrusive, the best solution is probably to seek a legislative exemption for the occasional fund-raising activities of churches and other nonprofit organizations. Camps, conference centers, and schools that regularly conduct feeding operations are unlikely to receive such exemptions.

Regulation of religious standards for food, such as kosher food, has been found by the New Jersey Supreme Court to be a violation of the establishment clauses of the state and federal constitutions.[84]

G. PUBLIC ACCOMMODATIONS

The Americans with Disabilities Act exempts "religious organizations or entities controlled by religious organizations, including places of worship" from its prohibition of discrimination against the disabled in public accommodations.[85] This broad exclusion protects virtually all organizations interested in the contents of this book from the public accommodations provisions of the act. However, churches and religious organizations that are concerned with maximizing the access to and utilization of their services, especially by the less fortunate, may want to examine their facilities to see what can be done within their means to accommodate the disabled. Employment discrimination against the disabled is discussed in chapter seven.

Other federal prohibitions against discrimination in public accommodations do not have a specific religious exemption. They are unlikely to apply to facilities run by religious organizations, however, since public accommodations are defined as "any inn, hotel, motel, or other establishment which provides lodging to transient guests."[86] Establishments that are not in fact open to the public are not covered by federal law.[87] State laws, however, need not follow the federal standards and must be examined for possibly broader applicability.

REFERENCES

Child Abuse

Child Abuse Prevention Handbook. Available from California Attorney General, Crime Prevention Center, P.O. Box 944255, Sacramento, CA 94244-2550.

Daly, Barbara, "Willful Child Abuse and State Reporting Statutes," 23 *University of Miami Law Review* 283 (1969).

Note: "The Clergy-Penitent Privilege and the Child Abuse Reporting Statute: Is the Secret Sacred?" 19 *John Marshall Law Review* 1031 (1986).

Taxation

Buzzard, Robert A., and Lynn R. Buzzard. *"Render unto Caesar": Unrelated Business Income Tax Liability of Churches and Ministries* (Buies Creek, N.C.: Church-State Resource Center, Norman Adrian Wiggins School of Law, Campbell University, 1990).

Buzzard, Lynn R., and Sherra Robinson. *IRS Political Activity Restrictions on Churches and Charitable Ministries* (Diamond Bar, Calif.: Christian Ministries Management Association, 1990).

Hammar, Richard R. *Church and Clergy Tax Guide, 1992* (Matthews, N.C.: Christian Ministry Resources, 1992). Published annually.

———. *Pastor, Church and Law,* 2d ed. (Matthews, N.C.: Christian Ministry Resources, 1991).

Internal Revenue Service Publication 557, *Tax Exempt Status for Your Organization,* revised, October 1988.

RISK MANAGEMENT ISSUES

CHAPTER 11

Organization and Governance

A. **An Overview of Organization and Governance**
B. **Should the Church Incorporate?**
C. **What Must a Religious Organization Do to Incorporate?**
D. **Governing Structure**
E. **Membership**
F. **Officers, Directors, and Trustees**
G. **Meetings**
H. **Powers**
I. **Merger, Consolidation, Dissolution**
J. **Incorporation of Subsidiary or Affiliated Organizations**

A. AN OVERVIEW OF ORGANIZATION AND GOVERNANCE

Risk management in a church or religious organization begins with the form in which it is organized and the manner in which it is governed. Issues as diverse as control of property and membership, exemption from property taxes or federal income taxes, and insulation from legal liability can turn on forms of organization and government. Chapter 4 discussed the history and contemporary forms of church organization and the general principles of court review of ecclesiastical decisions. This chapter considers whether a religious organization should incorporate, how it should structure its governance, and the responsibilities of its governing body. Managers of religious organizations should be attentive to these issues, not just at their inception but in the ongoing conduct of the ministry's affairs. The forms exist to produce a substantive

result, and the result may depend on adherence to the form.

Choose your form of organization and draft your church governance documents by at least considering doing the following:

1. Identify the theological view of the body regarding church organization. Does it believe itself to be subject to higher church authority? If so, to whom or what authority? If it is subject to such authority in some but not all matters, in what matters is it subject to such authority and in what matters is it not? If it believes particular issues are theologically bound to be determined in particular ways, what are the issues and how are they to be determined? If the church consists only of a local body without any broader affiliation, does it believe that the control of that body should be democratic and majoritarian, or does it believe there should be a hierarchical structure within the local body, for example, a pastor or board of elders whose membership or authority is not subject to democratic vote by the congregation? Do not confuse democratic notions of self-government and majority rule with religious doctrine.

2. Identify the options afforded by the law of the state in which the body is located or, if it is in more than one state, the state in which it will be incorporated. What are the advantages or disadvantages of each available form of organization? Is there anything in the requirements of state law that conflicts with the doctrine or tenets of the church with respect to its own governance? If so, does the state law

permit, or the state or federal constitution require, that the state law be superseded by the organization's own internal governance documents in this particular? Most state laws will provide broad leeway for a religious organization to create its own internal governance and will impose state law only in default of the church writing its own rules.[1]

3. Prepare church governance documents on the assumption that challenging situations will occur. Church governance is not an issue when there is no dispute. It is an issue when there are arguments over hiring or, more likely, firing a pastor; when admission or expulsion of people from membership becomes divisive; when the church splits over whether to join or withdraw from a denomination; when there is a dispute as to the expenditure of funds or undertaking of a financial burden; or when issues of doctrine, practice, or morality are understood differently within the body. In these and other matters in which a church schism divides the congregation, one or the other faction may have to abandon the church building and property that its members have helped to finance. These are the times that it matters what the documents say.

4. Consider including explicit dispute resolution procedures that are consistent with the church's biblical understanding in the corporate governance documents.[2]

B. SHOULD THE CHURCH INCORPORATE?

The answer to incorporation in almost all cases is Yes. Exceptions will be in states in which religious associations are not allowed to incorporate or states in which unincorporated religious associations are offered by state law most of the advantages of incorporation without sufficient correlative disadvantages. In the absence of state law providing otherwise, there are five major disadvantages to being unincorporated:

1. The inability to own property, at least in the organization's own name. Trustee ownership may be a solution to this, but it presents different problems.

2. Lacking existence as a legal person, the religious association cannot sue or be sued. Not only does this prevent the organization from recovering damages from parties who may be liable to it, but it also prevents the organization's own members from suing it for matters for which it might otherwise have liability to them, such as an injury in which the association was clearly negligent and against which it may even be insured. Similarly, the church or religious association cannot sue one of its own members for negligence that damages church property. Members of an unincorporated association are considered to be engaged in a joint enterprise with all of the members and cannot sue the association because it would be, in effect, a suit against themselves.[3]

3. An unincorporated association has no right to enter into contracts. Members who sign contracts for the benefit of the association may be personally responsible for the performance of them.

4. Most importantly, the members of an unincorporated association are personally liable for the debts of the association. That liability may be "joint and several," that is, each member is personally liable for the entire obligation. Obligations for which members may be liable include tort judgments for such claims as personal injury, defamation, or sexual misconduct of a church worker. Suits against churches are common today, and substantial judgments are occasionally rendered. This factor alone is a compelling reason for every religious organization to incorporate unless it is clear under state law that the members of an unincorporated religious association are as insulated from liability for the obligations of the association as if the association were incorporated. In modern corporate law, both business and nonprofit, unlike the historical era of the law merchant and the territorial parishes, the shareholders or members of a corporation are not, by virtue of their status as such, liable for corporate obligations.

5. Finally, corporate organization generally eases issues of succession and perpetuity of existence. While unincorporated asso-

ciations can use governing instruments to address such matters, they lack the formalities of corporate law to fall back on if it becomes necessary to deal with such issues because their own governing instruments fail to address them adequately. Rules of governance, in short, are likely to be clearer in an incorporated organization than in an unincorporated organization, either because of statutes that provide the rules—or at least the rules in default of rules made by the organization itself—or because the formalities of corporate structure encourage the organization to deal with rule-making issues itself.

C. WHAT MUST A RELIGIOUS ORGANIZATION DO TO INCORPORATE?

The particulars of the incorporation process will be determined by the state law under which the body is incorporating. Legal advice should be sought in connection with an incorporation to be sure the procedures are carried out correctly. Typically, the procedure requires preparation of a document which may be known as "articles of incorporation," or "articles of agreement." Articles of incorporation set forth certain identifying information about the organization, such as its name, its period of duration (which may be perpetual), the address of a registered office, the name and address of a registered agent, the purposes of the corporation, and the names and addresses of the incorporators. This incorporating document must be filed, sometimes in duplicate, and with a prescribed filing fee, with the secretary of state of the state of incorporation and sometimes with other officials, such as the town or city clerk of the town in which the corporation has its principal place of business. Upon the approval of the secretary of state and the issuance of a certificate of incorporation, the corporation exists.

Often the religious corporation can specify in its incorporation documents that it is organized for "charitable" or "educational" as well as religious purposes. While the religious purpose should be explicit in incorporation and all corporate governance

documents, inclusion of other appropriate purposes often allows a broader mission or has other advantages. Counsel should be consulted as to any possible disadvantages, and a conscious decision should be made as to breadth of purpose in the incorporation documents.

Organizing a corporation is a creative act. It brings into being a "juridical person," or legal entity, that did not exist before. Although there will be no physical distinction other than the existence of some pieces of paper that did not previously exist, this new legal person can own property, enter into contracts, sue and be sued, perpetuate its existence, organize its governance, and insulate its members from personal liability for its acts and activities.

Incorporation does not end the need to be concerned with the legal requirements of the form of organization. Most incorporation statutes require some sort of periodic reporting to remain in good standing. Religious organizations need to be familiar with the requirements of maintaining their corporate status as well as creating it. Failure to do so may result in involuntary dissolution of the corporation.

D. GOVERNING STRUCTURE

Church councils were held in the third century to avoid uneven treatment of penitents according to who the bishop was. The rules that developed from this are the foundation of canon law.[4] Some trace the origins of canon law back to apostolic times and the Scriptures themselves, citing the Christian legislation set forth in the Pauline letters and the resolution of issues pertaining to gentile converts by the Council of Jerusalem, described in Acts 15.

The Council of Nicaea in A.D. 325 addressed a number of points of practice and discipline, including procedures for the election of bishops, the organization of dioceses into provinces, rules and regulations for clergy, the sacraments, and other liturgical matters. These fundamental ecclesiastical norms were known as "canons," meaning "rule" or "measure" in Greek; and church law has become known as "canon law."

The most current revision of the Code of

Canon Law in the Roman Catholic church came into effect in 1983 and includes 1,752 canons.[5] The Episcopal church and the Orthodox churches have their own canon law. Other hierarchically organized denominations, whether or not they use the term, have documents that constitute church law, for example the Book of Discipline in the Methodist church and the Book of Church Order in the Presbyterian church.

With churches of a congregational polity, canon or church law is not a volume of rules developed over a period of time through the deliberations or promulgations of some higher church body. It is whatever the local congregation adopts for itself as its own rules of discipline, government, and practice. When those rules are developed, whether in the organization of a new church or the revision of long-neglected rules of an old church, the congregation is writing canon law.

In business and nonreligious nonprofit corporations, these rules are called by-laws. By-laws set forth more specific and detailed rules of governance than are set forth in the publicly filed incorporation document. In the local church or other religious organizations, the rules of governance may also be called by-laws, a constitution, a statement of faith, rules and regulations, or other names. Often they are contained in more than one document, although there is no legal reason to do this. It is not important what name is given to them or whether they are embodied in one document or several. They are, or at least contain, the church's canon law. These documents are referred to hereafter as "documents of church governance."

Local congregations often lack the time, personnel, or expertise to develop well-thought-out church governance documents. If they are affiliated with a larger association of churches, they may have access to model rules from the denomination. Too often, they are borrowed from another church with little thought, perpetuated from historical documents that do not accurately reflect the church's current practice or perhaps even belief, or borrowed from nonprofit corporate models that do not reflect the unique religious identity of the organization. To the extent that such rules

look like the by-laws of any secular organization, courts are likely to treat them as such ("if it looks like a duck . . .") and be more inclined to enforce them without concern for the religious nature of the organization. Even secular nonprofit organizations, however, are entitled to interpret the meaning of their own rules in the first instance, as long as they do so without fraud, collusion, or arbitrariness.

In drafting its church rules or canon law, the local congregation has an opportunity to think through what it really believes about itself as a part of the body of Christ, to consider biblical models with respect to church organization and the extent of their relevance to the organization of the church in modern American society, and to address core issues such as faith and doctrine, structure of power and authority, membership, church discipline, and responsibility for the ownership and management of property.

Some issues that should be clearly and unambiguously addressed in governance documents of religious organizations are:

1. Statement of faith. What does the body believe doctrinally and theologically?
2. Purposes of the organization. State this broadly but be clear as to religious purpose.
3. Locus of authority. What are the offices, boards, and committees? What are the duties of each? How do they relate to one another? Where does ultimate authority reside? How are power and authority divided among members, board or boards, pastor, and higher church bodies? Who reports to whom? Is there a religious basis for the division? Consider whether there are different focuses of authority with respect to spiritual versus secular matters. Are routine matters subject to a different authorizing or approval process than matters with a more profound effect on the church or organization? If so, whose approval is required for what? Is the pastor autonomous or subject to a hierarchy or church board, and, if so, in what respects? What acts require membership approval—budgets, election or filling vacancies in pastor or boards, the purchase or sale of property, borrowing money, merger, con-

solidation or dissolution, amending governance documents? Do any require more than a simple majority?

4. Rules for meetings of members and governing boards. What notice is required? How much notice is required? Must it be written? Who gives it? What kind of business requires notice of the nature of the business to be considered as well as the meeting? What is a quorum? What vote will decide a matter? Distinguish between majority of membership, majority of members present, and majority of members voting. Who presides? What records must be kept and by whom? What rules of procedure are to be followed? Can meetings be held or acts taken by teleconference or written consent?

5. Disposition of assets upon dissolution. Does a hierarchical body or denomination have any claim to them? Incorporate IRS requirements for tax-exempt organizations.[6]

6. Members. Who is a member? How does one become a member? How is membership terminated? Include both reasons and procedure. What are the rights and obligations of members? Does the church practice membership discipline? If so, on what basis, and by what procedure? Be clear on the acceptance of conditions of discipline and termination on becoming a member and the theological basis of such procedures.

7. How are the governance documents amended?

Other issues may be suggested by counsel, the organization's circumstances, experience, or theology, or may be mandated by the congregation's denomination.

E. MEMBERSHIP

In churches with congregational polities, ultimate authority usually resides in the membership. Members elect and depose clergy and church-governing bodies such as deacons, trustees, and the like, adopt or amend the governing documents, approve budgets, and authorize the purchase and sale of property. Even in hierarchical churches, members frequently possess some or all of these powers. Determining who is and is not a member and entitled to exercise the power of a member is an important function of the church documents.

Members are typically admitted to a church upon a profession of faith and agreement to adhere to the doctrines of the church and submit to its government. Courts frequently view membership as a contract or implied agreement by the member to the church rules. Churches are well advised, however, not to rely on a new member's implied agreement or to make his or her agreement to church rules and doctrine perfunctory, but, rather, to provide written copies of the church's governing documents with some opportunity for the member to be informed about them. This is particularly important with respect to the expectations that the church has of members and any provision for church discipline or expulsion from membership, the grounds for such action, and who is authorized to take it. Churches can best protect themselves from liability for such matters by being sure that the rules are clearly communicated to members when they join the organization.[7]

Similarly, it is important that a church clearly communicate to its new members what its church doctrines, beliefs, and tenets are and be sure that the new member accepts them as her or his own. When doctrinal issues arise, it will be important that the church has identified its doctrines and has a membership that has accepted them. Loose standards of membership are an invitation to schism when important issues arise.

In congregational polities, a majority of the membership normally governs in matters over which the members have authority, although the church may provide for a "super-majority," for example, a two-thirds or three-quarters vote, for certain important actions. Amendments to the church governance documents, the selection or termination of clergy, church officers or board members, or church members, sales or purchases of property, or consolidation or merger with another body are issues that are frequently subject to super-majority requirements.

Churches that wish to select a different authority structure than majority rule or to deprive members of any authority whatsoever, even if they are not part of a hierarchical denomination, are free to do so. The First Amendment almost certainly protects their right to do so even if state incorporation statutes for nonprofit or religious corporations set forth a different method of governance. A pastor or board of elders that is not subject to majority rule, with the occupancy of the office perpetuated through some means other than membership election, is not unlawful. There is no inherent reason why a church may not establish a hierarchy within a local body, just as larger church bodies have established more broad-based hierarchies.

Any church considering a hierarchical or authoritarian structure within a local church should, however, carefully consider the negative potential of such a structure.

In order to protect the integrity of church decisions, it is of obvious importance to know who the members are. Churches should maintain a complete and specific list of their members, which should be reviewed regularly for accuracy. If calling meetings or other church actions requires written notice to the members other than by posting in appropriate places on the church premises, the accuracy of addresses should be checked regularly as well. If such a written notice to members is required for any purpose, churches would be well advised to include in governance documents a provision that places the burden of notifying the church of a change of address on the member and to be sure that church action can be premised upon the votes of the appropriate percentage of members present rather than all members.

Provisions for termination of membership must be spelled out. Provisions conditioning membership upon participatory activities, such as attendance at services or financial support for the church, are problematic because they may be vague in nature, difficult to police, and bona fide members may fail to meet them through exigencies not in their own control, such as illness or impecuniousness. At the least, members should not be terminated for such vague reasons without being given notice

and some opportunity to explain their reasons. Reasons for termination and the procedure for termination should be clearly spelled out in the church's governing documents and meticulously adhered to. Similarly, if the church practices church discipline, it is imperative that the reasons, nature of, and procedure for discipline be spelled out in church governance documents and that the member be informed of them when joining.[8]

The issue of identifying who is a member most frequently reaches the courts in two contexts:

1. Membership expulsions or termination
2. Disputed votes on church issues in which the result turns on the question of whether or not certain voters were members and thus entitled to vote

Courts are likely to be much more deferential to the church's own determination of such questions in hierarchical churches than in churches with a congregational polity, perhaps from the sense that hierarchical churches have more built-in protections against abuse than local congregations, or perhaps because church governance documents in such churches look more ecclesiastical while church governance documents in nonhierarchical churches often resemble those of nonreligious organizations. Courts are also likely to be more deferential to church determinations of their own membership in cases involving issues other than a member's complaint about his or her own expulsion or excommunication, perhaps because of a sense of a greater need to protect the individual from arbitrary action in expulsion cases.

When membership termination, expulsion, or excommunication occurs, courts are unanimous in recognizing that they have no authority to review the issue if it is based on doctrinal or ecclesiastical considerations. In some states, the removal of church members has been viewed as an entirely ecclesiastical concern and subject to no further review by the civil courts. This position is based on (1) the First Amendment; (2) the contractual concept that a person uniting himself to a church agrees to abide by its rules, regulations, and authority and cannot dispute its own interpretation of them; and (3) the fact that the church itself is in the best position to determine the issues, having more expertise than a civil court.

In many states, however, courts are less deferential and more willing to review membership determinations that are not based on doctrinal matters. Such review is sometimes limited to making a sufficient examination of ecclesiastical authority to determine that the body which expelled the member was properly authorized to do so under the church's government; sometimes it goes further to insure that actions were taken in the procedural manner set forth in the documents with respect to such matters as notice and who was permitted to vote. Courts may, however, examine the propriety of such decisions if it is claimed they are the product of fraud or collusion; and some courts, at least if no purely ecclesiastical issues are involved, are willing to review membership excommunication matters if they affect "civil, contract, or property rights."[9]

The scope of these terms is unclear. Some courts have gone so far as to find that church membership itself is a property right because church members are entitled to the use of church properties, and that the civil rights of members who have been excommunicated were violated because of humiliation, injury to the excommunicated member's character, reputation, or feelings, and the like. Such cases betray a troubling tendency of civil courts to secularize matters of church governance. This is best combated by insuring that (1) governing church documents make clear the religious basis for admission and expulsion from membership; and (2) churches adhere meticulously to their own procedures in such matters.

F. OFFICERS, DIRECTORS, AND TRUSTEES

Most religious organizations are governed by officers and boards of individuals selected from time to time for the positions. In a typical nonprofit corporation, following the model of a business corporation, the members of the organization entitled to vote select a board of directors at an annual meeting; this board, in turn, elects or appoints the officers of the corporation. The officers have certain defined duties but report to the board and are subject to its direction. Board elections are often staggered so that one-third of the board, for example, is elected at each annual meeting to insure continuity and experience on the board. In churches, the function of the board of directors may be filled by a board or committee of a different name, or it may be divided between or among more than one body. The governing board or boards may be known as elders, deacons, trustees, wardens, vestry, or by some other term. In all cases, their manner of selection and removal from office are established by procedures in the documents of church governance and applicable state laws. The selection of church officials in violation of the procedures set forth therein can be challenged in court, as can removal of them. Removal from office can occur for cause, even if no specific provision is included in the church governance documents to that effect; and cause can include such matters as immoral conduct, incompetence, incapacity, and significant deviations from church doctrine.

The power and authority of such church officials to act are as set forth in the church governance documents or state statutes or as may be implied to do the things that are expressly empowered. Occupants of certain offices have inherent power, whether or not expressly granted, to do certain things, such as the inherent power of the president to preside at corporate meetings.

Church boards must normally take action at meetings that are held in accordance with the church governance documents or state statutes. The interchange and dialogue at a meeting presumably result in greater wisdom and better group decision making. State law sometimes permits action by written consent of a board without an actual meeting or by conference telephone call, and a board can always ratify retroactively an action taken outside a legal meeting. Meetings must comply with corporate governance documents or state statutes with respect to such matters as notice, presence of a quorum, and the like. As with membership meetings, a careful record should be kept of any action taken.

There have been relatively few cases in which claims of personal liability have been asserted against officers, directors, or board members of religious corporations. However, individuals occupying these positions should be aware that there has been lively litigation of such claims against officers and directors of business corporations, and more is beginning to be seen with respect to nonprofit and religious corporations.[10] Officers, directors, and board members of religious organizations, like those of other nonprofit or business corporations, have a duty of undivided loyalty to the corporation, that is, they may not act for their personal gain rather than in the best interest of the body. They must manage the corporation for its best interest and may be liable for disregarding it. They should not receive loans from the corporation or vote to grant them to other organizational insiders, at least without specific advice of counsel as to the propriety of the transaction. They should not induce the organization to enter into transactions in which they (or a business in which they have an interest) benefit without both full disclosure, insuring the transaction is fair and reasonable, and a proper authorizing vote from which they abstain.

Officers, directors, and board members also have a duty of care to the organization. They are not, however, individually liable for the debts or liabilities of the corporation unless they arise from a wrong that is personally committed by the individual. Judgments, votes, and decisions that are made in a good faith belief that they are in the best interest of the organization, after reasonable inquiry, and with such care as an ordinarily prudent person would take in a similar position under like circumstances do not render the individual liable even if they turn out poorly. Decisions not made by this standard can lead to liability.

Individuals who sign contracts or obligations on behalf of the organization, however, should be careful to do so expressly in their representative capacity, for example, "John Jones, as President of First Church Corporation" or "First Church Corporation by John Jones, President," so that no claim can be made that they are personally liable.

Individuals who occupy positions of responsibility in church or religious corporations should inform themselves of the responsibilities of their position and carry them out in good faith to the best of their judgment. Their judgments should be independent. They should not rubber-stamp the recommendations or decisions of the pastor, executive director, or staff without inquiry or information adequate to justify them. It is unwise, and an invitation to personal as well as organizational liability, for religious organizations (or any other) to be governed by boards that are obsequious or deferential to a strong executive figure. Nor should religious organizations be family corporations in which most members of the governing body are related. Independent judgment, exercised after appropriate inquiry in good faith, as the board member believes is in the best interest of the organization and its members, is the standard of conduct for a board member. Failure to so act may give rise to claims against individual officers, directors, or board members by public authorities, members, or creditors for neglect of the duties of their office. Such officeholders turn a blind eye to wrongdoing at their personal risk.

Governing officers and board members should be particularly alert to the management of corporate assets to insure that they are not being misused or misapplied. They should see that money handling is done with safeguards to protect the handlers against temptation and preserve organizational integrity. Many a church has discovered that a trusted treasurer who handled funds without supervision or controls fell victim to the opportunity of circumstance and pilfered thousands of dollars over the years. Such situations put the organization and its managers in the most difficult of dilemmas.

These situations occur with distressing frequency and are avoidable. A few simple steps should do. First, all cash (such as collection plate receipts) should be counted, handled, and accounted for by at least two unrelated people (who are also unrelated to the treasurer) working together. Second, all expenditures should be documented with receipts. Minor petty cash needs that may be allowed by board approval for the practical functioning of an office may be accounted for less formally. Reimbursement of expenses should always be based on documented receipts or written records of the date, nature, and business purpose of the expenses. Assume your records will be examined by the IRS or state attorney general. Third, the treasurer's bookkeeping procedures should be set up with the advice of an accountant to reflect good standard accounting and bookkeeping practices. Fourth, the books should be audited at least annually. This does not necessarily entail an expensive audit by an accounting firm. The board can have its own audit committee do the work, with some advice from an accountant, if needed, to get started. The important thing is to have a regular, independent review of the books to be sure they are accurate and that funds are being used for proper authorized purposes. Fifth, the organization should have an annual budget, approved by the board or membership as called for in its governance documents; and the budget should be monitored regularly and adhered to unless deviations are authorized by the body that approved it. Sixth, the board should examine budgets, treasurer's reports, and audit committee reports with diligence and should follow up on questionable items until satisfied. Seventh, it may be prudent to require two signatures on checks. Eighth, the treasurer can be bonded (insured) for faithful performance of duty.

The larger the organization, of course, the more internal controls are needed, the more likely inside or outside auditors and accounting services will be employed, and the more removed the board will be from the details of the system. Board responsibility then will be to insure that the organization has put in place sufficient controls and oversight to assure proper functioning through inside and outside auditors.

Specific situations should receive special attention. Funds given for specific purposes must be used for the purposes given.[11] Funds should not be expended or committed unless available. General funds should be used only for corporate purposes, never for private benefit or purposes other than those of the organization. Requirements for federal and local tax-exempt status should be rigorously respected.[12] Borrowing or deferred-giving devices to raise money should be done only with advice of counsel, careful attention to state and federal law, and protection of rights and expectations of lenders or donors. Securities law poses special problems and potential liabilities for individuals as well as organizations.[13] Organizations involved in profit-making activities should be particularly alert to appropriate forms of organization, tax requirements, and management necessities.[14]

In most states, some sort of public financial reporting is required. While religious organizations are commonly exempt from such reporting by legislative accommodation or for First Amendment reasons, they may become, or choose to become, subject to it, to receive either a benefit for which reporting is required, such as property tax exemptions, or constitutionally permissible governmental funding for nonreligious programs.[15] With such reporting comes accountability. If reports are inaccurate, public authorities may have remedies. And, whether or not such reporting is required or made, there is no doubt public authorities have the authority to act against religious organizations in cases of fraud. While the truth of religious doctrine cannot be made a basis of a fraud claim,[16] religious claims are not allowed to shield plain dishonesty. And in such cases, even personally innocent officers or directors who naively accepted someone else's assurance that all was well in the organizational bank account may find themselves the subject of a claim for reimbursement because they did not carry out the legal duties of the position with which they were entrusted.

The following excerpt from the opinion of the Bankruptcy Court in South Carolina in the PTL matter summarizes the obligation of corporate officers or directors:

> Good faith requires the undivided loyalty of a corporate director or officer to the corporation and such a duty of loyalty prohibits the director or an officer, as a fiduciary, from using this position of trust for his own personal gain to the detriment of the corporation. In this instance, there are no shareholders of the corporation; however, even though there are no shareholders, the officers and directors still hold a fiduciary obliga-

tion to manage the corporation in its best interest and not to the detriment of the corporation itself.[17]

The duty of the officers and directors in that case was violated by failing to inform the board of the true financial position of the corporation and to act accordingly, failing to supervise other officers and directors, failing to prevent the depletion of corporate assets, and violating the prohibition against self-dealing. In reaching its determination that the acts in question were not mere mistakes in judgment but gross mismanagement and neglect of the affairs of the corporation, the court cited such facts as the failure to require bids on construction projects; allowing capital expenditures to greatly exceed estimates despite warnings; rejecting warnings from financial officers about the dangers of debt financing; granting or accepting bonuses during periods of financial hardship of the organization; writing checks in excess of money on the books to cover them; persistent operation of programs at a loss; and a general failure to give attention to financial matters. The case, while extreme, illustrates the duties of good faith, due care, and loyalty owed by an officer or director to the corporation and demonstrates that persons occupying those positions can be legally accountable for their neglect. The court found that board members of nonprofit corporations "are liable for losses occasioned by their negligent mismanagement."[18]

The PTL case involved egregious conduct, but the principles involved can be applied in much less shocking circumstances. Another circumstance in which the law provides for liability of responsible officers and directors is when an organization, including a religious nonprofit organization, fails to pay withheld income taxes and the employees' share of FICA taxes to the IRS. Persons responsible for paying the money who willfully fail to do so are liable for the full amount under Section 6672 of the Internal Revenue Code. In order to be liable, the individual must be a responsible person, that is, one who is under a duty to collect, account for, and pay over the taxes; and the failure to pay the taxes must be willful. In one case, the court found four officers of a church-related charitable organization to be liable for more than $230,000 of unpaid taxes. The individuals were responsible persons within the meaning of the law, because they were both directors and officers, had authority to sign payroll and other checks, and were involved in routine business matters, including corporate funding, bookkeeping, salaries, hiring, and firing. That the corporation was nonprofit and the services were uncompensated was of no aid to them. They were also found to have acted willfully in the sense that the failure to remit funds to the IRS was voluntary, conscious, intentional, and not an accidental decision, notwithstanding the absence of any evil motive or intent to defraud: "The failure to investigate or to correct mismanagement after having notice that withheld taxes have not been remitted to the Government is deemed to be willful conduct."[19] Many church officers and directors are potentially liable for unpaid withheld federal income and Social Security taxes under this statutory interpretation.

Most states in recent years have enacted legislation of some sort to limit the liability of officers and directors of religious and other nonprofit corporations. Other state statutes allow corporations to indemnify officers and directors for personal liability under some circumstances, in both profit and nonprofit corporations. Specific votes or by-law provisions may be needed for indemnification.

There is no standard form for these statutes. In some states, liability-limiting statutes may protect all volunteers, in others only officers and directors of churches incorporated under the general, nonprofit corporation law. In some instances, the directors and officers must be uncompensated to be protected, which may be a reason to specify that the compensation of a pastor who is also an officer or board member of the church is entirely for pastoral duties and not for acting as an officer or director. Exceptions for conduct such as gross negligence or willful and wanton conduct are common.

Most of this sort of legislation is of recent vintage and is intended to encourage participation in nonprofit volunteer activities without the fear of legal liability. Most statutes have not been constitutionally tested. In some states, other legislative efforts to create special liability exemptions have been unsuccessful. Such statutes would do nothing to override liability under federal law for the failure of an organization to pay withheld income and Social Security taxes. Nevertheless, they may give comfort to volunteers who manage religious organizations. If liability considerations keep people from serving on boards, volunteer activity in this country will grind to a halt. The message to volunteers should be, "Don't say No. Just do the job you agree to do."

Finally, what should an individual in a position of responsibility do if he or she is convinced that the organization is acting improperly in some particulars and cannot be dissuaded from its actions? First, be sure that you fully express your dissent and that your dissenting vote is recorded. Second, resign from your position. Knowingly remaining in a position of responsibility in an organization that is acting improperly is an invitation to personal liability. If the organization is incorporated, there should be no liability risk to remaining a member to work for change.

G. MEETINGS

Important actions taken by churches are normally authorized at meetings. For such actions to be valid and effective, it is necessary that the meeting be properly called and conducted. The rules for properly calling and conducting of a meeting are found, in order, in:

1. Church governance documents, and if they do not appear therein, in
2. State statutes pertaining to the type of corporation or organization that the church is, and if they do not appear therein, in
3. The church's customary practice.

Since the rules for calling and conducting meetings can usually be ascertained by "neutral principles of law" and do not involve religious doctrines or tenets, most courts will be willing to examine the conduct of church business to see if it has complied with the rules.

Notice of a meeting includes both the necessity of informing the members and those who are entitled to vote at the meeting of the time and place, with reasonable lead time to enable them to be present. With respect to certain subjects of importance, there may also be a requirement of notice of the business to be transacted. Notice requirements should be strictly adhered to, and important issues should be set forth in the notice, as a matter of good practice, even it is not clear that it is required. Minor defects in notice procedure that do not actually prejudice the meeting, such as a notice signed by the wrong person but clearly communicated to the relevant people, who are in fact present, are sometimes overlooked by the courts. However, any failure to follow notice requirements jeopardizes the validity of actions taken at the meeting. Church governance documents should set forth specifically what the notice requirements are and what special business must be specifically noticed, if any. Church officers should follow these provisions with care.

The minimum number of members who must be present to transact business is known as a "quorum" and is often defined in the church governance documents or in state statutes. Churches are well advised to define a quorum in their governing documents in such a way that action is not impeded if members do not show up; some may in fact have moved away or be inactive. This can be as simple as stating a quorum to be a majority of those present at any properly called meeting.

The number of votes necessary to pass a measure should also be clearly defined in the church governing documents. Is a "majority," for example, a majority of all members, a majority of members present at the meeting, or a majority of members voting? Practical administration of church business would suggest the latter to be the best formulation, although it may result in minorities of actual membership taking significant action.

Church governance documents should also address such matters as when, if ever, a secret ballot is required, and whether or not absentee or proxy voting is permitted; and should specify if the church adopts Robert's

Rules of Order or any such specific set of parliamentary procedures.

Church officers responsible for calling and conducting meetings should inform themselves as to the appropriate means of doing so and may find help from denominational sources.[20]

H. POWERS

Since corporations exist by authorization of the state, they have only such powers as the state grants them. Religious organizations incorporated under the general non-profit corporation law or a religious corporation law will have a variety of specifically granted powers, including perpetual existence, the right to sue and be sued, the right to acquire and sell property, and the right to enter into contracts. State corporation law may allow the corporation in its charter to have other powers not specifically delegated, and corporations have implied power to take such actions as may be reasonably necessary to carry out the powers that are expressly granted by charter or statute. The power of a corporation to act is found in state statutes, the corporate charter, and such powers as may be reasonably implied to carry out the powers set forth therein.

Religious corporations that are part of hierarchical denominations may also have limitations imposed on their power or authority by the hierarchical body.

In some states, the powers of religious corporations are specifically restricted in certain areas, such as the amount, value, or kind of property the organization may own; the right to sell or encumber property without approval of a court or a specific percentage of member votes; and the right to receive testamentary gifts (gifts by will) either in amount or by instruments executed within a prescribed time before the death of the donor. Presumably these restrictions reflect the concerns, rooted in English and European history, that the church not accumulate greater property than is necessary for it to carry out its religious function and that the terminally ill be protected from overzealous solicitation by prospective religious beneficiaries at a time when they may be vulnerable to undue pressure or influence.

The purpose of such limitations on power as requiring judicial approval or a super-majority vote is to protect a body against hasty and ill-considered decision making on critical matters. The limits are probably constitutionally valid if not discriminatory or opposed to the church's theological views. Limitations on the amount or nature of property a church can own stand on a different footing. The concept is derived from the old English "mortmain" (dead hand) law which arose from a concern of Parliament that churches were acquiring so much land that they would monopolize the soil. There is little rationale for such statutes in this country.

The U.S. Supreme Court did, in the 1890 decision of *Late Corp. of the Church of Jesus Christ of Latter-Day Saints v. United States,*[21] uphold a mortmain statute passed by Congress that limited the real estate of a religious or charitable corporation in U.S. territories to $50,000. The decision was premised on the legislative authority to grant and withhold corporate charters, but the legislation and decision were plainly motivated by hostility to the Mormon practice of polygamy. The battle over this issue resulted in substantial amounts of Mormon property being forfeited to the government and the church ultimately abandoning the practice of polygamy. Apart from the issue of the appropriateness of state regulation of this practice, the episode involving the confiscation of Mormon property through legislative and judicial action is appropriately viewed today as a travesty of religious liberty arising from the inability of the government to separate its hostility to polygamy from the free exercise rights of the Mormon church. Mortmain statutes that remain on the books today, as they do in several states, are highly constitutionally suspect, and, if enforced, would be unlikely to survive.

I. MERGER, CONSOLIDATION, DISSOLUTION

Merger, consolidation, and dissolution are major corporate actions which require specific procedures to accomplish them in compliance with state statutes and corporate governance documents. Often they require super-majority votes.

Statutes concerning merger, consolidation, and dissolution are intended to achieve the following objectives:

1. To be sure that such major decisions with respect to corporate status and existence are considered decisions of the members of the corporation.
2. To insure the proper handling of corporate assets and liabilities, that is, that debts are paid, obligations met, and remaining assets transferred to an appropriate organization.
3. To provide a public notice or record of the changes in corporate status for the information of anyone who may require it.

Most states require some periodic reporting by religious or nonprofit corporations to maintain their corporate status. In some states that may be as infrequently as every ten years. Corporations have no memory, and it is incumbent upon those responsible for managing the affairs of any religious corporation to know the reporting requirements in their state and calendar them so that not only they, but their successors, will comply with them. Failure to comply with the periodic reporting requirements may result in the dissolution of the corporation either by force of law or by legislative act. Such dissolution may occur with no notice to the corporation. When the corporation is dissolved, it no longer exists, and all of its acts are without authority except to the extent that an unincorporated association may by force of state law have such authority. Its members may lose the insulation from liability that they had by virtue of the existence of the corporate entity.

Involuntary dissolution of nonprofit corporations for failing to comply with reporting statutes is so frequent that some states have revival statutes that enable a dissolved nonprofit or religious corporation, which acts within a specified period of time and with the proper formalities, to reestablish its corporate existence without beginning all over again. Involuntary and unknowing dissolution, however, is not an uncommon fate for religious organizations that have not attended to their reporting requirements.

Involuntary dissolution may occur for other reasons as well, including action by the state attorney general for fraudulent solicitation, for exceeding corporate authority, for management deadlocks that make it impossible for the corporation to function, and for action of a creditor when the corporation is unable to pay its debts.

Corporations may also dissolve voluntarily. Voluntary dissolution is governed by state statute and the corporate governance documents, including those of any hierarchical denomination of which the corporation is a part. The procedure is generally specific and detailed and contains such elements as notice to and vote of the members, notice to creditors, payment of liabilities, and filing of appropriate documents with the secretary of state or other authorities.

Upon dissolution, disposition of any corporate assets must be to another charitable or religious organization that has similar purposes. The IRS requires that a corporation recognized as tax exempt under the Internal Revenue Code includes specific provisions to that effect in its governing documents. In a hierarchical denomination, those assets may, by the documents of church governance, pass upward to the denominational organization. Absent such compulsory disposition, the church charter may specify the organization that will receive its assets on dissolution and, in the absence of any other dispositive provisions, courts have authority to direct the assets to an organization with similar purposes.

Religious corporations may also merge and consolidate, procedures that are technically different although the result may be the same. A merger occurs when one corporation is merged or absorbed into another, which maintains its corporate existence, while the corporation merged into it is dissolved. A consolidation occurs when two corporations join to form a new or third corporation, both of the predecessors being thereupon dissolved. Merger and consolidation must be conducted according to state law, which may provide the same or different procedures for them. The procedure is typically similar to that set forth above for dissolution, except that liabilities and assets are transferred to the new or surviving corporation instead of liabilities being paid off and assets being distributed to another organization of like purpose.

Precise compliance with statutory requirements is important, and legal advice should be sought and followed in carrying out any of these procedures. I encountered one situation in which two religious corporations, intending to merge, took all of the appropriate steps to do so including a vote of merger by both. Notice was given, meetings were held, unanimous votes were taken by both organizations, and everyone then thought the merger had been accomplished. State law required, however, that assets be transferred by formal instruments and that appropriate certified notice of the merger be recorded with the secretary of state and the town clerk. None of these follow-up acts had been done when the matter was revisited for the first time a decade later in connection with a review of title to real estate. Happily, all of the officers of both corporations were still alive and accessible, and we were able to get the appropriate instruments transferring title and certificates executed and recorded. Inattention to the legal requirements, however, can create unnecessary complications and frustrate good intentions.

J. INCORPORATION OF SUBSIDIARY OR AFFILIATED ORGANIZATIONS

Religious organizations often face the question of when and by what means they should separately incorporate various parts of their mission. A church may, for example, be running a school, day care center, counseling center, homeless shelter, soup kitchen, or church camp. Denominations must consider whether to separately incorporate regional organizations and affiliated denominational organizations such as camps, conference centers, publishing houses, colleges, universities, hospitals, nursing homes, or retirement centers. Highly structured churches must decide whether to separately incorporate each group at each level of the denomination from the local parish or congregation to the highest level of authority. The issue is both vertical and horizontal in the structure of religious organizations.

There is no universal answer or rule of thumb that can be used to judge when to separately incorporate a distinctive mission of a church or denomination. Every such mission must be judged on its own unique circumstances and a prudent decision made with appropriate legal advice. With respect to such large self-contained institutions with distinctive missions as colleges, universities, and hospitals, separate incorporation will be the norm in almost all cases. The question of whether the local church should separately incorporate its day care center is less obvious. Seven considerations should inform the judgment:

1. Insulation from liability. Some church missions, such as schools, day care centers, and camps, are inherently high-risk enterprises. In larger organizations, such as hierarchical denominations, the mere multiplicity of bodies and activities creates potential liability for the parent denomination. In most instances, separately incorporating and operating a mission or enterprise of the church separately will insulate the parent and related organizations from liability for the subsidiary or affiliated organization, at least if the organizations have separable missions and function separately.[22]
2. Maintenance of control. Subsidiary or affiliated organizations can be structured so that control is maintained in the parent or central organization through a variety of devices. Separate organizations with separate boards of directors, however, tend to become independent-minded, and any separate incorporation risks some level of loss of control. Indeed, some level of control separation may be necessary to achieve liability insulation.[23]
3. Regulatory and reporting requirements. It may be convenient or desirable to incorporate separately missions that are subject to particular regulatory requirements, scrutiny, or financial or other reporting so that the entire organization does not become subject to governmental or public scrutiny because one ministry is. Separating functions that generate taxable "unrelated business income"[24] from nonprofit organizations is often

desirable.[25] Units with smaller numbers of employees may not be subject to some employment regulations.[26] "Pervasively sectarian" organizations may not qualify for certain government aid that might be available to a less pervasively sectarian ministry if it is separately incorporated.

4. Geographical considerations. It may be useful or desirable to incorporate the mission or organization separately in each state in which it conducts activities. This may be for regulatory or reporting considerations, as noted in paragraph 3, or to ease compliance with the state law or qualify for state benefits. New Hampshire, for example, requires local municipalities to grant property tax exemptions to charitable organizations with respect to property owned, occupied, and used by them, if they are incorporated in the state. Out-of-state charities are only entitled to the exemption if they have a principal place of business in the state. While the definition of "principal place of business" has not been tested and discrimination against out-of-state corporations is constitutionally questionable, the provision illustrates the convenience, at least, if not the necessity, of separately incorporating within the state a religious organization that owns, occupies, and uses real property there.[27]

5. Management considerations. A different, perhaps more businesslike, management may be appropriate to some functions, especially those that may generate taxable income.

6. Public relations considerations. Inclusion of profit-making or controversial functions under nonprofit umbrellas may discourage contributions.

7. Maintenance of tax-exempt status. Lobbying or political involvement may jeopardize tax-exempt status. Such activities may need to be separately incorporated.[28]

In order to achieve insulation from liability by separate incorporation, the subsidiary or affiliated corporation must in fact be operated as more than a shell. The higher the level of control, however, the less likely it is that the separate incorporation will achieve the goal of insulating the parent from liability for acts of the subsidiary.

Some devices to maintain control, starting with those most likely to enable the parent to maintain liability insulation, are:

1. the right of the parent to amend, or veto amendments to, the corporate governance documents;
2. the right of the parent to select enough board members of the subsidiary to maintain control;
3. the right of the parent to select or veto the selection of the president or key officers of the subsidiary;
4. the right of the parent to enter into management by such acts as approving or vetoing the current operating budget or disposition of assets.[29]

Whatever control devices are used, the subsidiary should have its own board of directors and officers who should meet separately and not be identical with the parent, its own bank accounts in its own name, and its own employer identification number with the IRS. It should pay its own employees, meet its own liabilities, and maintain its own books and records. Property it occupies or uses should be owned in its own name or leased by it from the parent organization. The parent organization is not required to treat it in an arm's-length fashion, as if it were unrelated. It can make leased premises available free and provide financial support and the like, but if the separate corporation is a mere shell and the parent is in fact directly conducting the affairs of a corporation, the parent may be unable to avoid liability for it.

Much concern for the liability that may be associated with organizational structure was generated by the 1979 decision of a California intermediate appellate court in *Barr v. United Methodist Church*.[30] There the court held that the United Methodist church, an unincorporated connectional entity of Methodist regional conferences, could be held liable for the defaults of a bankrupt Methodist, nonprofit corporation that had operated a number of retirement homes. The case was ultimately settled at a cost to the church of some $21 million. *Barr* precipitated concern that the court had disregarded the church's own view of its polity in reaching the result and led to much reexamination of organizational structure by major denominations. The issues raised by *Barr* and subsequent similar cases and ways in which denominations can endeavor to avoid such sweeping attributions of liability are well addressed by E. M. Gaffney and P. C. Sorenson in their 1984 work, *Ascending Liability in Religious and Other Nonprofit Organizations*[31] and the follow-up *Planning Memorandum*.[32] While these brief but excellent works are aimed largely at denominational or other larger organizational structures, a review of them will reward all who are concerned with the problem of incorporating separate missions and organizations within or affiliated with a body of like-minded believers. The subject of liability of religous organizations for the acts of others is further discussed in chapter 6.

REFERENCES

American Bar Association. *Revised Model Nonprofit Corporation Act* (Clifton, N.J.: Prentice-Hall Law and Business, 1988).

Foshee, Howard B. *Broadman Church Manual* (Nashville: Broadman Press, 1973).

Gaffney, Edward McGlynn, and Philip C. Sorensen. *Ascending Liability in Religious and Other Nonprofit Organizations*, ed. H. Griffin (Macon, Ga.: Center for Constitutional Studies, and Mercer University Press, 1984).

Hammar, Richard R. *Pastor, Church and Law*, 2d ed. (Matthews, N.C.: Christian Ministry Resources, 1991).

Haugen, Edmund. *Mr./Madame Chairman—Parliamentary Procedure Explained* (Minneapolis: Augsburg Publishing House, 1963).

McCarty, C. Barry. *A Parliamentary Guide for Church Leaders* (Nashville: Broadman Press, 1987).

Moots, Philip R. *Ascending Liability: A Planning Memorandum* (Macon, Ga.: Center for Constitutional Studies, Mercer University Press, 1987).

Moots, Philip R., and Edward McGlynn Gaffney. *Church and Campus: Legal Issues in Religiously Affiliated Higher Education* (Notre Dame, Ind.: University of Notre Dame Press, 1979).

Morgan, Claude D. "The Significance of Church Organizational Structure in Litigation and Government Action," 16 *Valparaiso University Law Review* 145 (1981).

Myers, Marvin. *Managing the Business Affairs of the Church* (Convention Press, 1981).

Serritella, James E. "The Code of Canon Law and Civil Law," 29 *Catholic Lawyer* 195 (1984).

Venable, Giovan Harbour. "Courts Examine Congregationalism," 41 *Stanford Law Review* 719 (1989).

CHAPTER 12

Hiring, Supervising, and Firing Employees

A. THE EMPLOYMENT CONTRACT

The employment relationship is a consensual or contractual relationship and is governed, in general, by the same rules as other contracts. In order to be enforceable, (1) there must be an offer and an acceptance or meeting of the minds of the parties; (2) there must be consideration or value given; (3) and the contract must have a valid or lawful object or purpose. The requirements of offer and acceptance and consideration are normally met by the exchange of mutually beneficial promises, that is, the employee agrees to perform services in exchange for the employer's payment of wages and other benefits. The contract may be oral or in writing, and the conduct of the parties may create a contract or establish terms of the contract. The terms of the contract, to be enforceable, must be sufficiently definite so that a court can understand what the parties agreed to—the services to be performed, when and where they are to be performed, and for how much money. If actual services are rendered with the knowledge of the employer before agreement is reached on wages, the employee will be entitled to "reasonable compensation" for her or his services, which will be based upon compensation provided for similar services by the employer or similarly situated employers.

Clergy or other personnel who are self-employed or independent contractors are performing their services under a contract that is also subject to contract rules of law. If it is bona fide self-employment and not a self-classification by the parties of a relationship that is in reality an employer-employee relationship, it will be free of the considerations discussed in this chapter concerning employment contracts and other government regulation of employment relationships discussed in chapters 7, 13, and 14.

Employment contracts in religious organizations present two sets of issues on which they differ from other contractual relationships we have discussed. First, any employment contract with clergy or other personnel who perform functions that are integral to the religious mission of the organization (which may, for example, include teachers in religious schools) is subject to constitutional limitations on government interference discussed in chapter 3, section F, and in chapter 7 with respect to specific areas of government regulation. Courts will not intervene in contractual disputes that involve religious doctrine or polity. The rights of workers involved in religious employment are significantly limited by the discretion courts give to churches and religious organizations to be the judges of their own requirements of faith and practice. Religious organizations may be able to impose standards of morality and conduct upon their employees even when their functions are entirely secular.

Second, the employment relationship is one of the most highly regulated contractual relationships that exists within the American legal system. Federal and state statutes and even local ordinances regulate pay and hours, prohibit discrimination against various categories of people, and compel employers to participate in government tax and employee-benefit programs. Courts, in addition, have been increasingly willing to intervene in the employment relationship or the termination of that relationship to create protections for workers that did not previously exist. Statutory accommodations and constitutional religious freedom issues may limit or prevent the application of some of these regulations and restrictions in the context of certain religious employers. In other instances, full compliance is required. Every religious organization with employees, which is almost all of them, must have an understanding of the funda-

mentals of employment law. This chapter discusses the employment contract as such and general considerations in the hiring, supervision, and discharge of employees. Government regulation of employment in such areas as discrimination, wages and hours, and collective bargaining is treated in chapter 7. The church's obligation in payroll and working conditions, such as federal income tax withholding, Social Security and self-employment tax, workers compensation, and unemployment compensation, are covered in chapter 13. Chapter 14 discusses the pastor as taxpayer.

B. EMPLOYMENT AND TERMINATION OF CLERGY

The method of employing clergy will be determined by the organization or polity of the church. As discussed in chapter 4, churches are generally of either a hierarchical or congregational polity, although many church organizations have some mixture of congregational and hierarchical control in their church governance. In hierarchical denominations, the clergy may be designated or appointed by the denomination, selected by the congregation and the denomination together, or elected by the congregation. The denominational governance will determine the methodology.

Congregational churches select their clergy according to the procedures set forth in the church governance documents. Normally, that will require a majority vote of the membership of the congregation. If the church governance documents do not address the issue, then it will be determined in accordance with the state statutes governing the organization. In the absence of any other authority, the established practice or custom of the church will govern.

Selection of clergy, being an entirely ecclesiastical matter, is not normally subject to review by courts.[1] However, selection procedures that are, or are alleged to be, in plain violation of the governing procedures established by the church governance documents or state law may be reviewed by a court if it can do so without examining any issues of religious doctrine or polity. Such matters as the giving of proper notice and obtaining a proper vote, for example, may be subject to court review. If the parties in question were adequately informed for the purpose of the meeting, however, the failure to comply with formalities of notice is not always fatal.[2] Churches and religious organizations should never rely upon informal notice but should comply with their church governance documents or state law as applicable.

Termination of clergy will likewise be governed by the corporate governance documents or, where applicable, state law or church custom. Where church governance documents vest this authority in a denominational hierarchy, it will control the matter. Where church governance documents repose this authority in the congregation, it may terminate the employment according to its own procedures. If the termination is to occur before the expiration of a term that has been established by contract, congregational vote, or church governance documents, however, the termination must be based upon cause. Cause will include any specific breaches of the employment contract or grounds that may be implicit in the employment relationship, such as moral misconduct, significant deviations from church doctrine, or incompetence to perform the services required.

Clergy have been singularly unsuccessful in court challenges to their dismissal.[3] The reasons are well summarized in language that has often been quoted from the Fifth Circuit's 1972 decision in *McClure v. Salvation Army:*

> The relationship between an organized church and its ministers is its lifeblood. The minister is the chief instrument by which the church seeks to fulfill its purpose. Matters touching this relationship must necessarily be recognized as of prime ecclesiastical concern.[4]

Clergy will, however, be protected in the recovery of wages actually due them,[5] and clergy have been permitted to assert specific contractual provisions, such as a requirement of ninety-day notice for termination.[6] In one case involving age-discrimination claims, based on the law as well as the Methodist Book of Discipline (which disclaims age, among other things, as a basis for clergy appointments), the court refused to consider the discrimination claims, finding that it would involve the court in ecclesiastical matters. But the court did permit the pastor to assert an oral contract claim that he had been promised assignment to "a congregation more suited to his training and skills" in exchange for his continued work elsewhere.[7] This decision must be viewed as questionable, because it is hard to see how a court could evaluate the oral contract claims without getting into the ecclesiastical issues it sought to avoid. A less questionable decision allowed an associate pastor to press a claim of sexual harassment, which involved no issues of church doctrine, while dismissing her complaints about her employment termination.[8]

Religious organizations that enter into express employment contracts with clergy would be well advised to be as specific and comprehensive as possible in setting forth grounds for termination, to incorporate fully references to religious or ecclesiastical standards of conduct and doctrine into the contracts, and to identify who will decide when they have been breached. Religious employees engaged in specifically religious functions, such as teaching, counseling, and worship, or in other program leadership will generally be subject to the same limitations as clergy; and any contractual relationships with such employees should include the same provisions for doctrinal adherence, conduct, and authority to terminate the contract. Such employees are entitled, as are clergy, to enforcement of secular contract terms that can be implemented without requiring courts to evaluate religious doctrine, faith, or internal organization.[9] Contracts and employment relationships with clergy and other religious employees should also be managed according to the guidelines set forth hereafter with respect to nonreligious employees insofar as applicable.

C. EMPLOYMENT AND TERMINATION OF NONCLERGY EMPLOYEES

Religious employers are likely to be held to the normal contract rules of law that govern secular employment relationships to the extent that they employ persons for secular tasks, and these rules may also govern non-ecclesiastical employment relationships even with religious workers. Hence it is necessary that religious employers give the same attention to personnel practices and to their prospective liability as do other employers.

With the exception of specific areas of government regulation discussed in chapter 7, most liability concerns of employers relate to wrongful termination or discharge. In the legal climate of the 1990s, every involuntary termination of an employee must be considered a potential source of litigation, and the employer must be satisfied that it has conducted itself properly with respect to the matter. The rules of proper conduct are set forth in common-law decisions, in the contract between the parties, and in the specific statutory protections of workers, the more important of which on the federal level are discussed in chapter 7. State and local legislation may impose additional requirements.

The traditional common-law rule of employment, in the absence of a contractual provision to the contrary, is that employment is "at will," meaning that an employer or employee can terminate the relationship at any time, with or without cause, and incur no liability to the other for doing so. The majority of states have modified the "employment at will doctrine" in court cases, beginning in the 1970s, to provide greater protection to employees. The modifications have created a claim that blends notions of both tort and contract law, known as "wrongful discharge."

Olga Monge was a pioneer in the law of wrongful discharge. She refused to accept the right of her employer to harass and fire her after she refused her foreman's amorous advances. In her 1974 case, *Monge v. Beebe Rubber Company*, a wrongful discharge case, the New Hampshire Supreme Court found that employees "at will" had more rights than that:

> [T]ermination . . . motivated by bad faith or malice or based on retaliation is not in the best interest of the economic system or the public good and constitutes a breach of the employment contract.[10]

Subsequent New Hampshire cases have developed the wrongful discharge doctrine to require that an employee, in order to have a wrongful discharge claim, must show that a discharge (1) is motivated by bad faith, malice, or retaliation, and (2) is in violation of a public policy. Whether or not a public policy is violated is for decision by a jury.[11]

Most states, like New Hampshire, have adopted modifications of the employment at will doctrine that permit discharged employees to bring a claim based upon the factors set forth by the New Hampshire court or some variation thereof. Some may even require "cause" for discharge, rather than the absence of improper causes. Courts have allowed claims for discharges motivated by such factors as exercising a legal right to sue a supervisor for a non-work-related incident,[12] refusing to commit perjury,[13] filing a worker's compensation claim,[14] refusing to engage in illegal price fixing,[15] preventing an employee from collecting pension benefits, commissions, or other compensation,[16] refusing to support the employer's lobbying efforts,[17] and refusing to backdate or otherwise falsify records.[18]

If it is improper to fire an employee, it is equally improper to force an employee out by making working conditions so unpleasant that the employee feels constrained to leave. This is called a "constructive discharge" and will give the employee the same rights as if he or she was fired outright. In court, however, the effect is worse than an outright termination, because the facts of the constructive discharge case are likely to make the employer appear to be untrustworthy and hypocritical.

A "retaliatory discharge" of an employee who exercises a right given by law or refuses to engage in wrongful conduct is an invitation to a lawsuit which the employer is likely to lose. This rule can present a particular dilemma for religious organizations who adhere strictly to biblical principles of dispute resolution, which forbid taking such disputes to secular courts. Matthew 18:15-17 and 1 Cor. 6:1-8 are understood by many churches and religious organizations to preclude civil litigation between believers. Such disputes are to be resolved within the church, and believers are to consider it better to be wronged than to bring a lawsuit against another Christian. Suppose a religious organization whose doctrine includes adherence to these scriptural principles finds itself being sued or threatened with suit by an employee-believer. Can it discharge the employee for such a violation of doctrine? Or would that discharge be a retaliatory discharge forbidden to the church? Courts have reached different answers to this question. Two decisions by circuit courts of appeals illustrate the contrast.

In the 1982 decision of the Ninth Circuit Court of Appeals in *EEOC v. Pacific Press Publishing Association*,[19] the plaintiff worked for a nonprofit religious publishing house associated with the Seventh-Day Adventist church. The employer's board of directors was subject to authority from the church's General Conference, or governing body. The plaintiff claimed sex discrimination in pay and a retaliatory discharge. The discharge followed her complaints to the Equal Employment Opportunity Commission and was based, according to her employer, on her failure to adhere to biblical teaching and church authority with respect to the dispute with her church-affiliated employer.

The court recognized that the situation presented a real conflict with religious belief. But because the church did not claim a religious belief in pay discrimination against women, which underlay the dispute, the court did not view the case as an intrachurch dispute over religious doctrine and practice and did not find it was barred from considering it by the church autonomy cases discussed in chapter 4 above. The burden on religious doctrine, in the Ninth Circuit's view, was justified by the government's interest in equal employment opportunity. The court noted that although the claimant had administrative and discretionary duties, she was not a minister, seminary teacher, or author of religious texts, and did not occupy the type of critically sensitive position within the church that needed constitutional protection.

A contrasting case is *EEOC v. Dayton Christian Schools*, decided by the Sixth Circuit Court of Appeals in 1985.[20] There the religious school and parties associated with

it sought, under Section 1983,[21] to enjoin the Ohio Civil Rights Commission from exercising jurisdiction over a complaint by a pregnant, married teacher in a Christian school who had been informed that her contract would not be renewed for the following year because the school wanted to have mothers at home with preschool age children. After consulting an attorney who threatened legal action, she was terminated for failure to follow biblical dispute resolution procedures, which were alluded to in her employment contract. The school was "a pervasively religious institution in which religious considerations permeate all aspects of the educational process, govern the teacher selection process, and dictate parents' entrustment of their children's education to the school."[22] The court was impressed with the fact that the plaintiffs included parents whose children attended the school; the children were young and impressionable, and the teacher in question would serve as a role model for religious values. To compel the school to maintain her employment in the face of sincerely held religious beliefs that she had violated was too great a burden on the religious freedom interests of the parents and the school. Despite the sex discrimination and retaliatory discharge nature of the claims, the Sixth Circuit honored the religious freedom claims. The case was appealed to the U.S. Supreme Court, which reversed because the federal courts had acted before the state process was completed. The Supreme Court did not address the opinion of the Sixth Circuit on the substantive issue of whether the religious freedom claim should outweigh the sex discrimination and retaliatory discharge claims.[23]

Pacific Press and *Dayton Christian Schools* may not be as different as they appear to be on the surface. The employee in *Pacific Press* had a secular job for a religiously affiliated organization but was engaged in no specifically religious functions. The employee in *Dayton Christian Schools*, on the other hand, worked for a pervasively religious school in which she served as a role model for tender minds; and her employer was sensitive enough to the religious freedom issue of the use of the biblical dispute resolution procedures to have included a paragraph on the subject in her employment contract. Whether the Sixth Circuit is more sensitive to religious freedom claims than the Ninth in sex discrimination and retaliatory discharge cases, or whether the outcome of both cases is simply determined by their facts and would have been the same had each been litigated in the other circuit is an unanswerable question.

Religious employers who do not want employment disputes to be resolved in the secular courts have options. Alternative dispute resolution procedures such as arbitration are favored by the courts and, if selected by the parties by contract, will normally be honored[24] and will even override court jurisdiction given by statute over such claims as discrimination.[25] Such provisions would not necessarily have resolved the *Pacific Press* and *Dayton Christian Schools* issue. Employers may not by contract compel their employees to forgo rights given to them by law. Indeed, *Dayton Christian Schools* had at least an allusion to biblical dispute resolution in its employment contract. Such contract provisions require careful drafting to avoid requiring the courts to evaluate ecclesiastical matters in order to be enforceable.

The Christian Conciliation Service offers alternative dispute resolutions for biblical dispute resolution among believers or others who are willing to subscribe to its biblical principles for dispute resolution.[26] There is no reason why religious organizations could not include in employment contracts (or any other appropriate contract for that matter) mandatory biblical dispute resolution procedures and seek to have them honored by the courts.[27] The stronger the contract language and the more pervasively religious the institution and the nature of the employee's duties, the less likely it is that a court would permit government agencies or courts to override the employer's religious freedom interest.

The employment contract is, of course, whatever the employer and the employee have agreed to, so long as it is lawful, with respect to the terms and conditions of employment: what the employee will do, when and where he or she will work, what compensation and benefits will be received for the services. It may be oral or in writing.

Employers should be aware that in recent years, courts have increasingly found contracts in documents and statements that most employers might not have viewed as being of contractual force at all. Some of the most prolific sources of "contract" rights have been employee handbooks, personnel manuals, and similar documents that had traditionally been viewed as advisory rather than contractual. Virtually any piece of paper communicated to employees that has to do with the employment relationship may be found by a court to be part of the contract. While the rule is by no means universal,[28] employers must be conscious of the possibility that contract rights may be found in any document made available to employees and in documents that guide their personnel practices, whether or not they are formalized as part of an employment contract. Similarly, courts have found contractual rights in mere oral representations to employees, and even clergy have been allowed to assert oral contractual rights in some cases that seem to border on, if not intrude into, ecclesiastical concerns.[29] Statements in hiring interviews, such as, "As long as you do your job . . . you will be with the company,"[30] or that this job is one in which "[you] can stay and grow,"[31] have been found to limit the employer's ability to discharge at will and to require just cause.

D. RISK MANAGING THE EMPLOYMENT RELATIONSHIP

Good risk-management practices in the employment area will not prevent every lawsuit, but they will go a long way toward protecting a religious employer from liability and creating better relations between the employer and employees in the workplace. The following suggestions, while designed primarily for larger, secular employers, are useful, to the extent they are applicable, to all employers. Many religious organizations will find them useful; and some organizations operate affiliated enterprises that are not pervasively sectarian and for which these suggestions, in their entirety, may be applicable. Section 6— Special Considerations for Religious Employers—addresses some more specific concerns religious employers will have.

1. Hiring

Throughout the hiring process, whether in advertisements, applications, or interviews, avoid any references to prohibited discrimination as set forth in chapter 7. Issues to avoid include:

a. Marital status or intentions. Discrimination on the basis of marital status is often directly prohibited by state or local law. It may also be perceived as a subtle form of sex discrimination—to avoid, for example, the expense or inconvenience of an employee likely to get pregnant. Policies that prohibit employment of spouses of employees (which may be part of a general antinepotism policy) may violate laws against discrimination based on marital status. Employers whose policies preclude employment of family members of other employees should check with a local attorney on the state law applicable to such policies.

b. Gender. Unless there is a religiously based reason for gender discrimination in the particular situation, for example, if the church has a biblical belief that women should not serve as clergy, gender discrimination must be avoided. Height and weight requirements unrelated to business necessity may be treated as sex discrimination because of the "disparate impact" on gender and should not be included.

c. Pregnancy, child-bearing plans, or the number and ages of present children and child care arrangements. Religious organizations that do not believe in employing women with young children should get specific advice on their policies in the context of their religious beliefs and state and federal law.

d. Race, color, or national origin of the applicant, the applicant's spouse, or associates; physical, cultural, or linguistic characteristics of a particular group; membership or participation in organizations associated with a particular group; association of an individual's or spouse's name with a particular group; color of skin, eyes, hair.

e. Pre-hire photographs. These should not be required.

f. Citizenship. Avoid inquiring into an applicant's birthplace or that of his or her parents, spouse, or other relatives. Requests for birth or naturalization records should be avoided, except to comply with the Immigration Act of 1986, which requires verification of job eligibility within three days of hire (this is mandatory; see chapter 7).

g. Age or birthday, unless required by law.

h. Disabilities, except to the extent necessary to insure that the individual is not a direct threat to the health and safety of others in the workplace and that the job will not pose a significant risk of substantial harm to the individual. Pre-hire physicals must be limited to medical tests that meet the standards of the Americans with Disabilities Act. See chapter 7, section B.5.

i. Religion, except as it may be part of the job requirement for employment in many churches and religious organizations. In these cases, the expectations, including adherence to a statement of faith and standards of conduct, should be made explicit.

Certain inquiries or hiring requirements may have a "disparate impact"—that is, they may affect some groups protected by the antidiscrimination laws more than others—blacks, women, or national minorities, for example. In general, screen your application and interview or hiring processes to limit inquiries to matters pertaining to the job requirements. Disparate impact may occur when members of such groups are discouraged from applying as well as when they suffer in the hiring process. Be careful that inquiries into physical characteristics or preemployment physicals are only related to the ability to perform the job. Intelligence or other testing is suspect unless it is related to job requirements. Educational levels or fluency in English are unrelated to some jobs, and arrest (as opposed to conviction) records are rarely appropriate. Even being convicted of a crime can be suspected of having a disparate impact if it is used as a blanket disqualifier for all jobs, although it is obviously appropriate in certain circumstances.

Other requirements may be imposed by state and local law. Beyond these regulatory, antidiscrimination requirements, the employer can maximize its flexibility in employment by the following suggestions:

a. Advertisements

Advertisements for position vacancies should avoid such phrases as "permanent employment" or terms such as "guaranteed" or "tenured" that would imply anything but employment at will.[32]

b. The Application

The employment application should not include anything that might be interpreted as creating a permanent employer-employee relationship. It may be helpful to add a disclaimer to the application that employment is at will.[33]

c. The Interview

The interview poses innumerable opportunities for oral misrepresentations, such as those discussed in the previous section, that can later haunt the employer.

1. As a safeguard, have the applicant interviewed by two persons, such as a recruiter and a personnel manager or two representatives of the governing body. State clearly that the applicant can rely on the recruiter for information on the nature of the job but only on the personnel manager for information on the terms and conditions of employment. This can avoid problems caused by overeager recruiters who might tend to engage in "puffery" about the job.[34]
2. Construct and provide interviewers with a checklist to use during the interview. The list can help them avoid both improper questions and improper representations. The form should also leave ample space for the interviewer to record any questions asked by the applicant and the interviewer's response. This task should be completed during or immediately after the interview and kept in the applicant's personnel file, where it will be available if needed for future litigation.[35] Such checklists may be found in standard personnel management or human resource guides, or may come

from your attorney or through denominational resources.

d. The Offer Letter

If your organization uses offer letters, avoid such phrases as "we look forward to a long and successful career"[36] or offers of "permanent" or "lifetime" employment.[37] Do not attempt to list reasons for which an applicant may be fired. Describe the salary on a monthly, rather than an annual basis. As an alternative to offer letters, it may be better just to telephone successful applicants.[38] The important thing, in a letter or call, is not to make representations that might later be termed a contract for a set time period or that cannot be terminated without cause in court. Specify that the employment is "at will" and can be terminated without cause.

e. Probationary Periods

Be cautious in the use of probationary periods. If an employee is told that he or she can be fired without cause during the first 90 (or 30, or 120) days, this may be interpreted as providing security from discharge without cause once the probationary period is past.[39] Again, specify, preferably in writing, that the employment is "at will" and can be terminated without cause even after the probationary period.

2. Employee Manuals

Over thirty states have now recognized an employee manual as creating an employment contract of some type.[40] There are four steps you can take to avoid litigation arising from employment manuals:

a. Watch for Misleading Language. Employment manuals are no place for sloppy language. Do not say "permanent employment" when you mean "full-time employment." Do not say "subject to discharge for poor performance" when you mean "subject to discharge at management's discretion."[41]

Beware of vague statements such as "It is our policy to treat each employee fairly," which can be interpreted to mean almost anything.[42] In other words, make certain you truly intend, and are willing, to live up to *everything* in the manual.[43]

Try to read the manual from the employee's point of view. Will he or she interpret it the same way that you do?

b. Use Separate Manuals for Different Classes of Employees. The manual should make clear who (i.e., what class of employees) it applies to. Using separate manuals for different classes of employees allows you to specify different disciplinary or grievance systems, or different rights of privacy for an employee's work space, for management and hourly personnel.[44]

c. Have the Employee Sign the Manual. Have the employee sign that she or he has read and understands the material in the manual.[45] Provide an opportunity for questions, and write down questions asked and responses given.

d. Disclaimers. Disclaimers receive mixed reviews, but most experts recommend their use.[46] A few courts have upheld disclaimers in a manual to deny a terminated employee's claim that the manual created a contract.[47] Disclaimers should be as specific as possible. It may not do just to say, "This is not a contract."[48] You need to say more precisely what that means, for example, "Notwithstanding any statement or inference which may be drawn from this manual, all employees are subject to discharge at management's discretion, without cause." The disclaimer should also say that terms of employment are not and cannot be altered by the manual or by any employee or manager except for a specifically named individual—usually the company president—and that any such contract must be in writing.[49] Disclaimers should be provided to the applicant before hiring.[50] Even when all these safeguards are followed, the courts are likely to apply the disclaimer narrowly. Thus you may want to consider taking into account employee morale, possible union activity, or other factors in considering whether or not you wish to use a disclaimer.[51]

3. Maintaining the Employment Relationship

a. Nondiscrimination

Discriminatory practices that are forbidden in hiring are also forbidden with respect to other terms, conditions, or privileges of employment, including pay, promotion, and working conditions. The employer's obligations under the nondiscrimination laws discussed in chapter 7 do not end with hire.

Beyond the obvious requirement of treating all employees in all respects relating to employment on an equal basis, regardless of race, color, national origin, sex, age, citizenship, or disability, employers should create an atmosphere and supervisors set an example of nondiscrimination. Expressions of personal prejudice on the job, and even away from it, should be avoided. If you have any prejudices, keep them to yourself. Be sure that the people you supervise are treated fairly regardless of their race, sex, color, national origin, age, disability, or citizenship. Tolerate no personal prejudice, discriminatory behavior, or sexual harassment toward fellow employees by any employee or by outsiders, such as salesmen or independent contractors working on the premises; and report any such incidents to authorized persons. Make sure that all decisions concerning employment are based upon the employee's job performance and ability to perform, and not on any extraneous factors.

Guard against sexual harassment. It is a particular form of sex discrimination, as discussed in chapter 7. Refrain from inappropriate comments about personal appearance. Do not call your female secretary "my girl." Avoid physical contact, including patting, hugging, and squeezing. Keep the workplace free of sexually suggestive pictures or literature. Avoid suggestive jokes. And *never* request yourself or tolerate another employee's request for sexual favors from a subordinate.

Normal dating between unmarried persons when no employment conditions, privileges, or relationships are related to dating is not sexual harassment. When dating is between a subordinate and superior, however, be aware that misunderstandings can easily arise.

b. Employee Evaluations

Employee evaluations serve a variety of functions. They help fulfill employee expectations of feedback. This is important, because it can be difficult to fire an employee for nonperformance if the employee was not advised of problem areas or even all of the job requirements.

Evaluations allow the employer to demand performance. They are an opportunity to identify problem areas and resolve them. Perhaps most important, from the standpoint of avoiding wrongful discharge lawsuits, a well-written, candid evaluation is the best available evidence of failure to perform. Discharge for nonperformance when no written record exists is far more difficult to defend than one backed by solid documentation.[52]

1. Establish regularity. Have evaluations done regularly. Most experts recommend doing evaluations more than once a year.[53]
2. Use objective criteria. Where possible, include objective criteria, such as attendance, tardiness, productivity records, and references to specific incidents or performances. Such objective tests are more difficult to refute than purely subjective evaluations.[54]
3. Be candid. The most important thing in an evaluation is candor. There is a tendency for supervisors to give glowing evaluations as a means of maintaining peace in the workplace.[55] This, however, defeats the real goal of evaluations in improving worker performance and can actually hinder efforts to discharge poor employees. A series of favorable, or even neutral, evaluations can be very hard to refute when the decision to discharge is challenged in court.[56] Conversely, a well-documented, well-reasoned series of evaluations showing poor performance is powerful evidence in an employer's hands if it becomes necessary to discharge.

To avoid this "evaluation inflation":
• Supervisors should not check the same box on all categories.
• Supervisors should be counseled on the importance of evenhanded, candid evaluations.
• Where "evaluation inflation" persists, it may be worthwhile to require supervisors to give a certain number of high and low marks.[57]

4. Back up ratings in writing. Supervisors should back up ratings with written comments.
5. Have a supervisory review first. Before the evaluation goes to the employee, have the supervisor's supervisor approve it, add comments, then communicate it in writing to the employee.[58] This is an important step to avoid unfair evaluations based on personality conflicts.
6. Have the employee sign off. The employee should sign off to having read and discussed the review and should be allowed to add written comments and objections. If the review is unsatisfactory, written formal goals for improvement should be established. Advise the employee of the significance of the review and allow an appeal of a poor evaluation to higher management or the personnel department.[59]
7. Audit. Reviews should be audited, both generally, to avoid inflation and discrimination against protected groups,[60] and specifically. If ratings suddenly take a turn for the worse when the rating supervisor changes, the situation should be checked, and, if necessary, comments should be added to the file to support the reasons for the change.

c. Discipline

As discussed above, it can be difficult to discharge an employee for poor performance if there is no written record. Thus your disciplinary system serves the same important function as evaluations: it provides a record.[61] Do not be afraid to discipline early on. Not only are you building the record you may need for eventual discharge, but, more hopefully, early discipline will help catch and correct a problem before discharge is necessary.[62] Disciplinary policies should include a disclaimer that they are advisory and not contractual, and should allow management to disregard the policy when necessary.[63] While the policy should be generally adhered to, no written policy can handle every conceivable situation, so some flexibility is desirable.

d. Personnel Files

Maintain one complete, consistent personnel file in one place. You can make better decisions with a complete personnel file. Maintenance of multiple and/or incomplete files makes it tougher for you to take the best action. And should litigation ever result, you will want and need a complete file. You do not want to be forced to search for documents scattered in various files.

4. Counselors and Youth Workers: Special Concerns in Hiring, Supervision, and Retention

A church or religious organization has a responsibility to those who could be injured by the improper conduct of its employees to act in a reasonable and prudent manner, that is, without negligence (as discussed in chapter 6) in hiring, supervising, and retaining employees. The supervision referred to here is supervision of the employee, not supervision of the young people. Responsibility in this area includes the selection, supervision, and retention of volunteers, as well as people on the payroll. Failure to exercise this responsibility properly can lead to significant liability claims against the employer.

There are two features of this kind of claim that are worthy of note. First, the negligent hiring, supervision, or retention claim is different than a respondeat superior claim as discussed in chapter 6. In the respondeat superior claim, the employer *is* liable for the acts of the employee committed in the scope of her or his employment. There is no need to prove the employer is negligent or committed a tortious act if the employee has done so, because the employer is considered to be acting by or through the employee and is vicariously liable for whatever the employee has done. Litigation of the church's position in these cases is usually about (1) whether or not the individual really was an employee, and (2) whether the act in question was committed in the scope of employment and, therefore, binds the employer, as well as (3) whether there was any negligence by the employee. One reason for bringing a negligent hiring, supervision, or retention claim is that frequently the acts in question are not in the scope of employment and there is no vicarious liability, hence, the plaintiff seeks to prove negligence on the employer's part in putting the tortfeasor in a position to injure

people. The relevant negligence, then, in this sort of claim, is in placing an employee with a propensity to do harm, which the employer knew or should have known of, in a position in which to do that harm.

Second, because these claims almost invariably involve sexual misconduct, either by the molestation of minors or the seduction of a female counselee, they often present major challenges to the employer. The challenge derives from two factors: public attention and liability exposure.

Public attention is often drawn to sexual misconduct litigation by the media, whether or not the misconduct involves clergy or religious organizations. Because such conduct stands in such sharp contrast to the standards of the institution, it is the more newsworthy and the religious institution the more embarrassed by the attention. One case of sexual misconduct by clergy or religious workers is one too many.

The financial crisis arises because liability claims for sexual misconduct are often uninsured. Legal defense costs alone can be significant, and the exposure to loss if a claimant is successful, particularly for the sexual abuse of a minor, can be substantial and can involve punitive damages.

Claims with respect to hiring or firing clergy or others performing a religious function raise serious First Amendment issues. The courts have repeatedly declined on constitutional grounds to judge such matters.[64] Despite this refusal of the courts to judge disputes involving the hiring and firing of clergy, there is no argument to be made that sexual misconduct of clergy toward minors or counselees has First Amendment protection. It is, accordingly, unlikely that churches and religious organizations could shield themselves from such a negligent hiring claim based on their religious freedom protection in selection of clergy. With respect to employees or volunteers whose functions do not include specifically religious duties, the First Amendment argument, of course, disappears altogether.

A claim of negligent hiring requires showing that the employee is in fact incompetent or unfit to perform the job for which hired and that the employer knew or should have known of that incompetency or unfitness.[65]

*a. Hiring Counselors and
Youth Workers*

Religious institutions that engage in counseling and youth work at any level should be alert to the fitness and reliability of both paid staff and volunteers who work with counselees or minors in any way. Be aware that child molesters seek out institutions that deal with youth, including churches, and may use pseudonyms. Consider at least the following:

1. Use an application form prepared or reviewed by an attorney.[66] Some states have statutory requirements for hiring counselors. Your attorney or, possibly, denominational resources can direct you to these. Include a representation that the application is truthful, and a warning that a misrepresentation will be grounds for immediate discharge.
2. Require a complete job history and references from prior employers and youth work groups or agencies with whom the applicant has previously worked. Determine the references yourself—for example, immediate supervisor, senior staff person, and board chair of any youth-serving organization the applicant has been employed by or volunteered with for the past ten years. Check the references. Be sure to describe the work the applicant will be doing, including any counseling or work with youth or children. Ask the reference if they know of any reason the applicant would not be fit or trustworthy for the duties involved, what other organizations the applicant has worked for with similar duties, whom one might talk to in those organizations, and if there is anything else you ought to know about the applicant. Beware of hesitant or guarded responses, refusal to comment, or indications of an agreement between the applicant and former employer about what can be said. Get the applicant to give the former employer a release to provide records and talk freely if you are not getting satisfactory answers. Do not accept the applicant's account of why he or she left, without corroboration. Be alert to indications of a quiet resignation in exchange for the former employer forgoing investigation of charges that are, then, never proven. Make and keep a record of the reference contact.
3. Beware of gaps in the job history with vague explanations.
4. Get a history of church membership and attendance with the clergy identified. Check with them as with other references.
5. If the applicant is unknown to you, require identification. Consider requiring that volunteers be affiliated with the congregation for a period of time—six months or so—before giving them responsibility for young people.
6. Check with state authorities and police for any criminal record involving child abuse or molestation. Most states maintain a registry of child abuse complaints. It may be confidential, but employers or prospective employers may be able, with the employee's or applicant's authorization, to determine if his or her name is in it. Ask on the application for the date, court, and nature of offense for any criminal convictions other than minor traffic violations.
7. For critical positions, you may want to hire a service that does employment investigations. It may not be too expensive. You should get a written report from the service that will give the institution some confidence, as well as a level of liability protection, in the event a problem occurs.
8. Ask the individual directly, and include on your application form, whether he or she has any history of child abuse or sexual molestation of minors or, for counselors, of sexual relationships with counselees. While an actual abuser may be unlikely to answer these questions honestly, they may have a deterrent effect, alerting the individual that you are watchful for such problems, as well as demonstrating your prudent conduct if you are sued for negligent hiring. Keep a written record of the interview and responses to these questions.
9. Train your staff on child abuse–reporting laws in effect in your state,[67] and have a clear statement of policy, reviewed by an attorney and consistent with state law, of

your institution's opposition to such practices and the obligation to report them. Vigilant attention and publicity to the matter may also deter prospective child abusers from applying.

10. Do not assume that the only people you may have problems with are males or unmarried males. Neither assumption is consistent with case histories.

11. Provide in application forms that all employment is "at will."

12. Have a simpler interview and checklist for volunteers but use a written policy. Get references if the applicant is not well known to you, and ask, as standard policy, about any history of sexual misconduct toward minors.

13. Beware that most abusers were themselves abused as minors. Be especially alert if persons have a known history of being abused.

These matters must be addressed with discretion. It is not practical to have a police check of everyone who volunteers to watch over the church nursery, nor is it necessary to go through an extensive process for a grandmother who has been going to your church all her life and wants to teach Sunday School. The nature of the responsibility, the individual circumstances, and how well known the individual is to you will dictate the degree of caution that is appropriate.

While most negligent hiring cases involve sexual misconduct, this is not the only area of potential liability. It would be appropriate, for example, to check the driving record of someone who is going to be a bus driver; and a general criminal check of any employee is not out of place. Employers have been held liable for negligently hiring a janitor who commits a rape on the premises.

b. Supervising Youth Workers

Suppose you have made all of your reference checks and done everything right in bringing on employees or volunteers. Does your duty end there? The answer is "not necessarily." "Negligent supervision" refers to the notion that the employer has a responsibility or duty to the people its employees deal with to exercise some supervision to prevent injury. In our con-

text, we are primarily concerned with injury from sexual misconduct toward minors or counselees. Negligent supervision is frequently pleaded in cases of this sort, but in the absence of some information that comes to the employer's attention suggesting that there is a problem with the employee, it is much less frequently a basis for liability. There are actions you can take for risk management in this area:

1. Avoid placing youth workers in sole leadership positions. Sharing leadership reduces the risk factor, for obvious reasons. Having married couples share leadership is often desirable.

2. Be particularly alert to potential problems in one-on-one or overnight situations.

3. Keep in touch with youth activities by talking to the children involved. There is no need to be secretive or investigatory or to ask questions that imply suspicion. Simply having the pastor or supervisory personnel communicating regularly, freely, and informally with participants in child and youth programs gives one an opportunity to sense how the young people are feeling, how things are going, and to pick up any hints of problems. The sexual abuse of children occurs alone and is kept in the dark. Keeping adult company involved in youth activities is a healthy policy.

4. Be alert to any circumstances that seem unusual, such as a particular youth worker always giving the same child a ride to and from meetings or meeting with the child at times other than regularly organized group activities.

c. Counselors

Risk management in the area of supervision of counseling presents a different set of problems. The counselee is an adult and is legally capable of consenting to sexual relations. In some states, however, even consenting sexual relations with a counselee may be criminal, and the particular situation can give rise to serious legal liability for reasons set forth in chapter 18. Unlike youth leadership, the very nature of the counseling situation usually requires privacy. The counselee has come to the counselor because he or she has a problem and needs advice. Usually the problem is by its nature private, and a counselee does not want it broadcast to the world. The essence of the counseling relationship would be destroyed by having a supervisor sit in.

Much pastoral counseling involves a male counselor counseling a female counselee. The counselee is distraught, her defenses are down, and she is looking for an authority figure whom she trusts to guide her through her difficulties. Often the subject matter in the counseling involves marital or relational problems with a husband or boyfriend, thus introducing the topic of sex and sexuality. The female counselee may be young and attractive, the male counselor an authority figure. The stage is set for a problem. The pastoral counselor who behaves with the utmost circumspection may find that the counselee is inviting a more intimate relationship. Even if both parties are conducting the counseling sessions in perfect holiness, the very situation can give rise to suspicion on the part of others.

Pastoral counselors have addressed this situation in a number of ways. Some refuse to counsel women, calling on their wives or other women in the body to do so. This policy affords perfect protection at the price of (1) depriving women of counseling based on the pastor's training, experience, and spiritual insights, and (2) likely destroying the evidentiary privilege against compelled testimony in court, discussed in chapter 18. Other pastors may counsel women only with their wife or another woman present. This may meet the liability concern at the price of inhibiting the counselee from sharing her difficulties and, again, destroying the confidentiality of the communication if it becomes the subject of litigation. Still others practice the open-door policy of scheduling counseling only when their wives, the church secretary, or another female is on the premises nearby and doors are left open. This also may bear a price in inhibiting the counselee and may prove unsatisfactory if, for example, the counseling session is still going on at five o'clock when the church secretary goes home and there is no one on the other side of the open door.

There is no perfect solution to the dilemma of providing full and confidential counseling services to troubled members of the church and others who need it and also providing perfect insulation against potential liability. But it is fair for a governing board of a church or other religious body in which counseling is occurring to ask how the counselors are managing the situation and to establish policies with them to provide the best guidance and protection for them and the institution that they can devise for their circumstances. Some inquiry into the pastor's training, providing further education to the pastor, determining and subscribing to any standards or recommendations from the denomination or, if the church is independent, from a denomination or religious organization that shares the church's theological perspective, and being aware of ethical standards that guide religious counselors and secular therapists with respect to relationships with counselees can all assist.

From the counselor's perspective, any temptation to improper behavior on his or her part or suggestion of seductiveness on the part of the counselee should be immediately and uncompromisingly rejected. If the counselor is unable to maintain a counseling relationship without temptation, the relationship should be terminated and the counselee referred to someone else.

d. Negligent Retention

Negligent retention is the final kind of non-respondeat superior claim that is made to hold an employer liable for the acts of its employees. In order to have a negligent retention claim, there must be some showing that the employer had notice of the problem with the employee which led to the injury (which generally amounts to a negligent hiring or supervision claim). In the absence of some evidence that the employer had reason to know of a problem, it should not be liable for negligent retention.

Risk management against negligent retention claims consists of promptly investigating any claims of improper conduct by employees to a point of finality. If the alleged improper conduct is of a nature that could lead to serious harm to another, such as sexual abuse of minors, sexual seduction of counselees, reckless driving, or a propensity to assault, the employer should pursue the investigation to a point of finality and take appropriate action. It must do so keeping Potiphar's wife in mind (Genesis 39). Not every such accusation is accurate, and case histories reveal accusations of sexual impropriety made against pastors and counselors for a variety of other reasons. In some well-publicized cases in recent years, children have been shown to be highly suggestible, and vivid descriptions of bizarre conduct and even killings have, upon investigation, been devoid of any corroborating evidence. The reputation, job, income, and emotional and physical health of a person accused of such conduct may be at stake. Investigations should be conducted privately and confidentially, and a judgment made on the accuracy of any accusation. If the allegations are of child abuse, however, including sexual abuse, there may be a mandatory reporting obligation under state law.[68] If sexual or other misconduct that may cause significant harm has occurred, termination of the employee is usually the only viable option. To maintain him or her risks a devastating legal judgment in the event of a recurrence.

Can sexual offenders ever be given a second chance? The instincts of the church are to forgive and to seek healing and restoration, instincts that are supported by the claims of the mental health profession. From a legal perspective, however, the answer to this question must be a firm No. The best intended and most rehabilitated people can slip back into old habits when returned to old settings. It would be difficult, if not impossible, to defend a repeat offense. How can you explain to parents or a jury that you knew a person had a history of sexual abuse of children and yet put that person in a position to abuse another youngster?

The best the church can reasonably do for a rehabilitated offender would be to offer an employment opportunity in a situation that permitted no contact whatsoever with the kind of circumstances surrounding the original offense. Even that can be risky—any employee of a youth-serving institution is likely to have contact with the youth, even if not in a program or leadership position.

5. Termination

When termination is or may be necessary, be aware of the rules by which the relationship is governed. Is the employee an "at-will" employee? If so, are there any reasons for the termination that would be improper in your state for firing an at-will employee? Do you need "cause" to fire an at-will employee in your state? Is there a contract? If so, what provisions in it relate to termination? Then consider the following suggestions.

a. Substantive Fairness

Perhaps the best way both to avoid, or eventually win, a lawsuit is to treat discharges fairly. A few questions you should ask yourself before discharging an employee (a good plaintiff's lawyer will ask them, and a jury will consider them) are:

1. Did the employee have notice? Were the rule or standard and the consequences for failing to meet it stated clearly to the employee? (Remember the importance of evaluations and discipline, discussed above.) If notice was in writing, it is all the better.
2. Is the reason for discharge related to the orderly, safe, efficient operation of the employer?
3. How is the employer hurt by the conduct which is the cause for the termination?
4. Is the expected performance of the employee realistic?
5. Do termination, the reason for it, and the rule behind it make "common sense"?
6. Does the punishment fit the crime? Is termination "overkill"? Have other employees been terminated for the same misconduct? If not, what is the legitimate justification for treating this case differently?
7. Are there extenuating circumstances of personal crisis that should properly be considered, such as divorce or loss of a family member, and that may account for a temporary drop in performance? Such circumstances should not deter a termination for such causes as financial or sexual misconduct. But in cases in which cause is required and consists of less efficient job performance, a jury is likely to

hear and sympathize with such short-term behavior of someone who has otherwise been a good, long-term employee.

Asking these questions can not only help you avoid legal problems but may help you avoid making a personnel mistake that costs you a potentially valuable employee.

b. Procedural Fairness

Judges are used to dealing in a legal system that places particular emphasis on "due process," that is to say, does the process used to terminate an employee insure fairness, or does it seem arbitrary, discriminatory, or otherwise unlikely to produce a fair result, regardless of the substantive issues involved. Some of the issues involved in assuring due process, or procedural fairness, are:

1. Check—and follow religiously—any termination procedures set forth in the employee handbook, policy manual, circulars, etc. Failure to follow your own system may constitute a breach of contract even though the discharge was justified, and will create an impression of an arbitrary and unfair discharge.[69]
2. Investigate the problem.
   (a) Do not act too quickly. The decisiveness that marks sound business judgment in other settings can backfire with firings. If the situation seems to demand that the employee be immediately relieved of his or her duties or removed from the premises, you can suspend the employee with or without pay while investigating. If it turns out that firing is not warranted, you can explain the situation to the employee and bring him or her back with payment for the lost time.
   (b) Allow employees to tell their side. If an employee's story is different from management's, investigate the discrepancies.
   (c) Be fair and objective. Look for evidence that supports the employee's case as if you were the employee's attorney.
   (d) Obtain written statements where possible. For example, ask for written statements from witnesses and obtain copies of other relevant documents, such as police or insurance reports. Tape-recorded statements are acceptable but get specific permission, recorded on the tape or in writing, to do so.
   (e) Review the entire record in detail, including information gathered from the steps taken above, as well as the employee's personnel file, periodic evaluations, and application. Be aware that the better the employee's past record and the longer his or her service to the company, the more cause you may need to justify a discharge.[70] Also consider the level of the employee. The more discretion and judgment that go with the position, the greater the discretion that will be tolerated in a discharge.
   (f) Review the supervisor's file. Has the supervisor been criticized for personnel management? Is the supervisor's behavior erratic?
3. Share your decision in advance. The decision should be reviewed—*in advance*—by the employee's immediate supervisor, the next level supervisor, and, if possible, the personnel director. Agreement by two or three levels avoids mistakes and makes correct actions more defensible in court.
4. Document carefully.
   (a) State the real reasons for firing. Attempting to sugar coat the news can lead ex-employees (and their attorneys) to believe a wrongful discharge exists when one does not and may impair your credibility. You may win, but at a high cost. Be complete and thorough.
   (b) Document actions taken in compliance with statutory or in-house procedures.
   (c) Draft documents with care. Realize that documents related to the firing could eventually end up as court exhibits. Throw away all drafts, keeping only the final version of any memos or other documents.
5. Consider lesser penalties. In certain cases, a lesser penalty than discharge may be appropriate. Options include transfer, reprimand, suspension without pay, and demotion. Such actions should be selectively and carefully utilized.[71]

c. *"Red Flag" Cases*

Certain cases are more likely to result in lawsuits. The following is a laundry list of "red flag" cases that should always be investigated with extra care. In such cases, it may be wise to consult counsel before discharge.

- possible discrimination
- "whistle blowers" (employees who have reported violations of local, state, or federal rules or laws, who otherwise participate in court actions against the employer, or who refuse to carry out an illegal order)
- union activity
- workers' compensation claim filed
- sick leave, maternity, or disability claimed
- complaints about working conditions
- personality conflicts with supervisors
- imminent bonus, pension vesting, commissions, etc.
- nonwork-related reasons
- suspicious timing
- employees "wooed" away from competitors with promises of security or advancement

d. *Handling the Termination*

1. Demeanor. Have two management representatives present at all exit interviews.[72] Recognize that the termination should be handled discreetly, and the employee should not feel "ganged up on." The presence of a third person provides a witness to what is said on termination.

   You should be firm, unapologetic, candid, fair, and humane. Do not be angry or insulting, or embarrassing.

   Maintain your composure and do not invite problems by defamation or intentional infliction of emotional distress.

2. Terms.

   (a) Consider providing outplacement services to help the employee find another job.[73]

   (b) Consider allowing the employee the opportunity to resign, and promise not to contest any unemployment compensation application. This does not mean misrepresenting the reason for discharge but merely not actively opposing it and leaving it to the state agency to decide if unemployment compensation is warranted.

   (c) Be fair in the final paycheck. Allow full credit for vacation time, wages owed, and separation pay. Not only can employees have these benefits enforced through the state labor department, but employees who do so may also end up getting free advice on a wrongful discharge case.

   (d) Do not try to encourage the employee to resign by withdrawing responsibilities, privileges, etc. This can be interpreted as intentional infliction of emotional distress.

3. Releases. When there seems to be a prospect of litigation, consider a release. For a release or termination agreement to be valid, you must provide some consideration beyond wages or benefits already due the employee.[74] The employee should normally have some opportunity to bargain over terms (including having an attorney, if desired) and should understand the consequences of the agreement.[75] As the enforceability of a release depends on numerous factors, you should consult an attorney when considering whether and how to use a release.

e. *After Termination*

1. References. To avoid defamation suits, be circumspect about what you or your supervisors tell others about the fired employee. A good rule is to refuse to provide any information on former employees without a written waiver from the employee. Information provided should be factual and supported by documentation; it should not be opinions and speculation.

2. Monitor unemployment compensation proceedings. You should monitor any hearings with an eye to obtaining any useful evidence or admission.

6. Special Considerations for Religious Employers

Churches and many religious organizations have special employment requirements that are not applicable to secular employers. These requirements may apply only to clergy or those involved in direct religious ministries such as teaching, counseling, or leading worship or other program activities. Other organizations may view the religious ministry as applicable to all employees of the organization, including those whose principal function may appear to be secular, such as secretaries, janitors, kitchen staff, and the like. Still others will have employees whose jobs, even by the organization's self-understanding, are entirely secular, but will require certain standards for those employees. Some of the most common employment requirements may be:

1. That the employee be a member of the religious denomination or faith of the organization and subscribe to its statement of faith, or otherwise give evidence of satisfactory religious standing.
2. That the employee adhere to biblical standards of belief, practice, and personal conduct as understood by the organization.
3. That the employee abstain from certain specific conduct that the organization believes is proscribed for religious reasons, such as homosexual conduct, heterosexual sex outside of marriage, or consumption of alcohol or controlled drugs (in the case of Christian Science this may extend to all drugs or medications). Churches or religious organizations that adhere to biblical standards of conduct could expand the list substantially.
4. Organizational beliefs concerning the role of women in the workplace, for example, that they should not be employed if they have children younger than a certain age, should not occupy certain positions of religious leadership, or be ordained as clergy.
5. The organization's religious commitment to biblical dispute resolution with its employees.

Whatever these particular concerns may be for any given church or religious organization, the following nine suggestions may aid the organization to sustain them as employment conditions against attack by terminated or unhappy employees or government regulatory agencies:

1. Include in your statement of faith all beliefs that may be of particular application in the employment situation, such as those listed above. Be sure that this is provided to employment applicants *before* they are hired and reviewed with them during the hiring process, and that they sign an acknowledgment of their acceptance of it and an agreement to adhere to the standards as part of becoming employed.
2. If there is to be any separate, written employment contract, be sure it includes or specifically refers to the statement of faith and all of the special provisions which the church requires of its employees.
3. Ground any such requirements in Scripture, canon law, or other documents of church governance as specifically as possible to evidence the religious nature of the commitment.
4. Be sure that any faith-based rules that the organization wishes to adhere to are really that. There is nothing wrong with having policies that are based on good judgment rather than religious belief, but they will not be entitled to constitutional protection if they run afoul of government laws or policies, such as those banning sex discrimination.
5. Be sure that performance reviews, disciplinary action, or discharge which is based on religious considerations is specific on the religious ground of the evaluation or action and that this is communicated to the employee and included in any written record.
6. Review all of your personnel policies and practices to be sure they are in conformity with law. Be sure that you are not inadvertently or by unspoken presumptions engaging in sex discrimination, for example. If there is a bona fide religious reason why the organization feels a need to discriminate or otherwise engage in a personnel practice which is not in conformity with law, seek legal advice as to your position in the matter and be sure that you are adopting any policies that

do not conform to law out of sincere religious conviction. Testimony by a pastor, school administrator, or the like that the organization is opposed to the discrimination with which it is charged but does not think the government should have any jurisdiction to set it right will not be the most convincing defense.

7. Make specific provision in employment contracts for an alternative dispute resolution mechanism to be carried out in a church context, and insist upon following it when a dispute arises.[76]

8. Follow your doctrinal beliefs consistently. The credibility of a claim of interference with religious freedom is seriously impaired if the plaintiff can point to instances when you did not follow the principle you espouse.

9. If you have to litigate an employment case in which the organization's religious freedom position is at issue, be sure that your attorney understands and that you communicate clearly to the court the nature and depth of the religious issue involved in the case, why religious freedom will be impaired, and what the biblical or other religious basis is for your position. The judge may not agree with your religious position, but if she or he understands that it truly is a bona fide, sincere, and central religious belief, it is much more likely to be respected. Many cases have been lost because the organization's witnesses on the stand were simply not convincing in their testimony that religious freedom would be impaired by allowing the issue to be decided by a court or decided in favor of the complaining party.

REFERENCES

Bloss, Julie. *Employment Law: A Guide for Churches*. (Published by Church Management, Inc., P.O. Box 162527, Austin, TX. 78716). Excellent overview of important employment laws, particularly antidiscrimination laws. Does not deal with federal income tax or Social Security.

CHAPTER 13

The Church as Wagepayer

A. Federal Income Tax Withholding
B. Social Security
C. Workers' Compensation
D. Unemployment Compensation
E. Federal Employee Benefit Laws

A. FEDERAL INCOME TAX WITHHOLDING

All churches and religious organizations are obliged to withhold federal income taxes from the wages of their employees and to report them and pay them over to the Internal Revenue Service in accordance with the applicable rules. There is no religious exemption from this obligation, nor is there any limitation based upon whether or not a church or organization is engaged in commerce or has some minimum number of employees. One employee in the most local and purely religious endeavor will trigger the obligation as surely as a thousand employees engaged in a commercial enterprise across state lines.

There are some important qualifications. The most important from a church or religious organization's perspective is that the withholding obligation does not apply to wages paid for "services performed by a duly ordained, commissioned, or licensed minister of a church in the exercise of his ministry."[1] The meaning of this term is discussed in more detail in chapter 5, above. The exemption from withholding, however, does not exempt clergy from taxation. Many clergy prefer to have federal income taxes withheld, even though it is not required,

to eliminate estimating, quarterly reports, and potential penalties; and they may do so with the employer's consent by filing a completed Form W–4 (Employees Withholding Allowance Certificate) with the employer. Such voluntary withholding arrangements can be terminated unilaterally by either party or by mutual consent.

The second major qualification to the obligation to withhold, report, and pay over federal income taxes is that it applies only to employees, not to self-employed persons or independent contractors. The discussions of who is an employee for Social Security or liability purposes contained in chapter 6 and section B of this chapter are equally pertinent to the determination of employee status for purposes of federal income tax withholding. The presumption of self-employed status that applies to clergy for FICA purposes, however, does not apply for federal income tax purposes.

Constitutional attacks on the application of the federal income tax withholding requirements to churches and religious organizations have been uniformly unsuccessful.

Churches and religious organizations, like other employers, have a number of obligations in connection with administering the federal withholding tax procedure. These may be briefly summarized as follows:

1. The organization must have a federal Employer Identification Number (EIN), obtained by submitting Form SS–4 to the IRS.
2. Persons to whom funds are paid for services must be identified as employed or self-employed, and Social Security numbers must be obtained for each worker.

3. The organization must obtain a Form W–4 or W–4A for each employee in order to determine how much to withhold.

4. Based on Form W–4 or W–4A and the withholding tables (contained in IRS Publication 15 and Circular E), the amount to be withheld per pay period must be determined.

5. Churches that have not made a timely and qualified election to exempt themselves from Social Security taxes must withhold and pay FICA taxes on the wages of all nonminister employees.

6. Withheld taxes must be deposited as follows:

a. If less than $500 at the end of any month, deposit is not required.

b. If less than $500 at the end of any calendar quarter, the amount need not be deposited but can be paid directly to the IRS with Form 941 or 941E.

c. If the withheld taxes (including income taxes and employees' and employer's share of FICA) are $50,000 or less for a lookback period (7/1/91 to 6/30/92 for 1993), the taxes must be deposited within fifteen days after the end of the month at a financial institution qualified to act as a depository for federal taxes or the Federal Reserve Bank serving the area. You must use a federal tax deposit coupon (Form 8109).

d. If withheld income taxes and the employee's and employer's share of FICA taxes are over $50,000 during the lookback period taxes must be deposited semiweekly (the next Wednesday for Wednesday, Thursday, or Friday pay days, otherwise the next Friday), or by the next banking day if they are $100,000 or more.

7. Form 941 must be filed for each calendar quarter by the last day of the following month. It reports the number of employees and the amount of FICA and withheld taxes payable. A church with only one employee, who is the minister, need not file Form 941, even if the minister is treated as an employee, if the church is not withholding taxes. A church which has elected to be exempt from Social Security should file Form 941E.

8. All employees' wages and withheld income and FICA taxes are reported to the IRS on Form W–2 annually. The form is provided in triplicate to employees before February 1 of the following year, and an additional copy is filed with the Social Security Administration, along with a Form W–3 transmittal form. Special rules may apply to reporting employee business expense reimbursements.

9. Self-employed persons receiving nonemployee compensation of $600 or more receive a Form 1099–MISC, and persons receiving interest payments of ten dollars or more receive a Form 1099–INT before February 1 of the following year, with an additional copy submitted to the IRS before March 1 with a Form 1096 transmittal form. Churches will need to have Social Security numbers for self-employed persons to whom they make payments in order to properly complete this form. If the individual refuses to provide it, the church may be required to withhold 20 percent of the compensation as backup withholding. Visiting evangelists, guest speakers, musicians, and individual independent contractors who are paid for particular tasks performed at the church should receive Form 1099.

Careful compliance with federal income tax withholding requirements is important to both the organization and the individuals administering it. Employers are obligated to the government for wages that should have been withheld, whether or not they are. Improperly classifying an individual as self-employed who is later determined to be employed can result in a penalty. Failure to issue W–2s or 1099s is subject to a penalty of fifty dollars for each failure. An intentional failure results in a penalty of 10 percent of the total amount of unreported compensation. Finally, and importantly, any responsible person, such as a corporate officer, who willfully fails to withhold taxes and pay them over to the government may be personally liable for the taxes that should have been withheld. When an organization is having financial difficulty, sometimes the easiest place to find some money is the money set aside for withheld taxes or the employer's share of FICA when due. Resist the temptation to "borrow" this money. The price of this deviation from required procedure may come out of the wallet of the individuals responsible for it. This subject is discussed further in chapter 11.

The foregoing is a brief outline of major obligations with respect to federal income tax withholding and reporting by churches and religious organizations. With the exception of the exemption from the obligation to withhold federal income taxes from clergy compensation, even if the cleric is employed, they do not differ from the obligations of payroll administration in a secular organization. Individuals responsible for administering such organizations and these payroll procedures should consult one of the works listed in the References at the end of this chapter that deals with the subject on a detailed basis or an accountant, attorney, or other specialist in this area to insure that procedures are being correctly followed.

B. SOCIAL SECURITY

The Social Security system began in 1937, in the Great Depression, to provide protection to workers in certain circumstances. Benefits provided by the Social Security system include retirement benefits paid to insured persons, survivor benefits paid to the surviving spouse or dependent children of deceased workers, disability payments to certain permanently disabled workers, and the Medicare program, which provides certain medical and hospital benefits at age sixty-five. These benefits are financed through two separate tax systems, the Federal Insurance Contributions Act (FICA), which imposes a tax on a percentage of an employee's wages against both employers and employees; and the Self-Employment Contributions Act (SECA), which is imposed on the net earnings of self-employed persons.

A duly ordained, commissioned, or licensed minister is always considered self-employed for Social Security purposes with respect to services performed in the exercise of her or his ministry. Chapter 5 discusses in more detail when a cleric fits within these definitions. Application of the self-employment tax to ministers is discussed more fully in chapter 14.

When it began the Social Security sys-

tem exempted churches and other nonprofit organizations from coverage, an exemption that could be waived, since they were not able to pass the cost along to customers through price increases as could commercial enterprises. The exemption ended in 1984, and churches and religious organizations are currently subject to the Social Security tax on employees (except ministers who are deemed self-employed for Social Security purposes, as noted above). Churches have a one-time right to exempt themselves from Social Security if they are opposed to payment of the taxes for religious reasons. The exemption must be filed on Form 8274 prior to when the church would first be required to file a quarterly employer's tax return reporting its share of FICA taxes. Quarterly tax returns (Form 941) are due on April 30, July 31, October 31, and January 31. Since ministers are not covered, churches having no nonminister employees are not required to file the exemption until the due date of the first quarterly return after they hire a nonminister employee. Form 941 also reports compensation and federal income tax withholding, but an election is not barred by filing Form 941 for income tax purposes if there is no FICA tax obligation. Note that churches are not exempt from Social Security because they are churches. They are *only* exempt if their objection to Social Security is based on religious reasons *and* if they file a timely election. The exemption may not be claimed for economic or other nonreligious reasons. Most churches and religious organizations will probably not qualify for the exemption for lack of a *religious* reason to oppose payment of the tax.

Organizations that qualify for the election are not limited to churches. Conventions or associations of churches and elementary or secondary schools controlled, operated, or principally supported by a church, a convention, or an association of churches are qualified to make the election, because they are considered to be included in the term "church." Qualified controlled organizations may also make the election. This includes any church-controlled organization that is tax exempt under the Internal Revenue Code except those which offer goods, services, or facilities for sale other than on an incidental basis to the general public and normally receive more than 25 percent of their support from a combination of governmental sources and certain other receipts. Church-controlled hospitals would normally not qualify for the election, but seminaries or religious retreat centers and church auxiliary organizations, such as youth groups, women's auxiliaries, church pension boards, and fund-raising organizations, generally would be eligible. The qualification of church-run organizations such as orphanages and homes for the aged is likely to turn on their funding sources.

A timely election relieves the church and employee of the obligation to pay FICA taxes. However, individual employees are then treated as self-employed for Social Security purposes and must pay the SECA tax, which combines what would have been the employer's and the employee's share of the FICA tax. In short, the savings to the church is paid by the employee. There is a certain offsetting income tax deduction and SECA earnings reduction, but the employee will still bear some additional financial burden from being treated as self-employed. The employee will also be burdened with filing a quarterly estimated tax report and paying the self-employment tax in quarterly installments. This obligation can be avoided if the church or qualified church-controlled organization simply withholds the additional amount to cover the self-employment tax liability from each paycheck and reports it as additional income tax withheld on the church quarterly 941 forms. This becomes a credit against the self-employment tax that the employee may claim on his or her federal income tax return, in effect applied against self-employment tax responsibility. Absent such an arrangement agreed to by the church at the request of the employee, a church that has made a timely and proper election to exempt itself from FICA has no obligation to withhold Social Security taxes from its employees' compensation.

Effective with calendar quarters beginning after December 31, 1986, the election is irrevocable, although exemption forms that may still be in use from an earlier date (Form 8274) state to the contrary. If churches filed an election but continued to pay employment taxes through December 31, 1986, the IRS treats them as if they had not filed the election.

Some churches that have elected exemption have felt constrained to increase employee compensation to make up for the additional cost to the employee, thus leaving the church financially in the same position as if it had not elected the exemption. Constitutional attacks on this and other aspects of the Social Security system perceived as discriminatory with respect to religious organizations or intruding on religious freedom have been unsuccessful in court.[2]

Churches that have exempted themselves from FICA by timely election remain subject to income tax withholding and must continue to issue W–2 forms and file quarterly returns with the IRS for all nonminister employees and ministers who have voluntary withholding. The form used is 941E for quarterly returns. Nonexempt churches file Form 941. Failing to issue W–2 forms to employees for two years and disregarding an IRS request to do so can lead to a revocation of the church's exemption from Social Security coverage.

Churches and church-controlled organizations that have not filed a timely election to exempt themselves from FICA taxes must withhold the employee's share of FICA taxes and pay the employer and employee shares of persons who are employees. There is no obligation with respect to those who are self-employed or independent contractors.

The distinction between the self-employed or independent contractor and the employee is discussed in chapter 6. The test for Social Security purposes is essentially the same—an employer-employee relationship exists when a person for whom the work is performed has the right to control and direct the individual performing the work, not only as to the result but also as to the details and means by which the result is to be accomplished. Actual control is not necessary; it is sufficient if the employer has the right to control. The right to discharge is an important factor indicating that the requisite degree of control is present for an employer-employee relationship. Furnishing tools and a place to work is often also significant. Employees comply with instructions and have a continuous relationship with the employer, do the work personally, frequently work full time, can be dismissed, can normally leave the job without having a contractual liability to the employer, receive reimbursement for expenses, and receive training and work in a way that is integrated into the operation of the employer. Independent contractors are self-employed persons who employ their own assistants, determine when and how they will do their work, set their own hours, work for more than one party at the same time, get paid by the job, make their services available to the general public, have the opportunity for profit or loss in their endeavor, furnish their own tools, do work on their own or another's premises, and often make a substantial investment in their job. None of these criteria will apply in a hard and fast way to a given situation, but they are guidelines which must be observed to sort workers into the employed and self-employed categories for purposes of administering payroll taxes. Church secretaries, regular or full-time custodians, and paid organists and choir directors are likely to be employees. An individual or firm that enters into contracts for such things as church cleaning, snow removal, yard care, or other repair and maintenance activities is likely to be an independent contractor.

A detailed exposition on the application of payroll tax law and procedures is beyond the scope of this work. Church and religious organization administrators and personnel who administer payroll tax procedures are encouraged to acquire some of the specialized works listed at the end of this chapter to familiarize themselves with their obligations.

C. WORKERS' COMPENSATION

On-the-job injuries have always been a hazard and a problem in the employment relationship. In the American legal system, they caused a proliferation of job-based litigation between employer and employee which was expensive to both and yielded uneven results. Consequently, all fifty states have enacted workers', or workmen's, compensation laws to remove job-related injuries or illnesses from the system of litigation based on legal fault discussed in chapter 6. Workplace or job-related injuries or illnesses are placed in a separate administrative system in which compensation is assured if the injury or illness is employment-related but is rendered at fixed rates, usually a percentage of the compensation the employee was receiving. Employees are not permitted to sue employers and are sometimes also barred from suing fellow employees. The system is funded by insurance payments to a state workers' compensation fund, or, in some instances, by self-insurance by the employer. Job-related injuries or illnesses are thus treated as a cost of doing business and the ultimate burden is born by the consumers of the business.

Workers' compensation litigation addresses whether or not there was an employment relationship (as opposed to a self-employed or independent contractor relationship),[3] whether or not the injury or illness occurred during employment or is employment related, and the nature and extent of the disability.

The law of each state must be consulted to determine whether or not a church or religious organization is subject to the workers' compensation law of that state and what its responsibilities are under that law. Some states exempt churches or nonprofit organizations generally, and some exempt small employers. Absent qualifying for a specific statutory exemption, churches and religious organizations have generally been subject to workers' compensation; they may have to include in their coverage persons paid to do work as part of a charitable program for the needy.[4]

Constitutional arguments against requiring religious organizations to participate in workers' compensation programs have been unavailing. Under a *Catholic Bishop* analysis, workers' compensation is not viewed as raising serious First Amendment issues so as to require abstention from applying the statute. The claims that religious beliefs require the exclusive lordship of Christ over the church and the use of church funds solely for biblical purposes have not been successful in overriding the compelling government interest in the maintenance of a workers' compensation program.[5] The *Smith* case discussed in chapter 3, section F, will make it even more difficult to press a claim that religious freedom concerns should exempt churches and religious organizations from obligations of the workers' compensation system.

Churches that fail to comply with workers' compensation requirements may be subject to direct liability to employees for injuries. Churches that are not required to participate in a workers' compensation system may wish to determine whether or not they have the option of joining the system and may wish to do so for the protection of themselves and their employees. All churches and religious organizations that are subject to the workers' compensation law should be sure that they have purchased workers' compensation coverage and that they maintain it in force or otherwise keep themselves in compliance with state funding requirements.

D. UNEMPLOYMENT COMPENSATION

Unemployment compensation is another area of social legislation spawned by the Depression of the 1930s. Employers pay a federal unemployment tax on wages they pay on covered employment. State employment security laws in all states implement the federal minimum coverage standards and in some cases expand it. Employers are allowed a credit of up to 90 percent of the federal tax for contributions under state laws that are approved by the federal government.

While the federal unemployment tax does not apply to any religious, charitable, or other organization that is tax exempt under federal law,[6] the exemption has been narrowed somewhat with respect to state compensation plans by a federal religious exemption which is required of state plans as a condition of federal approval. States must cover all nonprofit organizations unless they are specifically exempted. Exempt services include:

1. Service in the employ of (a) a church, convention, or association of churches, or (b) an organization which is operated primarily for religious purposes and which is operated, supervised, controlled, or principally supported by a church, convention, or association of churches;
2. Service by a duly ordained, commissioned, or licensed minister of a church in the exercise of the ministry or by a member of a religious order in the exercise of duties required by such order.[7]

In the 1981 case of *St. Martin Evangelical Lutheran Church v. South Dakota*,[8] the U.S. Supreme Court held that employees of unincorporated church-controlled elementary and secondary schools are exempt from coverage as employees of churches. A school would also be exempt if separately incorporated and operated primarily for religious purposes and operated, supervised, or controlled, or principally supported, by a church, convention, or association of churches. Employees of churches, conventions, or associations of churches, and organizations operated primarily for religious purposes and operated, supervised, controlled, or principally supported by churches, conventions, or associations of churches are exempt whether or not their duties are religious.[9] Constitutional questions have been raised as to whether this exemption can be limited to religious schools associated with churches or denominations.[10] The constitutional issue of whether the unemployment compensation exemption can be limited to employees of religious organizations linked with churches or denominations as opposed to those which may have independent, interdenominational existence applies to a number of institutions. A troubling decision from the Supreme Court of Oregon illustrates the problem.

In the 1989 case of *Employment Division v. Rogue Valley Youth For Christ*,[11] the Oregon Supreme Court considered the constitutionality under the state constitution of making a distinction for unemployment tax purposes between church-affiliated and nonchurch-affiliated religious organizations. The federal statute conditions the credit against the federal unemployment tax on states covering all nonprofit organizations except those specifically exempted. The exemption, as noted above, appears by its terms to be limited to organizations affiliated with churches or denominations and to exclude independent, interdenominational religious organizations. To avoid the double taxation which would otherwise result to their employers if they lost the 90 percent federal credit, states follow the federal guidelines. The Oregon Constitution's guarantees of religious freedom, however, as interpreted by the Oregon Supreme Court, preclude distinctions between church-affiliated and nonchurch-affiliated religious organizations. Since the federal unemployment tax guidelines permit it to tax exempted religious organizations but not to exempt from coverage organizations which the federal law said should be covered, the Oregon Supreme Court avoided the double tax by allowing the taxation of all religious organizations. While this subjects religious organizations to tax that would otherwise be exempt, it does not subject them to double taxation since they would be fully exempt from the federal tax.

The effect of the Oregon ruling is to impose a direct tax on churches and religious organizations which, while constitutionally troubling, did not in the court's view override Oregon's interest in maintaining its unemployment compensation system and avoiding a double tax on the state's employers. This problem would be best addressed by amending the Federal Unemployment Tax Act to extend the permissible exemption to all religious organizations, not just those affiliated with a church or denomination.

While the imposition of a tax on a religious organization is a financial burden and necessarily has some burdening effect on religion, it does not interfere with belief or practice for most religious organizations, and it is not clear that it constitutes any more of a free exercise burden than the obligation of federal income tax withholding, Social Security taxes, or workers' compensation. Religious organizations that may fall in the gray area and be considering whether they should assert a constitutional challenge or seek exemption should consider the following questions:

1. Is the financial burden of the unemployment compensation tax on the organization sufficient to merit a challenge?

2. As a matter of responsibility to its employees, whom it may have to let go, does it wish to deprive them of the benefit of unemployment compensation?

While the language of state statutes will differ in detail, terminated workers generally may not collect unemployment compensation if the discharge was for good cause or due to work-related misconduct. In a 1989 Rhode Island case, a Catholic school employee's marrying outside the Catholic church was found not to be such "misconduct" as to preclude unemployment compensation.[12] A series of unemployment compensation cases has reached the Supreme Court concerning instances of secular employers discharging religious persons for alleged good cause or misconduct related to their adherence to their religious beliefs. These cases have been instrumental in shaping the law under the Free Exercise Clause of the U.S. Constitution and are discussed in chapter 3, section F.

E. FEDERAL EMPLOYEE BENEFIT LAWS

Employee benefit plans, including retirement and insurance programs, are also subject to federal regulation. The Employee Retirement Income Security Act of 1974 (ERISA) is the most important of these laws. Church plans are exempt from many ERISA requirements but are nevertheless subject to complex technical rules. Churches and religious organizations with retirement plans should obtain qualified, specialized advice to be sure their plans are in keeping with the law. Churches whose retirement plans are administered in accordance with the denomination's church pension board are probably not in violation of federal laws.

Another law known as the Consolidated Omnibus Budget Reconciliation Act of 1986, Continued Health Provision (COBRA) provides that certain employees, their spouses, and dependents are entitled to continue their group health insurance coverage at their own expense for a period of time after termination of employment for any reason. Moreover, they must receive notice of this right. Employers with fewer than twenty employees are exempt.

Church plans are also exempted from COBRA, including plans established and maintained for their employees (or their beneficiaries) by a church or by a convention or association of churches that is exempt from tax under Section 501 of the Internal Revenue Code. "Employee of a church" includes an employee of an organization, whether a civil law corporation or otherwise, that is exempt from tax under Section 501 and is controlled by or associated with a church, a convention, or an association of churches. "Associated with" means that the organization "shares common religious bonds and convictions with that church or convention or association of churches."[13]

Employees of organizations not exempt from COBRA must have a conversion privilege or right to continue coverage under the insurance contract on an individual basis when they leave employment. The right is terminated by their failure to do so or by obtaining alternative coverage.

Churches and religious organizations uncertain of what, if any, COBRA obligations they have, should consult a qualified attorney or other specialist.

REFERENCES

Hammar, Richard R. *Pastor, Church, and Law*, 2d ed. (Matthews, N.C.: Christian Ministry Resources, 1992).

Holck, Manfred, Jr. *Payroll Tax Procedures for Churches and Clergy* (Austin, Tex.: Church Management, Inc., 1989).

———. *Tax Planning for Clergy* (Austin, Tex.: Church Management, Inc., 1989).

Worth, B. J. *Income Tax Guide for Ministers and Religious Workers* (Winona Lake, Ind.: Worth Tax and Financial Service, 1990).

Compensation and Taxes

A. FEDERAL INCOME TAX

This chapter is an overview of the taxation of clergy. It will not instruct you on how to make out your tax return. Tax law, including tax law as it applies to clergy and churches, is a technical, complex set of rules, many of which are subject to interpretation in application. The rules change with nearly every session of Congress, sometimes substantially. A bewildering array of Revenue Regulations,[1] Revenue Rulings,[2] Revenue Procedures,[3] Letter Rulings,[4] and decisions of the Tax Court[5] and other courts confronts the taxpayer dealing with issues that arise in the gray area. More specialized advice is required than these pages permit, and advice changes so fre-

quently that constant update of preparation guidelines is essential. Happily, such information is increasingly available. Clergy and churches should take advantage of excellent new resources that address their tax responsibilities[6] and should consult competent tax advisors when necessary. The church should not be embarrassed by the inattention or sharp practices of its servants in tax matters.

1. Employee or Self-employed

The first issue that must be resolved for purposes of clergy tax reporting is whether the individual is an employee or is self-employed. This is important for a number of reasons. Employees will receive a Form W–2 from their employer, whereas self-employed individuals who receive at least $600 in compensation will receive a Form 1099–MISC. Employees will report their compensation directly as wages on Form 1040, whereas self-employed persons will report their compensation on Schedule C. Employees will deduct unreimbursed business expenses on Schedule A and only to the extent that such expenses exceed 2 percent of their gross income, with other limitations on business, meal, and entertainment expenses. Self-employed persons will report their business expenses on Schedule C without regard to the 2 percent limitation. Certain fringe benefits, such as medical insurance premiums, group term life insurance up to $50,000, and amounts payable on account of disability plans or cafeteria plans, which allow employees to choose among a variety of benefits or cash payments, are excludable only by employees.

Finally, Internal Revenue Service data indicates a substantially higher percentage of voluntary correct reporting of income by employees covered by mandatory withholding than by the self-employed—a difference of 99.5 percent to 13 percent, resulting in much greater IRS attention to self-employed persons' tax returns than to those of employees. Hence, the likelihood of a tax audit is much greater for clergy who report as self-employed.[7]

The test for determining whether clergy are employees or self-employed is the common-law test based on the right of the employer to control both the job goals and the means of achieving them. This test was discussed in chapter 7 with respect to respondeat superior liability of an employer for the acts of its employees.

Treasury Regulation 31.3401(c)–(b) summarizes the test as follows:

> Generally the relationship of employer and employee exists when the person for whom services are performed has the right to control and direct the individual who performs the services, not only as to the result to be accomplished by the work but also as to the details and means by which that result is accomplished. That is, an employee is subject to the will and control of the employer not only as to what shall be done but how it shall be done. In this connection, it is not necessary that the employer actually direct or control the manner in which the services are performed; it is sufficient if he has the right to do so. The right to discharge is also an important factor indicating that the person possessing that right is an employer. Other factors characteristic of an employer, but not necessarily present in every case, are the furnishing of tools and the furnishing of a place to work to the individual who performs the services. In general, if an individual is subject to the control or direction of another merely as to the result to be accomplished by the work and not as to the means and methods for accomplishing the result, he is not an employee.

The IRS has set forth a list of twenty criteria to aid in determining whether an individual is an employee under the common-law rules. These are included in Revenue Ruling 87–41, which is based on an examination of cases and rulings considering the issue. The importance of each factor is not equal in each situation, and the result cannot be determined by an arithmetic evaluation of the twenty criteria. A self-description of status by the parties is not determinative if the facts indicate a different relationship than the self-description. The criteria referenced in the Revenue Ruling are as follows:

1. Instructions. The requirement that one comply with instructions as to where, when, and how to do the work is a significant indicator of employee status.

2. Training. If the employer is training an individual or requiring that that the person have certain training in order to be engaged for the task, this would suggest employee status.

3. Integration. The extent to which the individual's services are integrated into the overall, ongoing program of the organization is an important indicator of employee status. Integrated work activity is likely to be subject to the direction and control of the employer.

4. Services rendered personally. The expectation that the individual will perform services on a personal basis tends to indicate employment rather than self-employment. The right of the employer to substitute other people to perform the service without prior approval would tend to support self-employment status.

5. Hiring, supervising, and paying assistants. If the assistants are hired, supervised, and trained by the employer, the person to whom they report is likely to be an employee. Self-employed people are likely to provide these services directly themselves with respect to their own assistants.

6. Continuing relationship. An ongoing relationship supports employee status.

7. Set hours of work. The self-employed generally set their own work hours, whereas employees are subject to their employer's requirement in this regard.

8. Full-time required. Full-time workers are usually employees. Self-employed persons can and do choose for whom they will work and for how much time.

9. Doing work on employer's premises. To the extent that work is done on the employer's premises that could be done elsewhere, this will indicate employee status.

10. Order or sequence of work. To the extent that the employer sets the order or sequence of work, the indication is that the worker is an employee.

11. Oral or written reports. The requirement of such reports tends to support an employer-employee relationship.

12. Payment by hour, week, month. Such payments support an employee-employer relationship, being in the nature of a wage or salary as opposed to a commission or lump-sum basis.

13. Payment of business and travel expenses. This would tend to indicate employee status as the self-employed are more likely to pay their own business and travel expenses and include that in a contract price.

14. Furnishing of tools and materials. Providing such helps to conducting the job as books, secretary, automobile, communion ware, and so forth supports an employee-employer relationship. Self-employed persons usually provide their own.

15. Significant investment. If the individual invests significant funds to get the job accomplished without reimbursement, self-employed status tends to be indicated; the opposite is true if the necessary facilities are furnished by the employers.

16. Realization of profit or loss. The risk of loss and opportunity for profit in a job tends to indicate self-employment. Employees do not normally realize profit or loss.

17. Working for more than one firm at a time. This factor would tend to indicate self-employment, although an individual could have part-time employment with more than one employer.

18. Making services available to the general public. This factor would support self-employment.

19. Right to discharge. Self-employed persons cannot ordinarily be discharged as long as they are performing the contract. The right to fire supports an employment relationship.

20. Right to terminate. If the individual can leave the job at any time without further responsibility, it supports an employee relationship. The self-employed have a responsibility to complete the job.

Applying these criteria, it is clear that most clergy serving local churches are employed rather than self-employed. Full-time evangelists, musicians, or speakers who earn their income by traveling from church to church and speaking or performing would, by contrast, be self-employed, as would employed ministers with respect to services they provide to others outside the scope of their employment for which they are paid directly, such as the performance of marriages or funerals. In most instances the IRS is likely to view a cleric who serves a local church as an employee.

Some clergy (or churches) may take the theological position that clergy are subject only to the direct authority of the Lord rather than that of a local church or governing body and, hence, that it is biblically incorrect for them to acknowledge subordination to local church authority by reporting themselves as employees. In such instances, it is important that the church governance documents and church conduct be consistent with this view if this position is to be sustained against a challenge by the IRS. The clergy should be, in fact, free of control by the church in the manner of job performance, and the employer should file its own tax documents consistent with this view, issuing 1099s rather than W–2s to the clergy and omitting reports of clergy earnings on quarterly 941 forms.

2. What Is Income?

Whether employed or self-employed, clergy must report their gross income, defined as simply "all income from whatever source derived."[8] Gross income is subject to certain exclusions and adjustments. Obviously, gross income includes compensation received for services rendered, whether as an employee or a self-employed independent contractor. Bonuses, although rare in religious organizations, would also be part of gross income.

Special-occasion gifts made by the church to the minister for Christmas, birthdays, anniversaries, or other occasions are almost always income and should be reported by the minister as such and included by the church on the minister's W–2 or 1099 form. The rule is the same whether the gifts came from general church funds or were collected by special offering. Churches, as nonprofit and tax-exempt organizations, are prohibited from distributing their funds except as payments in reasonable compensation for services or in direct furtherance of their exempt purposes. Tax-exempt, nonprofit organizations cannot make "gifts." Moreover, if the payments were truly gifts, the individual donors could not treat them as charitable deductions. Since most "gifts" made to the clergy are made in recognition of services rendered and with the expectation by the donors that the gifts are part of their charitable deduction, they are part of the cleric's gross income. An exception applies to a gift of a value so insignificant that it would be unreasonable or administratively impractical to account for it; you do not have to include the Thanksgiving turkey or nonmonetary Christmas presents of minimal value.

Churches that make special-occasion collections for their clergy should be sensitive to proper tax treatment of the proceeds. If the church intends a true tax-free gift, it should inform the parishioners that their contributions are not deductible and will be given directly to the pastor and that their checks should be made out directly to the pastor. If the church intends that gifts be deductible and includable in the pastor's income, then the process should be handled through the church, checks should be made payable to the church, and the church treasurer should understand the intent and report accordingly.

There is some dated authority that retirement gifts can be tax free rather than taxable compensation if (1) they were not made in accordance with any enforceable agreement, established plan, or past practice; (2) the pastor did not undertake to perform any further services for the congregation and was not expected to do so; (3) there was a closer personal relationship between the pastor and congregation than is normal in secular employment relationships; and (4) the amount paid was determined in light of the financial position of the congregation and the needs of the recipient, who had been adequately compensated for past services.[9] This would not include pension payments from a denomination;[10] and the adoption of Section 102(c) of the Internal Revenue Service Code, in 1986, that prohibits employers from characterizing payments to employees as tax-free gifts (with certain limited exemptions) prohibits treatment of a retirement gift as a tax-free gift with respect to minister employees.

Other items that are part of a cleric's gross income are:

1. Compensation received from others for performing services such as weddings, funerals, and baptisms.
2. Bargain sales, that is, property a minister is permitted to buy from his or her church at less than fair market value.
3. Income from writing, speaking, and the sale of books and tapes.
4. Contributions by the employer "in kind" as, for example, a car given by the church to the pastor. The fair market value of the car would be additional compensation.
5. Any amount paid by the church toward the cleric's obligation for Social Security or self-employment tax. Many churches do this because the pastor is treated as self-employed and therefore pays a higher Social Security tax than do employees, as discussed below. Such additional compensation to cover the pastor's additional Social Security obligation is taxable income and should be reported as such.
6. Moving reimbursements.
7. Premiums paid for term life insurance valued at more than $50,000 or for any permanent life insurance if the minister chooses the beneficiary.
8. Any unused portion of the housing or parsonage allowance (see section 3).
9. Expense allowances if the cleric is not required to submit records and receipts to the employer (see section A.5, below).
10. The value of personal automobile use for a vehicle provided by the employer.

11. The value of living quarters provided by the employer if the living quarters are not on the premises of the employer, if the living quarters are not provided for the employer's convenience, and if living in the quarters is not a job requirement.
12. Meals provided by the employer, with certain exceptions, such as when provided at the employer's place of business and for the employer's convenience, or when provided during working hours because meal periods are too short for the employee to be expected to eat elsewhere.
13. The benefit of low-interest or no-interest loans of $10,000 or more or of less than $10,000 if one of the principal purposes is tax avoidance may be regarded as additional compensation. State law often prohibits such loans to officers and directors, and this can also raise problems with a church's tax-exempt status.
14. Personal expenses of the pastor paid by the church.

In addition, clergy are subject to the same taxes as everyone else on a variety of other kinds of income, such as interest and dividends, rental income, certain retirement income and Social Security benefits, gains from the sale of property, canceled debts, and certain prizes and awards.

a. Tuition Reductions

Religious elementary or secondary schools or churches that run such schools can offer qualified tuition reductions to their employees or spouses and to dependent children of their employees. This is a reduction of tuition and does not need to be reported as income for federal tax purposes on Form W–2 or Form 1040 unless the employee is a "highly compensated employee." Highly compensated employees are defined by reference to formulas and definitions which will change from year to year. Hence specific advice should always be sought, and reviewed annually, before excluding tuition reductions from reported income. Highly compensated employees may exclude qualified tuition reductions if

the benefit is available on similar terms to other employees in a reasonably classified group on a basis that does not discriminate in favor of the highly compensated.

3. Housing Allowance

The amount of income on which taxes are paid is reduced by the devices of personal exemptions for the taxpayer and dependents, exclusions from income by adjustments to income, and deductions from income. One of the most useful and important such devices and one that is entirely unique to clergy is the housing allowance. To qualify for the housing allowance clergy must meet the criteria discussed in chapter 5. The cleric must be a licensed, commissioned, or ordained minister of a church. The allowance applies only with respect to services performed in the exercise of ministry.

The housing allowance allows a qualifying minister to exclude from income, that is, not to report as part of taxable income (1) the fair rental value of a church-owned parsonage which the minister occupies without payment of rent as part of the church's compensation to him or her; (2) the portion of compensation predesignated as a housing allowance, to the extent that it is actually used in maintaining the housing, including paying utilities and maintaining furnishings; (3) a portion of compensation predesignated as a rental allowance, to the extent that the cleric incurs actual rental expenses; and (4) the portion of compensation predesignated as a housing allowance, to the extent it is actually used to own and maintain a home, not exceeding the fair rental value of the home as furnished with utilities.

Note the following important principles with respect to the application of the housing allowance:

1. The principle of exclusion applies whether the cleric occupies a church-owned parsonage or rents or owns a home. The application of the rules differs somewhat, depending on the housing arrangements in question.
2. The allowance is available only to a cleric who meets the qualifications dis-

cussed in chapter 5 and only with respect to compensation paid by the church for services that are ordinarily the duties of a minister of the gospel; these duties are also discussed in chapter 5.

3. There is no requirement that the church take any special action to protect a minister's right to exclude the fair rental value of a church-owned parsonage in which she or he lives. The church *must,* however, designate *in advance* any part of the minister's compensation that is considered to be a housing allowance or a rental allowance, that is, for a minister's use in the purchase, rental, furnishing, or maintenance of a house, including expenses related to the occupancy of the church-owned parsonage. The clause of designation may be contained in an employment contract, the minutes, or a resolution by the church or its appropriate governing body, in the organization's budget, or in any other appropriate instrument evidencing the official action. To be sufficient, designation must permit a payment or part of a payment to be identified as such an allowance, as distinguished from salary or other remuneration. While there is no rule against an oral designation, written designation is always preferable to avoid problems of proof. A true oral designation, however, could be retroactively incorporated into a written record adopted to be effective as of the time of the oral designation. Issuing separate checks for the parsonage, housing or rental allowance, and salary is further documentation of the designation although it is not necessary if the church has adopted an appropriate designation.

4. Designation is ineffective if it has not been made in advance of the time of actual compensation. If a church has failed to make a housing allowance designation in advance of the current year, it can do so in the course of the tax year, but the designation will be effective only *after* it is made, for the balance of the year.

In such a situation, could the church or minister rear-end load the housing allowance so as to exclude from income any expenses incurred before the designation if the expenses are within amounts paid as housing allowances after the designation? For example, if a pastor is receiving a salary of $3,000 a month with no housing allowance designation, could the governing church board on September 1 vote an annual allowance of $12,000 and pay the pastor $3,000 a month, designated as housing allowance, for the balance of the year to cover expenses that were incurred in the first nine months as well as the last three months? There is no clear answer to this question. An aggressive tax position can be argued but may be challenged by the IRS. It seems probable that the minister would lose this position if challenged.

5. The housing allowance may include utilities and furnishings, whether or not the minister lives in a church-owned parsonage. Rental payments are covered by the allowance. Homeowners can include in the allowance mortgage interest and principal payments, down payments, property taxes, insurance, repairs and improvements, and yard care.

6. There is no limit on the amount of a pastor's compensation that may be designated as a housing allowance, provided the amount is not unreasonable compensation. To maximize the tax advantage to the pastor, it is wise to (1) make the allowance as generous as necessary to meet the pastor's needs; and (2) let the pastor request the amount that may be needed. As long as the pastor reports his or her taxes honestly on the tax return, the IRS suffers no loss if the church designates a housing allowance that turns out to be excessive.

7. The housing allowance is handled by the church by simply excluding it from the pastor's compensation as reported on his W–2 or 1099–MISC. The pastor, however, *may not* exclude from reported income any more of the housing allowance than is actually used. The cleric must report any excess housing allowance as "other income" on his or her tax return.

8. What if the pastor incurs an extraordinary, one-time expense, such as a down payment on a house? Should the church designate a high housing allowance that year to cover the down payment? The IRS has ruled that the housing allowance exclusion may not exceed the fair rental value of the pastor's home as furnished, including utilities.[11] In a given year, an extraordinary housing allowance to cover a down payment on a home or similar extraordinary housing expense is likely to bring the housing allowance above the fair rental value of the home for the year and, to the extent that it does so, the allowance would not be excludable according to the IRS ruling. The ruling itself is a questionable interpretation of the statute[12] but is ignored at the peril of a challenge by the IRS. One way of alleviating the problem is to borrow the amount of the down payment and then spread the payments out over a period of time to keep the total housing allowance within the fair rental value.

9. Clergy who are homeowners can have, in effect, a "double deduction." They are entitled to count their mortgage interest and real estate taxes as part of the housing allowance and exclude these amounts from their income, but they retain the tax deduction for these items like any other real estate–owning taxpayer.

10. Clergy who own their own homes and have paid off their mortgages will lose the benefit of the housing allowance to the extent of the mortgage payments. They are not entitled to exclude a "fair rental value" of a house which is not an actual expense.[13] The IRS has ruled that payments on home equity loans or on loans secured by a mortgage on a home that are not taken out to purchase or improve the home are not excludable from income as part of the housing allowance because they are not used to provide a home.[14]

11. While Section 107 of the Internal Revenue Code setting forth the housing allowance does not so specify, the housing allowance must be reasonable in amount so as not to jeopardize the tax-exempt status of the church by constituting unreasonable compensation to an individual. An IRS ruling has established that the housing allowance may not be excluded if it is unreasonable compensation.[15] Likewise, allowances may not be excluded when given for expenses actually paid directly by the church and not by the pastor.[16]

12. Housing allowances are exclusions only for federal income tax purposes. They are not exclusions for Social Security (FICA and SECA) tax liability. Both the fair rental value of the parsonage and any parsonage rental or housing allowance must be included on the minister's tax return for Social Security purposes. The fair rental value is the amount a comparable property would rent for in the area in an arm's-length transaction; it is not an arbitrary amount determined by the church. The best way to determine fair rental value is to have a professional appraisal done.

13. Churches may provide an equity allowance to a minister living in a church-owned parsonage to enable the minister to accumulate equity in order to afford a retirement home. Such allowances are not excludable income as parsonage rental or housing allowances. There are a variety of other devices available, however, that may enable funds to be set aside without subjecting them to current taxation. A church contemplating such a program should examine the options available with a qualified advisor.

14. Availability of the housing allowance does not depend on whether a minister is employed or self-employed. Self-employed ministers who receive compensation from a variety of sources, for example, traveling evangelists, will need either to (1) have each local church that compensates them designate in advance a portion of the compensation as a housing allowance, or (2) use other devices, such as the creation of a nonprofit corporation that would qualify to provide a housing allowance, in order to have this benefit.

15. Designations of housing allowances should be specific for each qualifying

minister on the staff. The designation should also be established for an indefinite time so that a minister does not lose the benefit because of oversight in a later tax year. Designations should be reviewed before the beginning of each new tax year, however, and updated as appropriate.

16. Ministers building a house while living in another one or in a church-owned parsonage are not likely to be able to exclude the construction cost of the new house until they occupy it, although the issue has never been specifically addressed by the courts or the IRS. To maximize the housing allowance benefit while building a new home, defer as much of the cost as possible until the time of occupancy.

17. Retired clergy are eligible for housing allowance exclusions according to an IRS ruling, if:

a. a portion of the pension is designated as a housing allowance by the trustees of a denominational pension plan;

b. the retiree has severed his or her relationship with the local church and is reliant upon the fund for a pension; and

c. the pension compensates the retired minister for past services to local churches of the denomination or to the denomination.[17]

Eligibility of retired clergy for housing allowance is under current study by the IRS.[18]

4. Lodging or Meals for the Employer's Convenience

The housing allowance should not be confused with another benefit that is important to some employees. The value of lodging furnished by an employer is excluded from gross income if (1) it is on the employer's business premises; (2) it is furnished for the employer's convenience; and (3) the employee is required to accept it as a condition of employment.[19] These provisions will be important to such institutions as camps and conference centers, often located in rural areas and with staff who live on the premises, and to secondary boarding schools and other live-in institutions that require employees to live on the premises for supervisory or other support purposes. Meals provided on the premises for the employer's convenience or during working hours because meal periods are too short for the employee to eat elsewhere are likewise excludable.

These benefits are available to employees who meet the qualifications without regard to their status as ordained, commissioned, or licensed ministers of a church and whether or not their services are performed in the exercise of ministry under the rules set forth in chapter 5.

5. Other Expenses

Clergy and other employees of churches or religious organizations incur a variety of business and professional expenses, such as travel expenses (including meals and lodging), compensation paid to others for services, rent paid for business property and equipment, professional dues and fees, entertainment, subscriptions, education, convention expenses, religious supplies and books, insurance, telephone, business gifts, and religious vestments and cleaning expenses for them. The tax treatment of these expenses does not depend upon a cleric meeting the qualifications discussed in chapter 5 and does not differ from treatment of comparable expenses of secular workers. The tax law allows a standard deduction to each taxpayer, and expenses will normally be itemized and deducted only if they exceed the standard deduction. Itemized and deductible expenses also include a number of expenses other than business and professional expenses, such as charitable contributions.

Self-employed ministers and other workers will deduct their ordinary and necessary business and professional expenses on Schedule C. Clergy and other employees will deduct unreimbursed business and professional expenses and nonaccountable reimbursed expenses as miscellaneous itemized deductions on Schedule A to the extent that they exceed 2 percent of adjusted gross income with an 80 percent limitation on deductibility of business meals and entertainment expenses.

The Internal Revenue Service, with the backing of the Tax Court,[20] considers unreimbursed business and professional expenses deductible to the extent that they are limited to the proportion of such expenses allocable to *taxable* income and nondeductible to the extent that they are allocable to the portion of income representing the excludable housing allowance. If one-third of a minister's compensation is attributable to the housing allowance, for example, the IRS would disallow one-third of the business and professional expense deductions. This rule applies only to unreimbursed expenses, which is a sound reason for adopting a full-reimbursement policy based on adequate accounting and the return of excess reimbursements, discussed below.

Needless to say, business and professional expense deductions must be limited to those which are in fact unreimbursed or reimbursed under a policy that requires reimbursement to be reported as income. One cannot receive reimbursement and also deduct it from taxes. Likewise the deductions must be true professional or business expenses, not personal ones.

Many employees of churches and religious organizations may be entitled to other exclusions and deductions not referenced here. One such deduction is a qualified tuition deduction for employer-provided educational assistance.[21] A number of special provisions apply to the various types of retirement plans. It must be emphasized again that full treatment of tax considerations for clergy and employees of churches and religious organizations is beyond the scope of this work. Such persons and organizations should obtain tax guides and advice for the particular issues relevant to their situations.

6. The Accountable Plan

Employed and self-employed ministers and others can avoid the problem of accounting for expenses on their tax returns if they account to the employing church or religious organization under a proper accountable plan. An "accountable plan" is one adopted by the employer that reimburses employees who submit an expense account or other required written statement to the employer that shows the date, place,

business nature, and amount of all the employee's expenses (including those charged directly or indirectly to the employer through credit cards or otherwise) and that requires any excess reimbursements (such as unused portions of a prepaid expense allowance) to be returned. Both accounting and return of excess reimbursements must be done within a reasonable time. As to such expenses as gifts, transportation, travel, and entertainment, an adequate accounting requires the submission to the employer of an account book, diary, statement of expense, or similar record maintained by the employee in which the information as to each element of expenditure (amount, time, place, business purpose, and business relationship) is recorded at or near the time of the expenditure, together with supporting documentary evidence, in a manner which conforms to all the "adequate records" requirements.

All income tax reporting requirements with respect to business expenses will be eliminated if a reimbursement policy is adopted by a governing board that requires the employee periodically to submit an expense account or other written statement showing the date, place, business nature and relationship, and amount of the expenses incurred by the employee or charged to the employer and that requires the employee to return any excess reimbursements received from the employer. Excess reimbursements must truly be returned; allowing the employee to keep them as a bonus will cause the plan to be treated as nonaccountable. Churches whose clergy receive reimbursed expenses under a reimbursement policy that provides for adequate accounting and return of excess reimbursements avoid the necessity for the church to include expense reimbursement on the employee's W-2 or 1099; and the employee need neither report the reimbursement income nor deduct expenses. This is the optimum way for churches to handle reimbursement of business expenses.

It is important that the accountable plan be adopted by the church. If the church has a nonaccountable plan, an employee cannot achieve the benefits of an accountable plan by voluntarily complying with the requirements of one.

Churches that provide a fixed expense

allowance or that reimburse expenses, requiring, in either case, no accounting for the expenses, must report the allowance or reimbursement as income to employees. The employees must include it in their returns as income and may deduct it on Schedule A to the extent that it exceeds 2 percent of their adjusted gross income and they are able to take advantage of itemized deductions. If a church requires the minister simply to pay business expenses out of his or her salary, whether or not the salary is increased from what it might otherwise be to take this into account, the church must include the full salary as income on the W–2, and the minister must report it as income on Form 1040 and use the Schedule A deductions to the extent possible to reduce his or her taxable income.

Reimbursement of expenses through salary reduction is not treated as an accountable plan. If a church agrees to pay a pastor x dollars per week, but treats any accounted-for expenses as a reimbursement in the next pay period by reducing the salary component of x by the amount of the expenses, the plan will not qualify, and the entire amount of payments must be treated as income. A church that wants to achieve the goal of such a plan must reduce the pastor's salary by an amount that will leave sufficient funds to cover estimated expenses.

A reimbursement policy solves all of these problems and is by far the most desirable approach. It can result in significant tax savings to employed ministers.

A reimbursement plan for self-employed ministers that requires adequate accounting and the return of excess reimbursements also has the effect of eliminating the need for the reimbursements to be recorded by the church as income on the 1099–MISC and for the minister to report the reimbursements as income on Schedule C and take the deductions. Reimbursement of business expenses is, however, one of the factors considered in determining whether an individual is an employee or self-employed (reimbursement suggests employment status), which may be a consideration for churches whose ministers are considered self-employed in deciding whether to adopt such a plan.

Internal Revenue Service guidelines with respect to accountable plans address the "reasonable time requirement" for substantiating business expenses and returning excess reimbursements. This may be done in either of two ways. The fixed-date method requires business expenses to be substantiated within sixty days after the expenses are paid or incurred and excess reimbursements returned within 120 days after the expenses are paid or incurred. Alternatively, the employer may give employees a periodic statement not less than quarterly that sets forth the amount by which reimbursements exceed the substantiated business expenses and request the employee to substantiate the difference or return it to the employer within 120 days. Substantiated expenses or returns during the 120-day period satisfy the reasonable time requirement.

There are particular record-keeping and other requirements with respect to expenses such as travel, entertainment, gifts, transportation, and personal computers. Automobile expenses can be accounted for alternatively by a standard mileage deduction (28 cents per mile in 1992) or a record of actual expenses. Clergy computing actual automobile expenses should consult a more specialized reference.[22]

7. Compensating a Spouse

In some churches the question may be raised as to whether the minister's spouse should be on the payroll. If salary is to be paid to a spouse, it should be reasonable and paid on the basis of actual services and time spent working for the employer. The decision to hire and pay the spouse should be made by an independent governing body with the best interests of the employing church in mind. Such payments should never be made personally by the minister.

There may be certain tax benefits to a second income. It can qualify the couple for child care credit for babysitting expenses incurred while both are at work, which would not be available as a professional expense deduction. If the couple has IRA accounts for retirement planning, they can contribute more when both receive a salary— a total of $4,000, compared to $2,250 if only one is employed. Professional expenses of both will be deductible if not reimbursed under an expense accounting plan by which the reimbursement can be kept out of income. Social Security earnings may be increased. Two semiretired salaries may be available without breaching Social Security's earnings limitations as retirement approaches.

B. SOCIAL SECURITY

1. Introduction

One of the consequences of being a duly ordained, commissioned, or licensed minister of a church is being treated as self-employed for Social Security purposes and, hence, subject to the Self-Employment Contributions Act (SECA) rather than the Federal Insurance Contributions Act (FICA) with respect to services performed in the exercise of ministry. Chapter 5 discusses who fits into this generic definition, which has other consequences in federal tax law. The origin of the treatment of clergy as self-employed regardless of their actual employment status is, like the origin of the housing allowance, somewhat obscure. The legislative history of the statute is said to be "meager and uninstructive."[23] Clergy were originally uncovered by Social Security, consistent with the treatment of other professionals, such as doctors and lawyers, and with the tradition in this country of considering all professional people to be self-employed. Social Security coverage through SECA later became optional for clergy and now is mandatory. Unlike other professions, however, all clergy who meet the definitions discussed in chapter 5 continue to be treated as self-employed.

Clergy who are subject to the self-employment tax must use the estimated tax procedure to report and prepay Social Security taxes. This is done on IRS Form 1040–ES. The estimate for Social Security purposes includes the housing allowance, although it is excluded for federal income tax purposes. Estimates are paid in quarterly installments due on the fifteenth days of April, June, September, and January of the following year, or on the following Monday if the fifteenth falls on a weekend. Installments are paid with payment vouchers contained on Form 1040–ES. If the cleric becomes liable for estimated tax payments

midway through the year, for example, if he or she begins a first pastoral assignment in mid-year, a payment voucher should be submitted by the next filing deadline accompanied by a check for the prorated portion of the tax liability for the year. If one's financial situation changes in the course of the tax year, it may be necessary to refigure estimated taxes and adjust quarterly payments appropriately. Actual taxes are computed and filed with the Form 1040 following the end of the tax year.

Clergy who meet the definitions discussed in chapter 5 are also exempt from federal income tax withholding for federal income tax purposes whether or not they are employees by common-law definitions. Consequently, they are responsible for the estimated tax procedure for their federal income tax withholding as well as their Social Security taxes although they may exclude the housing allowance in computing their federal income tax liability. Procedures and forms for complying with federal income tax withholding are as discussed above with respect to Social Security. Ministers may, however, agree to voluntary income tax withholding. This avoids the paperwork and financial discipline required for the estimated tax procedure. The cleric need only file a completed Form W–4 (Employee's Withholding Allowance Certificate) with the employer to put this into motion. Voluntary withholding arrangements can be terminated by mutual consent or by either party at any time. Such voluntary withholding would be inappropriate, however, for a cleric who claims self-employed status, as it would likely be construed as an admission that he or she is an employee. The procedure will not cover the self-employment tax, which is separate and additional, but clergy who wish to avoid the quarterly reporting requirement altogether, including the estimated tax procedure for Social Security taxes, can do so if they are in fact employees and they indicate on the Form W–4 an additional amount of cash to be withheld from each pay period sufficient to cover the SECA liability at the end of the year. Excess withholding becomes a credit against self-employment tax liability, which will be shown on Form 1040 when filed. This kind of voluntary withholding arrangement for both income and self-employment taxes is a major convenience and should be seriously considered by all clergy.

Self-employed ministers do not qualify for voluntary withholding for either income taxes or SECA, which must be reported on the church's Form 941 that documents the number of employees and the FICA taxes and withheld income taxes payable. Ministers may, however, enter into a withholding agreement with their churches; the church withholds an appropriate portion of compensation each week and deposits it in a church account (other than the one in which withheld taxes are deposited) and distributes it to the minister in advance of the due dates for quarterly estimated tax payments. This is done without W–4 forms and is not reported on Form 941, both of which pertain to the employed, not the self-employed.

2. Amount of the Tax

The Social Security tax rate has increased over the years. For 1992 the SECA tax is 15.3 percent, the same as the combined employer and employee shares of FICA of 7.65 percent apiece. The tax rate will be applied to the minister's net earnings from self-employment, which, for 1992, must be at least $400. Social Security income excludes certain deductions such as unreimbursed ordinary and necessary business and professional expenses incurred in the exercise of ministry. Clergy may be able to use deductions for SECA purposes that they cannot use for federal income tax purposes because they do not exceed the standard deduction or because they are reimbursed by nonaccountable reimbursement policies. The housing allowance or fair rental value of a church-owned parsonage, however, is included for Social Security earnings purposes, although it is excluded for federal income tax purposes. SECA earnings also include direct payment by the church of parsonage expenses such as utilities and other taxable fringe benefits. Social Security applies up to a maximum amount, also increased over the years, for 1993 $57,6000. Additional earnings up to $135,000 are subject to a 2.9 percent tax representing

the Medicare component of SECA. FICA taxes do not apply on amounts earned above this base.

To prevent the self-employed from paying more than the employee, self-employed persons, including clergy who are subject to self-employment status with respect to Social Security, are allowed to deduct one-half of the Social Security tax for purposes of computing both their Social Security income and their taxable income for federal tax purposes. Clergy who report their income tax as employees are also allowed to take these deductions.

The self-employment tax deduction phases out for higher-income taxpayers—in 1993 those whose earnings were $57,600 or more—and will cease altogether at a slightly higher level. The income tax deduction continues, however.

Special rules apply to members of religious orders who are under a vow of poverty. These rules are beyond the scope of this work.

3. Exemption from Social Security Coverage

a. Clergy

Ministers who meet the standards discussed in chapter 5 *may* also qualify for complete exemption from Social Security coverage, whether employed or self-employed. Ministers must (1) perform substantially all the religious functions of an ordained minister under the tenets and practices of their church or denomination;[24] (2) be ordained, commissioned, or licensed by an exempt religious organization;[25] and (3) be conscientiously opposed because of religious principles to accepting, for services performed as a minister, any public insurance that makes payments in the event of death, disability, old age, or retirement, or that makes payments for the cost of, or provides services for, medical care, including insurance systems established under the Social Security Act. The exemption application (Form 4361), affirming the minister's conscientious opposition to acceptance of such public insurance, must be filed in triplicate with the IRS.

To be exempt from Social Security taxes and benefits, the minister's opposition to accepting such benefits must be for *religious* reasons. The exemption *may not* be based on economic or other nonreligious reasons. The religious opposition must be to the *acceptance of benefits* rather than payment of the tax. Opposition need only be to public insurance programs; it does not preclude a minister from participating in private insurance programs. The application must be filed on or before the due date of the federal tax return for the second year in which the minister has net earnings from self-employment of $400 or more, any part of which is derived from services performed in the exercise of ministry.

For 1987 and succeeding years, an applicant for exemption must inform the ordaining, commissioning, or licensing body of the church or order that she or he is opposed to Social Security coverage. The exemption application form contains a statement that this requirement has been satisfied; hence, notification must be done prior to filing the exemption application. The purpose of the requirement of notification is to enable churches and denominations to provide exemption applicants with counseling on the desirability of taking the exemption, provide appropriate pension counseling, and make the applicant aware of the Social Security benefits that will be forfeited. Religious organizations and denominations should conduct such counseling, provide such information to clergy, and obtain their acknowledgment of the counseling and a release from any liability that may arise for financial loss that may follow a decision to opt out of the Social Security system.

Before approval, the exemption application also requires that the Internal Revenue Service and the Secretary of the Department of Health and Human Services, or a designated representative, has verified that the individual seeking the exemption is aware of the grounds on which he or she may receive the exemption and does seek the exemption on such grounds.[26] The verification requirement exists to insure that applicants for exemption present their application on proper grounds (i.e., religious opposition to the receipt of benefits rather than financial reasons). The IRS satisfies this requirement by sending the appli-

cant a statement listing the grounds on which the exception is available; and requiring the applicant to sign the statement, under penalty of perjury, claiming that he or she is seeking the exemption on available grounds and to return it within ninety days from the date originally mailed by the IRS. Exemption applications must be approved by an appropriate Internal Revenue officer and are not just filed. Ministers applying for the exemption should be sure they receive back an approved Form 4361; retain the form. A minister who does not receive an approved 4361 back from the IRS and fails to pay Social Security taxes can be assessed back taxes for three years if he or she filed a Form 1040 fully reporting all income. There is no limit on how far back taxes may be assessed if no Form 1040 is filed.

Social Security coverage exemptions are irrevocable. A one-time opportunity to reenter the system was created by the Tax Reform Act of 1986 but expired on April 15, 1988. The courts have consistently rejected attempts by ministers to file exemptions after the deadlines have passed, notwithstanding contentions of religious freedom abridgment.[27] Constitutional arguments have been unsuccessful in challenging the Social Security exemption of ministers.

The Social Security exemption applies only to compensation earned from the performance of services in the exercise of ministry, which is discussed more fully in chapter 5. Compensation for other services is subject to Social Security coverage and would generate resulting benefits.

b. Nonclergy

Individuals who do not qualify under the rules set forth in chapter 5 of this volume do not have the option to opt out of the Social Security system, regardless of their religious convictions about the receipt of public insurance benefits. They are subject to the FICA or SECA tax, depending on their employed or self-employed status under common-law rules, in the same manner as employees of secular organizations.

However, a self-employed person who is a member of a recognized religious sect opposed to the acceptance of Social Security benefits on the basis of established tenets or teachings to which the member adheres may opt out of the Social Security system. To do this, the person must file an exemption application by the due date of the first taxable year for which he or she has self-employment income. The exemption application must be accompanied by evidence of membership in the sect and adherence to the tenets or the teachings of the sect, and the person must waive all rights to all Social Security benefits. The government must find that the sect does in fact have established tenets or teachings in opposition to Social Security coverage, makes provision for the financial support of dependent members, and has been in continual existence since December 31, 1950. The exemption, if granted, is irrevocable unless the person leaves the sect or ceases to adhere to its teachings pertaining to participation in the Social Security system. This limited provision applies only to self-employed persons.[28] Employers or employees opposed to Social Security coverage on the basis of established religious beliefs qualify for the exemption, however, for tax years beginning in 1989, if the employer and employee are both members of the qualifying religious sect. Opposition to Social Security coverage on the basis of religious beliefs, absent membership in a sect of which such opposition is part of the established tenets or teachings, does not qualify one for the exemption.[29] This exemption presently can be obtained by filing a Form 4029 at any time, in contrast to the ministerial exemption, which must be claimed in a timely fashion as discussed above. Form 4029 and the individual exemption require that the individual be opposed to both public and private insurance.

c. Churches

Finally, churches or qualified church-controlled organizations which are opposed to the payment of Social Security taxes for religious reasons may elect not to be subject to such taxes.[30] This does not exempt the employee from responsibility for the tax if he or she would otherwise be subject to it. Employees of exempted employers must then do their own filing under the SECA system, although the church may withhold additional amounts to prepay their Social Security costs. Such churches must communicate to their employees the employees' responsibility for their own Social Security taxes on their Form 1040.

The church election is made by filing Form 8274. For churches that existed as of September 30, 1984, the filing was required by October 31, 1984. Churches created later must file before the first date on which a quarterly employment tax return would be due. Election can be revoked simply by filing a Form 941 on or before its due date for the first quarter for which the revocation is to be effective.

4. Retirement

Persons contemplating retirement can obtain estimates of their Social Security benefits from the Social Security administration and with the help of guides available on the subject.[31] Depending on the amount of retirement income, some part of Social Security benefits may be subject to income tax. Some retirement earnings may continue to be subject to Social Security. Retirees who receive Social Security benefits while continuing to have earnings may lose part or all of the benefits up to age seventy, at which time they are entitled to earn an unlimited amount without losing benefits.

Social Security income includes not only retirement benefits but also disability and survivor benefits. Benefits are also available under the Social Security Medicare program at age sixty-five. There are no further premiums for hospital insurance under Part A of Medicare, but Part B coverage requires a subject to enroll and pay a monthly premium for surgical and physicians' services. Clergy approaching age sixty-five should determine the benefits available to them under the Social Security Medicare program, as well as any denominational or other plans providing health coverage which they have or to which they have access.

Special rules, which are beyond the scope of this work, apply to missionaries serving overseas.[32]

REFERENCES

Hammar, Richard R. *Church and Clergy Tax Guide* (Matthews, N.C.: Christian Ministry Resources, 1992).

Holck, Manfred, Jr. A series of reprints or monographs by Holck are available from Church Management, Inc., P.O. Box 162527, Austin, TX 78716. Of interest to the subject matter of this chapter are: *Tax Planning for Clergy; Social Security for Clergy; Housing for Clergy; The Minister's Car Allowance and Expenses; Continuing Education Costs; Clergy Professional Expenses;* and *Payroll Tax Procedures for Churches and Clergy.*

Internal Revenue Service Publication 517. *Social Security for Members of the Clergy and Religious Workers for Use in Preparing 1989 Returns.* Available from sources listed in note 6.

Worth, B. *Income Tax Guide for Ministers and Religious Workers.* 1991 ed. Available from Worth Tax and Financial Service, Box 725, Winona Lake, IN 46590.

CHAPTER 15

Purchasing, Maintaining, or Altering Property

A. ACQUIRING PROPERTY

1. The Purchase and Sale Agreement

Most property is bought and sold under purchase and sale agreements that are signed before the title is transferred. These agreements may be drafted by the parties (i.e., their attorneys), or they may be standard form agreements that are commonly used in the area, are available from real estate agents or lawyers, and cover the normal issues in a real estate transfer in a customary manner. As with all contracts, review it with your lawyer *before*, not after, you sign. Once both parties have signed, the agreement is binding. A purchaser may be able to compel you to convey according to its terms; a seller may be able to keep your deposit or recover additional damages if you fail to complete the transaction; and a real estate agent may be able to charge you a commission.

It is prudent to evaluate the property subjectively before you sign an agreement: verify the condition of the buildings, improvements, mechanical systems, and the like. Consider hiring someone knowledgeable about building conditions to advise you.

Do not rely entirely on your attorney; read the agreement yourself, and be sure it contains everything you are expecting or relying on, and nothing with which you do not agree.

a. Conditions to Completing the Transaction

Most form contracts include a specific provision that the buyer may examine the title at the buyer's expense and is not obligated to purchase if the title is not marketable. If such a condition is not included, add it. Everything you understand as a condition of completing the transaction should be specifically listed in the agreement, and you should be able to withdraw without penalty if a condition is not met. Are you relying, for example, on obtaining financing or obtaining it on any particular terms? On zoning or planning approval, a building permit, or other regulatory license or action for a particular structure, improvement, or activity? On the sale of another property to finance the transaction? On the results of an environmental site assessment (which should be provided for in most cases for the reasons discussed in chapter 8 and section C, below)? On certain representations about the property that may not be visually self-evident, such as the nature of the water and sewer services available? On anything else? Add them to the agreement as conditions to your obligation to complete the purchase.

b. Nature of the Deed

In most instances, you will want a warranty deed, and the agreement should so specify. The warranty is, of course, only as good as the person giving it. If a title problem develops and the grantor is not around or has no assets, the warranty will be worthless.

c. The Title Search

Proper title searching requires training and should be done by an experienced professional. Do not rely on your own uninformed perusal of the records, however zealous. A title search should result in a title opinion by a responsible law firm as to the state of title and any limitations or exceptions to the attorney's opinion that title is good. Examine the document carefully, and review it with an attorney if you have any questions. Having the opinion is not enough; it must say the right thing. The opinion should verify that you are buying what you expect and without any encumbrances or burdens that are not acceptable.

In many areas, title insurance customarily covers the assurance of title. Instead of an attorney's opinion, you will receive an insurance policy (for which you pay a premium) that insures the title. The policy, however, is based on a title search done by the title company or a law firm it has hired and will contain the same exceptions an attorney would have put in a title opinion. Again, having the piece of paper is not enough. Read what it says, and be sure you are buying no surprises.

d. Down Payments

Down payments or deposits should be held in escrow by an attorney or a real estate agent. If something goes wrong, it may be easier to get the money back if it is held by a third party.

e. Description of the Property

The seller is not obligated to convey more than what the purchase and sale agreement describes. Hence it is important to be sure the agreement contains an adequate description of the property in question.

f. Authority to Sign

Be sure the agreement and the deed are signed by a person who is authorized to do so. An officer of a corporation who has neither by law nor board authorization the authority to sign may not bind a corporation.[1]

g. Time to Closing

Agreements usually set a time within which the closing will occur. If you need to close by a certain date or cannot close before a certain date, be sure the agreement is consistent with your needs.

h. Representations

Any representations about the property upon which you are relying but which are not visually self-evident, such as the absence of asbestos, petroleum contaminants, or hazardous waste on the property, should be included in the purchase and sale agreement, which should provide that they "survive the closing," that is, that they continue to bind the seller even after a deed has passed. Otherwise, any misrepresentations not detected before the closing may have no further effect when you accept a deed.

i. Environmental Assessment

The exposure to liability for environmental problems, discussed in chapter 8, mandates an environmental assessment whenever a church or religious organization is acquiring property. That assessment should be conducted by a firm that specializes in environmental consulting. As this is a rapidly growing and lucrative field, check the firm's credentials carefully. Some companies are attempting to break into this consulting field with inexperienced or marginally competent personnel. Select with care, and seek the advice of your attorney or other informed persons before hiring a consultant.

The assessment may be both of a building's interior, for the presence of asbestos, and of the property as a whole, for the presence of hazardous waste or petroleum contaminants. It should include a review of what is known of the history of use of the property and surrounding properties, a visual inspection for any evidence of disposal, and a sampling protocol of soil and groundwater to provide as much assurance as can reasonably be obtained that the organization is not buying a liability problem.

An environmental assessment should go a long way toward protecting a buyer from liability under CERCLA and other environmental statutes, but it is not a guarantee. As discussed above, it is also appropriate for the purchase and sale agreements to reflect the seller's representation that there is no hazardous waste or other contaminants on the property, or asbestos in the buildings, and that the seller will assume responsibility for any that may later be discovered.

j. Waste Disposal Systems

In rural areas where public water and sewer are not available, churches with buildings or parsonages, and other religious institutions, such as camps and conference centers, will have the additional environmental responsibility under state and local laws of insuring that their septic disposal systems are designed, constructed, and function in compliance with those laws and that they have obtained whatever permits or approvals may be necessary in this regard.

k. Zoning and Planning

Chapter 8 discusses zoning and other land-use controls. If you are facing a zoning issue in acquiring property or changing or expanding a use, consider the following issues:

(1) Is the use permitted by right in the zone
    (i) as a "church"?
    (ii) as an accessory use to a church?

    (iii) under any other permitted uses in the zone?
(2) Is the use permitted by a special exception or use permit if not as a matter of right? If so, can you meet the conditions for obtaining it?
(3) Can you qualify for a variance from the ordinance?
(4) Is the use an allowed continuation of a prior nonconforming use?
(5) If the ordinance prohibits your use, is it, in this respect:
    (i) a valid exercise of the police power?
    (ii) a denial of your state or federal constitutional free exercise right?
    (iii) a denial of your constitutional right to be treated equally with similar uses?
    (iv) a denial of your constitutional due process right because it bears no reasonable relationship to the purpose of the ordinance?
    (v) a taking of property without compensation?
    (vi) consistent with state enabling legislation?
(6) Seek out ambiguities in the ordinance and the administrative construction of the ambiguities that would support your use.

The legal issues pertinent to municipal planning requirements such as site plan review and subdivision controls will parallel many of the issues arising under zoning ordinances. Do they unreasonably burden the free exercise of religion in the absence of a sufficient governmental interest? Is the application of the regulation consistent with the enabling legislation and its own definitions? Is it being applied in a discriminatory fashion or for an improper purpose?

l. Property Taxes

If the property was acquired in the course of the tax year but was not exempt on the date of the beginning of the tax year, the property is subject to tax for the year, even though the purchasing organization would have been entitled to tax-exempt status for the property if it had owned it at the beginning of the year.[2] Thus, a church or religious organization purchasing property should take into account the prospective liability of property taxes for the year in question and address this issue in the purchase and sale contract.

2. Completing the Transaction

a. Meeting the Conditions

The time during which to insure that all conditions of the agreement are met is prior to the closing or title transfer. This is the time to arrange financing, do a title search, perform an environmental assessment if there is to be one, have a deed prepared and reviewed, and obtain land use or subdivision approvals. Be sure all the required bases are covered before paying your money and accepting a deed.

The environmental audit or assessment is particularly important for the reasons set forth in chapter 8 and section C of this chapter. Prudent purchasers of property today have an environmental audit or assessment done before buying to protect themselves against potential liability. Satisfactory completion of the assessment is a condition of the purchase. A consulting firm specializing in such matters conducts the audit or assessment.

b. The Closing

The deed is normally prepared by the seller's attorney and reviewed by the buyer's attorney. It must accord with the formalities required by state law. Be sure the names of both grantor and grantee are accurate on the deed. The church has a specific name, and it should be used. If your church is a corporation named "The First Church of Smithville, Inc." do not accept a deed to "The Smithville Church" or to "First Church, Inc.," for example.

The deed description must also be precise. It is the deed that determines the boundaries of your property, not a survey (although a survey may be helpful in locating the deed boundaries on the ground) or a tax assessor's map. Many old deeds have vague descriptions. Be sure your deed states your boundaries specifically and that you know where they are.

The closing should be conducted by legal counsel or a bank closing officer. A closing statement is prepared and reviewed and acknowledged by the parties to account for all funds. Transactions are usually closed in escrow so that a final title check can be done before recording the deed and turning over the purchase price. Last-minute liens or attachments may have intervened since the title was searched. The deed must be promptly recorded for the same reason: if someone records a lien or encumbrance against the prior owner after you have paid for the land, but before you record the deed, that action binds your land.

c. Deed Conditions and Restrictions

There are several devices to control private land use: covenants, conditions, and restrictions. These are provisions included in a deed that limit or restrict use of the property. They may be included by reference in the deed to a set of terms that are separately recorded. The restrictions may be common to a particular development and used to insure a specific level of uniformity or to exclude undesirable uses. Or they may be conditions in a deed, whether purchased or acquired by gift, that specifically limit the use of property. The limitations may be to protect neighboring property, or they may reflect the grantor's desire, particularly in deeds of gift, that the property continue to be used for the purposes given. Churches and religious organizations are particularly susceptible to such conditions because they often receive property by gift from religiously motivated donors.

The penalty for violating a covenant, condition, or restriction can vary, depending upon the nature of the violation, from being subject to a court order compelling compliance to actual loss of the property by reversion to the original grantor. Hence, it is important that religious organizations know and understand any covenants, conditions, or restrictions on the use of the property when it is acquired and that they carefully evaluate them when any changes in use are made.

Churches would be well advised to seek to minimize or eliminate any such restrictions on their use of property when accepting gifts of real estate. Restrictions that may seem innocuous at the time of a grant may be extremely burdensome years later. For instance, a religious organization may have a substantial investment in the premises which now have significant value, but because of changes in the circumstances of the organization or surrounding neighborhood, it now makes sense for the organization to sell the property for a nonreligious use and then itself use the cash to purchase property elsewhere to continue the religious use. Deed restrictions limiting the church's ownership of the property to the period of its use as a church may make it impossible to sell the property or liquidate the church's investment in it to acquire a new facility.

The nature of such restrictions may also be an issue in church property disputes in which a schism within a local congregation or a separation between a local congregation and a denomination raises the question of who owns the real estate. For example, in *Rhodes v. Westside Free Will Baptist Church*,[3] a 1987 Arkansas decision, a deed provided that "should this property cease to be used for religious purposes then it should revert to the grantors, their heirs and assigns." The court held that this restriction was not violated when the church, which previously had been independent, joined a denomination. Churches should be aware that deed covenants and restrictions that would require a court to make religious evaluations of matters of faith and doctrine in order to enforce them may be, as a result, unenforceable in court. Hence, any such provisions should be drafted with careful attention to prevailing Supreme Court decisions in this area.[4]

In conveyancing of property to or from a church or religious organization, one should always examine whether canon law or other church authority must be consulted to carry out the transaction properly. Conveyancing should also always identify any covenants, conditions, or restrictions that are appropriate to the property when the possibility exists of a dispute as to whether the property belongs to the denomination or the local church in the event of a church departure from the denomination.

B. PROPERTY TAXES

Churches and religious organizations should be alert to procedural requirements that may be necessary to obtain or preserve property tax–exempt status. In some jurisdictions, tax-exempt status is determined by the status of the property on a particular date, usually the beginning date of the tax year. It may be necessary to apply for tax-exempt status in advance, and an organization that purchases property, even from another tax-exempt organization, may have to submit its own application and not rely upon its predecessor's exemption.[5] The exemption application may have to be filed annually on or before a certain date, and failure to meet the filing date may preclude exemption. If taxes are assessed against the property, an appeal or appropriate procedure to protest the levying of the tax will have to be undertaken within a certain period of time, and time periods for such appeals are often short.

C. HAZARDOUS WASTE

If a hazardous waste or pollution problem is discovered on your property, you should:

1. Immediately obtain advice from a competent attorney and an environmental consultant. Prompt reporting or other specific action may be mandated by law to avoid substantial penalties.
2. Promptly report the matter to your insurer and to any other insurer that has provided coverage to you during the entire period in which the materials in question could have come onto or been present or released at the site. Earlier insurers may be liable for such events. A full review of insurance coverage with your counsel should also always be undertaken in such situations.
3. If it is not self-evident that the sole source of pollution is on your property, explore with your counsel and environmental consultant the potential liability of any neighbors who may have caused or contributed to the pollution. If it did originate solely on your site but before your ownership, explore the liability of prior owners. Many of the statutes we have been discussing, as well as common-law tort remedies which we have not covered specifically, will provide a

basis for recovering any damages you suffer from any other party that may have caused or contributed to the pollution.

4. Do not accept without examination any recommendations or remediation program from a governmental agency or other party. Government agencies or others who seek to impose liability on you may want a Cadillac for a remedy when a Chevrolet will do, and sometimes when no remediation at all is really necessary. Conversely, a party who may be liable to you for pollution is likely to look for the cheapest remedy possible, not necessarily the right one. And, as mentioned, consultants in this field have varying degrees of competence, and you cannot assume that the other party's consultant knows what he or she is doing. For all of these reasons, be sure you have your own competent advice on these matters.

D. PURCHASE OF GOODS

Perhaps your church is buying a new organ, refurnishing the church with pews, or furnishing a new building or facility. These and other transactions will require the church to enter into a contract which may involve the expenditure of significant sums of money. Here are a few suggestions to consider in making a major commitment for the purchase of goods:

1. The contract should be in writing. Most vendors in a major transaction for the sale of goods will have their own forms. Do not just blindly "sign on the dotted line." Examine the vendor's preprinted forms or written contract proposals with care. Take your time; no matter what someone might say, the goods are likely to still be available and at the same price later on. Be sure that the terms in the contract you sign are all actually agreeable to you, and do not sign unless they are. Insist on deleting anything you do not agree to and adding any representations of the vendor that you are relying upon. If the vendor will not accept reasonable modifications, find another vendor.

2. Make sure the contract fully, specifically, and unambiguously expresses everything that you believe you are getting, including any representations as to the nature, performance, and quality of the goods. Where the nature of the goods is appropriate, your order should contain specifications—the physical qualities, dimensions, materials, and so forth the goods must have, and the performance specifications they must meet. Where appropriate, you may wish to refer to a sample you have received or examined. If the vendor proffers a contract with reference to its own catalog model numbers or the like, be sure that the numbers refer to what you think you are buying. If there have been any guarantees or warranties given, be sure they are included. If there is an obligation to install or to maintain and repair for a given period of time at no extra cost, be sure that it is included. If a service is to be provided at a specific cost, be sure that is set forth. If the vendor or salesperson has told you anything that is important to you about the goods, be sure the representation is included in the contract.

3. Have the contract reviewed by an attorney *before* you sign it. People often come into our office seeking advice about contracts they have already signed. It is too late—the horse has left the barn. All a lawyer can advise you about then is what you have agreed to, not what you should have done to protect your interest. Seeing a lawyer before you make a major commitment may cost a few dollars, but it is an insurance policy against mistakes that could be much more costly later.

4. If you are part of a denomination that has access to denominational executives or other denominational professionals who have had experience with this sort of thing, consult them also before you sign. Their experience may help you to avoid costly mistakes.

5. Do not make large upfront payments. Once the money is in the vendor's hands, it is difficult to get it back if the goods are never delivered or are defective. If the vendor goes into bankruptcy,

your deposit is probably lost; you would be entitled to only a pro rata share of the vendor's net assets, along with all the other unsecured creditors, which is likely to be a very small share indeed.

6. Know your vendor. Recognize that vendors who are geographically distant from you and do not have places of business in your state may be difficult to pursue and collect a judgment from in litigation. Vendors who lack significant financial resources may be impossible to collect against. Get references and talk to others who have dealt with the vendor. Look for a track record of quality goods and satisfied customers, and a financially sound company.

7. Be sure you understand shipping obligations. Are you going to be charged additionally for the freight or is the cost of transportation included in the price?

8. There are some common terms in preprinted contract forms that you may want to think hard about:

    a. Warranties. Often the forms will contain exclusions or limitations of warranty that greatly reduce the vendor's responsibility to you. Contrary to what vendors will tell you, these terms are usually intended to limit, not expand, the rights that purchasers would have at law in their absence. Sometimes they conflict with verbal assurances given by a salesperson. These terms may not be negotiable, but, if they are not, you should at least understand them. A vendor who really wants your business should be willing to alter the terms at least to conform to the sales pitch.

    b. Costs of collection and attorney's fees. A vendor's preprinted forms will often provide that if it is necessary for the vendor to pursue you to collect the balances due, it will be entitled to interest, costs of collection, and attorney's fees. There is no reason that kind of provision should not be a two-way street. Suggest that the obligation to pay interest, costs of collection, and attorney's fees be made reciprocal in the event the goods are defective and the vendor ends up owing you money.

    c. Place of suit and governing law. Vendors' forms often state that any suit arising out of the contract can only be brought in the state or perhaps even the city in which the vendor is located and that the law of that state will govern. These are known as "choice of forum" and "choice of law" clauses, and they will usually be honored by courts if they refer to places that have a reasonable relationship with the contract. If they are not agreeable to you, change or delete them.

    d. Integration clause. This is contract language to the effect that no statements, warranties, or representations other than those contained in the contract are a part of the contract or are being relied upon by the parties. The clause is fine if it is true. If it is not true, be sure that any statements, warranties, or representations that have been made and upon which you are relying are included.

9. Be sure you and the contract clearly identify the contracting party. Because many corporate entities may be part of an affiliated organization or because of confusion between the parties to a contract, this is more often a problem than one might expect. One of the reasons businesses incorporate separate entities is to limit liability. You may think you are dealing with a large and prosperous organization and find that you are actually dealing with a small, marginally solvent subsidiary for whose contracts the prominent parent has no legal responsibility.

10. Be aware of when the risk of loss transfers. This will normally be when the goods are received at your premises. Be sure that your property insurance covers the goods against fire and other calamities as soon as you are responsible for them.

11. When the goods arrive, unpack them and inspect them promptly to be sure they conform to the contract. Do not sign any shipping or receipt documents that represent they are in conformity to the order or have been undamaged in transit unless you have actually inspected them and confirmed that this is so. If there is any problem with the goods, inform the vendor immediately and

make no further payment until the problem is made right.

12. If the goods are not delivered or are unsatisfactory and you are unable to get satisfaction from the vendor, minimize your damages by obtaining the most closely comparable goods at the best price you can.

13. If goods are rejected and are returned to the vendor or otherwise disposed of, be sure to preserve evidence, through the most appropriate means, of the reason the goods were rejected. This may include photographs, videotapes, written statements of persons who have inspected them, and keeping a sample. Consult your attorney at this time for suggestions before letting the goods out of your possession. Prompt action to preserve evidence is particularly important if the goods are perishable (for example, Christmas trees to be sold as a fundraiser).

14. Be sure the individual signing the contract, especially if it is you, on behalf of your institution, signs specifically in a *representative* capacity, such as "First Church, Inc. by John Jones, Treasurer" or "John Jones as Treasurer of First Church, Inc." Otherwise the signing party risks being personally liable for the contract. It is equally important to be sure that the person signing the contract is authorized to do so. If you have acted without authority from your organization, you may be bound personally by the contract and the organization may not. See the discussion in chapter 6, above.

15. For major purchases you may want to obtain authority from your congregation or ecclesiastical superior even if it is not legally required. Good relations within the church or denominational hierarchy may mandate getting the right people on board with your purchase as well as complying with the requirement of legal authority.

16. In appropriate circumstances, consider putting requests for purchases of goods out to bid. Do not obligate yourself, however, to accept the lowest bid. The vendor who makes the lowest bid may also be the least reliable.

17. It is often helpful before entering into a contract to set the forms aside and simply think through what you expect out of the contract. Then look the contract over to make sure that all of your expectations are expressly contained within it. Involve your legal counsel; tell your lawyer what your expectations are, and have your counsel read the contract to see if it conforms to those expectations.

18. Keep copies of everything.

19. Write down the names of everyone with whom you deal regarding the purchase (include phone sales and utility representatives) as well as the dates and times of the conversations. Details regarding the product's merits, seller's repair policies, warranties, and other representations are also important.

E. CONSTRUCTION CONTRACTS

Many churches, especially young and growing ones, will be dealing with construction contracts. The construction or major renovation of a building is a significant financial undertaking and should be done with proper attention to protecting the organization's legal rights and position. Major construction and related contracts (such as for architectural or engineering services) are frequently set forth in contract forms prepared by the American Institute of Architects. These are known as AIA forms and are standardized preprinted forms. There are different forms for different purposes, for example, for services of a design professional such as the architect or engineer, services of a contractor, services of a subcontractor, or services of a "clerk of the works" who monitors construction on behalf of the owner. The forms have been carefully developed over time and their meaning often litigated. Because they are prepared by the AIA, they are, not surprisingly, supportive of the position of the design professional. Nevertheless, they have been developed and used by professionals in the field and will cover many of the issues that contracts of this nature should cover, and for that reason they are often useful. Like the preprinted forms of vendors of goods, however, they should not be accepted and signed blindly. Many of the suggestions set forth under "Purchase of Goods," above are equally applicable to construction contracts. You should also be alert to other issues:

1. If AIA forms are used, be sure the appropriate forms are used for the purpose. I have not infrequently seen contractors confuse forms. When a form not designed for the purpose for which it is being used is signed without checking by the owner at the contractor's insistence, the result can be a contract form that is confusing and virtually useless.

2. Be sure that the parties to the contract are correctly identified and are who you think they are.

3. Be sure all the blanks are filled in as appropriate.

4. Construction contracts of any magnitude should have plans and specifications that identify exactly what is to be done. Plans are the written drawings or blueprints for the project. Specifications are the documents that set forth such things as the nature and quality of materials to be used, construction methods and standards, and the like. Review your plans and specifications to be sure, as much as you can within your expertise, that they describe what you believe you are getting.

5. Commonly the documents will call for "as-built" plans and specifications to be delivered to the owner by the contractor or design professional following completion of the project. These plans and specifications will reflect changes made during the project and will be invaluable to the owner later when repairs are needed or renovations or additions are undertaken. If your contract documents do not call for as-built plans and specifications, consider adding a requirement for them. When the contract documents do call for as-built plans and specifications, insist upon receiving them at the end of the project, and do not make final payment until you have. In my experience, as-built plans and specifications are more often than not overlooked at the end of the

project as the contractors and design professionals move on to their next job; and, unless the owner withholds money, they have nothing to gain by producing them. Owners often simply forget them until they are needed years later and it is discovered that the only plans and specifications available are the original ones that are inaccurate because of changes at the time of construction.

6. A major building project goes through a normal life cycle, which includes a planning stage, a design stage, the preparation of bid documents, bidding by prospective contractors, the construction phase, and the final phases of punch lists and building occupancy. The services of an architect or design professional are likely to be necessary to carry you through these stages. Your building committee or other responsible group should carefully monitor the process at every stage.

7. Be sure that all contractors and subcontractors working on the job have workers' compensation insurance to protect their workers (and you) for on-the-job injuries. Put the requirement in your contracts. Have them produce certificates of insurance to be sure they are in compliance.

8. Contractors should be bonded; that is, they should have insurance that protects you and assures that they will complete the job and pay their subcontractors and materials suppliers. In some jurisdictions, bonds may even be mandatory for a church construction project.[6] For major jobs, these bonds are commonly job specific, and there may be separate bonds for job performance and for labor and materials. The bonding process is simply the insurance of contractors that they will meet their obligations in carrying out their contract. The contract documents should require the contractors to produce bonds or evidence of insurance, and the owner should insist upon receiving this information.

9. As with any other contract, it is extremely important that the contract express fully, specifically, and unambiguously what the contractor is going to

do and for how much. The performance to be rendered is normally done by reference to the plans and specifications; hence, it is important to be sure that the contract provides fully for the job that needs to be delivered. Anything that is not included in the plans and specifications will not be implied. It will simply not be the contractor's obligation to deliver it, and you will be obliged to pay extra to receive it. Hence the importance of completeness.

10. Take the time to be sure that the contract documents, especially the plans and specifications, are well thought out and complete at the outset. Changes in the contract as you go along can be made but will result in price changes, usually upward.

11. Be sure the contract provides for the contractor to obtain building and occupancy permits and any other regulatory licenses or permits that need to be met, such as electrical or plumbing approvals. Zoning or other land-use approvals are normally the responsibility of the owner.

12. If the time of contract performance or completion is important to you, the contract should say so and say why. For example, if it is necessary to have a building completed by the first of August so that it can be moved into before the beginning of the next school year, the contractor should understand that and should be responsible for any additional cost from his failure to meet the obligation. You may not be able to hold a contractor to any timely completion standards in the absence of a specific contractual provision.

13. The design professional should, by contract, be responsible for the plans and specifications being in compliance with the building code, including any fire, safety, or similar regulations.[7] The contractor should have the same responsibility with respect to construction. The owner, of course, needs to be aware of any regulatory requirements for the building that would be unique to its use of it and be sure that the design professional has designed them into it. Standards for a church, for example, may be different and less stringent than standards for a child care center or school. If the building is to have a dual function, it should be designed for the most stringent standards of the contemplated use. The uses to which the building may be put and which the design must accommodate must be communicated to the design professional.

14. Shop small jobs and put large jobs out to bid. Know your contractors. Do not obligate yourself to select the low bidder if you are not satisfied with its ability to perform the contract.

15. Monitor the job in progress. Call any deficiencies immediately to the contractor's attention. If necessary, halt interim payments until deficiencies are corrected. On large jobs, owners may have a "clerk of the works" who is a part-time or full-time employee (or independent contractor) reporting to the owner with the responsibility of monitoring the job to insure compliance with the plans and specifications. He is *not* a job supervisor whose job is to tell the contractors or their employees how to perform the job. The distinction is important in determining who is responsible for job deficiencies. The clerk of the works is your eyes and ears on the job, not a construction boss. If the magnitude of the project does not justify having a clerk of the works, be sure that someone informed in the design and construction trades at least gives you some assistance in periodic job checks to make sure the job is coming together properly. Design professionals—architects and engineers—customarily have this responsibility on large jobs which they design. Continuous job monitoring is particularly important to be sure that proper materials are being used and building specifications followed as the job goes up. The very nature of building construction is such that much of the early work is "buried" or concealed by the ongoing construction and is invisible in the finished product. Foundation drains, driveway, roadway, and parking lot bases, the tying of structural steel, drainage in exterior masonry walls which depend upon construction tech-

niques within the wall, use of proper materials and construction techniques in water-resistant flat-roof construction are only a few areas where disregard of plans and specifications in the construction process may result in problems that will not be visible in the final product and will only become known when the failures and functional problems start occurring.

16. In larger contracts, provision is usually made for periodic payments at fixed intervals of percentage of completion of the job, with payment conditioned upon the architect's approval of the billing and certification that the job is done to the percentage completion represented by the bill. In smaller projects you may have to monitor the progress yourself with whatever level of assistance is appropriate to the situation. Do not let payments get ahead of job completion. The contractor's incentive to complete the job properly is to get his or her money.

17. There should be a retainage of 5 to 10 percent of bills as you go along, which is held until the job is certified to be complete and a certificate of occupancy issued by the building inspector or appropriate authorities. This should be written into the contract; if it is not, you do not have a right to do it unilaterally.

The purpose of the retainage is to assure punch-list completion. The punch list is the inevitable list of minor odds and ends at the end of the job needed for final completion. It should be made up by the contractor and a representative of the owner. Ideally, the architect or design professional and someone from the owner—say, the chairman of the building committee— walk through the job with the contractor and make up a specific written list of things that need to be done for job completion. The punch-list process may have to be repeated several times. A retainage should not be paid until all items on the final punch list have been taken care of.

18. Check all major operating items for proper functioning at the earliest opportunity. HVAC (heating, ventilat-

ing, and air conditioning) systems are particularly prone to difficulties and often need adjusting or "balancing" to function properly. All other mechanical or electrical systems should also be tested to be sure they perform satisfactorily at the earliest opportunity and monitored for a period of time to be sure they are working properly. Such systems may appear satisfactory by visual inspection. The real problems can only be discerned when they are operating.

19. Resolve any disputes with the contractor as you go along. The AIA contracts normally provide for a dispute-resolution procedure that gives certain authority to the architect but provides for the resolution of ultimate disputes by arbitration. For both practical and biblical reasons, it is best not to let the sun go down on issues but work them out promptly. If you conclude that you have made a mistake in selecting the contractor and that he cannot or will not meet contractual obligations, consult counsel and your design professional before you make a decision that you are justified in putting him off the job because he is in breach of contract. Any such situation presents the likelihood of litigation, whether in an arbitration forum or in court.

20. Dealing with members of the church or organization or other believers who provide professional design or contracting services should be done with caution. It is highly desirable to have people on a building committee who can render volunteer advice with the benefit of the expertise of their trade or profession. To expect them to do the job for you is another question, however. They rely on their trade for a living, and it is not fair of the church to expect them to give their services for nothing or at a cut-rate price. If they do, they may be tempted to cut corners to minimize their loss, which creates a bad situation for all parties. If the church contracts with them because they are Christians or church members without first putting a job out to bid or shopping it, it may find that they are not the

best-qualified people for the job or will not deliver it at the best price available. Contracting with church members on an arm's-length basis raises the same prospects of disagreement among believers that is present in dealing with nonbelievers in arm's-length construction work, which is an area fraught with the potential for disputes. Your church members who are design professionals or contractors probably are and should be insured or bonded with respect to their work, but the church may feel inhibited, for biblical reasons or due to personal relationships, from seeking to recover if their negligence or failure to perform their contract results in damage to the church. These things should be thought through in advance, not after the roof collapses under a snow load because your church member/architect did not design it right or your church member/contractor did not build it right—or a little of each.

21. If a building project is to be financed by borrowing, deferred-giving devices, or issuance of any kind of investment instrument, you must have legal counsel.[8]

22. Be slow to hire contractors on a time-and-materials basis rather than on a fixed-price basis. While a contractor bidding or offering a fixed price may take uncertainties or contingencies into consideration and make the price high enough to cover them, at least you know what to expect. Estimates made by contractors working on a time-and-materials basis are not binding and provide no basis for legal action unless they are fraudulent or totally unreasonable compared to what the contractor should have known and anticipated. I have rarely seen a job come in under an estimate when the contractor was working on a time-and-materials basis. The contractor, without being dishonest, will usually tend to understate the estimate to encourage the owner to hire him for the job.

23. In most significant construction projects there will be changes as the project progresses. Be clear on who can authorize changes. In a formal AIA contract,

these are evidenced by "change orders" issued by the architect to the contractor. Whether you are using an AIA contract or similar formal, written contract or not, changes should be documented in writing. Change orders usually require the contractor's agreement. If the contract reserves the unilateral right to issue them, the contractor is entitled to change the compensation to reflect the changes. Normally, this will be an increase, although occasionally, due to a decision to use a cheaper material or eliminate some construction shown in the original plans and specifications, it may decrease.

24. Read the contract with care. The AIA contract forms may contain a lot of provisions that are inapplicable to your situation or that you do not want to be applicable. If that is the case, make changes. Just because the contract comes with a preprinted form does not mean you must accept the form intact. Deletions and additions can be made to whatever extent the parties agree. Deletions can be made by crossing out sections and having all parties to the contract sign or initial the deletion. Additions can be made in a separate addendum attached to and forming part of the contract, again signed by all of the parties to it.

25. Rely on no representations, assurances, or guarantees of any sort that are not expressly contained in the contract. Think out what is important to you, and then be sure it is in the contract.

26. Take appropriate steps to protect against mechanic's liens. A mechanic's lien is a right provided by law in most states for subcontractors or suppliers of material to assert a lien against the owner's real estate if they are not paid. Thus the owner who pays the contractor may wind up paying twice if the contractor fails to pay its subcontractors and suppliers. Local counsel can advise you on the best way to protect yourself from this under the law of your state.[9]

Construction projects present the church with all of the same problems they present to secular owners. With the limited exception of the unique considerations that may be involved in dealing with church members or fellow believers as contractors, material suppliers, or design professionals, there is nothing unique to management of such a project by a sectarian owner. Significant construction projects present a myriad of opportunities for problems, misunderstandings, and disagreements, and require the most careful attention by the owner to insure management of church assets in a prudent and creditable manner.

F. PREMISES LIABILITY

Virtually all churches and religious organizations will own or at least occupy premises on which they will have meetings to which people will come from time to time for worship or other purposes. Invariably, injuries occur. People slip and fall on stairs, on icy walks and parking lots, on wet or slippery floors. Volunteers fall off ladders while doing painting or other construction or maintenance work. Neighboring children trespass on the property and get hurt. What is the church's responsibility in these situations?

Traditionally, courts have approached the question of premises liability by analyzing the status of the injured person. They are identified as "invitees," "licensees," or "trespassers"; and the landowner's duty differs as to each. Invitees are persons who are on the premises upon the business of the owner or occupier and are present upon her or his express or implied invitation to be there. As to such persons, the owner or occupier of the premises has a duty to use reasonable care to protect them against all known dangers and those dangers which might have been discovered with reasonable care. Invitees are the most protected category of plaintiffs.

Licensees are those whose presence is permitted or tolerated with the landowner's or occupier's knowledge or consent but without an express or implied invitation. The owner or occupier of the premises owes a lesser duty to a licensee than to an invitee: to warn the licensee of hidden dangers of which the owner or occupier is aware and to refrain from causing any intentional, willful, wanton, or reckless injuries to the licensee.

The lowest status of injured person is the trespasser, who is there with neither invitation nor permission. While landowners have no duty to trespassers, if aware of their presence they must refrain from willfully or wantonly injuring them and may have a duty to warn of concealed hazards.

The distinctions between invitees, licensees, and trespassers are often not obvious, and courts have reached different results in classifying, for example, people attending church services.[10] In recent years some courts have moved away from the invitee/licensee/trespasser distinction simply to examine the reasonableness of the conduct of the landowner or occupier in view of all of the circumstances, including the circumstances of the injured party. This rule seems more sensible and easier to administer, but few cases have arisen applying it to religious organizations.

Suppose your premises include a pond, a well shaft, or an abandoned structure. The neighborhood children love to play there. Sooner or later one of them drowns in the pond, falls down the well shaft, or is injured by falling through a floor in the abandoned building. Is the church liable? These situations have led to the development of a legal concept known as "attractive nuisance," which is recognized in most, but not all, states. It allows landowners to be found liable if they are aware of (1) the likelihood of trespass, (2) that the situation involves a foreseeable risk of harm, (3) that immature trespassers would not discover the harm or appreciate the dangers involved, and (4) that maintenance of the condition has little utility to the landowner compared to the risk to the child trespasser. The extent of the landowner's obligation to make the premises safe against such foreseeable trespassers and harm will depend on the circumstances. An owner is not required to child-proof the premises. A building under construction, for example, may be virtually impossible to protect from trespassers, but one should not leave dynamite caps lying around or well shafts uncovered.

In other variations of premises liability law, religious organizations have been held liable under state law for failure to remove snow and ice from abutting sidewalks[11] and for injuries that occurred on a carnival-type ride at a church fund-raising event even though the ride was owned and operated by an outside contractor.[12] The duties of an owner or occupier of property cannot be delegated to an outside contractor. A church may be liable for injuries to members or to guests of outside groups using the property.[13]

What can a church or religious organization do to avoid premises liability?

First, it should "risk manage" its property. Large institutions, such as universities and hospitals, are likely to have specialized employees whose job title or duties involve risk management. In most churches and religious organizations, risk management will be the task of the pastor or executive, the staff, the governing boards, and, ultimately, every member or person who cares about the organization and its mission. Risk management simply means being alert to the hazards involved in all of the operations and activities of the organization—making sure that stairs and stairwells are well lighted and have handrails; that walks and parking lots are cleared of ice and snow, and sanded and salted as appropriate; that glass doors have some warning of their presence; that floors and stairs are kept free of things that can cause people to slip and trip; that equipment that could cause injury is maintained in proper operating condition, has adequate guards, and is used only by those who know how to do so; that any areas of special hazard are secured; and that any situations that present potential hazards are corrected if correctable or, if not, that steps are taken to warn people of the danger or prevent them from accessing them. Your insurance company may be willing to inspect the premises and make suggestions.

Second, a church should be sure that it is adequately insured. While this does not avoid liability, it does transfer the financial burden to the extent that it has insurance coverage, at a cost of paying the insurance premiums. Liability insurance is discussed in chapter 20.

CHAPTER 16

Accounting for Funds and Trusts

A. The Mortmain Laws
B. Municipal Regulation of Solicitation
C. The Role of the State in the Enforcement of Charitable Trusts
D. Enforceability of Pledges
E. Revocation of a Gift after It Is Made: Fraud, Duress, and Undue Influence
F. Gifts in Trusts, Wills, and on Conditions
G. The Problem of Construction
H. The Cy Pres Doctrine
I. What Interest Is Created?
J. The Enforceability of Conditions, Restrictions, or Limitations involving Specifically Religious Conditions

Most churches and many other religious organizations have no income-generating capacity and depend for their existence on the voluntary contributions of their members and supporters. Such reliance is not misplaced: churches are consistently the leading objects of generosity of American citizens. In 1987, Americans gave $44 billion to religious organizations—an average contribution of $715 from 52.5 percent of American households. Religious giving is consistently just under half of all American philanthropic contributions, far exceeding any other category. It has increased more than fivefold since 1970, from $9.3 billion in that year to over $48 billion in 1988.[1] The concerns generated by that flow of wealth are the subject of this chapter. They include regulatory concerns, problems relating to the means of solicitation, and the issues

of the management or implementation of gifts, the terms of which are often left in unclear terms or outlive the meaningfulness of the conditions on which or objects for which they are given. Federal income tax considerations regarding giving are discussed in chapter 10. Donors of sufficient means or who make substantial contributions will need to obtain competent tax advice on the federal (and state, where applicable) gift and/or estate tax consequences of their gifts as well, a subject not addressed herein.

A. THE MORTMAIN LAWS

The struggle for power and wealth between king and church in feudal England resulted in the promulgation of mortmain ("dead hand") statutes designed to prevent the church from accumulating excessive wealth and depriving the king and lords of real estate. The American concern for the separation of church and state and hostility to the Church of England following the American Revolution led to the adoption of mortmain laws in many American states.

One form of mortmain law precludes religious organizations from accumulating more than a specified dollar value of assets. Such laws have been abandoned almost everywhere, although they may still exist in the private legislative charters of some churches that date back to the early nineteenth century. They are almost certainly unconstitutional by contemporary standards, and there is little record of attempts to enforce them within the past century.

A more persistent form of mortmain law involved gifts to clergy or churches made by a will written within a determined time before death. These laws had the additional rationale of purporting to protect the dying from importuning clergy who might be advantaged by the dying penitent's desire to maximize his or her position in the afterlife. The laws had a variety of forms: some invalidated all such gifts, some only those attacked by the heirs, perhaps limited to spouse or children; some had exceptions if the gift was similar to one made in a prior will.

The Supreme Court of Florida, one of the few states in which such statutes persisted, found the Florida mortmain law unconstitutional under both the state and federal constitutions in the 1990 case of *Shriners Hospitals v. Zrillac.*[2] The court determined that the ability to set aside gifts due to fraud or undue influence provided adequate protection and that the statute was unnecessary to accomplish its stated goals. Moreover, the differing treatment of gifts to charities and religious organizations compared to gifts to other donees violated their right to equal protection of the law. The statute also improperly interfered with a testator's right to devise property by will. The court identified Georgia, Idaho, and Mississippi as the only other states in which such laws persist.

B. MUNICIPAL REGULATION OF SOLICITATION

Municipalities may, as discussed in chapter 3, impose reasonable time, place, and manner regulations on public activities of religious organizations, including solicitation of funds. Some municipalities have registration or licensing ordinances for the solicitation of funds for charity and may or may not exempt religious organizations. Exemptions may apply only to certain religious organizations (such as 501(c)(3) organizations) or certain types of fund-raising (among members, at regular services, without using professional fund-raisers).

Such ordinances are constitutionally suspect. The Supreme Court has struck down as Establishment Clause or free speech violations ordinances that exempt only organizations that raise a certain percent of revenue from members or use a certain percent for charitable purposes.[3] Any discretionary

authority residing in municipal officials to permit or refuse to permit solicitation is clearly unconstitutional. Fraud can be prevented by other means than licensing and registration statutes, although government does have the authority to prevent fraud. Beyond reasonable, narrowly drawn means to protect against fraud, municipalities have little more authority to regulate religious solicitation than to impose the kind of time, place, and manner regulations acceptable to regulate any form of public communication.

C. THE ROLE OF THE STATE IN THE ENFORCEMENT OF CHARITABLE TRUSTS

States, usually through their attorneys general, have power both at common law and, in most states, by statute to exercise supervision over charitable trusts. Such provisions are intended to curb abuses. They typically require registration and the filing of periodic information and financial reports, and they authorize the state to engage in certain investigative procedures. Most state statutes contain a religious exemption which may be as narrow as trusts or trustees of churches, cemeteries, or orphanages operated in conjunction with churches, or as broad as any property held for any religious use.[4] Churches and religious organizations should be aware of the extent of the exemption in their state and be guided accordingly.

Where no religious exemption exists, churches and religious organizations need to be mindful of state and federal constitutional religious freedom protections that may make such regulatory statutes unconstitutional as applied to them.[5]

The state can be friend or foe in intervening under either statutory or common-law authority in matters pertaining to religious trusts and gifts. One instance of state intervention to protect a religious gift appears in the 1988 Georgia case of *Collins v. Citizens & Southern Trust Co.*[6] There the will had made provision for the distribution of funds to a charitable trust to feed starving people and give Bibles to those who need to know Jesus Christ. The family had challenged the will and worked out a settlement among themselves which excluded the trust. On intervention by the state through its director of revenue, however, the court protected the trust gift for religious use.

D. ENFORCEABILITY OF PLEDGES

Traditionally courts have viewed the pledge to make a gift as unenforceable as a matter of contract law because of the lack of any consideration, or quid pro quo, required to have an enforceable contract.[7] In many states, this is still the law.

Some courts, however, have adopted a theory of "detrimental reliance," finding the pledge enforceable on the theory that the donee has relied to its detriment on the pledge in planning its activities and making commitments to accomplish its goals. While this is largely fiction with respect to any given pledge, there is a certain rationale to the theory if one views pledges collectively and considers that if one pledgor can renege on a commitment, nothing prevents the rest from doing likewise. Sometimes detrimental reliance is described by courts as "consideration."

The most contemporary, and honest, view is probably that expressed by a New Jersey court in *Jewish Federation of Central New Jersey v. Barondess.*[8] Recognizing the questionable nature of the rationale of courts finding consideration and detrimental reliance, the *Barondess* court got to the bottom line: "The real basis for enforcing a charitable subscription is one of public policy—that enforcement of a charitable subscription is a desirable social goal."[9] The Jewish Federation of Central New Jersey collected its pledge.

Some states have enacted statutes which enable the personal representative of a deceased person (i.e., the fiduciary in charge of the deceased's estate) to honor an unsatisfied written charitable pledge, even if it is not legally binding, if in the personal representative's judgment the deceased would have wanted the pledge completed under the circumstances.[10] Absent such a statute, the ability to collect the pledge probably depends on whether it would be viewed as enforceable in the state in question if the pledgor were still alive.

E. REVOCATION OF A GIFT AFTER IT IS MADE: FRAUD, DURESS, AND UNDUE INFLUENCE

The law and the hazards to religious organizations of overzealous solicitation are well illustrated in the 1990 decision of the First Circuit Court of Appeals in *Dovydenas v. The Bible Speaks.*[11] The plaintiff was a well-to-do woman who had made contributions to the defendant church of more than six and a half million dollars, principally in three major gifts of one million dollars, five million dollars, and five hundred thousand dollars. Through family intercession, she recognized that she had believed a lie by the pastor—that through gifts, she had the power to influence events, such as curing illness and causing the release of an imprisoned Romanian pastor (he had been released before the gift was made). She undertook exit counseling and deprogramming treatment relating to cults and mind-control groups and then brought suit for the return of her gifts, claiming that they were obtained through undue influence.

The court noted that the Free Exercise Clause of the Constitution does not cloak fraud and "does not allow purely secular statements of fact to be shielded from legal action merely because they are made by officials of a religious organization."[12] The necessary elements of an undue influence claim under Massachusetts law were met: (1) a person who can be influenced, (2) the fact of deception practiced or improper influence exerted, and (3) the submission by the influenced person to the overmastering effect of such unlawful conduct. When a confidential relationship exists between the parties, as here, undue influence is easier to find. It can be inferred from such factors as disproportionate gifts made under unusual circumstances, the age and health of the donor, the existence of a confidential relationship, attempts by the recipient to isolate the donor from former friends and relatives, and the fact that the donor acted without independent and disinterested counsel or other advice. Based on these principles, the court invalidated most of the gifts.

The *Dovydenas* case was decided on the ground of undue influence. Fraud, duress, and undue influence are often asserted simultaneously as a ground for setting aside transfers improperly obtained. They are closely related concepts. Undue influence is defined in the *Dovydenas* case in a manner which would be accepted in most states. Fraud, by contrast, does not require a person to be particularly subject to influence, nor does it include the notion of submission to the overmastering effect of deceptive conduct. It simply requires (1) a misrepresentation of a material fact with the intent to induce reliance on it, and (2) that the person to whom the misrepresentation is made does in fact rely on it to his or her damage.

Duress presents the further variant of circumstances which deprive the individual of the ability to exercise free will. Duress is the "application of such pressure or constraint as compels man to go against his will and takes away his free agency, destroying the power of refusing to comply with unjust demands of another."[13] It has also been defined as including "any conduct which overpowers will and coerces or constrains performance of an act which otherwise would not have been performed."[14]

Fraud or misrepresentation claims are not limited to egregious circumstances such as the *Dovydenas* case. In the 1990 case of *Marcus v. Jewish National Fund,*[15] a New York court allowed such a claim when the charity had not spent the funds for the purposes for which it had solicited them. Duress and undue influence claims can, however, be difficult to prove and are often unsuccessful, particularly if the claim is brought by disinherited heirs who had little to do with the decedent, and if the decedent was in reasonable mental and physical health at the time of executing a will or making a gift.

Churches and religious organizations need not bow to spurious claims of fraud, duress, and undue influence, particularly when brought by disappointed heirs who are not dependent on the deceased and made little contribution to his or her welfare or happiness before death. They should, however, deal prudently with circumstances in which prospective donors are extremely elderly or in poor physical or mental health, or where the gift might deprive a spouse or children of funds that may be needed or reasonably expected. Prospective donee organizations should carefully avoid soliciting gifts through any representations that are even arguably false or through overbearing efforts to influence the giving process. The single, most prudent step that can be taken to protect the validity of a gift is to insure that the giver has independent, outside counsel and advice concerning the gift.

Major charitable and religious organizations often have planned-giving programs in which they produce, with the advice of their own counsel, structured or planned-giving arrangements that meet the requirements for federal tax deductibility and are otherwise drafted to comply with applicable law. Such arrangements, as well as the honest solicitation of prospective donors, are entirely proper. Organizations that solicit prospective donors need to understand, however, that their attorneys are not the donors' attorneys and should not be expected to act as such. We are occasionally asked by religious or other organizations if we would be willing to have the organization refer prospective donors to us for preparation of wills, trusts, or other donative arrangements. While we are happy to have such referrals, we have to explain to the referring agencies that we can only serve one master and that our master in such a situation would be the client for whom we were preparing the will or other donative instruments. While there is no reason for an attorney to discourage a client from making proper charitable or religious contributions by will or otherwise, the attorney's obligation is to provide independent and objective legal advice to the donor, not to be an advocate for the prospective donee, no matter how sympathetic the attorney may be to the donee or its objectives. Donee organizations will be best served by doing what they can to insure that their prospective donors receive such independent advice.

F. GIFTS IN TRUSTS, WILLS, AND ON CONDITIONS

A direct, unconditional gift to a church or religious organization, presuming it was not induced by fraud, duress, or undue influence or by the representation that it would be used for any specific purpose, is the ideal gift. The organization is the direct and full owner of the asset and is free to use it for any of its purposes. But gifts are often more complex. They may be made not only directly but by the mechanism of a trust. Both direct gifts and gifts in trust may be made either in the donor's lifetime (an *inter vivos* transfer) or by will (a testamentary transfer). Direct gifts, inter vivos trusts, and testamentary gifts or trusts may all contain various conditions or restrictions limiting the use of the asset in various ways and creating various consequences if they are not met. A brief description of trust law and the probate process may provide a useful contextualization of issues that churches and religious organizations deal with in this area. Always consult counsel when dealing with specific situations.

When an individual dies, it is necessary that his or her debts be paid and that property be transmitted to whoever becomes the rightful owner on death. The process of insuring that this happens is called "probate." It is controlled by statute and is subject to court supervision, often of a special court called a "probate court," or some similar designation, whose jurisdiction is limited to supervising decedents' estates, trusts, and such similar matters as may be allocated to it by state law.

A decedent can control the disposition of his or her property on death by writing a will. A will is a written instrument that expresses the decedent's wishes; it is executed with certain formalities to insure its validity. If you do not have a will (absence of a will on death is known as "intestacy"), the law will write your will for you in the form of state statutes that designate who will take your property. For married persons with lineal descendants, this will be their spouse and descendants. For unmarried persons, it will be their parents, if they survive them, and their siblings, if they do not; and if neither parents nor siblings survive them, it is the next most closely related person or persons. In the absence of any identifiable heir, the property will escheat (revert) to the state, a rare occurrence. Most married couples with children are surprised to learn that the spouse is not usually the sole heir in an intestacy but that the children will share some part of the estate regardless of their age or need. This is a sufficient reason for most couples to write a will when they begin a family.

A will should be drafted by an attorney and reviewed by an attorney whenever a move from one state to another occurs to be sure it is consistent with the laws of the new state of residence. If you do not have exceptional assets and complex estate-planning problems, having a will prepared is usually inexpensive. Since everyone's circumstances are different, using forms torn out of books purchased in the local bookstore is imprudent and deprives you of the personal legal advice you should receive when doing estate planning.

When an individual dies, the will, if there is one, is "proven," that is, filed, at the probate court and shown by the applicable state procedures to be the instrument it purports to be. The probate court will appoint a "personal representative," also referred to as the "executor" (male) or "executrix" (female), who is usually nominated by the decedent in the will and whose responsibility is to administer or manage the estate. If there is no will, the person with this responsibility may be known as an "administrator" or "administratrix." Notice is provided to those who are named in the will as prospective beneficiaries and normally to others who would have been heirs in an intestacy. Anyone who wishes to may challenge the will, usually on the grounds that the testator or testatrix was incompetent (i.e., lacked the mental capacity) to make a will at the time it was made, or, perhaps, on the theory that the decedent was subject to fraud, duress, or undue influence. This will require a "will contest," which is simply a trial to determine whether or not the will is valid and effective.

The administrator or executor, regardless of the provisions of the will, is responsible for insuring that the property of the decedent is identified and secured; that debts, taxes, and expenses of administering the estate are paid; and that whatever remains thereafter is distributed to those to whom it is given under the will or by statute in the case of intestacy. An inventory of the assets of the estate is taken at an early stage, usually by a formal means and filed with the court. Administrators and executors are often required to give a bond (i.e., a promise secured by an insurance policy) to guarantee the faithful performance of their duties. The size of the bond is likely to be determined by the size of the estate and in some instances may be waived by the heirs. Expenses of administration are also paid out of the estate. Some form of notice is also required, usually by newspaper, to enable those who have claims against the estate to assert them; and a fixed time will be provided by statute for the assertion of claims.

Once the process is complete—that is, the will has been accepted, notice has been given by required means to everyone who is entitled to it, all debts, taxes, and administrative expenses of the estate have been paid, issues as to the validity of any claims have been resolved, and the executor-administrator is ready to close the estate— he or she files a final account setting forth what was received, what was spent and for what purposes, and the amount to be distributed to the heirs. Estates that are not closed for extended periods of time may file interim accounts, usually annually. Each account is reviewed and approved by the appropriate judge, who may require the executor or administrator to show receipts or otherwise explain expenditures and who will specifically review and approve or disapprove administrative costs such as the fees for the executor-administrator or attorney's fees. When assets are distributed to heirs or beneficiaries of the estate, they will be required to sign receipts which must be filed with the probate court. In small estates the process may be simplified.

A number of special problems may arise in the course of administering an estate that may require particular actions by the executor or administrator with the approval of the probate court. These problems include selling estate assets rather than distributing them to heirs and making arrangements to continue the operation of a going business.

The purposes of the laws governing probate administration are simply to keep everybody honest in dealing with the decedent's assets and to be sure that the decedent's legitimate obligations are paid, and that the people who are supposed to receive the assets do so. While horror stories of abuse of the process by excessive fees occasionally appear in a few jurisdictions, it is a process that in most instances works well and achieves its purpose at a reasonable cost. Lawyers and other professional fiduciaries usually do most of the accounting and management of the estate through the probate process and do so more efficiently than an individual who is unfamiliar with the process could do because they have the expertise and systems in place to do so.

A "trust" is simply an arrangement in which assets are placed, either by will or by an inter vivos instrument, in the care or management of a trustee under a written instrument, the trust. The trust provides binding directions for the management of the assets: it identifies the beneficiaries, when and under what circumstances income or principal of the trust is to be paid out, what powers the trustee has with respect to investment and management of the assets, how the trustee can be replaced, and how and when the trust terminates. If the trust is inter vivos, it may be revocable, that is, the donor or the person creating the trust may retain the power to terminate it; or it may be irrevocable, in which case he or she has made the gift in trust without retaining the power to revoke it.

In addition to their specific statutory duties, executors, administrators, and trustees have certain common-law responsibilities with respect to the assets they manage and the beneficiaries of those assets. One such duty is "to display the skill and prudence which an ordinarily capable and careful man would use in the conduct of his own business of a like character and with objectives similar to those of the trust."[16] Persons who have represented that they possess exceptional capacity to conduct their responsibilities or actually have such abilities will be required to use the capacities they represented they had or the abilities they possess. Trustees and executors also have a duty of loyalty to the beneficiaries "to administer the affairs of the trust in the interest of the beneficiaries alone, and to exclude from consideration his own advantages and the welfare of third persons."[17] They are obliged to take possession of the trust or estate property, to defend it against attack, and to protect and preserve it. Executors and administrators will not normally invest assets since their ultimate obligation is to turn the assets over to the beneficiaries, but the trustees have a duty, subject to the provisions of the trust instrument and state statutes, to invest the trust property productively.

If your church or religious organization is the beneficiary of a trust or estate, it has the right to compel the executor, administrator, or trustee to manage the assets according to the terms of the governing instrument and law. In the case of an estate or testamentary trust which is subject to the jurisdiction of the probate court, the organization may wish to file an appearance, which is usually done by having an attorney file the appropriate papers with the probate court. The organization then will receive copies of papers filed by others, such as inventories, accountings, or motions to gain the court's permission to take particular action, and will have an opportunity to be informed or heard with respect to such matters. If those with an interest in the assets believe the meaning of the will or trust is unclear or that the fiduciary is not administering the estate or trust according to its meaning or is breaching obligations, they can have recourse to a court to take corrective action.

The 1988 Michigan case of *Matter of Green Charitable Trust* is illustrative.[18] The trustees of a charitable trust of which a local church and the Episcopal diocese were beneficiaries, had sold the major trust asset, a 315-acre estate and residence, for over three million dollars to meet trust expenses. The religious beneficiary went to probate court to challenge the sale, claiming that the trustees had breached their duties to inform the beneficiaries, obtain an appraisal, market the property adequately, and obtain an adequate sale price. The resulting decision of the probate court, upheld by a Michigan appellate court, was removal of the trustees from office and an award of $1.9 million in damages. The trustees, from the court's point of view, had breached their fiduciary duties to the beneficiaries to act with care, diligence, integrity, fidelity, and sound business judgment. These religious beneficiaries were well rewarded for their diligence in holding the trustees to proper trust administration.

G. THE PROBLEM OF CONSTRUCTION

The language in a trust or will is often ambiguous or unclear. It then becomes necessary to ascertain the meaning that will be acted upon in implementing the gift. Unless all of the beneficiaries or parties in interest agree with the fiduciary on the meaning, the proper manner of resolving the issue is to present the problem to the court that has jurisdiction over the matter and ask for instructions. The fiduciary should do so if she or he believes the resolution is not absolutely clear, even if the fiduciary has an opinion on the right result. If the fiduciary does not do so, an interested beneficiary may force the issue in the same manner.

To address problems of construing, or the construction of, the instrument, the court will follow some well-settled rules. It will first look at the "plain language" of the instrument to see if there really is ambiguity that requires construction. Just because someone asserts that there is does not mean that it is so. If the problem can be resolved "within the four corners of the instrument," there is no need to look further.

Usually the ambiguity is not so easily resolved. The court's task then is to ascertain the intent of the decedent or grantor of the trust. When it is unclear that he or she had any intention about the issue that has arisen, the next step may involve considering what the intent would likely have been had the donor considered the issue. To determine intent, the court will consider the trust instrument as a whole and all of the surrounding circumstances that may suggest what the donor's intent was or would have been. In all instances, courts will seek to achieve an end result that will be just and reasonable.

Religious beneficiaries have an advantage in cases that seek to determine the construction of a will or trust. Advancement of religion is uniformly held to be a valid charitable purpose in this country,[19] and charitable organizations and dispositions to them are "favorites of the law."[20] Gifts to charities are liberally construed, and "every presumption consistent with the language of the donor is employed to sustain them."[21]

An illustrative construction case is *Riegel v. United Methodist Church*,[22] in which a charity received a testamentary gift to be used to "build" within ten years, in default of which the funds were to go to a Methodist church. The charity proposed to use the funds to rebuild or remodel its existing facilities. The church challenged this construction of the will and was upheld by an Ohio court which found that to "build" did not include remodeling or refurbishing and that the church was to receive the funds unless a new facility was built by the charity within the ten-year limit.

In another construction case, the 1990 Tennessee case of *In re Estate of Jackson*,[23] an interesting construction problem was presented. The decedent had a $100,000 certificate of deposit which was claimed by both Eastminster Presbyterian Church and members of the deceased woman's family. The relevant will language read as follows: "I direct that my executor shall allow the members of my family to select such item or items from my clothing, jewelry, household goods, personal effects and all other tangible personal property not otherwise specifically bequeathed, except securities and cash on hand or on deposit, as each of them may desire or want . . . in the event that there is any of said personal property remaining, my executor is directed to sell the remaining property at public or private sale as deemed most appropriate by my executor, and the proceeds therefrom shall be paid to the Eastminster Presbyterian Church." A certificate of deposit would constitute personal property but would be in the category of "securities and cash on hand or on deposit," not tangible personal property. The Tennessee Appeals Court read this confusing will language to mean that "said personal property remaining" (the proceeds of which were to go to the church) was subject to the exception to the personal property to be divided by the family of "securities and cash on hand or on deposit" and deprived the church of the $100,000 certificate of deposit. The trial court from which the appeal had been taken had reached the opposite conclusion. As

American humorist Finley Peter Dunne (1867–1936) said, "An appeal is when ye ask wan court to show its contempt for another court."

Another somewhat different problem of interpretation, in this case not of a trust or will but rather of a donative situation, arose in the 1989 New York case of *Application of Troy Savings Bank*.[24] The Troy Savings Bank found itself in a situation not uncommon to churches, especially in smaller rural communities, when disaster strikes a family in the church or town. A fund had been started for the funeral expenses of a child who had been murdered; it raised about six times as much money as the actual expenses. The bank holding the fund properly asked the court how it should distribute the remaining funds. The court addressed the problem by sending a questionnaire to known donors and publishing a notice in local newspapers to attempt to reach donors who had been anonymous. Responding donors variously proposed that the funds go to the victim's family, that a permanent memorial fund be established, that the funds go to other charities, that a reward fund be created to find the murderer, that the money go to the victim's sisters, and that the money be returned to the donors. Although only 45 out of 742 donors responded, the court used the responses to formulate an order which followed the general principle of honoring the donors' intent so far as the court was able to ascertain the intent from the sample responses. It ordered a refund of the contributions of the few who specifically requested it and divided the remainder between the parents of the victim and a nonprofit local organization that assisted victims of child abuse and domestic violence.

H. THE CY PRES DOCTRINE

Suppose a donor leaves your church funds "for maintenance of the church building at 31 Park Street." Then the church at 31 Park Street is taken by eminent domain as part of an urban renewal project. Or the body outgrows the facility and needs to move on to larger quarters. What happens to the funds?

The problem presented by this simple

fact situation has a thousand common variations and is addressed by a legal principle known as "Cy Pres," from the Norman French "cy pres comme possible," meaning "as near as possible." It is a doctrine that enables courts to save charitable gifts when it is impossible, impractical, or illegal to carry out the donor's direct purpose; it does this by directing the charitable gift to another purpose as near as possible to the donor's objective, providing the objective is sufficiently general to allow the court to do so. The doctrine has an interesting history.

The origins of the notion of cy pres are at least as old as third-century A.D. Roman law and came into French and Spanish law from there. It is believed to have come into English law in decisions of the English chancery or equity court in the Middle Ages. The chancellors or judges were ecclesiastics, and most charitable gifts at the time (as today) were undoubtedly made for religious purposes and became subject to church control. The donor's objective in those days was to improve his position in the kingdom of heaven and provide penance for sins. Such gifts were often made by the dying. Whatever motive the ecclesiastical courts may have had to protect the church's interest in receiving the gift of the deceased, the cy pres doctrine was justified by the thought that the desire of the donor to obtain an advantageous position in heaven should not be frustrated due to an unexpected or unforeseen failure of his gift.[25] The cy pres doctrine was slow to be adopted in American law due to (1) the perception of American courts that it reflected the ecclesiastical court's exercise of power that actually belonged to the king, which was inappropriate in a democratic country; and (2) concern for abusive application of the principle.[26] In one notorious English case, *DeaCosta v. DePas,*[27] a testamentary disposition to establish a *jesupa,* for reading Jewish law and instructing people in the Jewish religion (gifts to promote Judaism being illegal at the time in England), was changed to support a preacher giving Christian instruction in a foundling home. Despite early reservations, however, the doctrine has been accepted today in virtually all American jurisdictions.

Cy pres requires that there be a general charitable intent or desire to benefit a particular purpose or objective, and not one which is limited to a specific purpose which has become impossible and impractical or illegal. The absence of an alternative gift in the instrument in the event that the gift in question fails at its purpose is one indicator of a general charitable purpose.

The 1990 Iowa case of *Matter of Trust of Rothrock*[28] was, like the *Riegel* case discussed above, a case in which funds were left in a testamentary trust to be used "solely for the building of a new church." Unlike *Riegel,* however, the testator had made no alternative provision for disposition of the assets. The church, which demonstrated to the court's satisfaction that it was impractical to carry out the decedent's purpose, asked the court under the cy pres doctrine to permit it to use the funds to remodel, improve, or expand existing facilities, purchase real estate as might be needed for future construction, and, to the extent that the fund generated income, for any purposes desired by the church board. Despite opposition by the heirs, who wanted the fund distributed to them, both the trial court and the state Supreme Court granted the church's wishes. The court noted the absence of any forfeiture or reversion clause and concluded that the church's intent fell within the general charitable intention of the decedent.

A common occasion for application of the cy pres doctrine is when the funds donated are either too small or too large to accomplish the expressed purpose. Such a case is the 1988 New Jersey case of *Sharpless v. Medford Monthly Meeting of the Religious Society of Friends.*[29] Both the trial and appeals courts found that it was impossible to use the excess income for the expressed charitable purposes and that application of the cy pres doctrine was appropriate and within the general charitable purpose of the donor to strengthen the institution to which the money had been entrusted.

Courts have divided on whether the proper cy pres remedy, when a trust administered by a public entity has an improper discriminatory purpose, is to replace the public trustee with a private fiduciary[30] or to change the offending provisions of the trust.[31] Faced with this issue in a case involving a trust for a scholarship for a "worthy Protestant boy," the New Hampshire Supreme Court chose to reform the trust to benefit a "student."[32]

The doctrine of cy pres is an extremely valuable tool for churches that are dealing with funds left for purposes for which it is not or no longer practical or possible to use the funds.

I. WHAT INTEREST IS CREATED?

It is not always clear whether a gift or disposition creates an absolute interest, a trust, a conditional gift, or some other property right.[33] Courts sometimes find that assets of charitable corporations or associations are held in trust even if not expressly given for a trust purpose. Gifts either outright or in trust may be subject to a variety of conditions that limit their use or disposition and raise issues of what happens if the condition is violated. The answers to the various legal questions raised may have such practical effect as whether or not the assets are available to the reach of creditors; whether the organization needs to qualify as a trustee or account for the property; whether property may be disposed of or used for general rather than specific purposes; whether the cy pres doctrine can be applied; whether property may be exempt from property taxation or gifts may be deductible for federal income, gift, or estate tax purposes; whether the property is lost if limitations or conditions are not met, and, if so, who gets it?

One authority describes these as among "the most thorny problems of construction in the field of charities."[34] Courts resolve these issues by applying a mix of principles of trust, corporate, and property law, but consistent guiding principles are not always easily ascertained. Courts have, however, tended to adopt constructions which will sustain or preserve the charitable disposition and have often resisted adopting a construction that would result in findings of violated conditions.[35] For example, in one Illinois case funds left in trust to maintain a building in a girls' school were conditioned on the school being operated as a strictly Protestant institution, in which no members

of the teaching staff or housing administration were of the Roman Catholic faith. The Court found that there was no violation of the condition, despite the fact that the school had employed housemothers of the Roman Catholic faith, by interpreting the trust language as being limited to the top policy-making executives of the organization.[36] In another case in Tennessee,[37] the court refused to allow a parsonage to revert to heirs and allowed the church to sell it to acquire a new one despite language in the deed granting the property for the purpose of a parsonage and prohibiting a pastor from occupying it who did not preach salvation by faith. The language, the court held, merely expressed the donor's purposes and did not require perpetual use of the property for the stated purposes to prevent the title reverting.

J. THE ENFORCEABILITY OF CONDITIONS, RESTRICTIONS, OR LIMITATIONS INVOLVING SPECIFICALLY RELIGIOUS CONDITIONS

Can a court constitutionally enforce specifically religious conditions to a gift in a will, trust, or deed when to do so might require the court to make judgments about religious doctrine, a responsibility the courts have generally avoided?

The first major U.S. Supreme Court decision involving issues of "church autonomy," the 1872 case of *Watson v. Jones*,[38] discussed, as one category of case coming before civil courts governing the rights to property held by ecclesiastical bodies, cases "when the property which is the subject of controversy has been, by the deed or will of the donor, or other instrument by which the property is held, by the express terms of the instrument devoted to the teaching, support or spread of some specific form of religious doctrine or belief."[39] The Court used as an example an instance in which "a pious man building and dedicating a house of worship to the sole and exclusive use of those who believe in the doctrine of the Holy Trinity and placing it under the control of a congregation which at the time holds the same belief, has a right to expect that the law will prevent that property from being used as a means of support and dissemination of the Unitarian doctrine, and as a place of Unitarian worship."[40] The Court had no doubt that such a provision was enforceable:

And though the task may be a delicate one and a difficult one, it will be the duty of the Court in such cases, when the doctrine to be taught or the form of worship to be used is definitely and clearly laid down, to inquire whether the party accused of violating the trust is holding or teaching a different doctrine, or using a form of worship which is so far variant as to defeat the declared objects of the trust.[41]

The discussion in *Watson* was dicta— unnecessary to deciding the question before it and hence not binding precedent. The Court has never faced that specific question in later decisions. In the 1969 decision of *Presbyterian Church v. Hull Church*,[42] Justice Harlan, in concurring with the Court's decision that Georgia's "departure from doctrine" approach to deciding a property dispute between a local church and a denomination was unconstitutional, was of the opinion that the Court's decision did not forbid:

civilian courts from enforcing a deed or will which expressly and clearly lays down conditions limiting a religious organization's use of the property which is granted. If, for example, the donor expressly gives his church some money on the condition that the church never ordain a woman as a minister or elder . . . or never amend certain specified articles of the Confession of Faith, he is entitled

to his money back if the condition is not fulfilled.[43]

In a footnote to the Court's most recent decision involving a church property dispute, the 1979 decision of *Jones v. Wolfe*,[44] the Court quoted *Watson v. Jones* for the proposition that regardless of the form of church government, it would be the "obvious duty" of the civil tribunal to enforce the "express terms" of a deed, will, or other instrument of church property ownership.[45] Hence, this was an apparent instance of application of the "neutral principles of law" approach favored by the *Jones* decision.

It thus appears that such specifically religious conditions or restrictions of gifts may be enforced, even though they require a court to examine questions of religious doctrine, without offending the Constitution. The Supreme Court's repeated reluctance, however, in cases not involving such express conditions in donative instruments, to examine such issues and make judicial decisions as to whether or not religious doctrine is being followed should lead donors, and churches and religious organizations to the extent they have any control over the matter, to draft donative instruments to avoid such specifically religious conditions wherever possible.

REFERENCES

Fisch, Edith, Doris Jonas Freed, and Esther R. Schachter. *Charities and Charitable Foundations* (Pomona, N.Y.: Lond Publications, 1974). Also see the 1990–91 cumulative supplement.

CHAPTER 17

Supervision of Children:
Social Events, Child Care, and Trips

When your camp or youth group is hiking in the mountains, your church or organization and each individual responsible for the situation has an obligation to the young people and their parents to exercise adequate supervision and provide all reasonable assurances of their safety. Such wilderness experiences are subject to hazards that the group leader must appreciate and prepare for—falls, sudden weather changes and lightning at high elevations, people getting separated from the group and lost. Whenever a minor is injured while under the supervision of a religious organization or its workers, there is a prospective legal claim for negligent failure to supervise.

When I lead a group of young people in the mountains, I have some rules. The first is that the group must stay together. The responsibility for keeping it together rests on those in front, not those in the rear. No individual should ever be out of sight of others in the group. The slowest hikers are put in the lead since it does not do much good to tell people who cannot keep up with the faster hikers and are lagging behind that they have to stay in sight of the group—they are doing the best they can. It is the faster hikers who must contain themselves. I make sure the members of the group are adequately dressed for the occasion, with cold-weather clothing, rain gear, and good footwear available even on what appears to be a nice summer day. This information has to be communicated before the young people even prepare for the trip, preferably in writing and to their parents. It does not do much good after a drive of several hours to get to the start of the trail and

find that everyone has dressed as if it was a day at the mall.

I also tell my hikers that if they should for any reason become separated from the group and lost, they have only one responsibility other than yelling to see if they can make voice contact with the group: to sit down. Most people who get lost wander around, and the more they wander, the more lost they get; often they are finally found a good distance away from where they started. But hikers who realize they are lost are likely not to be very far away from where they ought to be. The group will soon realize who is missing and backtrack to find them. Putting the responsibility on the group to locate a missing person rather than on the missing person to locate the group is almost always more effective.

When an electrical storm threatens above timberline, shelter is taken immediately, even if just by crawling under some nearby rocks, until the storm passes over. If no shelter is available, the hikers descend immediately off the exposed elevations. Finally, I count heads. The number of hikers that I have is fixed in my mind, and at every rest stop and periodically along the way, I count heads—over and over to be sure we are all together.

On one occasion I was climbing with a group in the mountains when several of the boys left me to descend from a mountain peak to the main trail that led on to our destination. I thought another adult leader was supervising the descent, but he was not. Several boys turned the wrong way when they got back to the trail juncture and started heading in the opposite direction from where the group was going. When I discovered what had happened, we had to send a runner after them to bring them back.

Canoe trips have a different set of hazards and are in some respects more difficult to supervise, since the participants are in vessels that can move apart fairly rapidly. There is a certain psychological elasticity of canoes on the water. They seem to stretch apart until an invisible rubber band, which is holding them together, is stretched to its maximum, and then they slowly pull back together again. Canoeing is a mixed experience of the solitary and the social, each with its own charms. But canoeing groups also have a responsibility to one another. Lakes and rivers can be wide, and islands and shorelines can be deceptive from a distance. Canoeists can get in trouble in a variety of ways, and if they are the last canoe and behind the bend and out of sight, no one will even know that they need help.

In our canoeing groups we designate a "lead" canoe and a "sweep" canoe. Both should be controlled by responsible canoeists. The lead canoe's responsibility is to be a cork in the group's bottle, keeping in mind those behind and not letting the group get too spread out or too distant from the rear canoe. The lead canoe will pick rest spots for lunch, snacks, and play, and will stop periodically to let the dawdlers in the group catch up and give them a chance to rest before pushing on. The sweep canoe should probably be the best canoe. The sweep's responsibility is simply to make sure that all of the canoes ahead of it are safe and on course. As a group leader, I always know how many canoes I have, and I count them as often as I count heads with my mountain climbers. And, naturally, everyone on the water must be wearing a life jacket. Whitewater canoeing is another level of adventure and should only be undertaken after training.

While mountain hiking and canoe trips may present extreme situations in which prudent and responsible supervision of young people is required, the principle is the same in every situation in which minors gather at an activity run or sponsored by a church or religious organization. It is true in the church nursery, at the Sunday School

picnic, at the youth group's trip to the beach, and in the denomination's summer camp. The degree of supervision that is required and the details of how it is carried out will depend on both the age of the children and the nature of the activity. In every situation, however, the church must be sure that there are an adequate number of supervisors to control the situation; that the supervisors are trained or instructed as to what is expected of them; and that there is a group leader who supervises the supervisors to make sure that it happens. In the examples of the mountain hike or wilderness canoe trip, the group leader should be someone with the training and experience necessary to appreciate the unique hazards of these situations. In the church nursery, a different kind of experience is needed. When I am in the nursery, I appreciate the sound advice and suggestions of the mothers and fathers who are more familiar with and comfortable in that environment than I am. In any situation where children or young people are supervised, consciousness of risk management is needed. When risk management fails, lawsuits follow.

Some organizations use permission or release forms for children involved in activities, at least if they involve trips or overnights. Such forms generally fall into three categories:

1. The permission slip. Parental permission for the child to go on the trip or activity has limited usefulness but is desirable for nonroutine activities. It at least assures that a parent knows where the child is and what he or she is doing and has assented to it. This does not protect the leader or church from liability for negligence but would protect against a claim that, for example, the church took the child into a dangerous situation to which the parent would not have consented if he or she had known—for example, a ski trip or an amusement park. Be aware that children have been known to sign their own permission slips. Communicate directly with the parents if at all possible. Any time youth activity involves anything that may present unusual hazards, you will want to be sure that parents are

expressly informed in writing of the nature of the activity. Such forms need not be complex, but you may wish to consult counsel or denominational resources if the activity involves any element of hazard that is not routine or obvious.

2. A medical release form. This form permits the leader or institution to authorize medical treatment for the child in the event that an injury or illness occurs that requires treatment and the parent cannot be located. It is advisable for summer camps or trips of longer duration, such as a week-long camping or canoe trip or travel to another location. It is standard operating procedure for institutions with custodial care of minors for a period of time, such as boarding schools and summer camps, to use these forms. They protect the institution and its representatives against a charge which in effect is assault and battery, that is, permitting medical treatment to the child's person without consent. All such forms should provide an opportunity for the parent to note particular medical needs or allergies the child has that should be known by care providers in the event treatment is required. Again, a form does not insulate anyone from negligence with respect to the injuries or the medical treatment. Camp administration manuals or materials and denominational resources are good resources for medical releases.

3. A liability waiver. In most states and in most circumstances, an agreement in advance to waive liability for negligence is not enforceable. It may be enforceable in some limited situations in which the hazard is apparent and inherent in the activity and the cost of liability insurance or other protection with respect to liability arising from the circumstances would be prohibitive. Ski trips and vehicle raceways may be examples of such activities. Consult local counsel for whether such a liability waiver is viable in your state and, if so, in what circumstances, and have it prepared by counsel.

Having signed releases or waivers of liability for all activities cannot, of course, do any harm. The worst result will be the same as not having them at all. But the forms should never be relied on, nor should they substitute for reasonable and prudent supervision and precautions.

CHAPTER 18

The Counseling Relationship and Church Discipline

A. INTRODUCTION

Counseling is part of the life of almost all churches and clergy in pastoral ministries. Church discipline in some form is practiced in many churches and may arise in situations where a need for counseling is perceived by church or clergy but not necessarily welcomed by the parishioner/counselee. These related situations are liability-prone relationships, the mishandling of which creates the specter of significant damage claims. Liability arising from counseling or church discipline situations is almost always tort liability, the general rules of which are

discussed in chapter 6. While claims are sometimes based on negligence, either by the counselor or by the employing institution in its supervision of the counselor, they are more commonly asserted as one or more intentional torts, each of which is defined by its own set of rules.

This chapter discusses the counseling relationship, negligence in the form of clergy malpractice and intentional torts that can arise out of that relationship, and church discipline. It also reviews several instructive cases in which actual claims against clergy or churches arising out of counseling or church discipline were decided by courts. See chapter 6 with respect to general principles of tort law and who is liable for torts of others. Consult chapter 10 with respect to the specific responsibility of the counselor and others to report abuse or neglect of children (and sometimes others). See chapter 12 with respect to hiring, supervising, and firing employees whose responsibilities in counseling and church discipline can expose the church to liability. And see chapter 20 concerning the protection of liability insurance.

As with most other legal issues pertaining to churches and religious organizations, one must always ask in a tort case whether the First Amendment or comparable provisions of state constitutions are implicated in a claim. In most ordinary negligence claims, such as motor vehicle accidents and injuries to people on the premises, the consideration will be short. There are rarely any religious freedom issues involved (although there may be in ascending liability questions, discussed in chapter 6). In claims unique to religious organizations, such as clergy malpractice or claims arising out of pastoral counseling and spiritual guidance or church discipline, religious freedom issues may be critical, however. Religious organizations and their attorneys should be sensitive to the religious freedom issues lurking in many claims brought against religious organizations that may be determinative of the outcome. An early defense based on religious liberty issues can avoid protracted, expensive, and often uninsured litigation.

B. COUNSELING

1. What Is Counseling?

Counseling may include giving spiritual advice, hearing confessions, and assisting counselees to deal with emotional issues. It may occur in a variety of settings which are not formally or traditionally thought of as counseling settings, including home visits, small group meetings, telephone advice, and informal settings. It may be rendered by ordained clergy who may or may not have licenses from the state to engage in any state-licensed activities, by staff members who may be neither ordained nor licensed, and by volunteers such as church elders or deacons. Do not restrict your thinking about counseling to the formal situation in which a parishioner makes an appointment with the pastor to come to the church office for advice on something that is personally troubling.

2. Licensing

Virtually all states license certain practitioners of mental health services other than psychiatrists, who are licensed physicians. Licensed practitioners include psychologists; marriage, family or child counselors; social workers; and clinical social workers. Some states may offer optional licensing to pastoral counselors.[1]

Clergy performing counseling services as part of their pastoral or professional duties are likely to be exempt from the licensing requirements. If they are not specifically exempted by statute, a serious First Amendment issue of state regulation of

pastoral counseling would result. Exemptions from licensing may be limited to ordained clergy, however. There may also be a question of whether unlicensed people practicing spiritual counseling can receive or accept a fee for their services. In addition, unlicensed personnel are likely to be barred from representing themselves as having the title identified by the licenses.

Clergy interested in improving their professional competence as counselors may seek secular training and licensing. In doing so, they may become subject to the same standards of care as secular licensees and thereby lose any statutory or constitutional protections with respect to their services. Most people seeking spiritual counseling will be doing so because of problems also addressed by secular counselors subject to licensing statutes, and clergy who have assumed secular licensing responsibilities cannot be assured that they will be constitutionally protected if a claim is made that they violated their obligations under the secular licensing statute. Purely spiritual counseling and receiving of confessions from the penitent, however, by clergy not licensed as counselors or therapists, will usually be assured of constitutional protection from state regulation.

Religious organizations that practice any form of counseling must be familiar with state law regulating the subject and be sure that their practices conform to it. If the practices do not conform to state law but are, in their view, religiously mandated, the organizations would be prudent to seek legal advice on how best to protect themselves with respect to any religiously mandated deviation.

3. The Testimonial Privilege

Suppose a cleric has learned something in the course of confidential communications from a parishioner or counselee that is relevant to litigation: innocence or guilt in a criminal charge, conduct relevant to decisions in divorce or child custody proceedings, and the like. When may—or must—the cleric testify about such matters?

The notion that clergy could not be compelled to testify as to confidential communications goes back to the obligatory duty to confess and the reciprocal obligation of the priest to maintain the inviolability of the confessional that developed over the first millennium of Christianity. With the Anglican break from Rome, confession ceased to be obligatory and the privilege was eroded. Early American common-law decisions were not consistent on the issue,[2] but most courts accepted the idea that the privilege of not testifying was one that had to be granted by statute. Confidentiality statutes or comparable court rules exist today in every American jurisdiction (although they are limited to marital counseling in West Virginia).[3] The privilege is justified as (1) protecting the benefit of open communication between clergy and counselees; (2) respecting individuals' rights of privacy in their relationships with their clergy; (3) a means of avoiding legal confrontations with the clergy; and (4) necessitated by the constitutional entitlement to free exercise of religion.

Depending upon the language of the statute or court rule in a particular state, the privilege may be that of the cleric, that of the penitent, or both. Thus in some states, if the penitent or communicant waives the privilege, the cleric can be required to testify. In other states the cleric may be entitled to refuse to testify even if the communicant requests that he or she do so. If a communicant waives the privilege and the cleric believes that there is a religious duty to keep the confidence anyway, unless state law extends the privilege to the clergy a constitutional issue is presented to which there is no definitive answer.

Another issue concerns to whom the privilege applies. Confessions may be made to other people than an ordained minister or clergyman. Again, case law differs in defining the scope of people to whom one can make a privileged confession. In general, the privilege is most likely to be upheld to the extent that the person to whom the confession is made can be shown to be functioning as a spiritual counselor or confessor with church authority to do so and acting under the supervision of a licensed or ordained cleric.[4]

The privileged conversation must be one that was made for the purpose of seeking religious advice, comfort, absolution, or other spiritual or pastoral care. The mere fact that a statement is made to a member of the clergy does not bring it within the privilege. The communication must, in fact, be confidential. The presence of third persons or other circumstances indicating that the person did not intend or expect confidentiality is likely to result in the loss of the privilege.

The scope of protected communication also varies. In some states it may be limited more strictly to penitential communications or confessions. Most states, however, would protect a much broader scope of communication with clergy, including marital counseling. Written records of the confidential communication would normally be entitled to the privilege, but other records of a religious organization are not.

A crisis arises when a cleric is subpoenaed to appear in court or at a deposition to give testimony. If the subject matter does or may involve questions that would require divulging confidential communications, the minister should consult counsel and be represented with respect to the matter. If in doubt as to whether or not the privilege applies, the privilege should be asserted. Assertion of the privilege should be based on counsel's advice, considering *both* the protection of the statute and federal and state constitutional rights that may exist independent of the statute. In the event that the court should rule against the clergy member and insist on a response to the questions, the cleric must consider whether religious conscience requires him or her to continue to refuse to divulge the confidential information. The minister can, of course, appeal the ruling of a trial judge but if the appeal is unsuccessful, a minister who continues to refuse to comply can be subject to sanctions which include imprisonment.[5]

A pastor can maximize the protection of the privilege against testifying by avoiding counseling situations at which third parties are present. If husbands and wives seek counseling together, the pastor may wish to have each sign an agreement that they will not seek the pastor's testimony. If the counselee insists on the presence of a third person, the pastor should advise the counselee that the third person's presence will probably destroy the privilege of confidentiality.

The church or denomination can support the pastor in maintaining confidentiality by adopting a formal policy that supports the confidentiality of communications made to the pastor on religious grounds and by formally assigning duties, supervising, and communicating the expectation of confidentiality with respect to any nonordained counselors.

4. When Must the Counselor Communicate Information to Others?

The situations in which a counselor is forced to communicate information are very limited, but there are some:

1. Information as required by state law pertaining to child abuse and, possibly, elder or other dependent abuse, if not within the privilege under applicable state law. As this information may come to the attention of the pastor or other church workers through other than counseling situations, this subject is treated in chapter 10.
2. Threat of harm to others. Whether there would be a religious reason for a pastor to make or withhold a disclosure must be determined by the counselor according to the doctrines and tenets of the denomination or by the pastor's personal faith, but the legal effect of a cleric's religious views should be determined with the advice of counsel. In some states mental health professionals have a legal duty to take action to protect a potential victim from harm if a counselee has communicated a serious threat of physical violence against a reasonably identifiable victim. Such an obligation may even pertain when the victim is not reasonably identifiable.[6] The duty may include communicating the threat to the intended victim(s) or communicating the threat to a law enforcement agency. It is unclear to what extent, if at all, these duties apply to a clergy counselor who is not licensed under any state statutes. Nevertheless, pastoral counselors should be aware that statutes in some states may require such disclosure and that case law may render certain counselors liable for failure to

make such disclosure if a victim is actually harmed. Whether the duty exists in your state in a given situation must be determined with the advice of counsel.
3. Information pertaining to minors. Beyond the child abuse–reporting requirements, there may be an exception to the general rule of nondisclosure of confidential information when it pertains to minors. In some instances, parents or other authorities have a right to know about certain kinds of problems the minor is experiencing. Although the duties in this area are typically imposed by statute and do not apply to clergy, and although there may be constitutional or other reasons why clergy would not be subject to such disclosure requirements, this is a sensitive area in which counselors should seek legal advice when they are unclear about their responsibilities. Suppose, for instance, that a minor is being sexually harassed, has been sexually assaulted, is engaged in substance abuse, is contemplating an abortion, is abusing alcohol, or is in such a mental or emotional condition as to be dangerous to himself or others. Any of these may require disclosure under certain circumstances. Know the rules in your state.

5. Confession of Crimes

Under the clergy-penitent privilege, disclosure of the true penitential communication is generally not required. Counselors should be aware, however, that it is illegal to assist someone who has committed a crime to avoid detection and to receive stolen property.

Counselees can be made aware of many of the issues of propriety in disclosure before they begin counseling by a written statement or an agreement they must sign. Such an agreement should be prepared with the advice of counsel and approved by the church governing board or superior religious authority. It should make specific reference to those situations in which the counselor is not bound by the duty of confidentiality; and it should be provided before the disclosures occur so that there can be no expectation of confidentiality on the part of the counselee.

C. CLERGY MALPACTICE

Malpractice is simply negligence by a professional person in performing the duties of his or her profession. It differs from other forms of negligence principally in that the standard of care is that of a reasonable and prudent practitioner of the profession, rather than the reasonable and prudent ordinary citizen who would not have the particular training and qualifications of the professional. It has long been familiar to the legal system in medical malpractice claims, and malpractice claims are now common against lawyers, dentists, accountants, architects, engineers, and other professionals. It was only a matter of time before it occurred to someone to bring malpractice charges against the clergy.

The concern for clergy malpractice rose and fell with the case of *Nally v. Grace Community Church* in California.[7] The facts of *Nally* were complex, and it should be said, in fairness to the church whose name appears in the case caption, that it appeared highly unlikely that the plaintiffs ever could have made a credible case against the church. Nevertheless, the central *allegation* was that a pastoral counselor at the church had negligently failed to refer a young man whom he knew or should have known was suicidal to secular therapists. The young man did commit suicide, and the suit was brought as a wrongful death claim by his parents. The case became a cause célèbre in the religious and legal worlds and one of the more written-about cases and topics in contemporary legal literature.[8] At least one insurance company began issuing clergy malpractice coverage policies.

The implications of liability for negligence in clergy counseling are far-reaching. How are the civil courts to determine the "standards of the profession" for the clergy, as they do for doctors and lawyers, when there is no uniformity of standards among the faiths that practice spiritual counseling? Are secular standards of psychological and psychiatric counseling to be applied to the spiritual guidance given by the clergy? Does the standard vary depending upon who is doing the counseling, the nature of the office held in the church, or the degree of training? And, if so, does this not require the courts to explore the spiritual duties of ecclesiastical officers and to interpret religious tenets? What if the religious community in question disagrees with the premises of mental health professionals and rejects cross-disciplinary referral as a matter of religious belief? Should mental health professionals reciprocally be required to determine when a spiritual problem exists and should they be held liable if they fail to refer a counselee to a spiritual counselor? And when is there a counselor/counselee relationship, anyway? The counselees in a pastoral setting rarely enter into contracts or pay fees. In some churches, counseling can occur in the confessional, which is sacramental; and it may occur in group settings, telephone calls, audio cassette tapes, even from the pulpit. How can its limits be defined?[9]

These questions were troubling not only to the religious community but also to the California courts. On the case's second trip through the California court system, the California Supreme Court put the issue to rest by deciding that the tort did not exist. There was no "duty to prevent suicide" or "general professional duty of care" on "a nontherapist counselor who offers counseling to a potentially suicidal person on secular or spiritual matters."[10]

The counselors in the *Nally* case were unlicensed spiritual or pastoral counselors. Those pastors or spiritual counselors who become licensed or certified under state statutes that regulate counselors or therapists are unlikely to be protected by the concepts articulated by *Nally* and can be expected to be held to the standards of the licensing statute.

While *Nally* is a leading and influential decision, it is binding only in California. Other state courts have also rejected claims of clergy malpractice. Alabama did so in the 1987 case of *Handley v. Richards*,[11] also a suicide case; and appellate courts in Missouri and Utah have reached the same conclusion in cases not involving sexual misconduct.[12] An Illinois appellate court has refused to recognize a malpractice claim against a Christian Science practitioner.[13] Other courts have both allowed and refused to allow claims labeled as clergy malpractice when the facts involved sexual seduction of counselees that in most states could be presented without creating a new tort,[14] usually dismissing clergy malpractice claims but allowing sexual seduction of counselee claims based on other theories.[15]

In summary, clergy malpractice remains an unrecognized tort except as a few courts have allowed a label to be put on sexual seduction cases that can usually be brought under other theories. Churches or pastors that have purchased insurance for clergy malpractice, however, should probably retain it because these claims will undoubtedly continue to be brought, defense costs can be significant, and the prospect that some court will permit such a claim is still open.

D. INTENTIONAL TORTS IN THE COUNSELING RELATIONSHIP

Counseling relationships, confidential communications, and church discipline are circumstances that frequently lead to intentional tort claims against churches. These issues are not mutually exclusive. Information obtained or conduct that occurs in a counseling relationship or confidential communication, for example, could in turn lead to conduct directed at clergy termination or church discipline of members. Because the kind of information relevant to matters of conduct among clergy and church members is often of great interest in the secular world, its inappropriate revelation can injure people's reputations, invade their privacy, and cause them a great deal of mental or emotional distress. The information is almost invariably the kind of information people would not want the public at large to know, such as sexual relationships outside of marriage, child or spousal abuse, or financial improprieties or irresponsibility.

When the church endeavors to deal with issues of conduct or holiness among its constituency, it walks on the margin, where religious belief intersects the requirements of the legal system. The misguided attempt to apply religious doctrine without considering the legal risks involved can quickly immerse the church in litigation. Since the conduct of the church in such matters is

almost always intentional, the lawsuits that result will be characterized as intentional torts. The plaintiff's attorneys will invoke as many different intentional tort theories or causes of action as an inventive mind can use to characterize the facts. Four intentional torts that are frequently alleged from the same set of facts are (1) defamation, (2) breach of privacy, (3) intentional infliction of emotional distress, sometimes called the tort of outrage or outrageous conduct, and (4) breach of fiduciary duty. We will review each of these briefly.

1. Defamation

The Bible condemns gossip and slander,[16] and so does the law. "Defamation" is the general term for "that which tends to injure reputation in the popular sense; to diminish the esteem, respect, goodwill or confidence in which the plaintiff is held, or to excite adverse, derogatory or unpleasant feelings or opinions against him . . ." and necessarily "involves the idea of disgrace."[17] Verbal or oral defamation is usually referred to as "slander." Written defamation is usually referred to as "libel." Both slander and libel require a communication of the defamatory statement to someone else. It is not, for example, defamation to make a remark only to the person involved. In most instances, in order to recover for defamation one must prove that one has suffered some actual damages, that is, that one's reputation was actually harmed or that there was some actual financial loss as a result of the remark. However, defamation that attributes to the defamed person a crime or a loathsome disease, or that affects the person's business, trade, profession, office, or calling can be the basis of a suit and the collection of damages without proof of any actual damage. The imputation of unchastity to a woman is also often considered to be in this category of "libel per se" in which the damage is presumed from the nature of the defamatory statement itself.

Defenses to a defamation action are called "privileges," and privileges are either absolute or qualified. An "absolute privilege" is one in which the motive and belief of the speaker are irrelevant; absolute privileges are generally limited to judicial and legislative proceedings, communications within or by the executive branch of the government, communications to which the plaintiff has consented, communications between husband and wife, and political broadcasts. The truth of the defamatory statement is sometimes permitted as an absolute defense, although many jurisdictions today limit the truth defense to situations in which there were good motives or justifiable ends.

All other privileges are conditional or qualified. Most "qualified privileges" can be described as situations in which the speaker or the persons to whom the communication is directed have a legitimate interest in the subject matter and the communication is fairly made to protect that interest. Qualified privileges must be exercised in a reasonable manner and for proper purposes. The privilege is lost if the defamatory communication (1) has no bearing on the interest to be protected; (2) is made to those whose hearing of it is not reasonably believed to be necessary or helpful to further the interest; or (3) is made with "malice," that is, from a motive of ill will or to achieve an improper purpose. In some jurisdictions, malice may include the absence of reasonable grounds for believing the truth of the statement.

First Amendment considerations led the Supreme Court in 1964 to add another defense in defamation cases—the "public figure" defense. The occasion was a suit against the *New York Times* that arose from articles it published pertaining to racial unrest in the South. An Alabama jury had awarded a large verdict against the newspaper in favor of a local public official. In *New York Times Co. v. Sullivan*,[18] the Court held that the First Amendment requirements of freedom of speech and press prevented a "public figure" from bringing a defamation action unless it could be shown that there was actual malice—that is, knowledge of the falsity of the statement or reckless disregard for a statement's veracity in the publication. The "public figure" rule has made it much more difficult for those in the public eye to recover in a defamation action.

Since the *New York Times Co. v. Sullivan* decision, case law has expanded the public figure concept to include persons of general fame or notoriety in the community, persons pervasively involved in the affairs of society, and persons who voluntarily inject themselves or are drawn into a particular public controversy. In the latter case, the person may be a public figure only with respect to the limited range of issues presented by the controversy. Religious leaders will occasionally be public figures under these criteria.

Claims of defamation directed at a religious organization or its personnel raise both common-law defenses and First Amendment issues. To the extent that the communications are made in pursuance of bona fide religious beliefs, they may be protected by the First Amendment. To the extent that they are in pursuance of the common interest of the organization and the speaker and are made with a proper motive and only to those who have a legitimate interest in the subject matter, they may be conditionally privileged communications and thus protected, apart from their religious motive. Courts may examine statements made in a religious setting to determine if they were made pursuant to a religious belief or if they cloaked a secular purpose, such as injuring a reputation. The claim of privilege that may be valid when statements relate to members of the church may not exist regarding nonmembers and may be lost, even as to members, if the defamatory statements are intended to injure.[19]

A doctrinal explanation of the grounds for divorce with respect to a prominent figure in a religious organization was given constitutional protection in the absence of a *New York Times Co. v. Sullivan* showing of malice.[20] Accusations of immoral conduct over a period of time made about a resigned member outside the denomination and to the general public have no privilege.[21] Statements made on a radio program and in a letter to a newspaper that the individual in question "lies a lot" and "spreads fear through outrageous lies" received no protection.[22]

It is possible to practice risk management with respect to defamation claims:

1. Confidential communications made to a pastor or church elder or leader, whether

in a specific counseling situation or otherwise, should be kept strictly confidential. They should not be communicated to any other person or group except for religious purposes and with the consent of the person making the communication.

2. Derogatory information about anyone should never be communicated to others unless there is some reasonable basis to believe that it is true and the hearer has a legitimate reason to be made aware of it.

3. When there is a legitimate reason to communicate derogatory information about others, communication should be strictly limited to those who have a legitimate interest in receiving it, and they should be cautioned against any further communication.

4. If it is necessary to present negative information about anyone at a church meeting—as, for example, in considering termination or discipline of clergy or members—be sure that only members are present. Personnel matters that do not require action by the congregation should be discussed by the governing body only in executive session, that is, in a private meeting.

5. Do not let personal motivations, your own or anyone else's, intrude and act to spur unnecessary or improper communications.

6. Do not presume the truth of every statement just because someone said it. Do not communicate gossip and other people's opinions. A speaker's honest opinion that contains no misrepresentations or distortions of the truth is not actionable against the *speaker*. But repetition of that opinion by others without a foundation to make it their own opinion is much less defensible.

2. Invasion of Privacy

The tort of invasion of privacy had an unusual birth. It began with an 1890 article in the *Harvard Law Review* by Samuel D. Horan and Louis D. Brandeis (later a Supreme Court justice) that advocated the tort's existence based on a broader principle that had been recognized in disguise in cases based on defamation, invasion of

property rights, and breaches of confidence or implied contracts.[23] The early cases that dealt with the issue involved commercial uses of people's names or pictures without their consent. The tort is now widely recognized and has several forms:

1. The appropriation, for the defendant's benefit or advantage, of the name or likeness of the plaintiff.

2. Intrusion on the plaintiff's physical solitude or seclusion in a way that would be offensive or objectionable to a reasonable person.

3. Public disclosure of private information that would be offensive and objectionable to a reasonable person of ordinary sensibilities. Such matters as publicizing the failure to pay a debt, disclosing the history of a reformed prostitute, or revealing embarrassing details of another's private behavior or physical characteristics fall in this category.

4. Placing a person in a false light in the public eye. This aspect often but not always overlaps with defamation. It frequently involves attributing to an individual an opinion, endorsement, or association with something with which the person in fact has no connection; an example would be using the face of an honest taxi driver in connection with a story about the cheating propensities of taxi drivers. Again, the disclosure must be one that would be objectionable to ordinary and reasonable people under the circumstances.

The third and fourth forms of breach of privacy, public disclosure of private facts and placing a person in a false light in the public eye, are the aspects most likely to be involved in claims made against churches and their personnel.

The defenses to breach of privacy claims are similar to those against defamation. Consent is one defense and, in the context of a church disciplinary procedure, could be found in the members' adherence to procedures specifically set forth in the organization's governance documents to which the member subscribed when joining. Similarly, information communicated on the basis of a legitimate common interest without improper purpose will generally not constitute an invasion of privacy.

Churches and clergy should be careful not to use the background or experiences of members of the congregation in sermons or as other forms of illustration without the consent of the individuals concerned. However sincere the conversion, reformed sinners do not necessarily want to have the congregation or other groups told about their past substance addiction, sexual misconduct, or criminal activities. It is best to let testimony of conversion experiences that have reformed previously sinful lives come from the converts themselves, and in no event should they be told without the consent of the subject.

Similarly, churches and clergy should be careful not to publish photographs of people without their consent, attribute opinions or beliefs to people that they may not hold, or force themselves on others' privacy by such things as persistent and unwanted telephone calls or unauthorized entry into a home.

3. Intentional Infliction of Emotional Distress: The Tort of Outrage or Outrageous Conduct

This is another tort of relatively recent origin. It consists of a showing of extreme or outrageous conduct intended to cause emotional distress or committed in reckless disregard of the probability of causing emotional distress when the conduct of the defendant actually caused the plaintiff to suffer severe emotional distress. Conduct must be "so outrageous in character, and so extreme in degree, as to go beyond all possible bounds of decency, and to be regarded as atrocious, and utterly intolerable in a civilized community."[24]

In an extreme case of intentional infliction of emotional distress, *Wollersheim v. Church of Scientology*,[25] a damage award of $5 million in compensatory damages and $25 million in punitive damages was made to a former member of the Church of Scientology. The award was later reduced to $500,000 in compensatory damages and $2 million in punitive damages.[26] The former member had been subjected to the church's "fair game" policy, which authorized coercive or punitive actions undertaken to ruin his social and business life, including making obscene phone calls to his employers, following him, and attempting to learn his new address from his relatives. An element in the award was the existence of a coercive environment that created the threat of physical, economic, and political reprisal if he left the group. Although the damage award was reduced by the appellate court, as noted, the award nonetheless illustrates the hazard a religious group faces when it behaves in an overbearing manner toward a departing member.

In another case involving a new religion (*Molko v. Holy Spirit Association*), the California Supreme Court allowed a claim of intentional infliction of emotional distress based on the fraudulent induction of an unconsenting individual into an atmosphere of coercive persuasion or "brain washing."[27] The court held that tort liability for religiously motivated acts can exist regardless of the authenticity of the teaching because it is the conduct, not the belief, that forms the basis for liability.

Outrageous conduct claims are not limited to coercive conduct. An outrageous conduct claim has also been allowed against a church and its priest for the priest's engaging in a sexual relationship with the wife of a couple that sought marital counseling from him,[28] for publicly reciting, in front of the congregation, the sexual conduct of a resigned member of the congregation in a church discipline proceeding,[29] and for failing to maintain confidence about a confession of adultery.[30]

4. Breach of Fiduciary Duty

The fiduciary duty is a duty that arises because of the nature of the relationship between the persons: one party has placed a special trust and confidence in another. That trust and confidence create, in the person in whom they are placed (the fiduciary), a special duty to exercise care, loyalty, and utmost good faith, and to act always in the best interest of the other. It includes the duty not to use information for one's own benefit or in competition with or to the injury of the other, whether by improper disclosure or by manipulative use to a sexual or financial advantage. Although clergy may not have a fiduciary duty toward their parishioners just because they are parishioners, when clergy act as counselors or spiritual advisors, they almost certainly do.

The duty of trustees, officers, and directors of religious and other organizations to the organization and its members, discussed in chapter 11, is also often said to be a fiduciary duty.

Many of the fact situations that lead to intentional tort claims such as defamation and breach of privacy can, if they arise out of facts that first became known in a counseling relationship, also be presented as breaches of fiduciary duty. The counseling situation, however, gives rise to another type of breach of fiduciary duty claim that occurs when the counselor takes advantage of the counselee's trust, confidence, and dependent emotional situation to manipulate the counselee into a sexual relationship.

E. CHURCH DISCIPLINE

The term "church discipline" may seem archaic to many twentieth-century Americans. They are accustomed to living in a world in which individual freedom and privacy have largely replaced community, institutional, and group commitments. Talk of church discipline conjures up notions of Hester Prynne wearing a scarlet letter in the seventeenth-century Massachusetts Bay Colony. Church discipline is actively practiced in many churches, however. Most major denominations retain provisions for church discipline in their canon law or denominational church governance documents. The provisions often apply differently to clergy than to laity. While the practice of church discipline of members in the United States may have its strongest contemporary vitality in conservative Protestant churches, it is a potential issue in almost all church settings.

Secular judges and juries may have difficulty understanding church discipline; they may see it as a classic example of the tort of outrage perpetrated by the very institution that should be the model of love and forgiveness. In order for them to discern the "elusive boundary between church and state" they must be given information "both historical and theological, unknown to most lawyers."[31] They must be informed about "the church's view as to its own nature and mission,"[32] the root of church discipline in the scandal of the cross, the real power the church has to provide the trapped and the burdened with resolution, forgiveness, and restoration. How then can a church maintain church discipline without incurring liability in secular courts for the causes of action we have discussed above—defamation, invasion of privacy, and intentional infliction of emotional distress?

First, the church must clearly identify its disciplinary beliefs and practices. These should be made explicit in the governing documents of the church by reference to biblical standards, canon law, hierarchical authority, or other specifically religious sources. Courts will usually defer to the church on disciplinary issues within the church when these issues are handled in accordance with the church's own religious doctrines.[33]

Second, the church can discipline only its own members. Members are considered to have freely chosen to associate with the church community and to have accepted the benefits and obligations of doing so:

A person who joins a church covenants expressly or impliedly that in consideration of the benefits which result from such a union he will submit to its control and be governed by its laws, usages and customs whether they are of an ecclesiastical or temporal character to which laws, usages, and customs he assents as to so many stipulations of a contract. The formal evidence of such contract is contained in the canons of the church, the constitution, articles, and by-laws of the society, and the customs and usages which have grown up in connection with these instruments.[34]

The church cannot prevent a member from resigning, and disciplinary action conducted after a member resigns is done at great risk of liability.[35] Some practices may, however, be protected,[36] for example, behavior established as the religious practices of a particular group—such as shunning—that are practiced only within the group and without communication to a larger public or with other intrusive or offensive conduct to injure the individual. Passive avoidance of contact or exclusion from community and communion are acceptable, in contrast to religiously motivated disciplinary measures that are meant to control and involve a person who has chosen to remove himself or herself from the community.[37]

In addition to developing a specific disciplinary procedure, incorporating it in church governance documents, and communicating it to new members, churches that practice church discipline should teach regularly on the subject, enforce church law consistently, and follow procedures carefully to protect church members against both invasions of privacy and public proclamations of unsubstantiated charges. Churches considering developing a church discipline program should carefully consider the biblical or other religious basis for their program and consult counsel and a more specialized work on this subject, such as L. R. Buzzard and T. S. Brandon's 1987 volume, *Church Discipline and the Courts*.[38] Although the disciplinary program should be designed with biblical and religious requirements in mind, courts will be most deferential to such programs if, in addition to implementing specific religious beliefs and doctrines, they also embody procedural and substantive fairness. To the extent it is consistent with religious requirements, members subject to discipline should have a fair opportunity to defend themselves, including the rights to confront accusers, to the assistance of counsel (not necessarily an attorney), and to an impartial fact-finding and decision-making tribunal.[39] Finally, a church discipline system should be administered with the conscious understanding that the ultimate objective is not punishment but repentance and restoration of the sinner.[40]

F. CASE HISTORIES

Some case histories may be helpful to illustrate how courts have actually handled recent intentional tort cases.

1. Hester v. Barnett[41]

The defendant Barnett was an ordained Baptist minister who was alleged to have visited the home of the Hesters, who were not members of his church. The Hesters' children were apparently having behavior problems. The Hesters claimed that Barnett assured them that their communication with him would be strictly confidential and that he invited them to confide in him. Despite the assurance of confidentiality, the pastor, they claimed, disclosed to church leadership and members of the community—and even from the pulpit—private information concerning their children's behavioral and disciplinary problems, accused the Hesters falsely and publicly of both theft and child abuse, instructed their children to lie about the parental discipline in their home so that they would be removed from the home, and publicly charged them with being irreligious and abusive parents. They also claimed that Barnett attempted to alienate the affections of the children from the parents and the husband and wife from each other, and that he had harassed, intimidated, and threatened employees of the family business and caused the employees to leave their employment.

Suit was brought on six claims of intentional tort, which were disposed of as follows:

1. Clergy malpractice. The clergy malpractice claim was dismissed because the allegations made against Barnett could be brought under existing theories of tort law not premised on a malpractice standard. To find a tort of clergy malpractice would presume that every cleric owed the same duty of care regardless of the particular tenets of conduct of her or his order.
2. Intentional infliction of emotional distress. This claim was dismissed because the kind of extreme and outrageous behavior required for such a claim was not present.
3. Alienation of affections. Alienation of affections is a common-law tort claim made when a person wrongfully interferes with the affection of a husband or wife for the other. It is commonly asserted

in cases of sexual seduction of married counselees by pastoral counselors. In most states it has been abolished either by statute or by court decision, but it was still allowed in Missouri. The *Hester* court was of the view that the allegations of interference with a marital relationship, when the allegations are based on a good faith pronouncement of doctrine or advocacy of religious faith, cannot be a basis for an alienation of affections suit. The court felt, rather, that the conduct in question here was malicious conduct intended to separate the wife from the husband and was not based on doctrine. It did, however, dismiss the alienation of affections claims between parents and children.

4. Defamation of character. The defamation claim was allowed. The court found that the various statements in question were not inherently and invariably expressions of religious belief or purpose that would be absolutely protected by the Free Exercise Clause, especially because the Hesters were not members of the church. As long as discipline was practiced in good faith, statements that chastened wayward members to keep with the liturgy, discipline, and polity of the church to which its members had presumably consented would not have been a basis for a suit. The privilege is lost if the church acts with an intent to injure a plaintiff's reputation, feelings, or profession. Although the child abuse–reporting statute would have protected Barnett from liability for reporting suspected child abuse, it was alleged that he knew that the child abuse claim was false; and this was sufficient to allow that aspect of the claim to go to trial.

5. Invasion of privacy. This claim was allowed to the extent that it alleged unreasonable intrusion into the Hesters' seclusion. The court concluded, however, that the allegations were insufficient insofar as they purported to set forth the breach of privacy claim of public disclosure of private facts or unreasonably placed another's private life in a false light.

6. Interference with contract. Interference with contract is a tort which, as the term suggests, involves a person interfering, without justification, with someone else's contractual relationship with another. This claim, stemming from the alleged activities that caused the Hesters' employees to leave their employment, was allowed.

The *Hester* case illustrates the importance of:

1. Employing church discipline only against church members who have expressly or impliedly consented to the church's practices.
2. Maintaining the confidentiality of communications made in confidence.
3. Limiting the disclosure of negative or derogatory information strictly to those who have a common interest or a good faith reason for being made aware of the information.
4. Limiting any activity directed toward errant church members to that which is strictly in keeping with the religious teachings of the church or denomination.

2. Destefano v. Grabrian[42]

The Destefanos sought marital counseling from a priest who thereafter engaged in adulterous conduct with the wife, resulting in the destruction of the marriage. Claims were brought by the husband and the wife for alienation of affections, breach of fiduciary duty, clergy malpractice, and outrageous conduct. Claims were also brought against the diocese in which the priest worked for negligent failure to supervise and train the priest, arguing there was actual or constructive knowledge of prior acts, and for liability under respondeat superior.

The Colorado Supreme Court did not allow the alienation of affections suit, because claims of this nature had been barred by statute in Colorado. It also dismissed the clergy malpractice claim, refusing to recognize that tort. And it dismissed the respondeat superior claim because the allegedly adulterous activity by the priest was by definition outside the scope of his employment.

The court did, however, allow the plaintiffs to proceed against the priest for breach of fiduciary duty and outrageous conduct, and against the diocese for negligent supervision. It also held that there could be no First Amendment protection for conduct that clearly fell outside of the beliefs and doctrines of the priest's religion.

The case illustrates the following points:

1. Sexual relations with a counselee can subject a clergy counselor to liability for intentional torts, even if clergy malpractice and alienation of affections claims are not allowed. '
2. Employer liability for sexual misconduct of church employees is likely to be limited to negligence in hiring, supervision, and retention. The case emphasizes the importance of supervision and of acting on any knowledge of prior misconduct by clergy or church employees who are in counseling or leadership positions.
3. The First Amendment will not provide a cover for wrongful conduct that has no religious justification merely because the conduct is performed by a cleric in a religious setting.

3. Guinn v. Church of Christ[43]

In this church discipline case, the plaintiff, a member of a local congregation, was confronted by three elders of the church about a rumor that she was having sexual relations with a man to whom she was not married. The church believed it was responsible for monitoring church members' conduct and confronting and discussing problems with people. The church member admitted the fornication, and the church leaders proceeded to follow Matthew 18 and confront her on three occasions during the next year, requesting that she repent and discontinue the relationship. After the third encounter, they sent her a letter advising her that a withdrawal of fellowship process would begin if she did not repent. This procedure, also based on Matthew 18, was to be carried out by the entire membership of the congregation. The process consisted of the elders reading aloud the violated Scriptures, and the members then withdrawing fellowship by refusing to acknowledge the presence of the miscreant.

The parishioner had observed a previous such incident and was aware that the church sought to encourage the transgressor to repent and return to fellowship and to maintain the holiness of the church. She contacted an attorney who wrote to the elders advising them that she withdrew her membership and requesting that they not expose her private life to the congregation. She wrote another letter to the elders asking them not to mention her name in church except to tell the congregation that she had withdrawn. These requests were ignored by the eldership, which advised the congregation to encourage her to repent and return and advised her that if she did not do so, the violated Scriptures would be read aloud to the congregation at the next service and the withdrawal of fellowship procedure would begin. When she met with one of the elders during the following week, she was told that withdrawal from membership was doctrinally impossible and could not halt the disciplinary process. The next Sunday, the Scriptures were recited to the congregation and she was identified as a fornicator. This same information was sent to four other Church of Christ congregations in the area to be read aloud during their services.

The lawsuit that followed claimed that actions of the church both before and after her withdrawal from membership had invaded her privacy by intruding on her seclusion and unreasonably publicizing private facts about her life, causing her emotional distress. A jury verdict awarded her $205,000 in actual, and $185,000 in punitive, damages.

The Oklahoma Supreme Court, acknowledging the U.S. Supreme Court's ban on civil court review of purely ecclesiastical matters, ruled that the First Amendment prevented suit for actions prior to the withdrawal of membership but that the church could be sued for actions thereafter.

The church's postwithdrawal activities presented a difficult legal problem. The church represented its religious doctrine as providing no means of withdrawal from membership; members remained a part of the congregation for life, like members of a family. The church claimed that it would be constitutionally impermissible state usurpation of religious discipline for a court to determine that the parishioner's withdrawal from membership terminated the church's authority.

The court, however, found that the right to freedom of worship under the First Amendment included the right, unhindered and unimpeded, to withdraw from a chosen form of worship. The court acknowledged that although the parishioner could waive this constitutional right to withdraw, she had not done so. A waiver is a voluntary and intentional relinquishment of a known right, and the parishioner had testifed that she had not been informed of the indissolubility of membership and, accordingly, could not have waived the right to leave the church by agreeing to it. The First Amendment does not shield a church from civil liability for imposing its will through a disciplinary scheme on one who had not consented to undergo the discipline. The court found that there was no conditional privilege of a common interest in the parishioner's behavior because she was not a present or prospective church member. The court considered the discipline in this case different from cases of shunning, in which a person was excluded from communion and the church simply instructed its members to avoid contact with that person.

Despite the adverse result of this decision to the church in question, the *Guinn* decision greatly clarifies the latitude of churches that engage in church discipline. It supports the constitutional right to discipline church members who have not withdrawn from membership, insulates prewithdrawal discipline from legal liability in most cases, and would allow a waiver of the constitutional right of a church member to withdraw from church membership if the waiver is made voluntarily and knowingly.

It also affirms the practice of passive discipline—simply turning away from a former member—even if not grounded in prior acquiescence. It further affirms the right of church members to knowledge of matters of common interest, and it allows for a greater common interest with respect to former clergy than would be the case with respect to former members. It stresses again the importance of limiting disciplinary activity to members and communicating clearly the expectations of church discipline when people join a body.

REFERENCES

American Bar Association. *Tort and Religion*, 1990. American Bar Association, Section of Torts and Insurance Practice, 750 North Lake Shore Drive, Chicago, IL 60611-4497.

Bush, John C., and William Harold Tiemann. *The Right to Silence: Privileged Clergy Communication and the Law,* 3rd ed. (Nashville: Abingdon Press, 1989).

Buzzard, Lynn R., and Thomas S. Brandon, Jr. *Church Discipline and the Courts* (Wheaton, Ill.: Tyndale House, 1987).

Buzzard, Lynn R., and Dan Hall. *Clergy Confidentiality: A Time to Speak and a Time to Be Silent* (Diamond Bar, Calif.: Christian Ministries Management Association, 1988).

Esbeck, Carl H. "Tort Claims against Churches and Ecclesiastical Officers: The First Amendment Considerations." 89 *West Virginia Law Review* 1–114 (1986).

Hammar, Richard R. *Pastor, Church and Law,* 2d ed. (Matthews, N.C.: Christian Ministry Resources, 1991).

Prosser, William L. *Handbook of the Law of Torts,* 4th ed. (St. Paul, Minn.: West Publishing Co., 1971).

Litigation

A. INTRODUCTION

Our ancestors resolved disputes that they could not negotiate to resolution by fighting. This was called "trial by battle." It had its place in medieval society, in the early settlement of the American West, and in the practice of dueling, which persisted into the nineteenth century. It is still the means employed by nations. Individuals have always realized, however, that battles are usually unproductive means of resolving disputes, and kings and priests have often served as judges over private disputes between their constitutents, as in the familiar story of King Solomon's decision as to which of two women was the mother of a baby claimed by both.[1]

An only slightly more refined step in the process of dispute resolution, known as "trial by ordeal," was usually invoked in criminal matters; here, the accused was exposed to a certain ordeal, such as being submerged in water for a period of time. Survival was considered proof of innocence.

Today, we resolve unsettleable disputes by litigation presided over by judges appointed or elected for the purpose of judging, with factual disputes resolved in appropriate cases by juries drawn at random from the venue served by the court. We preserve some vestige of the notion of the king as judge, however, in the power invested in presidents and governors to pardon criminals.

After battle and ordeal, litigation is usually the worst means of dispute resolution. It can be lengthy, expensive, and embittering to its participants. When disputes can be resolved on any reasonable basis without litigation, it is almost always preferable. Nevertheless, churches are regularly involved in litigation. Sometimes the lawsuit is forced on them when they are named as a defendant and find it necessary to protect their interests and assets. Sometimes government regulators or other parties may be abusing their rights in ways that make it important to take a stand to protect their position and that of other Christians in the political community. Sometimes the dictates of theology place churches in a position where they cannot accede to the demands of others with a clear conscience before God. For whatever the reason, the other cheek is not always turned, even in the most biblically devout churches, and the body of Christ is in fact, voluntarily or involuntarily, engaged in the dispute-resolution process on a regular basis. Understanding how lawsuits work will aid churches and religious organizations by familiarizing them with the process they may have to undergo and by assisting them in understanding the significance of reports received through the news media or religious or legal publications of particular claims filed and decisions made at various stages of a lawsuit.

B. THE ANATOMY OF A LAWSUIT

Lawsuits are organic; they have a natural life cycle. How they grow and develop to maturity and reach their end is shaped by the active tactics and strategy of the participants within the confines of a specific structure defined by statutes and rules of court. While Congress and the state legislatures have, and to some extent exercise, legislative authority to set the procedural rules for courts, they also provide by statute the power in courts to prescribe their own rules of practice, procedure, and evidence.[2] In the federal system, the rules of court are prescribed by the Supreme Court, which must submit them to Congress. With certain exceptions, rules prescribed by the Court become effective unless Congress takes action to the contrary.

The rules of proceeding in federal courts are known as the Federal Rules of Civil Procedure. For cases on appeal, there are also Federal Rules of Appellate Procedure. Some states have adopted rules similar or virtually identical to the Federal Rules of Civil Procedure, while others have more home-grown versions. In all state and federal courts, however, certain fundamental steps in a lawsuit will be recognizable.

1. Initial Pleadings

The term "pleadings" can encompass any papers filed with the court in the course of a lawsuit, other than papers filed as evidence at a trial or in conjuction with a hearing or motion in which evidence is appropriate. The initial pleadings are the documents filed by the parties at the outset of litigation which contain their basic claims and defenses.

The party initiating the lawsuit is generally called the "plaintiff," although in some proceedings terms such as "petitioner" may be used. The plaintiff sets forth his or her basic claims in a document usually called a "complaint" (or sometimes a petition, writ, declaration, or libel) which identifies the parties, the basis of the court's jurisdiction over the matter, the essential facts which form the basis of the complaint and how they violate legal rights, the particular legal theories or "causes of action" under which the suit is proceeding, and what relief is requested (i.e., money damages, an injunction, or other action by the court). The complaint must be served upon the adverse party, usually referred to as the "defendant" (or petitionee, respondent, or libelee) along with a court document known as a "writ" or "summons" which informs the defendant of (1) his or her obligation to answer the complaint, and (2) the time within which he or she must do so. The plaintiff is required to file proof with the court that he did indeed serve the defendant with the summons and complaint; the proof usually is in the form of an affidavit from the process server that it has been done in accordance with the governing statutes for giving proper notice. The statutes or court rules will provide for who must be served and in what manner, and they must be followed precisely.

Service on corporations, government entities, partnerships, and other forms of organization must be accomplished according to rules applicable to the particular defendant. State laws usually require that corporations or other organizations doing business in the state maintain a "registered agent," registered with the secretary of state, who is authorized to receive service of process on their behalf. State laws may also provide for service of process on agents who are designated by law to receive service in certain cases, such as service upon the secretary of state for an out-of-state corporation that has no registered agent in the state or for nonresident individuals who have committed acts in the state that subject them to service of process.

The defendant must, within the time designated in the writ or summons, file responses to the plaintiff's claims. The defendant may admit some, deny some, and respond to some with further explanations. The defendant may, and usually must, plead certain "affirmative defenses" that may provide a complete exoneration of him but that are not adequately set forth by simply denying the plaintiff's claims. A defendant may also have a claim against the plaintiff (known as a "counterclaim") and may, and in some instances must—particularly if the counterclaim arises out of the same transaction as that on which the plaintiff is suing the defendant—plead it as part of his answer. He must file his answer with both the plaintiff and the court but service of process is not normally necessary after the initial complaint is served upon the defendant. Thereafter, pleadings filed with the court are simply mailed to the attorney for the opposing party, or to the party himself if he is appearing *pro se* (without an attorney), with a certificate being added to the end of the pleading certifying to the court that a copy has been sent to the opposing party or his counsel.

If a counterclaim is pleaded, the plaintiff may be required to file a formal response to it. Otherwise, the initial pleadings are normally concluded at this stage although either party may seek to amend its initial pleadings from time to time as the lawsuit progresses to assert new claims or defenses or to reflect new facts of which they have become aware.

If you or your organization is served with process in a lawsuit it is extremely important that you do the following two things:

1. Be sure that you, or an attorney acting on your behalf, respond in the required manner *within the time set forth in the writ or summons*. Failure to do so may result in a default judgment against you (i.e., you lose the case before it begins by not contesting it in a timely fashion). If inadequate time is allowed for a proper response, your attorney may be able to obtain an extension of time within which you can respond. You should be sure this is properly done with the authorization of the court. Do not rely on a plaintiff's informal assurances that it will be all right to make a late response.

2. Notify your insurance company of the lawsuit and send it a copy of the papers served on you. This is most effectively done by counsel, but in all cases you must be sure the insurer gets prompt notice. Notice should be given to all insurers who had any insurance for you which may possibly be involved. If, for example, the allegations involve events that occurred over a period of time in which more than one insurance policy was in force, or if you maintain several insurance policies for different types of coverage (such as a bodily injury/property damage liability policy, errors and omissions coverage, and directors and officers coverage), all insurers for all relevant time periods should be contacted. This is often critical in, for example, pollution cases where an underground tank may have been leaking over an extended period of time and a number of insurers are potentially involved in the matter. The failure to give prompt notice to an insurance carrier may result in the loss of insurance coverage to which you would otherwise be entitled. All insurance policies require such notice.

Do not neglect contacting your insurer because your judgment is that there is no coverage, unless that conclusion is absolutely clear, as, for example, if you are being sued by a creditor to collect an unpaid bill. Coverage is often broader than you think, and your attorney may find policy language which provides coverage of which you were unaware.

One often reads about claims being made that seem unreasonable, even outrageous. Remember that the fact that claims are made by a plaintiff in a lawsuit does not mean that they are true or, even if they are true, that the plaintiff is entitled to recover on account of them. The initial claims or allegations in a lawsuit are simply what the plaintiff says. They should be given no more credence than any other unsubstantiated information.

Courts in recent years have made considerable efforts to curb abuses of the litigation process by parties and their attorneys who make unreasonable claims in pleadings, perhaps hoping to extract a settlement from a defendant faced with the expense of litigation or undesirable publicity. In the federal system, the effort is contained in Rule 11 of the Federal Rules of Civil Procedure, which requires that every pleading, motion,[3] and other paper filed by a party represented by an attorney must be signed by an attorney whose signature "constitutes a certificate by the signer that the signer has read the pleading, motion or other paper; that to the best of the signer's knowledge, information, and belief formed after reasonable inquiry it is well grounded in fact and is warranted by existing law or a good faith argument for the extension, modification, or reversal of existing law, and that it is not interposed for any improper purpose, such as to harass or to cause unnecessary delay or needless increase in the cost of litigation."[4] Violation of Rule 11 may cause the court to sanction the attorney; sanctions may include fines and paying the other parties reasonable expenses, including attorney's fees incurred because of the improper filing. Cases of courts enforcing Rule 11 violations are frequently reported in the legal literature.

2. Preliminary Motions

There are a number of preliminary defenses which a defending attorney may impose that, if successful, will stop the lawsuit at the outset. These are usually set forth in a motion called a "motion to dismiss" or "motion for judgment" on the pleadings or, in older legal parlance, a "demurrer." The more common preliminary motions would be based upon:

1. Lack of personal jurisdiction. A court must have jurisdiction of the parties, that is, some right to exercise its power over them. While parties may submit to the jurisdiction of the court even if not required to do so, and a plaintiff submits to the jurisdiction by filing a lawsuit, a defendant who does not agree to personal jurisdiction cannot be compelled to litigate in a court unless it is, in fact, present or "doing business" in the state, owns property in the state, or has engaged in

contractual or tortious activities in the state that subject it to jurisdiction. A Massachusetts resident who drives to California and is injured in an automobile accident caused by a California resident cannot go home and bring suit against the California resident in Massachusetts, thus forcing the defendant to litigate the claim on the opposite side of the country. The claim would have to be brought in California unless the California resident in fact had a presence in Massachusetts sufficient to subject her or him to personal jurisdiction in that state.

The U.S. Supreme Court has ruled that constitutional due process requires that there be some minimum contacts between a defendant and the state asserting personal jurisdiction and that "fair play and substantial justice" must guide decisions in this area. While courts have found relatively minimal contacts in a state to be sufficient to subject a defendant to the state's jurisdiction, particularly if the contacts had something to do with the subject matter of the lawsuit, personal jurisdiction should always be considered as a defense if the suit is outside the defendant's home state.

Personal jurisdiction is a defense that must be asserted at the outset of a lawsuit. If a party participates in the lawsuit, it will be considered to have consented to the court's jurisdiction over it and cannot raise the defense at a later date.

2. Lack of subject matter jurisdiction. Courts have jurisdiction only over the subject matter, as opposed to the parties, over which the statutes give them jurisdiction. In the federal courts, subject matter jurisdiction in civil matters usually arises from (1) federal questions, that is, the lawsuit involves questions of federal constitutional or statutory law, or (2) diversity jurisdiction, meaning that the litigation is between citizens of different states and involves an amount in controversy greater than a certain minimum fixed by statute (currently $50,000). To avoid splitting lawsuits between state and federal courts, a lawsuit in which some claims are properly brought in federal court as federal questions may also include related nonfederal claims which

may be heard by the court in the same suit, a concession to the economics of litigation known as "supplemental jurisdiction." Subject matter jurisdiction cannot be waived. If the court does not have jurisdiction to hear the subject matter of the action, the parties' consent to it is of no effect.

3. Failure to state a cause of action, or, as the Federal Rules put it, "failure to state a claim upon which relief can be granted."[5] Failure to state a cause of action may be called the "so what" defense. It asserts that even if everything the plaintiff has alleged is true, he is not entitled to recover the relief he seeks, that is, the facts alleged simply do not form the basis for a lawsuit. In ruling on such a motion, the court is required to assume for purposes of deciding the motion that the facts stated by the plaintiff are indeed true. It is a way of testing the legal viability of pleadings that seek to stretch the boundaries of existing law or that present factual situations that simply are not recognized by the law as constituting legal wrongs. There is no harm to a defendant in losing a motion to dismiss. The assumption that the pleaded facts are true is made only for purposes of passing on the motion; the defendant is free to contest them in later proceedings or at trial if the case is not dismissed.

There are a number of "affirmative defenses" which, if applicable, may be employed by a defendant. If the defenses are apparent on the face of the plaintiff's pleadings, they may also be the subject of a motion to dismiss. If they require establishing certain facts not apparent from the plaintiff's pleadings, they may become the subject of a later motion for summary judgment or a defense at trial. Some special affirmative defenses which may provide a basis for an early dismissal are:

1. The statute of limitations. Most civil and criminal claims are subject to statutes of limitations; that is to say, the right to press the claim lapses if it is not brought within a period of time. This period of time is fixed by statute, although there is an equitable doctrine called "laches," which indicates that in equitable cases not governed by any specific statute of limitations, the claim must be brought within a "reasonable" time. Generally, courts hearing equity matters will follow the statute of limitations unless some different time appears reasonable under the circumstances of the case.

Statutes of limitations are statutory, as the name implies, and not part of the common law (except for the laches doctrine). There are very few statutes of limitations in federal law, and in almost all instances, the applicable period of limitations is determined by state statute. Hence, the time period varies from state to state, but in most instances is not longer than six years and is usually less— typically two or three years. The statute of limitations is not necessarily the same for all actions. Most states have a general statute of limitations but may adopt different statutes of limitations for particular kinds of claims that vary from the general statute.

The statute of limitations is sometimes extended by what is known as the "discovery rule," or "fraudulent concealment." These are common-law rules, occasionally adopted by statute, that protect people who have no reason to know of the wrongdoing of which they complain. If your car was negligently designed, manufactured, or repaired, you may not be aware of it until the accident happens. If there is a defect in the wiring in your house, you may not know it until the house burns down. If the doctor leaves a sponge in your stomach in an operation, you may not know it until further problems cause it to be discovered. In cases like these, most courts have held that the statute of limitations begins to run from the time of "discovery" of the defect, or the time the plaintiff knew or should have known that the problem existed. The fraudulent concealment rule is similar but applies in instances where the defendant was aware of the wrongdoing that ultimately caused the plaintiff damage but did not reveal it. A party who is aware of a problem, however, has an obligation to initiate legal action within the applicable statute of limitations or that right is lost.

Statutes of limitations were established for two reasons. First, people should not have claims hanging over their head indefinitely.

Second, lapses of time can be prejudicial to a fair trial of claims. Witnesses die, move, or are lost track of; records are destroyed; memories fade; physical evidence is altered or disappears (e.g., the intersection where the accident happened is redesigned). The further away from the event one is, the less likely it is that a trial will reach a just determination of responsibility.

2. Res adjudicata and collateral estoppel. Res adjudicata means that the "res," or thing (case or action), has been adjudicated. In the interest of finality, parties can have only one lawsuit over the claims arising out of a single set of facts. They cannot try one theory and then, if they lose, go back for another bite at the apple with another. If the essential claims have been litigated to a point of finality between the same parties, the res adjudicata defense would apply.

Collateral estoppel is a variation of res adjudicata. It usually applies when (1) one of the parties has in fact litigated and lost an essentially identical claim in another lawsuit which may not have involved the adverse party of the present lawsuit, or (2) litigation occurred over a different subject but one in which the essential contested issue in the present lawsuit was in fact at issue and decided. In one case, I represented the owner of a mobile home park in a claim for a relatively minor amount of money by a single tenant. The claim involved the owner's initial deposit policies. When the judge inquired why the owner was appearing with counsel in what was a relatively trivial claim, I pointed out that there were hundreds of other tenants who would have identical claims if the first tenant were successful and the owner would probably be collaterally estopped from contesting them. The judge immediately understood the importance of a careful decision on the first claim.

Res adjudicata and collateral estoppel rules developed in the interest of economy and finality of litigation. Every party is entitled to a day in court, but no one is entitled to retry the issue in question on numerous other days in court.

3. Discovery

After the initial pleadings and preliminary motions phases, the lawsuit goes into the discovery phase. Discovery is the right of a party to have the other party provide information in its control that may be relevant to the lawsuit. It is not limited to evidence that may be admissible in trial if it "appears reasonably calculated to lead to the discovery of admissible evidence."[6]

Discovery is accomplished by several means. The most important are:

(a) Written interrogatories. A written interrogatory is simply a written question or series of written questions given by one party to the other in a formal document known as a "set of interrogatories," which requires a written response within a fixed period of time, usually thirty days. The response is submitted under oath and signed by the other party; it may be used in court to the extent that it presents admissible evidence, just as if it were testimony in court.

(b) Requests for production of documents and objects. Either party can require the other to produce for inspection and copying documents that are relevant to the subject matter of the lawsuit, to allow inspection of property or tangible objects that may be relevant to the lawsuit, and to allow independent medical examination of parties claiming injuries.

(c) Depositions. A deposition is the taking of the testimony of a witness by counsel for a party outside the courtroom. Unless arrangements are made by agreement, it requires that formal notice be given to the other parties to the lawsuit. The witness is sworn to give his or her answers under oath. A court reporter or stenographer is present and makes a verbatim transcript of the attorneys' questions and the witness's answers. Regardless of which party requests or serves notice of a deposition, attorneys for all of the parties in the lawsuit have the right to be present and to make their own inquiries. The persons deposed may be parties or other witnesses. Recalcitrant witnesses can be subpoenaed to appear in a deposition, and procedures exist for attorneys to compel depositions outside the state of the court in which the lawsuit is pending.

(d) Requests for admission. A party who believes that certain information vital to the case is not seriously contested by the adverse party can file a formal request of the adverse party to admit the truth of various matters, including the genuineness of documents. If the adverse party disputes the requested admission, it must do so for stated reasons.

In addition to these and some other less commonly used means of formal discovery of the other party, both parties can and normally will engage in their own investigatory activity with respect to the events pertaining to the lawsuit—interviewing witnesses; reviewing documents; engaging experts or consultants for evaluation and advice where appropriate; examining accident scenes, damaged vehicles, or other tangible objects or products involved in the event; and other appropriate activities.

Parties engage in discovery for several reasons. First, they want to avoid surprise; that is, they want to know what the other side's case is and not hear it for the first time in the courtroom. This enables the attorney and client to prepare adequately to respond to evidence that the adverse party can be expected to present, and to evaluate the case properly for purposes of settlement negotiation. A second reason is to establish the elements of or evidence favorable to one's own case that may be in the possession or control of the other side. A third reason is to pin the adverse party and its witnesses down to a story so they cannot vary it to meet the circumstances. Lawyers often suspect that witnesses, with or without the encouragement of their counsel, adapt their story to conform to the exigencies of the legal situation. Such adaptation is not necessarily intentional deceit; selective recall, or the tendency to recollect facts that support a view one wants to maintain and to forget contradictory facts, is a well-known psychological phenomenon. Memory can be "filled in" by later sources of information; vague recollections can become precise by being rehearsed; and recollections that apply to one situation can be transferred in the mind to another.[7] A thorough early deposition can fix a witness's story in place before he becomes sufficiently educated or selective in his recall that his answers more effectively serve his interest.

It is vital that parties in litigation provide their attorneys thorough and complete information to respond to discovery directed at them. It is at best embarrassing, and sometimes worse, to turn up information late in the lawsuit that should have been given to the other side in response to an earlier discovery request. If such information is helpful to the litigant, it may even be kept out of evidence by the judge if the adverse party objects to its admission. Litigants who intentionally frustrate the discovery process by providing incomplete or evasive responses or by a lack of response are subject to penalties by the court, including the ultimate remedy of dismissing the action if the defending party is a plaintiff or entering a default judgment against a defendant.

Parties are sometimes reluctant to provide their attorney with information that is damaging to their position, especially because they fear the attorney will release it in discovery. Withholding such information prevents an attorney from giving, and prevents you from receiving, the best advice available as to your legal situation. No competent attorney will release information damaging to his or her client unless it is required by the discovery process. To withhold such information if it is subject to a proper discovery request is unethical and worse, for both you and your attorney. If a knowingly inaccurate answer is given under oath, as in a deposition or answer to interrogatories, it may be criminal. And in any event, if it comes to light it will have a devastatingly negative impact on the offending party's litigation position. Responses to discovery should be approached like a tax return. You do not need to give more than the law requires, but to evade giving up what is due is dishonest and will get you in trouble. To be sure, there are a lot of gray areas regarding what may or may not need to be disclosed in discovery, often generated by the vagueness and imprecision of the other party's request. Give your attorney all the information and let her decide how it must be handled.

4. Summary Judgment

A motion for summary judgment represents to the court that there is no genuine issue of material fact and that the party filing the motion for summary judgment is entitled to judgment as a matter of law. It differs from a motion to dismiss or a motion for judgment on the pleadings in that it does not rely solely on the pleadings but incorporates additional supportive factual material such as documents or affidavits. A motion for summary judgment is only appropriate when the party filing it believes that it is entitled to win the case based on *uncontested* facts. Summary judgment is not a procedure for determining whose version of the facts is correct. The other party can defeat a motion for summary judgment by filing affidavits, documents, or other evidentiary materials that demonstrate that there is in fact a contest over some genuine issue of material fact important to resolving the case.

A motion for summary judgment can be filed at any stage of the proceedings prior to trial but is usually not filed immediately because it requires some investigation or discovery to establish the facts necessary to support it. It has the highly useful function of avoiding the necessity and expense of a trial when there is no real fight about the facts, only about the legal consequences that flow from them.

Motions for summary judgment may be filed on a partial basis, that is, to determine certain issues but not the entire case, when there are issues that can be disposed of on the basis of undisputed facts. Even if a trial is still necessary, the partial summary judgment can be useful in shortening the trial and avoiding expense and uncertainty.

Sometimes both parties agree that summary judgment is appropriate but differ on who should prevail. In such cases, the parties often file cross motions for summary judgment; that is, each of them asks the court for summary judgment in its favor. The case can then be disposed of one way or the other by the trial judge based on the motions if the judge agrees that the undisputed facts entitle one or the other party to prevail.

5. The Trial

The trial is the climax, although not necessarily the conclusion, of the litigation process. The parties appear in court represented by their lawyers and surrounded by their witnesses, exhibits, and evidence, and make their presentation to the judge and jury. As noted in chapter 2, not all cases involve a jury. For those that do, there will be a process of jury selection from a panel of prospective jurors summoned to be available for that purpose for a fixed period of time. In some jurisdictions, lawyers interrogate the individual prospective jurors in a process called "voir dire." Whether the lawyers get to voir dire or not, the judge will ask the jurors a standard set of questions to determine if they have any biases or reasons why they cannot fairly hear and decide the case. Jurors who have some connection with the facts or parties or some reason why they cannot fairly hear the case are excused for cause. Each side will also be allowed a certain number of "peremptory" challenges, that is, the opportunity to excuse selected jurors without specifying any cause. In England, historically, jurors were chosen from the contestants' village or neighborhood and often brought to their task a knowledge of the facts and the litigants and, hence, some basis for rendering their judgment other than what they heard in the courtroom. Today, such people would be excluded from any jury in America for cause; we seek jurors who are ignorant of the facts and parties and require them to make their decisions based only on what they hear and see in the courtroom.

Once the jury is chosen, the lawyers make their opening statements, in which they give the jury a preview of the evidence they expect to present. In cases in which the jury is going to view a site outside the courtroom, such as an accident scene, the view is usually taken before the opening statements.

Following the opening statements, the plaintiff presents its evidence first, and each witness is subject to cross-examination by defense counsel before retiring. When the plaintiff has completed presenting all the evidence it wishes, it "rests." The defendant may then move for a directed verdict, which is a trial version of the "so what" defense. In essence, it says to the judge that even if all of the plaintiff's evidence is believed and all reasonable inferences are drawn from it, the plaintiff is not entitled to prevail. Granting a directed verdict terminates the case in favor of the defense. Directed verdicts may be issued on some but not all issues, thereby limiting but not terminating the trial. In federal courts the motion is now termed a "motion for judgment as a matter of law" and may be made at any time during a trial when the adverse party has been fully heard on an issue.

Assuming that a directed verdict is denied, as it usually is if the case has progressed this far, the defendant then presents its evidence in the same fashion as the plaintiff did, with its witnesses subject to cross-examination by plaintiff's counsel before retiring. At the conclusion of the defendant's case the plaintiff may make its "so what" motion and claim that the defendant's evidence, taken in its best light, does not establish a defense and the judge should direct a verdict in favor of the plaintiff. At the same time the defense may renew its motion for a directed verdict against the plaintiff.

After everybody's motions are denied, counsel present their final arguments summarizing the evidence presented; the judge instructs the jury on the law applicable to the case; and the jury retires and deliberates until it renders its verdict.

If the case is heard by a judge without a jury, the procedures will become abbreviated accordingly. There is usually no opening statement or final argument, and the parties submit written memoranda that summarize the evidence and their view of the applicable law, with requests that the judge make certain specific rulings of law and findings of fact on the matter in addition to reaching a conclusion.

Following the rendering of a verdict or judgment, the parties have an opportunity to ask the judge to overrule the jury verdict (a "judgment notwithstanding the verdict") or reconsider his or her decision. Such motions must be submitted within a relatively brief period of time, usually in a week or ten days. Once any such post-trial motions have been disposed of, there will be a fixed period of time, typically thirty days, for appeal to the next higher court.

6. The Appeal

The appeal process may be one of right, or the appellate court may be permitted to select which appeals it will consider. The appeal will require (1) the submission of selected portions of the record relevant to the issues appealed—a transcript of the testimony and the evidence or exhibits—(2) the submission of legal briefs by the parties setting forth their positions and arguments on the issues appealed, and (3) oral argument by the attorneys before the appellate court. In normal circumstances, the parties cannot present new evidence to the appeals court, nor may they come up with new legal theories or arguments that they did not present at the trial. The purpose of the appellate process is to enable the reviewing court to determine if the trial court made any errors, not to create a forum for the parties to have a new trial.

There are many aspects of the litigation process not covered by the foregoing brief outline. Each lawsuit has a life of its own and often takes twists and turns in directions neither party contemplated at the outset. In cases in which monetary damages are sought, parties may seek to make attachments at the outset to preserve the assets of the defendant. In cases in which circumstances may change so as to defeat the object of the litigation, a plaintiff may ask a court to enter a temporary restraining order or preliminary injunction to preserve the status quo or to prevent the defendant from taking some action which would be irreparable, at the outset of the lawsuit. Parties may file motions asking the court to rule on any number of issues that may arise in the course of the lawsuit that do not fit neatly within the preceding outline. Court rulings on motions at various stages, such as motions to dismiss, motions for summary judgment, or motions for directed verdict, are subject to appeal. Similarly, courts may deny such motions, but the parties filing them may prevail in trial.

During the period leading up to the Persian Gulf war in early 1991, the public was deluged with ominous information. A protracted ground war was predicted by some against a dug-in enemy whose elite troups were hardened by eight years of a previous war and armed with chemical and biological, if not nuclear, weapons. Tens of thousands of body bags reportedly had been shipped to Saudi Arabia, and in the case of a ground war, American and allied casualties were predicted in the thousands. When the shooting started, however, the war was won after forty days of aerial attack and one hundred hours of ground war, with a few hundred allied deaths, many of them from accidents or friendly fire. The enemy surrendered in great numbers and put up only occasional and ineffective resistance.

The accuracy of information the public receives about lawsuits is often similar to the early predictions of the course of the Persian Gulf war. News media and even legal periodical reports are often not of final outcomes but of allegations made or motions filed by one party or the other, or of decisions made by judges on various motions or issues before them that may have little to do with the final result. Juries may award a verdict for the defendant in cases that began by claiming millions of dollars, and jury verdicts for plaintiffs for millions of dollars may be whittled down or overturned by appellate courts. In lawsuits, as in baseball, "it ain't over till it's over." Read your legal news and follow your own case with this in mind.

C. ALTERNATIVE DISPUTE RESOLUTION

1. In General

The cost and delay inherent in litigation have led many to seek other means of resolving disputes. These other means are collectively referred to as "alternative dispute resolution." When disputes arise among believers who take seriously the instructions of the apostle Paul in 1 Cor.

6:1-8, alternative dispute resolution is not only desirable for all of the reasons it may be desirable in a secular context but may even be biblically mandated.[8]

The most common form of secular alternative dispute resolution is *arbitration*. Federal law and statutes in most, if not all, states expressly authorize it. It is often provided for as a means of dispute resolution in standard contracts such as American Institute of Architects contracts pertaining to the design and construction of buildings and other improvements; securities industry contracts; and provisions for uninsured or underinsured motorist coverage in liability insurance contracts. It is the normal method of dispute resolution in disputes that arise under labor union collective-bargaining contracts. Commercial contracts may also provide for it. Parties drafting their own contracts may include an arbitration clause, and disputants are always free to agree to submit a dispute to arbitration after it has arisen, whether or not it arises under a contract that mandates arbitration.

Agreements to arbitrate can be agreements for binding arbitration, that is, an agreement that the parties will be bound by whatever the results of the arbitration. Or arbitration can be nonbinding and engaged in to give the parties an independent perspective on their dispute in the hope that it will enable them to resolve their differences.

Parties to a contract that calls for dispute resolution by arbitration are free to waive the arbitration and proceed in court, either by an express agreement or simply by the implicit waiver of one party filing a lawsuit and the other responding to it without invoking the arbitration clause. If either party insists upon the dispute being resolved by arbitration, however, the court will refuse to hear the dispute and order the parties to proceed with arbitration. Arbitration is favored by the courts as a means of relieving congested dockets and encouraging expeditious dispute resolution without cost to the government. Arbitration agreements will be enforced even when the claim to be arbitrated is created by a statute that expressly gives jurisdiction over that type of claim to courts (as in discrimination claims under federal law).[9]

Parties are free to establish their own arrangements for arbitration, and there are private firms that provide arbitration and other alternative dispute resolution services to parties for a fee. There is a well-established system of labor arbitrators who resolve disputes under collective bargaining agreements. Perhaps the most common form of arbitration is arbitration that occurs under the auspices of the American Arbitration Association (AAA), which maintains offices in many cities, publishes a set of arbitration rules, including specialized rules for arbitration in, for example, construction industry disputes or commercial disputes, and maintains a roster of arbitrators that can be called upon to hear disputes. Arbitration is initiated by filing a demand for arbitration with the AAA, on a form the AAA provides. In the demand, the party identifies the adverse party and the nature of the dispute. The adverse party is notified and given an opportunity to assert any claims it may have and wish to submit to the arbitration. The AAA submits to both parties a list of proposed arbitrators and a calendar, and each party returns the list after deleting any arbitrators to whom it does not wish to submit the matter and dates on which it is unavailable. After receiving both parties' responses, the AAA assigns the arbitrator, who sets a date and place for the arbitration. In some instances there may be more than one arbitrator hearing the matter.

Federal law and arbitration law in most states permit parties to engage in discovery in conjunction with an arbitration hearing. In most arbitrations, however, discovery is less formal and less extensive than in litigated matters. While the parties have the same right to engage in discovery, there seems to be something about the nature of matters heard in arbitration or the psychology of an arbitration proceeding that minimizes the extensive discovery often conducted in court litigation.

The arbitration hearing differs from a trial in court in several important respects. Unless the parties have made arrangements to do so at their own expense, there will be no official record, although the arbitrator or the parties may provide for a tape-recorded record. Testimony in arbitration proceedings is, however, required to be sworn and the case is presented and controlled by the attorneys. The rules of evidence that apply in a courtroom do not apply in arbitration. Hence, the proceedings are much less formal. The parties are, however, free to object to the introduction of evidence and to refer to the rules of evidence that would apply in court, but the arbitrator is not bound to follow them and may use his or her discretion in admitting evidence that might not be admissible in court. As an example of the informality of the arbitration format, in one arbitration I was involved in, a party asked for and received the permission of the arbitrator to telephone a witness who was not present. The witness was allowed to testify to the arbitrator over the telephone, with each counsel permitted to ask her questions and represent the answers she gave to the arbitrator.

A decision in a binding arbitration is enforceable by a court, and arbitrators' decisions are not subject to the usual rules of appeal. In the absence of a showing of fraud, collusion, extreme bias, or some other egregious conduct, courts will almost never reexamine an arbitrator's decision, even for errors of law.

Another, typically prearbitration form of alternative dispute resolution is *mediation*. In mediation, the mediator will meet with the parties, often both together and separately, and seek to assist them in resolving their dispute. Often he or she will serve the useful function of "reality testing" the parties' positions and helping them to explore from a neutral perspective some means of coming together.

Alternative dispute resolution has become so popular that even courts are getting into the act. Some courts require nonbinding arbitration hearings in at least certain types of cases. Typically this requires the parties to submit their cases and important evidence in written form, followed by a brief hearing, at which they can make an oral presentation to the judge or arbitrator who provides a nonbinding opinion on the outcome. Another alternative dispute resolution format used in federal and some state courts is the summary jury trial. In a summary jury trial, each party is given an abbreviated time period, such as an hour, in which to present its entire case to a jury panel. Most of the presentation will be done orally by the attorney, who may refer to specific evidence, charts, and so forth. The jury then renders its verdict, which, again, is nonbinding. Both the nonbinding arbitration and summary jury trial procedures serve the useful function of giving the parties a neutral view of the probable outcome. Results of actual jury trials are often similar to the results reached in a summary jury trial and nonbinding arbitration, so settlement is encouraged after these procedures. Since actual jury trials can take days, weeks, and sometimes months, summary jury trials and nonbinding arbitration save enormous time and expense for both the court and the parties if they lead to a settlement.

What are the advantages and disadvantages of arbitration? Here are some considerations:

1. Expense. Arbitration is usually perceived as, and in most cases probably functions as, a cheaper alternative than litigation. This result is not, however, foreordained. Because discovery is equally available in arbitration, if the parties in fact engage in the same discovery that they would have engaged in if the case were litigated in court, there are no savings. And, while an arbitration hearing itself is usually much more expeditious than a court hearing because there is no jury and the rules of evidence do not apply, if the case is a lengthy and complex one, it may be heard more efficiently in court. Once a court trial begins, the parties normally have the undivided attention of the court until it is over. This is not necessarily true in arbitration. Arbitrators are normally people with schedules and obligations other than the arbitration. Hence, if the arbitration cannot be completed in a day, it may require the parties to come back on additional, widely separated days to continue it. Every return to the arbitration hearing requires the parties and their counsel to get back up to speed on the case and gives both parties all of the intervening time to work on the case and to think of things they can do to enhance their posi-

tions. Some arbitration cases have gone on for months and even years on an intermittent basis. No lawyer involved in them would have claimed they were cheaper or more expeditious than trying the same case in a courtroom.

2. Speed of resolution. Most courts have significant backups in their docket. The time from filing a suit to a trial is likely to run from one to several years, depending on the court and jurisdiction and the state of the docket at the time. Arbitration can happen quickly because the parties do not have to wait in line in the same fashion and can have their case heard whenever they and the arbitrator can agree to get together to do it. However, the same factors that can drive up the cost of arbitration can delay an arbitrated resolution. Hence, arbitration, while usually more expeditious, can be as delayed as a court trial.

3. Fairness of the process. While most arbitrators undoubtedly strive to be fair and impartial in conducting the hearing process and reaching their decisions, and may indeed reach the same result a judge or jury would have reached, parties to an arbitration proceeding should realize that they do not have the same protections that they have in court. Since the arbitrator is not obliged to follow the rules of evidence, he or she may give attention to evidence that would not be admissible in court and, a party may feel, should not be considered. The informality of the process may allow a party to get away with conduct that the other party may view as prejudicial to its case and not that would be allowed in court. The tendency to a reduced level of discovery, or the unavailability or reduced availability of discovery under some state arbitration laws, may allow the other party to conceal evidence adverse to its position, make exploration of the facts in advance of hearing more difficult, and allow parties to gain an advantage by surprise in the evidence presented.

4. Resolution of issues of law. When the result of a proceeding turns on the resolution of legal, as opposed to factual, issues, parties should realize that many arbitrators are not attorneys and that it

is extremely difficult to appeal from an arbitrator's decision, even if he or she makes a wrong ruling on an issue of law. If determination of legal issues is of the essence in the proceeding, you are usually better off in court.

5. The need for collateral orders. In many court proceedings, it is important to have access to the enforceable authority of a court order, particularly when dealing with a difficult or recalcitrant adverse party. Attachment of assets to preserve them for judgment, orders to compel compliance with discovery requests, and early dismissal of claims without merit are only a few of the available court remedies that are difficult or impossible to obtain in the arbitration process. If the ultimate relief sought is an injunction (an order that a party do or refrain from doing something), obtaining the order from a court makes it immediately enforceable. Arbitrators have no enforcement power in and of themselves; their orders are only enforceable by presenting them to a court in a further proceeding and obtaining a court order to enforce them.

6. Fees. Apart from attorney's fees and other costs associated with either litigation or arbitration, fees paid to a court are nominal since the facilities and personnel are maintained at the expense of the government. Arbitration, however, is private dispute resolution, and the parties must pay for the services they receive. This is usually based on a sliding scale of fees, depending upon the amount involved, payable to the arbitration association. There may be a separate fee payable to the arbitrator, depending upon the amount of time he or she is required to devote to the matter. In cases of significant value, arbitration fees can be a significant aspect of the cost consideration.

In general, arbitration is a good solution for routine disputes in which an early and less expensive resolution is more important than maximizing the rights of the parties. Cases that turn on factual disputes and not legal issues and that can be resolved with an evidentiary hearing that will take no more than a single day are the best candidates for arbitration. More complex matters or matters in which the parties are relying on legal precedent or the resolution of legal issues may be more effectively handled in court.

2. Christian Conciliation

In the late 1970s, Christian attorneys concerned about the proliferation of litigation and the importance of dispute resolution in a biblically faithful model (Matt. 18:15-17; 1 Cor. 6:1-7) began an experiment in Christian conciliation as an approach to conflict resolution. The experiment has been blessed by the Lord for its faithfulness to biblical commands and today exists as the Association of Christian Conciliation Services, with a referral network of dozens of organizational and individual members throughout the country. It has a set of procedural rules, an administrative fee schedule, forms to use for the various purposes appropriate to mediation and arbitration, standards of conduct, a code of ethics, and a training and certification program for conciliators. It also publishes a newsletter and other resources for biblical peacemaking.[10]

A review of the rules of procedure for Christian conciliation followed by the Association of Christian Conciliation Services reveals an outline for mediation and arbitration proceedings that in many respects parallels those of the American Arbitration Association and other private, alternative dispute resolution organizations. Its initial purpose, however, reveals its deeper roots:

> The purpose of Christian Conciliation is to glorify and serve God by helping people to resolve disputes in a conciliatory rather than an adversarial manner. In addition to facilitating the resolution of substantive disagreements, Christian Conciliation seeks to reconcile those who have been alienated by conflict and to help them learn how to change their attitudes and behaviour to avoid similar conflicts in the future. These Rules shall be interpreted and applied in a manner consistent with this purpose.[11]

Arbitrators and mediators are referred to as "conciliators." They are instructed to consider all laws brought to their attention by the parties, "but the Holy Scriptures [the Bible] shall be the supreme authority governing every aspect of the conciliation process."[12]

Conciliation may be postponed until the parties have made reasonable efforts at private resolution or, with the help of their churches, resolution pursuant to Matt. 18:15-20.[13]

The mediation process may involve initial meetings to "assess the parties' attitudes and needs, to teach relevant Biblical principles, and to assign homework that will facilitate the mediation process."[14] Mediation proceedings include opening prayer; discussion, sometimes initially in private, of each party's responsibility for the dispute; the application of relevant biblical principles; and closing prayer. Private Bible study and prayer of the conciliator with the parties separately is also provided for.[15] Conciliators reserve the right to discuss with church leaders cases of parties who profess to be Christians and to ask church leaders to participate actively in resolving the dispute. The rules provide that the parties recognize that churches may institute discipline with respect to parties who refuse to repent of sin and cooperate in the process and that the conciliation service may cooperate with the church during such processes in a way that is consistent with Scripture.[16] Parties to an arbitration proceeding, if the issue is not resolved by mediation, may submit briefs or written position papers that set forth their understanding of scriptural as well as legal and factual issues.[17]

Among the useful and scripturally faithful work done by the Association of Christian Conciliation Services are recommended provisions for Christian conciliation to be inserted in contracts and wills (see Appendix C).

A discussion of the theology of reconciliation is beyond the scope of this work.[18] While the Association of Christian Conciliation Services is not so widely represented in the country as to guarantee that its services will be available to all, its procedures are designed to be available to churches and other Christian bodies that wish to resolve disputes in accordance with its principles. Before permitting any disagreement to go to court and if the adverse party is a fellow believer or is willing to be bound by its terms, every Christian believer who takes the Bible as his or her guide to matters of faith and practice should prayerfully consider the Christian Conciliation Service model of biblical dispute resolution.

D. HIRING A LAWYER

Litigation is a situation for which a lawyer should always be engaged. A perusal of this book will identify many other occasions when the church may need a lawyer.

There are nearly one million lawyers in the United States, and American law schools continue to pump another fifty thousand lawyers a year into a supersaturated profession. Some of them may be members of your congregation or religious organization. Some of them are members of your faith or denomination or simply fellow believers, whatever their denominational affiliation may be. How do you choose the right one for your needs when you need to hire a lawyer?

1. Structure of the Profession

It may help in answering the question to have some understanding of the structure of the legal profession. The delivery of legal services is as varied as many other trades and professions, such as health care or food distribution. There are "national" law firms with hundreds of lawyers and offices in a number of cities around the country, sole practitioners serving a very local clientele, and everything in between. Some law firms are "boutiques," that is, specialty firms whose practice is limited to a particular field of law such as trademark, immigration, or admiralty law; or they may specialize in somewhat broader concerns such as personal injury recovery, personal injury defense, labor law, municipal and government law, or real estate conveyancing. There are very few religious boutiques, although there are lawyers and even firms with a high degree of specialized knowledge in representing religious organizations or particular religious clients.

More typically, law firms serve their clients' legal needs in a broad range of fields of law, and individual attorneys within the firm specialize in particular areas. Individual attorneys frequently limit their practice to broad fields such as litigation, real estate practice, business and taxation, or probate, trust, and estate planning. Almost no lawyer today is a true generalist who is competent or will endeavor to serve the needs of any client with respect to any legal problem. Some lawyers, most commonly in smaller or more rural communitites, may still be the equivalent of the family doctor and will attend to a broad range of common or minor legal problems but will refer more complex matters to specialists.

2. Cost

Lawyers' fees are usually determined by an hourly rate applicable to the particular attorney working on the matter. The hourly rate of the particular attorney in turn depends upon a number of factors appropriate to setting the cost of services, such as experience, degree of specialization, reputation, competitive rates in the geographical area of practice, and, sometimes, on the nature and complexity of the matter involved. Most attorneys will have a standard hourly rate or rate range depending upon these factors.

Plaintiffs' personal injury cases are customarily handled on a contingency fee basis, that is, the attorney collects a percentage of the proceeds actually recovered for the plaintiff and if the attorney is not successful in recovering anything, he or she collects nothing except out-of-pocket disbursements for which the client normally remains responsible. Some matters are customarily handled in some areas on a fixed-fee basis, irrespective of the value of the transaction or the time it takes; and some commercial transactions are handled for a fee that is a percentage of the amounts involved but is not contingent on outcome.

Hourly rates for lawyers may range from as low as $40 or $50 for beginning lawyers in rural areas to many hundreds of dollars an hour for senior lawyers in large firms in major cities. It is fair and reasonable for you to ask your attorney for an estimate of the cost of the undertaking. Do not be surprised if the estimate is expressed as a range

or is a little vague. It is a much less precise art to determine how many hours it is going to take to conduct a lawsuit than it is for an experienced contractor to determine how long it will take to build a building.

The earlier discussion of the anatomy of lawsuits and some of the variabilities therein makes the difficulty apparent. Lawsuits may be terminated at an early stage by settlement or actions dismissing the suit, or they may be extended beyond any expectation the parties had when they started. Litigation is not in the control of one party. Each party must respond to the demands of the other, as well as those imposed by the court. Trials get scheduled, forcing lawyers to prepare for them, and then continued so they have to prepare again. Issues arise in the course of the litigation that were not apparent at the outset and require additional attention. Clients often request additional action. A lawsuit is like a war—a dynamic, unfolding event that can never be fully assessed at the beginning.

Other legal services may be easier to estimate more precisely. It is a rare legal service, however, that does not have inherent variability. While you can and should get general cost estimates before hiring legal services, be aware of their limitations. The best protection you can have against excessive charges for legal services is to hire a lawyer in whom you have confidence. If his or her bills are higher than you expected, at least you can be assured that it is because your needs required the additional investment and not because you are being taken advantage of.

It is a popular impression that lawyers are grossly overcompensated. Senior partners at large firms in major metropolitan areas may earn hundreds of thousands of dollars per year, but they are a small group at the top of a large profession. Most lawyers today, as Daniel Webster observed, "work hard, live well and die poor." The average sole practitioner in the United States earns less than $60,000 per year, and the average lawyer in firms with up to twelve lawyers earns under $100,000.[19] In general, lawyers in larger metropolitan areas and in larger firms earn more than their counterparts in more rural areas and smaller firms.

While these levels of compensation are certainly comfortable, they belie the exaggerated views of lawyer wealth held in some quarters. As much as 60 percent of law-firm revenue is spent to maintain the office—staff salaries, occupancy costs, equipment, reference material, insurance, and so forth—before any revenue is available for lawyer compensation. While younger lawyers have made compensation gains over the past decade, compensation of partners or more senior lawyers has barely kept pace with inflation or has even declined.

3. Legal Ethics

Lawyers (or experts or teachers of the law) do not fare well in the Gospel narratives, although the references are to professionals in Mosaic, not civil, law—the Jewish canon lawyers of the time. A believer known as Zenas the lawyer, however, who may have been a Roman jurist, was with Titus on Crete and is referred to approvingly by Paul in Titus 3:13.

"The first thing we do, let's kill all the lawyers" is an oft-quoted line from Shakespeare's *Henry VI* that is invariably used as part of the popular lawyer bashing of our day. Anti-lawyer jokes are on every tongue, and collections of them are appearing in books. The bad press has become legendary. But, remember, the lawyers to be killed in *Henry VI* are in danger because they stand in the way of those who would destroy the ancient rights of Englishmen, overthrow the government, and establish dictatorship.

Most people who do not like lawyers do not like someone else's lawyer. Rarely do they feel that way about their own advocate. Regrettably, some clients come to an attorney looking for a dirty street fighter and expecting to find someone who will "lie, cheat and steal" to protect their client's interest. I have had more than one client say to me, "You just tell me what to say and I'll say it." Such clients are genuinely disappointed when they find that their attorney is not trained in the practice of unethical conduct and will not countenance it in the client.

The legal profession, like every other trade or calling, has its heroes and its villains. There would be no gain in expounding here on their virtues or their treachery. The profession is to some extent unique, however, in that it operates under rules of ethics or professional conduct imposed by courts that are enforced to the point of disbarring attorneys for egregious violations. The threat is not idle; one need only read the newspapers to be aware of the regularity of the fate of transgressors. The professional ethics code to which attorneys are bound requires them to have an absolute loyalty to their clients and to honor client confidences (except in limited situations such as the threat of a crime to be committed); to refrain from self-dealing or taking advantage of the client in any transaction that benefits the attorney personally; to avoid any conflict of interest by not representing clients who may have opposing interests with respect to a matter; to inform clients fully concerning their cases; and to deal honestly with the courts, clients, and adversaries. The overwhelming majority of the hundreds of lawyers I have personally known and practiced with (and against) have been conscientious, ethical practitioners. While the profession has its problems, clients should not fear that they are in danger of being victimized by every lawyer they meet.

Christian lawyers bring another dimension entirely to the practice. The pages of periodicals such as the *Christian Legal Society's Quarterly* and the *Catholic Lawyer* are filled with articles by practicing attorneys that address the issues of faith in practice and how to integrate the Lordship of Christ over their lives with their professional careers. The words of the Lord to the apostle Paul in Corinth could well be spoken of the legal profession: "I have many people in this city."[20]

4. Finding a Reference

It is relatively easy to find out what an attorney's field of specialization or particular competence is. It is much more difficult to find out how competent he or she really is. As in every other trade or profession, the skill level and effectiveness of attorneys vary and depend on a combination of factors—experience in both years of practice and specialization in the area in question, personality, intelligence, judgment, other personal factors, and how hard the attorney works at it, both in addressing your particular problem and in maintaining skills in the area of specialization. It is often very difficult for clients who are not sophisticated consumers of legal services (and sometimes even for those who are) to recognize quality in legal services when they receive it, much less identify where they are going to get it before they receive it.

There are legal directories, with which lawyers are familiar, that give extremely broad ratings to attorneys and in which most attorneys, at least those who practice in firms, will be listed. The most prominent of these is known as *Martindale Hubble* and is available in most law offices and law libraries. Its ratings are based on confidential peer surveys by other attorneys who are in the best position to make a judgment. Its A-, B-, and C-level ratings of overall professional competence are gross characterizations that may tend to underrate younger lawyers and many solo or small-town practitioners who may not be listed in the directory at all.

The single best source of reference for finding the right lawyer is another lawyer. Lawyers work with lawyers and form professional opinions about one another's competence and skill levels. They also talk to other lawyers to add to their store of knowledge. A lawyer's reputation and ability are most accurately perceived by professional colleagues. If you have a lawyer whom you can use as a resource to identify the right lawyer to hire, do so. The second best source of reference is a satisfied client, particularly a client whose program or problem is similar to yours. If you know colleagues who have dealt with a similar problem in similar organizations, ask them who their lawyers were and how they felt about the services.

As a general proposition, obtain your services at the most local level at which you can find an attorney who is competent to provide them and in whom you have confidence. Many firms and lawyers increasingly are attempting to practice across state lines as growth in numbers in the profession and economic slowdowns increase pressure for economic survival. While competence is not measured by geographic location and some legal services may be so specialized that you need someone outside the jurisdiction to provide them, there are advantages that more local attorneys can bring to a situation. In a litigation situation, they will know the clerks of court and will have appeared before the judges and know their predilections. They will know the local rules of court and the customs and practices, and may have dealt with their professional adversary many times before. These advantages also apply in administrative agencies. Local attorneys are likely to know the people who staff the agencies, to have appeared before hearing officers or boards and commissions, and to bring with them some local knowledge and expertise as well as their own reputation and credibility. Local land-use planning boards may also be more comfortable with local attorneys. Often an out-of-state attorney will be required to associate himself or herself with a local attorney in order to practice before a court in a state.

How local is local enough? It depends on the state and area you are in. In smaller states, most attorneys may practice on a state-wide basis, particularly those in the larger firms in the state's metropolitan areas. In larger states, the practical divisions may be different, depending upon geography and location of population.

5. Managing the Attorney-Client Relationship

Tell your lawyer everything you can think of about the matter you have entrusted to him or her. Give him all the documents. Tell her the bad news as well as the good. Unless you are about to commit a crime, your lawyer is obliged to keep the information confidential. You will not get the best advice or handling of the matter if you have held back information that is damaging to your case or that puts you in a bad light.

Make sure your attorney has time to do the job. Attorneys are largely dependent for their sustenance on people who come in the door, and they are understandably reluctant to turn away business. No matter how busy they are, they are always afraid that next month no clients will appear and they will have nothing to do. Consequently, some attorneys take on more work than they can reasonably handle and then delay or ignore responding to client needs for which they are responsible. This is one of the greatest sources of client dissatisfaction.

If your project has time needs, tell your attorney what they are and ask directly if the attorney has the time available to do the work within the time schedule required. If your project is a crisis and requires the attorney to set other matters aside to give it emergency attention, or if it is something that will require the attorney to decline other work for a period of time, be willing to pay a little extra for the service.

Your relationship with your attorney is a professional relationship that should be imbued with trust and confidence. If you have entrusted your work to an attorney who does not return your phone calls or communicate with you about it, retrieve the file and find an attorney who can give you the service you need. Seek out an attorney in whom you can repose trust and if you do not maintain it, find another.

6. Considering an Attorney Who Shares Your Faith

The ideal attorney for a religious organization would be the attorney who understands and shares their organization's faith and its unique needs and views and who is also competent in the particular field of law in which the services are needed. A Christian attorney who specializes in real estate practice and has never been in a courtroom should not become your trial lawyer just because she or he is a Christian or a member of the church, nor should the litigator who handles no real estate transactions become your real estate lawyer because of shared faith. If you do not know an attorney's area of specialization or field of particular competence, ask. And if you have confidence in the attorney but recognize that the particular need that you have is outside of his or her area of competence, ask for a reference.

The single greatest failing in legal services rendered to religious organizations is the tendency of lawyers, even those who may be people of faith themselves, to be insensitive to the unique religious freedom rights of religious organizations and believers under both federal and state constitutions in the American legal system. Often the organizations and believers themselves are insensitive to these rights. Issues of church autonomy, the right of religious organizations to manage their own internal affairs without government interference, and the right of believers to practice their beliefs without such interference make religious clients different from secular clients. Lawyers who are not experienced in handling such matters and are not familiar with the constitutional jurisprudence that has grown up around religious freedom issues in this country are likely to treat religious organizations with legal problems like any secular client. If the lawyer is not a believer, his or her view may be colored by a personal belief that what the organization or individual wants to do is improper or that the religious freedom protection should not transcend some government regulation. It is here that religious organizations and religious people most need a lawyer with experience and sensitivity to their religious needs—not just because the lawyer is a believer but because believers may have rights unique to their religious situation. It is my hope that this book will make religious organizations and believers more aware of those rights. They should be sure their attorneys are equally aware of them.

Do not expect the lawyer who happens to be a member of your church or denomination or a fellow believer to provide you with free or reduced-fee advice on significant matters. It is good practice to have attorneys on the boards of churches and religious organizations, and their training and experience can be invaluable as volunteers in guiding the affairs of such organizations. But, to quote Abraham Lincoln, "A lawyer's stock in trade is his time and his advice." It is not reasonable to presume on the attorney or assume that because the client is religious the attorney must donate services. Christian attorneys may and often have contributed thousands, even tens and hundreds of thousands, of dollars of free services to religious clients, particularly in litigating religious freedom issues for clients who could not afford the normal fee. The decision to do so must be the attorney's. Churches and religious organizations with budgets and income should normally expect to pay the attorney's usual and customary charges for services rendered.

Many believers may, for a variety of reasons, feel more comfortable having the counsel of a Christian attorney with respect to their legal problems, whether or not the problems are related to faith. Christian or believing attorneys may be more likely to understand and be in sympathy with the unique concerns and problems of their religious client. I have, for example, written wills for believers that made separate provisions, depending on whether the rapture occurred before their death.[21] My partners who specialize in estate planning would most likely have been mystified by these believers' concerns. A Christian attorney may be able to better understand and deal with Christians' concerns about biblical faithfulness in resolving disputes among believers (Matt. 18:15-17; 1 Cor. 6:1-7) or whether the obligation to love one's enemies and turn the other cheek (Matt. 5:38-48) precludes using the civil legal system to enforce obligations. The effect of liability insurance (discussed in chapter 20) on these obligations, as understood by the believer, may be more effectively sorted out with the advice of an attorney who understands the client's perspective. The better a lawyer knows a client, whether that client is secular or religious, the more effective he or she is in serving the client.

Christians should beware, however, of substituting spirituality for competence and knowledge in the field of expertise. Lawyers who are available to the organization and share its faith position may not be specialists in the area in which it needs services. Spirituality is not a substitute for competence, and religious organizations have many legal problems that require no unique religious or spiritual understanding to be handled effectively by counsel. The legal needs of a construction project for a religious organization, with the limited possible exceptions discussed in chapter 15, for example, are not likely to differ from those of a secular owner. Select attorneys who are competent to the task.

E. MANAGING THE CRISIS

Let us assume that a crisis has occurred and that it is of the worst kind—a charge of sexual molestation or abuse of one or more minors by a church staffperson or volunteers. How do you respond?

In managing the crisis after it has occurred, you have a number of constituencies or interest groups to consider: (1) the victim and his or her family; (2) the accused molester; (3) the members of the congregation; (4) your insurer; and (5) the general public.

Many of the issues we have discussed will present less acute crises than accusations of child molestation, and all of the suggestions that follow will not be equally applicable to each of them.

Here are some suggestions for crisis management:

1. Take all allegations seriously. Even if you do not think they are true, or if upon investigation they turn out not to be true, you cannot assume that in advance.

2. Support the victim and the victim's family. Too often the church or its leadership—motivated either by disbelief of the allegations and support for the alleged offender or by concern for liability—will close ranks against the accuser. The victim then becomes victimized a second time by being made to feel an outcast. This aggravates the problem and increases the likelihood of litigation. The victim's parents are often more interested in truthfulness and honest investigation, assurance of steps taken to prevent future offenses, healing, and reconciliation than in monetary damages. A lawsuit may reflect the failure of the church to respond to the victim's distress. Once the matter is in the hands of a plaintiff's attorney, however, it is unlikely to be resolved without the payment of a significant amount of money. You can help the victim and the

victim's family by (1) providing free medical care and counseling; (2) assuring the family of a full, fair, and honest investigation; and (3) instituting measures to prevent a recurrence.

3. Notify your insurer immediately. If the events in question have occurred over a period of time, notify every insurer that has provided coverage within the time period in question, as well as the insurer providing coverage at the time of reporting.

   Provide your notice to the insurer immediately by telephone followed by written notice sent by certified or registered mail with a return receipt requested. Read your policy for an address to which to provide notice.

   Provide notice to the local insurance agency issuing the policy as well.

4. With respect to liability issues, cooperate fully with the insurer and allow it to manage liability aspects of the matter.

5. If the insurer denies coverage, do not accept the denial at face value but have your attorney review the facts and the policy if a claim is asserted by the victim or the victim's family. Insurers will read the policy in terms most favorable to them, but your attorney may be able to find coverage, or establish it through litigation, that is not initially acknowledged by the company.

6. With or without the participation of the insurer, conduct a full investigation into the allegations. Pursue the matter to a point of closure; i.e., reach an internal judgment as to whether the allegations are well founded; then take appropriate action. This aspect of the matter should be handled by counsel or with the advice of counsel with the potential liability implications in mind. In no circumstances, however, should you ignore the allegations.

7. Protect the rights of the alleged perpetrator by:

   (a) Being sure that (1) your investigation does not presume the truth of the allegations but provides the alleged perpetrator a full and fair opportunity to present information on his or her own behalf; and (2) the investigation is approached in an unbiased manner. For example, interviews with witnesses should solicit information in a neutral fashion, not with leading questions asking them to assent to information provided by the interrogator. Questioning should be in the nature of "What happened?" "What did you see?" "Who was there?" "What was said?" "What happened next?" rather than "Did Mr. X touch Bobby or Sally in a wrong place?" Interviews with minor witnesses, especially young children, are especially susceptible to being colored by the interviewee's perception of what the interviewer wants to hear. Having interviews conducted by counsel or, in the case of minors, by a trained specialist is particularly useful, given the problem of bias in the investigation.

   Obtain written or tape-recorded statements where possible. Do not audio- or videotape statements without the express consent of the interviewee; the consent should be recorded on the tape.

   (b) If the alleged perpetrator is an employee, review the employment contract (if any exists), any personnel policy manual or procedures established by the organization, the employee's personnel file and job history, and any other documentation that may be material at an early stage of the investigation and before deciding on the appropriate disciplinary sanction, if any.

   (c.) Maintain the correct balance regarding who is made privy to the information and investigation. This requires:

   i. Being sure that those who should be involved in the investigatory or decision-making process are given pertinent information. A pastor should not, for example, conduct a sensitive investigation without first consulting his or her governing board or ecclesiastical superior. Decisions to discipline or terminate an employee are most defensible if the facts are reviewed and the decision shared by a larger body or higher level of authority. Peremptory decisions made on the spot by an immediate superior are more vulnerable to attack.

ii. On the other hand, information should be limited to those who have a legitimate reason to know and to be involved in the decision making. These persons should be cautioned not to spread the information.

8. Release information to church members prudently and with advice of counsel. Certain circumstances will, for example, call for some explanation, for instance, when the occurrence has become more public—is reported in the newspaper, etc.—or when something is happening that calls for explanation, such as a significant staff person suddenly leaving a post. In some circumstances, the announcement that is made or the information that is released may be negotiated with the individual or individuals concerned. This is desirable as long as the information is truthful and not misleading. Often that will not be possible and you must formulate your own statement which must be carefully worded so as to be truthful and not misleading, but will not defame the individual.

9. If the matter has become the subject of media attention or you anticipate receiving a number of questions about it from members or other interested persons, consider either:

(a) Identifying a single person to act as the spokesperson and have everyone else in authority refer inquiries to that individual. This avoids the possibility of members of governing boards or involved individuals making statements that are inconsistent, poorly informed, defamatory, or otherwise inappropriate. The fewer people discussing the issue publicly, the less likely something will be said that will cause a problem.

(b) Formulating a written statement and responding to all questions by reference to it.

(c) Making, in appropriate cases, a statement that an investigation is being undertaken and assurance that the church will take appropriate action based on the results.

10. Where serious allegations have been made but you are unsure of their truth, a suspension of the alleged perpetrator (with pay, if employed) will often be in order to enable you to alleviate people's concerns and any fear of further liability-creating incidents until the matter is resolved.

11. In addition to investigating the truth or falsity of the immediate allegation and taking appropriate action based on the result, review all of your policies and procedures with a view to what changes need to be made to prevent a recurrence (or occurrence if you conclude that the allegations are not well founded) of the events complained of.

12. If the individual chooses to resign rather than face an investigation, you cannot prevent the resignation. There may be several good reasons, however, to proceed with your investigation anyway. Should a legal claim be brought, you may be in the best position to identify information which would tend to exculpate the church from organizational liability while memories of the event are fresh and personnel available. You may learn information that is useful in preventing future recurrences. And the victim and victim's family may be less likely to pursue a legal claim if they believe the church took the allegation seriously and took appropriate measures to prevent a recurrence. If the investigation is conducted properly, it should not provide a foundation for liability that does not already exist.

13. Be wary of negotiating deals to induce the resignation of an alleged perpetrator that have any hint of a cover-up, such as providing references or letters of recommendation that would enable the perpetrator to obtain future employment in a similar situation.

14. Follow your obligations under the child abuse–reporting law.

15. No matter how serious the allegations and how obvious it is or how persuaded you are that they are truthful, treat the perpetrator with dignity. If employment termination is necessary, be firm, candid, and unapologetic, but also be fair and humane. Do not be angry, insulting, or embarrassing. Be fair in the final paycheck.

16. Consult resources of your denomination or judicatory for assistance.

17. If the investigation is inconclusive and you decide, after consulting counsel, that you are unable to terminate the employee, monitor and supervise carefully thereafter.

REFERENCES

Association of Christian Conciliation Services, 1537 Avenue D, Suite 352, Billings, MT 59102, has a variety of publications available on Christian conciliation.

Buzzard, Lynn R., and Laurence Eck. *Tell It to the Church* (Elgin, Ill.: David C. Cook Publishing Co., 1982).

Sandee, C. Ken. *The Peacemaker—A Biblical Guide to Resolving Personal Conflict* (Grand Rapids: Baker Book House, 1991).

CHAPTER 20

Liability Insurance

A. THE NEED FOR LIABILITY INSURANCE

The liability system described in this book is, to some extent, a fortuity. Good planning, prudent hiring, training, and supervision of staff and volunteers, risk management, and other sound administrative approaches can reduce the risk of the fortuity but not eliminate it. Every church and religious organization is exposed to the liability of an unforeseen motor vehicle accident, injury on the premises, or other contingency. Sometimes they can be catastrophic. Consider the number of times a church or religious organization transports groups of children or adults in a motor vehicle—even someone's private car, not necessarily a van or bus. One missed stop sign by an inattentive driver can result in multiple deaths, serious physical injuries, and millions of dollars of prospective liability. Neither state nor federal constitutions will protect the church from the liability associated with this fortuity. A religious organization that lacks the funding to meet a judgment is subject to the seizure of its assets, including the church itself, by a successful plaintiff; and some plaintiff's lawyers have stated that they would not mind owning a church.[1] Legal judgments can also be paid off, by court order, in periodic installments in some states. But how enthusiastic is a congregation going to be to contribute its funds knowing that they will be used not for the ongoing ministry of the organization but to pay off a legal judgment that the donors did not bring about and have no particular motive to fund?

Churchgoers and supporters of other religious organizations contribute their offerings to further the missions of these organizations of worship, teaching, evangelism, and serving the needy. These ministries are dependent for their existence on the ongoing flow of support. With this support, the church acquires and builds its places of worship, church schools, camps, retreat centers, and other institutions. Prudent management does not put these assets and ministries at risk for a fortuity.

The only protection for the fortuity of a tort judgment is liability insurance. It serves the same function for churches and religious organizations that it does for individuals, commercial organizations, and other kinds of entities—it spreads the risk over a large base of participants, funds the payment by the insurance premiums paid by all of the participants, and reduces the exposure of the organization's assets and income to the relatively predictable cost of insurance premiums. While one court has held that there is no duty on the part of a church-operated school to purchase insurance,[2] and in at least one state a limitation on charitable immunity is conditioned upon an institution having liability insurance,[3] unless a religious institution is large enough to self-insure and has done so on a planned and well-advised basis, liability insurance should be considered routine and mandatory.

There is a second reason to purchase liability insurance. While the legal system is imperfect, tort judgments are normally awarded to people who have genuinely suffered injuries at the hands of the organization or its personnel who were carrying out its ministry. The responsibility to deal fairly with people suffering such injuries, while recognized by and enforceable within the legal system, is not merely a legal responsibility. Churches and religious organizations should recognize the moral responsibility to those injured by their negligence or other conduct to make them whole. Liability insurance also serves this purpose.

Every injury does not, of course, merit compensation. Claims may be spurious or damages inflated. Often the organization and its personnel were not in fact negligent and did not breach any legal duty to the injured person. But even in such cases, liability insurance serves a further purpose. When suit is brought by an injured person, defense costs alone can be tens of thousands of dollars—and even higher in serious cases. A victory in the courtroom or in an appellate court may be bought at a very high price. Liability insurance will pay the defense costs of victory and thus protect the church against claims that are not well founded.

Liability insurance is not a panacea for tort claims. Many churches and religious organizations have liability insurance policies that do not provide adequate coverage or the kinds of coverage that they should have. Other kinds of exposure cannot be insured at any price. But even the smallest church or religious organization should understand what its liability insurance does and does not cover and should make intentional choices with its insurance agent as to what coverage it wishes to buy.

Check with your denomination or judicatory—some will have coverage available that may be more extensive or less expensive than individual churches can buy on their own.

B. THE AMOUNT OF LIABILITY INSURANCE

Many religious organizations should carry more insurance than they do. Claims of sexual molestation of minors can yield verdicts in the six- or seven-figure range. A single motor vehicle accident that results in death or serious physical injuries can cause liability exposure in the millions of dollars. One lawyer of my acquaintance told me that he would not have less than five million dollars of personal liability coverage since he often drives around with several other lawyers in his car. He has been around the liability system enough to recognize that in one bad accident he could incur seven-figure liability very easily. The right amount of insurance will depend upon the nature of the religious organization, the laws of the state in which it is located posing any limitations on liability or tying such limitations to the purchase of liability insurance, and the advice of its attorney and insurance agent. Adding extra dollars of insurance coverage is not usually high-cost protection and is well worth the investment for the protection against catastrophe that it provides.

C. PERSONS COVERED BY THE INSURANCE POLICY

An insurance policy is a contract, and the scope of coverage will be determined by the terms of the contract. While courts may be sympathetic to people who have difficulty understanding the sometimes-obscure contract language, there is no excuse for not reading the contract and understanding its plain terms.

It is important to understand whether your liability policy covers individual church employees and volunteers as well as the organization itself. Corporations act only through individuals and, when an accident happens, the individual or individuals whose conduct is thought to be responsible for it are frequently sued along with the employing organization, which is alleged to be liable on the basis of respondeat superior (see pp. 88–92). The individual employee or volunteer's personal policy may not provide coverage for acts done in the service of the church. If they are not covered by the church's policy, they may be exposed to the damage claim.

Liability policies are often unclear about who is covered. Frequently, companies issue policies to churches and religious organizations that are designed for commercial enterprises. The policy language simply does not fit. Coverage may be extended, for example, to "executive officers," but it may be unclear in a church context who would be considered an "executive officer." Officers and directors may be covered but the church governing bodies may use different terminology.

When the individual employee or volunteer is sued on account of an injury that occurred when he or she was acting in the scope of carrying out the church's ministry and the insurance policy does not provide coverage, the church is in a dilemma. In most instances, it will have no legal obligation to provide a defense or pay a judgment for the individual. To undertake that obligation may be expensive, even ruinous. On the other hand, if it leaves the employee or volunteer to face the legal system alone, it can cost the organization the services of that individual and others and leave abiding ill will and morale problems.

The best resolution of the dilemma is to be sure your policy covers all employees and volunteers as well as the organization itself. This should not add significantly to the exposure of the insurance company since the respondeat superior doctrine will make the church, and hence its insurer, responsible for the acts of the employees and volunteers in the course of employment, and usually the organization is sued along with the individuals. Thus it should not cause a significant increase in premium.

If your policy's language is unclear, you should clarify it with your insurer. If you receive oral assurances from the insurance agent that certain coverage is provided, confirm it in writing so there will be a record.

D. CLAIMS COVERED BY INSURANCE

Most insurance policies distinguish between "bodily injury" and "personal injury." By "bodily injury" the insurance contract will likely refer to physical injuries or physical manifestations, the kind of things for which you see a doctor. If bodily injury is the only kind of injury to individuals that is covered, there will be no coverage for emotional distress, mental suffering, and the like, at least unless they are accompanied by or lead to physical manifestations.

"Personal injury" is often defined more broadly and may include emotional or mental injuries and damages from such acts as defamation, invasion of privacy, and the like that do not normally result in bodily injury.

For churches and religious organizations, it is important to have the broader coverage afforded for "personal injuries" as well as bodily injury coverage.

Policies normally cover property damage as well. Liability policies apply to damage caused by the insured to the property of others, not to its own property. Naturally, any organization should have adequate property insurance to cover damage to its own property.

Be sure that your liability policy is a general liability policy and includes, for example, employees operating automobiles. Some policies may be limited to premises liability and may not extend coverage to motor vehicle accidents that happen off the property.

There is an important distinction in insurance contracts between "claims made" and "occurrence" policies. The former insures only claims made during the policy period, the latter only occurrences within the policy period. The significant language is usually in the section of the policy called the "insuring agreement." The distinction is particularly important to be aware of when switching policies. If you go from a claims made to an occurrence policy, there will be no coverage for occurrences before the new policy period for which no claim was made during the former policy period. Some protection can usually be asserted in this situation by reporting all events which might give rise to a claim, even if no claim has been asserted, and purchasing a "tail" or extended reporting period, in which newly reported claims for occurrences during the earlier policy period will be covered.

E. CLAIMS NOT COVERED BY INSURANCE

The language of the policy will determine what is covered and what is not. A policy will include an insuring agreement that makes a general statement as to what is covered. It will also include definitions that will be important to understanding the scope of the terms in the insuring agreement. Definitions of, for example, the "insured" and "bodily injury" are important in determining who and what kind of injuries are covered.

The policy will also contain a list of "exclusions." Read these with care. There may be some things that you thought were covered that in fact are removed from coverage by the exclusions.

Most policies will exclude coverage for intentional acts, either by the way the insuring agreement is phrased, by definitions of terms used in the insuring agreement, or by specific exclusions. Thus, acts such as sexual misconduct or molestation of minors, physical assaults, and the like may be outside of coverage. Some companies write specific exclusions for such acts, although you may be able to purchase specific coverage for such things as sexual misconduct. But be aware that some of the most significant liability-generating events may be uninsured and uninsurable. The exclusion for intentional acts will further reinforce noncoverage of such claims as defamation or invasion of privacy unless the policy provides specific coverage for such claims.

Many policies also contain exclusions for criminal conduct. Sexual molestation of minors is also likely to be excluded from coverage by such a provision unless specific coverage for such acts is provided.

Contractual obligations will normally not be covered by insurance.

Subsidiary or affiliated organizations and certain specific activities such as schools and day care centers also may not be covered under a church or religious organization's policy (be sure you know) and need to have separate coverage.

Many policies contain exclusions for professional conduct, in effect a malpractice exclusion. Clergy malpractice is likely not to be covered by a normal liability insurance policy unless special coverage is purchased to provide for it. Despite the theories of court decisions that reject the tort of clergy malpractice in several states, the purchase of clergy malpractice insurance is probably still advisable. Some states and courts have allowed such claims to proceed, at least when the alleged conduct would be tortious in the absence of a specific clergy malpractice tort, as, for example, in cases of sexual misconduct. And even if the claim is not accepted as a valid tort, the defense of the claim can be expensive and insurance will cover the defense costs.

A variation of "malpractice" coverage for organizations and individuals not normally thought of as providing "professional" services is "errors and omissions" insurance. Such coverage is often held by service companies such as insurance or real estate offices; it insures their liability for injuries from their negligence that are usually economic and not covered by liability policies that only cover property damage and bodily or personal injury. Errors and omissions coverage is appropriate for some religious organizations. One parochial school was glad it had purchased it; a court found that the policy covered a damage claim for marital discrimination under state law when it discharged a husband after his wife had resigned.[4]

Another coverage some religious organizations may wish to consider is directors and officers insurance. While directors and officers will be covered under most property damage/bodily or personal injury liability policies, such policies will not cover them for liability for other types of damages attributable to neglect in performing the duties of their office, as, for example, if their neglect of duty causes the organization's assets to be wasted. Suits of this nature are more common in business organizations in which the shareholders who have invested in the corporation are the owners and the persons to whom the directors and officers are ultimately accountable. In a religious organization, however, there may be members or public authorities who can hold the leadership accountable. Directors and officers insurance has been expensive and sometimes difficult to obtain in recent years. Consult your counsel and insurance agent as to the need and availability of such coverage for your organization.

F. WHAT TO DO WHEN AN ACCIDENT HAPPENS OR A PROSPECTIVE CLAIM ARISES

All insurance policies require that the insured give notice of claims or prospective claims. Some policies require that notice be given whenever the insured has reason to believe that circumstances have arisen which may lead to a claim. Others may not require notice until the claim is asserted, which may be done by the injured person or his attorney and does not necessarily mean when suit is filed. You may, however, be able to bring the claim within the policy by giving notice of the facts even if no claim is asserted—a particular concern if you are changing policies. The reasons for the notice provisions are to give the insurer (1) the opportunity to investigate the facts of the claim before they become difficult to reconstruct and (2) the best opportunity to manage and defend a claim properly on your behalf.

Notify your insurance company of the claim as soon as you are aware of the circumstances which may have created it. Whenever someone is injured on the property or in connection with any of the organization's activities, notice should be given to the insurance carrier. Moreover, whenever any circumstances arise which you suspect could give rise to a lawsuit later on, notify the insurance carrier.

Notice should be prompt and by telephone as soon as the claim occurs so that if circumstances warrant an insurance adjustor can make an immediate investigation. It should be followed up, in all instances, with a written notice, preferably by registered or certified mail with return receipt requested so that you have evidence that the notice was given. Insurance carriers who have not been given reasonable and timely notice of a claim may not be obligated to defend it or pay a judgment.

All insurance policies also contain a cooperation clause requiring the insured to cooperate with the insurer in defense of the claim.[5] In practical terms this means that you should (1) turn the management of the claim over to the insurance carrier; (2) not interfere with it in any way or do anything to compromise it or make it more difficult to defend; (3) provide the insurance company with all information and documents that it needs to investigate and defend the claim; and (4) appear in court or at depositions as requested by the insurance company in the conduct of the defense. When you have purchased liability insurance, you have protected yourself by turning the management of liability claims over to the insurer. If you try to take it back again, you risk losing your coverage for the claim. Even if the injury is to a member of the congregation or the church feels a moral obligation to be sure the individual is adequately compensated, it should not interfere with the insurance company's management of the process or do anything to compromise the claim. Insurers are in the business of evaluating, settling, and, when necessary, litigating claims. They are the professionals in this business, not you. They are highly experienced in determining what a claim is worth and the likelihood that a plaintiff will be successful in court. To interfere with a claim management process may not only jeopardize your insurance coverage, it may also be simply bad management.

The obligation to cooperate with the insurance company is of course an obligation to cooperate only in an honest and truthful fashion. If the facts of the accident are helpful to the plaintiff and not to the church, no one expects you, from a legal as well as a moral point of view, to misrepresent them.

G. BIBLICAL DISPUTE RESOLUTION AND INSURANCE

Churches that believe in and practice biblical dispute resolution, discussed in chapter 19, may find themselves in a genuine dilemma when a claim involves a member of their own congregation or another believer. You cannot impose a biblical dispute resolution procedure on an insurance contract that does not provide for it or on a claimant who has not agreed to it. When the parties do want it in an insured claim, the insurer is a necessary party to any financial implementation. Consider thoughtfully and prayerfully whether you view an insured claim, even if by a church member or fellow believer, to be subject to biblical dispute resolution procedures or whether the reality of the dispute is not between the injured party and the insurance company. The insurer needs no reconciliation and forgiveness from the injured party. It will handle the matter based on a business judgment of the cost of defense, the probability of the plaintiff's success, and the likely amount of judgment, not on the basis of biblical principles, no matter how important those principles may be to the church in the internal management of the issue.

If you believe that, despite insurance coverage for the injury, your religious beliefs mandate a biblical dispute resolution procedure, you may have to manage the claim outside the insurance process and risk losing the protection of your insurance contract.

H. SUMMARY OF INSURANCE CONCERNS

1. Carry enough liability insurance. Consult your attorney and insurance agent for the appropriate amount. A million dollars is not excessive.
2. Cover your governing body, pastor, employees, and volunteers while working for the church, not just the church for their acts. This may require policy amendments or clarification in writing of who is covered.
3. Carry "personal injury" as well as "bodily injury" and "property damage" coverage.
4. When changing policies, consult your attorney and insurance agent to avoid coverage gaps.
5. Consider buying insurance that will cover sexual misconduct toward minors, which is often not covered by normal liability insurance policies.
6. Consider buying clergy malpractice coverage. Even though most courts have not allowed the claim, many states have not addressed it, and the insurance will cover defense costs for such claims.
7. Be sure any subsidiary or affiliated organizations or activities are adequately insured—schools, day care centers, counseling centers, and the like.
8. Review with your insurance agent and attorney the need for other forms of coverage such as "errors and omissions" and "directors and officers" coverage.
9. Notify your insurer promptly (and keep a record) of any claims or potential claims.
10. Let your insurer handle claims covered by insurance.

Weaving Law and Church Together

Yet I reserve seven thousand in Israel—
all whose knees have not bowed down to
Baal and all whose mouths have not
kissed him. (1 Kings 19:18)

The origins of this book lie in my conviction that those who shepherd the church in
America today need to understand the
shape and nature of the American legal system—not just as a bundle of rules but how
it was formed, how it operates, and how it
integrates with and impacts upon the work
they do for God's kingdom.

Before I began writing, I corresponded
with a number of Christian attorneys and
solicited their experiences. Their comments
confirmed my conviction and reflected the
depth and breadth of concern. How, they
wrote, does the church structure itself to
assure a membership that shares and maintains a continuity of belief? What should
the authority structure be between pastor,
boards, and members; and how do you
express it? How does the church protect
itself from liability for the acts of errant
leaders? Does a church have a greater obligation than other employers to investigate
the fitness of its clergy because it encour-
ages parishioners to look to them for counsel or even forgiveness? Must the church
bookstore collect sales taxes? What uses
qualify for property tax exemption? Who
can receive a tax-free housing allowance?
How does receipt of federal funding impact
religious freedom? How should a church
manage restricted gifts? Can the health
department keep the church from selling
homemade chili at the annual bazaar?

This book is not the definitive answer to
these and the multitude of other legal issues

confronting the church. At most, it can raise
awareness of the issues and provide context
for the answers. Each problem is a little different and must be worked out by the
churches and religious organizations
involved with the advice of their counsel.
Often the questions are in gray areas of the
law where judgments must be made in
the absence of definitive guidelines.

One of the personal blessings during the
time I have devoted to this work has been
the opportunity to make the acquaintance,
if sometimes only through the written word,
of a cadre of believing attorneys and law
professors who are working to fill the voids
in legal knowledge available to the church.
Many of their names appear in footnotes
and references herein. They include Sam
Ericsson, who successfully litigated the
Nally clergy malpractice case and later
served as executive director of the Christian Legal Society; Sam Casey, dean of the
Simon Greenleaf School of Law, who left a
prosperous position as a partner in a California firm to become the director of the
Western Center for Law and Religious
Freedom and who shared with me over
lunch his vision of raising a generation of
Christian lawyers who would serve the wid-
owed, orphaned, and needy of society out
of love of Christ; such committed writers as
Lynn Buzzard and his colleagues at the
School of Law at Campbell University in
North Carolina, who have prepared monographs on clergy confidentiality and aspects
of federal tax law; Assembly of God counsel Richard Hammar whose book *Pastor,
Church, and Law* covers a wide range of
legal issues of interest to churches and
clergy and whose guides to tax and copy-

right law for church and clergy are invaluable; Michael McConnell of the University of Chicago, who authored the epic examination of the history of the Free Exercise Clause published in the *Harvard Law Review* in 1990; Edward McGlynn Gaffney, Jr., dean of Valparaiso University School of Law, and his colleagues who have worked on the difficult issues of ascending liability and other matters of concern to churches and religiously affiliated organizations; and Carl H. Esbeck of the University of Missouri, who tracked the history and theology, as well as the jurisprudence, of church discipline in his 1990 masterpiece published in the *West Virginia Law Review*. These works are more than scholarship or commercial publishing ventures; they are works of love and caring for the church of Jesus Christ. These works of his servants will aid the church to honor him by being holy and blameless in the world and by setting an example above criticism for those whose way of life calls out for redemption.[1]

Oliver Wendell Holmes, in his essay "The Common Law," wrote, "The life of the law has not been logic: it has been experience."[2] So is the life of the law as it applies to religious organizations the life of their experience. It is the experience of Bridget Mergens, a teenager from Nebraska, whose stand before the Omaha School Board led to the Supreme Court ruling upholding the constitutionality of the Equal Access Act that allowed Bible clubs to meet in public schools; of Amish parent Jonas Yoder, who protected his right to educate his children as the Amish faith teaches; of the Boston Jesuits who resisted surrendering control of their church to the local landmark commission; and of thousands of other believers across the land who have stood against the antireligious tide and encroaching new religions in the public schools, maintained the presence and good news of the gospel on public and private campuses where adherence to Judeo-Christian morality is often perceived as a phobia or hate crime, and wrestled with all of the questions discussed within these covers.

It is sometimes difficult to see how it all fits together, but it does. Michael Woodruff, former director of the Center for Law and Religious Freedom, spoke to a gathering of Christian attorneys at Sandy Cove, Maryland, in the fall of 1989, about what he called "the view from thirty thousand feet." He recalled the pattern of the tribes of Israel camped around the tabernacle in the Sinai desert, each with thousands of people organized and arranged, and how the representatives of the tribes came in to make their offerings at the tabernacle, each at his time and in his turn to fulfill the instruction of the law. To the single Israelite camped out in the midst of the pack, the arrangement and movement of the people and tribes would look like uncoordinated confusion, with no order or reason. But to an observer of this mass of humanity looking down from thirty thousand feet, all would be in perfect harmony, reflecting a design and pattern intended by a loving Creator and law giver.

My prayer, in concluding this book, is that God will place it where it can be used by His servants to bring honor and glory to Him in rightly ordering the relations of His church with the secular world in which it dwells until His kingdom comes.

Constitution of the United States of America

We the People of the United States in order to form a more perfect Union, establish Justice, insure domestic Tranquillity, provide for the common defence, promote the general Welfare, and secure the Blessings of Liberty to ourselves and our Posterity, do ordain and establish this CONSTITUTION for the United States of America.

ARTICLE I.

SECTION 1. All legislative Powers herein granted shall be vested in a Congress of the United States, which shall consist of a Senate and House of Representatives.

SECTION 2. 1. The House of Representatives shall be composed of Members chosen every second Year by the People of the several States, and the Electors in each State shall have the Qualifications requisite for Electors of the most numerous Branch of the State Legislature.

2. No Person shall be a Representative who shall not have attained to the Age of twenty five Years, and been seven Years a Citizen of the United States, and who shall not, when elected, be an Inhabitant of that State in which he shall be chosen.

3. Representatives and direct Taxes shall be apportioned among the several States which may be included within this Union, according to their respective Numbers, which shall be determined by adding to the whole Number of free Persons, including those bound to Service for a Term of Years, and excluding Indians not taxed, three fifths of all other Persons. The actual Enumeration shall be made within three Years after the first Meeting of the Congress of the United States, and within every subsequent Term of ten Years, in such Manner as they shall by Law direct. The Number of Representatives shall not exceed one for every thirty Thousand, but each State shall have at Least one Representative; and until such enumeration shall be made, the State of New Hampshire shall be entitled to chuse three, Massachusetts eight, Rhode-Island and Providence Plantations one, Connecticut five, New-York six, New Jersey four, Pennsylvania eight, Delaware one, Maryland six, Virginia ten, North Carolina five, South Carolina five, and Georgia three.

4. When vacancies happen in the Representation from any State, the Executive Authority thereof shall issue Writs of Election to fill such Vacancies.

5. The House of Representatives shall chuse their Speaker and other Officers; and shall have the sole Power of Impeachment.

SECTION 3. 1. The Senate of the United States shall be composed of two Senators from each State, chosen by the Legislature thereof, for six Years; and each Senator shall have one Vote.

2. Immediately after they shall be assembled in Consequence of the first Election, they shall be divided as equally as may be into three Classes. The Seats of the Senators of the first Class shall be vacated at the Expiration of the second Year, of the second Class at the Expiration of the fourth Year, and of the third Class at the Expiration of the sixth Year, so that one-third may be chosen every second Year; and if Vacancies happen by Resignation, or otherwise, during the Recess of the Legislature of any

State, the Executive thereof may make temporary Appointments until the next Meeting of the Legislature, which shall then fill such Vacancies.

3. No Person shall be a Senator who shall not have attained to the Age of thirty Years, and been nine Years a Citizen of the United States, and who shall not, when elected, be an Inhabitant of that State for which he shall be chosen.

4. The Vice President of the United States shall be President of the Senate, but shall have no Vote, unless they be equally divided.

5. The Senate shall chuse their other Officers, and also a President pro tempore, in the Absence of the Vice President, or when he shall exercise the office of President of the United States.

6. The Senate shall have the sole Power to try all Impeachments. When sitting for that Purpose, they shall be on Oath or Affirmation. When the President of the United States is tried, the Chief Justice shall preside: And no Person shall be convicted without the Concurrence of two thirds of the Members present.

7. Judgment in Cases of Impeachment shall not extend further than to removal from Office, and Disqualification to hold and enjoy any Office of honour, Trust or Profit under the United States: but the Party convicted shall nevertheless be liable and subject to Indictment, Trial, Judgment and Punishment, according to Law.

SECTION 4. 1. The Times, Places and Manner of holding Elections for Senators and Representatives, shall be prescribed in each State by the Legislature thereof; but the Congress may at any time by Law make or alter such Regulations, except as to the Places of chusing Senators.

2. The Congress shall assemble at least once in every Year, and such Meeting shall be on the first Monday in December, unless they shall by Law appoint a different Day.

SECTION 5. 1. Each House shall be the Judge of the Elections, Returns and Qualifications of its own Members, and a Majority of each shall constitute a Quorum to do business; but a smaller Number may adjourn from day to day, and may be authorized to compel the Attendance of absent Members, in such Manner, and under such Penalties as each House may provide.

2. Each House may determine the Rules of its Proceedings, punish its Members for disorderly Behaviour, and, with the Concurrence of two thirds, expel a Member.

3. Each House shall keep a Journal of its Proceedings, and from time to time publish the same, excepting such Parts as may in their Judgment require Secrecy; and the Yeas and Nays of the Members of either House on any question shall, at the Desire of one fifth of those Present, be entered on the Journal.

4. Neither House, during the Session of Congress, shall, without the Consent of the other, adjourn for more than three days, nor to any other Place than that in which the two Houses shall be sitting.

SECTION 6. 1. The Senators and Representatives shall receive a Compensation for their Services, to be ascertained by Law, and paid out of the Treasury of the United States. They shall in all Cases, except Treason, Felony and Breach of the Peace, be privileged from Arrest during their Attendance at the Session of their respective Houses, and in going to and returning from the same; and for any Speech or Debate in either House, they shall not be questioned in any other Place.

2. No Senator or Representative shall, during the Time for which he was elected, be appointed to any civil Office under the Authority of the United States, which shall have been created, or the Emoluments whereof shall have been encreased during such time; and no Person holding any Office under the United States, shall be a member of either House during his Continuance in Office.

SECTION 7. 1. All Bills for raising Revenue shall originate in the House of Representatives; but the Senate may propose or concur with Amendments as on other Bills.

2. Every Bill which shall have passed the House of Representatives and the Senate, shall, before it become a Law, be presented to the President of the United States; If he approve he shall sign it, but if not he shall return it, with his Objections to that House

in which it shall have originated, who shall enter the Objections at large on their Journal, and proceed to reconsider it. If after such Reconsideration two thirds of that House shall agree to pass the Bill, it shall be sent, together with the Objections, to the other House, by which it shall likewise be reconsidered, and if approved by two thirds of that House, it shall become a Law. But in all such Cases the Votes of both Houses shall be determined by yeas and Nays, and the Names of the Persons voting for and against the Bill shall be entered on the Journal of each House respectively. If any Bill shall not be returned by the President within ten Days (Sundays excepted) after it shall have been presented to him, the Same shall be a Law, in like Manner as if he had signed it, unless the Congress by their Adjournment prevent its Return, in which Case it shall not be a Law.

3. Every Order, Resolution, or Vote to which the Concurrence of the Senate and House of Representatives may be necessary (except on a question of Adjournment) shall be presented to the President of the United States; and before the same shall take Effect, shall be approved by him, or being disapproved by him, shall be repassed by two thirds of the Senate and House of Representatives, according to the Rules and Limitations prescribed in the Case of a Bill.

SECTION 8. The Congress shall have Power 1. To lay and collect Taxes, Duties, Imposts and Excises, to pay the Debts and provide for the common Defence and general Welfare of the United States; but all Duties, Imposts and Excises shall be uniform throughout the United States;

2. To borrow Money on the credit of the United States;

3. To regulate Commerce with foreign Nations, and among the several States, and with the Indian Tribes;

4. To establish a uniform Rule of Naturalization, and uniform Laws on the subject of Bankruptcies throughout the United States;

5. To coin Money, regulate the Value thereof, and of foreign Coin, and fix the Standard of Weights and Measures;

6. To provide for the Punishment of counterfeiting the Securities and current Coin of the United States;

7. To establish Post Offices and post Roads;

8. To promote the Progress of Science and useful Arts, by securing for limited Times to Authors and Inventors the exclusive Right to their respective Writings and Discoveries;

9. To constitute Tribunals inferior to the supreme Court;

10. To define and punish Piracies and Felonies commited on the high Seas, and Offences against the Law of Nations;

11. To declare War, grant Letters of Marque and Reprisal, and make Rules concerning Captures on Land and Water;

12. To raise and support Armies, but no Appropriation of Money to that Use shall be for a longer Term than two Years;

13. To provide and maintain a Navy;

14. To make Rules for the Government and Regulation of the land and naval Forces;

15. To provide for calling forth the Militia to execute the Laws of the Union, suppress Insurrections and repel Invasions;

16. To provide for organizing, arming, and disciplining, the Militia, and for governing such Part of them as may be employed in the Service of the United States, reserving to the States respectively, the Appointment of the Officers, and the Authority of training the Militia according to the discipline prescribed by Congress;

17. To exercise exclusive Legislation in all Cases whatsoever, over such District (not exceeding ten Miles square) as may, by Cession of particular States, and the Acceptance of Congress, become the Seat of the Government of the United States, and to exercise like Authority over all Places purchased by the Consent of the Legislature of the State in which the same shall be, for the Erection of Forts, Magazines, Arsenals, Dock-Yards, and other needful Buildings;—And

18. To make all Laws which shall be necessary and proper for carrying into Execution the foregoing Powers, and all other Powers vested by this Constitution in the Government of the United States, or in any Department or Officer thereof.

SECTION 9. 1. The Migration or Importation of such Persons as any of the States now existing shall think proper to admit, shall not be prohibited by the Congress prior to the Year one thousand eight hundred and eight, but a Tax or Duty may be imposed on such Importation, not exceeding ten dollars for each Person.

2. The Privilege of the Writ of Habeas Corpus shall not be suspended, unless when in Cases of Rebellion or Invasion the public Safety may require it.

3. No Bill of Attainder or ex post facto Law shall be passed.

4. No Capitation, or other direct, Tax shall be laid, unless in Proportion to the Census or Enumeration herein before directed to be taken.

5. No Tax or Duty shall be laid on Articles exported from any States.

6. No Preference shall be given by any Regulation of Commerce or Revenue to the Ports of one State over those of another: nor shall Vessels bound to, or from, one State, be obliged to enter, clear, or pay Duties in another.

7. No Money shall be drawn from the Treasury, but in consequence of Appropriations made by Law; and a regular Statement and Account of the Receipts and Expenditures of all public Money shall be published from time to time.

8. No Title of Nobility shall be granted by the United States: And no Person holding any Office of Profit or Trust under them, shall, without the Consent of the Congress, accept of any present, Emolument, Office, or Title, of any kind whatever, from any King, Prince, or foreign State.

SECTION 10. 1. No State shall enter into any Treaty, Alliance, or Confederation; grant Letters of Marque and Reprisal; coin Money; emit Bills of Credit; make any Thing but gold and silver Coin a Tender in Payment of Debts; pass any Bill of Attainder, ex post facto Law, or Law impairing the Obligation of Contracts, or grant any Title of Nobility.

2. No State shall, without the Consent of the Congress, lay any Imposts or Duties on Imports or Exports, except what may be absolutely necessary for executing it's inspection Laws: and the net Produce of all Duties and Imposts, laid by any State on Imports or Exports, shall be for the Use of the Treasury of the United States; and all such Laws shall be subject to the revision and Controul of the Congress.

3. No State shall, without the Consent of Congress, lay any Duty of Tonnage, keep Troops, or Ships of War in time of Peace, enter into any Agreement or Compact with another State, or with a foreign Power, or engage in War, unless actually invaded, or in such imminent Danger as will not admit of Delay.

ARTICLE II.

SECTION 1. 1. The executive Power shall be vested in a President of the United States of America. He shall hold his Office during the Term of four Years, and, together with the Vice President, chosen for the same Term, be elected, as follows

2. Each State shall appoint, in such Manner as the Legislature thereof may direct, a Number of Electors, equal to the whole Number of Senators and Representatives to which the State may be entitled in the Congress: but no Senator or Representative, or Person holding an Office of Trust or Profit under the United States, shall be appointed an Elector.

The Electors shall meet in their respective States, and vote by Ballot for two Persons, of whom one at least shall not be an Inhabitant of the same State with themselves. And they shall make a List of all the Persons voted for, and of the Number of Votes for each; which List they shall sign and certify, and transmit sealed to the Seat of the Government of the United States, directed to the President of the Senate. The President of the Senate shall, in the Presence of the Senate and House of Representatives, open all the Certificates, and the Votes shall then be counted. The Person having the greatest Number of Votes shall be the President, if such Number be a Majority of the whole Number of Electors appointed; and if there be more than one who have such Majority, and have an equal Number of Votes, then the House of Representatives shall immediately chuse by Ballot one of them for President; and if no Person have a Majority, then from the five highest on the List the said House shall in like Manner chuse the President. But in chusing the President, the Votes shall be taken by States, the Representation from each State having one Vote; A quorum for this Purpose shall consist of a Member or Members from two thirds of the States, and a Majority of all the States shall be necessary to a Choice. In every Case, after the Choice of the President, the Person having the greatest Number of Votes of the Electors shall be the Vice President. But if there should remain two or more who have equal Votes, the Senate shall chuse from them by Ballot the Vice President.

3. The Congress may determine the Time of chusing the Electors, and the Day on which they shall give their Votes; which Day shall be the same throughout the United States.

4. No Person except a natural born Citizen, or a Citizen of the United States, at the time of the Adoption of this Constitution, shall be eligible to the Office of President; neither shall any Person be eligible to that Office who shall not have attained to the Age of thirty five Years, and been fourteen Years a Resident within the United States.

5. In Case of the Removal of the President from Office, or of his Death, Resignation, or Inability to discharge the Powers and Duties of the said Office, the same shall devolve on the Vice President, and the Congress may by Law provide for the Case of Removal, Death, Resignation or Inability, both of the President and Vice President, declaring what Officer shall then act as President, and such Officer shall act accordingly, until the Disability be removed, or a President shall be elected.

6. The President shall, at stated Times, receive for his Services, a Compensation, which shall neither be encreased nor diminished during the Period for which he shall have been elected, and he shall not receive within that Period any other Emolument from the United States, or any of them.

7. Before he enter on the Execution of his Office, he shall take the following Oath or Affirmation:—

"I do solemnly swear (or affirm) that I will faithfully execute the Office of "President of the United States, and will to the best of my Ability, preserve, protect and defend the Constitution of the United States."

SECTION 2. 1. The President shall be Commander in Chief of the Army and Navy of the United States, and of the Militia of the several States, when called into the actual Service of the United States; he may require the Opinion, in writing, of the principal Officer in each of the executive Departments, upon any Subject relating to the Duties of their respective Offices, and he shall have Power to grant Reprieves and Pardons for Offences against the United States, except in Cases of Impeachment.

2. He shall have Power, by and with the Advice and Consent of the Senate, to make Treaties, provided two thirds of the Senators present concur; and he shall nominate, and by and with the Advice and Consent of the Senate, shall appoint Ambassadors, other public Ministers and Consuls, Judges of the supreme Court, and all other Officers of the United States, whose Appointments are not herein otherwise provided for, and which shall be established by Law: but the Congress may by Law vest the Appointment of such inferior Officers, as they think proper, in the President alone, in the Courts of Law, or in the Heads of Departments.

3. The President shall have Power to fill up all Vacancies that may happen during the Recess of the Senate, by granting Commissions which shall expire at the End of their next Session.

SECTION 3. He shall from time to time give to the Congress Information of the State of the Union, and recommend to their Consideration such Measures as he shall judge necessary and expedient; he may, on extraordinary Occasions, convene both Houses, or either of them, and in Case of Disagreement between them, with Respect to the time of Adjournment, he may adjourn them to such Time as he shall think proper; he shall receive Ambassadors and other public Ministers; he shall take Care that the Laws be faithfully executed, and shall Commission all the officers of the United States.

SECTION. 4. The President, Vice President and all civil Officers of the United States, shall be removed from Office on Impeachment for, and Conviction of, Treason, Bribery, or other high Crimes and Misdemeanors.

ARTICLE III

SECTION 1. The judicial Power of the United States, shall be vested in one supreme Court, and in such inferior Courts as the Congress may from time to time ordain and establish. The Judges, both of the supreme and inferior Courts, shall hold their Offices during good Behavior, and shall, at stated Times, receive for their Services, a Compensation, which shall not be diminished during their Continuance in Office.

SECTION 2. 1. The judicial Power shall extend to all Cases, in Law and Equity, arising under this Constitution, the Laws of the United States, and Treaties made, or which shall be made, under their Authority;—to all Cases affecting Ambassadors, other public Ministers, and Consuls;—to all Cases of admiralty and maritime Jurisdiction;—to Controversies to which the United States shall be a Party;—to Controversies between two or more States;—between a State and Citizens of another State;—between Citizens of different States,—between Citizens of the same State claiming Lands under Grants of different States, and between a State, or the Citizens thereof, and foreign States, Citizens or Subjects.

2. In all Cases affecting Ambassadors, other public Ministers and Consuls, and those in which a State shall be Party, the supreme Court shall have original Jurisdiction. In all the other Cases before mentioned, the supreme Court shall have appellate Jurisdiction, both as to Law and Fact, with such Exceptions, and under such Regulations as the Congress shall make.

3. The Trial of all Crimes, except in Cases of Impeachment, shall be by Jury; and such Trial shall be held in the State where the said Crimes shall have been committed; but when not committed within any State, the Trial shall be at such Place or Places as the Congress may by Law have directed.

SECTION 3. 1. Treason against the United States, shall consist only in levying War against them, or in adhering to their Enemies, giving them Aid and Comfort. No Person shall be convicted of Treason unless on the Testimony of two Witnesses to the same overt Act, or on Confession in open Court.

2. The Congress shall have Power to declare the Punishment of Treason, but no Attainder of Treason shall work Corruption of Blood, or Forfeiture except during the Life of the Person attainted.

ARTICLE IV.

SECTION 1. Full Faith and Credit shall be given in each State to the public Acts, Records, and judicial Proceedings of every other State. And the Congress may by general Laws prescribe the Manner in which such Acts, Records and Proceedings shall be proved, and the Effect thereof.

SECTION 2. 1. The Citizens of each State shall be entitled to all Privileges and Immunities of Citizens in the several States.

2. A Person charged in any State with Treason, Felony, or other Crime, who shall flee from Justice, and be found in another State, shall on Demand of the executive Authority of the State from which he fled, be delivered up, to be removed to the State having Jurisdiction of the Crime.

3. No Person held to Service or Labour in one State, under the Laws thereof, escaping into another, shall, in Consequence of any Law or Regulation therein, be discharged from such Service or Labour, but shall be delivered up on Claim of the Party to whom such Service or Labour may be due.

SECTION 3. 1. New States may be admitted by the Congress into this Union; but no new State shall be formed or erected within the Jurisdiction of any other State; nor any State be formed by the Junction of two or more States, or Parts of States, without the Consent of the Legislatures of the States concerned as well as of the Congress.

2. The Congress shall have Power to dispose of and make all needful Rules and Regulations respecting the Territory or

other Property belonging to the United States; and nothing in this Constitution shall be so construed as to Prejudice any Claims of the United States, or of any particular State.

SECTION 4. The United States shall guarantee to every State in this Union a Republican Form of Government, and shall protect each of them against Invasion; and on Application of the Legislature, or of the Executive (when the Legislature cannot be convened) against domestic Violence.

ARTICLE V.

The Congress, whenever two thirds of both Houses shall deem it necessary, shall propose Amendments to this Constitution, or, on the Application of the Legislatures of two thirds of the several States, shall call a Convention for proposing Amendments, which, in either Case, shall be valid to all Intents and Purposes, as Part of this Constitution, when ratified by the Legislatures of three fourths of the several States, or by Conventions in three fourths thereof, as the one or the other Mode of Ratification may be proposed by the Congress; Provided that no Amendment which may be made prior to the Year one thousand eight hundred and eight shall in any Manner affect the first and fourth Clauses in the Ninth Section of the first Article; and that no State, without its Consent, shall be deprived of its equal Suffrage in the Senate.

ARTICLE VI.

1. All Debts contracted and Engagements entered into, before the Adoption of this Constitution, shall be as valid against the United States under this Constitution, as under the Confederation.

2. This Constitution, and the Laws of the United States which shall be made in Pursuance thereof; and all Treaties made, or which shall be made in Pursuance thereof; and all Treaties made, or which shall be made, under the Authority of the United States, shall be the supreme Law of the Land; and the Judges in every State shall be bound thereby, any Thing in the Constitution or Laws of any State to the Contrary notwithstanding.

3. The Senators and Representatives before mentioned, and the Members of the several State Legislatures, and all executive and judicial Officers, both of the United States and of the several States, shall be bound by Oath or Affirmation, to support this Constitution; but no religious Test shall ever be required as a Qualification to any Office or public Trust under the United States.

ARTICLE VII.

The Ratification of the Conventions of nine States, shall be sufficient for the Establishment of this Constitution between the States so ratifying the Same.

DONE in Convention by the Unanimous Consent of the States present the Seventeenth Day of September in the Year of our Lord one thousand seven hundred and Eighty seven and of the Independence of the United States of America the Twelfth **In Witness** whereof We have hereunto subscribed our Names,

Go. WASHINGTON—
Presidt and Deputy from Virginia

NEW HAMPSHIRE

John Langdon,   Nicholas Gilman.

MASSACHUSETTS.

Nathaniel Gorham,   Rufus King.

CONNECTICUT

Wm. Saml. Johnson,   Roger Sherman.

NEW YORK

Alexander Hamilton.

NEW JERSEY

Wil: Livingston,   David Brearley,
Wm. Paterson,   Jona. Dayton.

PENNSYLVANIA

B. Franklin,   Thomas Mifflin,
Robt. Morris,   Geo: Clymer,
Thos. Fitz Simons,   Jared Ingersoll,
James Wilson,   Gouv: Morris.

DELAWARE

Geo: Read,   Gunning Bedford, Jun.
John Dickinson,   Richard Bassett,
Jaco: Broom.

MARYLAND

James McHenry,   Dan: of St. Thos. Jenifer,
Danl. Carroll.

VIRGINIA

John Blair,   James Madison, Jr.
I.- 47

NORTH CAROLINA

Wm. Bount,   Rich'd Dobbs Spaight,
Hu. Williamson.

SOUTH CAROLINA

J. Rutledge,   Charles Cotesworth Pinckney,
Charles Pinckney,   Pierce Butler.

GEORGIA

William Few,   Abr. Baldwin.

            Attest: WILLIAM JACKSON,
                                          Secretary

ARTICLES
IN ADDITION TO, AND AMENDMENT OF,
THE CONSTITUTION OF THE UNITED STATES OF AMERICA.

Proposed by Congress, and Ratified by the Legislatures of the Several States, Pursuant to the Fifth Article of the Original Constitution.

(ARTICLE I)

Congress shall make no law respecting an establishment of religion, or prohibiting the free exercise thereof; or abridging the freedom of speech, or of the press; or the right of the people peaceably to assemble, and to petition the Government for a redress of grievances.

(ARTICLE II)

A well regulated Militia, being necessary to the security of a free State, the right of the people to keep and bear Arms, shall not be infringed.

(ARTICLE III)

No Soldier shall, in time of peace be quartered in any house, without the consent of the Owner, nor in time of war, but in a manner to be prescribed by law.

(ARTICLE IV)

The right of the people to be secure in their persons, houses, papers, and effects, against unreasonable searches and seizures, shall not be violated, and no Warrants shall issue, but upon probable cause, supported by Oath or affirmation, and particularly describing the place to be searched, and the persons or things to be seized.

(ARTICLE V)

No person shall be held to answer for a capital, or otherwise infamous crime, unless on a presentment or indictment of a Grand Jury, except in cases arising in the land or naval forces, or in the Militia, when in actual service in time of War or public danger; nor shall any person be subject for the same offence to be twice put in jeopardy of life or limb; nor shall be compelled in any Criminal Case to be a witness against himself, nor be deprived of life, liberty, or property, without due process of law.

(ARTICLE VI)

In all criminal prosecutions, the accused shall enjoy the right to a speedy and public trial, by an impartial jury of the State and district wherein the crime shall have been committed, which district shall have been previously ascertained by law, and to be informed of the nature and cause of the accusation; to be confronted with the witnesses against him; to have Compulsory process for obtaining Witnesses in his favour, and to have the Assistance of Counsel for his defence.

(ARTICLE VII)

In Suits at common law, where the value in controversy shall exceed twenty dollars,

the right of trial by jury shall be preserved, and no fact tried by a jury, shall be otherwise re-examined in any Court of the United States, than according to the rules of the common law.

(ARTICLE VIII)

Excessive bail shall not be required, nor excessive fines imposed, nor cruel and unusual punishments inflicted.

(ARTICLE IX)

The enumeration in the Constitution, of certain rights, shall not be construed to deny or disparage others retained by the people.

(ARTICLE X)

The powers not delegated to the United States by the Constitution, nor prohibited by it to the States, are reserved to the States respectively, or to the people.

(ARTICLE XI)

The Judicial power of the United States shall not be construed to extend to any suit in law or equity, commenced or prosecuted against one of the United States by Citizens of another State, or by Citizens or Subjects of any Foreign State.

(ARTICLE XII)

The Electors shall meet in their respective states, and vote by ballot for President and Vice President, one of whom, at least, shall not be an inhabitant of the same states with themselves; they shall name in their ballots the person voted for as President, and in distinct ballots the person voted for as Vice-President, and they shall make distinct lists of all persons voted for as President, and of all persons voted for as Vice-President, and of the number of votes for each, which lists they shall sign and certify, and transmit sealed to the seat of the government of the United States, directed to the President of the Senate; —The President of the Senate shall, in presence of the Senate and House of Representatives, open all the certificates and the votes shall then be counted;—The person having the greatest number of votes for President, shall be the President, if such number be a majority of the whole number of Electors appointed; and if no person have such majority, then from the persons having the highest numbers not exceeding three on the list of those voted for as President, the House of Representatives shall choose immediately, by ballot, the President. But in choosing the President, the votes shall be taken by states, the representation from each state having one vote; a quorum for this purpose shall consist of a member or members from two-thirds of the states, and a majority of all the states shall be necessary to a choice. And if the House of Representatives shall not choose a President whenever the right of choice shall devolve upon them, before the fourth day of March next following, then the Vice-President shall act as President, as in the case of the death or other constitutional disability of the President.—The person having the greatest number of votes as Vice-President, shall be the Vice-President, if such number be a majority of the whole number of Electors appointed, and if no person have a majority, then from the two highest numbers on the list, the Senate shall choose the Vice-President; a quorum for the purpose shall consist of two-thirds of the whole number of Senators, and a majority of the whole number shall be necessary to a choice. But no person constitutionally ineligible to the office of President shall be eligible to that of Vice-President of the United States.

AMENDMENT XIII

SECTION 1. Neither slavery nor involuntary servitude, except as a punishment for crime whereof the party shall have been duly convicted, shall exist within the United States, or any place subject to their jurisdiction.

SECTION 2. Congress shall have power to enforce this article by appropriate legislation.

AMENDMENT XIV

SECTION 1. All persons born or naturalized in the United States and subject to the jurisdiction thereof, are citizens of the United States and of the State wherein they reside. No State shall make or enforce any law which shall abridge the privileges or immunities of citizens of the United States; nor shall any State deprive any person of life, liberty, or property, without due process of law; nor deny to any person within its jurisdiction the equal protection of the laws.

SECTION 2. Representatives shall be apportioned among the several States according to their respective numbers, counting the whole number of persons in each State, excluding Indians not taxed. But when the right to vote at any election for the choice of electors for President and Vice President of the United States, Representatives in Congress, the Executive and Judicial officers of a State or the members of the Legislature thereof, is denied to any of the male inhabitants of such State, being twenty-one years of age, and citizens of the United States, or in any way abridged, except for participation in rebellion, or other crime, the basis of representation therein shall be reduced in the proportion which the number of such male citizens shall bear to the whole number of male citizens twenty-one years of age in such State.

SECTION 3. No person shall be a Senator or Representative in Congress, or elector of President and Vice President, or hold any office, civil or military, under the United States, or under any State, who, having previously taken an oath, as a member of Congress, or as an officer of the United States or as a member of any State legislature, or as an executive or judicial officer of any State, to support the Constitution of the United States, shall have engaged in insurrection or rebellion against the same, or given aid or comfort to the enemies thereof. But Congress may by a vote of two-thirds of each House, remove such disability.

SECTION 4. The validity of the public debt of the United States, authorized by law, including debts incurred for payment of pensions and bounties for services in suppressing insurrection or rebellion, shall not be questioned. But neither the United States nor any State shall assume or pay any debt or obligation incurred in aid of insurrection or rebellion against the United States or any claim for the loss or emancipaton of any slave; but all such debts, obligations and claims shall be held illegal and void.

SECTION 5. The Congress shall have power to enforce, by appropriate legislation, the provisions of this article.

AMENDMENT XV

SECTION 1. The right of citizens of the United States to vote shall not be denied or abridged by the United States or by any State on account of race, color, or previous condition of servitude.

SECTION 2. The Congress shall have power to enforce this article by appropriate legislation.

AMENDMENT XVI

The Congress shall have power to lay and collect taxes on incomes, from whatever source derived, without apportionment among the several States, and without regard to any census or enumeration.

AMENDMENT XVII

The Senate of the United States shall be composed of two Senators from each State, elected by the people thereof, for six years; and each Senator shall have one vote. The electors in each State shall have the qualifications requisite for electors of the most numerous branch of the State legislatures.

When vacancies happen in the representation of any State in the Senate, the executive authority of such State shall issue writs of election to fill such vacancies; *Provided,* That the legislature of any State may empower the executive thereof to make temporary appointments until the people fill the vacancies by election as the legislature may direct.

This amendment shall not be so construed as to affect the election or term of any Senator chosen before it becomes valid as part of the Constitution.

AMENDMENT XVIII

SECTION 1. After one year from the ratification of this article the manufacture, sale, or transportation of intoxicating liquors within, the importation thereof into, or the exportation thereof from the United States and all territory subject to the jurisdiction thereof for beverage purposes is hereby prohibited.

SECTION 2. The Congress and the several States shall have concurrent power to enforce this article by appropriate legislation.

SECTION 3. This article shall be inoperative unless it shall have been ratified as an amendment to the Constitution by the legislatures of the several States, as provided in the Constitution, within seven years from the date of the submission hereof to the States by the Congress.

AMENDMENT XIX

The right of citizens of the United States to vote shall not be denied or abridged by the United States or by any State on account of sex.

Congress shall have power to enforce this article by appropriate legislation.

AMENDMENT XX

SECTION 1. The terms of the President and Vice President shall end at noon on the 20th day of January, and the terms of Senators and Representatives at noon on the 3d day of January, of the years in which such terms would have ended if this article had not been ratified; and the terms of their successors shall then begin.

SECTION 2. The Congress shall assemble at least once in every year, and such meeting shall begin at noon on the 3d day of January, unless they shall by law appoint a different day.

SECTION 3. If, at the time fixed for the beginning of the term of the President, the President elect shall have died, the Vice President elect shall become President. If a President shall not have been chosen before the time fixed for the beginning of his term, or if the President elect shall have failed to qualify, then the Vice President elect shall act as President until a President shall have qualified; and the Congress may by law provide for the case wherein neither a President elect nor a Vice President elect shall have qualified, declaring who shall then act as President, or the manner in which one who is to act shall be selected, and such person shall act accordingly until a President or Vice President shall have qualified.

SECTION 4. The Congress may by law provide for the case of the death of any of the persons from whom the House of Representatives may choose a President whenever the right of choice shall have devolved upon them, and for the case of the death of any of the persons from whom the Senate may choose a Vice President whenever the right of choice shall have devolved upon them.

SECTION 5. Sections 1 and 2 shall take effect on the 15th day of October following the ratification of this article.

SECTION 6. This article shall be inoperative unless it shall have been ratified as an amendment to the Constitution by the legislatures of three-fourths of the several states within seven years from the date of its submission.

AMENDMENT XXI

SECTION 1. The eighteenth article of amendment to the Constitution of the United States is hereby repealed.

SECTION 2. The transportation or importation into any State, Territory, or possession of the United States for delivery or use therein of intoxicating liquors, in violation of the laws thereof, is hereby prohibited.

SECTION 3. This article shall be inoperative unless it shall have been ratified as an amendment to the Constitution by conventions in the several States, as provided in the Constitution, within seven years from the date of the submission hereof to the States by the Congress.

AMENDMENT XXII

SECTION 1. No person shall be elected to the office of the President more than twice, and no person who has held the office of President, or acted as President, for more than two years of a term to which some other person was elected President shall be elected to the office of the President more than once. But this Article shall not apply to any person holding the office of President when this Article was proposed by the Congress, and shall not prevent any person who may be holding the office of President, or acting as President, during the term within which this Article becomes operative from holding the office of President or acting as President during the remainder of such term.

SECTION 2. This article shall be inoperative unless it shall have been ratified as an amendment to the Constitution by the legislatures of three-fourths of the several States within seven years from the date of its submission to the States by the Congress.

AMENDMENT XXIII

SECTION 1. The District constituting the seat of Government of the United States shall appoint in such manner as the Congress may direct:

A number of electors of President and Vice President equal to the whole number of Senators and Representatives in Congress to which the District would be entitled if it were a State, but in no event more than the least populous State; they shall be in addition to those appointed by the States, but they shall be considered, for the purposes of the election of President and Vice President, to be electors appointed by a State; and they shall meet in the District and perform such duties as provided by the twelfth article of amendment.

SECTION 2. The Congress shall have power to enforce this article by appropriate legislation.

AMENDMENT XXIV

SECTION 1. The right of citizens of the United States to vote in any primary or other election for President or Vice President, for electors for President or Vice President, or for Senator or Representative in Congress, shall not be denied or abridged by the United States or any State by reason of failure to pay any poll tax or other tax.

SECTION 2. The Congress shall have power to enforce this article by appropriate legislation.

AMENDMENT XXV

SECTION 1. In case of the removal of the President from office or of his death or resignation, the Vice President shall become President.

SECTION 2. Whenever there is a vacancy in the office of the Vice President, the President shall nominate a Vice President who shall take office upon confirmation by a majority vote of both Houses of Congress.

SECTION 3. Whenever the President transmits to the President pro tempore of the Senate and the Speaker of the House of Representatives his written declaration that he is unable to discharge the powers and duties of his office, and until he transmits to them a written declaration to the contrary, such powers and duties shall be discharged by the Vice President as Acting President.

SECTION 4. Whenever the Vice President and a majority of either the principal officers of the executive departments or of such other body as Congress may by law provide, transmit to the President pro tempore of the Senate and the Speaker of the House of Representatives their written declaration that the President is unable to discharge the powers and duties of his office, the Vice President shall immediately assume the powers and duties of the office as Acting President.

Thereafter, when the President transmits to the President pro tempore of the Senate and the Speaker of the House of Representatives his written declaration that no inability exists, he shall resume the powers and duties of his office unless the Vice President and a majority of either the principal officers of the executive department or of such other body as Congress may by law provide, transmit within four days to the President pro tempore of the Senate and the Speaker of the House of Representatives their written declaration that the President is unable to discharge the powers and duties of his office. Thereupon Congress shall decide the issue, assembling within forty-eight hours for that purpose if not in session. If the Congress, within twenty-one days after receipt of the latter written declaration, or, if Congress is not in session, within twenty-one days after Congress is required to assemble, determines by two-thirds vote of both Houses that the President is unable to discharge the powers and duties of his office, the Vice President shall continue to discharge the same as Acting President; otherwise, the President shall resume the powers and duties of his office.

AMENDMENT XXVI

SECTION 1. The right of citizens of the United States, who are eighteen years of age or older, to vote shall not be denied or abridged by the United States or by any State on account of age.

SECTION 2. The Congress shall have power to enforce this article by appropriate legislation.

NOTE: A prospective 27th Amendment received the necessary number of state approvals in May of 1992. Becaue it was first proposed as part of the original amendments to the Constitution in 1789 and did not secure the necessary number of state approvals for over two hundred years, doubt remains about its validity. It reads: "No law varying the compensation for the services of the Senators and Representatives shall take effect, until an election of Representatives shall have intervened."

Legal Citations

Opinions of the United States Supreme Court and the highest court of each of the states are in writing and published in books known as "court reporters." Most opinions of the federal Circuit Courts of Appeals and the intermediate appellate courts in those states that have intermediate appellate courts are also published in court reporters. Selected significant written decisions of the United States district courts and some state lower courts are also published, but the majority are not. There are three reporters for U.S. Supreme Court opinions: *United States Reports* (U.S.), *Supreme Court Reports* (S.C.), and *Lawyer's Edition* (L. Ed.)

In addition to the court reporters, there are companies that collect and publish decisions or summaries of decisions in special-interest areas (for example, employment or tax) that are not published in regular court reporters. The only specialized reporters dealing with cases pertaining to religion are the *Religious Freedom Reporter* (published monthly by the Church-State Resource Center, Norman Adrian Wiggins School of Law, Campbell University, P.O. Box 505, Buies Creek, NC 27506, telephone 800–334–4111) and *Church Tax and Law Report* (published bimonthly by Christian Ministry Resources, P.O. Box 1098, Matthews, NC 28106, telephone 704–846–2507). Both of these publications publish summaries of cases rather than entire opinions.

Court cases are cited by the name of the case (e.g., Lemon v. Kurtzman), followed by an abbreviated reference to the court reporter or reporters in which the opinion appears, designated by a conventional abbreviation (403 U.S. 602). The numeral preceding the abbreviation of the court reporter represents the volume, and the number following is the page on which the opinion begins. Thus, 403 U.S. 602 tells us that the case of *Lemon v. Kurtzman* is published in the 403rd volume of the *United States Reports,* beginning on page 602. The final element of the citation is a parenthetical reference which includes the year of the decision and an abbreviated identification of the court that made it if it is not self-evident from the court reporter. In our example, one would only include the date (1971) since the *United States Reports* publishes only decisions of the United States Supreme Court.

Publishers of court reporters, after a certain number of volumes have accumulated, often begin a second (or third or fourth) series. Hence, some reporters will be identified by a 2d, 3rd, or 4th following them, such as F. 2d for the second series of the *Federal Reporter,* publishing decisions of Federal Courts of Appeal.

Most Supreme Court references are to only one of the three reporters (*United States Reports, Supreme Court Reporter,* and *Lawyer's Edition*). In this book I have generally used the U.S. reference as it is the official reporter, except in the case of decisions too recent to have a complete U.S. reference. The *Supreme Court Reporter* and the *Lawyer's Edition* will cross-reference to the citation in the *United States Reports.* The reverse is not true.

Decisions of the U.S. Circuit Courts of Appeals are published in the *Federal Reporter* (Fed.), which has a second series (F. 2d). Published decisions from the United States District Courts are published in a series known as the *Federal Supplement* (F.Supp.).

Thus, *Corporation of the Presiding Bishop v. Amos*, 483 U.S. 327 (1987) is a reference to a case of that name which appears in the 483rd volume of the *United States Reports,* beginning at page 327, and was decided in 1987. *EEOC v. Pacific Press Pub. Association*, 676 F. 2d 1272 (9th Cir. 1982) refers to a case of that name decided by the Ninth Circuit Federal Court of Appeals in 1982 which is published in the 676th volume of the second series of the *Federal Reporter,* beginning at page 1272. *Dolter v. Wahlert High School*, 483 F.Supp. 260 (N.D. Iowa 1980) refers to a case of that name decided by the United States District Court for the Northern District of Iowa in 1980 which was published in the 483rd volume of the *Federal Supplement,* beginning at page 260.

State court decisions are usually published in two reporters, the official state reporter and a series of seven regional reporters published by the West Publishing Company, which specializes in legal publications. Some states have adopted the *West Reporter* as their official state reporter and do not publish their opinions separately. The *West Reporter* cross-references the official state reporter citation, but the reverse is not true. Regional reporters are the *Atlantic* (Atl., A. 2d); *Pacific* (Pac., P. 2d); *North Eastern* (N.E., N.E. 2d); *South Eastern* (S.E., S.E. 2d); *Southern* (So., So. 2d); *South Western* (S.W., S.W. 2d); and *North Western* (N.W., N.W. 2d). There are also special reporters for California, known as the *California Reporter* (Cal. Rptr., Cal. Rptr. 2d), and New York, known as the *New York Supplement* (N.Y.S., N.Y.S. 2d). Thus the citation *Lowndes Prods., Inc. v. Brower*, 259 S.C. 322, 191 S.E. 2d 761 (1972) refers to a case of that name decided by the Supreme Court of South Carolina in 1972 which is published in the 259th volume of the *South Carolina Reports* beginning at page 322 and also in the 191st volume of the second series of the *South Eastern Reporter* beginning at page 761. If the citation is given only to the West Reporter, it would be given as *Lowndes Prods., Inc. v. Brower*, 191 S.E. 2d 761 (S.C. 1972) to identify the decision as being from the South Carolina Supreme Court.

If a case has a history of being reported at one level and then appealed to another level with the higher opinion reported, and the citation is to a lower court decision, then the subsequent history in the higher court is given with a standardized phrase to indicate how the higher court dealt with it (e.g., affirmed, reversed, reversed on other grounds). Thus *Dayton Christian Schools v. Ohio Civil Rights Comm'n*, 766 F. 2d 932 (6th Cir. 1985), reversed on other grounds, 477 U.S. 619 (1986) refers to a case of that name decided by the Sixth Circuit Federal Court of Appeals in 1985 which was reversed by the United States Supreme Court in 1986 but for reasons other than the proposition for which the Sixth Circuit opinion is being cited in the text. Case names often get reversed on appeal. The *Dayton Christian Schools* case in the U.S. Supreme Court appears as *Ohio Civil Rights Comm'n. v. Dayton Christian Schools*.

There is a complex series of standard conventions for abbreviations and stating case names followed by legal periodicals and publishers that is not important to the lay readers. These and other rules for legal citations in professional publications are contained in *A Uniform System of Citations,* published and distributed by the Harvard Law Review Association.

A number of standard and well-recognized legal texts set forth the law in particular areas, such as the works on torts by Prosser and on contracts by Corbin. Some of these appear in multiple volumes. There are also legal "encyclopedias," such as *American Jurisprudence* (Am.Jur.) and *Corpus Juris Secundum* (C.J.S.), which set forth the law on numerous subjects arranged alphabetically. There are also publications known as annotations, the most prominent of which is the American Law Reports (A.L.R.) series, which selects contemporary cases dealing with subjects of interest and publishes them in full followed by an "annotation" or summary, organized by subject matter, of other cases dealing with the issue of interest in the published opinion.

Most of the legal literature containing more reflective or conceptual analyses of cases and legal subjects is published in journals or periodicals known as "law reviews."

Most law reviews are published by law schools, and most law schools have a law review. The prestige of the law review is closely associated with the prestige of the school itself. Law reviews are student-edited publications; they publish both extensive analytical articles, usually written by law professors, and shorter "notes" or "comments," which are student-written pieces analyzing contemporary court decisions or a subject of interest. Student editors of law reviews are selected either by a competitive writing or on the basis of grades and are, generally speaking, the more able and ambitious students in their peer group. Law review articles can be influential, particularly when they are in-depth analyses by respected law professors. They are not infrequently cited by courts in explaining the reasons for their decisions. The name of the author is given if the reference is to an article by a professor. Student-written pieces do not include the name of the author. The method of citations to writings that appear in law reviews is similar to court citations. Thus, Douglas Laycock, "A General Theory of the Religion Clauses: The Case of Church Labor Relations and the Right to Church Autonomy," 81 *Columbia Law Review* 1373 (1981) refers to an article of that name by Professor Douglas Laycock published in 1981 in the 81st volume of the *Columbia Law Review* beginning at page 1373. For the convenience of readers without a legal education, I have not abbreviated law review references herein.

Court reporters and law reviews are available in law libraries but are rarely available in general libraries. All lawyers and law firms necessarily maintain law libraries, the size, extent, and contents of which will naturally vary with the size, location, and practice specialties of the firm.

Federal statutes are known as the United States Code, the major publications of which appear in two series known as the United States Code Service (U.S.C.S.) and the United States Code Annotated (U.S.C.A.). Each prints the statutes followed by an annotation or summary of cases that have been decided pertaining to the statute, organized by subject matter. The statutes are organized by chapter and section. Thus, 42 U.S.C.S. Section 1981 refers to Section 1981 of the 42d chapter of the United States Code as it appears in the United States Code Service.

The method of referring to state statutes is not standardized and varies by state.

Conciliation Provisions for Contracts and Wills

In order to encourage people to resolve their disputes out of court, the ACCS [Association of Christian Conciliation Services] recommends that the following mediation/arbitration clauses be inserted in contracts and wills. The contract clause will be legally enforceable in most states. The will clause, though not legally enforceable in most states, will often encourage people who have disagreements over a will to settle their differences in a conciliatory manner rather than through litigation.

For Contracts:

"Any claim or dispute arising out of or relating to this agreement shall be settled by mediation and, if necessary, arbitration in accordance with the *Rules of Procedure for Christian Conciliation* of the Association of Christian Conciliation Services, and judgment upon an arbitration award may be entered in any court of competent jurisdiction."

This clause may be used in employment, construction, commercial, and any other agreements that could someday give rise to a lawsuit. If you begin using it today, when your contract relationships are positive, you may avoid a great deal of unnecessary stress and expense should unforeseen problems arise in the future. The legal requirements for mediation/arbitration clauses vary from state to state (e.g., some states require that notice of arbitration provisions be printed on the front page of the contract in capitalized, underlined letters). Therefore, it is wise to get advice from an attorney when you first begin to use such clauses in your agreements.

For Wills:

"I ask that any questions or disputes that may arise during the administration of my estate be settled by mediation and, if necessary, arbitration in accordance with the *Rules of Procedure for Christian Conciliation* of the Association of Christian Conciliation Services."

This request may carry more weight if it is accompanied by an explanation of the writer's intentions and desires. For example it could be preceded by these words:

"I believe that God wants Christians to make every effort to live at peace and to resolve disputes with one another in private or within the church (see Matt. 18:15-20; 1 Cor. 6:1-8; Eph. 4:1-3). I believe that obedience to these principles honors and pleases God, leads others to believe in Christ, and benefits those involved. With these thoughts in mind, and trusting that those who will receive my property will honor my beliefs, . . ."

For Church or Organizational By-laws:

Similar mediation/arbitration provisions may be included in church or other organizational laws to require members to settle disputes between themselves and the organization through mediation and arbitration. For further information on such provisions, contact a local CCS or the Association of Christian Conciliation Services.

Bibliography

Throughout this work I have cited cases, law review articles, and other sources that may be of interest to the reader. A list of references follows each chapter. Some of the contemporary sources, which contain more extensive and specific information, are here listed.

General Texts

The Center for Church/State Studies, DePaul University College of Law, 25 East Jackson Boulevard, Chicago, IL 60604, anticipates 1994 publication of its Centerpiece Project, a three-volume study of the legal structures in which church organizations conduct their activity, which aims at developing a jurisprudence for the legal structures of religious organizations. The work will cover subjects such as real estate, taxation, employment, tort liability, charitable solicitation, educational institutions, health care institutions, and social service agencies.

Eidsmoe, John. *The Christian Legal Advisor* (Milford, Mich.: Mott Media, 1984).

Hammar, Richard R. *Pastor, Church and Law,* 2d ed. (Matthews, N.C.: Christian Ministry Resources, 1991).

Topical Monographs or Short Works

Adams, Arlin M., and Charles J. Emmerich. *A Nation Dedicated to Religious Liberty* (Philadelphia: University of Pennsylvania Press, 1990).

American Bar Association. *Tort and Religion* (1990). Available from American Bar Association.

American Bar Association, *Tort Liability for Charitable, Religious and Non-Profit Institutions* (1992). Available from the American Bar Association.

Association of Christian Conciliation Services. *Christian Conciliation: A Better Way to Settle Conflicts* (1989). Available from Association of Christian Conciliation Services, 1537 Avenue D, Suite 352, Billings, MT 59102.

Bloss, Julie L. *Employment Law: A Guide for Churches* (1990). Available from Church Management, Inc. P.O. Box 162527, Austin, TX 78716.

Buzzard, Lynn R., and Sherra Robinson. *IRS Political Activity Restrictions on Churches and Charitable Ministries* (1990). Available from Christian Ministries Management Association, P.O. Box 4368, Diamond Bar, CA 91765.

Buzzard, Robert A., and Lynn R. Buzzard. *"Render Unto Caesar": Unrelated Business Income Tax Liabilities of Churches and Ministries* (1990). Available from Church-State Resource Center, Norman Adrian Wiggins School of Law, Campbell University, Buies Creek, NC 27506.

Church Management, Inc. (P.O. Box 162527, Austin, TX 78716) has a number of publications available on federal taxation for churches and clergy, including "Tax Planning for Clergy," "Legal Matters (Estate Planning for Ministers)," "Social Security for Clergy," "Housing for Clergy," "How to Deduct the Cost of Continuing Education," "Car Allowance and Expenses," "Professional Expenses," and "Payroll Tax Procedures for Churches and Clergy."

Gaffney, Edward McGlynn, Jr., and Philip C. Sorenson. (Griffin ed.) *Ascending Liability in Religious and Other Nonprofit Organizations* (Macon, Ga.: Mercer University Press, 1984).

326

Hammar, Richard R. *Church and Clergy Tax Guide.* Published annually for current tax returns by Christian Ministry Resources, P.O. Box 2301, Matthews, NC 28106.

———. *The Church Guide to Copyright Law,* 2d ed. (1990). Available from Christian Ministry Resources, P.O. Box 2301, Matthews, NC 28106.

Moots, Philip R. *Ascending Liability: A Planning Memorandum* (Macon, Ga.: Mercer University Press, 1987).

Moots, Philip R., and Edward McGlynn Gaffney, Jr. *Church and Campus: Legal Issues in Religiously Affiliated Higher Education* (Notre Dame: University of Notre Dame Press, 1979).

Sande, Ken C. *The Peacemaker: A Biblical Guide to Resolving Personal Conflict* (Grand Rapids, Mich.: Baker Book House, 1991).

Worth, B. J. *Income Tax Guide for Ministers and Religious Workers.* Published annually for current returns by Worth Tax and Financial Service, Box 725, Winona Lake, IN 46590.

Periodicals

Church Law and Tax Report. Published bimonthly by Christian Ministry Resources, P.O. Box 1098, Matthews, NC 28106.

Religious Freedom Reporter. Published monthly by Church-State Resource Center, Norman Adrian Wiggins School of Law, Campbell University, P.O. Box 505, Buies Creek, NC 27506.

Notes

Introduction
Religion and Its Legal Context

1. F. F. Bruce, *The Canon of Scripture* (Downer's Grove, Ill.: InterVarsity Press, 1988), 19; Sinclair B. Ferguson, David F. Wright, and J. I. Packer, eds., *New International Dictionary of Theology* (Downer's Grove, Ill.: InterVarsity Press, 1988), 173.

2. Some of these give great insight into the practices of the time and, by their unique nature, give testimony to the authenticity of the text. The story of Abraham's purchase of a field for the burial of Sarah from Ephron the Hittite, as told in Genesis 23, may illustrate both the custom of negotiation and Hittite land law, which would have bound Ephron to continue to meet certain financial and social obligations if he had sold less than the entire field to Abraham. By yielding to Ephron's insistence that he buy the whole piece of land rather than just the cave he desired for the burial, Abraham relieved Ephron of those obligations.

3. A. James Casner, ed., *American Law of Property*, vol. 1 (Boston: Little, Brown & Co., 1952), secs. 1.2–1.4.

4. See chapter 2.

5. C. Zollman, *American Church Law* (St. Paul, Minn.: West Publishing Co., 1933), sec. 533.

6. Ibid., secs. 534–35.

7. Ibid., sec. 536.

8. The Council of Chalcedon, in A.D. 451, dealt with defining the nature of Christ to respond to developing heresies. Jesus, the Council declared, was "one and the same Son, perfect in Godhead and perfect in manhood, truly God and truly man . . . acknowledged in *two natures* unconfusedly, unchangeably, indivisibly, inseparably; the difference between the two natures is in no way removed because of the union, but rather the peculiar property of each nature is preserved, and both combine in one person. . . ." T. Ware, *The Orthodox Church* (London: Penguin Books, 1964), 34.

The Monophysites saw Jesus as having a single nature in which the divine swallowed up the human. The Nestorians separated Christ's human and divine nature so severely that they seemed to have two persons in one body. The Monophysite church, largely Semitic and located in Egypt and Syria, but with Armenian, Ethiopian, and Indian churches, never accepted the verdict of Chalcedon. Neither did the Nestorian church, which was located primarily in Persia beyond the bounds of the Roman and Byzantine Empires.

9. Ware, *The Orthodox Church*, 62 (quoting a letter from Pope Nicholas in A.D. 865).

10. Stone v. Graham, 449 U.S. 39 (1980).

Chapter 1
Pre-Constitutional History

1. Iain H. Murray, *Jonathan Edwards: A New Biography* (Edinburgh: The Banner of Truth Trust, 1987), xv.

2. Samuel Eliot Morison, *The Oxford History of the American People* (New York: Oxford University Press, 1965), 191.

3. Ibid.

4. Ibid., 207.

Chapter 2
The U.S. Constitutional System

1. Roy P. Fairfield, ed., *The Federalist Papers* (Garden City, N.Y.: Doubleday, 1961), 160–62.

2. Authority to seize persons or goods of subjects of a nation that is denying justice to subjects of another nation oppressed and injured by subjects of the nation denying jus-

tice. Congress has the power to grant such letters under Article I, Section 8 of the U.S. Constitution.

3. Article I, Section 2.

4. E.g., zoning laws discussed in chapter 8.

5. McCulloch v. Maryland, 17 U.S. (4 Wheat.) 316 (1819).

6. Article I, Section 7.

7. 301 U.S. 1 (1937).

8. 301 U.S. 37.

9. Pennsylvania v. Nelson, 350 U.S. 497, 501–505 (1956).

10. The delegated powers of the federal government could, of course, be removed by amending the U.S. Constitution.

11. See chapter 3, pp. 49–57.

12. See chapter 3, pp. 40–43.

13. See chapter 10.

14. See chapter 8.

15. See chapters 10, 13 and 14.

16. See chapters 7 and 12.

17. A "member of a society of radical democrats in France during the revolution of 1789: Their meetings were held in the Jacobin friars' convent hence 'an extreme political radical'" (*Webster's New World Dictionary,* 3d College ed., 1988).

18. A writ of *mandamus* is a court order directing an officer to perform a nondiscretionary duty.

19. "Original jurisdiction" refers to suits that can be initiated in the Supreme Court, as opposed to cases that reach the Court by appeals from lower courts.

20. 304 U.S. 64 (1938).

21. 410 U.S. 113 (1973).

22. 410 U.S. 153.

23. 381 U.S. 479 (1965).

24. 410 U.S. 154.

25. 410 U.S. 163.

26. 410 U.S. 164.

27. 462 U.S. 416 (1983).

28. 476 U.S. 747 (1986).

29. 492 U.S. 490 (1989).

30. Decided June 29, 1992. The opinion appears in 60 *U.S. Law Week* 4795, a journal that reports decisions before they are available in other court reports.

Chapter 3
The Religion Clauses of the
First Amendment

1. F. Makower, *The Constitutional History and Constitution of the Church of England* (1895), 86, quoted in Michael W. McConnell, "The Origins and Historical Understanding of Free Exercise of Religion," 103 *Harvard Law Review* 1409, 1421 (1990).

2. Michael W. McConnell, "The Origins and Historical Understanding of Free Exercise of Religion," 103 *Harvard Law Review* 1409, 1425 (1990), quoting Act Concerning Religion of 1649, reprinted in *The Founders' Constitution,* vol. 5, ed. P. Kurland and E. R. Lerner (1987), 49, 50.

3. McConnell, "Origins," 1425–27.

4. Ibid., 1432–33, quoting John Locke, *A Letter Concerning Toleration,* in *Works of Locke,* vol. 6 (London, 1823; reprint, 1963), 12–13, 19.

5. Article I, Section 3, Clause 6 (Senate sitting in an impeachment trial); Article II, Section 1, Clause 7 (swearing in of president); Article VI, Clause 3 (state and federal legislators, executive and judicial officers).

6. Reprinted in Arlin M. Adams and Charles J. Emmerich, *A Nation Dedicated to Religious Liberty* (Philadelphia: University of Pennsylvania Press, 1990), 104–7.

7. Samuel Eliot Morison, *The Oxford History of the American People* (New York: Oxford University Press, 1965), 314.

8. Archibald Cox, *The Court and the Constitution* (Boston: Houghton Mifflin Co., 1987), 184–87.

9. 302 U.S. 324–25 (1937).

10. 310 U.S. 296 (1940).

11. 330 U.S. 1 (1947).

12. 403 U.S. 602, 614 (1971).

13. Cox, *The Court and the Constitution,* 375.

14. Abington v. Schemp, 374 U.S. 203 (1963) (objective study of the Bible as a literary or historical work, rather than for religious purposes, is permitted in public schools, as is such study of religious music and art and comparative religion).

15. Engle v. Vitale, 370 U.S. 421 (1962); Lee v. Weisman, 60 *United States Law Week* 4723 (1992).

16. Wallace v. Jaffree, 472 U.S. 38 (1985) (a moment of silence law would probably be constitutional if not instituted for the purpose of encouraging prayer or with specific encouragement of students to pray. That students who are so minded may use it to pray does not make it unconstitutional).

17. Epperson v. Arkansas, 393 U.S. 97 (1968).

18. County of Allegheny v. American Civil Liberties Union, 492 U.S. 573, 106 L. Ed. 2d 472 (1989); Board of Trustees v. McCreary, 739 F. 2d 716 (2d Cir. 1989), affirmed by an equally

divided court, 471 U.S. 83 (1985); Lynch v. Donnelly, 465 U.S. 668 (1984).

19. County of Allegheny v. American Civil Liberties Union, 492 U.S. 573, 106 L. Ed. 2d 472, 518, 519 (1989), quoting Lynch v. Donnelly, 465 U.S. 693 (1984).

20. Lynch v. Donnelly, 465 U.S. 675–78 (1984); Allegheny, 492 U.S. 624–25, 106 L. Ed. 2d 515 (O'Connor concurring).

21. Zorach v. Clauson, 343 U.S. 306, 393 (1952).

22. 403 U.S. 602 (1971).

23. 403 U.S. 614 (1971).

24. Lynch v. Donnelly, 465 U.S. 687, 689 (1984). For discussion of the endorsement concept as part of the *Lemon* test, see Note, "A Controversial Twist of Lemon: The Endorsement Test as the New Establishment Clause Standard," 65 *Notre Dame Law Review* 671 (1990).

25. 463 U.S. 783.

26. Walz v. Tax Commission, 397 U.S. 664 (1970).

27. 343 U.S. 313–14.

28. 456 U.S. 288.

29. 175 U.S. 291.

30. 487 U.S. 589.

31. 487 U.S. 609.

32. 487 U.S. 610, quoting Hunt v. McNair, 413 U.S. 734, 743 (1973).

33. 487 U.S. 610.

34. 487 U.S. 613.

35. 42 U.S.C. 9858 et. seq.

36. 330 U.S. 1 (1947).

37. Roemer v. Maryland Board of Public Works, 425 U.S. 736 (1976); Hunt v. McNair, 413 U.S. 734 (1973); Tilton v. Richardson, 403 U.S. 671 (1971).

38. Witters v. Washington Department of Services for the Blind, 474 U.S. 481 (1986).

39. 333 U.S. 203 (1948).

40. 343 U.S. 306 (1952).

41. 330 U.S. 1 (1947).

42. 443 U.S. 229 (1977).

43. 473 U.S. 373 (1985).

44. Wolman v. Walter, 433 U.S. 229 (1977).

45. Ibid.

46. Committee for Public Education and Religious Liberty v. Regan, 444 U.S. 646 (1980).

47. Wolman, above, n. 44.

48. Aguilar v. Felton, 473 U.S. 402 (1985).

49. Board of Education v. Allen, 392 U.S. 236 (1968).

50. Wolman v. Walter, 433 U.S. 229, 252–55 (1977).

51. 413 U.S. 825 (1973).

52. 413 U.S. 756.

53. 463 U.S. 388 (1983).

54. Douglas Laycock, "A Survey of Religious Liberty in the United States," 47 *Ohio State Law Journal* 409, 446 (1986).

55. See section H of this chapter.

56. 20 U.S.C. Section 4071–74 (In U.S.C.S. Supp. IV) (1986).

57. Walz v. Tax Commission, 397 U.S. 664 (1970). See chapter 8.

58. Texas Monthly v. Bullock, 489 U.S. 1, 103 L. Ed. 2d 1 (1989). See pp. 164–65, below.

59. Corporation of the Presiding Bishop v. Amos, 483 U.S. 327 (1987). See chapter 7, sec. B.1.

60. See nn. 57–59, above.

61. Letter to a committee of the Danbury Baptist Association, 1802, quoted in Adams and Emmerich, *A Nation Dedicated to Religious Liberty,* 112.

62. See pp. 32–33, above.

63. People v. Phillips, Court of General Sessions, City of New York (June 14, 1813), quoted in McConnell, "Origins," 1504–5.

64. Simon's Executors v. Gratz, 2 Pen. & W. at 414 (1831) quoted in McConnell, "Origins," 1508.

65. Late Corporation of Church of Jesus Christ of Latter-Day Saints v. United States, 136 U.S. 1 (1890); Davis v. Beason, 133 U.S 133 (1890); Reynolds v. United States, 98 U.S. 145 (1878).

66. Sherbert v. Verner, 374 U.S. 398 (1963).

67. Wisconsin v. Yoder, 406 U.S. 205 (1972).

68. 406 U.S. 205, 215–16.

69. 367 U.S. 488 (1961).

70. 367 U.S. 495, n. 11.

71. It should be noted that there has been other litigation, some of which has reached the Supreme Court, in the area of conscientious objection under laws pertaining to military service which have extended the "religious" conscientious objector exemption to one who "deeply and sincerely holds beliefs that are purely ethical or moral in source and content but that nevertheless impose upon him a duty of conscience to refrain from participating in any war at any time," which "beliefs certainly occupy in the life of that individual 'a place parallel to that filled by . . . God' in traditionally religious persons." When such beliefs "function as a religion in his life," the individual is entitled to religious conscientious objector status (Welsh v. United States, 398 U.S. 333, 340 [1970]). While the Court undoubtedly had First Amendment issues in mind in addressing the issue under the draft

exemption law, these cases should not be understood as reading "religion" out of the religion clauses. While theistic belief may not be necessary to be religious, a purely philosophical belief system will not qualify.

72. Frazee v. Illinois Department of Employment Security, 489 U.S. 829, 103 L. Ed. 2d 914 (1989).

73. Thomas v. Review Board, 450 U.S. 707, 714–16 (1981).

74. Article I, Section 3, Clause 6 (Senate sitting in an impeachment trial); Article II, Section 1, Clause 7 (swearing in of the president); Article VI, Clause 3 (state and federal legislators, executive and judicial officers).

75. Thomas v. Review Board, 450 U.S. 207 (1981); Hobbie v. Unemployment Commission, 480 U.S. 136 (1987); Frazee v. Illinois Dept. of Employment Security, 489 U.S. 829, 103 L. Ed. 2d 914 (1989).

76. Lyng v. Northwest Indian Cemetery Protective Association, 485 U.S. 439 (1988).

77. Bowen v. Roy, 476 U.S. 693 (1986).

78. Employment Division v. Smith, 494 U.S. 872, 108 L. Ed. 2d 876 (1990).

79. Reynolds v. United States, 98 U.S. 145 (1978).

80. 494 U.S. 872, 890.

81. Edward McGlynn Gaffney, Douglas Laycock, and Michael W. McConnell, "An Answer to Smith: The Religious Freedom Restoration Act," *Christian Legal Society Quarterly* 11, no. 4 (Winter 1990), 17.

82. Michael W. McConnell, "Religious Freedom: A Surprising Pattern," *Christian Legal Society Quarterly* 11, no. 1 (Spring 1990), 5, 8. Congress, for example, enacted legislation (10 U.S.C. Sec. 774 [1988]) to nullify the Supreme Court's decision in Goldman v. Weinberger, 475 U.S. 503 (1986), which allowed expulsion of an Orthodox Jew from the military for wearing a yarmulke under a uniform cap.

83. 462 N.W. 2d 383.

84. 462 N.W. 2d 397.

85. 409 Mass. 38, 564 N.E. 2d 571 (1990).

86. 2 Cal. Rptr. 2d 32 (Cal. App. 2d Dist. 1991).

87. 605 A. 2d 63 (Me. 1992).

88. 268 U.S. 510 (1925).

89. Kentucky State Board for Elementary and Secondary Education v. Rudasill, 589 S. W. 2d 877 (Ky. 1979), *cert. denied,* 446 U.S. 938 (1980).

90. For discussion of constitutional issues involving church-related day care centers, see Note, "Dilemma in Day Care: The Virtues of Administrative Accommodation," 57 *University of Chicago Law Review* 573 (1990); Note, "Day Care and the Establishment Clause: The Constitutionality of the Certificate Program in S.5, the 'ABC' Bill, 12 *Geo. Mason University Law Review* 317 (1990).

91. See North Valley Baptist Church v. McMahon, 696 F. Supp. 518 (E.D. Cal. 1988); State v. Corpus Christi People's Baptist Church, 683 S.W. 2d 692 (Texas 1984); Department of Social Services v. Emmanuel Baptist Pre-School, 150 Mich. App. 254, 388 N.W. 326 (1988).

92. Emmanuel Baptist, *supra* n. 91.

93. Prov. 13:24.

94. Emmanuel Baptist, *supra* n. 91; North Valley Baptist, *supra* n. 91.

95. Henry J. Abraham, *The Judiciary: The Supreme Court in the Governmental Process,* 8th ed. (Los Angeles: William C. Brown, 1991), 86.

96. See pp. 46–49.

97. United States v. Ballard, 332 U.S. 78 (1944).

98. Board of Airport Commissioners v. Jews for Jesus, 482 U.S. 569 (1987).

99. International Society for Krishna Consciousness v. Lee, 925 F. 2d 576 (2d Cir. 1991).

100. Heffron v. International Society for Krishna Consciousness, 452 U.S. 640 (1981).

101. Frisby v. Schultz, 487 U.S. 474 (1988) (anti-abortion picketing of an abortionist's residence).

102. McCreary v. Stone, 471 U.S. 83 (1985), affirming by a 4-4 vote the Second Circuit decision at 739 F. 2d 716 (1984).

103. Grayned v. City of Rockford, 408 U.S. 104 (1972).

104. Widmar v. Vincent, 454 U.S. 263 (1981). Charles Alan Wright, "The Constitution on the Campus," 22 *Vanderbilt Law Review* 1027 (1969).

105. See p. 55.

106. Marsh v. Alabama, 326 U.S. 501 (1946).

107. Tucker v. Texas, 326 U.S. 517 (1946).

108. Lloyd Corporation v. Tanner, 407 U.S. 551 (1972) (general distribution of religious literature at shopping center may be banned).

109. Amalgamated Food Employees Union v. Logan Valley Plaza, 391 U.S. 308 (1968) (union picketing of store in labor dispute allowed).

110. Pruneyard Shopping Center v. Robins, 447 U.S. 74 (1980) (California Constitution).

111. Widmar v. Vincent, 454 U.S. 273–76.

112. Adams and Emmerich, *A Nation Dedicated to Religious Liberty,* 94.

113. Ibid., 40.

114. See discussion in ibid., 41 and notes therein.

115. Michael A. Paulsen, "The First Amendment Religion Clauses: Two Sides of the Same Coin," *Christian Legal Society Quarterly* 8, no. 2 (1987), 14; idem, "Religion, Equality, and the Constitution: An Equal Protection Approach to Establishment Clause Adjudication," 61 *Notre Dame Law Review* 311 (1986).

116. 397 U.S. 664, 668–69 (1970).

117. Abington School District v. Schempp, 374 U.S. 203, 222 (1963).

118. Zorach v. Clauson, 343 U.S. 306 (1952).

119. 483 U.S. 327 (1987).

120. 483 U.S. 334, quoting Hobbie v. Unemployment Appeals Comm. of Fla., 480 U.S. 136, 144–45 (1987).

121. 483 U.S. 334, quoting Walz v. Tax Commission, 397 U.S. 664, 673 (1970).

122. 483 U.S. 334, quoting Walz, 397 U.S. 669.

123. 483 U.S. 334–35, quoting Hobbie, 480 U.S. 145.

124. Zorach v. Clauson, 343 U.S. 314.

125. 483 U.S. 335.

126. 397 U.S. 669.

127. 454 U.S. 263 (1981).

128. 741 F. 2d 538 (3rd Cir. 1984), vacated on other grounds, 475 U.S. 534 (1986).

129. 741 F. 2d 555 and 561.

130. 20 U.S.C. Sections 4071–74, Supp. IV (1986).

131. 496 U.S. 226, 110 L. Ed. 2d 191 (1990).

132. 496 U.S. 250, 110 L. Ed. 2d 216.

133. 496 U.S. 250, 110 L. Ed. 2d 215–16.

134. Rethford v. Norman Public School System, 11 Religious Freedom Rptr. 74 (1991).

135. 11 Religious Freedom Rptr. 181 (1991).

136. Hoppock v. Twin Falls School District No. 411, 772 F.Supp. 1160 (D. Ida. 1991).

137. Garnett v. Renton School District No. 403, 772 F.Supp. 531 (W.D. Wash. 1991).

138. Burlington Assembly of God Church v. Zoning Board of Adjustment, 238 N.J. Super. 634, 570 A. 2d 495 (1989). The church, however, was unable to prove any loss of property value, and collected no damages, 588 A. 2d 1297 (N.J. Super. 1990).

139. 896 F. 2d 1082 (7th Cir. 1990).

140. 41 U.S.C. Section 1988.

141. Smith v. Wade, 461 U.S. 30 (1983).

142. Kentucky v. Graham, 473 U.S. 159 (1985).

Chapter 4
Ecclesiastical Organization and the Courts

1. U.S. Department of Commerce, *1990 Statistical Abstract of the United States*, referred to in *Church Law and Tax Report* 4, no. 5 (Sept./Oct. 1990), 13.

2. See J. Gordon Melton, *The Encyclopedia of American Religions* (Detroit: Gale Research Co., 1987).

3. See Frank S. Mead, *Handbook of Denominations in the United States,* rev. by S. Hill, 9th ed. (Nashville: Abingdon Press, 1990).

4. Harry G. Henn, *Law of Corporations* (St. Paul, Minn.:West Publishing Co., 1970), sec. 5.

5. Ibid.

6. Ibid., sec. 6.

7. Paul G. Kauper and Stephen C. Ellis, "Religious Corporations and the Law," 71 *Michigan Law Review* 1500, 1507 (1973).

8. Ibid., 1529.

9. Ibid., 1541.

10. Ibid., 1538.

11. See chapter 6 for a more general discussion of contract law.

12. See Howard B. Foshee, *Broadman Church Manual* (Nashville: Broadman Press, 1973).

13. See *Proceedings of the 24th National Meeting of Diocesan Attorneys*, April 25–26, 1988, Office of General Counsel of United States Catholic Conference, pp. 52–72.

14. See chapter 3, sec. F.

15. 443 U.S. 595 (1979).

16. Presbyterian Church v. Hull Church, 393 U.S. 440 (1969).

17. 443 U.S. 602.

18. Ibid.

19. Ibid., 604.

20. Ibid.

21. Ibid., 607.

22. Ibid., 616.

23. Serbian Eastern Orthodox Diocese v. Milivojevich, 426 U.S. 696 (1976).

24. 215 N.J. Super. 589, 522 A. 2d 497, appeal after remand, 239 N.J. Super 229, 570 A. 2d 1297 (1990), *cert. granted*, 122 N.J. 195, 584 A. 2d 253, affirmed 125 N.J. 404, 593 A. 2d 725 (1991).

25. 522 A. 2d 683 (Pa. Comm. 1987).

26. 739 P. 2d 167 (Alaska 1987).

27. 544 N.Y.S. 2d 955.

28. 763 P. 2d 522 (Ariz. App. 1988).

29. 828 F. 2d 718 (1987).

30. Milivojevich, n. 23 above.

31. See, e.g., Bethlehem Missionary Baptist Church v. Henderson, 522 So. 2d 1339 (La. Ct. App. 1988); First Union Baptist Church v. Banks, 533 So. 2d 1305 (La. App. 1988).

32. Virgis v. Rock Creek Baptist Church, 734 F.Supp. 30 (District of the District of Columbia 1990).

33. See Mt. Olive Baptist Church v. Williams, 529 So. 2d 972 (Ala. 1988).

34. 533 So. 2d 1305 (La. App. 1988).

35. 443 U.S. 603–4.

36. 443 U.S. 604, quoting Presbyterian Church v. Hull Church, 393 U.S. 440, 449 (1969).

37. 443 U.S. 606.

38. 80 U.S. 666, 678.

Chapter 5
Legal Privileges and Obligations
of Clergy

1. C. Zollman, *American Church Law* (St. Paul, Minn.: West Publishing Co., 1933), sec. 533.

2. 92 T.C. 12 (1989).

3. The Tax Court is a court established by Congress to hear taxpayers' petitions to redetermine a proposed deficiency asserted by the Internal Revenue Service. Most of its judges have extensive experience in taxation, often with background in government agencies. Its jurisdiction may be invoked by the taxpayer as an alternative to paying the tax and suing for a refund in the U.S. district courts or claims court. Its principal office is in Washington, but its judges hear cases in many cities throughout the country. Appeals from its decisions may be taken to the U.S. Courts of Appeals.

4. Technical Advice Memorandum 89-15001.

5. Wingo v. Commissioner, 89 T.C. 922 (1987).

6. Richard R. Hammar, *Pastor, Church, and Law,* 2d ed. (Matthews, N.C.: Christian Ministry Resources, 1991), 61–65.

7. See, e.g., Lawrence v. Commissioner, 50 T.C. 494 (1968).

8. Private Ruling 88-25025, discussed in *Church Law and Tax Report* 4, no. 1 (January/February 1990), 14.

9. 46 T.C. 190 (1966).

10. 57 T.C. 727 (1972).

11. Revenue Ruling 72–606.

12. Technical Advice Memorandum

90–33002, discussed in *Church Law and Tax Report* 4, no. 6 (November/December 1990), 13; Private Letter Ruling 89–22077, discussed in *Church Law and Tax Report* (September/October 1989), 13; Revenue Ruling 70–549.

13. Revenue Ruling 57–129.

14. Blair v. Commissioner, 69 T.C. 521 (1977).

15. Private Letter Rulings 88–26043 and 89–30038, discussed in Richard R. Hammar, *Church and Clergy Tax Guide* (Matthews, N.C.: Christian Ministry Resources, 1989).

16. IRC Section 3309(b).

17. 50 U.S.C. App. Sec. 456(g).

18. See "The Status of Clergy under the Selective Service Act," in *Church Law and Tax Report* 5, no. 2 (March/April 1991) for a summary of law in this area.

19. 8 U.S.C. Section 1101(a)27(C).

20. Hammar, *Pastor, Church, and Law,* 140.

21. First Albanian "Teqe Bektashiane" in America v. Salhi, 231 F.Supp. 516 (E.D. Mich. 1964).

22. Re: Rhee, Immigration and Naturalization Interim Decison no. 2682 (1982).

23. 49 U.S.C. Section 10723.

24. Cimijotti v. Paulsen, 219 F.Supp. 621 (N.D. Iowa), appeal dismissed, 323 F. 2d 716 (8th Cir. 1963).

25. In re: Verplank, 329 F.Supp. 433 (C.D. Cal. 1971).

26. People v. Diercks, 88 Ill. App. 3rd 1073, 411 N.E. 2d 97 (1980).

27. Knight v. Lee, 80 Ind. 201 (1881).

28. In re: Murtha, 115 N.J. Super. 380, 279 A. 2d 889 (1971).

29. Federal Rules of Evidence 501.

30. Hammar, *Pastor, Church, and Law,* 109–10.

31. Zorach v. Clausen, 343 U.S. 306, 313 (1952).

32. Zollmann, *American Church Law,* sec. 451–52.

33. Hammar, *Pastor, Church, and Law,* 118–19.

34. Ibid., 139.

35. Ibid., 141.

36. Zollmann, *American Church Law,* sec. 457, pp. 430–31.

37. McDaniel v. Paty, 435 U.S. 618 (1978).

Chapter 6
Liability for Contracts and Torts

1. See the discussion in chapter 16.

2. See Daniel Webster Council v. St. James

Association, 129 N.H. 681, 553 A. 2d 329 (1987), where a land sale contract signed by a church treasurer and secretary was unenforceable when they had no authority to make the contract under either the church by-laws or board resolution.

3. *Black's Law Dictionary,* 6th ed. (St. Paul, Minn.: West Publishing Company, 1990).

4. Ibid.

5. 248 N.Y. 339, 162 N.E. 99 (1928).

6. Restatement, Second Torts, Section 402A (1965).

7. Restatement, Second Agency, sec. 220 (1958).

8. Ibid.

9. Malloy v. Fong, 232 P. 2d 241 (Cal. 1951).

10. 758 P. 2d 219 (1988).

11. 530 So. 2d 801 (1988).

12. 52 Wash. App. 688, 763 P. 2d 1237 (Wash. App. 1988).

13. Restatement, Second Agency, sec. 228 (1958).

14. William L. Prosser, *The Law of Torts,* 4th ed. (St. Paul, Minn.: West Publishing Co., 1971), sec. 70, pp. 460–61.

15. See Byrd v. Faber, 57 Ohio St. 3d 56, 565 N.E. 2d 584 (1991); Milla v. Tamayo, 187 Cal. App. 3rd 1453, 232 Cal. Rptr. 685 (Cal. App. 1986); Dunn v. Gracia, 768 P. 2d 419 (Or. App. 1989) (national and regional Boy Scout organizations are not vicariously liable for sexual seduction of minor boy by female scout leader).

16. Doe v. Samaritan Counseling Center, 791 P. 2d 344 (Alaska 1990).

17. Erickson v. Christenson, 99 Or. App. 104, 781 P. 2d 383 (Or. App. 1989); M.V. v. Gulf Ridge Council of Boy Scouts of America, Inc., 529 So. 2d 1248 (Fla. App. 2d Dist. 1988) (scout camp case).

18. An excellent discussion of ascending liability and related issues appears in Edward McGlynn Gaffney and Philip C. Sorenson (Howard R. Griffin, ed.), *Ascending Liability in Religious and Other Nonprofit Organizations* (Macon, Ga.: Center for Constitutional Studies, and Mercer University Press, 1984).

19. Charles M. Whelan, "'Church' and the Internal Revenue Code: The Definitional Problems," 45 *Fordham Law Review* 885, 903 (1977).

20. See, e.g., Eckler v. The General Council of the Assemblies of God, 784 S.W. 2d 935 (Tex. App. 1990); Pentecostal Holiness Church, Inc. v. Mauney, 270 So. 2d 762 (Fla. App. 1972), *cert. denied,* 276 So. 2d 51 (Fla. 1973).

21. 784 S.W. 2d 935 (Tex. App. 1990).

22. 90 Cal. App. 3d 259, 153 Cal. Rptr. 322. See discussion in Chapter 11, pp. 193–94.

23. See discussion by Edward McGlynn Gaffney, Jr., "Piercing the Veil of Religious Organizations," in ABA National Institute on Tort and Religion, June 14–15, 1990.

24. 477 So. 2d 1060 (Fla. App. 1985).

25. Revenue Procedure 80–27.

26. Exod. 26:31-33; Matt. 27:52; Mark 15:38; Luke 23:44; Heb. 10:19-22. See discussion in Gaffney, "Piercing the Veil," 3–5.

27. See, e.g., Massachusetts General Laws, Annotated Chapter 231, Section 85K; South Carolina Code Section 33–55–210; Texas Code of Civil Practice and Remedies, Supplement, Chapter 84.

28. See, e.g., Carson v. Maurer, 120 N.H. 925, 424 A. 2d 825 (1980), striking down a New Hampshire statute limiting liability for medical malpractice.

29. English v. New England Medical Center, 405 Mass. 423, 541 N.E. 2d 329 (Mass. 1989); Doe v. American Red Cross Blood Services, 297 S.C. 430, 377 S.E. 2d 323 (1989). The cases and Massachusetts, Texas, and South Carolina statutes are discussed in *Church Law and Tax Report,* 4, no. 1 (January/February 1990), 1–5.

Chapter 7
The Church as Regulated Employer

1. See chapter 3, sec. E.

2. 440 U.S. 490 (1979).

3. 440 U.S. 502.

4. 440 U.S. 503.

5. Douglas Laycock, "A General Theory of the Religion Clauses: The Case of Church Labor Relations and the Right to Church Autonomy," 81 *Columbia Law Review* 1373 (1981).

6. Bruce N. Bagni, "Discrimination in the Name of the Lord: A Critical Evaluation of Discrimination by Religious Organizations," 79 *Columbia Law Review* 1514 (1979).

7. Ohio Civil Rights Commission v. Dayton Christian Schools, Inc., 477 U.S. 619 (1986); Sacred Heart School Board v. Labor and Industry Review Commission, 460 N.W. 2d 430 (Wis. App. 1990).

8. See, e.g., Convent of the Visitation School v. Continental Casualty Co., 707 F.Supp. 412 (D. Minn. 1989), dealing with insurance coverage for a claim of marital discrimination under Minnesota law when a husband was fired following his wife's termination.

9. 42 U.S.C. Section 2000e–2.

10. 42 U.S.C. Section 2000e(b)(h).

11. 42 U.S.C. Section 2000e(b).

12. 42 U.S.C. Section 2000e–1.

13. 42 U.S.C. Section 2000e–2(e)(II).

14. McClure v. Salvation Army, 323 F.Supp. 1100 (N.D. Ga. 1971), affirmed, 460 F. 2d 553 (5th Cir.), *cert. denied*, 409 U.S. 896 (1972).

15. Feldstein v. Christian Science Monitor, 555 F.Supp. 974, 978 (D. Mass. 1983).

16. Fike v. United Methodist Children's Home of Virginia, 747 F.Supp. 286, 290 (E.D. Va. 1982).

17. Little v. Wuerl, 929 F. 2d 944 (3rd Cir. 1991).

18. 483 U.S. 327 (1987).

19. 483 U.S. 336.

20. Larsen v. Kirkham, 499 F.Supp. 960 (District of Utah 1980).

21. 42 U.S.C. Section 2000d(j). The employer need only offer a reasonable accommodation, not show that all of the employee's alternative accommodations would cause undue hardship. The extent of the hardship is only at issue when the employer claims it can offer *no* reasonable accommodation without undue hardship. Philbrook v. Ansonia Board of Education, 479 U.S. 60 (1986).

22. Thornton v. Caldor, Inc., 472 U.S. 703 (1985).

23. Larsen v. Kirkham, 499 F.Supp. 960 (District of Utah 1980).

24. 42 U.S.C. Section 2000e–2(e)(I).

25. Pilne v. Loyola Univ. of Chicago, 803 F. 2d 351 (7th Cir. 1985).

26. 42 U.S.C. Section 2000e(k).

27. 29 U.S.C. Section 206(d)(1).

28. The Fair Labor Standards Act is discussed in section D of this chapter.

29. EEOC v. Pacific Press, 676 F. 2d 1272 (9th Cir. 1982).

30. EEOC v. Fremont Christian School, 781 F. 2d 1362 (9th Cir. 1986).

31. DeSantis v. Pacific Telephone, 608 F. 2d 327 (9th Cir. 1979); Madsen v. Irwin, 395 Mass. 715, 481 N.E. 2d 1160 (1985). See section G of this chapter.

32. McClure v. Salvation Army, 460 F. 2d 553 (5th Cir.), *cert. denied*, 409 U.S. 896 (1972); Rayburn v. General Conference of Seventh-Day Adventists, 772 F. 2d 1164 (4th Cir. 1985).

33. McClure v. Salvation Army, 460 F. 2d 553 (5th Cir.), *cert. denied*, 409 U.S. 896 (1972); Scharon v. St. Luke's Episcopal Presbyterian Hospitals, 736 F.Supp. 1081 (E.D. Mo. 1990) (applying a *Catholic Bishop* analysis), affirmed 929 F. 2d 360 (8th Cir. 1991) (based on a free exercise analysis).

34. EEOC v. Southwestern Baptist Theological Seminary, 651 F. 2d 277 (5th Cir. 1981).

35. EEOC v. Mississippi College, 626 F. 2d 477 (5th Cir. 1981).

36. Dole v. Shenandoah Baptist Church, 899 F. 2d 1389 (4th Cir. 1990) (decided under Fair Labor Standards Act).

37. Chambers v. Omaha Girls Club, Inc., 834 F. 2d 697 (8th Cir. 1987).

38. Dolter v. Wahlert High School, 483 F.Supp. 266 (N.D. Iowa 1980).

39. 766 F. 2d 932 (1985).

40. See discussion in chapter 12, section C.

41. 42 U.S.C. Section 1981. The section guarantees all persons "the same right . . . to make and enforce contracts . . . as is enjoyed by white citizens." It has been interpreted to apply to hiring but not discharge claims. Williams v. First Union National Bank of N.C., 920 F. 2d 232 (4th Cir. 1990), *cert. denied*, 59 United States Law Week 3726 (1991).

42. 8 U.S.C. Section 1324a.

43. Bob Jones University v. United States, 461 U.S. 574 (1983).

44. 29 U.S.C. Sections 621–34. The act was amended in 1990 to specifically include employee benefits and establish minimum standards for the validity of waiver of ADEA claims.

45. 29 U.S.C. Section 623(a).

46. 29 U.S.C. 630(b).

47. 440 U.S. 490 (1979). See section A of this chapter.

48. Ritter v. Mt. St. Mary's College, 814 F. 2d 986 (4th Cir. 1987); Soriano v. Xavier University, 687 F.Supp. 1188 (S.D. Ohio 1988); Usery v. Manchester East Catholic Regional School Board, 430 F.Supp. 188 (D. N.H. 1977).

49. 717 F.Supp. 1413 (E.D. Mo. 1989).

50. Minker v. United Methodist Church, 894 F. 2d 1354 (D.C. Cir. 1990).

51. Scharon v. St. Luke's Episcopal Presbyterian Hospitals, 736 F.Supp. 1081 (E.D. Mo. 1990), affirmed, 929 F. 2d 360 (8th Cir. 1991).

52. 42 U.S.C. Sections 12101–12213. Sections 12111–12117 deal with employment discrimination.

53. 29 U.S.C Section 794(a).

54. See chapter 3, section E.3 with respect to Establishment Clause issues of receipt of government funds by religious organizations.

55. At least one court, however, has found to the contrary, McGlotten v. Connelly, 338 F.Supp. 448 (District of District of Columbia 1972).

56. 20 U.S.C. Section 1681(a).

57. 20 U.S.C. Section 1681(a)(3).

58. 29 U.S.C. Section 794.

59. 29 U.S.C. Section 706(8)(B).

60. Blackwell v. United States Department of Treasury, 656 F.Supp. 713 (District of District of Columbia 1986).

61. 29 U.S.C. Section 706(8)(c).

62. District 27 Community School Board v. Board of Education, 502 N.Y.S. 2d 325 (1986).

63. See section B.4 of this chapter.

64. 42 U.S.C. Section 2000d.

65. 465 U.S. 555 (1984).

66. Dodge v. Salvation Army, 48 Employment Practices Decisions (Commerce Clearing House) 38,619 (S.D. Miss. 1989).

67. 42 U.S.C. Section 9858 et seq.

68. 38 U.S.C. Section 2012.

69. 29 U.S.C. Sections 151–68.

70. See chapter 2, section A.

71. 440 U.S. 490 (1979).

72. 29 U.S.C. Section 152(VII).

73. 29 U.S.C. Section 152(VI).

74. NLRB v. St. Louis Christian Home, 663 F. 2d 60 (8th Cir. 1981).

75. NLRB v. World Evangelism, Inc., 656 F. 2d 1349 (9th Cir. 1981).

76. NLRB v. St. Louis Christian Home, 663 F. 2d 60 (8th Cir. 1981); Tressler Lutheran Home for Children v. NLRB, 677 F. 2d 302 (3rd Cir. 1982).

77. St. Elizabeth Community Hospital v. NLRB, 708 F. 2d 1436 (9th Cir. 1983); Bon Secours Hospital, Inc., 248 National Labor Relations Board 115 (1980).

78. Mid American Health Services, Inc., 247 National Labor Relations Board 752 (1980).

79. 29 U.S.C. Section 169.

80. Wilson v. National Labor Relations Board, 920 F. 2d 1282 (6th Cir. 1990). See discussion of Larson v. Valente, 456 U.S. 228 (1982) in chapter 3, section E.2.b.

81. 815 F. 2d 219.

82. See discussion of preemption in chapter 2, section B.2.

83. Catholic High School Association v. Culvert, 753 F. 2d 1161 (2d Cir. 1985).

84. In re Hill-Murray Federation of Teachers v. Hill-Murray High School, 487 N.W. 2d 857, 61 United States Law Week 2075, 1992 WL 171587 (Minn. 1992).

85. For an excellent discussion of the application of the Fair Labor Standards Act to religious organizations and their employees, see *Church Law and Tax Report* 5, no. 4 (July/August 1991), 1.

86. 29 U.S.C. Sections 201–19.

87. See section B.2 of this chapter.

88. 29 U.S.C. Section 206(a).

89. 29 U.S.C. Section 203(s)(1); Donovan v. Shenandoah Baptist Church, 573 F.Supp. 320 (D. Va. 1983).

90. 29 U.S.C. Section 213(a)(III).

91. 29 U.S.C. 213(a)(I); 29 Code of Federal Regulations Section 541.

92. 471 U.S. 290 (1985).

93. 471 U.S. 292.

94. 471 U.S. 299.

95. Mitchell v. Pilgrim Holiness Church Corp., 210 F. 2d 879 (7th Cir. 1954).

96. 899 F. 2d 1389. A similar case is DeArmont v. Harvey, 932 F. 2d 721 (8th Cir. 1991).

97. New Hampshire Revised Statutes Annotated 279:1 V.

98. Pilgrim Pines Conference Center Wage Adjustment Decision, New Hampshire Department of Labor, November 1, 1989.

99. Brock v. Wendell's Woodwork, Inc., 867 F. 2d 196 (4th Cir. 1989).

100. 8 U.S.C. Sections 1324a and b.

101. Intercommunity Center for Justice and Peace v. Immigration and Naturalization Service, 910 F. 2d 42 (2d Cir. 1990); American Friends Service Committee v. Thornburgh, 718 F.Supp. 820 (C.D. Cal. 1989), affirmed, 941 F. 2d 808 (9th Cir. 1991).

102. Section B.3 of this chapter.

103. 29 U.S.C. Sections 651–78.

104. 29 U.S.C. Section 652(V).

105. 29 U.S.C. Section 652(III).

106. Massachusetts, Wisconsin, Hawaii, and Connecticut at this writing, with similar legislation proposed in other states.

107. Madsen v. Erwin, 395 Mass. 715, 481 N.E. 2d 1160 (Mass. 1985) (lesbian employee of the *Christian Science Monitor,* which is treated as part of the Christian Science church); Walker v. First Presbyterian Church, 22 Labor Relations Rptr. (Bureau of National Affairs) 762 (1980) (dismissal of unrepentant homosexual organist upheld despite San Francisco ordinance); Murphy v. Buchanan, 21 Labor Relations Rptr. (BNA) 696 (1979) (pastor's withdrawal of employment offer after learning applicant was homosexual upheld despite St. Paul, Minnesota, ordinance).

Chapter 8
The Church as Property Owner

1. See chapter 2.

2. Edward H. Ziegler, *Rathkopf's the Law of Zoning and Planning* (New York: Clark Boardman Co., 1990), sec. 1.01[2].

3. 272 U.S. 365 (1926).

4. 348 U.S. 26 (1954).

5. 348 U.S. 33.

6. 416 U.S. 1 (1974).

7. 416 U.S. 9.

8. See chapter 2, sec. B.3.

9. "Fire inspections, building and zoning regulations, and state requirements under compulsory school-attendance laws are examples of necessary and permissible contacts" (between church and state). Lemon v. Kurtzman, 403 U.S. 602, 614 (1971).

10. 223 N.J. Super. 55, 537 A. 2d 1336 (1988).

11. 896 F. 2d 1221 (9th Cir. 1990).

12. 859 F. 2d 820 (10th Cir. 1988).

13. Cornerstone Bible Church v. City of Hastings, 740 F.Supp. 654 (D. Minn. 1990), reversed, 948 F. 2d 464 (8th Cir. 1991).

14. North Syracuse First Baptist Church v. Village of North Syracuse, 524 N.Y.S. 2d 894 (1988).

15. Neddermeyer v. Ontario Planning Board, 548 N.Y.S. 2d 95 (1989).

16. 671 F.Supp. 515. The same reasoning was rejected by the federal District Court in Minnesota in the *Cornerstone Bible Church* case.

17. Islamic Center of Mississippi v. Starkville, 840 F. 2d 293 (5th Cir. 1988); Church of Jesus Christ of Latter-Day Saints v. Jefferson County, 741 F.Supp. 1522 (N.D. Ala. 1990).

18. 7 Religious Freedom Rptr. 64.

19. Wilkenson v. LaFranz, 9 Religious Freedom Rptr. 299 (Civil District Court for the Parish of Orleans, La. 1989).

20. Our Saviour's Evangelical Lutheran Church of Naperville v. City of Naperville, 186 Ill. App. 3rd 988, 542 N.E. 2d 1158 (Ill. App. 1989); Orthodox Minyan of Elkins Park v. Cheltenham Township Zoning Hearing Board, 552 A. 2d 772 (Pa. Commonwealth 1989).

21. Lakeshore Assembly of God Church v. Village Board of the Village of Westfield, 764 S.W. 2d 647 (Mo. 1989).

22. Greentree at Murray Hill Condominium v. Good Shepherd Episcopal Church, 550 N.Y.S. 2d 1981 (Supreme Court 1989).

23. Burlington Assembly of God Church v. Zoning Board, 238 N.J. Super. 634, 570 A. 2d 495 (N.J. Super. 1989).

24. Gallagher v. Zoning Board of Adjustment, 32 Pa. District and County 2d 669 (Pa. 1963).

25. Compare City of Concord v. New Testament Baptist Church, 382 A. 2d 377 (N.H. 1978) (allowing a church school in conjunction with the church) with Bethel Evangelical Lutheran Church v. Village of Merton, 201 Ill. App. 3rd 858, 559 N.E. 2d 533 (Ill. App. 1990) (denying unlimited enrollment for church school with preexisting capacity limit, by special use permit, of seventy-five).

26. Church of the Saviour v. Zoning Hearing Board, 568 A. 2d 1336 (Pa. Commonwealth 1989).

27. Needham Pastoral Counseling Center, Inc. v. Board of Appeals, 29 Mass. App. Ct. 31, 557 N.E. 2d 43 (Mass. App. 1990).

28. 17 Conn. App. 53, 549 A. 2d 1076 (1988).

29. 161 Ariz. App. 406, 778 P. 2d 1302 (Ariz. Ct. of App. 1989).

30. Richard R. Hammar, *Pastor, Church, and Law,* 2d ed. (Matthews, N.C.: Christian Ministry Resources, 1991), 704–5.

31. Community Synagogue v. Bates, 154 N.Y.S. 2d 15 (1956).

32. Portage Township v. Full Salvation Union, 318 Mich. 693, 29 N.W. 2d 297 (1947); Independent Church of the Realization of the Word of God, Inc. v. Board of Zoning Appeals, 437 N.Y.S. 2d 443 (1981); State Ex Rel. B'nai B'rith Foundation v. Walworth County, 59 Wis. 2d 296, 208 N.W. 2d 113 (1973); see Hammar, *Pastor, Church, and Law,* 260–65.

33. Nichols v. Planning and Zoning Commission of the Town of Stratford, 667 F.Supp. 72 (District of Conn. 1987).

34. Larkin v. Grendel's Den, Inc., 459 U.S. 116 (1982).

35. City of Renton v. Playtime Theaters, Inc., 475 U.S. 41 (1986).

36. City of Stanton v. Cox, 207 Cal. App. 3rd 1557, 255 Cal. Rptr. 682 (Cal. App. 1989); Amoco v. New Castle County, 101 Federal Rules Decisions 472 (D. Del. 1984); City of Whittier v. Walnut Properties, 149 Cal. App. 3rd 633, 197 Cal. Rptr. 127 (1983).

37. 7 Wis. 2d 275, 96 N.W. 2d 356 (1959).

38. See "Zoning Ordinances, Private Religious Conduct and the Free Exercise of Religion," 76 *Northwestern University Law Review* 786 (1981).

39. Employment Division v. Smith, 494 U.S. 872 (1990). See chapter 3, sec. F.

40. City of Sumner v. First Baptist Church, 97 Wash. 2d 1, 639 P. 2d 1358 (1982); Faith Assembly of God v. State Building Code Commission, 416 N.E. 2d 228 (Mass. App. 1981).

41. Congregation Beth Sholom v. Building Commissioner, 27 Mass. App. Ct. 276, 537 N.E. 2d 605 (1989).

42. 42 U.S.C. Section 12187.

43. 114 Wash. 2d 392, 787 P. 2d 1352 (1990).

44. Employment Division v. Smith, 494 U.S. 872 (1990); see chapter 3, sec. F.

45. 113 L. Ed. 2d 208 (1991) on remand, 840 P. 2d 174 (Wash. 1992).

46. 914 F. 2d 348 (2d Cir. 1990).

47. Society for Ethical Culture v. Spatt, 68 Appellate Division 2d 112, 416 N.Y.S. 2d 246 (1979), affirmed, 51 N.Y. 2d 449, 415 N.E. 2d 922, 434 N.Y.S. 2d 932 (1980); St. Bartholomew's Church v. City of New York, 914 F. 2d 348 (2d Cir. 1990).

48. 409 Mass. 38, 564 N.E. 2d 571 (1990).

49. Giamboi and Sylvia, *Primer on Environmental Issues for Diocesan Attorneys, Proceedings—26th National Meeting of Diocesan Attorneys,* 1990, p. 103.

50. 42 U.S.C. Sections 9601–9675.

51. Public Law 99–499, 100 United States Statutes at Large 1615 et. seq. (1986). The SARA amendments are codified within 42 U.S.C. Sections 9601 et. seq. and other statutes.

52. 42 U.S.C. Section 9607(b).

53. 42 U.S.C. Section 9601(35).

54. 42 U.S.C. Sections 9601(35)(A)(i), (B).

55. 42 U.S.C. Section 9601(20)(A).

56. United States v. Fleet Factors Corp., 901 F. 2d 1550 (11th Cir. 1990); United States v. Mirable, 15 Environmental Law Rptr. (Bureau of National Affairs) 20,992 (E.D. Pa. 1985).

57. United States v. Maryland Bank and Trust Co., 632 F.Supp. 573 (D. Md. 1986).

58. 42 U.S.C. Sections 9603(b), 9609(c).

59. 42 U.S.C. Section 6991(I)(A)(B).

60. 42 U.S.C. Sections 7401–7642 (1983 and Supp. 1990).

61. 15 U.S.C. Sections 2601–2671 (1983 and Supp. 1990).

62. 15 U.S.C. Sections 2641 et. seq. See also The Asbestos School Hazard Detection and Control Act, 20 U.S.C. Sections 3601–3611.

63. Giamboi and Sylvia, *Primer on Environmental Issues,* 103.

64. United States v. Geppert Brothers, 638 F.Supp. 996 (E.D. Pa. 1986).

65. First United Methodist Church v. U.S. Gypsum, 882 F. 2d 862 (4th Cir. 1989).

66. Lev. 25:23.

67. Escheat is the right of the sovereign to property that has no lawful heir or claimant.

68. Kohl v. United States, 91 U.S. 367, 371, 372 (1876).

69. Article I, Section 8, Clause 18.

70. United States v. Gettysburg Electric Railway Co., 160 U.S. 668 (1896).

71. Constitution of the United States, Amendment 5: "nor shall private property be taken for public use, without just compensation."

72. 181 Colo. 411, 509 P. 2d 1250 (1973).

73. 509 P. 2d 1253.

74. Denver Urban Renewal Authority v. Pillar of Fire, 552 P. 2d 23 (Colo. 1976).

75. 186 Colo. 367, 527 P. 2d 804 (1974).

76. Kelly v. Romney, 316 F.Supp. 840 (S.D. Ohio 1970).

77. 858 F. 2d 855 (1988).

78. First English Evangelical Lutheran Church of Glendale v. County of Los Angeles, 210 Cal. App. 3rd 1353, 258 Cal. Rptr. 893 (Ct. App. 1989).

79. 271 Md. 265, 316 A. 2d 807 (1974).

80. 35 N.Y. 2d 121, 359 N.Y.S. 2d 7, 316 N.E. 2d 305 (1974).

81. Pogue v. White Stone Baptist Church, 554 So. 2d 981 (Ala. 1989).

82. The antidiscrimination provisions are contained in Title VIII of the Civil Rights Act of 1968, codified as 42 U.S.C. Sections 3600–3620.

83. Dignity Twin Cities v. Newman Center and Chapel, 11 Religious Freedom Rptr. 121, reversed, 472 N.W. 2d 355 (Minn. Ct. App. 1991).

84. Hammar, *Pastor, Church, and Law,* 798; Gen. 47:26.

85. 397 U.S. 664 (1970).

86. 397 U.S. 676–77.

87. 397 U.S. 681.

88. Alton Bay Camp Meeting Association v. Alton, 109 N.H. 44, 242 A. 2d 80 (1968) (conference center and youth camp); Christian Camps and Conferences v. Town of Alton, 118 N.H. 351, 388 A. 2d 187 (1978) (youth camp); Appeal of C.H.R.I.S.T., 122 N.H. 982, 455 A. 2d 106 (1982) (rehabilitation facility).

89. Benedictine Sisters of the Sacred Heart v. Department of Revenue, 155 Ill. App. 3rd 325, 508 N.E. 2d 470 (Ill. App. 1987).

90. Lutheran Child and Family Services of Illinois v. Department of Revenue, 160 Ill. App. 3rd 420, 513 N.E. 2d 587 (Ill. Ct. App. 1987).

91. Council Rock School District v. G.D.L. Plaza Corporation, 496 A. 2d 1298 (Commonwealth Court of Pennsylvania 1985) (residential construction tax).

92. Foursquare Tabernacle Church of God in Christ v. State Board of Tax Commissioners, 550 N.E. 2d 850 (Ind. Tax Ct. 1990).

93. Scripture Union v. Deitch, 572 A. 2d 51 (Pa. Common 1990).

94. Evangelical Lutheran Good Samaritan Society v. Board of Equalization, 430 N.W. 2d 502 (Neb. 1988).

95. Church Contribution Trust v. Mendham Borough, 224 N.J. Super. 643, 541 A. 2d 249 (N.J. App. 1988).

96. The Dominican Nuns v. City of La Crosse, 142 Wis. 2d 577, 419 N.W. 2d 270 (Wisc. App. 1987).

97. Bexar County Appraisal Review Board v. First Baptist Church, 800 S.W. 2d 892 (Tex. Ct. App. 1990).

98. Salvation Army v. Department of Revenue, 8 Religious Freedom Rptr. 463 (Ill. Ct. App. 1988).

99. Community Christian Church v. Board of Tax Commissioners, 523 N.E. 2d 462 (Tax Court of Indiana 1988).

100. LeSea Broadcasting Corp. v. Board of Tax Commissioners, 525 N.E. 2d 637 (Tax Court of Indiana 1988).

101. Baptist Health Care Corp. v. Okmulgee County Board of Equalization, 750 P. 2d 127 (Okla. 1988).

102. Appeal of Lutheran Social Services, 539 A. 2d 895 (Pa. Common 1988).

103. Matter of Worley, 377 S.E. 2d 270 (N.C. App. 1989).

104. Pickens County Board of Tax Assessors v. Atlanta Baptist Association, 191 Ga. App. 260, 381 S.E. 2d 419 (Ga. App. 1989).

105. Markham v. Broward County Nursing Home, Inc., 540 So. 2d 940 (Fla. App. 1989); Dallas County Appraisal District v. The Leaves, Inc., 742 S.W. 2d 424 (Tex. App. 1987).

106. Illinois Conference of the United Church of Christ v. Illinois Department of Revenue, 165 Ill. App. 3rd 200, 518 N.E. 2d 755 (Ill. App. 1988).

107. Evangelical Alliance Mission v. Department of Revenue, 164 Ill. App. 3rd 431, 517 N.E. 2d 1178 (Ill. App. 1987).

108. Congregation Brith Emeth v. Limbach, 33 Ohio St. 3rd 69, 514 N.E. 2d 874 (Ohio 1987); Hausman v. First Baptist Church, 513 So. 2d 767 (Fla. App. 1987).

109. Maurer v. Young Life, 779 P. 2d 1317 (Colo. 1989).

110. Waushara County v. Graf, 157 Wis. 2d 539, 461 N.W. 2d 143 (Wis. Ct. App. 1990).

111. 83 Md. App. 599, 576 A. 2d 224 (1990).

Chapter 9
Copyright Law and the Church

1. United States Constitution, Article I, Section 8, Clause 8.

2. 17 U.S.C. Section 301(a).

3. Harper & Row, Publishers, Inc. v. Nation Enterprises, 471 U.S. 539, 558 (1985) quoted in P. Goldstein, *Copyright,* 3 vols. (Boston: Little, Brown & Co., 1989), 1:6.

4. 17 U.S.C. Section 502.

5. 17 U.S.C. Section 503.

6. 17 U.S.C. Section 504.

7. 17 U.S.C. Section 505.

8. 17 U.S.C. Section 102.

9. 17 U.S.C. Section 102(b).

10. 17 U.S.C. Section 401.

11. 17 U.S.C. Section 407.

12. 17 U.S.C. Section 408.

13. 17 U.S.C. Sections 101 and 201(b).

14. 17 U.S.C. Section 106.

15. 17 U.S.C. Section 101.

16. 17 U.S.C. Section 107. A discussion of the four fair use factors in the context of a biography of a religious leader appears in New Era Publications International v. Carol Publishing Group, 904 F. 152 (2d Cir. 1990).

17. The guidelines are reproduced in the House Report on the Copyright Act of 1976 (pp. 68–70) and are summarized and reproduced in part in Hammar, *The Church Guide to Copyright Law,* 2d ed. (Matthews, N.C.: Christian Ministry Resources, 1990), 85–92.

18. 17 U.S.C. Section 109(c).

19. 17 U.S.C. Section 109(d).

20. 17 U.S.C. Section 101.

21. 17 U.S.C. Section 110(1).

22. 17 U.S.C. Section 110(3).

23. 17 U.S.C. Section 110(4).

24. Hammar, *Church Guide to Copyright Law.* Appendix 1 contains the copyright policies of thirteen publishers of religious music.

25. Goldstein, *Copyright,* sec. 5.2.1.4. See Apple Computer, Inc. v. Formula International, Inc., 594 F.Supp. 617 (Central District of Cal. 1984); Micro-Sparc, Inc. v. Amtype Corp., 592 F.Supp. 33 (District of Mass. 1984).

26. Goldstein, *Copyright,* sec. 10.2.2.3. See Sony Corp. of America v. Universal City Studios, Inc., 464 U.S. 417 (1984); Williams and Wilkins Co. v. United States, 487 F. 2d 1345 (Court of Claims), affirmed by an equally divided Court, 420 U.S. 376 (1975) (per curiam).

27. 17 U.S.C. Section 101.

28. 17 U.S.C. Sections 106 and 101.

29. 17 U.S.C. Section 110(1).

30. 17 U.S.C. Section 110(1); Goldstein, *Copyright,* sec. 5.8.1.

31. 17 U.S.C. Section 110(3).

32. Goldstein, *Copyright,* sec. 5.7.2.1.

33. Hammar refers the reader to Motion

Picture Licensing Corporation, 1177 Summer Street, Stamford, CT 06905–0838, telephone 203–353–1600, which is said to offer a blanket license for churches to use some 2,000 videos at an annual fee of $100 (*Church Guide to Copyright Law,* 156).

34. 17 U.S.C. Section 115.

Chapter 10
Other Government Regulation

1. Walz v. Tax Commission, 397 U.S. 664 (1970).

2. See IRS Publication 575, which sets forth procedures for group exemption letters. See also Revenue Procedure 80–27.

3. Internal Revenue Code Section 6033.

4. See Revenue Procedure 86–23.

5. Comments of IRS Spokesperson J. H. Rotz, *New York Times,* January 9, 1991, p. A–12.

6. For criticisms of certain restrictions on tax-exempt organizations, see Lynn R. Buzzard and Sherra Robinson, *IRS Political Activity Restrictions on Churches and Charitable Ministries* (Diamond Bar, Calif.: Christian Ministries Management Association, 1990), 3–5; and Edward McGlynn Gaffney, "On Not Rendering to Caesar: The Unconstitutionality of Tax Regulation of Activities of Religious Organizations Relating to Politics," 40 *DePaul Law Review* 1 (1990).

7. Bob Jones University v. United States, 461 U.S. 574 (1983).

8. Church of Scientology v. Commissioner of Internal Revenue, 823 F. 2d 1310 (9th Cir. 1987). See Buzzard and Robinson, *IRS Political Activity Restrictions on Churches and Charitable Ministries.*

9. Truth Tabernacle Church, Inc. v. Commissioner of Internal Revenue, 57 Tax Court Memorandum 1386, Tax Court Memo 1989–451.

10. Heritage Village Church and Missionary Fellowship, Inc. 92 Bankruptcy Reporter 1000 (District of South Carolina 1988).

11. The discussion of political activity herein is a summary and overview of a complex and technical area of tax law. I recommend that churches and religious organizations dealing with concerns about political activity restrictions with respect to their exempt status consult counsel and familiarize themselves with the governing principles. An excellent resource is Buzzard and Robinson, *IRS Political Activity Restrictions on Churches and Charitable Ministries,* available from Christian Ministries Management Associa-

tion, P.O. Box 4638, Diamond Bar, CA, 91765. This eighty-four-page monograph provides an in-depth analysis of political activity restrictions on religious organizations.

12. See United States Catholic Conference v. Abortion Rights Mobilization, Inc., 487 U.S. 72 (1988).

13. Internal Revenue Code Section 501(c)(3).

14. Slee v. Commissioner Internal Revenue Service, 42 F. 2d 184 (2d Cir. 1930). See Buzzard and Robinson, *IRS Political Activity Restrictions on Churches and Charitable Ministries,* 37.

15. Ibid.

16. 461 U.S. 540 (1983).

17. In 1991, the Court reached the same conclusion with respect to activities funded by the government, upholding the ban on use of federal funds for abortion counseling in family-planning clinics. Rust v. Sullivan, 500 U.S.___, 114 L. Ed. 2d 233 (1991).

18. Internal Revenue Code Section 4911 (d)(I).

19. Revenue Procedure 71–39.

20. Buzzard and Robinson, *IRS Political Activity Restrictions on Churches and Charitable Ministries,* 53–54.

21. Haswell v. United States, 500 F. 2d 1133 (Court of Claims 1974); Khron v. United States, 246 F.Supp. 341 (D. Colo. 1965).

22. This section provides a summary overview of the complex and technical issues involving unrelated business income. I recommend that churches and religious organizations with unrelated business income issues obtain advice of counsel and familiarize themselves with the legal intricacies of the subject. A particularly valuable resource is Robert A. Buzzard and Lynn R. Buzzard, *"Render unto Caesar": Unrelated Business Income Tax Liabilities of Churches and Ministries* (available from the Church-State Resource Center, Norman Adrian Wiggins School of Law, Campbell University, Buies Creek, NC 27506). This 119-page monograph with sample tax forms and documents is an invaluable resource providing an in-depth examination of the issues surrounding unrelated business income and analyzing application of the law in a number of practical situations faced by churches and religious organizations.

23. Internal Revenue Code Section 513.

24. Internal Revenue Code Section 513(c).

25. Higgins v. Commissioner, 312 U.S. 212 (1941).

26. Veterans of Foreign Wars v. Commissioner, 89 T.C. 7 (1987).

27. See discussion in chapter 4.

28. General Counsel Memorandum 39752; Private Letter Ruling 8121164.

29. Waco Lodge No. 166 v. Commissioner, 696 F. 2d 372 (5th Cir. 1983).

30. Shiloh Youth Revival Centers v. Commissioner, 88 T.C. 565 (1987).

31. Revenue Regulation Section 301.7611-1.

32. St. German of Alaska Eastern Orthodox Catholic Church v. United States, 840 F. 2d 1087, 88-1 United States Tax Court paragraph 9201 (2d Cir. 1988).

33. H.R. Report No. 861 (Conf. Rep.) 98th Cong. 2d Sess. 1112. See Zoe Christian Leadership Inc. v. United States, 89-1 United States Tax Cases paragraph 9236 (Central District of California 1988).

34. United States v. Church of Scientology of Boston, Inc., 739 F.Supp. 46 (D. Mass. 1990), affirmed, 933 F. 2d 1074 (1st Cir. 1991).

35. Tax Court Memo 1990-41, CCH Tax Court Memorandum Decisions, 46, 344(m), affirmed 927 F. 2d 335 (8th Cir. 1991).

36. Commerce Clearing House Tax Court Memorandum Decisions, p. 1286.

37. The standard mileage rate for charitable travel is currently twelve cents per mile.

38. Summers v. Commissioner, 33 Tax Court Memorandum 695 (1974).

39. Wineberg v. Commissioner, 326 F. 2d 157 (9th Cir. 1964).

40. 490 U.S. 680.

41. 495 U.S. 472, 109 L. Ed. 2d 457.

42. Peace v. Commissioner, 43 T.C. 1 (1964); Revenue Ruling 62–113.

43. Private Letter Ruling 8916041.

44. Revenue Ruling 62–113.

45. Revenue Ruling 83–104.

46. McFadden v. Commissioner, 57 Tax Court Memorandum 152 (1989).

47. Burns v. Commissioner, 56 Tax Court Memorandum 703, TC Mcmo 1988–536.

48. Easter Lutheran Church v. Commissioner of Revenue (Minnesota T.C. unpublished opinion 1989), *Church Law and Tax Report* (May/June 1990), 14–15.

49. 50 Ohio St. 3rd 76, 552 N.E. 2d 908 (1990).

50. 493 U.S. 378 (1990).

51. Murdock v. Pennsylvania, 319 U.S. 105 (1943); Follett v. McCormick, 321 U.S. 573 (1944).

52. Quill Corp. v. North Dakota, 504 U.S. ___, 119 L.Ed. 2d 91 (1992); National Geographic Society v. California Board of Equalization, 430 U.S. 551 (1977); National Bellas Hess, Inc. v. Department of Revenue, 386 U.S. 753 (1967).

53. See, e.g., Quill Corp. v. North Dakota, 504 U.S.___, 119 L.Ed. 2d 91 (1992); National Geographic Society v. California Board of Equalization, 430 U.S. 551 (1977); National Bellas Hess, Inc. v. Department of Revenue, 386 U.S. 753 (1967); Nelson v. Sears, Roebuck & Co., 312 U.S. 359 (1941); Nelson v. Montgomery Ward & Co., 312 U.S. 373 (1941).

54. Freeman v. Hewit, 329 U.S. 249, 253 (1946).

55. National Bellas Hess, 386 U.S. 758.

56. 430 U.S. 551 (1977).

57. Miller Brothers Co. v. Maryland, 347 U.S. 340, 344–345 (1954).

58. Quill Corp. v. North Dakota, 504 U.S. ___, 119 L.Ed. 2d 91 (1992).

59. 489 U.S. 1 (1989).

60. Former Texas Tax Code Annotated, Section 151.312 (1982).

61. Walz v. Tax Commission of New York, 397 U.S. 664 (1970).

62. See, e.g., California Penal Code, Article 2.5, Sections 11165.7, 11165.8, and 11166.

63. New Hampshire Revised Statutes Annotated 169–C:29.

64. 114 Wash. 2d 353, 788 P. 2d 1066 (1990).

65. Former Revised Code of Washington 26.44.020(8).

66. New Hampshire Revised Statutes Annotated 169–C:29.

67. See, e.g., California Welfare and Institutions Code, Sections 15600–15754.

68. Herbert v. State, 526 So. 2d 709 (Fla. App. 4th Dist. 1988).

69. Department of Social Services v. Father and Mother, 366 S.E. 2d 40 (S.C. App. 1988).

70. State v. Grover, 437 N.W. 2d 60 (Minn. 1989); State v. Motherwell, 114 Wash. 2d 353, 788 P. 2d 1066 (1990).

71. See Fischer v. Metcalf, 543 So. 2d 785 (Fla. App. 1989).

72. Thomas v. Chadwick, 274 Cal. Rptr. 128 (Cal. App. 1990); Cream v. Mitchell, 264 Cal. Rptr. 876 (Cal. App. 2d Dist. 1989) (California law provides absolute immunity to reporters).

73. Hester v. Barnett, 723 S.W. 2d 544 (Mo. Ct. App. 1987).

74. Mendive v. Children's Services Division, 102 Or. App. 317, 794 P. 2d 807 (Or. App. 1990).

75. State v. Motherwell, 114 Wash. 2d 353, 788 P. 2d 1066 (1990).

76. Employment Division v. Smith, 494 U.S. 872 (1990). See discussion in chapter 3, section F.

77. Securities and Exchange Commission v. World Radio Mission, Inc., 544 F. 2d 535, 538

(1st Cir. 1976) quoting United Housing Foundation, Inc. v. Forman, 421 U.S. 837, 852 (1975).

78. Uniform Securities Act, Section 401(l), adopted in many states.

79. Securities Act of 1933, Section 3(a)(4).

80. 544 F. 2d 535 (1976).

81. 544 F. 2d 539.

82. 544 F. 2d 540.

83. April 1990 newsletter, St. Andrews Church, Connecticut.

84. Ran-Dav's County Kosher, Inc. v. State, 129 N.J. 141, 608 A. 2d 1353 (N.J. 1992).

85. 42 U.S.C. Section 12187.

86. 42 U.S.C. Section 2000a (b)(1).

87. 42 U.S.C. Section 2000a (e).

Chapter 11
Organization and Governance

1. See Gipson v. Brown, 749 S.W. 2d 297 (Ark. 1988), which allows church polity and practice to override state statutes with respect to election of directors and church disclosure of financial records to members.

2. See chapter 19, section C.

3. Crocker v. Barr, 367 S.E. 2d 471 (S.C. App. 1988).

4. John McManners, ed., *The Oxford Illustrated History of Christianity* (Oxford: Oxford University Press, 1990), 45.

5. James H. Coriden, Thomas J. Green, and Donald E. Heintschel, eds., *The Code of Canon Law: A Text and Commentary* (New York: Paulist Press, 1985).

6. See chapter 10.

7. See chapter 18.

8. Ibid.

9. Richard R. Hammar, *Pastor, Church, and Law*, 2d ed. (Matthews, N.C.: Christian Ministry Resources, 1991), 357–59.

10. See *Church Law and Tax Report* (Jan./Feb. 1988), 6–8, for a summary of the legal liability of church board members.

11. See chapter 16.

12. See chapter 10.

13. See chapter 10, sec. E.

14. See chapter 10, sec. A.2. As to unrelated business income, see Robert A. Buzzard and Lynn Buzzard, *"Render unto Caesar": Unrelated Business Income Tax: Liabilities of Churches and Ministries* (Buies Creek, N.C.: Church-State Resource Center, Norman Adrian Wiggins School of Law, Campbell University, 1990).

15. See chapter 3, sec. E.

16. See chapter 3, sec. F.

17. Heritage Village Church and Mission-

ary Fellowship, Inc., 92 Bankruptcy Reporter 1000 (District of South Carolina 1988), quoted in *Church Law and Tax Report* 3, no.4 (July/August 1989), 9.

18. Ibid.

19. Carter v. United States 89–2 U.S. Tax Court para. 9446 (S.D. N.Y. 1989), quoted in *Church Law and Tax Report* 3, no. 6 (November/December 1989), 16–17.

20. See, e.g., Edmund B. Haugen, *Mr./Madame Chairman—Parliamentary Procedure Explained* (Minneapolis: Augsburg Publishing House, 1963); C. Berry McCarty, *A Parliamentary Guide for Church Leaders* (Nashville: Broadman Press, 1987).

21. 136 U.S. 1 (1890).

22. See chapter 6.

23. See chapter 6.

24. See chapter 10, sec. A.2.

25. Buzzard and Buzzard, *"Render unto Caesar": Unrelated Business Income Tax*.

26. See chapter 7.

27. New Hampshire Revised Statutes Annotated 72:23(V).

28. See Lynn R. Buzzard and Sherra Robinson, *IRS Political Activity Restrictions on Churches and Charitable Ministries* (Diamond Bar, Calif.: Christian Ministries Management Association, 1990).

29. Philip R. Moots and Edward McGlynn Gaffney, *Church and Campus: Legal Issues in Religiously Affiliated Higher Education* (Notre Dame, Ind.: University of Notre Dame Press, 1979), 7–8, 13.

30. 90 Cal. App. 3d 259, 153 Cal. Rptr. 322 (1979).

31. Edward McGlynn Gaffney and Philip C. Sorensen, *Ascending Liability in Religious and Other Nonprofit Organizations*, ed. H. Griffin (Macon, Ga.: Center for Constitutional Studies, and Mercer University Press, 1984).

32. Philip R. Moots, *Ascending Liability: A Planning Memorandum* (Macon, Ga.: Center for Constitutional Studies, Mercer University Press, 1987).

Chapter 12
Hiring, Supervising, and Firing Employees

1. Kedroff v. St. Nicholas Cathedral, 344 U.S. 94 (1952).

2. Owens v. Second Baptist Church, 516 N.E. 2d 712 (Ill. App. 1987).

3. See McClure v. Salvation Army, 460 F. 2d 553 (5th Cir.), *cert. denied*, 409 U.S. 896 (1972); Natal v. Christian and Missionary Alli-

ance, 878 F. 2d 1575 (1st Cir. 1989); Owens v. Second Baptist Church, 516 N.E. 2d 712 (Ill. App. 1987); United Methodist Church v. White, 571 A. 2d 790 (District of Columbia 1990); O'Connor Hospital v. Cleu, 240 Cal. Rptr. 766 (Cal. App. 1987).

4. 460 F. 2d 553, 558-59 (5th Cir. 1972).

5. Bodewes v. Zuroweste, 303 N.E. 2d 509 (Ill. 1973).

6. Salzgaber v. First Christian Church, 10 Religious Freedom Rptr. 20 (Ohio Ct. App. 1990).

7. Minker v. Baltimore Annual Conference of United Methodist Church, 894 F. 2d 1354 (D.C. Cir. 1990).

8. Black v. Snyder, 471 N.W. 2d 715 (Minn. Ct. App. 1991).

9. Reardon v. Lemoyne, 122 N.H. 1042, 454 A. 2d 428 (1982).

10. Monge v. Beebe Rubber Company, 114 N.H. 130, 133, 316 A. 2d 549 (1974).

11. Cloutier v. A & P Tea Co., 121 N.H. 915, 436 A. 2d 1140 (1981); Howard v. Dorr Woolen, 120 N.H. 295, 414 A. 2d 1273 (1980).

12. Fulford v. Burndy Corp., 623 F.Supp. 78 (D. N.H. 1985).

13. Peterman v. Teamsters, 174 Cal. App. 2d 184, 344 P. 2d 25 (1959).

14. Frampton v. Indiana Gas Co., 297 N.E. 2d 425 (Ind. 1973).

15. Tameny v. Atlantic Richfield, 610 P. 2d 1330 (Cal. 1989).

16. Savodnick v. Korvette's, 488 F.Supp. 822 (E.D. N.Y. 1980); Fortune v. National Cash Register, 364 N.E. 2d 1251 (Mass. 1971).

17. Novosel v. Nationwide Insurance, 114 Labor Relations Reference Manual 3105 (3rd Cir. 1983).

18. Russ v. Pension Consultants Company, Inc., 538 N.E. 2d 693 (Ill. App. 1989).

19. 676 F. 2d 1272 (9th Cir. 1982).

20. 766 F. 2d 932 (6th Cir. 1985).

21. See text at chapter 3, section I.

22. 766 F. 2d 938.

23. Ohio Civil Rights Commission v. Dayton Christian School, Inc., 477 U.S. 619 (1986). The procedural ground of reversal was the Abstention Doctrine established by Younger v. Harris, 401 U.S. 37 (1971). The Abstention Doctrine says that a federal court should not enjoin a pending state proceeding unless there is a very unusual situation in which the injunction is required to prevent great and immediate irreparable injury. Essentially it requires federal courts to let state administrative agencies and courts work out constitutional issues on their own and not burden federal courts

with them before the state administrative and judicial system has reached a point of finality in dealing with them. In a case such as Dayton Christian Schools, it forces the religious organization to go through the litigation process, which itself is very intrusive and entangling, in order to demonstrate that it should be free of it, although such cases can be addressed by motions filed at an early stage; see chapter 19, passim.

24. See chapter 19, sec. C. See also Alicea v. New Brunswick Theological Seminary, 244 N.J. Super. 119, 581 A. 2d 900 (N.J. Super. App. Div. 1990), in which the court abstained from passing on a seminary faculty member's claim that there was an agreement to put him on a tenure track but required the seminary to apply its established grievance procedure.

25. Gilmer v. Interstate Johnson Lane Corporation, 500 U.S.___, 114 L. Ed. 2d 26 (1991).

26. See chapter 19, sec. C, and Appendix C.

27. See Appendix C for sample contract clauses from the Association of Christian Conciliation Services.

28. See Rosby v. General Baptist State Convention of North Carolina, Inc., 370 S.E. 2d 605 (N.C. App. 1988) (unilaterally promulgated employment manuals or policies do not become part of the employment contract unless expressly included in it).

29. See Minker v. Baltimore Annual Conference of United Methodist Church, 894 F. 2d 1354 (D.C. Cir. 1990) (the allegation that the conference would provide him with a congregation more suited to his training and skills in exchange for continued work at another church states a contractual relationship).

30. Toussaint v. Blue Cross/Blue Shield, 292 N.W. 2d 880 (Mich. 1980).

31. Forman v. Bir Corp., 532 F.Supp. 49 (E.D. Pa. 1982).

32. Andrew D. Hill, "Wrongful Discharge" and the Derogation of the At-Will Employment Doctrine (Philadelphia: Wharton School, Industrial Research Unit, University of Pennsylvania, 1987), 161.

33. Ibid., 162.

34. "How to Avoid 'Wrongful Discharge' Suits," 5 Lawyers Alert 272 (1986).

35. Ibid.

36. Hill, "Wrongful Discharge," 162.

37. Paul I. Weiner, Stuart H. Bompey, and Max G. Brittain, Jr., Wrongful Discharge Claims: A Preventive Approach (New York: Practicing Law Institute, 1986), 87. See also, e.g., Novosel v. Sears, Roebuck & Co., 495 F.Supp. 344 (E.D. Mich. 1980).

38. "How to Avoid 'Wrongful Discharge' Suits," 272 n. 4.

39. Weiner, Bompey, and Brittain, *Wrongful Discharge Claims,* 73. See also Hill, *"Wrongful Discharge,"* 163.

40. See, e.g., Toussaint v. Blue Cross/Blue Shield, 292 N.W. 2d 880 (Mich. 1980); Wooley v. Hoffman-LaRoche, 99 N.J. 2984, 491 A. 2d 1257 (1985); Liekveld v. Valley View Hospital, 688 P. 2d 170 (Ariz. 1984); Weiner v. McGraw Hill, 433 N.E. 2d 441 (N.Y. 1982); contra Reid v. Sears, Roebuck, 790 F. 2d 453 (6th Cir. 1986); Garcia v. Aetna Finance Co., 752 F. 2d 488 (10th Cir. 1984); Heideck v. Kent General Hospital, 446 A. 2d 1095 (Del. 1982); Gates v. Life of Montana, 638 P. 2d 1063 (Mont. 1982).

41. "How to Avoid 'Wrongful Discharge' Suits," 272.

42. Ibid.

43. See Lex K. Larson and Philip Borowsky, *Unjust Dismissal* (New York: Matthew Bender & Co., 1988), sec. 8.02, for a review of court decisions on what is and is not binding in manuals. Though employers frequently win in court when the suit is over broad policy statements (e.g., Patrowich v. Chemical Bank, 470 N.Y.S. 2d 599 [1984]), the costs and risks can be alarming.

44. Hill, *"Wrongful Discharge,"* 165–66.

45. Ibid., 166.

46. Ibid., 162.

47. See, e.g., Dell v. Montgomery Ward & Co., 811 F. 2d 970 (6th Cir., Feb. 17, 1987); Batchelder v. Sears, Roebuck, 114 Labor Relations Reference Manual 3467 (E.D. Mich. 1983).

48. "How to Avoid 'Wrongful Discharge' Suits," 273.

49. Hill, *"Wrongful Discharge,"* 163.

50. "How to Avoid 'Wrongful Discharge' Suits," 273.

51. Larson and Borowsky, *Unjust Dismissal,* sec. 1.01.

52. Hill, *"Wrongful Discharge,"* 170.

53. "How to Avoid 'Wrongful Discharge' Suits," 273.

54. Weiner, Bompey, and Brittain, *Wrongful Discharge Claims,* 87. See also, e.g., Novosel v. Sears, Roebuck & Co., 495 F.Supp. 344 (E.D. Mich. 1980).

55. Hill, "Wrongful Discharge," 169–70.

56. See Sacred Heart School Board v. Labor and Industry Review Commission, 460 N.W. 2d 430 (Wis. App. 1990); and Brown Transport Corp. v. Commonwealth of Pennsylvania, 578 A. 2d 555 (Pa. Comm. 1990), where a terminated Jewish employee who had objected to religious materials in the company newsletter and Bible verses on payroll checks refuted the employer's claim of inconsistent job performance by showing good job evaluations prior to the discharge.

57. "How to Avoid 'Wrongful Discharge' Suits," 273.

58. Ibid.

59. Weiner, Bompey, and Brittain, *Wrongful Discharge Claims,* 101.

60. Ibid., 103.

61. Ibid., 114.

62. Ibid.

63. Ibid., 111.

64. See sec. B, above.

65. See, e.g., Byrd v. Faber, 57 Ohio St. 3rd 56, 565 N.E. 2d 584 (1991) (claim of sexual misconduct of clergy in counseling).

66. A sample form that may be considered for work with children or youth is reproduced in *Church Law and Tax Report* 3, no. 4 (July/August 1989), 7.

67. See chapter 10.

68. Ibid.

69. Larson and Borowsky, *Unjust Dismissal,* sec. 8.04.

70. Henry H. Perritt, Jr., *Employee Dismissal Law and Practice* (New York: Wiley Law Publications, 1984), sec. 4.8.

71. See Weiner, Bompey, and Brittain, *Wrongful Discharge Claims,* 112–15.

72. Ibid., 107.

73. Hill, *"Wrongful Discharge,"* 171–72.

74. Weiner, Bompey, and Brittain, *Wrongful Discharge Claims,* 126.

75. Hill, *"Wrongful Discharge,"* 173.

76. See chapter 19, sec. C, and Appendix C.

Chapter 13
The Church as Wagepayer

1. Internal Revenue Code 3401(a)(IX).

2. See Bethel Baptist Church v. United States, 822 F. 2d 1334 (3rd Cir. 1987).

3. See chapter 6.

4. Hoppmann v. Workers Compensation Appeals Board, 226 Cal. App. 3rd 1119, 227 Cal. Rptr. 116 (6th Dist. 1991).

5. South Ridge Baptist Church v. Industrial Commission of Ohio, 676 F.Supp. 799 (S.D. Ohio 1987); Victory Baptist Temple v. Industrial Commission, 442 N.E. 2d 819 (Ohio 1982), *cert denied,* 459 U.S. 1086 (1982); Greenway Baptist Church v. Industrial Commission, 636 P. 2d 1264 (Ariz. App. 1981); Tepesch v. Johnson, 296 N.W. 740 (Iowa 1941); Schneider v. Salvation Army, 14 N.W. 2d 467 (Minn. 1944).

6. Internal Revenue Code Section 3306 (c)(8).

7. Internal Revenue Code Section 3309(b).

8. 451 U.S. 772 (1981).

9. Hickey v. District of Columbia Department of Employment Service, 448 A. 2d 871 (D.C. App. 1982).

10. Salem College and Academy v. Employment Division, 659 P. 2d 415 (Or. App. 1983).

11. 770 P. 2d 588 (Or. 1989) *contra*, Claim of Klein, 563 N.Y.S. 2d 132 (Supreme Ct. 1990).

12. St. Pius X Parish Corporation v. Murray, 557 A. 2d 1214 (R.I. 1989).

13. Internal Revenue Code, Section 414.

Chapter 14
Compensation and Taxes

1. Revenue Regulations are the administrative regulations promulgated by the Treasury Department by its authority under Section 7805(a) of the Internal Revenue Code. They provide meaning in application for complex statutory provisions.

2. Revenue Rulings are interpretations by the IRS of the application of tax law to particular fact situations which are of general interest.

3. Revenue Procedures are descriptions of IRS internal management operations as interpretations of various statutory provisions; they often have an impact on taxpayers' rights and duties.

4. Letter Rulings are the IRS's response to a taxpayer's request for advice on the tax consequences of a particular set of facts. They do not have precedental value but are a useful indicator of the IRS's approach to problems.

5. See chapter 5 n. 3, with respect to the Tax Court. Tax Court decisions not officially published but available through private services are called *memorandum decisions* and are cited as TCM or Tax Ct. memo. If the Tax Court decides a case against the IRS, the Commissioner may issue a notice of acquiescence, meaning the IRS accepts the decision, or nonacquiescence, meaning it does not and will continue to challenge taxpayers on the issue. Tax Court decisions are binding only with respect to identical facts in cases in the circuit in which the case arose. They are appealable to the federal Courts of Appeals.

6. I recommend Richard R. Hammar, *Church and Clergy Tax Guide,* published annually, for current-year returns. It is available from Christian Ministry Resources, P.O. Box 2301, Matthews, NC 28106. The same publisher produces a bimonthly newsletter, *Church Law and Tax Report,* which updates tax information, contains a tax calendar, includes regular articles on legal subjects of interest to clergy and religious organizations, and reviews current legal developments. Other helpful guides are B. J. Worth, *Income Tax Guide for Ministers and Religious Workers,* available from Worth Tax and Financial Service, Box 725, Winona Lake, IN 46590; a series of tax-related publications by Manfred Holck, Jr., available from Church Management, Inc., P.O. Box 162527, Austin, TX 78716, including "Tax Planning for Clergy"; "Housing for Clergy"; "Social Security for Clergy"; "Payroll Tax Procedures for Church and Clergy"; "How to Deduct the Cost of Continuing Education"; "Professional Expense"; and "Clergy Car Allowance and Expenses"; and publications available from the IRS including Publication 17, *Your Federal Income Tax,* and Publication 517, *Social Security for Members of Clergy and Religious Workers.* IRS forms and publications are available in most public libraries and can be ordered from the nearest of the following IRS forms distribution centers: Rancho Cordova, CA, 95743-0001; P.O. Box 9903, Bloomington, IL 61799; P.O. Box 258661, Richmond, VA 23289; or V.I. Bureau of Internal Revenue, Lockharts Garden, No. 1A, Charlotte Amalie, St. Thomas, Virgin Islands 00802.

7. Hammar, *Church and Clergy Tax Guide,* 24.

8. Internal Revenue Code Section 61(a).

9. Revenue Ruling 55-422; Schall v. Commissioner, 174 F. 2d 893 (5th Cir. 1949); Mutch v. Commissioner, 209 F. 2d 390 (3rd Cir. 1954); Kavanagh v. Hershman, 210 F. 2d 654 (6th Cir. 1954); Abernathy v. Commissioner, 211 F. 2d 651 (D.C. Cir. 1954).

10. Perkins v. Commissioner, 34 T.C. 117 (1960) (United Methodist church pension payments).

11. Revenue Ruling 71–28.

12. Internal Revenue Code Section 107. See Hammar, *Church and Clergy Tax Guide,* 82.

13. Swaggart v. Commissioner, 48 Tax Court Memorandum 759 (1984).

14. Private Letter Ruling 9115101. See *Church Law and Tax Report* 5, no. 4 (July/August 1991), 9.

15. Revenue Ruling 78–448.

16. See Heritage Village Church and Missionary Fellowship, Inc., 92 Bankruptcy Reporter 1000 (District of South Carolina 1988), the PTL bankruptcy case, for a discussion of unreasonable compensation and the parsonage allowance.

17. Revenue Ruling 75–22.

18. Revenue Procedure 89–54.

19. Internal Revenue Code Section 119(a).

20. Dalan v. Commissioner, 55 Tax Court Memorandum 370, Memo 1988–106; Deason v. Commissioner, 41 T.C. 465 (1964).

21. Internal Revenue Code Sections 117(d) and 127.

22. See Hammar, *Church and Clergy Tax Guide* (1992), 94ff.; and Holck, "Clergy Car Allowance and Expenses," for a detailed analysis of transportation expenses.

23. Colbert v. Commissioner, 61 T.C. 449, 455 (1974).

24. Revenue Ruling 78–301.

25. Revenue Ruling 80–59.

26. Internal Revenue Code Section 1402(e)II.

27. E.g., Ballinger v. Commissioner, 728 F. 2d 1287 (10th cir. 1984).

28. United States v. Lee, 455 U.S. 252 (1982).

29. Varga v. United States, 467 F.Supp. 1113 (D. Md. 1979); Palmer v. Commissioner, 52 T.C. 310 (1969).

30. Internal Revenue Code Section 3121(w).

31. See Holck, "Social Security for Clergy."

32. See B. J. Worth, *Income Tax Guide for Ministers and Religious Workers,* 59–62.

Chapter 15
Purchasing, Maintaining, or Altering Property

1. Daniel Webster Council v. St. James Association, 129 N.H. 681, 553 A. 2d 329 (N.H. 1987).

2. Bethany Baptist Church v. Deptford Township, 225 N.J. Super. 355, 542 A. 2d 505 (1988).

3. 292 Ark. 250, 729 S.W. 2d 171.

4. See discussion in chapters 4 and 11.

5. St. Mark Coptic Orthodox Church v. Colorado State Board of Assessment Appeals, 762 P. 2d 775 (Colo. Ct. App. 1988).

6. See General Electric Supply Co. v. Downtown Church of Christ, 746 S.W. 2d 386 (Ark. App. 1988).

7. In Congregation Beth Sholom v. Building Commissioner, 537 N.E. 2d 605 (Mass. 1989), a congregation had to install a sprinkler system after a remodeling job at twice the cost it would have incurred if done during the remodeling.

8. See discussion in chapter 10, section E.

9. See Corporation of the President v. Seymour Electric Supply, 558 So. 2d 88 (Fla. App. 1990), where a bond protected the church.

10. Compare McNulty v. Hurley, 97 So. 2d 185 (Fla. 1957) and Autry v. Roebuck Park Baptist Church, 229 So. 2d 469 (Ala. 1969) (persons attending religious services are licensees) with Fleischer v. Hebrew Orthodox Congregation, 504 N.E. 2d 320 (Ind. App. 1987) (person attending religious service is an invitee).

11. Brown v. St. Venantius School, 111 N.J. 325, 544 A. 2d 842 (1988).

12. Kendzorek v. Guardian Angel Catholic Parish, 178 Mich. App. 562, 444 N.W. 2d 213 (1989).

13. St. Casimir Church v. Frankiewics, 563 N.E. 2d 1331 (Ind. App. 1990).

Chapter 16
Accounting for Funds and Trusts

1. U.S. Department of Commerce, *1990 Statistical Abstract of the United States,* 372.

2. 563 So. 2d 64 (Fla. 1990).

3. Larson v. Valente, 456 U.S. 228 (1982); Village of Schaumburg v. Citizens for a Better Environment, 444 U.S. 620 (1980).

4. Edith Fisch, Doris Jonas Freed, and Esther R. Schachter, *Charities and Charitable Foundations* (Pomona, N.Y.: Lond Publications, 1974), and idem, 1990–91 Cumulative Supplement, Sec. 685.

5. See, e.g., Larson v. Valente, 456 U.S. 228 (1982) (unconstitutional to exempt from registration only religious organizations more than half of whose income was from members); Village of Schaumburg v. Citizens for a Better Environment, 444 U.S. 620 (1980) (Free Speech Clause protects charitable appeal for funds); Heritage Village Church and Missionary Fellowship v. State, 263 S.E. 2d 726 (N.C. 1980) (state may not constitutionally deny exemption to religious organization).

6. 258 Ga. 665, 373 S.E. 2d 612 (1988).

7. See chapter 6.

8. 234 N.J. Super. 526, 560 A. 2d 1353 (N.J. Super. 1989).

9. 560 A. 1354.

10. See Fisch, Freed, and Schachter, *Charities and Charitable Foundations,* sec. 70; 1990–91 Cumulative Supplement; and, e.g., Arizona Revised Statutes (1975) Sec. 14–3715; Nebraska Revised Statutes (1989), Sec. 30–2476(4).

11. 869 F. 2d 628 (1st Cir. 1990).

12. 869 F. 2d 645.

13. *Black's Law Dictionary,* 6th ed. (St. Paul, Minn.: West Publishing Co., 1990).

14. Ibid.

15. 557 N.Y.S. 886 (App. Div. 1990).

16. Bogert, *Law of Trusts,* 5th ed., sec. 93 (St. Paul, Minn.: West Publishing Co., 1973).

17. Ibid., sec. 95.

18. 172 Mich. App. 298, 431 N.W. 2d 492 (Mich. App. 1988).

19. Fisch, Freed, and Schachter, *Charities and Charitable Foundations,* sec. 272.

20. Ibid., sec. 133.

21. Ibid.

22. Riegel v. United Methodist Church (Ohio App. unpublished opinion 1989), reported in *Church Law and Tax Report* (May/June 1990).

23. 793 S.W. 2d 259 (Tenn. App. 1990).

24. 146 Miscellaneous 2d 173, 549 N.Y.S. 2d 910 (Supreme Court, Rensselaer County).

25. Fisch, Freed, and Schachter, *Charities and Charitable Foundations,* secs. 562, 563.

26. Ibid., sec. 565.

27. 1 Ambler's English Chancery Reports 228, 7 Vesey, Junior, English Chancery Reports 76 (1754).

28. 452 N.W. 2d 403 (Iowa 1990).

29. 228 N.J. Super. 68, 548 A. 2d 1157 (N.J. Super. 1988).

30. Matter of Estate of Wilson, 465 N.Y.S. 2d 900, 452 N.E. 2d 1288 (1983).

31. Commonwealth of Pennsylvania v. Brown, 392 F. 2d 120 (3rd Cir.), *cert. denied,* 391 U.S. 921 (1968).

32. In re: Certain Scholarship Funds, 133 N.H. 227, 575 A. 2d 1325 (1990).

33. Fisch, Freed, and Schachter, *Charities and Charitable Foundations,* sec. 134.

34. Ibid., p. 130.

35. Ibid., secs.134, 61.

36. State Bank & Trust Co. v. Park Ridge School for Girls, 34 Ill. App. 2d 396, 181 N.E. 2d 204 (1962).

37. Mitchell v. Jerrolds, 1991 Tenn. App. Lexis 201, 11 Religious Freedom Rptr. 85 (1991).

38. 80 U.S. 679 (1872). See discussion in chapter 4.

39. 80 U.S. 722.

40. 80 U.S. 723.

41. 80 U.S. 724.

42. Presbyterian Church in the United States v. Mary Elizabeth Blue Hull Memorial Presbyterian Church, 393 U.S. 440 (1969).

43. 393 U.S. 452.

44. 443 U.S. 595 (1979).

45. 443 U.S. 603.

Chapter 18
The Counseling Relationship and Church Discipline

1. See, e.g., N.H. Revised Statutes Annotated 330.A:16–c.

2. See chapter 3, section F.

3. Lynn R. Buzzard and Dan Hall, *Clergy Confidentiality: A Time to Speak and a Time to Be Silent* (Diamond Bar, Calif.: Christian Ministries Management Association, 1988), 8.

4. See chapter 5.

5. Keenan v. Gigante, 390 N.E. 2d 1151, 47 N.Y. 2d 160, 417 N.Y.S. 2d 226 (1979) (ten-day prison sentence for criminal contempt for a priest who refused to answer questions in a Grand Jury investigation of prison conditions).

6. Tarasoff v. Regents of the University of California, 17 Cal. 3rd 425, 551 P. 2d 334, 131 Cal. Rptr. 14 (1976); Petersen v. State, 100 Wash. 2d 421, 671 P. 2d 230 (1983), California Civil Code, Section 43.92; California Evidence Code, Section 1024.

7. 47 Cal. 3rd 278, 763 P. 2d 948, 253 Cal. Rptr. 97 (1988).

8. Some of the numerous articles addressing the Nally case and the theory of clergy malpractice appear in references accompanying the various papers in the ABA National Institute on Tort and Religion, 1990. See, e.g., Samuel E. Ericsson, "Clergy Malpractice: Ramifications of a New Theory," 16 *Valparaiso University Law Review* 163 (1981); Carl H. Esbeck, "Tort Claims against Churches and Ecclesiastical Officers: The First Amendment Considerations," 89 *West Virginia Law Review* 1 (1986). Over fifty articles on clergy malpractice have appeared in legal periodicals.

9. Esbeck, "Tort Claims against Churches and Ecclesiastical Officers," 82–84.

10. 253 Cal. Rptr. 110.

11. 518 So. 2d 682 (Ala. 1987).

12. Hester v. Barnett, 723 S.W. 2d 544 (Mo. App. 1987); White v. Blackburn, 787 P. 2d 1315 (Utah App. 1990).

13. Baumgartner v. First Church of Christ, Scientist, 141 Ill. App. 3rd 898, 490 N.E. 2d 1319 (1986).

14. Destefano v. Grabrian, 763 P. 2d 275 (Colo. 1988).

15. Compare Byrd v. Faber, 57 Ohio St. 3rd 56, 565 N.E. 2d 584 (1991) (disallowing clergy malpractice claim) with S.P. v. Mitchell (Henapin County Court, Minnesota) (jury verdict reported in *Lawyers Alert,* vol. 9, no.

17 [June 11, 1990], p. 1). In Schmidt v. Bishop, 779 F.Supp. 321 (S.D. N.Y. 1991), a New York federal district court concluded that the cause of action did not exist in New York.

16. 2 Cor. 12:20.

17. William L. Prosser, *Handbook of the Law of Torts,* 4th ed. (St. Paul, Minn.: West Publishing Co., 1971), 739.

18. 376 U.S. 254 (1964).

19. Hester v. Barnett, 723 S.W. 2d 544 (Mo. Ct. App. 1987).

20. McNair v. Worldwide Church of God, 197 Cal. App. 3rd 363, 242 Cal. Rptr. 823 (1987).

21. Gorman v. Swaggart, 524 So. 2d 915 (La. Ct. App. 1988).

22. Rajneesh Foundation International v. McGreer, 303 Or. 371, 737 P. 2d 593 (1987).

23. Samuel D. Horan and Louis D. Brandeis, "The Right to Privacy," 4 *Harvard Law Review* 193 (1890).

24. Restatement, Second Torts Section 46, comment d (1965).

25. 212 Cal. App. 3rd 872, 260 Cal. Rptr. 331 (1989).

26. 6 Cal. Rptr. 2d 532 (Cal. App. 2 Dist. 1992).

27. Molko v. Holy Spirit Association, 179 Cal. App. 3rd 450, 224 Cal. Rptr. 817 (1986).

28. Destefano v. Grabrian, 763 P. 2d 275 (Colo. 1988); and see Erickson v. Christenson, 99 Or. App. 104, 781 P. 2d 383 (1989).

29. Guinn v. Church of Christ, 775 P. 2d 766 (Okla. 1989).

30. Snyder v. Evangelical Orthodox Church, 216 Cal. App. 3rd 297, 264 Cal. Rptr. 640 (1989).

31. Esbeck, "Tort Claims against Churches and Ecclesiastical Officers," 39.

32. Ibid.

33. See, e.g., Paul v. Watchtower Bible and Tract Society of New York, 819 F. 2d 875 (9th Cir.), *cert. denied,* 484 U.S. 926 (1987).

34. Rosicrucian Fellowship v. Rosicrucian Fellowship NonSectarian Church, 39 Cal. 2d 121, 132, 245 P. 2d 481 (1952), quoting Zollman, *American Church Law* (St. Paul, Minn.: West Publishing Co., 1933), sec. 328.

35. Guinn v. Church of Christ, 775 P. 2d 766 (Okla. 1989); Wollersheim v. Church of Scientology, 212 Cal. App. 3rd 872, 260 Cal. Rptr. 331 (1989).

36. Paul, n. 33, above.

37. Guinn v. Church of Christ, n. 29, above.

38. Lynn R. Buzzard and Thomas S. Brandon, Jr., *Church Discipline and the Courts* (Wheaton, Ill.: Tyndale House, 1987).

39. See chapter 19 on the subject of alternative dispute resolution mechanisms, which may be useful in this context.

40. Matt. 18:15; 2 Cor. 2:5-11.

41. Hester v. Barnett, 723 S.W. 2d 544 (Mo. Ct. App. 1987).

42. Destefano v. Grabrian, 763 P. 2d 275 (Colo. 1988).

43. Guinn v. Church of Christ, 775 P. 2d 766 (Okla. 1989).

Chapter 19
Litigation

1. 1 Kings 3:16-28.

2. 28 U.S.C. Section 2072 contains that authority for the federal court system.

3. A "motion" is simply a request by a party that the court make some particular ruling in the course of a lawsuit. Except for motions made in the course of a trial, they are usually in writing, supported by affidavits and legal briefs or memoranda. They may address any subject pertinent to the lawsuit.

4. Federal Rules of Civil Procedure 11.

5. Federal Rules of Civil Procedure 12(b).

6. Federal Rules of Civil Procedure 26(b)(1).

7. Elizabeth Loftus and Katherine Ketcham, *Witness for the Defense* (New York: St. Martin's Press, 1991).

8. 1 Cor. 6:1-8 reads: "If any of you has a dispute with another, dare he take it before the ungodly for judgment instead of before the saints? Do you not know that the saints will judge the world? And if you are to judge the world, are you not competent to judge trivial cases? Do you not know that we will judge angels? How much more the things of this life! Therefore, if you have disputes about such matters, appoint as judges even men of little account in the church! I say this to shame you. Is it possible that there is nobody among you wise enough to judge a dispute between believers? But instead, one brother goes to law against another—and this in front of unbelievers!

"The very fact that you have lawsuits among you means you have been completely defeated already. Why not rather be wronged? Why not rather be cheated? Instead, you yourselves cheat and do wrong, and you do this to your brothers."

9. Gilmer v. Interstate Johnson Lane Corporation, 114 L. Ed. 2d 26 (1991).

10. The Association of Christian Conciliation Services may be contacted at 1537 Avenue D, Suite 352, Billings, MT 59102.

11. Rules of Procedure for Christian Conciliation, Rule 1.

12. Ibid., Rule 4.

13. Ibid., Rule 5.B.

14. Ibid., Rule 19.

15. Ibid., Rule 20.

16. Ibid., Rule 22.

17. Ibid., Rule 36.

18. The reader is referred to C. Ken Sande's book on this subject, *The Peacemaker—A Biblical Guide to Resolving Personal Conflict* (Grand Rapids: Baker Book House, 1991). The author is the president of the Association of Christian Conciliation Services. Another useful work on this subject is Lynn R. Buzzard and Lawrence Eck, *Tell It to the Church* (Elgin, Ill.: David C. Cook Publishing Co., 1982).

19. *National Law Journal,* March 26, 1990, p. S.12.

20. Acts 18:10.

21. The "rapture" is the event spoken of in 1 Thess. 4:16-17 and 1 Cor. 15:51-52, believed by many Christians to describe a return of Jesus, in which he will rapture or remove believers from the earth before the terrible times of the tribulation and his Second Coming, spoken of in, e.g., Matthew 24 and Revelation.

Chapter 20
Liability Insurance

1. Cleary, *Special Problems: Tort Liability for Churches* (ABA National Institute on Tort and Religion, 1990), 1.

2. Wicina v. Strecker, 242 Kan. 278, 747 P. 2d 167 (1987) (no duty by school to purchase medical insurance or advise parents to do so in the context of quadriplegic football injury).

3. Texas Code of Civil Practice and Remedies, Supplement, Section 84.997(g).

4. Convent of the Visitation School v. Continental Casualty Co., 707 F.Supp. 412 (D. Minn. 1989).

5. See Church of St. Matthew v. Aetna Casualty and Surety Co., 554 N.Y.S. 2d 563 (Appellate Division 1990) for a discussion of a church's obligations under the cooperation clause.

Conclusion
Weaving Law and Church Together

1. See 1 Peter 1:13-19.

2. Holmes, *The Common Law* (Boston: Little, Brown & Co., 1963), 5.

Index